8e

Small Business:
An Entrepreneur's Business Plan

J.D. Ryan
Emeritus, Irvine Valley College

Gail P. Hiduke
Saddleback College

SOUTH-WESTERN
CENGAGE Learning™

Australia • Brazil • Japan • Korea • Mexico • Singapore • Spain • United Kingdom • United States

SOUTH-WESTERN
CENGAGE Learning™

Small Business: An Entrepreneur's Business Plan, Eighth Edition
J.D. Ryan, Gail P. Hiduke

Vice President of Editorial, Business:
Jack W. Calhoun

Editor-in-Chief: Melissa S. Acuña

Sr. Acquisitions Editor: Michele Rhoades

Developmental Editor: Elizabeth Lowry

Marketing Communications Manager:
James Overly

Executive Marketing Manager: Kimberly
Kanakes

Marketing Manager: Clinton Kernen

Marketing Coordinator: Sarah Rose

Sr. Content Project Manager: Holly Henjum

Managing Media Editor: Pam Wallace

Media Editor: Rob Ellington

Frontlist Buyer: Doug Wilke

Permissions Account Manager/Images:
Don Schlotman

Permissions Account Manager/Text:
Mollika Basu

Production Service/Compositor: Pre-PressPMG

Senior Art Director: Tippy McIntosh

Cover and Internal Designer: Mike Stratton,
Stratton Design

Cover Image: Philippe Poulet/Mission,
Getty Images

Main Image, Internal: Daisuke Moita/Photodisc,
Getty Images

Secondary Image, Internal: Photodisc,
Getty Images

For product information and technology assistance, contact us at
Cengage Learning Customer & Sales Support, 1-800-354-9706

For permission to use material from this text or product,
submit all requests online at **http://www.cengage.com/permissions**.
Permissions questions can be emailed to
permissionrequest@cengage.com

ExamView® is a registered trademark of eInstruction Corp.

© 2009 Cengage Learning. All Rights Reserved.

Library of Congress Control Number: 2008932623

ISBN-13: 978-0-324-59102-6

ISBN-10: 0-324-59102-0

South-Western Cengage Learning
5191 Natorp Boulevard
Mason, OH 45040
USA

Cengage Learning products are represented in Canada by Nelson Education, Ltd.

For your course and learning solutions, visit **http://www.academic. cengage.com**.

Purchase any of our products at your local college store or at our preferred online store, **http://www.ichapters.com**.

Printed in the United States of America
2 3 4 5 6 7 12 11 10 09

brief contents

contents

preface

Welcome to the eighth edition of *Small Business: An Entrepreneur's Business Plan.* We created our book for the thousands of dreamers like you who want to create their own businesses. Most first-time entrepreneurs start out with little more than an idea. By combining your talents with a practical approach, we will show you how to take your idea and form it into a functional Business Plan.

Every great adventure begins with a map; this book serves as your map and navigator. The Action Steps provide you with direction and tasks to accomplish along the way, while the vignettes give you a first-hand look at the trials, tribulations, and successes of other entrepreneurs.

By following the Action Steps, you will learn how to develop a Business Plan from the inception of the idea to identifying and locating your Target Customers and determining how to market to them successfully. Fasten your seatbelt and prepare to embark on your great entrepreneurial adventure!

ORGANIZATION

Target the Chapters that Call to You

The Action Steps are spaced out across 15 chapters, from Chapter 1, "Your Great Adventure," to Chapter 15, "Pull Your Plan Together."

- Chapters 1, 2, and 3 help you focus on yourself and your ideas; they explain how to develop and test your ideas in the marketplace before you risk your money. If you are just exploring entrepreneurship, concentrate on these chapters and the accompanying Action Steps. Remember, you are designing not only your Business Plan but also your life plan.
- Chapters 4, 5, and 6 help you locate several of the keys to success in small business: your Target Customer and the right location.
- Chapter 7 helps you reach out to your Target Customer with promotional tools.
- Chapter 8 plunges you into numbers—how much you will need to start up and how much you will need to keep going. Chapter 9, "Shaking the Money Tree," helps you find the money to take your dream from the drawing board to reality.
- Chapter 10 focuses on copyrights, trademarks, and patents to help you keep control of your intellectual property. This is especially helpful if you are a creative person trying to peddle an invention or book.
- Chapter 11 helps you build a winning team.
- Chapter 12 guides you through insurance, taxes, and ethical dilemmas.
- Chapter 13 offers tips and advice if you want to buy an ongoing business. If you want to join the franchise movement, read Chapter 14 first. There are franchisees around every corner in the United States, but not all of them

are happy with their lot. If your goal is to be a happy franchisee, complete a Business Plan for your franchise to see if it lives up to the hype.

- Chapter 15 asks you to gather all of your Action Steps together to form the basis of your Business Plan—your business's launching document.
- Appendix A is a Fast-Start Plan for a smaller business that has an owner with few employees, or where additional work is contracted out and the loss of investment will not sink the ship.
- Appendix B showcases Annie's Business Plan Proposal for a chocolate and candy store located at Sea World.
- Appendix C contains forms to assist you in your entrepreneurial planning: personal budget, Small Business Administration loan forms, and other helpful and time saving documents.

KEY FEATURES

Action Steps

More than 70 Action Steps take you through every phase of a start-up, from the initial dream to developing marketing strategies and finally to building and implementing the completed Business Plan.

Entrepreneurial Vignettes

Throughout the text we present you with case studies full of strategies and real-world applications that provide insight into entrepreneurial minds and ventures. We have modified the stories for simplicity and clarity. Some vignettes are compilations of several case studies, and other vignettes are based on entrepreneurs we have known.

Business Plans

Featured Business Plans include *Yes, We Do Windows: A Fast-Start Plan* (located in Appendix A), applicable for very small businesses requiring minimal capital, and *Annie's* (found in Appendix B), an in-depth Business Plan Proposal for a chocolate store to be located at Sea World.

Entrepreneurial Links

Our featured resources are available online, where each chapter's resources include highlighted books, magazines, journals, Web sites, and associations that will help guide you through the entrepreneurial maze to a wealth of information.

Community and Incredible Resources

Recognizing that the entrepreneurial life can be lonely and scary at times, we encourage you to reach out to available community resources for support, guidance, and direction. From entrepreneurial organizations in Chapter 1 to the Stanford University entrepreneurial podcasts in Chapter 5 to the Angel Capital Association in Chapter 9, we encourage you to seek out like-minded individuals dreaming the same dream as you.

Global Resources

To encourage entrepreneurs to reach beyond the U.S. market, we provide global statistics and resources such *http://www.Alibaba.com* and information on global franchising throughout the text.

Passion

In each chapter we highlight a passionate entrepreneur, one who exhibits his or her passion for products, locations, or markets. Not all entrepreneurs are passionate solely about money; in fact, few are. We highlight passionate entrepreneurs like Melissa Marks Papock, who developed a line of sun-protective clothing for women and children after being diagnosed with melanoma. Another passionate entrepreneur is synthetic biologist Timothy Lu, whose current mission is to destroy antibiotic–resistant bacteria.

NEW AND REVISED FOR THE EIGHTH EDITION

New resources and Web sites have been added throughout the chapters. Approximately 40 percent of the entrepreneurial vignettes, Community Resources, Incredible Resources, Passions, and Global Village highlights have been updated or replaced with new information.

To reflect the changes in our society, we have highlighted social entrepreneurship throughout the book by highlighting social entrepreneurs such as Jock Brandis, who developed a peanut-shelling machine, and groups such as Scientists Without Borders.

Chapters 2 and 3 highlight many new trends and opportunities for entrepreneurs. We feature such hot topics as water shortages, rising natural resource prices, the laptop generation, and artificial body parts. We also explore such large and forceful markets as aging baby boomers and "millennials."

Chapters 4 and 6 expand the use of Claritas data for product positioning and location decisions. We also have expanded the location chapter to include more in-depth information on distribution.

Competitive analysis and strategy have been expanded in Chapter 5, allowing the reader to utilize the research information gained in Chapters 2 through 4 and develop more thorough, competitive plans and strategies to meet his or her Target Customers' needs.

We have discussed the melding of promotion, distribution, and location decisions as the Web's impact is part of almost all entrepreneurial decisions today. To help promote your business on the Web, we have included information on search engine optimization and Web promotion alternatives.

Chapter 8, "Start-Up Concerns and Financial Projections," has been expanded with more thorough pricing strategies.

Chapter 10 has the latest information available on patents, trademarks, and copyrights.

Chapter 12 introduces open-book management.

Chapters 13 and 14 recognize and address the large number of entrepreneurs who decide to purchase an ongoing business or franchise. We have included more in-depth information on franchise brokers, as well as social networking franchising Web sites.

PLANNING FOR SUCCESS

The reason we wrote this book was to provide you with a Business Plan workbook. We supply the steps, and you supply the effort to chart a course for your dream business. Writing a Business Plan sharpens your focus. When you sharpen your focus, you see more clearly. Seeing more clearly raises your confidence. In the big world of small business, as in life, confidence helps you keep going when the going gets tough. There is an adage in the business world: If you fail to plan, then you are planning to fail.

Before you write a Business Plan, you should study the form. From the outside, a Business Plan looks like a stack of paper: for the short plan it is a thin stack; for the long plan, it is a thick stack bound together to look like a book. However thick the stack, your plan will be a document with a beginning, middle, and end and should remain a living and ever-evolving document.

There are two good plans in this book that serve as a guide and many more good plans floating out there in cyberspace for you to peruse, and we lead you to those. We have tried to provide current material, but Internet sites will come and go, and government programs will take new forms. Because of the dynamic nature of business today, we urge you to keep current by checking both the Internet and our Web site for their vast resources at *http://academic. cengage.com/management/ryan*.

Because laws and tax issues are constantly in flux, consult your legal counsel and tax advisors rather than relying only on the material contained in this text or on any Internet site. All forms have been provided as examples only and should not be used without benefit of legal counsel. Our society is highly litigious, and you must be diligent if you want to stay out of court. Never skimp on legal fees!

We hope you can open one of the three entrepreneurial doorways: starting your own business from scratch, franchising, or buying a business. We encourage you to find success along with over 200,000 fellow entrepreneurs who have followed the Action Steps provided. Good luck!

INSTRUCTOR'S RESOURCE MATERIALS

Instructor's Manual and Test Bank

The Instructor's Manual, prepared by Ross Mechum at Virginia Tech University, includes teaching aids such as learning objectives, lecture outlines, and suggestions for guest speakers and class projects. The Test Bank is full of true/ false, multiple-choice, and short-answer questions.

Voxant Newsroom Videos

Video segments from Voxant's Newsroom are located at *http://academic. cengage.com/management/ryan* and include content from major content providers, such as CBS and Reuters. Questions for each video are included in the Instructor's Manual.

PowerPoint Slides

The PowerPoint presentation, prepared by Ross Mechum at Virginia Tech University, is colorful and varied and was designed to hold students' interest and reinforce each chapter's main points. The PowerPoint presentation is available only on the Web site.

Web site

Visit our Web site at *http://academic.cengage.com/management/ryan*, where you will find a complete listing of the "Entrepreneurial Links" and margin definitions found in the text; links on management topics, careers, and time management; and other valuable resources for both the instructor and student.

Acknowledgments

First and foremost we want to thank the thousands of entrepreneurs we have met whose grit, determination, passion, and hard work have served as an inspiration to us. Many of their personal stories have been woven throughout this book. In addition, we have attempted to address many of the problems and issues they have faced. Thus, many of the stories throughout the text are composites of entrepreneurs we have met in our journeys.

A special thank-you goes to founder and president of Caterina's, Josie Reitkerk, for the real-world retailing and franchising experience she shared. Her invaluable insight will save you thousands of dollars as you embark on your venture.

We appreciate John Galati, an entrepreneurial accountant, who reviewed and improved Chapter 8. We also wish to acknowledge the material integrated into the text from the late Ron Knowles, author of the Canadian edition of this book.

We want to extend a thank-you to the reviewers whose insightful comments helped to shape this edition:

Lou Firenze	*Northwood University–Midland*
Mark Zweig	*University of Arkansas–Fayetteville*
Cathy Lewis-Brim	*Warner Southern College*
Carol Carter	*Louisiana State University*
Dennis Pitta	*University of Baltimore*

We also thank the book team: Michele Rhoades, Elizabeth Lowry, and Holly Henjum.

Without the support, patience, and love from Troy and Casey, the journey would not have been as easy or as sweet.

Gail Hiduke
Joe Ryan

chapter 1

Your Great Adventure
Exploring the Right Fit

Action Step 1

Adventure Notebook

If you are a typical entrepreneur, you probably write 90 percent of your important data on the back of an envelope. That might have been okay in the past, but now that you are doing this for real, purchase an organizer and some type of container—a shoebox, a briefcase, a folder—in which to store your information. Organize your data in an **Adventure Notebook,** something with pockets and files, so that you can keep track of small items such as articles, advertisements, and business cards. For some, a notebook computer or PDA may work best for the written parts. Your Adventure Notebook will become the heart of your Business Plan, and it should include:

1. Twelve-month calendar
2. Appointment calendar
3. List of priorities
4. All Action Steps, #5 in front
5. An idea list—continue to add items to this throughout your search
6. A "new eyes" list for keeping track of successful and not-so-successful businesses you come across, plus notes about the reasons for their success or failure
7. A list of possible team members
8. Articles and statistics you gather that serve as supportive data for your Business Plan
9. A list of helpful Web sites
10. A list of experts who might serve as resource people when you need them, such as lawyers, CPAs, bankers, successful businesspeople, and so on
11. A list of potential customers
12. A list of names and phone numbers of contacts for goods and services

Entrepreneur A visionary self-starter who loves the adventure of a new enterprise and is willing to risk his or her own money

Adventure Notebook Dream to reality with collection of Action Steps and information

---

Life is short, and you only go around once. So you want to make sure you are getting what you want, having fun, making money, and being the best person you can be. How do you do that? Some people do it by going into business for themselves. If you are thinking about owning your own business, this book is for you.

Try this line of thought: What do you want to be doing in the year 2015? In 2025? What is the best course of action for you right now? What might be the best business for you? What are your strengths? What do you want out of life? What are your dreams? And most of all, what are your passions? This chapter will help you address these questions, and their answers should stay in the forefront of all the decisions and steps you take in making your dreams come true.

This is the age of the **entrepreneur.** According to the Small Business Administration (SBA), *http://www.sba.gov,* there are 25–35 million small businesses out there. Each year, more than a million new businesses are started. If you are thinking about starting a small business, you are among the 7 million budding entrepreneurs currently dreaming the same dream. Statistics from the Entrepreneurial Research Consortium show that one in three U.S. households has been involved in small business. Most new jobs in the private sector are created by firms with fewer than 20 employees. Yes, it is a great time for an entrepreneur. You could have the time of your life. Come along with us!

BUILDING YOUR ROAD MAP

This book, with its **Action Steps,** can be your personal road map to success in small business. Beginning with Action Step 1, the book will guide you through the bustling marketplace—through trends, Target Customers, and promotions; through shopping malls, spreadsheets, and hushed gray bank buildings; through independent businesses that are for sale; through franchise opportunities— all the way to your own new venture.

Along the way you will meet fascinating people and have fantastic adventures and fun. Furthermore, by completing the Action Steps, you will be drawing a customized road map (Figure 1.1) for your personal and small-business success. The elements for your complete **Business Plan** will emerge to evaluate and illuminate your opportunity for entrepreneurial success. Each Action Step draws you deeper into your business and will light the way to your final, presentable Business Plan.

You will start your journey by taking a careful look at yourself and your skills. What kind of work pleases you? How secure is your present job? How long does it take you to get organized? What internal drive makes you believe that you are an entrepreneur? What do you value? How do you like to work? With whom do you like to work? What customers or clients would you like to work with? What are your dreams? What are your talents? What do you want to accomplish?

Next, you will step back and look at the marketplace. What is hot? What is cooling down? What will last? Where are the long lines forming? What are people buying? What distinguishes the up-and-comers from the

figure **1.1**

Entrepreneurial Road Map

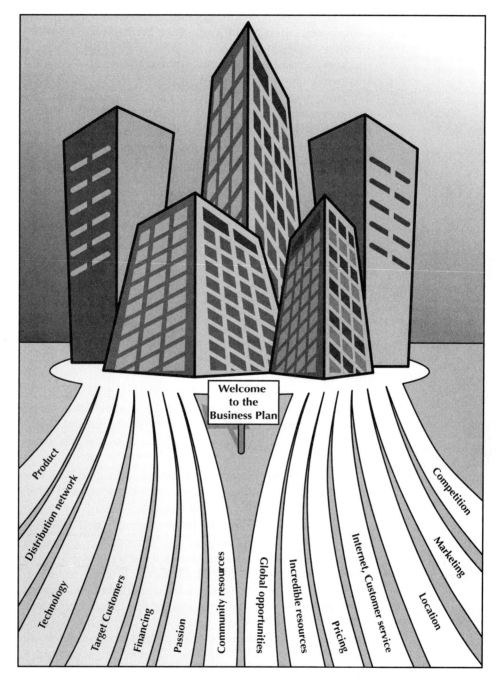

Welcome
to the
Business Plan

Product

Distribution network

Technology

Target Customers

Financing

Passion

Community resources

Global opportunities

Incredible resources

Pricing

Internet, Customer service

Location

Marketing

Competition

down-and-outers? You will **brainstorm** a business that will fit into an industry niche, toss around numbers to get a feel for how they turn into money, and keep having fun.

Then it will be time to profile your Target Customer, assess the competition, figure out clever promotional strategies, and scout locations. By that time, you will know where you are going, and you will feel that you are in control of your own destiny. Next, you will move on to pricing structures,

Action Steps Activities to prepare you to write a Business Plan

Business Plan A working blueprint outlining finances and direction for a new start-up or expansion

Brainstorm Unlock your brain to possibilities

cash-flow statements, distribution strategies, and building a winning team. By the time you reach Chapter 15, you will have gathered enough material to write a complete Business Plan for showcasing your business to the world—that is, to bankers, vendors, lenders, venture capitalists, credit managers, key employees, family, and friends. Your finished plan will be a working and ever-evolving blueprint for your business. It will provide a walk-through of your industry, generate excitement in potential investors, demonstrate your competence as a thoughtful planner, and underline the reasons customers will clamor for your product or service. Your plan will also serve as a means of channeling your creative energies.

Let us think about that for a moment. One reason you are reading this book is that you are creative. You like to build, to pull things together, to plant seeds and watch things grow, to develop projects, to produce. When your mind is racing, you probably come up with more ideas than you can process. That is when you need a plan to help keep your entrepreneurial energies on track while the creative steam rises. Perhaps you have always dreamed of working for yourself and being your own boss. Well, you can realize that dream—*if you are prepared.*

Preparing yourself takes time, energy, and the willingness to reach out to the larger business community within which you will operate. Once you begin, and once you possess basic knowledge about your industry and markets, you can reach out to entrepreneurs, associations, inventors' forums, and Web site communities. Throughout the text, we highlight many Community Resources, which are only the tip of the iceberg. Show your tenacity and search out the best sources for yourself and your business. You will be glad you did.

We hope to kick-start our readers into thinking internationally by highlighting global information within the Global Village boxes. The opportunities are limitless, yet few entrepreneurs take the global path. Be a pioneer in your industry or market, and reach out to over 6 billion people who live outside the United States.

Incredible Resource boxes focus on individual Web sites, books, associations, and programs that provide excellent sources of information and assistance usually available at no or low cost.

More than anything, we believe strongly that without passion, you will not succeed. Ten- to fourteen-hour workdays, no vacations, stress, tension, employee problems, misplaced cash, loan turndowns, and frustrations beyond belief will be too much to handle unless you are passionate about your business. Throughout the text, we have highlighted entrepreneurs who are passionate about their products and services, employees, markets, or ideas and dreams. Read their stories and search your soul. Believe in yourself and your passions, because those beliefs will lead you to achieve entrepreneurial success. Hadzima's following article highlights the importance of passion for entrepreneurs.

INTERNET LINKS

The links in this book hook you into the Internet, your key to keeping up with what is happening in business and the world. All of the links included in our text are listed on our Web page at *http://academic.cengage.com/management/ryan*. The Internet links you to business and general publications, statistics, associations, and other resources available and continually updated through our home page. Throughout the text, we will highlight many useful sites.

Pinpointing That Critical Entrepreneurial Spark

So you want to start a company. Do you think you are an entrepreneur?

Do you have a passion to succeed?

Entrepreneurs are driven to succeed. They will figure out ways to go over, under, around, or through obstacles to reach their goal. Entrepreneurs leave the impression that they are going to succeed, that their train is leaving the station and they will be on it, one way or another.

Ask yourself whether you are leaving your current position because of something there, or because you have the passion to do something innovative.

Can you focus on success and set clear goals and accomplish them?

Because nothing succeeds like success, are you capable of sacrificing the perfect situation to generate some near-term successes that you can leverage?

Entrepreneurs usually are not distracted by details that are not important to achieving the task at hand. That is usually the opposite of what it takes to succeed in a larger, more rigid organization. Warning: Those who have this trait should make sure they get someone working with them who will worry about the details.

Can you deal with STRESS?

Start-ups can be very stressful. One of my start-up clients is a company founded by a former Digital employee and a former Data General employee, both in their 40s. Each held very responsible positions with their prior employers, and both worked long hours. They admit that they did not really understand stress until they started their own company. "At DEC, I never woke up in the middle of the night in a sweat, unable to get back to sleep," says one entrepreneur.

Not all founders face that level of stress, but the question is this: Are you ready for stress and, perhaps more important, are your spouse and children ready?

A roller coaster metaphor is appropriate for several reasons. A roller coaster provides highs and lows. Are you capable of managing such extremes? The ups and downs of a roller coaster usually come in rapid succession. Start-ups can also face rapid changes, and you have to be ready for them.

Are roller coasters risky? They are thrilling, perhaps, but not commonly thought of as risky. Jumping out of an airplane without a parachute—now that is risky!

Although people often say that entrepreneurs are risk takers, most entrepreneurs do not jump out of airplanes without knowing what they are doing. While they are not afraid to undertake projects that might fail, they also work to minimize risk.

Are you an innovator?

Entrepreneurs look at problems and craft new ways of doing things. Jonathan Harber was a cofounder of Digital Video Applications (DiVA), a company that developed and marketed digital video editing software for the Macintosh. At a seminar series organized for entrepreneurs at MIT, Harber told how he set a "zero budget" marketing policy for DiVA. "If it cost money, we wouldn't do it," he said proudly.

The result? DiVA managed to attend trade shows by appearing at other companies' booths. DiVA also got Ben & Jerry's to beta test DiVA's product and donate ice cream bars as a promotion for DiVA at the trade shows. A larger corporation using traditional approaches to

(continued)

(continued)

marketing would probably have spent $100,000—without achieving the same impact.

Can you build a team?

Entrepreneurs often think and act differently, but the most successful ones are not loners. MIT Sloan Professor Ed Roberts in his book *Entrepreneurs in High Technology* (Oxford Press) reports on research that shows that entrepreneurial teams of three or more have a higher probability of success.

Are you capable of identifying your strengths and weaknesses? Are you capable of finding and motivating people with complementary skills?

Are you a control freak?

Many people leave larger companies because they want to be their own boss. The simple fact is that no one is *really* his or her own boss. An entrepreneur must answer to many people, including customers, investors, and employees. Entrepreneurs, however, probably will have more control over their situation than they would in a larger company, but they should not look to control for the sake of controlling. Ask yourself, "Am I a control freak?" If so, ask whether you would like to work with, and for, somebody like you.

If you have answered these questions to your satisfaction, and have not been dissuaded from starting a new venture, here are five homework assignments:

1. Hang out with people interested in entrepreneurial ventures. For example, attend the MIT Enterprise Forum, the WPI Forum at Worcester Polytech, and other similar groups.
2. Read extensively about entrepreneurial efforts in newspapers.
3. Join an entrepreneurial network. Talk to people. Get on mailing lists from the big accounting firms, law firms, and so on.
4. Read biographies, not only of today's entrepreneurs but also of those who have innovated in the past. Ask yourself what traits the person had that enabled him or her to succeed. How did the person handle failure?
5. Above all, constantly plumb your soul and consider what motivates you to start and grow a company.

DISCLAIMER: This column is designed to give the reader an overview of a topic and is not intended to constitute legal advice as to any particular fact situation. In addition, laws and their interpretations change over time, and the contents of this column may not reflect these changes. The reader is advised to consult competent legal counsel as to his or her particular situation.

By Joseph G. Hadzima, Jr., Senior Lecturer, MIT Sloan School of Management, Chair MIT Enterprise Forum, Inc., Managing Director, Main Street Partners LLC. Article originally appeared in the "Starting Up" column of the *Boston Business Journal*.

Source: *http://enterpriseforum.mit.edu/mindshare/startingup/print/entrepreneurial-spark.html* (Accessed January 10, 2008). Copyright 1994, *Boston Business Journal*.

However, remember that the Internet's resources are limited only by the amount of time you have available to look for them.

As you read through this book and work through the Action Steps that lead you to a Business Plan, you will access a wealth of information, ask questions of experts, communicate with fellow entrepreneurs, and discover marketing and financial resources on the Internet. For example, if you had typed in the Internet address *http://www.sba.gov*, you would have reached the home page of the SBA, from which you could access their basic sample Business Plan outline

(Figure 1.2). If you type in an address and come up empty—Web sites on the Internet come and go at warp speed—persevere and you will find your desired site or one that replaced it.

Web Link Starting Points

- *http://www.eventuring.com*
- *http://www.microsoft.com/smallbusiness/hub.mspx*
- *http://www.brint.com*
- *http://www.entrepreneurs.about.com*
- *http://www.allbusiness.com*
- *http://www.inc.com*
- *http://www.fastcompany.com*
- *http://www.nfib.com*
- *http://www.smartbiz.com*

We will be linking to the Internet as we move through the phases of the book, addressing personal assessment, trends, location, number crunching, legal issues, and writing a plan. For example, if you would like to review sample Business Plans now, turn to the last chapter and the appendices in this book. Or, you could link to the Internet at *http://www.businessplans.org* or *http://www.bplans.com*. The Web offers numerous examples—some free, some for sale—of how to blueprint your business. This book shows you how to sharpen your vision so that you can write the Business Plan you need to succeed in a fast-changing world. As you follow the Action Steps, you will be building your own personal Business Plan for your great adventure.

— figure **1.2**

Basic Business Plan Outline

SBA Elements of a Business Plan
Agenda should include an executive summary, supporting documents, and financial projections. Although there is no single formula for developing a business plan, some elements are common to all business plans. They are summarized in the following outline:

1. **Cover sheet**
2. **Statement of purpose**
3. **Table of contents**

I. The Business
   A. Description of business
   B. Marketing
   C. Competition
   D. Operating procedures
   E. Personnel
   F. Business insurance

II. Financial Data
   A. Loan applications
   B. Capital equipment and supply list
   C. Balance sheet
   D. Break even analysis
   E. Pro-forma income projections (profit and loss statements)

   F. Three-year summary
   G. Detail by month, first year
   H. Detail by quarters, second and third years
   I. Assumptions upon which projections were based
   J. Pro-forma cash flow

III. Supporting Documents
   A. Tax returns of principals for the last three years and personal financial statements (all banks have these forms)
   B. For franchised businesses, a copy of franchise contract and all supporting documents provided by the franchisor
   C. Copy of proposed lease or purchase agreement for building space
   D. Copy of licenses and other legal documents
   E. Copy of resumes of all principals
   F. Copies of letters of intent from suppliers

Sample Plans
One of the best ways to learn about writing a business plan is to study the plans of established businesses in your industry.

For more information, see *http://www.sba.gov/smallbusinessplanner/plan/writeabusinessplan/SERV_WRRITINGBUSPLAN.html* (Accessed January 10, 2008).

Knocking at the Entrepreneurial Doors

There are three doorways to small-business ownership. Doorway 1 is buying an ongoing business: You search, locate a business that you like, and buy it. Sounds pretty easy, doesn't it? A business broker will make it sound even easier, so beware!

Doorway 2 is buying a franchise: You find a logo you like—one with national visibility—and buy it. In exchange for your money, the franchisor may or may not supply you with inventory, advice, training, buying power, a shorter learning curve, and a product or service that is well known in the marketplace. Sounds pretty easy, doesn't it? A slick franchisor will make it sound even easier. In addition to franchising, many individuals will reach out and become part of the vast number of people who are part of multilevel marketing business opportunities.

Doorway 3, our favorite, is starting a new business, one that is compatible with your interests, skills, and passions that is also backed up by careful research that demonstrates strong customer need and willingness to purchase. Entering the world of small business by any of these doorways demands a carefully designed Business Plan—words and numbers written out on paper that guide you through the gaps, competition, bureaucracies, products, and services. The Action Steps presented in this book will provide you with the necessary elements to complete a Business Plan. We hope to show you how to have fun as an entrepreneur as you collect the essential pieces for your plan.

What about These Three Doorways?

More than two thirds of all entrepreneurs enter the world of small business by buying an existing business or investing in a franchise operation. When these people have gained some business experience, many of them decide to start a totally new business from scratch. Few entrepreneurs are happy with just one business. They start up, they sell, and they start up again.

No matter which doorway you choose, you will need a Business Plan. If you buy an ongoing business, you may inherit the seller's Business Plan. However, it is advisable to write one of your own. Ask the seller, again and again if necessary, for the data you need to write your own plan before you finalize the sale. Do not take any figures for fact: Do your own research. Check out the seller's claims of huge potential profits and endless goodwill before you commit to a purchase.

If you invest in a franchise, you will be buying a Business Plan from the franchisor. But until you see it, you will not know for certain what additional research you will need to conduct to determine how the franchise will fit into your particular community. If you do not understand the franchisor's plan, ask questions; and by all means, write your own plan addressing the needs of your particular customers, community, and marketplace. Writing a Business Plan is a lot cheaper than plunking down money on a franchise that may not be successful. If you start your own business through any of the three doorways, a Business Plan is an absolute must. That plan stands between you and success or failure.

If you want to quickly explore the options of franchising, buying a business, and multilevel sales, read Chapters 13 and 14 now.

The world is changing, and you must assess the changes and act accordingly. You want to survive. You want to have fun. You want your life to have

incredibleresource

SBA Free Online Courses

Knowledge is power. Improve your ability to compete by participating in one or more of the short, self-paced courses and workshops listed below. Many of these courses are also available in Spanish. Available courses, identified by topic, are self-paced and each should take about 30 minutes to complete. Most of the courses require a brief online registration.

Starting a Business

1. Small Business Primer: Guide to Starting a Business
2. My Own Business (A free course) *http://app1.sba.gov/sbtn/registration/index.cfm?CourseId=6*
3. Starting Your Small Business
4. Business Plan Workshops
5. Identify Your Target Market
6. How to Start a Business on a Shoestring Budget
   Trump University

Business Planning

1. The Beginning: Developing a Successful Business Plan
2. How to Write a Business Plan
   Trump University
3. Business Plan Workshops
4. Creating a Strategic Plan
5. Strategic Planning & Execution
   PA SBDC – Kutztown University
6. Developing a Business Plan (en español)
   PA SBDC – Kutztown University
7. My Own Business (A free course with a planning section)

Business Management

1. Managing the Digital Enterprise
2. Developing a Successful Business Plan
3. Business Plan Workshops
4. Maintaining an Agile Company
   South-West Texas SBDC
5. Smart Steps for Managing Business Credit
   Dun & Bradstreet

Financing & Accounting

1. How to Find Start-up Funding
   Trump University
2. Assessing Financial Needs
   South-West Texas SBDC
3. Cash Flow
4. Accounting 101: The Fundamentals
   PA SBDC – Kutztown University

Marketing & Advertising

1. Building Your Brand
2. Marketing for Small Business
   Maine SBDC
3. E-Mail Marketing
4. Marketing 101: The Fundamentals
   PA SBDC – Kutztown University
5. Conduct a Marketing Analysis
   PA SBDC – Kutztown University

Government Contracting

1. Guide to Government Contracts
2. INSIGHT: Guide to the 8(a) Business Development Program

Risk Management & Cyber Security

1. Computer Security

E-commerce

1. Building Your Web site
   South-West Texas SBDC
2. Managing the Digital Enterprise

International Trade

1. Breaking into the Trade Game
2. A Primer on Exporting
3. International Business Opportunities

Federal Tax Training

1. Understanding Taxes
2. Tax & Accounting Basics
3. Small Business Tax Center

Small Business Retirement

1. Retirement Planning

Source: *http://www.sba.gov/services/training/onlinecourses/index.html* (Accessed January 10, 2008).

meaning. You want substance and honesty and security and success. So, to decide which road to take, begin your research and keep your eyes and ears wide open.

Personal financial security obtained by employment in large companies continues to wane. Many people are recognizing that self-reliance through one of the three doorways described often provides the most secure and rewarding career option. Our text is written to help you take control of your business and personal life and prepare you to enter one of the three doorways.

THE AGE OF THE ENTREPRENEUR

If the business world is changing faster and faster—revving up like a high-speed motor—what do you do? If life is not what you imagined it would be when you were in high school, what do you do? If the big firm you targeted as your dream employer is busy downsizing, if the job you trained for is now obsolete, if the position you now have is spoiled by office politics—what do you do?

If you have a great idea for a product but your employer does not believe in it, what do you do? If you have found a great location for a small, unique restaurant on your last vacation to Sun Valley, what do you do? If you saw a great product on your trip to Hungary and think it would sell well in Cedar Falls, Iowa, what do you do?

Get up to speed. Upgrade your computer. Surf the Internet for opportunities. Figure out who you are and what you want from life. Think with your pencil and spreadsheets while you figure out how much you are willing to pay for the "good life." How much time are you willing to spend? How much money? How much sweat? How much risk can you handle?

REV UP

Small companies, those with fewer than 100 employees, employ more than half of the private-sector workers in the United States. New start-ups create new jobs, and these jobs are created by an absolutely unique partnership—the marriage of money, risk, and hard work. The money comes from savings, friends, family, credit cards, second mortgages, bank loans, venture capitalists, and angels. Hard work, faith, and passion come from the driving force of the entrepreneur and from those who trust the entrepreneur. Entrepreneurship should grow and blossom with the fields—biotechnology, nanotechnology, surveillance technology, organic agriculture, green technology, and others—so ripe and ready for the harvest. Plant early. You are in the Age of the Entrepreneur and age is no barrier.

Ready to Start?

First, you need to become organized, starting with your Adventure Notebook in Action Step 1. Some people believe organization stifles creativity. Jan Wilkes was like that until she saw the value of using her Adventure Notebook in developing a new Internet travel business—Romantic California Escapes.

Romantic California Escapes—From Adventure Notebook to Internet Travel Business

During her 5 years working as a travel agent for three different travel agencies, Jan kept a notebook, listing what seemed to be important elements of the travel business, her contacts, news and magazine articles, ideas, competitors' ads, websites, and business cards. Her Internet guru friend, Pat Perk, tired of working for other people, enthusiastically agreed to be her partner in starting up a new company of their own.

After reviewing her notes, Jan looked for a gap in the marketplace. She realized that many of her clients were looking for short breakaway escapes. With both husband and wife working full-time, week-long escapes were more and more difficult for her clients. Therefore, Pat suggested to her partner that they tap into the Internet by focusing on using Web sites that offered weekend discounts on cars, hotels, and airfares within California. After extensive research, Jan and Pat repackaged these deals into great California weekend escapes. By adding extras such as dinners, flowers, theater tickets, and limousine services, Romantic California Escapes emerged. The extras added value to the trips and removed all the planning hassles that busy couples today have little time or inclination for.

Next, Jan and Pat had to determine how to reach their market. They were fortunate in that Jan had retained most of her past clients' phone numbers and addresses. She and Pat sent postcards announcing their new online Internet service and requested all to come online and provide their e-mail addresses for a chance to win a wonderfully romantic trip to Big Sur's Post Ranch Inn, one of the most exclusive private resorts in California. Surprisingly, 30 percent responded. Once online, respondents were asked to fill out detailed questionnaires about their travel desires for weekend escapes.

Every Tuesday at noon, Romantic Escapes posted their weekend escapes. Tuesday through Friday, Jan and Pat were busy booking trips. Within 6 months, they were profitable, and, fortunately, customers quickly became repeat customers. Sales rapidly increased due to word of mouth and excellent publicity through a travel column that highlighted romantic rendezvous. Romance was in the air, and money was in the bank for Pat and Jan.

Why Do You Want to Be an Entrepreneur?

For some, becoming an entrepreneur is a lifelong dream; for others, it is buying a job. It is the excitement of an unlimited income or a way to pay the bills. It is the dream of never having a boss or the dream of being the boss. It is the desire to leave a legacy, the joy of producing the perfect product, the thrill of developing a new service. Becoming an entrepreneur is manifesting the desire to live out your dreams and passions.

One entrepreneur opened her retail store to keep an eye on her three teenagers. Fifteen years later, she owns six stores. One of her former teenagers, now 30, manages several stores; another, now 28, manages the chain's finances and two new retail outlets. She has built not only a chain of stores but also a legacy for her children. Not willing to stop at this point, she and her daughter are already designing several new store concepts.

Action Step 2

Why Do I Want to Be an Entrepreneur?

1. In your Adventure Notebook, make a list of all the reasons why you want to become an entrepreneur.

2. Assess how those reasons above will fit your desired personal, family, financial, and professional lifestyles and your social, spiritual, and ego needs.

3. Spend a few minutes now and many, *many* hours throughout the next few months reviewing how various businesses would fit into your prioritized list. What fits? What does not?

4. Review your current job situation. Are you happy? Are you excited about going to work each day? Is there something else you would rather be doing?

5. If money were no object, what would you do?

6. Make a list of all the reasons you do not want to become an entrepreneur. Review the list. What can you do to minimize these issues? When you honestly review the advantages and disadvantages of being an entrepreneur, you will see that they often are flip sides of each other. Many people want to become entrepreneurs to be their own boss and find out they now have many bosses—employees, customers, suppliers, and investors.

Be sure to look realistically at your lists and keep refining them as you seek fulfillment of your passions and dreams. As you explore various businesses, continue to return to your answers, and focus on whether your selected business ideas will meet your personal goals as well as your entrepreneurial focus and passion.

Another entrepreneur wanted to improve children's lives. He researched businesses that served children and located and purchased an educational tutoring franchise. Now with three franchise stores, his business and profits have grown and now allow him to provide free scholarships for needy students.

Complete Action Step 2 to discover your entrepreneurial motives. Your job situation can change quickly; your life situation may change, or your job and personal desires may change—like Sally Honeycutt Binson's did.

Marketer to Writer

When she turned 30, Sally Honeycutt Binson took a good look at her life. Sally lived in Charleston, South Carolina; had a fine job as a marketing director of a restaurant chain; and earned a good salary. Her home—sunny with a view of the water—was wonderful. But Sally paid a price for the "good life" with endless meetings, squabbles with her boss, and lots of air miles.

To plot her future, Sally drew a mind map (Figure 1.3). When she put herself inside a bubble in the center of the page, she did not get anywhere. When she added "writing" inside a bubble, she found a new career: freelance writer. Sally had a degree in English literature and read constantly. Knowing she wanted to write full-time eventually, Sally created a home office and began to write. Her first effort was rejected by agents and publishers. Sally then researched her local bookstore and was struck by how large the romance, mystery, and science-fiction sections were. Using her marketing background, she took bookstore managers to lunch and asked: What was selling? What did readers want? What did editors want? Which books received the most promotion? She also spent many hours researching books and reviews on Amazon.com and Powells.com.

Armed with information about book sales and target readers, Sally enrolled in a writing course at her local community college. The instructor was a published author. With his guidance, Sally studied the mystery genre.

Before she began writing her second book, Sally checked out Web sites for anything related to mystery. At http://www.MysteryNet.com she found a homepage for mysteries with information on writing, selling, readers' groups, and webzines. Sally joined two organizations: Mystery Writers of America and Sisters in Crime. A contact from Sisters in Crime connected Sally to several literary agents.

A Book Is a Product

Before she developed her product, she engaged in intensive research and development (R&D) by analyzing ten mystery novels. Using the analytical techniques she learned in her writing class, Sally discovered the secret of mystery writing: conceal and then reveal. Following her instructor's advice, the setting of her first mystery was a location Sally was familiar with: an island off the coast of South Carolina. Because she could relate easily to her own gender's thinking patterns, Sally's main characters were female: the sleuth, the victim, and the killer.

In one year, Sally had a manuscript. Although her agent connections through Sisters in Crime did not work out, Sally did find an agent through the Internet and mailed a plot outline and the first three chapters. The agent sold the book to a publisher. And when the royalty checks were enough to provide her with 6 months' financial security, Sally tendered her resignation. By then, her second book was underway: Murder on Amelia Island.

— figure **1.3**

Mind Map for Mystery Writer Sally Honeycutt Binson

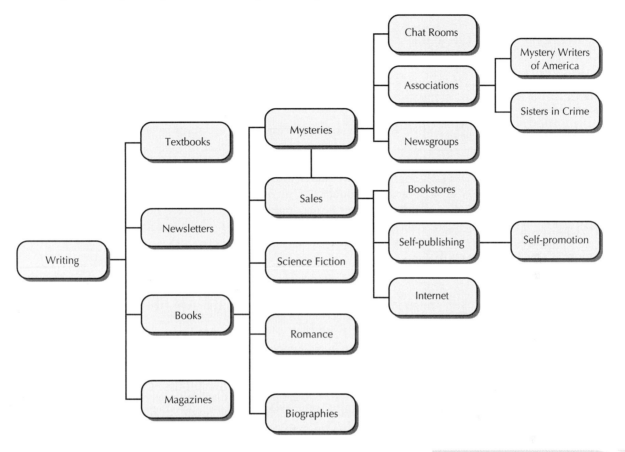

WHAT IS YOUR CURRENT FAMILY AND FINANCIAL PICTURE?

Action Step 3 will help you assess your current situation as you prepare for the future. Is your family dreaming the same dream? If so, great. If not, ask what they are willing to do to help. An essential element to achieving a successful entrepreneurial lifestyle is family support. Spend a great deal of time understanding the demands on both you and your family from both time and financial standpoints.

Review your current financial picture. Complete the personal financial statement and budget in Appendix C. Sit down with your family and review how you can reduce expenses. For many, short-term financial pain is worth long-term gain; for others, it is not. Before leaping into the new venture, decide what you and your family are willing to sacrifice.

Meeting with a professional financial planner may also be of help to you and your family. Fee-only planners will meet with you to discuss your situation without the pressure to purchase financial products. In addition, a planning meeting with your accountant may also prove very helpful, as some businesses can be structured to provide tax breaks.

A major impediment to entrepreneurship is the ability to obtain affordable health insurance for you and your family. This issue should not be taken

Action Step 3

Review Your Financial and Family Picture

Sit down with your family to discuss how starting your own business may affect the family's financial future. Complete the Personal Financial Statement and Personal Budget, which can be found in Appendix C. You will need these figures later to determine your financial needs and also to assess the financial contribution you will be able to make to your business.

After completing the above, consider the following:

1. Can I live on less? How much less?
2. What can I cut from my budget? Go through each line item in the budget to assess where you can cut expenses.

(continued)

Action Step 3

(continued)

3. How long can I continue to cut my budget before I feel too deprived? How long before my family feels deprived?
4. Your personal financial statement will show your assets and liabilities. Which of your assets can you access easily, and what amount of your net worth (assets minus liabilities) are you willing to put at risk?
5. Talk with your family about the time and money sacrifices that may be involved in developing your new venture.
6. Meet with a fee-only financial planner and your accountant to discuss your unique financial issues.

A business is a living, breathing entity, and it takes time for the golden egg to hatch. Be prepared to wait awhile. The following Web sites will assist you in preparing budgets and will answer many questions about financial planning issues.

http://www.finance.cch.com

http://www.kiplinger.com

http://financialplan.about.com

lightly and should be addressed *before* you take the leap. Check out COBRA insurance from your current employer, your spouse's insurance, associations' insurance offerings, and private health insurance through an HMO or PPO. Also, look into policies with lower rates that provide catastrophic coverage. Depending on your current health and that of your family members, obtaining insurance may be very difficult and or exorbitantly expensive. Some entrepreneurs have found that working 20 hours a week at one of the few firms that provide insurance to part-time employees is one alternative. You must be willing to be creative and work hard on this important area to protect yourself and your family.

Believing in your dream opens your eyes to endless sacrifices and possibilities. Living at home for an extra year to save cash, working a part-time job to support your fledgling business, or moving to a less-expensive area of the country all become realistic options if you believe in your own dream. Amilya Antonetti, founder of Soapworks, and her husband were willing to leave their jobs, sell their home, and risk everything for their dream of providing hypoallergenic, nontoxic cleaning products. What are you willing to give up for your dream?

WHAT DOES IT TAKE TO BE AN ENTREPRENEUR?

To find out if you have what it takes to make it in small business, first profile yourself as an entrepreneur in Action Step 4, and complete the questionnaire in Table 1.1. You will not be a perfect fit on any of the questionnaires, because there is no such thing. On the SBA's Web site, at *http://www.sba.gov/assessmenttool/index.html*, an additional entrepreneurial test can be found, and many others like it can also be found on the Internet. These assessment tools will bring up many issues that you should consider before entering the world of entrepreneurship. Share your responses and concerns with those who know you well and want the best for you.

Entrepreneurship requires persistence, hard work, commitment, reliability, decisiveness, risk, and failure management. As an entrepreneur, your challenges will include balancing family and work, maintaining focus, reaching emotional and monetary goals, and dealing with the initial exhaustion and stress inherent in almost any entrepreneurial venture.

In addition to a strong work ethic and the ability to handle stress, an entrepreneur must possess basic business skills. Review Table 1.2 to determine where your strengths and weaknesses lie in the areas of sales, marketing, financial planning, and so on. If you find yourself questioning your abilities in any one area, search out college classes, books, online seminars, and mentors to fill your skill gaps before making the entrepreneurial leap. Also, the Key Points in the Another View feature at the end of the chapter explores the various roles you will play as an entrepreneur.

Exploring your passions and needs in this first chapter starts you on the Business Plan journey. Complete the Action Steps throughout the text, and you will benefit more from this book, because you mentally immerse yourself in a new and exciting venture. Even if you do not end up following through with your Business Plan, you will have learned the process. One never knows when the entrepreneurial passion will start to burn, and when it does, you will already know the process and be able to follow your dream through with a Business Plan. Entrepreneurship is not for everyone, and even if it is for you, you will need help along the way. Keep your mind open and your pencil sharp. The opportunities are unlimited.

—————————————————————————— table **1.1**

25 Questions to Answer to See if You Have What It Takes to Be an Entrepreneur

So you want to start a business on your own, be your own person, be an entrepreneur. To find out if you are cut out for all that, answer the following 25 questions. If you really have what it takes, you should be able to answer yes to most of the following questions.

1. When you have been disappointed, have you dealt with it and come back with a positive state of mind?
2. Do you like to be the center of attention and sell yourself or the business you are in?
3. Is it easy for you to be organized?
4. Do you know how to take control of your life and be disciplined?
5. Are you a risk taker?
6. Do you have a vivid imagination and know how to express your creative side?
7. Are you able to take what seems like a detriment and turn it into an opportunity?
8. Are you courageous and patient?
9. Is your family in a position to cope with the lack of freedom you will experience when you start your new business?
10. Do you know how to fight for what you believe in?
11. Do you like people?
12. Have you ever had any management experience?
13. Do you dread routine?
14. Are you reliable and self-confident?
15. Do you ignore the judgment of others when you really believe in someone or something?
16. Do you have a knack for influencing others?
17. Do others describe you as an enthusiastic person, full of life?
18. Do you like the idea of working alone most of the time?
19. Do you enjoy being on the telephone and talking to strangers?
20. Do you wake up early in the morning with a positive attitude?
21. Is your financial situation stable? (You should have enough money to get by for at least a year before you venture out on your own.)
22. Have you done your homework and studied all materials that cover the business you are going to start?
23. Do you know how to laugh at yourself?
24. Is it easy to control your temper with others?
25. Do you get bored easily?

If these are easy questions, you are a born entrepreneur!

Source: *http://www.smartbiz.com* (Accessed April 4, 2001).

Action Step 4

Self-Assessment

Complete the questionnaires in Table 1.1 and Table 1.2. With your entrepreneurial juices flowing, go online to the following pages and complete their assessments: *http://app1.sba.gov/sbat/index.cfm?Tool=4* (Small Business Readiness Assessment Tool), *http://www.sric-bi.com/VALS/presurvey.shtml* (psychographic profiling), and *http.www.authentichappiness.sas.upenn.edu.Default.aspx* (VIA Signature Strength questionnaire). From the above questionnaires and tests, you should be able to answer the following questions:

1. What do you love to do?
2. What skills have you acquired through the years?
3. What are you good at doing?
4. What makes you happiest?
5. What type of businesses might offer you the fulfillment you desire?
6. What personality traits will help you in your own business?
7. What personality traits might hinder you in your own business?
8. What do you value?
9. What are your financial dreams?
10. What are your passions?

In Action Step 5, you will be pulling together all your information. Add new information to the answers whenever it occurs to you. Keep your information current and continue to refine your answers as you continue to work on your Business Plan and talk to others.

"Successful founders can be gregarious or taciturn, analytical or intuitive, risk averse or thrill seeking," according to Amar Bhide (Harvard School of Business), who also believes that there is no "ideal" entrepreneurial personality.

The entrepreneur who succeeds is one who works incredibly hard. But Jeff Bezos has joked in the case of Amazon.com's success, "half of it was timing, half of it was luck, and the rest of it was brains. The fact of the matter is, the odds are stacked against any start-up. Heavily so. There's a huge amount of luck and timing involved."

Entrepreneurial Success

Starting a business allows you to design your own successful lifestyle. Action Step 5 asks you to design your "entrepreneurial lifestyle." Warren Bennis

Action Step 5

"Inc. Yourself"

Mind map your way to a picture (see Figure 1.3) of what you want you to become, your product—yourself. There is no such thing as a wrong idea or a wrong direction. So far you have looked at why you want to be an entrepreneur and what success means to you, and you have reviewed your skills, accomplishments, and passions. It is now time for you to mind map the life *you* want.

1. Review your answers to Action Steps 2 through 4 and define success for yourself by reviewing the checklist below and also add any additional items that signify success to you.

Success Checklist

A. Do you measure success in dollars? If so, how many?
B. Do you measure success in other ways?

- Being able to enjoy a certain lifestyle
- Dealing with friendly customers who appreciate your service
- Power, recognition, and/or fame
- Being able to live and work where you want
- Providing employment and training for others
- Being the best business in your area
- Having time to enjoy your children and hobbies
- Participating in teamwork
- Building a legacy
- Early retirement
- Making people's lives safer and better
- Helping others directly or indirectly

2. Draw a circle in the middle of a piece of paper. Write your name inside the circle. Close your eyes for a few minutes, and allow your imagination to take over. Think of yourself as a product. In 5 to 10 years, where and what do you want

(continued)

table 1.2

Strengths and Weaknesses Skill Checklist

The chart below will help you identify your strengths and weaknesses and will give you a better idea of whether you are ready to become a small-business owner. Examine each of the skills areas listed in the chart. Ask yourself whether you possess some or all of the skills listed. Rate your skills in each area by circling the appropriate number, using a scale of 1 through 5; use 1 for low, 2 for between low and medium, 3 for medium, 4 for between medium and high, and 5 for high.

Skills		Rating	
	Low	Medium	High
Sales • pricing • buying • sales planning • negotiating • direct selling to buyers • customer service follow-up • managing other sales reps • tracking competitors	1	2 3	4 5
Marketing • advertising/promotion/public relations • annual marketing plans • media planning and buying • advertising copy writing • marketing strategies • distribution-channel planning • pricing • packaging	1	2 3	4 5
Financial Planning • cash-flow planning • monthly financials • bank relationships • management of credit lines	1	2 3	4 5
Accounting • bookkeeping • billing, payables, receivables • monthly profit and loss statements/ balance sheets • quarterly/annual tax preparation	1	2 3	4 5
Administrative • scheduling • payroll handling • benefits administration	1	2 3	4 5
Personnel Management • hiring employees • firing employees • motivating employees • general management skills	1	2 3	4 5
Personal Business Skills • oral presentation skills • written communication skills • computer skills • word-processing skills • fax and e-mail experience • organizational skills	1	2 3	4 5

(continued)

———————————————————————— table **1.2**

Strengths and Weaknesses Skill Checklist (*continued*)

Intangibles					
• ability to work long and hard					
• ability to manage risk and stress					
• family support	1	2	3	4	5
• ability to deal with failure					
• ability to work alone					
• ability to work with and manage others					
Total					

After rating yourself in each area, total up the numbers and apply the following rating scale:
- If your total is less than 20 points, you should reconsider whether owning a business is the right step for you.
- If your total is between 20 and 25, you are on the verge of being ready, but you may be wise to spend some time strengthening some of your weaker areas.
- If your total is above 25, you are ready to start a new business.

Source: Reproduced with permission from CCH Business Owner's Toolkit™, *http://www.toolkit.cch.com*, published and copyrighted by CCH Tax & Accounting.

Action Step 5

(continued)

to be? What do you want your product to be? What do you want—personally, socially, spiritually, financially, and as a lifestyle—and what are your material wants and needs? You can predict your future as well as anyone else; all you need to do is mesh the information with your imagination and go for it! Your final mind map should represent your desired entrepreneurial and personal lifestyle.

and Patricia Ward Biederman, authors of *Organizing Genius* (Perseus Books, 1997), developed a four-question test aimed at anyone seeking success. The questions are:

1. Do you know the difference between what you want and what you are good at?
2. Do you know what drives you and what gives you satisfaction?
3. Do you know what your values and priorities are, what your organization's values and priorities are, and can you identify the differences between the two?
4. Having measured the differences between what you want and what you are able to do, between what drives you and what satisfies you, and between your values and those of your organization, are you able to overcome those differences?

Source: Fast Company, *http://www.fastcompany.com/magazine/09/one.html* (Accessed January 8, 2008).

Bennis concludes that the key to success is identifying talents unique to you and then finding the right arena in which to use them.

Success is personal and subjective, whereas income and return on investments are measurable. Success wears many faces. You need to think about this as you start your adventure, because being an entrepreneur is the best chance you will have at defining personal and professional success. Action Step 5, and a review of the following Killer and Success Factors for Entrepreneurs, will help you.

The Ten Killer Factors for Entrepreneurs

1. **Weak personality:** The lack of psychological or emotional strength at the head of a company leads to failure 50 percent of the time. If company founders cannot cope with the many challenges they must confront, and if they have private problems as well, a collapse is predetermined.
2. **The loner syndrome:** Loners have a difficult life. Because they don't discuss their problems with colleagues or professionals, they lose that perspective and critical distance from their projects. They flounder with closed eyes into failure.

3. **Nebulous business ideas:** Losers don't know how to make their ideas work. They do not familiarize themselves with the market and don't know their competition or their potential customers.

4. **No plan:** If a clear concept is missing, one false decision follows another. When requested, a Business Plan is submitted to the bank, but it seldom has anything to do with reality. It is written just to be convincing.

5. **Too little financial backing:** There are always young entrepreneurs who succeed without beginning capital. But then modesty is called for. Many founders use too much money too early for private purposes. Too little financial substance leads immediately to problems. A general rule of thumb has it that one third of the balance or two thirds of the fixed assets should come from one's own capital.

6. **Cash-flow troubles:** Entrepreneurs without knowledge of business management and who fail to exercise cash-flow management are responsible for their own downfall. Many naively believe that their customers will pay within 30 days, but the opposite is true. If salaries and suppliers cannot be paid, any attempt to save the sinking ship comes too late.

7. **No marketing strategy:** According to statistics, one third of young entrepreneurs disappear from the market because of insufficient marketing. An amateurish marketing approach undermines credibility, and a lack of trust results in a lack of business.

8. **No control:** Ignoring the need for a good evaluation system usually results in realizing too late that something has gone wrong, so it's virtually impossible to turn the situation around and correct it.

9. **The wrong people:** Hiring the wrong people is the quickest way to lose a lot of money fast.

10. **Underestimating the competition:** Good ideas are not the perfect guarantee for getting a good hold in the market. The competition is not sleeping. It takes the offensive and tries to make up for opportunities it missed. New developments that are undertaken without first checking out their chances on the market simply cost a lot of money.

The Ten Success Factors for Entrepreneurs

1. **Willingness to succeed:** Successful entrepreneurs spare no expense. They must be prepared to work 50 to 60 hours a week and give up holidays. For that, they need the support of their families.

2. **Self-confidence:** Only those who believe in themselves will achieve their goals. That calls for optimism and trust in the future. Founders must take on challenges and confront constant changes, and they should not be afraid of making mistakes.

3. **A clear business idea:** The idea has to be right. The heads of companies know their strengths and weaknesses and their competition. They know the reason for their success, whether it's because they have better products, better service, or a more intelligent sales and marketing approach.

4. **The Business Plan:** The Business Plan is the key to building up a company. This instrument, which is always being adapted to the latest developments, makes it possible to proceed with a systematic plan of action and recognize problems in their early stages so that the proper corrective measures can be taken in plenty of time.

5. **Exact control of finances:** A young entrepreneur doesn't have to be swimming in money. But success usually doesn't come as quickly as anticipated, which is why financial resources should be calculated somewhat generously. An entrepreneur must understand something about business management, know how to react quickly, and have finances and cash flow under control. Any profits are reinvested in the company.

6. **Targeted marketing:** Only entrepreneurs who have a clear concept about how to introduce a product or service to the market will be able to succeed.

7. **A step ahead of the competition:** Success must be worked on constantly. It includes a plan for research and development so that an advantage in the market isn't lost. Acting instead of reacting will supply the advantage.

8. **Management support:** Young entrepreneurs' powers increase if they can fall back on the knowledge of experienced entrepreneurs. Possible advisers to call on would be financiers or successful colleagues who are also entrepreneurs. This can also open doors for company founders that might otherwise be closed.

9. **Cooperation:** No one is tops in every field. Building up a network of cooperation often provides access to additional know-how that would otherwise cost a lot of money.

10. **Clear company structure:** A successful company has a clear structure. The employees are motivated and know exactly what their responsibilities are. The customers know who to contact.

Source: *http://new.innonet.ch* (Accessed May 1, 1999).

Defining Business Success

Action Step 6 is optional but fun. Thinking about business success can be stimulating and enlightening. What makes a business successful or unsuccessful? How do you measure success? How do your friends measure success?

GLOBAL VILLAGE

World Economic Data to Ponder

From World Development Indicators Database, World Bank

Country (209 listed)	GNI Per Capita 2006 Atlas Method and PPP/US Dollars*	World Rank
Luxembourg	$76,040	1
United States	$44,970	10
Japan	$38,410	19
New Zealand	$27,250	34
Czech Republic	$12,680	57
Chile	$6,980	76
Belize	$3,650	101
China	$2,010	129
India	$820	161
Kenya	$580	174
Malawi	$170	204

*** World Bank Atlas Method**

"The World Bank's official estimates of the sizes of economies are based on gross national income (GNI) converted to current U.S. dollars using the Atlas method. GNI takes into account all production in the domestic economy (i.e., GDP) plus the net flows of factor income, such as rents, profits, and labor income from abroad. The Atlas method smoothes exchange rate fluctuations by using a three-year moving average, price-adjusted conversion factor."

According to the recent World Bank Development Data Group, approximately one sixth of the world's people produce 78 percent of the world's goods and services and receive 78 percent of the world's income—an average of $70 a day. Three fifths of the world's people in the poorest 61 countries receive 6 percent of the world's income—less than $2 a day.

As you venture around the world as a potential global entrepreneur, you need to be aware of the economic conditions that will preclude selling medium- and high-ticket items in many countries. Considering the statistics above, you will recognize that a huge market for basic products and services, clean water, electricity, communications, and infrastructure exists throughout the world.

The global entrepreneur will view the above statistics as an opportunity, not a threat, to their business ventures. The economies of China and India are exploding. How can you take advantage of their growth?

Half of U.S. exporters employ fewer than five people, so explore and find the right opportunity for you. The possibilities are endless.

Based on 2006 Data.

Source: *http://siteresources.worldbank.org/DATASTATISTICS/Resources/GNIPC.pdf* (Accessed January 10, 2008).

Action Step 6

Survey Your Friends about Business Success

1. The next time you are at a party or with a group of your colleagues and there is a lull in the conversation, pass out paper and pencils and ask them to list three to five small businesses they perceive as successful. Then ask them to list the signs of those firms' success and the reasons for their success. If this cannot be done in person, email several individuals for their responses.
2. Group the negative thinkers together in a "devil's advocate" group, and have them list unsuccessful businesses and point out the reasons why those firms are losing.

If you continue to assess businesses in your selected industry and other industries, you will begin to recognize success and failure factors that are constant throughout. Keep your eyes and ears open at all times.

communityresource

Sharing Your Passions and Your Dreams

The Young Entrepreneur's Resource Guide

Joining a networking organization can be an easy way to build valuable contacts and expand your business knowledge. Consider the following:

Collegiate Entrepreneurs Organization (*http://www.c-e-o.org*)

Group seeks to inform, support, and encourage college students' entrepreneurial ventures, serving over 30,000 students in over 400 collegiate organizations.

Students in Free Enterprise (*http://www.sife.org*)

International nonprofit organization with presence on over 1,600 college campuses in 45 countries and awards over $1,000,000 in prize money each year.

Business Owners' Idea Café (*http://www. businessownersideacafe. com*)

Site designed to appeal to young self-starters with how-to articles, sample Business Plans, and profiles of young entrepreneurs. Try out the Cyberschmooz message boards and chat with fellow young entrepreneurs.

National Collegiate Inventors & Innovators Alliance (*http:// www.NCIIA.org*)

Group presents entrepreneurship workshops for technology-oriented ventures on college campuses, and it attempts to link program participants with technology professionals. In addition, grant proposals are received for funding. The Alliance has developed an excellent online *Guide for Getting Started as an Entrepreneur.* They have also authored a thorough online manual for operating a Student Entrepreneurship Club, *The ENTRECLUB Handbook.* The organization includes excellent information about **social entrepreneurship**.

Entrepreneurs' Organization (*www.eonetwork.org*)

More than 6,600 young entrepreneurs whose companies have revenues of over one million dollars belong to this well-regarded group, which runs educational forums and support groups for entrepreneurs in 38 countries, provides monthly webcasts, and produces the online magazine *Octane.* In addition you can find the organization at *www.youtube.com/eonetwork.*

Social entrepreneurship Solving a social problem through entrepreneurship

You and your friends can merely speculate about which businesses are doing well financially. Only a detailed examination of each business's books will give the whole picture, but we urge you to exercise your marketplace intuition. For example, next time you dine out, try to estimate:

- The number of customers in the restaurant
- The total number of customers the restaurant serves each day
- The average price per meal

- The number of employees in the front and in the kitchen
- The number of cars in the parking lot
- The approximate cost of the food on your plate
- The cost of advertising
- The overhead cost, which would include utilities and rent

Cost of goods sold (COGS) Expenses directly attributable to production

Next, multiply the average per-meal price by the total number of daily customers. Perform your estimates on different days of the week and at different hours, and do this type of analysis for other businesses you patronize. Soon you will have the feel for which businesses are losing customers and which are winning them. Success factors will begin to emerge.

Now, attempt to develop a business's profit profile. In the course of your interviews (see Action Step 7), try to ascertain key numbers, such as gross sales, cost of goods sold, rent, salaries (owner, management), and how much is spent on marketing (advertising, commissions, promotions, and so on). You can estimate the other expenses and arrive at a range that will give you perspective when the time comes to work with your own numbers.

For example, suppose a business has $500,000 in sales. The cost of goods sold (COGS) averages 53 percent, rent is $2000 a month, and total salaries are 15 percent of gross sales. The company spends 6 percent of their gross on marketing. Based on these numbers, you can estimate benefits, including FICA (social security) costs, at 20 to 30 percent of salaries; other expenses—supplies, utilities, accounting, legal, auto, entertainment, and so on—also can be estimated at 8 to 12 percent. Combining what you have been given with your estimates yields the profit profile.

On the high side, the profit profile is slightly better than 10 percent, or $51,000. On the low side, it is slightly below 5 percent, or $23,500. (That $23,500 may not be as low as it appears if the owner has already taken salary, auto, and entertainment expenses.) Taxes would still be owed.

Looking at the profit potential of any business is absolutely essential, because many entrepreneurs fall in love with an idea or a product and do not take the time to see if the venture would be profitable. Without profits your venture will be very short lived.

	High Side	**Low Side**
Sales	$500,000	$500,000
COGS (53% of Sales)	$265,000	$265,000
Gross Profit	$235,000	$235,000
Marketing (6%)	$30,000	$30,000
Salaries (15%)	$75,000	$75,000
FICA/benefits	$15,000	$22,500
Rent ($2000/mo.)	$24,000	$24,000
Other expenses	$40,000	$60,000
Net profit before taxes	$51,000	$23,500

Interviewing Successful Entrepreneurs

Action Step 7 encourages you to interview entrepreneurs primarily within your selected industry. As you continue to explore, we recommend you also interview your competitors, potential customers, distributors, suppliers, and wholesalers. Too much information never hurts, but too little usually does.

Action Step 7

Interview Entrepreneurs

1. Interview at least three people who are self-employed, one in your area of interest. If you are a potential competitor, you may need to travel to find an interview subject willing to help you.

   Successful entrepreneurs love to tell how they achieved success. Be up front about the type of information you need and why you want it. Then make appointments with them at their convenience. Look for the passion behind their success.

2. Prepare for your interviews by making a list of open-ended questions which leave room for embellishment. Some suggestions are:

   - What were your first steps?
   - How did you arrange financing?
   - If you had it to do all over again, what would you do differently?
   - How large a part does creativity play in your business?
   - What are your tangible and intangible rewards?
   - What was your best marketing technique?
   - What portion of gross sales do you spend on advertising?
   - Did you hire more employees than you originally expected?
   - What makes your business unique?
   - How did you formulate your Business Plan?
   - Are gross profits what you expected them to be?

   (continued)

Action Step 7

(continued)

Depending on how you relate to your subject, you might be able to think of these first interviewees as sources of marketplace experience. They may provide you with contacts for later recommendations you will need for your "taxi squad"—your lawyer, accountant, banker, insurance agent, and so on.

It helps to take notes during interviews. If you use a recorder, be sure to ask permission. Do not worry about evaluations. The information will assemble into patterns sooner than you think. Be sure to send a handwritten thank-you note. You will be amazed at how much help you receive from fellow entrepreneurs, because they love to talk about "their babies."

SUMMARY

Throughout this chapter, you have reviewed your financial situation, personal goals, passions, strengths, and weaknesses, and you have worked on defining your desired new entrepreneurial lifestyle. Take the time to review your answers to these Action Steps and questionnaires with several people who know you well. Their input will be invaluable as you come to grips with the reality and challenges that face you in your entrepreneurial quest.

According to Jim Collins, author of *Built to Last* (Harper Business, New York, 2002) it is best to look at developing a business that looks at the intersection of three circles: 1) what you are good at, 2) what you stand for, and 3) what people will pay you for. You have answered the first two with the action steps throughout this chapter that have asked you to search your soul, your pocketbook, and your family's needs and desires. In Chapter 2, you will be looking at your changing world for opportunities. In later chapters, you will discover the right target market: people who possess the dollars and willingness to purchase your product or service.

Your Adventure Notebook should be filling up now with information, concerns, and wonderful ideas. Entrepreneurship is difficult but rewarding for many. The risks and rewards can only be measured by each individual entrepreneur.

Earl Graves, Sr., founder of Black Enterprise, says the secret of start-up success is a pit-bull-like refusal to give up. "You have to have a junkyard dog mentality." Before you open your own business, know yourself well, and ask yourself if you are a junkyard dog.

In addition to tenacity, a positive outlook will help drive your success. Jeff Bezos, founder of Amazon.com, was highlighted as one of the 25 Most Fascinating Entrepreneurs by *Inc.* magazine due to his outlook that "optimism is essential." During his interview, he said, "I believe that optimism is an essential quality for doing anything hard—entrepreneurial endeavors or anything else. That doesn't mean that you're blind or unrealistic, it means that you keep focused on eliminating your risks, modifying your strategy, until it is a strategy about which you can be *genuinely* optimistic. People think entrepreneurs are risk-loving. Really what you find is successful entrepreneurs hate risk, because the founding of the enterprise is already so risky that what they do is take their early resources, the small amounts of capital that they have, whatever assets they have, and they deploy those resources systematically, eliminating the largest risk first, the second-largest risk, and so on, and so on."

Also, echoing one of this book's themes, he reminds us, "You don't choose your passions, your passions choose you."

THINK POINTS FOR SUCCESS

Remember:
- We are entrepreneurs. Work is fun. We seldom sleep.
- Even though you may not be in business yet, you can intensify your focus by writing down your thoughts about the business you think you want to try.
- Stay flexible.
- Change is accelerating everywhere, and change provides you with opportunities to follow your dreams.
- To find the doorway into your own business, gather data and keep asking questions.

- Get reckless on paper before you get reckless in the marketplace.
- Brainstorm.
- Draw mind maps.
- Confirm your venture with numbers and words.
- Write a Business Plan.
- Follow your passions.

KEY POINTS FROM ANOTHER VIEW

Roles You'll Be Expected to Play

Here's a look at some of the roles you can expect to play if own your own business:

- Tax collector — If you sell goods at the retail level, you're responsible for collecting a sales tax for various government entities; also, if you have employees, you're responsible for collecting payroll taxes from them.
- Manager/boss — If you have employees, you'll be responsible for all of the human resources-related functions, including recruiting, hiring, firing, and keeping track of all the benefits information; you'll be the one filling out all the insurance forms, answering employee questions and complaints, and making the decisions about whether you should change the benefits package you offer your employees.
- Sales/marketing/advertising executive — In addition to having to plan your marketing or advertising campaign, you'll have to carry it out; you may write advertising copy, do some preliminary market research, visit potential customers, and make sure existing customers stay happy; depending upon the type of business you own, you may have to join business groups, attend various breakfasts, lunches, and dinners, and just generally network with anyone who could help your business prosper.
- Accountant — Even if you have an accountant, you'll have to know a lot about accounting; you'll have to know which records to keep and how to keep them; if you don't have an accountant, you'll also have to prepare all of your tax forms, and you'll have to know how to prepare and interpret all of your own financial statements.
- Lawyer — Even if you have a lawyer, you'll have to know a lot about the law; if you don't have a lawyer, you'll have to prepare all of your own contracts and other documents and understand all of the employment laws if you have employees or want to hire someone.

- Business planner — As you own your business, you'll inevitably want to make changes, perhaps to expand the business or add a new product line; if you want to make a change, it'll be your responsibility to do it; you'll have to plan it and execute it, and you'll have to consider all of the ramifications of your decision.
- Bill collector — When customers don't pay, it'll be up to you to collect from them; you'll have to know what you can and can't do when collecting; you'll have to decide how best to collect from them and when to give up.
- Market researcher — Before you start your business, you'll have to find out who your customers are and where they're located; you may also have to conduct market research at various times during the life of your business, such as when you are considering introducing a new product.
- Technology expert — As a small business owner, you will probably come to depend upon your computer; you'll have to fix it when it breaks, install upgrades, and load software; you'll also have to keep up with the newest products and the latest changes in technology.
- Clerk/receptionist/typist/secretary — Even if you have clerical help, you'll inevitably do some of your filing, some of your typing, some of your mailing, and some of your telephone answering; even if you have someone else, for example, keep track of overdue accounts, you'll have to know how to do it so that you can teach them what to do.

Don't make the mistake of underestimating the cost, in hours, of being in business for yourself. A person who spends 40 hours a week focused on his or her work will have to work a lot more hours as a business owner to get in 40 hours of activity directly relating to providing customers goods or services. And during the startup period, you'll probably be the busiest you'll ever be.

Source: Adapted from *http://www.toolkit.com/small_business_guide/sbg.aspx?nid=P01_0250* (Accessed January 10, 2008). Reproduced with permission from CCH Business Owner's Toolkit™ *(http://www.toolkit.cch.com)* published and copyrighted by CCH Tax and Accounting.

chapter 2

Spotting Trends and Opportunities
Opening Your Eyes

Where can you find a business idea that will really pay off? One that fulfills your passions? One that will make you rich? One that will make you famous? One that will make you happy? What are the best ventures for you to pursue today?

Only you can answer these questions, because the best opportunity for you is one that you will enjoy, and one that makes money. The best business for you uses those experiences, passions, skills, and aptitudes that are unique to you. The Action Steps in this book are designed to help you discover what is unique about you: Who are you? What are your skills? What turns you on? What special knowledge do you have that distinguishes you from other people?

OPENING YOUR EYES AND MIND TO VAST OPPORTUNITIES

Look around, and check out the new businesses in your town or industry. Which new firms are operating in your selected industry? What new target markets are developing? What could you sell on the Internet? How can you meet the needs of the aging **baby boomers**? What about the **echo boomers**? What needs do you have? What needs do your friends have? Is there a product you could repurpose? Are there any products you could put together to increase their value?

Baby boomers Persons born between 1946 and 1963

Echo boomers Persons born between 1977 and 1994

As you seek opportunities and formulate your business, consider if your business opportunity possesses the following six Forbes ASAP leading success factors:

1. Responsiveness to change: How well can your company respond to market change?
2. Market opportunity: How big is the potential market for your company's products?
3. Marketing expertise: How good will your company be at selling and marketing into the previously mentioned opportunity?
4. Human capital: Can you build strong management, marketing, sales, and support?
5. Alliances and partnerships: Can you build strong partnerships and relationships?
6. Prospects for growth: How fast is the company growing, and can it continue to ramp up quickly?

Chapter 2 is designed to help you recognize opportunities in **market segments** so you can define the gaps in the marketplace. You want to be sure your business serves a need, that people are willing to pay for it, and that you enter the marketplace from a position of strength. It is time to look at our changing world and your selected industry to spot trends and opportunities.

Market segments Identifiable slices of a larger market

Be a trend spotter and ride your way to a successful business. Do not forget to add blood, sweat, tears, energy, enthusiasm, money, passion, to your good idea. When we began working with entrepreneurs some 25 years ago, we handed out sage advice, like "Just find a need and fill it." Now we say, "Examine the marketplace thoroughly for flaws and opportunities, and use technology to keep track of your customer's needs continually." We also used to say, "If you're doing business now the same way you did 2 years ago, you're probably doing many things wrong." Now we say, "If you're doing business today the same way you did 6 months ago, you should think about a new strategic plan."

Use your marketplace radar to choose a growth segment of a growth industry to ride the crest of the wave. Choosing the hot growth sector is usually the right way to begin before the trend turns down. Occasionally, however, the trend sours quickly. Twenty years ago, you could ride a trend for 5 to 10 years; now that time is greatly compressed, and reaching a profit sooner rather than later is essential for continuing your business.

If you are already in a small business, or thinking about getting into one, make it easy on yourself by first identifying industries in the growth phase of their life cycle. Play "marketplace detective."

Look around you. When you focus in on a particular business, do you sense growth over the long term? Or is it involved with a fad that will not last? For your business, you want a growth industry that will generate new customers quickly, allowing you to build a repeat customer base.

As a small-business owner, one of the things you must have going for you is fast footwork, so you can adjust to change quickly; it is one of your best weapons in the marketplace. But you can benefit from fast footwork *only if you operate from a position of knowledge*; stay in touch with customers and keep your ear tuned to the marketplace. We recommend you follow your competition closely and keep abreast of the broad changes in society and technology.

Look before you leap. Brainstorm with your family, friends, colleagues, and competitors; and, most importantly, interview your potential customers. Study the marketplace. Read industry journals. Use your new eyes. With trained eyes, you will be able to see the big picture. When conducting your research, start with the big picture and work down into your industry and then your competitors and specific marketplace. To jump-start your mind, complete Action Step 8. You may not open a business after taking this class or reading this text, but by keeping an open mind and training your intuition over the next few years, an incredible opportunity may be placed in front of you and you will be prepared to act. Allow yourself to dream.

It's a Dynamic World

- Computers and telecommunications create a global neighborhood.
- Health care technology changes at lightening speed.
- Software is developed around the clock with 8-hour shifts in three countries: India, the United States, and Ireland.
- Industry deregulation creates incredible opportunities.
- Competition is everywhere and more intense than ever.

ENVIRONMENTAL VARIABLES

Changes within the business and social world occur within five major environmental variables. Your challenge is threefold: 1) constantly be aware and follow the big picture, which consists of the five major variables; 2) recognize the changes occurring within each variable; and 3) identify opportunities for products or services as changes occur.

1. **Technology:** biotechnology, the Internet, nanotechnology, personal genomics, universal translation
2. **Competition:** deregulation, impact of "box stores," international
3. **Social/cultural:** immigration, single parents, religion, ethnic shifts, aging population
4. **Legal/political:** who is in power, tax laws, changing rules (international, federal, state, and local)
5. **Economics:** recessions, inflation, changing income levels, cost of housing, food, and renewable energy

Each change in the environmental variables and the subsequent trends affect how products are manufactured, marketed, and delivered to customers.

Life cycle The progression through stages—from birth to death—of a product, business, service, industry, location, target market, and so on

New eyes Observation with intuition

Shelf velocity The speed at which a product moves from storage to shelf to customer

Action Step 8

Opening Your Mind to New Information

Your community and workplace are your marketing labs. It is time to open your mind to all the information around you. Time to head out! Yes, you could also do this on the Internet, but why not get some fresh air and be around people?

1. **First stop:** large bookstore with lots of magazines. Select and read five distinctly different magazines that you have never read before. What did you learn? Did you read about a target market that you did not know existed? Next, review the top ten best sellers: fiction, nonfiction, children's, trade, and paperbacks. What do they tell you about your current world? Did you see any new genres?
2. **Second stop:** music area of large bookstore. What's hot? What's not? Are there any new music styles?
3. **Third stop:** local mall. What new stores are opening? Which department store has the best service? Highest prices? Best selection? Which restaurants are hot? Where are the longest lines?
4. **Fourth stop:** visit your favorite store. Compile a list of all the products and services that were not there 1 year ago; if you are visiting a computer store, shorten the time to 3 or 6 months. Can you guesstimate **shelf velocity**? What's hot? What's not?

(continued)

GLOBAL VILLAGE

Why Go Global? Look at the Numbers!

World Population by Region and Growth

Major area	Estimated population in year 2003 (millions)	Projected population in year 2050 (millions)
World	6,301	9,191
More developed regions	1,203	1,245
Less developed regions	5,098	7,946
Least developed countries	718	1,742
Other less developed countries	4,380	6,204
Africa	851	1,997
Asia	3,823	5,266
Latin America and the Caribbean	543	769
Europe	726	664
Northern America	326	445
Oceania	32	49

Source: Population Division of the Department of Economic and Social Affairs of the United Nations Secretariat (2003). *World Population Prospects: The 2006 Revision Highlights.* New York: United Nations.

Our world has grown from 3 billion to over 6 billion in only 40 years. Asia and Africa are predicted to comprise 80 percent of the population in 2050. "The increase in the world population over the next 40 years is equivalent to the total world population in 1950." Only 1 in 20 people in the world live in North America today, and only 1 in 25 will in 2050. Is it any wonder why huge multinational firms are heading off to the rest of the world? You can too!

Which products and services will those who live outside of the United States need? What resources are available? What cultural, financial, and legal obstacles must be overcome to meet the needs of 2050's estimated 9 billion people, two thirds of whom will live in urban areas? Potential international customers are being born each minute, and so are potential international entrepreneurs. Is it time for you to search out opportunities overseas? To find out, start with Internet resources, which are most helpful because they are constantly updated—in the rapidly changing international marketplace, current information is essential.

To begin research on specific countries start with two federal government websites and resources:

http://www.state.gov/r/pa/ei/bgn (U.S. Department of State: *Background Notes*): Factual publications that contain information on all the countries of the world with which the United States has relations. They include facts on each country's land, people, history, government, political conditions, economy, and relations with other countries and the United States. The *Notes* are updated/revised by the Office of Electronic Information and Publications of the Bureau of Public Affairs as they are received from regional bureaus and are added to the database of the Department of State.

https://www.cia.gov/library/publications/the-world-factbook/index.html (CIA Factbook): Provides country-specific demographic, government, economic, and infrastructure information.

In addition to Internet resources, search out federal and state trade offices, local colleges with international programs, consulates, embassies, and international chamber of commerce organizations.

Action Step 8

(continued)

5. **Fifth stop:** your television set. Spend 1 hour watching *CNN World Report*. Make a list of the stories. Did any surprise you? Did you spot any opportunities?
6. **Final stop:** log on to the Internet. For at least 2 to 4 hours, surf topics you know nothing about. What did you learn? What opportunities did you find?

Your brain should now be in high gear—and suffering from information overload! Use what you learned as you continue to explore opportunities.

Buy and read *Newsweek, Time, Wired,* and *Fast Company;* peruse industry journals and newspapers; begin to learn how to spot the changes. *Future Survey* from the World Future Society constantly scans the environment for trends and predicts the future. Figure 2.1 lists ten forecasts that *Future Survey* views

figure 2.1

The Futurist's Top Ten Forecasts for 2008 and Beyond

Each year since 1985, the editors of *The Futurist* have selected the most thought-provoking ideas and forecasts appearing in the magazine to go into our annual **Outlook** report. Over the years, **Outlook** has spotlighted the emergence of such epochal developments as the Internet, virtual reality, and the end of the Cold War. Here are the editors' top 10 forecasts from **Outlook 2008:**

1. The world will have a billion millionaires by 2025. Globalization and technological innovation are driving this increased prosperity. But challenges to prosperity will also become more acute, such as water shortages that will affect two-thirds of world population by 2025. —*James Canton, author of "The Extreme Future," reviewed in* The Futurist *May–June 2007, p. 54*

2. Fashion will go wired as technologies and tastes converge to revolutionize the textile industry. Researchers in smart fabrics and intelligent textiles (SFIT) are working with the fashion industry to bring us color-changing or perfume-emitting jeans, wristwatches that work as digital wallets, and running shoes like the Nike +iPod that watch where you're going (possibly allowing others to do the same). Powering these gizmos remains a key obstacle. But industry watchers estimate that a $400 million market for SFIT is already in place and predict that smart fabrics could revitalize the U.S. and European textile industry. —*Patrick Tucker, "Smart Fashion," Sep–Oct 2007, p. 68*

3. The threat of another cold war with China, Russia, or both could replace terrorism as the chief foreign-policy concern of the United States. Scenarios for what a war with China or Russia would look like make the clashes and wars in which the United States is now involved seem insignificant. The power of radical jihadists is trivial compared with Soviet missile capabilities, for instance. The focus of U.S. foreign policy should thus be on preventing an engagement among Great Powers. —*Edward N. Luttwak, "Preserving Balance among the Great Powers," Nov–Dec 2006, p. 26*

4. Counterfeiting of currency will proliferate, driving the move toward a cashless society. Sophisticated new optical scanning technologies could, in the next 5 years, be a boon for currency counterfeiters, so societies are increasingly putting aside their privacy fears about going cashless. Meanwhile, cashless technologies are improving, making them far easier and safer to use. —*Allen H. Kupetz, "Our Cashless Future," May–June 2007, p. 37*

5. The earth is on the verge of a significant extinction event. The twenty-first century could witness a biodiversity collapse 100 to 1,000 times greater than any previous extinction since the dawn of humanity, according to the World Resources Institute. Protecting biodiversity in a time of increased resource consumption, overpopulation, and environmental degradation will require continued sacrifice on the part of local, often impoverished communities. Experts contend that incorporating local communities' economic interests into conservation plans will be essential to species protection in the next century. —*World Trends & Forecasts, Nov–Dec 2006, p. 6*

6. Water will be in the twenty-first century what oil was in the twentieth century. Global fresh water shortages and drought conditions are spreading in both the developed and developing world. In response, the dry state of California is building 13 desalination plants that could provide 10 to 20 percent of the state's water in the next two decades. Desalination will become more mainstream by 2020. —*William E. Halal, "Technology's Promise: Highlights from the TechCast Project," Nov–Dec, p. 44*

7. World population by 2050 may grow larger than previously expected, due in part to healthier, longer-living people. Slower than expected declines of fertility in developing countries and increasing longevity in richer countries are contributing to a higher rate of population growth. As a result, the UN has increased its forecast for global population from 9.1 billion people by 2050 to 9.2 billion. —*World Trends & Forecasts, Sep–Oct 2007, p. 10*

8. The number of Africans imperiled by floods will grow seventyfold by 2080. The rapid urbanization taking place throughout much of Africa makes flooding particularly dangerous, altering the natural flow of water and cutting off escape routes. If global sea levels rise by the predicted 38 cm by 2080, the number of Africans affected by floods will grow from 1 million to 70 million. —*World Trends & Forecasts, July–Aug 2007, p. 7*

9. Rising prices for natural resources could lead to a full-scale rush to develop the Arctic. Not just oil and natural gas, but also the Arctic's supplies of nickel, copper, zinc, coal, freshwater, forests, and of course fish are highly coveted by the global economy. Whether the Arctic states tighten control over these commodities or find equitable and sustainable ways to share them will be a major political challenge in the decades ahead. —*Lawson W. Brigham, "Thinking about the Arctic's Future: Scenarios for 2040," Sep–Oct 2007, p. 27*

10. More decisions will be made by nonhuman entities. Electronically enabled teams in networks, robots with artificial intelligence, and other noncarbon life-forms will make financial, health, educational, and even political decisions for us. Reason: Technologies are increasing the complexity of our lives and human workers' competency is not keeping pace well enough to avoid disasters due to human error. —*Arnold Brown, "'Not with a Bang': Civilization's Accelerating Challenge," Sep–Oct 2007, p. 38*

Source: "Top Ten Forecasts for 2008 and Beyond," World Future Society, *http://www.wfs.org/Nov-Dec%20Files/TOPTEN.htm* (Accessed April 20, 2008).

as "significant probable developments that deserve wide attention." As you review their forecast, what opportunities do you see? Action Step 8 opened your mind to new information, and now it is time to evaluate the information and search for opportunities. Action Step 9 will help you to do that.

CHANGING FAMILIES

How does your world differ from the world your parents experienced? How will your children's world differ from yours? You may recognize how your world differs from your parents', but the real business opportunities will result when you focus on how your children's world will differ from yours.

The traditional "Beaver Cleaver" family of a working dad, stay-at-home mom, and two children exists for very few today. The opportunities to serve the diverse family structures that exist are vast: day care, after-school care, recreation programs, errand services, and college-planning programs. If you compiled a list of all the services June and Ward Cleaver provided to keep their household running, you would discover that all those services *and many more* are still needed today; but service-oriented businesses are doing them, not June and Ward.

Who else is in need of these services? The elderly? Single parents? The disabled? The chronically ill? Grandparents raising grandchildren? Couples who both work? All of these groups are ability and time starved. In fact, many say real wealth today is *time*.

Service businesses generated 68 percent of our 2006 GDP, government services generated about 12 percent, and manufacturing 20 percent. People are thus buying time. Do you see a need for a service? Do any of your friends or colleagues have the same need? Are people willing to pay for this service? If so, what will they pay? Can you provide this service and get the word out? If you answered yes, go for it! In many instances, service-oriented businesses can begin out of the home with low capital investment, few or no employees, and a great idea that fills a need. According to Andrew Carnegie, *"Making money shouldn't be your first goal. Fill a need, and if you're good enough at it, the money will come."*

People are marrying later, having fewer children and having them later, and remarrying and reformulating new families with greater frequency. Twenty-two percent of homes today are purchased by single women, something almost unheard of just 30 years ago. Figure 2.2 breaks down the household family structures based on the 2000 Census, making it apparent that Beaver Cleaver

---

Action Step 9

Discover how changes = trends = opportunities

Pick up the last six issues of *Time* or *Newsweek*—your local library should have copies—and your notes from Action Step 8, and start reading. What is happening in the world? Fill in the chart with the areas that are changing within each environmental variable. If you are fortunate and have done your research, you will spot the changes before trends start to develop. Being at the forefront of trends has made business-savvy people rich. Remember when the biotechnology industry began? How about the cell phone industry? How about digital photography? If you had spotted the changes within these technologies, hopped on board, and rode the opportunities to success, where would you be today? Under each of these factors will be many changes, trends, and opportunities. All you need to do is find one!

Social/cultural
  Changes:
    Trends:
      Opportunities:

Competition
  Changes:
    Trends:
      Opportunities:

Technology
  Changes:
    Trends:
      Opportunities:

Legal/political
  Changes:
    Trends:
      Opportunities:

Economics
  Changes:
    Trends:
      Opportunities:

---

figure **2.2**

Changing U.S. Household and Family Structures, 2000

Household Type	Percentage of Population
Married couple with children	23.5
Married couple without children	28.1
Female-headed household with children	7.2
Female-headed household without children	5.1
Male-headed household with children	2.1
Male-headed household without children	2.1
Non-family household, single person	25.8
Non-family household, two or more persons	6.1

Source: Social Science Data Analysis Network, *http://www.censusscope.org/us/chart_house.html* (Accessed February 8, 2005).

families are in the minority. Are there any opportunities here for you? Each change and trend in our society represents threats and opportunities to current businesses. If current businesses do not expand and change, new businesses will move in. Your firm's success depends on *you* recognizing changes and capitalizing on them.

What opportunities can you envision from the above information? What gaps are in the marketplace that you can fill? How can you help these time-starved families? What services can you provide for them? The changing family is only one social change; there are many others, such as people living longer and healthier lives, rising incomes, younger children with large spendable incomes and greater influence on family buying habits, and so on. What other changes do you see? What opportunities open up? Follow how one entrepreneur parlayed his love of chess into a business focusing on after-school programs for the children of time-deprived working parents.

Checkmate!

Chess had changed Sammy Wong's life, and he wanted to change others' lives too. At most grade schools, chess is not considered a trendy game. But Sammy knew he could make chess cool. After graduating from college, he worked with local elementary schools, volunteering his time to teach chess with four free, half-hour lessons. After providing incredibly fun lessons—bishops being conked on the head, three-foot-tall chess pieces, double chessboards, and lots of laughter—Sammy was ready to launch after-school chess classes at $7 per class per child. In some schools more than 30 percent of the kids took his classes, and currently, several thousand children are involved in his programs.

Yes, Sammy wrenched kids away from Playstation 3 and the Internet! Parents were thrilled. They had been looking for an activity without a joystick or keyboard that would challenge their children's minds. Few envisioned chess would be the answer. Sammy was riding the trend of parents seeking alternatives to television, computers, and video games.

Many of the moms and dads in the upscale community where Sammy lived were programmers, engineers, and scientists who had played chess as children but could not find the time to teach their own kids. Sammy came to the rescue. In addition, Friday-night chess tournaments, traveling chess teams, chess camps, and chess champs were born when Sammy Wong listened to his customers—parents and kids.

Sammy started his business for less than $1,000. Can you do the same? Action Step 10 asks you to explore the business opportunities open to you if you had only $1,000 and a working car or pickup truck. In good times and bad times, there are *always* opportunities to make money. Not everyone has a nest egg or a rich uncle; most entrepreneurs are just regular people. After completing this assignment, you may discover an opportunity you never recognized before; at the least you will have a list ready and waiting for the next friend who complains about not having any money. Your list can show the way to dollars. As students have shared their lists in our classes, we have seen light bulbs go on. One student with less than $200 started an incredibly successful window-washing business. Two students joined together using their interior design skills to offer computerized interior designs in addition to their monthly trips to the Furniture Mart with their clients. And yet another offered personal training and shooting hoops to overweight teenage boys. Complete Action Step 10 *after* you have finished reading the chapter.

Action Step 10

$1,000 and a Working Vehicle

Quickly, can you think of a business to start with little capital and no employees? Place yourself in the position of having to make money within 1 week. You *have* to start a business, and you have only $1,000. You have a working car or pickup truck; an apartment, garage, or dorm room; and a phone. Remember, the business must be legal!

1. Ask friends what they need. Drive through local neighborhoods and towns. Jump on the Internet. Read local papers in other areas. Find out what other people are accomplishing with what appears to be a small investment. What did you find? What opportunities can you explore further?

2. Can you purchase products at a warehouse for resale at a swap meet or online? If time visit a swap meet and explore online selling at eBay and Yahoo.

3. Could you tap a skill you already possess? Remember Sammy's chess skills?

4. Compile a list of all the business opportunities you have discovered and share them with your friends, colleagues, and potential customers. What are they willing to pay for your products and services? How often would they purchase? Who are your competitors?

P.S.: Apple Computer started with $1,350. Dell Computer started with $1,000. Nike started with $1,000.

P.P.S.: Walt Disney started in his garage!

CHANGING WORKFORCE AND DEMOGRAPHICS

"According to the Bureau of Labor Statistics, the U.S. now has more choreographers (16,340) than metal-casters (14,880), and more people make their livings shuffling and dealing cards in casinos (82,960) than running lathes (65,840). There are three times as many security guards (1,004,130) as machinists (385,690). Whereas 30 percent of Americans worked in manufacturing in 1950, fewer than 15 percent do now," *New York Times* writer Christopher Caldwell pointed out in a recent article, stressing that we are not moving to a service economy, we are already there.

Education and training will play a leading role in preparing and retraining the workforce, and opening many opportunities for tutoring services, career planners, test-preparation services, and employment agencies. Also, we will continue to see online education programs skyrocketing as overcommitted individuals find it difficult to attend traditional learning programs.

It is estimated that **Generation Y** individuals will have eight to ten different careers in their work lives. Training and retraining will be part of their lives and will provide opportunities for entrepreneurs. Ken Dychtwald, a leading researcher on the baby boomers, predicts that our life will follow a "Cyclic Life Plan where people in the future will learn, work, relax, learn some more, work in a different role, play differently, go back to school, work in a new calling."

Generation Y Individuals born between 1977 and 1994

Immigration will play a leading role in the future growth of the United States. According to the Pew Research Center, "If current trends continue, the population of the United States will rise to 438 million in 2050, up from 296 million in 2005, and 82 percent of the increase will be due to immigrants arriving from 2005 to 2050 and their U.S.-born descendants." Opportunities abound to meet the social and business needs of the changing consumers and the workforce. See Table 2.1 to view the population changes by racial and ethnic groups. What opportunities do you see in these changes?

The Pew Research Center's U.S. Population Projections: 2005–2050 notes a startling fact on the nation's future "dependency ratio," the number of children and elderly compared with the number of working-age Americans. There were 59 children and elderly people per 100 adults of working age in 2005. That will rise to 72 dependents per 100 adults of working age in 2050. With this study in hand, one can recognize the potential labor shortage and the wealth of opportunity, along with the need to increase productivity through the use of technology. Who will take care of the frail elderly and the small children when there are so few potential employees?

Boomer Explosion

The Boomer generation identified with the Iron Curtain, the Berlin Wall, the Cold War, Sputnik, transistor radios, calculators, computers, a man on the moon, hula hoops, *Leave It To Beaver,* Mouseketeers, doo-wop, R&B, *American Bandstand,* Elvis, Little Richard, Chuck Berry, Motown, Beach Boys, Haight-Ashbury, hippies, VW bugs, peace, love, LSD, Woodstock, California Dreamin', hot tubs, TM, platform shoes, bell-bottoms, miniskirts, hot pants, bikinis, tie-dye, flower power, communes, Nehru jackets, the Beatles, the Rolling Stones, Chelsea, King's Road, Carnaby Street, bohemians, the Mods, the Rockers, Liverpool, Twiggy, the fall of the Berlin Wall, Pan Am, and $5.00 a day in Europe.

Source: *http://hometown.aol.com/boomersint/bindex/html* (Accessed July 23, 2001).

table 2.1

America Is Changing

Pew Research Center Publications
Immigration to Play Lead Role In Future U.S. Growth

By Jeffrey Passel and D'VeraCohn, Pew Research Center

February 11, 2008

Executive Summary

If current trends continue, the population of the United States will rise to 438 million in 2050, from 296 million in 2005, and 82% of the increase will be due to immigrants arriving from 2005 to 2050 and their U.S.-born descendants, according to new projections developed by the Pew Research Center.

Of the 117 million people added to the population during this period due to the effect of new immigration, 67 million will be the immigrants themselves and 50 million will be their U.S.-born children or grandchildren.

Among the other key population projections:

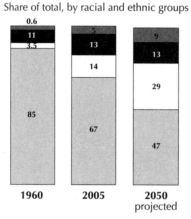

U.S. Population 1960-2050
Share of total, by racial and ethnic groups

☐ White   ☐ Hispanic   ■ Black   ■ Asian

- Nearly one in five Americans (19%) will be an immigrant in 2050, compared with one in eight (12%) in 2005. By 2025, the immigrant, or foreign-born, share of the population will surpass the peak during the last great wave of immigration a century ago.

- The major role of immigration in national growth builds on the pattern of recent decades, during which immigrants and their U.S.-born children and grandchildren accounted for most population increase. Immigration's importance increased as the average number of births to U.S.-born women dropped sharply before leveling off.

- The Latino population, already the nation's largest minority group, will triple in size and will account for most of the nation's population growth from 2005 through 2050. Hispanics will make up 29% of the U.S. population in 2050, compared with 14% in 2005.

- Births in the United States will play a growing role in Hispanic and Asian population growth; as a result, a smaller proportion of both groups will be foreign-born in 2050.

- The non-Hispanic white population will increase more slowly than other racial and ethnic groups; whites will become a minority (47%) by 2050.

- The nation's elderly population will more than double in size from 2005 through 2050, as the baby boom generation enters the traditional retirement years. The number of working-age Americans and children will grow more slowly than the elderly population, and will shrink as a share of the total population.

The Center's projections are based on detailed assumptions about births, deaths and immigration levels—the three key components of population change. All these assumptions are built on recent trends. But it is important to note that these trends can change. All population projections have inherent uncertainties, especially for years further in the future, because they can be affected by changes in behavior, by new immigration policies, or by other events. Nonetheless, projections offer a starting point for understanding and analyzing the parameters of future demographic change.

The Center's report includes an analysis of the nation's future "dependency ratio"—the number of children and elderly compared with the number of working-age Americans. There were 59 children and elderly people per 100 adults of working age in 2005. That will rise to 72 dependents per 100 adults of working age in 2050.

Source: *http://pewresearch.org/pubs/729/united-states-population-projections*, (Accessed April 25, 2008).

figure **2.3**

Boomer Impact

Where Boomers Have Been

- Boomers didn't just eat food—they transformed the snack, restaurant, and supermarket
- Boomers didn't just wear clothes—they transformed the fashion industry
- Boomers didn't just buy cars—they transformed the auto industry
- They didn't just date—they transformed sex roles and practices
- They didn't just go to work—they transformed the workplace
- They didn't just get married—they transformed relationships and the institution of marriage
- They didn't just borrow money—they transformed the debt market
- They didn't just go to the doctor—they transformed health care
- They didn't just use computers—they transformed technology
- They didn't just invest in stocks—they transformed the investment marketplace

Where Boomers Are Headed
The rising "age wave" will continue to produce many demographically motivated revolutions in the consumer marketplace. As the boomers pass through their middle years and on to maturity, five key factors will reshape supply and demand:

1. Concern about the onset of chronic disease and boomers' desire to do whatever is possible to postpone physical aging.
2. Increasing amounts of discretionary dollars—for some but not all—as a result of escalating earning power, inheritances, and return on investments.
3. Entry into new adult life stages including empty nesting, care giving, grandparenthood, retirement, widowhood, and rehirement—each with its own challenges and opportunities.
4. A psychological shift from acquiring more material possessions toward a desire to purchase enjoyable and satisfying experiences.
5. The continued absence of "disposable time" due to complex lifestyles.

Source: Ken Dychtwald, "The Age Wave Is Coming," *http://www.agewave.com/agewave.shtml* (Accessed February 8, 2005), Courtesy of Age-Wave.com, 2004.

Baby boomers, a major economic and social force in our society for decades (see Figure 2.3), are aging, much to their dismay. As they approach their 50s and 60s, they are redefining aging and retirement. What products will they need and want? Where will they buy them? How can you reach them?

Between the end of World War II and 1965, 78 million baby boomers were born, and they now control over 70 percent of the financial assets in America. In addition, they account for over 50 percent of discretionary income. With 27 percent of the population in their peak earning and spending years with teens in college, they are the major gorilla in the marketplace, and their impact is felt throughout almost every industry. They purchase over 41 percent of all cars and over 48 percent of all luxury cars. Looking at traveling, investing, saving, planning for retirement, investing in second homes, and reinventing retirement, their impact and dollars provide incredible business opportunities. Figure 2.3 highlights the past changes of the baby boomers. Your goal is to identify and capitalize on the future changes.

The *Business Journal of Phoenix* recently cited a Robert Half International survey of 150 senior executives working within the nation's largest companies and found the executives considered "the retirement of baby boomer employees to have the greatest impact on the workplace in the next generation." What opportunities lie here for entrepreneurs?

By 2030 half of all U.S. adults will be 50 or older. According to many sources, the boomers will *not* "go gentle into that good night." They will fight the aging process with every dollar they have. Ken Dychtwald, founder of AgeWave, a consulting firm guiding Fortune 500 companies and government groups reaching out to boomers, explains where the baby boomers have been and where they are headed in Figure 2.3. Dychtwald also notes that "two thirds of people in the history of the world who have lived past age 65 are still alive today!" And as these Boomers look toward their final years, they make clear that they fear going into a nursing home three times more than they fear dying.

One cannot look at past generations to predict the buying habits of this group. Boomers are wealthier and more educated, have fewer children, and are in "new family" structures. Firms are going right to the source, asking boomers what they want. The boomer research of Puelte Homes/Del Webb, a premier developer of retirement communities, showed not only a need for retirement communities in sunny climates, but also the need for retirement communities in the East and Midwest to serve boomers who choose to retire closer to home.

Scrutinize boomers—from the tops of their heads to the bottoms of their feet—to determine if you can develop products or services to make money. Brainstorm away! If you are twenty-something, look at your folks; if you are forty-something, look in the mirror. Be as creative and wild as you can be. The following should help get you started:

- **Hair:** Toupees, hair implants, wigs, great hats, special sunscreen for bald spots
- **Eyes:** Eye drops, cool magnifiers, trifocals, refractive surgery, eyelid lifts, eyelash growth enhancers, reading sunglasses
- **Face:** Plastic surgery, skin creams, Botox, skin cancer checkups, facial exercise classes, facial massages, makeup formulated for aging skin, creams for brown spots

Every doctor, dentist, lawyer, accountant, travel agent, and financial planner waits in the wings for boomers to break down the door. Estate planners, trust attorneys, and eldercare attorneys are presenting workshops everywhere to capture this exploding marketplace's dollars. Opportunities are enormous for those who want to capitalize on and meet the boomers' needs. The "sandwich generation," those who both care for teenagers and elderly parents" are in special need of help as they are overwhelmed with responsibilities and time pressures. Another segment developing for the first time due to our extended life span consists of elderly people caring for the frail elderly. The need for assistance is vast.

AARP The Magazine (formerly *Modern Maturity*), the largest distributed subscription magazine targeted at those over age 50—and distributed free to American Association of Retired Persons (AARP) members as part of their membership dues—may have one of the hottest Web sites of the future, *http://www.aarpmagazine.org*. Legally, politically, and economically those over age 50 have always been a strong force. With the power of the Internet, real social, political, and economic change is not only possible but also inevitable.

As the boomers age, will they all be alike? Not according to Yankelovich's MindBase, a marketing tool created to answer the questions "Who will buy?" and "Why?" There are two major groups of older people: One group is the Renaissance Masters, "financially secure individuals who are vitally connected to community and to life . . . upbeat about their future, and (who) remain interested in personal development." The other group is the Maintainers, "mature individuals who use the past as their point of reference. The Maintainers group is sedentary and resource constrained." In addition, Yankelovich further segments each of these groups based on attitudes, personalities, values, and motivations. The opportunities to capitalize on the needs of older people are vast, but do not make the assumption that they are all the same.

To explore your chosen target market, and to spot the emerging trends and opportunities, complete Action Step 11.

Millennials Rising

"This is the first generation to grow up digital—coming of age in a world where computers, the Internet, video games, and cell phones are common, and where expressing themselves through these tools is the norm. Given how present these technologies are in their lives, do young people act, think, and learn differently today? And what are the implications for education and for society?" commented President Jonathan Fanton of the MacArthur Foundation, one of the nation's largest private philanthropic foundations which launched a $50 million digital media and learning initiative in 2006.

Figure 2.4 shows the evolution of digital communications, and Figure 2.5 targets the devices that millennials, the techno-savvy generation, "cannot live without." Your challenge will be to meet the millennials where they shop, search, travel, play, and learn.

According to Tunheim Partners in their presentation Marketing to Millennials, the lifestyle of a 12- to 24-year-old may be described as follows:

- *Will never read a newspaper but attracted to some magazines*
- *Will never own a land-line phone*
- *Will not watch television on someone else's schedule*
- *Trusts unknown peers more than experts*
- *For first time (2005), willing to pay for digital content—never before*
- *Little interest in the source of information and most information aggregated*
- *Community at the center of Internet experience*
- *Less interested in television than any generation before*
- *Wants to move content freely from platform to platform with no restrictions*
- *Wants to be heard (user generated)*
- *Uses text messaging and IM. Thinks e-mail is for their parents.*

When viewing the figures and the information above, what new products and services can you think of to provide to this market as they begin to enter college and the workforce and start purchasing homes? A Nickelodeon study conducted in 2002 concluded that millennials have "more choices, more freedom, and more empowerment possibly than any other generation." In addition,

Action Step 11

Spotting Trends in Your Selected Target Markets

1. Select a target market of your choice—**Millennials**, healthy and active seniors, frail and elderly, soccer kids, preteens. Search the net for statistics and information. Start with census data at *http://www.census.gov* and continue using search engines.
2. Using your statistics, intuition, and knowledge of the target market, work back through the baby boomer starting points on page 34 and go through a day in the life of your selected target market. What trends do they identify with? What products and services do they desire? How can you best meet their needs?
3. Next, review the list of products, ideas, and services baby boomers identified with. Compile a similar list for your Target Customer. As you continue through this book, you will learn how to further refine your target market.

Millennials Persons born between 1977 and 1994

---

figure **2.4**

Evolution of Digital Communities

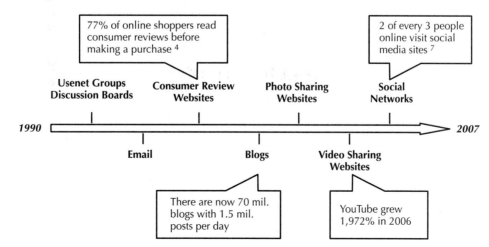

Source: *http://www.cymfony.com/files/pdf/Making_the_case_social_media_2007.pdf* (Accessed April 20, 2008).

figure **2.5**

The Millennial Value Pyramid

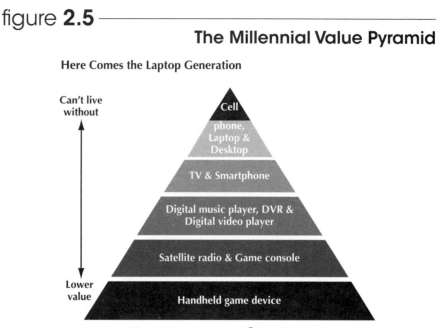

Here Comes the Laptop Generation

Source: Millennial Strategy Program®, Frank N. Magid Associates

Miami University entrepreneurship professor Jay A. Kayne notes that millennials "have an aversion to being ordinary." Marketing to millennials requires you to prove that your product or service is relevant to their lives more so than in any past generation. And you will need to be constantly aware of changing technologies and communication patterns of the millennials. Not only will millennials play a significant role in the workforce, but we believe their impact through entrepreneurship will be even stronger.

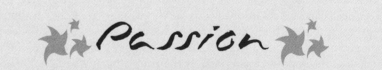

Build Your Future, Inc.

Redefining a life and living with passion

For years Patti Moir dreamed of her *own* business with her *own* schedule, her *own* office, and her *own* clients. When she turned 55, Patti knew it was time for her to spread her wings and fly into a new life, where she would not only help high school students build their futures but also build her own new future. It would be a future that would include time for herself, her grandchildren, exercise, golf, and most of all time to enjoy the few sun-filled days in Lake Oswego, Oregon. Patti was passionate about finding the correct fit and balance in her life. After passionately teaching, tutoring, and counseling for more than 30 years, and with a secure pension in hand, Patti's vast experience and counseling reputation at one of the leading high schools in the country spurred her to open an educational counseling service business.

Patti's passion for helping millennials find their way through the college-planning process is a welcome relief to parents and teens. With the National Association for College Admission Counseling reporting a 315 to 1 student ratio, the trend toward stiffer admissions requirements, and a much more competitive atmosphere, many parents and teens require a specialist like Patti to maneuver through the admission maze. Patti has definitely found her passion for sunlight and students, and as a side benefit, has increased her income substantially.

The Splintering of the Mass Market

Today's consumers are informed, individualistic, and demanding. Their buying habits are often difficult to isolate, because they tend to buy at several levels of the market. For example, high-fashion, high-income consumers may patronize upscale boutiques but buy their household appliances at Wal-Mart. They may shop at Williams-Sonoma for specialty Sprinkles cake mixes but buy their flour in bulk at Costco.

For the consumer, three key factors have splintered the mass market:

1. **A shrinking middle class:** The income of the wealthiest fifth of the population has grown by approximately 20 percent, and that of the poorest has stagnated or dipped, according to U.S. census data. In 2008, about 22 percent of all children in the United States lived below the federal income guidelines for poverty of $21,200 for a family of four. Two distinct marketing strategies are developing to reach customers at both ends of the population.

2. **Ethnic groups shifting and growing throughout the United States:** According to census data, 50 percent of the country's over 36 million Hispanics reside in California and Texas. California, New York, and Hawaii are the home of half of the over 12 million Asians in the United States. Over 70 percent of Blacks live in the South and the Northeast. The greater Los Angeles area, already the most ethnically diverse population in the world, has television stations available in Korean, Spanish, Chinese, Farsi, and Vietnamese. In one Orange County, California school district, the students speak more than 50 languages. Although ethnic groups have been concentrated, ethnic diversity is rapidly expanding throughout the United States.

3. **Living arrangements are changing and evolving:** The U.S. population comprised of stepfamilies, dual-career families, single parents, grandparents raising grandchildren—according to 2000 Census data, they number over 2,000,000—three-generation households, and increasing population of the frail elderly. Skyrocketing housing prices around the country have more adult children returning to the nest, and baby boomers are even moving in with elderly parents.

If you look with new eyes, you can see additional major segments emerging, growing, and becoming more powerful: affluent 80-year-olds, the rising Hispanic upper class, and preteen consumers. Take a few minutes to surf *http://www.mediafinder.com* and *http://www.mrmagazine.com*. Within minutes, you will discover hundreds of very narrow target markets reached by magazines. Although many predicted magazines would be folding under the pressure of the Internet, 389 magazines were launched in 2007. We found three interesting magazines launched recently that are narrowly focused:

Lofts: "*Lofts* magazine's mission is to explore the urban lifestyle anywhere, capitalizing on a sweeping national movement toward a new urban aesthetic and city living. *Lofts* combines this density-conscious, preservation-oriented lifestyle aimed at efficient and ecologically-minded living with the propensity for beautiful, eclectic, and diverse interiors."

Stretching Canvas Magazine: "*Stretching Canvas* is a quarterly publication from the editors of *International Tattoo Art* which covers work by tattoo artists. Tattoos have become increasingly popular and are now regarded as art. *Stretching Canvas* takes it a step further by showing tattoo artists as complete artists with work in art galleries."

Miller-McCune: "*Miller-McCune,* heavy on information and light on fluff, is distributed bimonthly and harnesses current academic research with real-time reporting to address social, political, and economic concerns. Contentwise, this publication is closer to a research journal."

Today's technology allows us to define ever-smaller target markets. With the power of the Internet and the right software, we achieve one-to-one target marketing. If you order product B, and 50 percent of customers who order product B also order product Z, information or an advertisement for product Z will pop up on your screen automatically—basically, a salesperson in a box. Amazon.com's incredible software provides an excellent example of one-to-one marketing and sales promotion.

FRANCHISERS RESPOND TO SOCIAL AND CULTURAL CHANGES

Take a look at the top ten new franchises for 2008 according to *Entrepreneur* Magazine, and see how they are meeting the needs of a changing society. Massage Envy, Snap Fitness, Super Suppers, Mathnasium, and Instant Tax Service serve the time starved and stressed out.

Entrepreneur Magazine's Top Ten New Franchises for 2008

1. Instant Tax Service (Retail tax preparation and electronic filing)
2. Massage Envy (Therapeutic massage services)
3. Snap Fitness (24-hour fitness center)
4. System4 (Commercial cleaning)
5. One Hour Air Conditioning & Heating (HVAC replacement and services)
6. Super Suppers (Do-it-yourself home meal preparation)
7. Mathnasium Learning Centers (Math learning center)
8. The Growth Coach (Small-business coaching and mentoring)
9. Play N Trade Franchise (New and used video games)
10. N-Hance (Wood floor and cabinet renewal systems)

Source: *Entrepreneur* Magazine's 2008 Franchise 500, *http://www.entrepreneur.com/franchises/toptenlists/index.html* (Accessed April 20, 2008).

The following list includes *Entrepreneur's* fastest-growing franchises for 2007–2008 based on straight growth in the number of franchises verified in *Entrepreneur's 29th Annual Franchise 500* listing. With three of the leading franchises being tax services, one recognizes the complexity of our tax system. According to *Entrepreneur,* "The following list is not intended to endorse any particular franchise but simply to provide a starting point for research. Perhaps after a careful investigation of these franchises, you may find a franchise that can put you on the fast track to success."

Entrepreneur Magazine's Top Ten Fastest-Growing Franchises for 2008

1. Jan-Pro Franchising International
2. 7-Eleven, Inc.
3. Subway
4. Jani-King
5. Dunkin' Donuts
6. Jackson Hewitt Tax Service
7. Bonus Building Care
8. Instant Tax Service

9. Liberty Tax Service

10. RE/MAX International, Inc.

Source: *Entrepreneur* Magazine's 2008 Franchise 500, *http://www.entrepreneur/com/ franzone/fastestgrowing.index.html* (Accessed April 20, 2008).

INFORMATION EXPLOSION

If some days you feel like you are on information overload, you are! The average person today receives more information from their big-city Sunday newspaper than a person living during the Middle Ages received in an entire lifetime. The wants and needs of the American consumer are screaming, "Faster! Pare it down! Train me!" They demand quality over quantity, they want to earn lots of money, and pile on the excitement. Generation Y does not take their tents to the mountains and veg out for the week. They take their mountain bikes and mountain climbing equipment. They plan their vacations on the Internet while talking in chat rooms, find the best climbing sites, jump in the Prius with their friends in the back watching DVDs, and use a GPS system to guide them to their destinations. No vegging out is allowed at any point. And REI, a major outdoor retailer, is there to meet their needs.

Instead of turning to the TV for our news, we turn to vlogs, blogs, You-Tube, and Yahoo! News. Instead of turning to maps to find our way, we turn to MapBlast or our GPS. Instead of calling a friend for a restaurant recommendation, we log on to tripadvisor.com. Instead of calling a travel agent, we log on to Fodor's, and instead of calling a doctor, we log on to Web MD. With all this information at our fingertips, we are overloaded and sometimes overwhelmed with our options. We *need* personal information managers. Could that be a potential service business?

Figure 2.6, Online Publishers Association's 2008 Internet Activity Index, breaks down how we spend our time on the Internet. Our private lives and

figure **2.6**

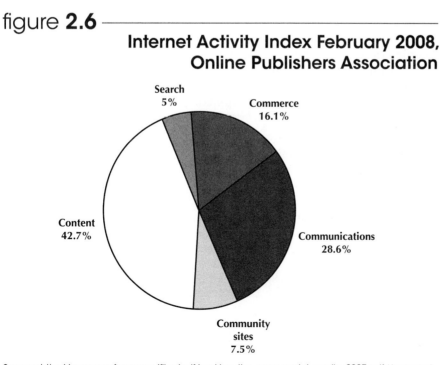

Internet Activity Index February 2008, Online Publishers Association

Search 5%

Commerce 16.1%

Content 42.7%

Communications 28.6%

Community sites 7.5%

Source: *http://www.cymfony.com/files/pdf/making_the_case_social_media_2007.pdf* (Accessed April 25, 2008).

Action Step 12

Have Some Fun Identifying Problems and Opportunities

1. Form a focus group of your friends or colleagues and ask them about their wants and needs. It is likely that you will discover gaps in the marketplace. Do not judge the answers you receive; you are only seeking information, and the more you get, the better. Ask participants to respond to questions such as the following:

   - What frustrates you most about your daily life? Banking? Dating? Buying a car? Grocery shopping? Clothing shopping? Buying textbooks? Registering for class?

   - What products or services do you need or want but cannot find?

   - What products or services would enhance your quality of life?

   - How could you increase your productivity without working more hours?

2. If you are dealing with a nonconsumer product or service, change the questions to fit your market. Make a list of the gaps that the group identifies, then project the list out as far as you can into the marketplace and follow the wants, needs, and frustrations of your friends. Are any of their needs national in scope? Are they global?

work lives are converging. With technology, our workplaces can be in contact with us 24/7 wherever we are in the world. We spend less time at home and more time at work, becoming more dependent on the workplace to provide us with financial-planning classes, travel services, company concierges, dry cleaning, child and adult day care, and so on. Each change becomes an opportunity for the enterprising entrepreneur. How can you help your customer manage information overload? And how can you manage the appropriate amount of contact your customer wants to have with you?

Have some fun now with a group of people and complete Action Step 12. Remember, the more problems you spot, the more opportunities arise. With each problem, you move one step closer to your Business Plan.

TECHNOLOGY REVOLUTION

The inexpensive microchip that runs a 2008 Sony PlayStation3 today cost $1,000 in 1993 and powered high-end servers. The computer has changed every facet of modern life. We rarely reach a human being when we telephone a business. When frustrated, we look up their Web site and send an e-mail message or a text message. Computer-to-computer communication is now a way of life. Handwritten letters seem to be a thing of the past. We use videophones, teleconferencing, iPhones and send jokes via e-mail to our friends. What impact will technology have on your business? What opportunities are just waiting for someone to exploit them?

The Human Genome Project mapped the 30,000 genes that make up human DNA. But now the quest is on to discover the roles hundreds of thousands of proteins play in making us human. Possibilities for products and services are mind-boggling and will come at an incredible pace. Will there be genetic testing centers cropping up in every city? Will people go to one of these centers before getting married to have potential mates evaluated? How far will we go to customize our children? Will there be franchised centers?

Embedded microchips are common in veterinary medicine, giving veterinarians instant access to a pet's medical history. Will it be long before people also have embedded microchips? One restaurant recently encouraged customers to have embedded chips so that they could automatically be charged for food and drinks. Can you discover any other new uses for embedded chips? What about in appliances? Clothing? Furniture? Sports equipment?

Keep up on technology news by watching technology-oriented programs on television, surfing the Internet, reading *Forbes ASAP* and *Scientific American,* and checking out MIT's and CalTech's Web sites. Reviewing MIT's Media Lab site at *www.media.mit.edu* on April 25, 2008 brought up a phenomenal array of research projects, several of which are highlighted below. Further information on their current research projects can be found at *www.media. mit.edu/research*.

MIT Media Lab

<u>City Car</u>, a stackable, electric, environmentally friendly, shared-use, two-passenger city vehicle that integrates with a city's existing transportation infrastructure and power grid to change the way we travel in dense urban areas.

The **world's first powered ankle-foot prosthesis,** which successfully mimics the elegance of nature, propelling the wearer forward with each step, and providing mechanical behavior closer to natural walking, increasing both speed and normality of gait for amputees.

The **Huggable,** a robotic teddy bear for use in children's hospitals, nursing homes, or for early education. Equipped with full-body sensate skin and a series of sensors, it responds to a person's presence and touch, and can act as a medical monitoring device.

Scratch, a new programming toolkit that makes it easier for kids to manipulate graphics, images, and sounds to create animated stories, video games, and interactive art. Just as children can build physical structures with LEGOs, they can "construct" computer creations with Scratch.

The Media Laboratory provides a unique environment for exploring basic research and applications at the intersection of computation and the arts. Research at the Media Lab comprises interconnected developments in an unusual range of disciplines, such as software agents; machine understanding; how children learn; human and machine vision; audition; speech interfaces; wearable computers; affective computing; advanced interface design; tangible media; object-oriented video; interactive cinema; digital expression—from text, to graphics, to sound; and new approaches to spatial imaging, nanomedia, and nanoscale sensing.

Source: MIT Media Lab, *http://www.media.mit.edu/?page_id=110* (Accessed April 25, 2008).

The future of integrating science into all areas of our lives as shown above through the innovative and creative ideas of MIT researchers proves that the future holds incredible improvements for our lives. As entrepreneurs work with technology experts and researchers, we will see more of our problems solved and our needs met through their efforts.

With artificial body parts and transplanted organs an everyday occurrence, will cancer, Parkinson's, Alzheimer's, and heart disease become distant memories because of advances in biotechnology? If these diseases were cured, what could you do with the empty doctor's offices? Medical buildings? Equipment? One enterprising entrepreneur in Southern California follows the changes in medical equipment and then scoops up the "old" technology equipment, services it, and sells it to third-world countries.

Surgeons provide online instructions in real time to operating rooms throughout the world. When a patient's chest is open and a surgeon must cut in a precise spot, Dr. Sam Melia from Syracuse is ready to assist—not only for his own patients in Syracuse, but also for doctors and patients in places like Bolivia. Doctors monitor patients at home with products previously available only at a hospital. This saves untold hospital bed space and doctor visits. Do you know someone with a chronic illness? How could technology help him or her?

New high-tech materials from the aerospace industry allowed Van Phillips, founder of the Flex-Foot, to invent, design, and market innovative lower-limb prosthetic devices constructed of 100 percent carbon fiber. Amputees are now benefiting from the use of incredible new materials and design capabilities (see Figure 2.7). New materials used creatively have allowed many businesses to produce products for industry and consumers. Technology has revolutionized the lives of the disabled, and the future holds even more promise.

In a past edition, we listed *Forbes ASAP's* "25 Cool Things You Wish You Had . . . and Will." Amazingly, many things that seemed incredible just 10 years ago are now available, such as powerful personal digital assistants,

figure **2.7**

Flex-Foot Technology Sends Athlete Flying

Source: *http://www.flexfoot.com/lisalib/getfile.aspx?itemid=11190* © Ossur 2002–2004.

wearable computers, e-books, toxin testers, and common-cold detectors. Will the earthquake detectors and digital spines predicted become common in the next 5 years?

The Greening of the World

In response to the global warming problem, the Greening of the world has been accepted. One of the largest research facilities in the United States, Battelle, manages thousands of projects for both industry and the government with over 7,000 scientists, engineers, and support specialists. Battelle projects the following Green technologies over the next 13 years.

What Can Green Do for You?

In 1970, Kermit the Frog (voiced by Jim Henson) crooned, "It's not that easy being green, having to spend each day the color of the leaves."

Welcome to the 21st century, Kermit, a time when you could be the mascot for an entire movement. Green is now synonymous with sustainability and environmentally friendly practices. Green, as everyone knows, is the hottest thing going, so it's much easier to be Green today than it was 40 (or fewer) years ago.

1. **Increased Use of Renewable and Sustainable Fuels for Electric Power Generation:** In the future, population growth and economic expansion, particularly in China and India, will mean an increased use of electricity. While electricity is a clean form of energy, the fuels often used to generate it are not, especially burning coal that has numerous emissions, including carbon dioxide, a principal greenhouse gas.

   That's why our panel anticipates a dramatic increase in such Green fuels as wind power, solar power, fuel cells, biofuel, and clean coal technologies. Renewable and sustainable fuels for electric power generation could greatly reduce carbon emissions and other greenhouse gas emissions by reducing the current reliance on coal-burning, central-station power plants. Such fuels also offer an alternative to nuclear power.

2. **Water Resource Management, Including Reuse and Recycling of Water:** Efforts to conserve water will become more important, as will new technologies addressing desalination. Clean water technologies will improve the quality and supply of fresh water to people around the world and help limit the expansion of deserts and waste areas.

   Graywater is neither fresh (potable) nor heavily contaminated—it comes from our houses, from showers and baths, laundry, sinks, and dishwashers. It may still, however, contain microorganisms that must be treated, but it may be possible in the future to treat graywater at the point of use rather than in municipal water treatment plants.

3. **Carbon Regulations and Policy:** It is highly likely that the U.S. will join with other countries in the future to limit and reduce carbon use. States and regions across America are adopting climate policies, such as the development of regional greenhouse gas reduction markets, the creation of state and local climate action and adaptation plans, as well as increasing renewable energy generation. These are ways of cutting greenhouse gas emissions to reduce the growing threat of global climate change.

   In the next 12 years, there may be regulations on vehicle carbon emissions, taxes on carbon emissions, and credits given to those who meet their carbon emission standards, and these credits can be sold on commodity markets that already exist. These regulations will require the development and large-scale adoption of cleaner, advanced energy systems.

4. **Green is Good Business:** It's happening already—doing some good for the environment while still making money. Green technologies can reduce industrial waste and energy use and make it cheaper to manufacture a product, which benefits everyone. Many companies may show greater concern about their environmental practices in response to their concerns about the well-being of their customers and the sustainability of their processes and products for long-term corporate growth.

   Additionally, there is a movement toward Green labeling of products in Europe that will likely come to the U.S. in the future, such as our current nutritional labeling for food products. It is probable that product labels will increasingly provide information about environmental impacts of the product.

5. **The Greening of Transportation:** At least a third of greenhouse gas emissions come from vehicles, and more cars and trucks are being built every day. The development of renewable and sustainable fuels for automobiles and trucks, including ethanol and many other types of biofuels now being explored, will have importance in the future.

   The Battelle panel expects the further deployment of hybrid cars, the development of the "plug-in" electric vehicle, and fuel cell cars. It also sees an increased use of fuel cells and advanced batteries as auxiliary power units for automobiles and trucks, reducing the consumption of fuels for cooling and electronics. On the back end, new technologies will emerge to reduce carbon emissions from cars and trucks—perhaps even allowing the capture and storage of carbon.

6. **Increasing Availability of Green Products and Services:** While the panel noted in its fourth entry the importance of Green being good business, that is only the supply side point of view. There is another trend that dovetails with it—consumers will want to buy Green products and services in the future.

   Consumers will become better educated and more informed about the environmental attributes of what they buy, and they will clamor for variety. Because there will be more information available to them, especially through the Internet, they also will have more choices and are likely to prefer Green products and services. More products will be designed for eventual disposal with each product having a disposability plan. More products will be designed for reduced greenhouse gas emissions and other types of waste effluents, and packaging will be reduced to avoid more solid waste.

7. **A Systems Approach to Environmental Analysis:** At first glance, this one has a high hurdle of understanding. But think of it this way—the trend in the past has been to evaluate the environmental qualities of products, processes, and plants at the local level without looking at the broader ecology of production, distribution, and consumption.

   In the future, we will evaluate products, services, and processes at the macrosystem level. When we look at the advantages of biofuels, such as ethanol from corn, we also will have to consider the entire system that includes the chemicals used for pesticides, herbicides, and fertilizers; the water consumption and the energy needed to grow corn; let alone the impacts of ethanol on corn prices going into the food chain.

   As computing capabilities increase, so will our ability to understand holistic systems.

8. **Increasing impact of the world's growing urban population on resources:** An increase in people throughout the world will mean more consumers, wasters, and polluters, therefore an expanding global population and its implications are a Green trend.

9. **Information and Communication Technologies (ICT) Used in Place of Traveling:** In the 1968 Stanley Kubrick movie *2001: A Space Odyssey,* Dr. Heywood Floyd (William Sylvester) calls his young daughter on Earth from a space station videophone to wish her a happy birthday. This is what we're talking about with our No. 9 entry.

   Today there are at least 16.5 million telecommuters or e-lancers in the U.S.—people who work from home or other locations by computer, the Internet, and telephone. These people are assumed to be consuming less gasoline by not having to physically commute into a central workplace five times a week.

Action Step 13

Investigate New Technologies

If you are a tech expert, share your insights with others to bring them up to speed. Technology affects every aspect of small business today—distribution, marketing, products, and so on. So if you are not tech savvy, it is time to get up to speed.

1. Read *Wired* either online at *http://wired.com* or in hard copy. What new technologies did you find? What new opportunities did you discover?

2. Surf the Internet and locate five to ten articles on new technologies. Can you discover any trends developing? Future opportunities? Share your findings with others. Remember a technological breakthrough in one industry will often lead to a breakthrough in another industry.

3. Read several copies of *The Futurist, Science,* or high-tech magazines in your selected industry. List all the new, developing technologies. What trends and opportunities can you find?

4. Log on to research university Web sites, such as the MIT site noted in this chapter.

With information in hand, you will be better prepared to focus on the opportunities within these changing technologies. As you go forth with your business idea, never stop reading and being aware of emerging technologies.

It has been estimated that at least 33 million Americans today could telecommute to work, saving 67 million metric tons per year of potential greenhouse gas emissions and reducing gasoline consumption to a point where U.S. imports of oil could decline.

In addition to telecommuting to work, an increasing number of people around the world are using the Internet for shopping, recreation, and socialization, thereby avoiding physical transportation and reducing energy costs and pollution.

10. **Green Buildings:** In the future, architects and other designers will give much greater consideration to how a building operates. New construction methods will be developed to reduce greenhouse gas emissions. Designs for Green buildings will integrate and optimize heating, cooling, lighting, and water systems.

Large urban building programs in countries such as China are increasingly sensitive to environmental impacts on the land and surrounding water and air. There also is emerging a new concept of Eco-cities planned to increase energy efficiency and reduce emissions.

Planned communities in the future may offer smaller office buildings and stores with smaller environmental footprints and more green spaces for recreation and socialization based on fewer people doing work at offices and shopping at stores.

Green building codes will likely be in force in the future, and Green buildings will increasingly incorporate alternative energy systems, especially solar power, fuel cells. geothermal energy, and possibly wind power.

Source: Battelle.org, "What Can Green Do For You?" Battelle Top Ten List Forecasts Emerging Green Technologies, *http://www.battelle.org/SPOTLIGHT/4-21-08emerginggreen.aspx* (Accessed April 25, 2008).

What opportunities do you see in the growth of Green technology for your community, business, products and services, and a changing marketplace and markets? Where will all these incredible trends presented above lead? What products and services will become obsolete? How will our jobs and lives change? We ask you not only to follow technology but to take chances and explore the incredible possibilities.

Some individuals make a business of trend watching. Among these are leading trend watchers Nicholas Negroponte, cofounder of the MIT Media lab and Chairman of the One Laptop per Child nonprofit; Ken Dychtwald, founder of AgeWave, an expert in the aging population (see Figure 2.3); and Faith Popcorn, author and founder of the Brain Reserve. Popcorn stated in a recent interview with Women.com, "At Brain Reserve, my marketing consulting company, we braille the culture. We read every imaginable magazine, newspapers from all over the world, we watch television, we go the movies, and we read books. And from all of our brailling, we start gathering information and looking at things that keep reoccurring in different industries in the culture, and these things point us to trends." Throughout this book, we will continue to ask you to "braille the culture," not only before you start your business, but as you continue to run and prosper in your business.

Locate your "industry gurus" and read *everything* they write. In addition to individual trend watchers, major market research firms Nielsen and Burke provide extensive studies, many of which are available on the Net. Action Step 13 asks you to explore new technologies in depth.

INFORMATION IS EVERYWHERE

Market research Collection and analysis of data pertinent to current or potential viability of a product or service

It is hoped that the information presented so far has your creative juices flowing. If you want to learn more and explore several opportunities and potential markets, you will need **market research**, creativity, and intuition to discover the right opportunity for you. Conducting research is easier with the advent of the greatest information data bank ever—the Internet. Research data previously available only to large corporations with big R&D budgets are now available to you free, or for only a few dollars. If you keep your eyes wide open, your intuition and creativity will blossom.

Secondary Research

Researching industries and markets takes three forms: secondary, primary, and "new eyes" research. **Secondary research** should be your starting point. When you read what someone else has discovered and published, you are carrying out secondary research. Using the Internet and asking Google to search for census data and locating newspaper articles containing information you think will be helpful are both forms of secondary research. For instant access to U.S. and international newspapers and other publications, use *http://www. newspapers.com* or *http://www.newsdirectory.com*.

Secondary research Reading and using previously published (primary) research

Keeping your eyes open not only to your industry but to other industries is vital, because many times services and products from one industry can be adapted to another. Also, ideas and research currently being explored within one function of a company can be adapted into another function, such as computer software. Reinventing the wheel is not necessary for entrepreneurs to succeed. One can choose to improve the wheel's looks, speed, or function or to reduce the cost—all can be highly lucrative.

Conducting good, thorough secondary research will prepare you to perform targeted primary research, because you will be better prepared to ask focused questions and thus get to the heart of any issue much more quickly. Also, by continuing to flood your brain with information, you will start to build your intuition; then your "new eyes" will work even better.

Contact **trade associations** such as the National Restaurant Association (Figure 2.8) for industry, supplier, distributor, and customer information. Trade associations conduct research, publish **trade journals**, and offer books and courses. They may also provide data to project how much money one can net in small business. Good research techniques here will save lots of footwork. Never underestimate the information available through associations. Their primary goal is the success of their members, so they listen and are attuned to their members' information needs. Early on in your research, national and local association chapters often can provide you with invaluable contacts for further primary research. Begin with the Internet Public Library's listing of associations at *http://www.ipl.org/div/aon*. Many associations offer student memberships at a reduced cost, offering access to Web sites and specialized research. Also, take time to ask people in your industry which associations they belong to and which magazines and websites they use.

Trade associations Groups dedicated to meeting the needs of a specific industry

Trade journals Narrowly focused magazine on specific industry or activity

Next, move on to *http://www.mediafinder.com* to find magazines that reach your **target market** and trade journals in your industry. Many have online access to their research and periodicals. Magazines develop **media kits**, many available online, that provide statistics on their readership for their advertisers. This is one of the quickest ways to get a quick read on the marketplace. Reading magazines and media kits will show you competitive products, interests shared by your customers, and industry and product trends; and it will provide you with extensive **demographic, psychographic,** and usage information.

Target market Segment of a market most likely to purchase the product or service. Possesses desire, dollars, and authority

Media kits Readership profiles, ad information, and market research developed by magazines for potential advertisers

Demographic Quantifiable data on population, race, age, education, income, gender, and so on

Sometimes highly technical journals are not easy to locate online or in stores. If this is the case, ask your library to help you locate the corporate libraries within your local area and industry. Many corporate libraries will

Psychographic Descriptive information on values, attitudes, and lifestyles

figure **2.8**

Homepage for Restaurant.org

Source: *http://www.restaurant.org*. Courtesy of National Restaurant Association, 2008.

(in**credible**resource

State of the Nation

http://www.stat-usa.gov, 1–800-STAT-USA, (202) 482–1986: STAT-USA's *State of the Nation* scours the government information vaults, assembles that information in one location, and delivers it via advanced computer technology. The information is available by subscription online for $200 per year or $75 per quarter. In addition, individual reports can be purchased without a subscription. For free access to the information, locate your local federal depository library at *http://catalog.gpo.gov/fdlpdir/FDLPdir.jsp*, and complete your research. *State of the Nation* data is compiled by the Economics and Statistics Administration within the U.S. Department of Commerce.

Both historical and current economic and financial data are available along with Consumer Price Index (CPI), housing, employment, manufacturing, economic policy, and general economic indicators. This impressive collection of data is easy to use and provides excellent statistical backup data for a Business Plan. Remember, bankers live and die by numbers, and this is where you may find the numbers to support your business ideas and dreams.

allow individuals access to their facilities. In addition, their trained librarians can be an invaluable resource, not only in locating information but in searching out faculty members who are conducting research applicable to your business venture.

In fact, as you begin your research, you would also do well to locate the best research librarian in your college or local library. In many universities, individual libraries exist within certain specialties, such as pharmacy or biomedical engineering. Check the Internet to locate university faculty members throughout the world who may be conducting research applicable to your business venture. Throughout the next few chapters, we will be introducing you to many additional secondary sources, but it is now time to begin your industry research with Action Step 14.

Primary Research

After you learn the basics about your industry, customers, suppliers, and competitors through secondary research, you are ready to conduct primary research, interacting with the world directly by talking to people and perhaps interviewing them. It is time to find out exactly what your potential customer wants: Do not make assumptions! Do not give them what you want to give them—*give them what they want and will pay for*. Go out and ask questions:

- What brands do you wish your favorite clothing store would carry?
- How likely are you to use the Internet to make dinner reservations?
- How much do you usually spend each month on fast-food meals?
- How would your ideal automobile dealer behave?
- What would you not buy on the Internet?

Ask vendors and suppliers: What advertising works best in businesses like ours? What products are hot? What services are being offered? What are the biggest problems for suppliers in the industry? Ask small-business owners: With whom do you bank? Where did you obtain your first financing? What percentage of sales do you spend on advertising? How do you deal with shipping charges? How do you encourage repeat customers?

New Eyes Research

New eyes research provides a variety of fresh ways to look at a business. Based on your knowledge, experience, and intuition, play detective. You might become a "mystery shopper" to check out your competition. You might sit in your car and take telephoto pictures of a business you are thinking about buying; when **Target Customers** appear, photograph them so that you can profile them later. Stand in a supermarket aisle and, trying not to look nosy, observe what is in people's shopping carts. For example:

Hamburger + chips + Popsicles + apples + *Redbook* = busy family with young active children; probably driving a van or SUV

Protein bars + steak + *Runner's World* + GQ + asparagus + pesto = Single man who is athletic, clothes- and weight-conscious, and probably likes to cook

Profiling your Target Customer demographically and psychographically is necessary for you to gain a handle on your customers' needs and wants.

Action Step 14

Launch Your Industry Research

1. Use the Internet to locate the names of trade associations your business would be part of and make note of the addresses, phone numbers, and Web sites. Contact the associations and request information. Because you are a potential member, they should send you an enormous amount of information and provide membership details. If you mention you are a student conducting research, they may be surprisingly helpful and may even offer student memberships. Also, to enhance your research, contact associations your suppliers and customers may belong to. Combining this information will provide you with an incredible amount of data to sift through.

2. Locate a local chapter of a national association relevant to your business and attend a local meeting as a guest or student.

3. Use *http://www.mediafinder.com* to locate magazines or journals within your selected industry, magazines or journals that reach your Target Customers, and magazines or journals for your suppliers. Spend some time on the Net or in the library researching your list and delving deeper into the information.

4. Select at least one magazine or journal from each of the categories and locate their media kit online. Media kits generally provide an excellent start for your specific research. Complete this Action Step before moving on; you will need the information to complete the Action Steps in Chapters 3 through 5.

Target Customers Persons who have the highest likelihood of buying a product or service

Action Step 15

Decode the Secrets of the Shopping Cart

1. Use your "new eyes" to uncover the lifestyle of your customer by analyzing the contents of a supermarket shopping cart. Play detective the next time you are in a supermarket and make some deductions about lifestyles as you observe the behaviors of shoppers.

2. Give each subject a fantasy name, perhaps associated with a product (Chad Cereal, Steve Steak, and Sally Sugar) so that you can remember your insights. What can you deduce about each shopper's lifestyle? What do their shoes say? Their clothes? Their jewelry? Their hairstyle? Their car?

3. Put these deductions together with a demographic checklist (sex, age, income, occupation, socioeconomic level), and then decide if any of these shoppers are potential Target Customers for your business.

4. Trained marketers look for a category of buyer known as a "heavy user." A heavy user of apples would eat 7 to 10 apples a week. A heavy user of soda would drink four a day. A heavy user of airlines—called a "frequent flyer"—flies 10 to 30 times a year. Can you determine who the heavy users are in your business?

Niche A small, unique slice of an industry

Industry segment Potential slice of industry market share

Profiling will be covered thoroughly in later chapters, but start training your observation faculties by completing Action Step 15.

New eyes research is fun. Combined with books, magazines, trade journals, publications (*The Wall Street Journal,* for example), and talking to people, it will get you all the way to your Business Plan. And the Business Plan will either lead you to success or show you that your idea is not worth any more of your time.

Train your mind. Remain open to new ideas, new information, new statistics, new people, and a changing world. Observe everything. Keep your ideas in your Adventure Notebook. The more ideas that pour in, the more likely you are to find the right fit for you and your target market. Alex Rusch, the founder of the largest audio-books firm in Switzerland, RuschVerlag, said he kept a notebook, and when he had 200 ideas, he sat down and reviewed them all before launching his firm. Chapter 3 will help you sort through your ideas.

THE BIG PICTURE

A Business Plan begins with the "big picture"—the industry overview. Industries go through life cycles. Products and services within industries also progress through the stages of the cycle: embryo, growth, maturity, and decline. At the same time, target markets experience major cyclical changes. The industry overview in your Business Plan helps you gain perspective on your **niche** and helps the reader, the potential lender or investor, understand why you have chosen to pursue this particular segment of the market.

To be successful in small business, you need to know what business you are really in and where your business is situated in its life cycle. Entrepreneurs tend to be in a big hurry. They want to push on, to get on with it, to throw open the doors to customers, and read the bottom line—and that is not all bad. But before you charge into the arena, step back and examine what is going on in your **industry segment.** Where are the lines forming? In what part of your community do you see "Going Out of Business" signs? Where are the start-ups? What is hot? What is cooling down? Which business segments will still be thriving 3 years from now? If you opened the doors of your new business today, how long would it be before your product or services were no longer valuable or wanted?

Let us back up and get the big picture. Before the Industrial Revolution, most people were self-employed. Farmers and sheepherders were risk takers because they had to be; there were few other options. The family functioned as an entrepreneurial unit.

Today's growth of megacorporations should not be viewed as a threat to the small venture but as an opportunity. First, most large corporations are dependent on small business to produce support products and services. Second, bigger is not always better. Many small businesses—even those whose markets are expanding rapidly—are barely noticed by large corporations. And therein lies the opportunity! If you are lucky, you will hit on a high-tech idea and be bought out for millions by Bill Gates!

So look before you leap. Brainstorm with your family, friends, colleagues, and suppliers. Interview potential customers; they will tell you what they want and need. If you have done your research, your new eyes will be in full gear, and you will be able to recognize the opportunities and understand the risks. Continue to study the marketplace with your new eyes and never stop reading.

communityresource

The Global Consortium of Entrepreneurship Centers (GCEC)

Throughout the United States, over 200 entrepreneurship centers are ready, willing, and able to help you start up or expand your venture. Many of the centers are headquartered at universities and may include small-business development centers (SBDCs), small-business innovation research centers (SBIRs), innovation institutes, and franchise management institutes.

The centers serve the needs of their respective communities and thus are quite variable. Inexpensive or free workshops, consulting, short-term coursework, competitions, degree programs, and specialized programs are available.

To locate a center in your area, log on to the Web site for the Global Consortium of Entrepreneurship Centers at *http://www.nationalconsortium.org.* Several Entrepreneurship Centers are highlighted below.

DePaul University Coleman Entrepreneurship Center

> College of Commerce
> DePaul University
> 1 East Jackson
> Chicago, IL 60604
> Phone: (312) 362–8353

Programs and activities: Speakers Series, degree programs, assists entrepreneurs in exploring, launching, growing, and evolving their businesses; offers individual strategic management consulting.

Entrepreneurship Center

> Miller College of Business
> Ball State University
> 2000 University Avenue
> Muncie, IN 47306
> Phone: (765) 285–9002

Programs and activities: Business plan challenge, award program for entrepreneurs, assists emerging entrepreneurs as well as maturing businesses.

Center for Entrepreneurship

> Appalachian State University
> Appalachian Enterprise Center
> 130 Poplar Grove Connector
> Boone, NC 28608
> Phone: (828) 262–6196
> Web site: *http://www.entrepreneurship.appstate.edu*

Programs and activities: Association of Student Entrepreneurs, The Carole Moore McLeod Entrepreneur Summit, The Martha Guy Summer Institute for Future Business Leaders. In addition, the Center offers business start-up, capital formation, and intellectual property workshops, as well as mentoring and support to entrepreneurs through university professors and local successful entrepreneurs.

MIND MAPPING YOUR WAY INTO SMALL BUSINESS

Snowboard Express

Annie and Valerie loved to snowboard. For 7 years, they snowboarded every chance they had—Mammoth, Vail, Tahoe, Snowbird. They kept looking for ways they could make a living snowboarding. At school Annie and Valerie discovered the technique of mind mapping [see Figure 1.3]—a method of note taking using clusters and bubbles—to let information flow along its own course. They could mind map their way into the snowboarding business!

In the center of a large sheet of paper they wrote "snowboarding." In a bubble next to "snowboarding" they wrote "travel." Momentum built up. They wrote "segments," "beginners," "preteens," "teens," "college students," and "families." Then they wrote "clothes and accessories," "gloves," "pants," "jackets," "goggles," "boots," and "socks." Then they let their imaginations go even further and wrote "Europe," "East Coast," "California," "Utah," "contests," "lessons," "trips," "fun," "exciting," "skateboarders," "transportation," "buses."

"This is great fun!" Annie said.

"This smells like money and fun!" Valerie exclaimed.

The two friends kept on mapping until they developed an idea for their business—Snowboard Express—roundtrip weekend bus transportation to mountain ski resorts from five local pickup points surrounding Salt Lake City. Different resorts were selected each weekend.

Two or three weeks after they began booking their trips, they went back to their mind map and the words "clothes and accessories" jumped out at them. They went to one of the major manufacturers and bought out their seconds and sold them all to Snowboard Express customers at 100 percent over cost within 4 weeks.

After they had been in business for only 2 months, a few women asked if Valerie and Annie could provide weekday trips so they could have the mountains to themselves while their children were in school—and a new market segment was uncovered, and a gap was filled. They listened to their customers and began "Slope Thursdays."

Sometime in April, the riders began asking what Annie and Valerie were going to do for the summer. They responded by asking, "What are you doing this summer?" The answer they kept hearing was, "I'm going mountain biking." Valerie and Annie were off to explore the regional mountain bike trails. Afterward they talked to their bus drivers to determine how they could transport all the bikes on the buses. With their answers in hand and market research completed, "Mountain Bike Express" was born.

Brainstorming Techniques

In addition to mind mapping with a partner as did Valerie and Annie, you can gather a group of people together for a simple exchange of ideas, which can later lead to mind mapping sessions. If you gather around you people with wit, spark, creativity, positive attitudes, knowledge, and good business sense, the result will almost always surprise you and could lead to company growth, expanded profits, or perhaps the formation of a new business idea. With limitless possibilities, the trick is to structure brainstorming sessions in a way that maximizes creativity. You want members to encourage each other, to be able to stretch their minds, and to set their competitive instincts aside. A few suggestions follow.

When Gathering Participants and Planning Your Meeting

1. Try to find imaginative people who can stretch their minds and who can set their competitive instincts aside for awhile.
2. Remember, in brainstorming sessions, "no" is a no-no. You are not implementing yet. Skepticism will kill a session.
3. Find a neutral location and eliminate interruptions.
4. Encourage the members of the group to reinforce and believe in each other and also to challenge ideas.

5. Consider recording a brainstorming situation. If not, have someone record your ideas on a laptop or flip chart.

6. Pick a time that is convenient and not rushed to make it relaxed for all involved.

7. Invite 10 to 15 people; some will drop out, and you should allow for no-shows.

8. Schedule the starting time. Relax, serve tasty food, and begin after about a half-hour.

9. Allow time for self-introductions. Tell participants not to be modest. They are winners, and they want to be seen as winners. Have them speak in terms of accomplishments, problems, activities, and interests.

Tips

- Have everyone arrive with a business idea or a problem.
- Before the close of the first meeting, cast a vote to select two or three hot ideas and ask participants to prepare a one-page checklist summarizing and analyzing the ideas.
- Get together again within 2 weeks and brainstorm the hot ideas. Make it clear that the basic purpose is to get energy rolling, not to form a huge partnership.
- The best brainstorming sessions occur when you connect brain-to-brain with other creative, positive people; it helps remind you that you've still got it. Brain energy is real, and you need to keep tapping it.

LIFE-CYCLE STAGES

Economically, socially, technically, and financially, our world is changing at incredible speed. The world is at warp speed—a revolution. There are Internet coffeehouses in Africa with telecommunication satellites circling, China is exploding, Russian capitalistic entrepreneurs are expanding their reach, and opportunities abound.

Review past Action Steps and make a list of all the trends, products, services, and markets you unearthed. Divide these into four groups according to their current stage in the life cycle (Figure 2.9). If a trend is just beginning and is in its formative stage, label it *embryo*. If it is exploding, label it *growth*. If it is no longer growing and is beginning to wane, label it *mature*. If it is beyond maturity and feeling chilly, label it *decline*. Think through these life-cycle stages often. Everything changes—products, needs, technology, and neighborhoods. Complete Action Step 16.

Market signals are everywhere—in the newspaper (classified ads, bankruptcy notices, display ads), in the queues at the theater, in the price slashing after Christmas, and in discount coupons, rebates, closings, and grand openings. With practice, you can follow a product or target market through its life cycle. Which items have you seen go through their life cycle from upscale to deep discounts? Looking at the life-cycle diagram, you can see that the auto industry as a whole is very mature. Nonetheless, some of its segments remain promising; for example, convertibles, upscale imports, and hybrid vehicles. In the wealthiest suburbs, you see Porsches and Mercedes everywhere. Despite traffic jams, people are still driving, but the cars they drive reflect changing lifestyles. In some suburbs, drivers have weekend or lifestyle vehicles in addition to their main transportation.

Today, product life cycles are measured in terms of months and years rather than decades and generations, as seen in Figure 2.9. Few of us today could imagine life without the Internet. What will be the next big thing we will

Action Step 16

Match Trends with Life-Cycle Stages

1. Throughout this chapter, you should have discovered many trends, new products, and services. Pull out your notes and past Action Steps. Review Figure 2.9, draw a life-cycle chart, and place the trends, products, and services you have found in their appropriate stages. How many lie in the embryo/birth stage? In the growth stage? In the maturity stage?

2. It is now time to move forward and to try to discover possible opportunities within the embryo or growth stage What opportunities exist?

If you are entering the embryo stage, be prepared to "beat the pavement" for new business. If you are entering a mature or declining market, be ready to meet and beat the competition head on.

figure **2.9**

Life-Cycle Stages and Products

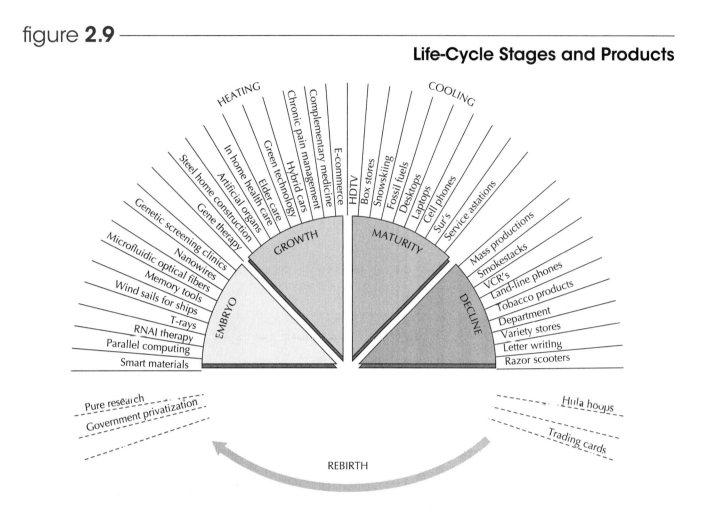

not be able to live without? Rapid technical and societal changes offer great opportunity but also pose increased risk if you make the wrong decision. The market no longer allows you years to test and prove your product or idea.

SUMMARY

Two tools will help you chart trends: researching—secondary, primary, and new eyes; that is, playing marketplace detective—and applying the life-cycle yardstick to products, industries, and so on. A life cycle has four stages: embryo, growth, maturity, and decline. Before you open the doors of your small business, you need to be aware of what stage your product is in.

Information on trends surrounds you—on the freeways, in the headlines and classifieds, at government agencies, and in the many trade associations. This information provides you with the big picture if you know how to look for it.

For your Business Plan, you will need to demonstrate your knowledge and understanding of the business opportunity you will pursue. Investors look for opportunities within growth segments of growth industries, and you should too. Investors look for solid data supporting your business idea. Be sure to file any hard data you find and include it in the appendices of your Business Plan.

You have looked at who you are and what you want in Chapter 1. You became a trend spotter in this chapter. Now it is time for you to put your research and ideas together to generate the right opportunity for you as you continue to pursue opportunities in Chapter 3.

THINK POINTS FOR SUCCESS

- The most valuable tool you have for charting trends is new-eyes research combined with extensive secondary and primary research.
- Keeping your eyes open, not only to your selected industry but also to developments in other industries that may impact yours, will keep you one step ahead.
- The life-cycle yardstick helps you discover a growth industry, decide what business you're really in, and uncover promising gaps and segments.
- Trends don't usually develop overnight. The signs are out for all to read months, sometimes years, in advance.
- Try to latch on to a trend that will help you survive in style for the next 3 to 5 years.
- Keep an eye out for new trends at all times. Don't assume that because you have caught one trend, that another one won't nip at your heels down the road.

- Once you know what segment you're in, focus your research.
- Save time and money by accessing valuable resources, such as trade associations and periodicals.
- Read everything you can and talk to everyone you can. The opportunities will appear endless.
- Trends are like customers. You can spot some by standing outside and others by staring through a window. Still others won't show up until you're in business, working and sweating away, wondering whether or not you'll make it.
- You're now a great trend spotter, so it's time to analyze the opportunities you have unearthed.

KEY POINTS FROM ANOTHER VIEW

EIGHT TECHNOLOGY TRENDS TO TRACK IN A WEB 2.0 WORLD

Technology alone is rarely the key to unlocking economic value: companies create real wealth when they combine technology with new ways of doing business. McKinsey and Company, a leading consulting firm, identifies eight technology-enabled trends that will shape businesses and the economy in coming years. The following is an expanded commentary on those trends.

1. Distributing co-creation

Co-creation is the process of allowing outsiders, connected via the Internet and other networking technologies, to participate in product development. In other words, companies can now outsource innovation to business partners, contract employees, and the like. Co-creation is a value chain and the networked distribution of product innovation both reduces costs and allows for products to be marketed sooner.

2. Consumers as co-creators

McKinsey looks at Threadless, the online clothing store, which asks visitors to its website to contribute t-shirt designs. This co-creation strategy has much in common (and is certainly influenced by) the free encyclopedia Wikipedia.com, which allows anyone to contribute articles and edit them—and, not identified by McKinsey—the various distributions of open-source software such as Linux and FreeBSD operating systems and OpenOffice, the office application suite that compares to Microsoft Office.

Indeed, it is Wikipedia that offers a succinct definition of this process, where co-creation is the practice of product or service development that is collaborative

and executed by developers and *stakeholders* [emphasis added]. The term was popularized by management writers C. K. Prahalad and Venkat Ramaswamy in *The Future of Competition* (2004).

They hold that value is co-created by the firm and the customer—not just inside the firm. To that dyad can be added the other stakeholders, too: freelancers, business partners, even government. What they suggest, of course, is business that is less "a private concern." Nevertheless, unlike working with contracted suppliers and partners, "managing" consumers and what they contribute presents numerous challenges about productivity, quality assurance, ownership, compensation, and the like.

3. Tapping into a world of talent

More than ever the world has become a pool of human resources and intelligence. McKinsey notes that the networking technology and the collaboration that it facilitates mean that "companies can outsource increasingly specialized aspects of their work and still maintain organizational coherence."

This is an important distinction because where co-creation decentralizes product development, it engenders new avenues of management and control as well as creativity and freedom. Management can now "parcel out" work to freelancers, other companies, legal departments, indeed, a host of shareholders in the development and vetting of a product—and manage numerous individuals all over the globe with everything from email to online teleconferencing.

The book you are reading was written on a college campus, managed by a publisher in a city far from that campus, produced by numerous individuals and its electronic files sent more than halfway around the world before it comes back as the finished book you bought in a college bookstore. The individuals who worked on the book belonged to small and large firms. Others were self-employed. McKinsey and other consultants see even more possibilities as technologies improve.

4.   The value chain of interactions

This an ongoing and increasingly important consideration for management in the future. The modalities of "wikis," "virtual team environments," "videoconferencing," not to mention ever increasing bandwidth, has made it possible to interact over a broad spectrum of activities ranging from front office to back office.

Making an Academy Award-winning film, for example, in New Zealand, with its computer animators in L.A., would not have been possible without the technology and the new management of interactions that companies not only have learned but are keeping to themselves in order to compete.

5.   Expanding the frontiers of automation

Everything from purchasing a product to making and distributing it before that purchase has been automated by the Internet. As these processes are standardized and interconnected, the range of possibilities for transformational and transactional activities increases. The task of finding a car part with one database and ordering it from another is only seamless because we are building in, at the get-go, the ability to exchange and use data in common. "Companies, governments, and other organizations have put in place systems to automate tasks and processes," McKinsey notes. Now these systems are "talking" to each other in the form of "forecasting and supply chain technologies; systems for enterprise resource planning, customer relationship management, and HR; product and customer databases; and websites."

6.   Unbundling production from delivery

"Technology helps companies to utilize fixed assets more efficiently," using them as components freed from the "monolithic systems" they were intended to serve to create value on their own. An example would be a fleet of trucks repurposed into hauling the product of another company—a product entirely different from the brand and picture painted on the van body. Only with the networking technologies now available can such capacity be tracked and used. Unbundling, however, has been met with some resistance when it is ordered from the top down. This happened when German utilities were ordered to introduce ownership unbundling to other companies by the EU. U.S. and state governments have also attempted this to benefit American consumers by unbundling energy assets.

As one observer noted, what McKinsey is onto here is not unlike the man in a village with the only cell phone. He learned how to rent out the phone when he was not using it.

7.   Putting more science into management

What McKinsey really means here is the access and use of vast amounts of information by managers. It points to how Amazon.com can track the tastes of its diverse customer base (its "customer segmentation") and thereby create a user interface—its webpage—virtually customer specific. The science here is database science and the correlation of purchase histories to web design. Indeed, with the arrival of the Web 2.0, consumers—not agencies and marketers—will have an enormous hand in the success and failure of a product or service.

Other companies that don't sell books and CDs, but simply information, have learned to do this, too. Ancestry.com sells subscriptions to its online genealogical research. As the user gradually establishes an account, he or she soon finds it more customized to his or her informational needs.

8.   Making businesses from information

Ancestry.com has already been mentioned. McKinsey's paradigms show a broader view of what is meant by this trend. Real estate websites that serve the house buyer can provide information that sellers and their agents might not want them to know. Armed with the "supply curve" and what housing really sells for, a potential homebuyer can have the advantage. In contrast, a supermarket can utilize the data from its security cameras—the raw footage—to redesign displays, end caps, and entire departments based on the traffic patterns they see in their honest clientele.

This trend can also be seen in the rise of businesses such as Carbonite, which offers a 24/7 connected backup service to protect valuable information on subscribers' hard drives to both businesses and private individuals. This could only be achieved with the Internet and the increased bandwidth now available to virtually every home that has a telephone, cable, or satellite connection.

Sources: "Technology alone is rarely the key to unlocking economic value: companies create real wealth when they combine technology with new ways of doing business" from the *McKinsey Quarterly*, Special to *CNET News.com*, 26 December 2007; C. K. Prahalad and Venkat Ramaswamy, *The Future of Competition* (Cambridge, Mass.: Harvard Business Press, 2004); David Niles, "German Energy Utilities: Resistance to Asset Unbundling," *Energy Business Review*, 30 January 2007; "Unbundling production from delivery can change the world," *The Sunjay Times*, 29 January 2008, http://times.jayliew.com; and Serdar Yegulalp, "Review: Five Online Backup Services Keep Your Data Safe," *InformationWeek*, 9 April 2007.

- Mesh your personal and business objectives with one of the many opportunities in the marketplace.
- Understand that your business objectives provide a positive and unique thrust to your business.
- Narrow your industry research until viable gaps appear.
- Gain insight into markets using the life-cycle yardstick.
- Discover how problems can be turned into opportunities.
- Understand how to use the North American Industrial Classification System (NAICS).
- Research your favorite industry using secondary and primary data.
- Discover the incredible association resources at your fingertips.
- Brainstorm creative solutions with mind mapping.
- Use a matrix grid for blending your objectives with your research findings to produce a portrait of a business.
- Define your business.
- Begin to develop your "elevator speech."

chapter 3

Opportunity Selection
Filtering Your Ideas

As you head for one of the three doorways to small business, you may feel weighed down with information; that is part of life in the Information Age. You may also be feeling exhilaration. Opportunities exist that were unheard of 2 years ago and, in some instances, 2 days ago. The speed of change is overwhelming. If you have done the research in Chapter 2, you understandably are experiencing information overload. Despite the fact that you are a creative, wound-up, and ready-to-charge person, unless you live vigorously for 200 years, you will never be able to follow up on all the changing trends you have discovered.

What you need is a filtering system, something like a wine press or a Mouli mill (the kitchen machine that turns apples into applesauce) to get rid of peels (segments that are not growing), stems (markets where barriers to entry are too high), and seeds (opportunities that do not mesh with your personal objectives).

After completing the Action Steps in Chapter 3, you will have amassed valuable information and identified several well-defined business opportunities, and you will be further along on your Business Plan.

WELCOME TO OPPORTUNITY SELECTION

Conducting research will help you exploit gaps, which are untapped segments in the marketplace. Research shows you what new skills you will need to develop. It aims the power of your mind at a particular segment and opportunity: It opens up the world. In fact, we suggest you always keep open to exploring global opportunities; the information in the Global Village box on page 69 that focuses on growing world markets may be just the information you need to send you researching further into exporting to Korea, Hungary, or Poland.

If you have been completing each Action Step as you read through this book, you are now ahead of the game. If you are not doing the Action Steps, go back and start. Here is a quick preview of the seven steps needed to achieve effective opportunity selection:

1. Keep personal and business objectives in mind throughout the filtering process.
2. Learn more about your favorite industry.
3. Identify three to five promising segments.
4. Through research, identify problems that need solutions.
5. Brainstorm for solutions.
6. Mesh possible solutions with your objectives.
7. Concentrate on the most promising opportunities.

At this point you have just begun to plan. The marketplace is open, filled with excitement and confusion. The most important thing is not to lose your momentum which is related to confidence, and confidence helps you win. Keep your personal and business objectives in the forefront as you search and evaluate opportunities.

Opportunity selection is like a huge funnel equipped with a series of filters (Figure 3.1). You pour everything into the funnel: goals, personality, problems,

figure **3.1**

Opportunity Selection Funnel

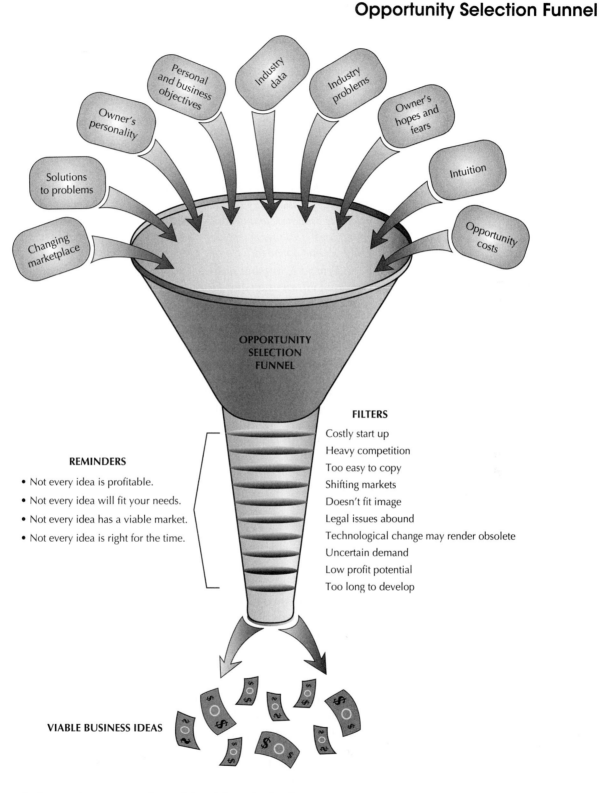

REMINDERS

- Not every idea is profitable.
- Not every idea will fit your needs.
- Not every idea has a viable market.
- Not every idea is right for the time.

FILTERS

Costly start up

Heavy competition

Too easy to copy

Shifting markets

Doesn't fit image

Legal issues abound

Technological change may render obsolete

Uncertain demand

Low profit potential

Too long to develop

hopes, fears, industry data, research, and intuition. And, after you narrow the choices, viable businesses filter through to the bottom. Carrying out this process gives you the knowledge of where you are going. And knowledge is power.

International Freelancer and Soloist

After Eric Duke graduated from law school, he freelanced as a lawyer while planning his wedding and yearlong European and Asian honeymoon with his new wife, Christy, who had just earned her accounting degree from the University of Minnesota. While planning the trip, Eric and Christy realized their true dream was to live overseas for several years. They figured now was the time to experience overseas living—no kids, no car payments, and no mortgage.

On researching the overseas job market, Eric and Christy recognized that continuing to freelance might be the best choice. Eric spent a great deal of time on the Internet and in the library researching opportunities. One day he found an article about a nearby conference for private investment abroad. Eric signed up, and after paying $2,500, he was ready to begin his primary research.

At the conference he came into contact with 50 lawyers from around the world. Eric made the best use of every meeting and break by finding out each lawyer's interests and needs. By the end of the meeting, he had set up three meetings for the following week. In addition, Eric had a handshake deal with a Greek lawyer and a new idea for one of his current clients for an international office.

Eric's $2,500 was well spent. Without the international research background information and his goals clearly in his mind, Eric would have not been able to respond to the opportunities. Although it may seem that some people fall into opportunities, most "lucky" people are fully prepared.

Before you begin your industry research, review Action Step 5, which asked you to "Inc. Yourself." Think back to what is important to you. Keep this picture in the front of your mind at all times. Stay focused on what you want your life and your business to become. As you begin to explore the vast opportunities within your selected industry, you will discover that some will mesh better than others. Making your business work for you and your customers will bring you the most satisfaction. Hold on to your business objectives, personal skills, passions, and strengths as you begin to follow the unending research threads.

INDUSTRY RESEARCH

Searching for trends in Chapter 2, you probably found several industries that sounded interesting. Next, you will be brainstorming, mind mapping, funneling, and matrixing ideas and opportunities throughout this chapter. It is time now to focus in on one industry in more depth and, by the end of the chapter, you will define your main business idea. The industry that interests you most might be genetics, robotics, infotainment, food service, travel, education, publishing, construction, manufacturing, or information services. Select an industry for which you know you can maintain interest and passion.

As you moved through your favorite industry collecting information from your previous Action Steps, what problems did you find? What are the solutions? How can you explore these further?

While Chapter 2 focused on the broader picture—trends and problems—the focus of Chapter 3 is on the industry and opportunity you select. Cabana Life's founder Melissa Papock (see the Passion box) needed to find a solution to her desire to be in the sun and her need for skin protection. In searching for a solution, she found a way to produce 100 percent protective clothing using patented High-IQ Sun Protection fabric, and she developed Cabana Life.

Melissa combined the sense of fashion she developed while working in merchandising, her desire for alternative sun protective clothing, and her

Malignant Melanoma Drives Entrepreneur

Cabana Life

"After being diagnosed with a malignant melanoma—the deadliest form of skin cancer—at age 26, I discovered something very important about the clothing that I thought was protecting me. Ordinary, light-weight clothing is often the equivalent of SPF 5! That is when my doctor informed me that sun protective clothing exists. I wondered why I hadn't heard of sun protective clothing, but when I saw the available options, I knew exactly why.

"Sun protective clothing is only helpful if you wear it, and I realized there was a need to develop STYLISH, 100% cotton, UPF clothing for my fellow fashion-conscious friends. The cotton collection offers a variety of beach-essentials including hats, cover-ups, tunics, shirts, and pants using pat-ented High-IQ Sun Protection for boys, girls, women, and expecting moms.

"So with the help of my loving husband (who also battled skin can-cer), we formed Cabana Life. The recent birth of our daughter has helped fuel our desire to protect and educate children and parents alike.

"Trust me, I never expected to hear the "C" word, and at such a young age! But if we can use our experiences help you protect yourself or loved ones, we've accomplished our goal. Since you can't escape the sun, protect yourself from its harmful rays while looking fabulous. That is what Cabana Life is all about.

"Cabana Life is a socially-conscious company that strives to in-crease skin cancer education through numerous strategic partnerships with nonprofit organizations such as Huntsman Cancer Institute, the Skin Cancer Foundation, Women's Dermatologic Society, Live4Life, and many others."

Source: *http://www.cabanalife.com* (Accessed May 3, 2008).

entrepreneurial drive to start Cabana Life. Her industry research led her to develop an entire line of clothing and accessories. In Melissa's case, she knew her target market's needs and researched the industry to determine how to meet those needs in light of current and potential competition. In Chapter 4 you will profile your specific target market, and in Chapter 5 you will further identify and analyze your competition.

With melanoma growing rapidly, especially among young adults, Melissa recognized a problem and identified the market. As Vinad Khosla of Kleiner Perkins Caufield & Byers shares, "Any big problem is a big opportunity. If there is no problem, there is no solution and no reason for the company to ex-ist. No one will pay you to solve a problem that doesn't exist."

You are now looking for an accurate picture of opportunities in your se-lected industry. With research you may even be lucky and come across an incredible opportunity for capital. In the Incredible Resource box on page 67, we highlight the iFund, which seeks to fund new products for the iPhone and iTouch platform.

If you conduct technology research, the resources from the Small Business Innovation Research (SBIR) offices (see Community Resource) may prove beneficial in targeting your research to a government agency that needs your services and will help fund your research.

Conducting secondary and primary research does not eliminate risk, but it definitely reduces it. You need to learn what is breaking, what is cresting, and what is cooling down. You also need to be aware of potential industry changes on the horizon. Action Step 14 in Chapter 2 asked you to start researching by finding at least one association and one periodical associated with a selected industry. Now it is time to explore your selected industry in greater depth:

- What role is technology playing in the industry?
- Who are the key players?
- What are the trends?
- Are there barriers to entry? If so, what are they?
- What are the niches?
- Where are the gaps?
- What is the cost of **positioning** yourself?
- Are there distribution changes underway?
- Who are the industry leaders? What makes each successful?
- What is required to succeed?
- Can the market handle another player?
- Is the industry regulated? Are any new regulations coming down the pike?
- How long does it take to bring a product to market?
- What role does the Internet play in marketing and distribution?
- Are the markets reachable?
- What is the competition?
- What role does international competition play?

Later, after you have gathered data, you can use these and other emerging questions as filters for the Opportunity Selection Funnel (see Figure 3.1). In addition, you are building background information and statistical data for your Business Plan. Remember, bankers and investors want to see back-up data; your research should provide facts and figures that demonstrate the need for your product or service in your selected industry or area.

One of the reasons you were asked to look at the big picture in Chapter 2 was to be sure you kept your eyes open to technology and changes throughout the business world. For example, publishers continually keep an eye out on the progress of e-books and downloadable books off the Internet. And as computers become cheaper and printers become faster, potential for even greater change exists in the book market. What will be the future for textbook manufacturers, local and chain bookstores, writers, graphic artists, and paper manufacturers? Change is inevitable; but if one views only the threats, one might not see the incredible opportunities. Keep your eyes wide open, or be left in the dust!

Find an industry segment where there is room for growth. In addition to growth, look for industry **breakthroughs**. What in your selected industry or segment is really humming? Early computers' memory banks filled large rooms and read data from punched cards. The first industry breakthrough was the printed circuit, the second was the microchip processor, and the third was the Internet. What is the fourth? What breakthroughs are now occurring in your selected industry? Does your business idea capitalize on the latest advances in technology and imagination?

Positioning Where a firm or product lies in the buyer's mind compared to other products

Breakthrough A new way through, over, under, or around an obstacle

communityresource

Small Business Innovation Research (SBIR)—Research and Development Funding

According to the SBIR Gateway, "The SBIR program is a highly specialized form of funding for small firms (less than 500 employees) to perform cutting-edge R&D that addresses the nation's most critical scientific and engineering needs. These needs span the technology spectrum—from aviation and agriculture to medicine and manufacturing.

SBIR is a federal government program administered by ten federal agencies for the purpose of helping to provide early-stage R&D funding to small technology companies (or individual entrepreneurs who form a company). Solicitations are released periodically from each of the agencies and present technical topics of R&D that the agency is interested in funding.

Companies are invited to compete for funding by submitting proposals answering the technical-topic needs of the agency's solicitation. Each of these ten agencies has various needs and flavors of the SBIR program, and you can learn more about them by visiting their sites. A list of SBIR Federal Agency sites and links follows, and all can be accessed through *http://www.zyn.com/sbir*."

SBIR FEDERAL AGENCY PROGRAM LINKS
Dept. of Agriculture:
    USDA SBIR Home Page
Dept. of Commerce:
    DOC-NOAA SBIR Page
    DOC-NIST Home Page
Dept. of Defense:
    DOD SBIR Home Page
    Air Force SBIR/STTR
    Army SBIR/STTR
    DARPA SBIR Program Home Page
    DTIC-Defense Technical Information Center
    MDA SBIR Program Home Page
    DTRA-Defense Threat Reduction Agency
    Navy SBIR/STTR
    NGA-National Geospatial Intelligence Agency
    SOCOM-Special Operations Command
Dept. of Education:
    ED IES
    ED OSERS / NIDDR
Dept. of Energy:
    DOE SBIR Home Page
Department of Health & Human Services
    NIH SBIR Home Page
Department of Homeland Security
    DHS S&T Directorate
    DHS DNDO
Dept. of Transportation:
    DOT SBIR Home Page
Environmental Protection Agency:
    EPA SBIR Home Page
National Aeronautics & Space Administration:
    NASA SBIR Home Page
National Science Foundation:
    NSF SBIR Home Page
Small Business Administration:
    SBA SBIR Home Page

Source: *http://zyn.com/sbir/#agsites* (Accessed May 2, 2008).

Growth industry Annual sales increase well above average

Competition A contestant in the same arena who is fighting for the business; everyone is fighting for customers' dollars

Market share Percentage of total available market

CONDUCTING SECONDARY RESEARCH FOR YOUR SELECTED INDUSTRY

Chapter 2 introduced secondary, primary, and new-eyes research. You may have stumbled across a wonderful opportunity with your new eyes, and now it is time to develop industry-specific knowledge. Is someone else already conducting a similar business? Is there a market? Are you in a **growth industry**? Will enough people pay for your product or service? What do you need to know before leaping? The first place to start is with secondary research. If you are lucky, it will provide you with excellent free background information from which to do further research.

Industry Research Using NAICS/SIC Codes

Almost all government statistics, business research, and tracking use the North American Industry Classification System (NAICS). NAICS replaces the U.S. Standard Industrial Classification (SIC) system and provides comparable statistics for businesses throughout North America. To locate your selected industry's NAICS code, and those of your potential customers and suppliers, refer to the government's NAICS manual—available at your library—or contact the NAICS Association at *http://www.naics.com*. Both systems will be in use for some time. NAICS is a numerical system that assigns a number to almost every identifiable industry. The structure of the new system is:

XX Industry sector (20 major sectors)
XXX Industry subsector
XXXX Industry group
XXXXX Industry
XXXXXX U.S., Canadian, or Mexican national specific industry

North American Industry Classification System

An example of this coding system follows:
31 Manufacturing
315 Apparel Manufacturing
3151 Apparel Knitting Mills
31511 Hosiery and Sock Mills
315111 Sheer Hosiery Mills
315119 Other Hosiery and Sock Mills
31519 Other Apparel Knitting Mills
315191 Outerwear Knitting Mills
315192 Underwear and Nightwear Knitting Mills
3152 Cut and Sew Apparel Manufacturing
31521 Cut and Sew Apparel Contractors
315211 Men's and Boys' Cut and Sew Apparel Contractors
315212 Women's and Girls' Cut and Sew Apparel Manufacturing
31522 Men's and Boys' Cut and Sew Apparel Manufacturers
315221 Men's and Boys' Cut and Sew Underwear and Nightwear Manufacturing
315222 Men's and Boys' Cut and Sew Suit, Coat, and Overcoat Manufacturing
315223 Men's and Boys' Cut and Sew Shirt (except Work Shirt) Manufacturing
315224 Men's and Boys' Cut and Sew Trouser, Slack, and Jean Manufacturing
315225 Men's and Boys' Cut and Sew Work Clothing Manufacturing
315228 Men's and Boys' Cut and Sew Other Outerwear Manufacturing

NAICS and SIC codes help you:

- Discover what industry you are in for statistical purposes.
- Define the boundaries of that industry.

Action Step 17

Research Your Selected Industry Segment through Secondary Data

1. Which industry segments really attract you?
2. What magnetic pull can you not resist? To help you get started, recall what you discovered in Action Steps 8, 9, 11, 12, 13, and 15. Keep your views wide-angled by looking at two or three segments that you find especially promising and interesting.
3. After you have decided on your segment, research it in depth. Organize your research by categorizing trends, target markets, **competition**, industry breakthroughs, and **market share**. For now, while looking for opportunities, focus primarily on the industry segment and its changes, and be sure to file or bookmark all extraneous data for upcoming Action Steps.
4. If you are working alone, write an industry overview. If you are working with a team, have each team member write an overview, and then meet to hash out your final draft after you have shared your perspectives.

This is a never-ending Action Step. Once you are in business, you have to be as diligent in keeping up with the segment as you were in your initial research—even more so, because now your money is on the line!

- Locate customers, suppliers, and competitors.
- Access the number of potential customers and potential market.
- Reach out to other industries thoughtfully and systematically.
- Track customer sales.

Once you have researched your NAICS codes, you are ready to use all the resources available to categorize your industry. Action Steps 17 and 18 should be reviewed now and worked on throughout the chapters.

Libraries

Make your public or school library your first research stop. Many large cities and universities offer libraries focused on business information, and excellent technical expertise is available—librarians love helping people find needles in haystacks. An excellent reference librarian can be one of your best and cheapest resources. Always ask lots of questions, and never underestimate a librarian's ability to help focus your research. In addition, research librarians will lead you to sources that you would never find on your own or those you would only find after many fruitless searches. The Internet is fabulous, but an experienced research librarian's expertise will make your future Internet searching more productive and less time consuming—so start at the library.

Technical and specialized journals (print and database), which may reach only a small number of readers and may be very expensive to purchase, may be readily available only through private corporate libraries. Use your local librarian to help you generate a list of these libraries. Many corporations will allow you access without charge, so contact their librarians, who are research experts. Also, certain trade groups and associations may have private libraries. When researching the horse racing industry, one student located a private library in Los Angeles. With one phone call and a plea, he was in. After driving 120 miles to the library and meeting the librarian, he realized there was no other place in the United States with the wealth of information now at his fingertips.

In addition, more than 1,250 federal depository libraries that offer a wealth of free government information are available throughout the United States. Find the one closest to you at *http://catalog.gpo.gov/fdlpdir/FDLPdir.jsp*.

Trade Associations

Your next research stop should be the trade associations within your selected industry and the industries of your customers and suppliers, as introduced in Chapter 2. Detailed information about these associations is provided in the *Directory of Associations,* or at *http://www.ipl.org/div/aon*. Select four or five associations that look the most promising and visit their Web sites. Many of their studies are available only to members, but membership fees for startups and students are usually low. Associations provide vast resources—always start research with your association.

Throughout the text, we have highlighted many of the resources available through one association, the National Restaurant Association (NRA), *http://www.restaurant.org*, which represents the restaurant and hospitality industry. Be aware that many other associations provide similar, incredible resources for your particular industry.

Do you want to know what the industry experts think the latest trends will be? Do you want an in-depth analysis of the industry? What about information concerning workforce trends and the emerging restaurant consumer? Need statistics on sales by restaurant group? If so, the NRA will happily sell you their yearly *Restaurant Industry Forecast* (Figure 3.2), and for a mere $79.95, this information can be in your hands. Throughout the next few chapters

figure **3.2**

2008 Restaurant Industry Forecast: Table of Contents

Table of Contents

The *2008 Restaurant Industry Forecast* was prepared by the National Restaurant Association Research Department

Bruce Grindy
Chief Economist

Alexandra Karaer
Director, Research Projects

Hudson Riehle
Senior Vice President, Research & Information Services

Denise Roach
Editor

Tim Smith
Art Director

NATIONAL RESTAURANT ASSOCIATION.

National Restaurant Association
1200 17th Street NW
Washington, DC 20036
(800) 424-5156
www.restaurant.org

© 2007 by the National Restaurant Association

ISBN 1-931400-63-6

Source: Courtesy National Restaurant Association, 2008.

we highlight the NRA and their vast resources as an example. We want you to find your association and get a leg up, and know the industry inside and out before you leap.

Secondary information, such as the *Forecast*, always provides you with a starting point for your research. For example, after reading a report on national and statewide trends in food and menu prices, your primary research on specific trends and pricing in your local area will be much easier to conduct. Your questions to those in the industry will now become focused, targeted, and productive. Secondary information sharpens intuition as well.

"Ranked as the number one challenge for restaurant operations, recruiting and retaining employees will be an industry priority for 2008," according to NRA's recent *Forecast*. Dealing with an industry that employs millions of people and encompasses hundreds of thousands of businesses leads the NRA to spend an incredible amount of money and time developing products, information, and services for their member organizations, as do most large associations. For example, the NRA provides members access to an information service professional, who aids members in their search for hiring practice information, legal changes, statistical data, and financial information. In exchange for this and numerous other services, a typical Idaho restaurant with sales of $500K to $1 million would pay would pay $440 yearly in NRA and Idaho Lodging and Restaurant Association membership fees. Student fees of $75 covers two years membership to the NRA.

In reviewing the information from the *Forecast*, you will see that there may be untapped food markets or a niche you never knew existed, such as community centers, colleges, clubs, prisons, and recreational camps. What about in-transit restaurant services and commercial cafeterias? Your key to locating and tapping markets may lie within the data and human sources at your respective associations.

For specific training opportunities, associations present online courses and classes throughout the United States that help entrepreneurs get up and running quickly and efficiently, saving time, money, sweat, and tears. If you cannot attend classes and workshops offered through your association, check out possible online courses; for example, the NRA offers training for employees and managers. Seminars and workshops are also offered locally, statewide, or regionally. In addition, many associations offer start-up manuals with incredibly detailed and well-researched advice and information. Some would-be entrepreneurs are cocky and will not take advice from others. Do not make this mistake! Developing expertise takes time, energy, and money. Be open and willing to learn from others.

To learn about gross sales, profit, and operating expenses, Restaurant.org provides a yearly *Industry Operations Report*, which can be purchased for $60 for members and $125 for non-members. In addition, online you can learn all about opening up a restaurant by surfing subjects such as catering, décor, food safety, and technology. Only a click away are a how-to series, a buyers' guide, and lists of associations, magazines, books and Web sites to continue your research. One wonders why anyone would open a restaurant without stopping here first.

Do you know about the Juice and Smoothie Association? How about the American Correctional Foodservice Association? If you are producing frozen foods, the American Frozen Food Institute is there to serve you. These and about 100 more associations are linked through Restaurant.org.

In addition to associations, outside publications are an incredible source of information on retailers, wholesalers, consumers, and your competition. Restaurant.org links to over 100 restaurant, foodservice, and hospitality industry publications (Figure 3.3) as *El Restaurante Mexicano*, a bilingual magazine for Mexican, Tex-Mex, Southwestern, and Latino Restaurants, and *Restaurant Startup and Growth*, a monthly magazine focusing on new ventures.

Keeping up on the latest food industry changes is easy with Restaurant.org's "In the News" Web page. Recent headlines included information on health plans for small businesses, organic/natural foods, and minority restaurant operators. Keeping up on food safety and nutrition would be a full-time job, but with the site's Web page devoted to these issues, you can be assured you are receiving the latest information. Since government and legal issues have a great impact on food service, clicking to the Government and Legal Web page will keep you abreast of employment laws and potential regulatory changes. Direct links to state and local resources are also included.

A challenge for many start-up restaurants is locating suppliers. Through the Restaurant.org Web site, you will be able to access thousands of providers in over

figure **3.3**

Restaurant, Foodservice, and Hospitality Industry Publications

Source: Courtesy National Restaurant Association, 2008.

Action Step 18

Determine NAICS Code

1. Find the NAICS codes for your:
   a. Industry segment (for example, retail candy store)
   b. Suppliers
   c. Wholesalers
   d. Customers (if applicable)

2. Determine through your research the size of your market in dollars and volume.

3. What percentage of the market would you need to capture to make your venture profitable?
   a. Is that possible?
   b. Is it probable?

4. Locate future sales projections for your industry.
   a. What is the growth rate?
   b. Are you in a **growth segment?**

Growth segment An identifiable slice of an industry that is expanding more rapidly than the industry as a whole

800 categories. The National Restaurant Association (NRA) is representative of many of the incredible organizations that strive to help make their members' businesses strong and successful. It is now time for you to explore your industry in depth through Action Step 18. Start your search for information with the best associations that deal with your venture, and maybe you will be fortunate enough to find a goldmine like Restaurant.org.

Trade Shows

Another way to research your selected industry is to attend trade shows—events at which manufacturers and service providers in a common industry demonstrate their wares to potential distributors, wholesalers, and retailers. While there, research your competition, pick up literature, talk to everyone you can, and soak it all in. Most trade shows are open only to firms within the industry. If you cannot gain access as a member of the trade, ask if you can attend for a guest fee; if that is not possible, network your way to a friend or acquaintance that can take you as a guest.

Over 500 firms presented their wares and services at The WasteExpo 2008 Conference and Trade Show, attended by over 8,000 people. For 3 days in May, Chicago's McCormick Place teemed with sellers trying to capture the eyes and ears of buyers from throughout the world. Product and service providers reached out to those involved in the $43 billion solid waste and recycling market.

In addition to all the exhibits, about 16 wide-ranging, free educational workshops and programs were offered. These were some of the topics:

- Food Waste: New Frontiers in Collection and Composting
- Truck Fires: Causes and Solutions
- Top Trends in Tracking and Communications
- Bringing Glass, Steel, and Aluminum to the Best
- You Stink as a Leader

To locate trade shows for your industry, log on to *http://www.tsnn.com*, where the database can be searched by event name, industry, date, city, state, and country. You will be hyperlinked to one of the thousands of trade shows held throughout the world each year. In addition, the Web site will help you locate trade show suppliers for over 50 product categories, such as tents, lighting, traffic builders, and trade show bags, many of which you can use when you are ready to sponsor your own tradeshow booth.

Additional Resources for Research and Opportunity Gathering

- **Newspapers:** Several trend watchers monitor more than 6,000 regional and daily newspapers. Follow their lead and study local newspapers for business and other news. For a broader picture, read the *Wall Street Journal* or the *Christian Science Monitor*. Thousands of daily, weekly, national, and college papers are linked at *http://www.newslink.org*. Many

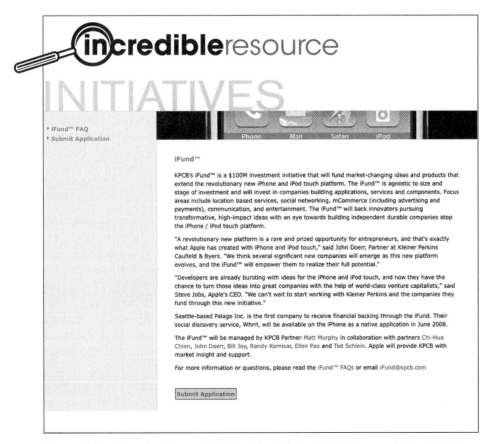

Source: *http://www.kpcb.com/initiatives/ifund/index.html,* (Accessed May 2, 2008).

metropolitan newspapers sell specialized research studies at modest prices. If you are exploring a service business, research other towns' papers to see if someone is currently providing such a service; phone the owners, and ask good questions. Remember, people love to talk about their "babies."

- **Magazines:** Reviewing magazines keeps you up to date. The ads tell you what is hot and where the money is flowing. Visit *http://www.mediafinder.com* or *http://www.newslink.org* to locate appropriate magazines for your target market, competitors, and suppliers. For the broadest in world coverage, consider reading The *Economist*.
- **Trade journals and magazines:** These are valuable resources, once you know the industry you want to enter. Many journals are also available online for a reasonable fee. Search *http://www.mla.org/bib_periodicals* to locate journals.
- **Banks:** Banks make money by loaning money. Large corporate banks have staffs of economists, marketing experts, and others who research and write forecasts and reports on economic trends.
- **Brokerage firms:** These service-oriented companies have staff analysts who survey specific industries. The analysts gather earnings statistics, attend corporate and stockholder meetings, read annual reports, and publish reports about individual companies and industry overviews. These reports, which predict the direction an industry is taking, are available to clients of the firms and are sometimes available at libraries. Contact the report authors for further information and insight.
- **Planning offices:** Cities and counties employ planners to chart and plan future growth. Check city and county offices' listings in the phone book to locate these offices. For the best service, you will need to visit the office, make friends with the staff, and be pleasant and patient. If you are planning a retail establishment or a manufacturing facility, these visits are essential. You also may need to attend city council meetings, or at least read all of the meeting minutes to be aware of upcoming changes and long-range planning.
- **Reports from colleges and universities:** State universities publish annual and semiannual reports on economic conditions in the states where they are established. Private institutions of higher learning with special interests also publish research reports. Cutting-edge leaders in their fields conduct a vast amount of technical research at universities throughout the world. Also, search directly on the Internet for experts in your field and e-mail them with questions.
- **Online communities, chat rooms, and message boards:** Keep abreast of all those who are working in the industry. Search here for information on your field and also through blogs, online newsletters, YouTube, Facebook, and the ever present and helpful Google. Many of these sites will allow you to post queries to others or to post ideas and ask for feedback.
- **Real estate firms:** Large commercial and industrial real estate firms have access to developers' site research. The more specific your request, the easier it will be for these firms to help you. Familiarize yourself with the dynamics of the area. Which firms are going into business? Which firms are relocating? Where is expansion occurring?
- **SBA:** The Small Business Administration of the U.S. government has an excellent Web site at *http://www.sba.gov* that provides access to thousands of resources, including franchising, financing, start-up costs, and federal and state programs.
- **Chambers of Commerce:** Check your local Chamber for research and contacts.

- *http://www.census.gov*: This Web site provides access to 100 current industrial reports on more than 5,000 manufactured products and is a treasure chest of data.
- **Bureau of Labor Statistics at** *http://www.bls.gov*: Economic and employment statistics can be obtained in hard copy or downloaded from this Web site.
- *http://www.brint.com*: One of the most extensive general business sites on the Internet. It searches the Internet for forums, books, articles, announcements, and comprehensive indexes of magazines, journals, and publishers.
- **Web sites:** To locate industry information on the Internet, begin searching under your selected industry and follow the never-ending thread. Search your competitors', suppliers', and potential customers' Web sites for information. Chapter 5 will delve deeper into researching competitors.
- **Standard & Poor's Industry Surveys may be accessed online at their Web site,** *http://sandp.ecnext.com*: This site provides an overall review of industry and its major players.
- **Company directories on the Internet:** Hoover's covers 10,000 firms *(http://www.hoovers.com)*; Dun & Bradstreet provides free, brief profiles *(http://www.dnb.com/us)*; ThomasNet has information on manufacturers in North America *(http://www.thomasnet.com)*.
- ABI/INFORM, Standard & Poor's NetAdvantage, Predicasts, Wall Street Journal Index, Guideline, Small Business Sourcebook—all are excellent starting points.

GLOBAL VILLAGE

Market Potential Index for Emerging Markets—2008

Countries	Market Size		Market Growth Rate		Market Intensity		Market Consumption Capacity		Commercial Infrastructure		Economic Freedom		Market Receptivity		Country Risk		Overall Index	
Hong Kong	25	1	9	35	1	100	1	100	4	96	2	95	1	100	2	88	1	100
China	1	100	1	100	25	9	20	44	18	41	27	1	17	6	13	47	2	89
Singapore	27	1	2	49	10	53	14	53	5	89	5	80	2	84	1	100	3	76
Taiwan	11	5	20	16	7	58	5	81	1	100	4	80	6	30	3	83	4	62
Korea, South	6	11	24	10	6	61	2	92	2	97	7	75	10	19	6	64	5	59
Czech Rep.	23	1	22	15	15	48	4	82	3	96	3	81	9	20	5	65	6	51
Hungary	26	1	25	4	3	68	3	89	7	83	6	75	8	21	9	60	7	48
Mexico	7	11	16	21	9	54	22	29	15	52	9	64	3	83	12	51	8	45
Israel	24	1	27	1	2	72	9	68	8	78	8	70	4	39	7	63	9	45
Poland	15	4	21	16	12	52	7	72	6	85	11	63	16	8	8	60	10	42
India	2	39	3	46	23	22	13	56	24	26	18	43	25	2	16	40	11	40
Russia	3	27	19	19	22	26	12	59	10	63	26	11	19	6	15	41	12	28
Turkey	9	7	8	37	14	48	15	49	14	53	17	45	20	6	19	28	13	25
Malaysia	20	3	14	23	24	19	18	44	9	67	16	46	5	32	11	52	14	25
Chile	21	2	23	14	18	39	24	9	13	55	1	100	12	13	10	60	15	22
Thailand	17	4	10	34	19	39	16	47	17	48	21	32	11	19	17	39	16	22
Argentina	13	5	6	37	5	61	21	33	11	59	14	49	23	3	26	2	17	19
Philippines	12	5	13	23	4	67	19	44	22	33	19	43	13	13	23	18	18	17
Indonesia	5	12	12	25	20	37	10	63	23	30	20	43	21	4	24	15	19	17
Saudi Arabia	14	4	17	21	27	1	8	69	12	56	24	17	14	9	4	65	20	16
Egypt	16	4	7	37	16	45	11	61	21	35	22	16	18	6	20	28	21	16
South Africa	8	7	11	49	17	49	27	1	25	19	10	64	7	22	14	46	22	14
Brazil	4	22	26	4	21	37	25	8	16	49	13	51	27	1	18	32	23	12
Pakistan	10	6	18	20	8	56	6	73	26	18	22	22	26	1	25	9	24	9
Peru	22	2	4	46	17	39	23	24	27	1	12	57	24	2	22	22	25	5
Colombia	19	3	15	22	11	53	26	3	20	40	15	48	22	4	21	23	26	4
Venezuela	18	3	5	41	26	4	17	47	19	41	23	18	15	8	27	1	27	1

Source: *http://globaledge.msu.edu/resourceDesk/mpi/* (Accesed April 30, 2008).

Market Potential Index for Emerging Markets - 2008

Global marketing is becoming more and more important along the years with the increasing trend in internationalization. Having too many choices, marketers face the challenge of determining which international markets to enter and the appropriate marketing strategies for those countries.

The focus of this study is ranking the market potential of countries identified as "Emerging Markets" by *The Economist* magazine. These emerging economies comprise more than half of the world's population, account for a large share of world output, and have very high growth rates; all indicators of enormous market potential.

This indexing study is conducted by *MSU-CIBER* to help companies compare the Emerging Markets with each other on several dimensions. *Eight dimensions* are chosen to represent the market potential of a country over a scale of 1 to 100. Each dimension is measured using various indicators, and are weighted in determining their contribution to the Overall Market Potential Index.

Dimensions and Measures of Market Potential for 2008

Market Size	10/50	• Urban population (million) -2006[1] • Electricity consumption (billion kwh) - 2005[2]
Market Growth Rate	6/50	• Average annual growth rate of primary energy use (%) - between years 2001–2005[2] • Real GDP growth rate (%) – 2006[1]
Market Intensity	7/50	• GNI per capita estimates using PPP (US Dollars) - 2006[1] • Private consumption as a percentage of GDP (%) - 2006[1]
Market Consumption Capacity	5/50	• Percentage share of middle-class in consumption/income (latest year available)[1]
Commercial Infrastructure	7/50	• Main Telephone lines (per 100 habitants) - 2006[3] • Cellular mobile subscribers (per 100 habitants) - 2006[3] • Number of PC's (per 1000 habitants) - 2007[4] • Paved road density (km per million people) - 2007[4] • Internet users (per 100 habitants) - 2006[3] • Population per retail outlet – 2007[4] • Percentage of Households with TV - 2007[4]
Economic Freedom	5/50	• Economic Freedom Index – 2007[5] • Political Freedom Index - 2007[6]
Market Receptivity	6/50	• Per capita imports from US (US Dollars) – 2007[7] • Trade as a percentage of GDP (%) - 2006[1]
Country Risk	4/50	• Country risk rating - 2007[8]

Source: Adapted from *http://globaledge.msu.edu/resourceDesk/mpi*.

Locating Private Database Vendors

A number of private database service firms have emerged, and many of them are frequent advertisers in *Advertising Age Magazine*, (*http://www.adage.com*). Some vendors specialize in niche markets, such as boomers, healthcare, and t'weens. Others provide data for accessing manufacturers, site selection, and locating foreign markets. A list of potential vendors and a short synopsis of their capabilities follows. Many of these vendors supply free analyses in addition to their paid studies, research, and data CD-ROMs.

1. GFK Custom Research North America helps you "gain perspective on what consumers need" (*http://www.gfk.com/north_america/index.en.html*).
2. Easy Analytic Software (*http://www.easidemographics.com*) provides excellent affordable demographic information.
3. Claritas (*http://www.claritas.com*) is a very thorough source for market research, analysis, and site selection data.

4. Mediamark Research (part of GFK *http://www.mediamark.com*) can be used to determine more about your customer: "who they are, what they buy, how they think, and how to reach them".

5. InfoUSA (*http://www.infousa.com*) advertises "powerful analytics made affordable."

You never know what you will encounter while searching the Internet. Many researchers and writers can be reached directly via the Internet through articles and references within articles. University Web sites also lead you to researchers in your specific field, which is crucial for those involved in high-tech or manufacturing. First visit home pages, if they are available. Your questions may be answered there. Additional links to sources may also aid you. If not, send an e-mail requesting information. *Never* be afraid to reach out.

You may be lucky and find an online community such as *http://www.foodonline.com*, a site providing a virtual vertical community and marketplace for professionals and vendors in the food equipment and ingredients industries. This Web site saves time in locating products, proposals, and regulations, and it provides online chat rooms in which to locate additional information. Jump on the Internet and locate your **virtual community**, which can give you access to thousands of experienced people. Start tossing out questions in the chat rooms, and you may gain access to free consultants.

Foodonline.com also sends individual weekly and biweekly, targeted newsletters for the beverage, dairy, food ingredients, and packaging industries, among others. These newsletters provide an easy way to keep up to date on the industry, new products, and your competitors.

Janet Shore, a successful entrepreneur, had only 3 days to complete a retail store proposal requiring only California food and gift products. She jumped on the Internet, completed the proposal, and won the contract. After awarding Janet the contract, the mall owner inquired how she was able to pull the proposal together in 3 days. She enthusiastically replied, "Hard work, diligence, experience, and information!"

It is time for you to head onto the Internet and into the library to complete Action Step 19. Note: If you are developing a product and need patent information, read Chapter 10 before going further.

PRIMARY RESEARCH ON YOUR SELECTED INDUSTRY

After spending days or weeks researching your favorite industry, whittle down the opportunities to two or three by using the Opportunity Selection Funnel (Figure 3.1) and the Action Steps throughout this chapter to help you.

Get off the Internet and get out of the library! It is time to step out and talk directly with people involved in the industry: salespeople, developers, manufacturers, competitors, suppliers, and customers. By now you have developed a strong knowledge base and a million questions. Ask away, and take notes. Now is the time to set your ego on the shelf. Listen to everything people say. Remember, your goal is to provide a service or product that *your* market needs and wants, not a product you want to give them.

Recently, two business owners were offered the opportunity to open a retail store. As they searched for a concept that would work in the location, they discovered that a children's clothing store could be profitable. The future owners then walked the streets and visited mall stores throughout their region discovering potential suppliers, pricing, product lines, and spending hours talking with children's clothing storeowners. To their amazement, they found many customers willing and able to spend $75 to $100 on children's toys and untold amounts on children's clothing. Neither

---

Action Step 19

Net Research Assignment

Action Step 19 asks you to complete several industry-specific research assignments. This Action Step should take you many hours to complete if done correctly and thoroughly.

1. Research at least three associations in your industry.
   a. What services do they offer? What classes and publications do they offer?
   b. What research can they provide?
   c. What is the cost to join? Where are their local meetings? When will you attend one?
2. Use *http://www.tsnn.com* to locate and research trade shows for your selected industry. Can you attend any of these? If so, when and where? And at what cost?
3. Using *http://www.newslink.org*, find publications where you can research your industry and customers. If you have a technical product, you will need to research it through specific databases found in the library and online.
4. Try to read at least four or five industry journals. This will be time well spent. If they are not readily available, locate someone in your desired line of business and ask if they will loan you copies.
5. Go to *http://www.census.gov* and begin to explore applicable census data. Future chapters will cover this in more depth.
6. Using Standard and Poor's, Hoover's, or Dun and Bradstreet, profile several of your competitors.
7. Locate virtual communities or newsgroups for your business.

Virtual community Group of firms engaged in similar industry

Action Step 20

Brainstorming Solutions

Okay, here is where you need to be creative. Brainstorm solutions with everyone you meet. If your business idea is fairly well developed, you should be presenting it to people and asking them to brainstorm with you as to its fit in the marketplace. If not, you should be working on developing an idea that meets people's needs—one they are willing to pay for.

You will generate better ideas and solutions now that you have completed your secondary research. Have fun at this stage as you continue to develop your ideas. Write down everyone's input. You may want to take a tape recorder. After brainstorming ideas, ask yourself the following questions:

1. Which niches can you own?
2. Which niches might be the most profitable?
3. Which niches will be easiest to reach?
4. What can you do to be unique?
5. What are people willing to pay for your product/service?

Return to the Opportunity Selection Funnel (Figure 3.1). What additional filters could you add for your specific situation? Which ideas are filtering through?

Confidentiality agreement Deal between two or more parties not to disclose information

of the owners would be willing to spend this amount of money themselves for children's products, but they were not opening the store for themselves; they were opening it for their potential customers, who had high incomes and were free spending.

Primary research can be conducted via telephone, mail, and face-to-face interviews as discussed in Chapter 2. Select research methods based on your needs, time, and available money. When conducting personal interviews, listen carefully and read between the lines. Ask intelligent follow-up questions. Probe the psyche of your interviewee as well.

It is time to start sharing your business ideas with others, and it may be scary. Action Step 20 will help you define your opportunity further. Many entrepreneurs are afraid to share their ideas for fear someone will steal them. It can happen. But if you do not share your idea, how can you turn it into a business? Online you may find a sample **confidentiality agreement** to use, which may make you feel more comfortable.

INDUSTRY SEGMENTATION AND GAP ANALYSIS

Industry segmentation breaks down potential markets into as many "digestible" segments as possible, just as is done with NAICS codes. The more you learn about an industry, the better you will be at isolating opportunity gaps and seeing combinations of gaps that may constitute markets. Figure 3.4 illustrates a mind map that "explodes" one segment of the food industry. This is the kind of thinking we want you to do in Action Step 21, another brainstorming activity. Have fun!

Susan's Healthy Gourmet

Susan Johnson, founder of Susan's Healthy Gourmet, searched for gaps and opportunities by taking a look at a major, far-reaching trend—the meal replacement market. People want fresh, high-quality food, but they do not want to cook. The "time bind" is fueling this market change.

Frozen dinners have been available since 1953, but these cannot be compared to the freshly prepared, nutritionally balanced meals from Susan's Healthy Gourmet. These include Buffalo burgers, cucumber salmon salad, dragon lady pork, and Kung Pau tofu.

After coming home to face cooking one time too many, Susan realized that there had to be many other busy individuals hoping for a hot, wonderful healthy gourmet meal as they opened their front doors. With unemployment at less than 5 percent, there were many others with the same need and available cash.

In researching her selected industry, Susan recognized that no one was producing fresh, made-from-scratch, calorie-controlled gourmet meals that met the guidelines of the American Heart Association, the American Cancer Society, and the American Dietetic Association. Others merely produced frozen meals, diet replacement drinks, take-out food, and so on.

Quality meals that were convenient and nutritionally balanced represented a gap Susan knew she could fill. With currently over 20 employees and a varied menu of 1 to 21 meals per week, and home delivery pickup points twice a week, she developed a product and service that met her customers' needs.

Susan's Healthy Gourmet was located in the heart of a growing, high-tech community whose demographics included the young, highly educated, physically fit, and health conscious (Chapter 4 delves deeper into Susan's target market). Requests for diet fare led Susan to include low-carb options for breakfast, lunch, and dinner.

As she continues to meet the needs of the changing marketplace, she now offers a full vegetarian menu as well as kids' meals. Her latest additions include family meals, senior, diabetic, and antiaging purification packages. Not one to rest, she is now looking forward to shipping her meals beyond the Southern California marketplace.

Thirteen years after opening her doors, Susan is grossing more than she ever dreamed, serving over 250,000 meals a year throughout Los Angeles, San Diego, Orange County, and Riverside.

In business, one needs to segment markets and then differentiate products or services to meet the target market's needs. By requiring no minimum orders, Susan enabled busy people to access their product on their own terms without preset requirements.

Find gaps in the marketplace and take advantage of those gaps by developing products and services that fulfill the needs of the marketplace. Listen closely to your customers. They will lead you in the right direction.

Wrap your product around your target market through pricing, product development, marketing, advertising, and location. Many times, opportunities in the market arise not because there is a need for a new product or service, but because there are new target markets. As a result, a product can be delivered differently, priced lower, or offered in combination with another product or service.

When you write your Business Plan, explain why you have selected a particular industry segment, or gap and back your decision with hard data from your secondary and primary research. If you have chosen a promising segment and have communicated your excitement about it, you will have developed a "hook" for the banker or venture capitalist who will read your plan.

More Brainstorming for Possible Solutions

Brainstorming is a process used by many groups—think tanks, middle management, small businesses, and major corporations—to generate fresh ideas. The goal is to come up with many ideas, some that may seem far out or even erroneous, and then to see how concepts develop as momentum grows. The key to brainstorming is to reserve judgment initially so that creativity is not stifled.

What follows is a recap of a brainstorming session held by the founders of the Entrepreneurs' Computer Specialists when they began to transform problems into business opportunities. As you read, consider not only the information gathered but also the process involved.

Gamers' Dream

Three friends listed ideas for businesses that had come to them during the earlier steps of an opportunity selection process. One wanted to start a company to design computer games. Another, a graphic designer with game design experience, said he could certainly help with the artwork. Another wanted to design computer systems for entrepreneurs.

On a flipchart, Derek wrote "Design Computer Games."

"Here's another," Robert said. "Let's take over Sony!"

Phil yelled out, "Teenagers and video games!"

Action Step 21

Mind Mapping Your Business

Narrow the Gaps; Watch Your Target Customer Emerge

Consider all the secondary and primary information you have gathered. Take out paper and pencil and start a mind map (see Figure 3.4). Review all the ideas you have researched. Sketch out your mind map, focusing on the specific segment that you have chosen. You need to stay with this segment until you know whether or not it will work for you.

Ideas will come together as you place opportunities next to each other. Through this exercise, you will be able to identify the most promising gap in your selected industry.

figure **3.4**

Susan's Healthy Gourmet Mind Map

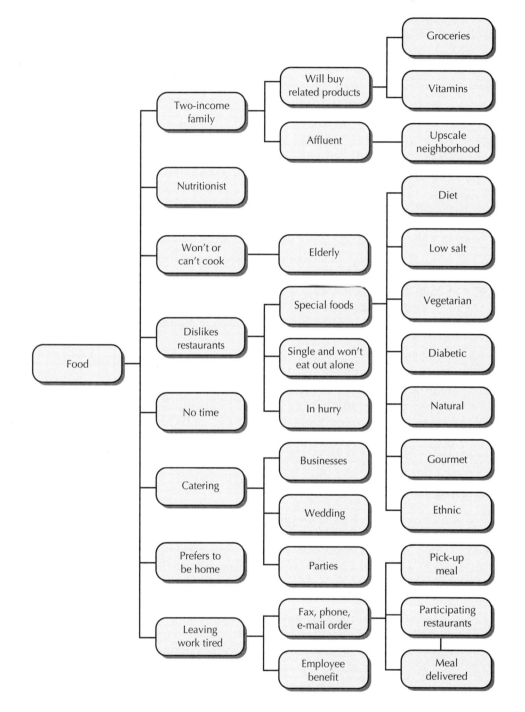

For a half hour they transferred their ideas—game design, software design, retailing, end-user training, hardware and software system designs, computer repair, and consulting—onto the flip chart. Robert, who was turning into a mad inventor, wanted to design a computer program that boiled down all election data into a single voter, who then made the decision on who became President. The 2008 election had gone on too long for Robert!

"Time for a break," Derek said.

When they came back from their break, Phil flipped to a clean sheet on the chart and proceeded to draw a mind map. As they developed the mind map, five areas emerged: entrepreneurial software, computer gaming software, gamers' paradise, and consulting.

Further refinements of the mind map brought gamers' paradise and game design into the foreground. All three men grew up playing video games and still were big fans and gamers. They also had many friends and nieces and nephews who were into gaming.

Excitement built up in the room as the ideas flowed, and soon all three friends were standing at the flipchart, adding their ideas and amendments to the mind map. As the brainstorming session wound down, they had identified two main areas to explore: game design and gamers' paradise.

The first area was game design. They could do this in their homes but felt if they were all together working, it would be beneficial. Discussions led to developing games for the growing t'ween, teen, and adult markets.

The second area was gamers' paradise, a place where people could come and work on the latest computers with the latest games, where the players could have LAN parties or rent out the facility for their groups of friends.

Robert, who knew there were many parents concerned about gaming, thought maybe a safe place for teens could be offered for after-school and weekend gaming. They could charge an hourly fee or even sell memberships.

Phil said, "I want to design games, so being around my Target Customers would be great, and we could have testers in the other room if we set up a design studio in the back room of a facility.

There was a silence.

"So," Phil said, "We've got several options that look pretty good. How do we decide?"

"How about a matrix?" Derek suggested.

"A what?"

"It's a way of weighing what you really want. I learned about it from one of my inventor buddies. He called it an Opportunity Matrix."

"Let's try it," they said.

It is helpful to summarize after a brainstorming session so that you can identify the most useful ideas. Let us summarize what happened in this session:

1. Using the mind mapping device, the team identified problems and possible solutions.
2. They decided all ideas were good ideas.
3. The two ideas that looked best were gamers' paradise and designing games.
4. They asked whether they could do both at once, or if one would have to go on the back burner.

Matrix Analysis

Whereas some people like to use lists, mind maps, or opportunity funnels for arriving at conclusions, others prefer a more systematic numeric method. A **matrix grid** can provide a desired structure to serve as another type of

Matrix grid Measurement tool with which ideas are screened and evaluated in order to find solutions

Action Step 22

Matrix Grid

Mesh Possible Solutions with Objectives

A matrix analysis helps you focus, especially if you are working with a group and have diverse objectives to satisfy. If you prepare a large grid and put it on the wall, all members of the team can participate.

1. Down the left side, list business goals brainstormed earlier.
2. Along the top, list the business opportunities you have discovered.
3. Select a rating system to use for evaluating the match of each possible solution with each objective. It could be a 10-point scale or a plus zero-minus system.

    Plus (+) = 3

    Zero (0) = 2

    Minus (−) = 1

4. When you have rated all the combinations, find the total for each column. The totals will indicate your best prospect. The rest is up to you.

figure 3.5

Opportunity Matrix Grid for Future Gamers' Paradise

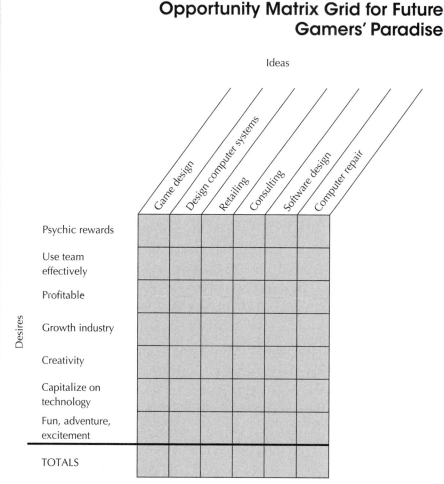

filter. After you have brainstormed some possible solutions, you need to improve your focus on those solutions and evaluate them. The matrix grid in Figure 3.5 helped the gamers focus their energies and talents.

At their next meeting, the gamers rated each possible solution on the objectives, which they had designated earlier. On review, gamers' paradise and game design received the highest total of points from the group. The key people saw these as areas in which their teamwork skills within a fast-growing industry could be used best. In addition, the cost to develop a gamers' paradise was feasible, because Derek's family owned an empty office building with high street visibility and the rent was very low.

There was no direct competition within 30 miles, and the team's enthusiasm and excitement about their idea ran high. In addition, one member suggested that as soon as they developed the gamers' paradise, it would not be long before they could begin to design games as well.

In developing their business, they decided to:

Build a psychological cushion: *The founders would start a gamers' club. Anyone who joined for 6 to 12 months would have full access to a gaming computer and could reserve their time online. Discounts on facility rental*

Psychological cushion A unique, untouchable rung on the ladder in your Target Customer's mind

would also be included, along with an opening game-day party invitation for members only when new games were released.

Charge reasonable fees: *Since the major market would be teens and t'weens, charges would need to be reasonable and competitive with options such as movies.*

Stress fun in a safe environment: *If gamers are having fun, they will play for hours and hours. With any luck, they will spread the word to all their fellow gamers via viral marketing.*

Taking Stock

What have you learned about opportunity selection? Before you answer this, take a minute to rethink what you want to achieve with your business. If you feel a little uneasy about how fast you have run the last couple of laps, perhaps it is because you have not identified your industry or the right opportunity for you. If it does not feel like home, you should sense it now.

Have you used the Opportunity Selection Funnel from Figure 3.1? Have you whittled down the list from hundreds of trends to industry segments to the one opportunity that emerged through all your research? Does it feel like home? If so, you are ready to define your new business.

DEFINE YOUR BUSINESS

Watch a carpenter framing a new house. He works close to the wood, nailing with quick strokes of his hammer. However, to get a view of the total house—the structure that will become someone's home—he must walk across the street. He has to step back from his detailed work to see the shape of the whole. What business is the carpenter in? Is he in the nail-driving business, the framing business, or the home-building business? Or is he in the business of satisfying the age-old dream of home ownership?

Only by stepping back can you answer the very important question: What business am I in? You can move forward, once you know who your customers are and what internal and external needs your product or service is satisfying. Mary Clark's stable experience illustrates the importance of understanding exactly what business you are really in.

Clark's Stables

Mary Clark, a 30-year-old software engineer, had always been more interested in riding her prize-winning quarter horses than in programming. When her grandmother died and left her $500,000, Mary made a down payment on a boarding stable and left the corporate world forever—or so she thought.

The boarding stable was run down. It had stalls for 50 horses, but only 25 stalls were occupied. Mary did everything she could think of to make the place better for the horses. She spent $200,000 rebuilding, painting, and grading, which made Clark's Stables a very attractive place. She bought the highest quality feed and gave the horses the best care money could buy.

When owners began to move their horses to other stables after 9 months, Mary could not understand why. She had not increased her fees, and she treated the horses like friends. After 12 months, only six paying customers remained. After 15 months, Mary was behind on her mortgage payments. In her eighteenth month, Mary sold the stable at a great loss. Luckily, she was able to return to her old programming job.

Mary had made the simple mistake of thinking horses were her customers. Her real Target Customers were young girls between the ages of 7 and 14 and their parents. Mary thought she was in the business of stabling horses. Actually, she should have seen that she was in the business of providing girls a fun, social activity, and offering parents a safe after-school activity for their daughters. The girls wanted recreation, training, and social events. Mary's customers left because other stables provided parties, barbecues, and horse shows with lots of ribbons and trophies. The girls wanted prizes and activities, but Mary was more interested in satisfying her horses than the young girls and their parents.

What Business Are You Really In?

Now that you have a specific industry segment, it is time to define what you do. Naming anything is a game of words, and a small business is no exception. The following examples can help you define your business. If you are hesitant about defining at this early stage, remember what happened to Clark's Stable. When defining your business, ask yourself why people buy the product. People do not buy products or services. They buy what the product or service will do for them: enhance their lives or make life easier, safer, or more fun. Cosmetics firms frequently say they are in the business of selling "hope in a jar." Use the following examples to help zero in on defining what business you are truly in.

If You Are a	Try Saying
Personal financial planner	"I'm in the peace-of-mind business."
Small-business teacher	"I'm in the dream-to-reality business."
Cosmetic plastic surgeon	"I'm in the do not-grow-old business."
Porsche salesperson	"I'm in the ego-gratification business."
Gourmet cookware salesperson	"I help people be Wolfgang Puck."
Personal trainer	"I keep you feeling young, fit, and buff."
Coffeehouse owner	"I provide a place to relax and people watch."

Business definition A clear picture of the enterprise

Keep honing your definition of your business. Your **business definition** should be a work in progress as you further explore your target market and competition. Four of our favorite business definitions or mission statements follow:

Fast Company: "*Fast Company* is where best practice meets big ideas; new talent meets innovative tools; the emerging business community meets the emerging conversation about the future of business."

Deux Amis Needlepoint: "We believe there is nothing so beautiful as an exquisitely painted canvas or the enjoyment, satisfaction, and relaxation derived from fine handwork and stitching a lovely design with beautiful threads on fine canvas."

Chicken Soup: "We're selling stories that encircle the heart and penetrate the soul and cuddle up to make you feel better."

Travel + Leisure: "*Travel + Leisure* is the source for people who make travel their quest in life. Our authentic stories motivate readers, making us the catalyst for what is next and setting trends. Being the authority, we get there first."

DEVELOP YOUR ELEVATOR PITCH

In addition to looking at what business you are really in, you should also consider how your business definition could impress not only your customer but also potential suppliers and investors. Along with developing your mission statement you may also need to develop an **elevator pitch**, a brief speech designed to hook your listener into responding, "Tell me more."

The Tech Coast Angels, a venture capital organization in Orange County, California, sponsor a yearly "Fast Pitch" competition. Hundreds of applicants apply for spots to receive private coaching and practice sessions for one month before the competition, in which 12 entrepreneurs vie for the top pitch. One winning pitch follows:

> My name is Jack Syagen, and I am the founder and CEO of Syagen Technology. Syagen has developed, under an FAA contract, the fastest and most sensitive bomb detector for airport security. However, our best commercial opportunity involves applying this high-speed analysis technology to red-hot markets in pharmaceuticals and proteomics.
>
> Our detection system is ten times faster than the competition and won a major industry award. We have also signed a deal with Agilent to provide one of our core technologies for their top selling instrument and are in negotiations with two other industrial leaders for a similar agreement.
>
> We have raised over $5M from investments and government funding to develop the technology and are now seeking capital to ramp up commercial development.
>
> Syagen is a profitable 4-year old company with strong patents and a first rate management and technical team.

> —Jack Syagen, founder/CEO of Syagen Technology

The previous pitch was well crafted and developed, and by the time you reach Chapter 15, your pitch should be just as strong and focused. While you are developing your Business Plan, keep in mind that you should be working on your pitch at all times. You will want to impress not only future customers, but suppliers and—most important—potential investors.

Your pitch should be delivered in 50 to 75 seconds with about 150 words. Write and rewrite it as you develop your business idea. According to Louis Villalobos, founder and director of the Tech Coast Angels, "To craft an effective pitch, identify your venture's key points and organize them into an effective story, edit to eliminate fluff, make each word serve a purpose, and then practice your delivery." Villalobos shares additional insight in Figure 3.6.

According to Richard Koffler, also a Tech Coast Angel, your pitch should "1) show passion 2) show an understanding of the business and its customers 3) offer industry perspective 4) add "magic dust" and 5) tell who you are and why you need the money."

Complete Action Step 23 by revisiting the Opportunity Selections Funnel, narrowing your focus, and developing your business definition with a first draft of your pitch.

Being in business today is all about satisfying needs and providing benefits. You find a need, you satisfy it, and then you translate the results into a benefit for your customer. This new era of knowledge- and experienced-based marketing involves two key principles. First, all of a firm's efforts should be focused on satisfying the needs of a customer at a profit. Second, the name of the game is to create or develop your own niche; that is, own the market as opposed to sharing it with competitors. You create and develop your market niche or segment by changing your product or service as dictated by the

Elevator pitch Clear, concise description of your business idea

Action Step 23

Define Your Business and Begin to Develop Your Pitch

1. Brainstorm what business you are really in. Let your mind play at this, and sum it up in one phrase. Remember your customers' comments when you were probing their psyches.
2. Next, think of yourself riding up 50 floors in an express elevator. You have 30 to 60 seconds to explain to a stranger what your business is about. What will you say? Can you dazzle him or her, so they will ask for more? Include your product or service's benefits, your target market, distribution, and why customers will buy from you. Review the information from Figure 3.6 and the examples in the text before you begin.
3. Review and refine your pitch one more time using Richard Koffler's rules:
   a. Show passion
   b. Show an understanding of the business
   c. Offer industry perspective
   d. "Magic dust"
   e. Tell who you are and why you need the money

figure **3.6**

Elevating Your Pitch

Nothing may have more impact on your chances of getting funded by angels or VCs than a great "elevator pitch"—the ability to capture an investor's interest quickly. Depending on the situation and context, "quickly" may be a few seconds, a minute, or a simple paragraph of text. Angels fund fewer than 5% of ventures that approach them; VC funds are even more selective, funding between 1-in-100 and 1-in-300. If you fail to ignite their interest immediately, investors will often tune out the rest of your presentation or relegate your plan to the "later" pile, which never gets read. Consider the following when crafting your elevator pitch.

1. **Grab them or lose them:** You may have a dynamite team, unassailable market niche, revolutionary product, disruptive technology. But investors may never hear of them. You must lead with the 4–6 points that differentiate your venture and that make it an attractive investment. The elevator pitch should be the first content slide in your PowerPoint, and the lead paragraph in your exec summary.
2. **Authors of best-selling novels understand:** Of the year or more that authors of best-sellers take to write one, about 10% of that time is spent on the first sentence, and another 10% on the balance of the first paragraph. Why? Because people go to the best-seller rack, take down a book, read the first sentence, and if that grabs them, read the rest of the paragraph, and if that grabs them they usually buy; but if either fails to engage them, they turn to the next book. Investors are like that.
3. **Say it in English for laypeople:** Unless your audience can explain your venture to someone else, you have lost them. Do you think investors ever tell their associates or spouses: "I saw this great venture today, but can't explain what they do"—they don't.
4. **Exclude fluff and hype:** Replace all superlatives ("unique," "revolutionary," "best," "fastest," etc.) with specifics; e. g. "priced 40% below market leader" is informative, whereas "lowest cost" says little. This is how Michael Moritz of Sequoia Capital puts it: "Factors like market size and intellectual property clearly play into our decisions, but there are no absolutes in the world of venture capital. The only thing that leaves me cold during a pitch from a startup is the use of the drop-dead words or phrases: 'synergy,' 'no-brainer,' and 'slam dunk.'"
5. **Relevance:** Avoid the unimportant (e.g., founded in May, offices in Los Angeles, Delaware C-Corporation). Make sure it's not only unique but relevant; that the names of all six founders start with 'J' may be unique, but it is hardly relevant.
6. **There is no pat answer:** Often I am asked what should be included in the elevator pitch, as if there were a standard set of points. Focus on what differentiates your venture and makes it an attractive investment. Below is a list of just a few of the items to consider:

Results (actual)	Team	Barriers to Entry and Niche to Dominate
• Cash flow	Spin-out from leader	Blocking patent
• Profit	Track record	Picket fence patents
• Revenues	Domain expertise	Exclusive agreements
• Sales	Tech wizard	Key customer(s)
• Bookings	Marketing guru	Vanity 800 number
• Key contacts	Sales star	Lead time
• Customers	Board	Regulatory permits
• Beta site(s)	Advisors	Trade secrets
• Proven concept	Degrees	

Source: Reprinted from "Suggestions and 6 Years of Winning Pitches" © 2007 Luis Villalobos, Founder and Board of Governors—Tech Coast Angels, with the permission of Luis Villalobos.

"It's an OK concept but not worth talking about at 15 cents a minute."

Source: Tribune Media Services, Inc. All Rights Reserved. Reprinted with permission.

customer. Marketing today emphasizes networking, creativity, associations, and partnerships; it requires:

1. Integrating customers' needs and desires and your strategies into the development of the product. Market needs drive the product.
2. Focusing your knowledge and experience on a specific and targeted customer segment or niche. The idea is to own the niche. The old concept of sharing a market is obsolete for small business ventures.
3. Creating customer, supplier, and even competitor relationships that will sustain and grow your customer base. Cooperation is the key.

Marketing encompasses everything a business does to get products and services from the manufacturer to the customer so that the consumer is satisfied and the seller has met his or her objectives.

SUMMARY

You have found the industry that interests you, explored associations, conducted secondary and primary research, and found a niche. You have applied the life cycle to learn what stage the industry and products are in and how long you have to make your business go. You have defined your business, and you got a head start on your elevator pitch.

Looking back on the Opportunity Selection Funnel in Figure 3.1, review one more time your business and personal objectives to determine if the viable business ideas you have developed through your research fit as well as you need them to.

If you found your current skills and knowledge do not exactly guarantee success, you are sure of at least three things: you know where to acquire the skills and knowledge you need, you know how long it will take, and you are exploring the marketplace in every way you can.

You have brainstormed your business objectives and reviewed the interlocking concepts—life cycle, competition, and industry breakthrough. A business idea should be emerging for you.

According to Thomas Davenport, professor of information technology and management at Babson College, "All big ideas share at least one of three business objectives: improved efficiency, greater effectiveness, or innovations in products or processes. In a way, it's an exhaustive set of possibilities. You do things right, you do the right thing, or you do something new. Nobody wants to hear about a 'me too' business. Stress your differentiation and translate features into market-hungry benefits. It is important to prove you have an edge over the competition. Try to think in terms of a 'personal niche monopoly.'"

THINK POINTS FOR SUCCESS

- Build your business around your likes, strengths, and passions while connecting with customers.
- Direct the power of your mind toward a particular industry segment through opportunity selection.
- Spend time early on learning about the industry, its major players, and its trends.
- Use all secondary data available so that when you move out to conduct primary data research, you will be in a position of knowledge and strength.
- Find a gap and take advantage of it. This is much easier and brings more success than being a "me too" competitor. If someone else owns the niche, find another—unless you are willing to hold on and fight the competition with your deep pockets.
- Recognize that not all opportunities are equal.
- Acknowledge that not all opportunities can be profitable.
- Do not fall in love with a product or a market.

- Know that there has to be a compelling reason for the customer to change.
- Dare to be different in your approach.
- Define your business. Dazzle in 150 words or less. Make them beg for more.
- Research! Research! Research! And never stop!

KEY POINTS FROM ANOTHER VIEW

Intuit Study: Next-Gen Artisans Fuel New Entrepreneurial Economy

Artisans, historically defined as skilled craftsmen who fashioned goods by hand, will reemerge as an influential force in the coming decade. These next-gen artisans will craft their goods and shape the economy—through upswings and downturns—with an effect reaching far beyond their neighborhoods, or even their nations. They'll work differently than their medieval counterparts, combining brain with brawn as advances in technology and the reaches of globalization give them greater opportunities to succeed.

That's one of the conclusions in the third installment of the Intuit Future of Small Business Report, which looks ahead 10 years and examines the prospects, influences, and profiles of small business. The report is sponsored by Intuit, Inc. (INTU) and authored by the Institute for the Future.

"No longer confined to a Main Street store front, tomorrow's small businesses will increasingly collaborate with big businesses, gain access to big business infrastructure, and take full advantage of a global marketplace," said Rick Jensen, senior vice president and general manager of Intuit's small business group. "The next generation of entrepreneurs will be knowledge artisans, yet in many ways look very similar to their pre-industrial age counterparts."

Three Trends Influence New Entrepreneurial Economy

The study identified three emerging trends that reveal how small businesses, equipped with advanced technology and unprecedented social networks, will amplify their reach and capabilities.

—Brain Meets Brawn to Create Opportunities for Small Business—The emergence of barbell-like economic structures will drive new business collaborations, creating greater opportunity and profitability for small business.

—Barriers Down, Small Business Opportunities Up—Access to big business infrastructure will expand, making their sophisticated technologies available to small and personal businesses, at lower risk, with a variable cost structure.

—The Next Wave of Globalization Will be Driven by Small Business—Muted trade barriers, improved technology, and professional and social networks across borders will facilitate small business access to new markets.

Brain Meets Brawn to Create Opportunities for Small Business

The first trend is based on the concept of barbell economics. It envisions a barbell structure for most industries, with a few giant corporations on one end, a relatively small number of mid-sized firms in the middle, and a large group of small businesses balancing the other end. As this structure becomes more prevalent, there will be increasing opportunities for small business to flourish in niches left untouched by the global giants. In addition to the physical skills that are the foundation of many small businesses, there will be greater opportunities for entrepreneurs to use their business savvy as well, to increase profits by collaborating with their larger counterparts in areas such as specialized services, innovation, and outsourcing. As a result:

—Small businesses will be better positioned than large corporations to provide customers with highly targeted, customized, and relevant products. Given their size and agility, small businesses are extremely well positioned to serve niche markets.

—Outsourced innovation from big business will increase opportunities for small business. Simply put, large corporations will increasingly tap small business for collaboration, fueling the number of small business innovators.

Barriers Down, Small Business Opportunities Up

The second trend foresees dramatically lowered barriers to big business infrastructure, giving way to lightweight technologies that make running small and personal businesses easier than ever. As a result:

—Small businesses will reclaim manufacturing, fueling small-scale and specialized production. Tools such as computer-aided design and desktop manufacturing systems will transform the manufacturing process and change the very nature of producing goods.

—Plug-and-play infrastructures will make small businesses more competitive and successful. With the ability to access world class, large-scale infrastructure and new technologies, small businesses will expand their reach and address industries formerly served only by big business.

—The shift to variable cost structures for core business operations will reduce risk and increase opportunities for small businesses. As startup and operating costs decline, the risks associated with starting and running a small business will decrease, allowing for greater operating speed, agility, and flexibility.

The Next Wave of Globalization Will Be Driven by Small Business

The number of U.S. small businesses trading globally will substantially increase, fueled by cross-border business opportunities, technological advances leading to broader social networks, and reductions in export costs. More specifically:

—Almost half of U.S. small businesses will be involved in global trade by 2018. As the costs associated with doing business globally continue to decrease, small businesses will make no distinction between domestic and international commerce.

—Social networks will fuel borderless commerce. Online and offline social networks will help remove soft trade barriers, such as language and cultural differences. These networks will introduce small businesses to new markets and facilitate cross-border trade.

—Globalization will increase small business diversity and amplify its economic value. Small business diversity will help increase market growth in the U.S. and abroad and will unlock new opportunities for all small business owners.

The Future Resembles the Past

With the removal of technological and geographical limits, entrepreneurial artisans will reassert some of the force and influence they lost to the industrial revolution and the growth of manufacturing industries, the study found.

"Like their medieval predecessors in preindustrial Europe and Asia, these next-gen artisans will ply their trade outside the walls of big business, making a living with their craftsmanship and knowledge," said Steve King, senior advisor at the Institute for the Future and study co-author.

"But there also will be marked differences. In many cases, brain will meet brawn; software and technology will replace hard iron and hard labor. As a result, small businesses will increasingly serve international markets and customers as easily as they serve their local customers today."

Source: Copyright 2008 BusinessWire (Accessed May 3, 2008).

—learning objectives

- Draw a magic circle around your Target Customer.
- Understand that your key to survival in small business is your Target Customer.
- Learn how to use media kits to profile Target Customers.
- Identify primary and secondary Target Customers.

- Interview, observe, and survey to gain insight into your Target Customer.
- Understand lifestyle factors.
- Explore various profiling systems.
- Develop your customer-profiling ability into a reflex.
- Visualize your Target Customer by preparing a Target Customer collage.

chapter 4

Profiling Your Target Customer
Research to Discover Customer Needs

Chapters 4 and 5 go together. Your best strategy is to read both chapters quickly, grasping the heavy connection between your Target Customer (Chapter 4) and competition and product differentiation (Chapter 5). Then read the chapters again, taking notes, doing research, and completing the Action Steps for both chapters. Your Target Customer is the lifeblood of your business—your resource base. You provide customers a product or a service they need, and in return they support your business by purchasing your product or service.

Competition occurs when someone else—another entrepreneur or corporation—wants your resource base enough to wage war. This could be a price war. Your competitor cuts the price of the same or competing product or service to steal away your Target Customers. It could be a quality war: The competitor has a superior product or better service. The war could be waged with a smear campaign: Your product is not environmentally sound, so the competition brings this to the attention of the public.

The best defense against competition is to know your Target Customer. Chapter 4 focuses on profiling your Target Customer through secondary, primary, and "new eyes" research.

By conducting ongoing market research you will:

- Minimize the risk of doing business
- Uncover opportunities
- Identify potential problems and solutions
- Be guided to customers

The prime concerns covered in Chapter 3 can be summed up by two questions you should ask yourself: "Do I have a product or service that is in a growth segment of a growth market?" and "Are the business goals consistent with my own personal goals?" By now we hope you have a solid idea of what business opportunities are hot for you, because it is time to establish whether there is a market for those products or services. If there is a market, are buyers willing to pay for your product or service?

THE POWER OF PROFILING

Understanding your Target Customer is your key to survival in small business. Profiling draws a "magic circle" around your Target Customer. Placing the customer in the center of that circle transforms the whole arena into a target at which you can aim your product or service. Nothing happens without customers; every segment of your Business Plan must begin with complete knowledge of their wants and needs. Profiling is the instrument used to uncover the wants, needs, and behaviors of your customers. Generating this profile requires a combination of geographics; demographics, or statistical analysis; and psychographics, or firsthand intuitive insight and research into lifestyles, buying habits, patterns of consumption, and attitudes. In this chapter, we focus on specific profiling techniques and resources that will help you get a handle on that elusive customer.

Market niche A small, focused area of a market segment

Customer relationship marketing The development of long-term, mutually beneficial, and cost-effective relationships with your clients.

It is often useful to ask prospective customers what one aspect of your product or service they would change. If you talk to enough people, a pattern will emerge that reveals a gap in the marketplace. Effective market research can help you target rich niches and avoid stagnant ones. For example, a plumber who was ready to leave his day job with a construction company asked his friends what would make them more likely to use his plumbing services. Their replies were almost universal: "Can you come during evening or weekend hours, so I won't have to stay home from work?" In response, he called himself the "Off Hours Plumber" and worked from 4:00 to 8:00 PM, Monday through Friday and all day Saturday, without charging overtime rates. He was an immediate success, because he had profiled his customers and found a **market niche** with his positioning. There is an old and true saying: "There are riches in niches."

Two social workers found a niche by listening to their clients who were unable to visit their loved ones in prison. The clients had limited resources, no access to cars, and no access to any public transportation that served prisons. Visits to husbands, wives, adult children and siblings were therefore nearly impossible. The social workers believed, as did the families, that frequent contact was necessary for future rehabilitation of the prisoners and for keeping families together.

On locating a used 15-passenger van, the social workers began Family Express: They offered weekend roundtrips to one prison for $25 a passenger. Not only were they supplying a service, they were also providing a community for their riders. Developing long-term relationships and community beyond the product or service is essential in today's competitive marketplace as customer loyalty and retention become the keys for firms that practice **customer relationship marketing (CRM)**.

With more than 2 million people in the U.S. prison and jail system today, the opportunity to serve family needs is vast. What other needs do you envision? How can you meet them? And one key question for any business idea is this: Will people be willing to pay enough for this product or service for the idea to be profitable?

Where receiving adequate payment to cover costs does not exist, some individuals decide to address the problem through developing a nonprofit organization. To reduce the recidivism rate of 66 percent among the 600,000 prisoners released each year in the United States, one social entrepreneurial non-profit organization has arisen. The Prison Entrepreneurship Program (PEP) headquartered in Texas provides entrepreneurship training to inmates and provides subsequent services as they transition back into the community. This unique program has reduced recidivism of their clients to only 3 percent!

There are many market niches, which have been ignored for far too long, and your idea may fit into one of those special niches. Your goal is to locate a market niche and use data to build a profile of potential customers within a market segment. One leader who chooses to look at the numbers within those niches, Alicia Morga, founder and CEO of Consorte Media (see Key Points from Another View), tells us her secret: "Data works. There's so much of the anecdotal in this (Hispanic) marketplace." Lorena Arnold, highlighted in this chapter's Passion box, conducted research to find her niche.

When profiling your Target Customer, it is likely that several different prospective segments will be discovered. Further analysis will be required to focus on only the most worthy. These should then be separated by sales estimates, competitive factors, potential for repeat business, and the costs associated with reaching each segment.

Identifying the unmet need—your niche—and clearly explaining the market potential for your concept can make or break a Business Plan. Before profiling in depth, take a look at various Target Customers. We will focus on primary

incredibleresource

The Source Book of Multicultural Experts 2007/2008

As you focus on your target market, you may recognize the need for experts who have experience with your very specific Target Customers. The annual sourcebook will lead you to statistics, market experts, business leaders, and a deeper understanding of your market. The Source Book is published by Multicultural Marketing Resources and edited by Lisa Skriloff, and the firm can be reached at *http://www.multicultural.com.*

Table of Contents

The African-American Market

- "Managing Your Brand's Strategy in the African-American Market," by Howard Buford, Prime Access, Inc.
- "African-American Market Experts and Business Leaders"

The Asian-American Market

- "The Asian-American Market: Will Your Brand Be a Leader or a Follower?" by Saul Gitlin, Kang & Lee Advertising
- Asian-American Market Experts and Business Leaders

The Hispanic Market

- "When Reaching Latinos, Relevance Rules" by Alex López Negrete, López Negrete Communications
- Hispanic Market Experts and Business Leaders

The Multicultural Market

- "Passing Your Cultural Literacy Test" by William R. Ortiz, Global Works Group
- Multicultural Market Experts and Business Leaders

Other Market Experts and Business Leaders

Chinese-American Consumer Buying Behavior

- "Understanding the Asian-American Viewer and Consumer" by Michael Sherman, KTSF-TV

The Disability Market

- "Disability as Diversity . . . Connecting the Dots" by Tari Hartman Squire, EINSOF Communications

Diversity

- "The Opportunity Most Companies Are Missing: Understanding"
- "Cross-Cultural Communications" by Luke Visconti, Diversity, Inc.

The Gay and Lesbian Consumer Market

- "Today's Gay Consumer Market: A Competitive Advantage" by Howard Buford, Prime Access, Inc.

Multicultural Market Research

- "The Changing Face of America: Multicultural Market Research–Nuts and Bolts" by Michael Halberstam,

Interviewing Service of America

Listing by Industry Expertise

Alphabetical Listing by Company (with Contact Information and Profiles)

About Multicultural Marketing Resources, Inc.

Source: *http://www.multicultural.com/book/sourcebook.html* (Accessed May 18, 2008).

Latino Marketing

Hola Images

Lorena María Arnold is the Founder of Hola Images and serves as its President. Immersed in the stock photography industry for over 11 years, Lorena María is driven to lead Hola Images as the premier resource for Latino creativity. Her purpose is to be the premiere supplier of Hispanic stock imagery, focusing specifically on the Latino way of life. Hola Images provides creative imagery produced by Hispanic-driven artists for the high-end advertising market using both rights-managed and royalty-free models. She oversees the development and implementation of Hola Images' strategic course.

After studying photography at Cal Poly–San Luis Obispo, Lorena María began her career as an account executive for Getty Images in Los Angeles, where she managed key advertising agency accounts and became one of the top negotiators in licensing rights-managed imagery. As Director at Workbook Stock, she launched the stock imagery business unit from its inception. Throughout her 10 years at the stock image portal, Lorena María has been an essential asset, representing the company and developing its business strategies. She has initiated and implemented worldwide distribution channels for image collections and maintains relationships as the main contact with domestic and international distributors that include Getty Images, Photolibrary, Mauritius, Wide Group, and 33 other distributors of rights-managed and royalty-free collections. Her networking within the stock industry has formed lasting business connections throughout the world.

Lorena María is proud of her origins. It has always been her dream to merge her passion for the Hispanic community with her love of photography. Born in California to a Puerto Rican mother and a Caucasian father from Bakersfield, she has a passion for her heritage, visiting her family in Puerto Rico no less than twice a year. Although Lorena María is a Puerto Rican-American, her cousins insist that she is 95 percent Puerto Rican. She gives directions by pointing you to the *panadería* at the corner instead of using street names, and she dances salsa and loves eating *lechón con morcilla*.

Source: *http://www.holaimages.com/html/sobrehola.php* (Accessed May 16, 2008).

and secondary Target Customers, because these are the only customers that you can see right now. However, once you open your business, a new customer may arrive on the scene, and you must always be ready to change so that you can take advantage of new opportunities.

You are also going to have to think about whether you are going to sell directly to consumers or to businesses. These two areas are called business-to-consumer (B2C) marketing and business-to-business (B2B) marketing. B2B profiling is unlike the segmentation of consumer markets in that it is most effectively performed using geographic factors, customer-based segmentation, company size, order size, and end-user applications.

Entrepreneurs should watch for at least three Target Customer groups.

Primary: This Target Customer group is perfect for your business and could be a heavy user. They possess the resources to purchase your product; they have a need or desire, or you can create the need or desire, for your product; and they have the authority to purchase the product. In addition, they are reachable through some form of advertising or promotion at a reasonable cost.

Secondary: This group almost slips away before you can focus the camera. Keeping good customer records will help you identify your secondary group and your primary group. Sometimes your secondary Target Customer group will lead you to a third customer who is invisible at first.

Invisible: These customers appear after you have the courage to open the doors and talk to whomever walks in.

WHAT CAN WE LEARN FROM MEDIA SOURCES?

An easy way to understand the power of profiling is to analyze media sources that are aimed at different target markets. For example, what would you find if you compared information on the readers of three different entertainment magazines? What clothes do they wear? How much money do they spend on concerts? How much money do they spend on music yearly?

Most if not all of the major media sources have conducted extensive research to develop demographic and psychographic profiles of their Target Customers. In many cases these profiles are available through media kits from the advertising departments of the media sources. A media kit includes a copy of the magazine, a reader profile, distribution figures, a **rate card** (specifications for advertisements and costs), an editorial calendar (monthly proposed content schedule), and an audited bureau circulation statement (ABC statement). Usually kits can be found online.

Rate card A magazine's advertising prices and details for ad placements

The key here is to know which media sources your Target Customer reads, listens to, and watches. In-depth profiles from media companies are compiled for potential advertisers who are evaluating which advertising vehicle would best meet their Target Customer.

Think of the differences and similarities among the readers of women's online and print magazines, such as *O, Redbook, Cosmopolitan,* and *Family Circle,* each aimed at a different segment of the women's market. What about the differences between the readers of *Sports Illustrated* and the *Sporting News?*

In this chapter, we will focus primarily on magazines, both online and print versions. Figure 4.1 highlights both types of readers for *Surfing.* We could just as easily expand our discussion to include TV programs, radio stations, Internet sites, and, to a lesser extent, books and movies.

We often walk past magazines without giving them a glance. That is unfortunate, because magazines hold the answer to many questions about customers. One way to view a magazine is as a glossy cover wrapped around pages of advertisements and editorial copy. With new eyes, however, you can see that a mass-market magazine exists because it is a channel to the subconscious of a certain type of reader. That knowledge is power. What can you learn about target markets, consumption patterns, and buying power from the advertisements and feature articles in a magazine?

Put yourself in an analytical frame of mind, and begin by counting the advertisements. Then note the types of products that dominate the advertisements;

figure **4.1**

Surfing Magazine Media Kit Information

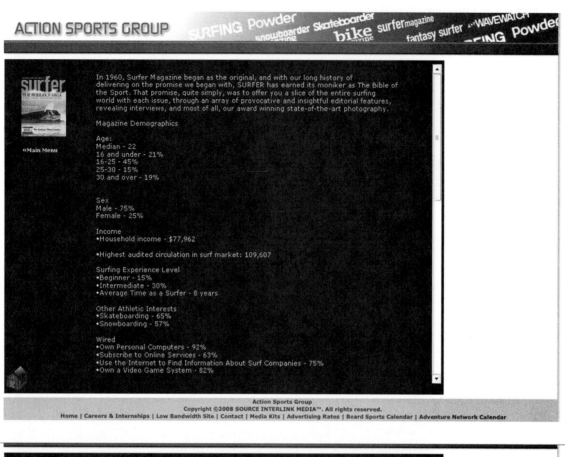

Source: *http://www.actionsportsgroup.net* (Accessed May 16, 2008).

these advertisements are probably aimed at the heavy users of those products. Next, study the models; they are fantasy images that the Target Customer is expected to identify with, aspire to, connect with, and remember. The activities pictured in the advertisements enlarge the fantasy, and the editorial links it to real life. A good advertisement becomes a slice of life—a picture that beckons the customer inside, toward the product.

We took an issue of *Surfing* and did a new-eyes analysis for a board shorts manufacturer. After we looked at the articles and the advertisements, we completed a trial profile. We developed categories as we went along. (One of the nice things about new-eyes research is that you can expand the model as you collect data.) We looked for:

- Total number of advertisements a half-page or larger Models represented
- Advertisements aimed at heavy users, the type of products that are advertised the most
- Large advertisements of two or more pages
- Lifestyle and demographics
- Main activities depicted in advertisements
- Content of magazine articles

Reviewing the Media Kit

The issue of Surfing we studied contained 180 pages, 100 of which were advertisements. These advertisements, mostly full-page and two-page spreads, covered almost 60 percent of the magazine. There were four main categories: clothing, surfboards, sunglasses, and shoes.

The advertisements predominantly depicted the surfer lifestyle. Professional surfers were showcased in several of the advertisements. The remaining models were primarily blond, surfer types between age 15 and 20. Text, content, and advertisements almost meld together.

After our initial profiling, we reviewed the information supplied by *Surfing*'s advertising department (Figure 4.1). From the following reader profile provided by *Surfing* magazine, the magazine's content, and what we know about their customer, we agree with *Surfing*'s customer profile:

> They shun the pretension for innovation and excellence, astutely seeking both value and "the latest." Upwardly mobile, educated or being educated, idealistic, and stoked on their number-one passion (surfing), they are the first to try new maneuvers, new music, or new technologies they deem appropriate. Fashion and change leaders, they are the ones others turn to for advice.

The next step in profiling your Target Customer is to compare the profiles of the readers of all the magazines aimed at your target market to determine which best represents your customer. Look not only at demographics and psychographics but the spirit of the reader as well. Another surfing magazine editor defined his target reader as the "soul-surfer, one who lives to surf!" Complete Action Step 24 to focus more clearly on your Target Customer.

Changing Profiles

In the past we viewed segmentation of the market like slices of pie. Each business tried to aim their products at their slice, and slicing the pie was primarily based on demographic segmentation. As technology advanced and media outlets and marketing researchers conducted extensive studies on customers, we suggested to our readers that they try to aim for a single blueberry in a slice of blueberry pie. With the Internet and the explosion of relatively inexpensive independent target-market studies, we now suggest you aim for the

Action Step 24

Media Kit Assignment— Target Customer

1. Choose five magazines that you believe your Target Customer reads. (Return to Action Step 14 in Chapter 2 for the list you previously researched.)
2. Find each magazines' publisher online and locate a media kit for each.
3. Compare the magazines by first reviewing the content and the advertisements using your new eyes. Define who you believe the target market is for each.
4. Next, compare your new-eyes profile with the demographic and psychographic information provided. Then rank the five magazines from 1 to 5, with 1 being the magazine that best targets your customer.

In the beginning, you may not be able to advertise in these magazines because of cost, but you may very well be able to keep an eye on your competitors, and your target market, by following these magazines.

GLOBAL VILLAGE

The World's Biggest Value Gaps

According to a recent study, "Remapping the World of Consumers" by Roper Starch, "Some values exhibit hugely polarizing trends from culture to culture, giving a great amount of insight into those countries and cultures." Understanding the culture of a country is vital before an entrepreneur enters the global marketplace.

Culture Value	Where It's In	Where It's Not
	(Rank out of 60)	(Rank out of 60)
Respecting ancestors	Vietnam (1)	Germany (46)
Faith	Indonesia, Egypt, and Saudi Arabia (1)	France (45)
Friendship	Germany (1)	South Africa (46)
Freedom	Argentina, France, Italy, and Spain (2)	China (40)
Knowledge	India (2) and Singapore (3)	Egypt (34)
Stable relationships	United Kingdom and Japan (3)	Venezuela (43)
Self-reliance	Mexico (3) and Russia (4)	Saudi Arabia (33)
Ambition	Egypt (6) and Saudi Arabia (7)	Italy (55)
Romance	Thailand (9)	India (56)
Looking good	Egypt (13)	Japan and China (54)

Source: *http://www.americandemographics.com/publications/ad/00_ad/ ad0010roper.htm* (Accessed December 11, 2000).

One-to-one marketing Meeting customer needs on a personal and individual basis

seeds in the blueberry. If you add your intuition, demographics, geographics, psychographics, and extensive observation of your target market, you will accomplish **one-to-one marketing:** meeting the needs of the "seeds."

Thirty years ago, there was usually only one bookstore owner in town, and he knew exactly what each of his customers wanted and would provide personal recommendations and reviews. He was in the business of one-to-one marketing just as Amazon.com is now when it recommends books to you online. In essence, Amazon.com has not created a new way to market, but is just adopting an old method using today's technology. The bookstore owner's brain has thus been replaced by the collective reviews of thousands of readers. Computer databases and the information they provide to online customers serve as salespeople today. Recently, Amazon.com sent an email to clients who had purchased an author's first book, suggesting that they might also be interested in the author's second book. Local bookstores might send the same note to their hundreds of customers but Amazon.com will be able to send an email to millions.

Society's fragmentation allows you to focus directly on the needs of your particular market segment. Rather than focusing only on demographic and geographic segmentation, you now also look for *lifestyle segments,* such as the differences between the purchases of 40-year-old first-time parents and the purchases of 40-year-old parents who have just sent their youngest child off to college. Below, LifeMatrix by NOP World identifies five parenting segments—each with their own set of financial needs, dreams, and outlooks.

- **Dynamic duos**—These are high-income parents who have digital-age lifestyles. They are extremely optimistic about the future and have high consumer confidence. They have many different drivers, though they are less likely to hold modesty, duty, obedience, and traditional gender roles as core values.

- **Home soldiers**—These are more traditional families with young children. These parents are home-centric, motivated by wealth, power, status, romance, and adventure. They are armchair warriors, more likely to dream of the perfect vacation than they are to travel.
- **Priority parents**—These are family-focused individuals with traditional values. Usually the parents of small children, they spend most of their time with their children and on family activities. Priority parents are fairly pessimistic about the financial outlook.
- **Renaissance women**—These are high-energy moms. They balance work and family and visit museums and cultural institutions with their children. They are motivated by freedom, creativity, curiosity, knowledge, and self-reliance. These women have an optimistic financial outlook.
- **Struggling singles**—These are single parents, very worried about money and making ends meet. They hold a very pessimistic view of their financial future. They aspire to have wealth, status, power, and possessions.

Source: NOP World, 2004.

With information like this, an entrepreneur can begin to understand the "soul" of their customer. NOP World believes in combining life-stage information, personal values, and lifestyles through its LifeMatrix product, allowing entrepreneurs to create messages that resonate with the target market.

Know your client and then focus marketing efforts. Use customer research data to focus on your customers, determine what products and services they want, and how to reach them with the right message at the right time. Then decide what pricing points will spur your customer to purchase from the ideal channel of distribution.

The largest provider of lifestyle segmentation data, Claritas divides the market into 66 lifestyle groups, which are then grouped into 11 broader life-stage groups, as shown in Figure 4.2. First make lists of restaurant chains, clothing stores, and car manufacturers. Then study Figure 4.2 to determine which group or groups each of these firms may be targeting. Now take your business idea and the list of your competitors and determine which lifestyle groups each is targeting. Are there some areas where competition is very stiff? Is there a group that no one is targeting? If so, does that provide you with any opportunities? Sometimes offering the same product in a different place or at a different price, aiming your promotion differently, or changing the product slightly will allow you to compete in a slightly different arena. **Product differentiation** includes changing any one or all four of these "P variables." Your goal is to wrap the four Ps around your target market as tightly as you can, and continue to change and rewrap as the target market, products, competition, and environment evolve. From profiling your "blueberry seed" in Chapter 4 you will move into Chapter 5 where you will develop a competitive strategy aimed toward your well-developed "blueberry seed." Chapter 6 will guide you in promoting your product or service and Chapter 7 will help you select the best distribution strategies while focusing on relevant demographic, geographic, and lifestyle issues.

Product differentiation Manipulating price, product, promotion, and place—to wrap around Target Customer.

PROFILING IN ACTION

Susan Johnson made a decision to locate Susan's Healthy Gourmet business in Orange County, California. Let us review the secondary data resources available to aid her in profiling her target consumer market. Many of the sources

figure **4.2**

PRIZM Lifestage Groups

Lifestage Groups

YOUNGER YEARS	FAMILY LIFE	MATURE YEARS
Y1 **MIDLIFE SUCCESS** 03 Movers & Shakers 08 Executive Suites 11 God's Country 12 Brite Lites, Li'l City 19 Home Sweet Home 25 Country Casuals 30 Suburban Sprawl 37 Mayberry-ville	**F1** **ACCUMULATED WEALTH** 02 Blue Blood Estates 05 Country Squires 06 Winner's Circle	**M1** **AFFLUENT EMPTY NESTS** 01 Upper Crust 07 Money & Brains 09 Big Fish, Small Pond 10 Second City Elite
Y2 **YOUNG ACHIEVERS** 04 Young Digerati 16 Bohemian Mix 22 Young Influentials 23 Greenbelt Sports 24 Up-and-Comers 31 Urban Achievers 35 Boomtown Singles	**F2** **YOUNG ACCUMULATORS** 13 Upward Bound 17 Beltway Bloomers 18 Kids & Cul-de-Sacs 20 Fast-Track Families 29 American Dreams	**M2** **CONSERVATIVE CLASSICS** 14 New Empty Nests 15 Pools & Patios 21 Gray Power 26 The Cosmopolitans 27 Middleburg Managers 28 Traditional Times
	F3 **MAINSTREAM FAMILIES** 32 New Homesteaders 33 Big Sky Families 34 White Picket Fences 36 Blue-Chip Blues 50 Kid Country, USA 51 Shotguns & Pickups 52 Suburban Pioneers 54 Multi-Culti Mosaic	**M3** **CAUTIOUS COUPLES** 38 Simple Pleasures 39 Domestic Duos 40 Close-In Couples 41 Sunset City Blues 43 Heartlanders 46 Old Glories 49 American Classics
Y3 **STRIVING SINGLES** 42 Red, White & Blues 44 New Beginnings 45 Blue Highways 47 City Startups 48 Young & Rustic 53 Mobility Blues 56 Crossroads Villagers	**F4** **SUSTAINING FAMILIES** 63 Family Thrifts 64 Bedrock America 65 Big City Blues 66 Low-Rise Living	**M4** **SUSTAINING SENIORS** 55 Golden Ponds 57 Old Milltowns 58 Back Country Folks 59 Urban Elders 60 Park Bench Seniors 61 City Roots 62 Hometown Retired

HIGH — $ — LOW

Source: © Nielsen Claritas

used throughout this chapter are available both on the Internet and in print form at libraries. Some of the research firms will allow you to tap into their databases free to receive excellent and detailed information, but if you desire a great deal of in-depth and current information, you will need to pay a monthly or per-search fee. In evaluating your Business Plan, many lenders will request demographic, geographic, and psychographic statistics to support your Target Customer numbers. We have therefore included just a small sample of the services that provide such numbers.

Healthy Gourmet now serves the Tech Coast of Orange County, San Diego, Los Angeles and Riverside. For illustration purposes, we focus on customers in the Newport Beach coastal area of Corona Del Mar (zip code 92625).

Chapter 7 discusses additional issues in Susan's choice of physical location. Her initial research identified Orange County as an excellent location as a result of its high-income demographics, high level of dual-career couples, and propensity for large expenditures on restaurant meals. In addition, this location is centralized between Los Angeles and San Diego. Susan would be able to use the Orange County location as her main commissary kitchen, serving areas to the north and to the south, and eventually to the east.

Focusing on the demographics of their Corona Del Mar customers, the first stop is U.S. Census data, *http://www.census.gov* (the last Census figures available are for 2000). You can search the U.S. Census Bureau's American Fact Finder database by hundreds of different variables: education, employment, family household size, income, race, sex, age groupings, and so on. If your area is one that is growing and changing rapidly, consider purchasing information from providers who project and measure changes within their databases. In addition, information can be obtained through *http://quickfacts. census.gov*, where one can compare county and state statistics, as shown in Table 4.1.

Your next stop is *www.easidemographics.com*, one of the easiest online databases to use. Searching on Corona Del Mar, California, produces a report on relevant variables based on 2000 Census data (Table 4.2). Additional updates are available for a fee.

Using Claritas' PRIZM NE lifestyle segmentation systems database, found at *http://www.claritas.com*, provides insight into your customers' psyches. PRIZM ConneXions' NE defines every zip code and drills down to zip code + 4, which is a geographical area that encompasses 10 to 12 households, clustering people into 66 distinct clusters. Lifestyle profiles focus on lifestyle, retail, financial, and media variables, and ConneXions focuses on the use of communications by each group. The five major clusters for Susan's 92625 neighborhood in order are Executive Suites, Movers & Shakers, New Empty Nests, Pools & Patios, and Upper Crust, two of which are highlighted in Figure 4.3.

Primarily college graduates with median household incomes around $100,000, these customers enjoy traveling and driving very nice cars. Marketing and promotion materials should be focused specifically on meeting the needs of these time-strapped and status-oriented individuals.

Continuing on with the search for data brings us to Values and Lifestyles Segment™ profiles (VALS). A quick check of the VALS segmentation diagram (Figure 4.4 on p. 102) shows eight profiles: Innovators, Thinkers, Achievers, Experiencers, Believers, Strivers, Makers, and Survivors. According to SRI Consulting Business Intelligence:

> Consumers buy products and services and seek experiences that fulfill their characteristic preferences and give shape, substance, and satisfaction to their lives. An individual's primary motivation determines what in particular about the self or the world is the meaningful core that governs his or her activities. Consumers are inspired by one of three primary motivations: ideals, achievement, or self-expression. Consumers who are primarily motivated by ideals are guided by knowledge and principles. Consumers who are primarily motivated by achievement look for products and services that demonstrate success to their peers. Consumers who are primarily motivated by self-expression desire social or physical activity, variety, and risk.

Source: *http://www.sric-bi.com/VALS/types/shtml* (Accessed June 5, 2008).

table **4.1**

Orange County/California QuickFacts

U.S. Census Bureau
State & County QuickFacts
Orange County, California

People QuickFacts	Orange County	California
Population, 2006 estimate	3, 002,048	36,457,549
Population, percent change, April 1, 2000 to July 1, 2006	5.5%	7.6%
Population, 2000	2,846,289	33,871,648
Persons under 5 years old, percent, 2006	7.4%	7.3%
Persons under 18 years old, percent, 2006	26.3%	26.1%
Persons 65 years old and over, percent, 2006	10.8%	10.8%
Female persons, percent, 2006	50.0%	50.0%
White persons, percent, 2006 (a)	78.8%	76.9%
Black persons, percent, 2006 (a)	1.9%	6.7%
American Indian and Alaska native persons, percent, 2006 (a)	0.8%	1.2%
Asian persons, percent, 2006 (a)	16.1%	12.4%
Native Hawaiian and Other Pacific Islander, percent, 2006 (a)	0.4%	0.4%
Persons reporting two or more races, percent, 2006	2.0%	2.4%
Persons of Hispanic or Latino origin, percent, 2006 (b)	32.9%	35.9%
White persons not Hispanic, percent, 2006	47.4%	43.1%
Living in same house in 1995 and 2000, pct 5 yrs old & over	48.0%	50.2%
Foreign born persons, percent, 2000	29.9%	26.2%
Language other than English spoken at home, pct age 5+, 2000	41.4%	39.5%
High school graduates, percent of persons age 25+, 2000	79.5%	76.8%
Bachelor's degree or higher, pct of persons age 25+, 2000	30.8%	26.6%
Persons with a disability, age 5+, 2000	434,000	5,923,361
Mean travel time to work (minutes), workers age 16+, 2000	27.2	27.7
Housing Units, 2006	1,022,937	13,174,378
Homeownership rate, 2000	61.4%	56.9%
Housing units in multi-unit structures, percent, 2000	33.2%	31.4%
Median value of owner-occupied housing units, 2000	$270,000	$211,500
Households, 2000	935,287	11,502,870
Persons per household, 2000	3.00	2.87
Median household income, 2004	$58,605	$49,894
Per capita money income, 1999	$25,826	$22,711
Persons below poverty, percent, 2004	10.2%	13.2%

Business QuickFacts	Orange County	California
Private nonfarm establishments, 2005	87,905	860,866[1]
Private nonfarm employment, 2005	1,452,733	13,382,470[1]
Private nonfarm employment, percent change 2000–2005	5.4%	3.9%[1]
Nonemployer establishments, 2005	245,266	2,609,258
Total number of firms, 2002	285,242	2,908,758
Black-owned firms, percent, 2002	1.2%	3.9%
American Indian and Alaska Native owned firms, percent, 2002	1.0%	1.3%
Asian-owned firms, percent, 2002	16.1%	12.8%
Native Hawaiian and Other Pacific Islander owned firms, percent, 2002	0.3%	0.2%
Hispanic-owned firms, percent, 2002	10.6%	14.7%
Women-owned firms, percent, 2002	27.9%	29.9%
Manufacturers shipments, 2002 ($1000)	40,080,953	378,661,414
Wholesale trade sales, 2002 ($1000)	109,881,218	655,954,708
Retail sales, 2002 ($1000)	35,736,615	359,120,365
Retail sales per capita, 2002	$12,205	$10,264
Accommodation and foodservices sales, 2002 ($1000)	5,592,425	55,559,669
Building permits, 2006	8,303	160,502
Federal spending, 2004 ($1000)	13,834,698	232,387,168[1]
Geography QuickFacts	**Orange County**	**California**
Land area, 2000 (square miles)	789.40	155,959.34
Persons per square mile, 2000	3,607.5	217.2
FIPS Code	059	06
Metropolitan or Micropolitan Statistical Area	Los Angeles-Long Beach-Santa Ana, CA Metro Area	

(continued)

—— table **4.1**

Orange County/California QuickFacts *(continued)*

1: Includes data not distributed by county.
(a) Includes persons reporting only one race.
(b) Hispanics may be of any race, so also are included in applicable race categories.
D: Suppressed to avoid disclosure of confidential information.
F: Fewer than 100 firms
FN: Footnote on this item for this area in place of data
NA: Not available
S: Suppressed; does not meet publication standards
X: Not applicable
Z: Value greater than zero but less than half unit of measure shown

Source U.S. Census Bureau: State and County QuickFacts. Data derived from Population Estimates, Census of Population and Housing, Small Area Income and Poverty Estimates, State and County Housing Unit Estimates, County Business Patterns, Nonemployer Statistics, Economic Census, Survey of Business Owners, Building Permits, Consolidated Federal Funds Report
Last Revised: Wednesday, 02-Jan-2008 15:09:13 EST
Source: *http://quickfacts.census.gov/qfd/states/06/06059.html* (Accessed May 16, 2008).

—— table **4.2**

Professional Demographics Report (Abbreviated) From Easidemographics

Zip Code: 92625
Post Office Name: Corona Del Mar
County FIPS Code: 06059
City Name: Newport Beach, CA
County Name: Orange, CA
State Name: California
CBSA Name: Los Angeles-Long Beach-Santa Ana, CA
Area Code: 949

Description	Value	EASI Score	EASI Rank of 39480
Non-family population	3,619	A	786
Female householder, no husband present with children under 18	72	D	24,841
1-person household	2,132	A	968
2 Vehicles	2,741	A	401
Rent $2,000+	380	A	75
Occupied structure trailer	0	E	33,520
Owner-occupied home value			
Median value ($)	788,628	A	33
$750,000 to $999,999	1,042	A	4
Households by income			
$35,000 to $49,999	590	D	25,856
$200,000 and over	1,430	A	46
Industry (Pop 16+)			
Agriculture	12	D	26,371
Professional, scientific, management., administrative, etc.	1,342	A	372
Educational, health and social services	1,153	B	12,287
Manufacturing	696	C	16,870
Public administration	82	D	28,059
Education			
Less than high school	275	D	29,082
College	4,163	A	48
Graduate degree	2,571	A	361

EASI Rank: based on the concentration of the variable with a "1" being the highest rank and the number of areas in a geography being the lowest rank.
EASI Score: arranges the EASI Rank into a quintile frequency distribution ranging from "A" (the highest concentration group and top 20%) through "E" (the lowest concentration group and bottom 20%).
U.S. Avg = 100 indicates an index value that has a range of 0 (low) to 200 (high).
Easy Analytic Software, Inc. (EASI) is the source of all updated estimates. All other data are derived from the U.S. Census and other official government sources.
All estimates are as of 4/1/2000 unless otherwise stated.

Source: *http://www.easidemographics.com* (Accessed May 16, 2008).

figure **4.3**

Sample Segments from PRIZM

communityresource

U.S. Census Bureau American FactFinder

Reference Shelf

Reports and Publications

- Rankings and Comparison Tables from Census 2000—A series of tables covering a wide variety of topics including race, Hispanic or Latino origin, group quarters, and ancestry.
- 4 Easy Steps to Census 2000 Data (PDF—17.3 MB)—Simple instructions to find Census 2000 data in American FactFinder.
- American FactFinder Brochure (PDF—1.71 MB)—An overview of features available in American FactFinder.
- American Community Survey Congressional Tool Kit—A collection of documents explaining how and why the survey is conducted, its benefits, and how to obtain additional information.
- Census 2000 Basics (PDF—634 KB)—The importance of the Census: what it is used for and why.
- Census 2000 Briefs—Access analyses focusing on the most important aspects of Census topics as well as exploration of geographic distribution for each topic.
- Census Bureau Publications—A resource guide to the programs and services of the U.S. Census Bureau.
- The Decennial Censuses from 1790 to 2000—A great historical resource about measuring America.
- Demographic Profiles—Select "Census 2000 Profiles" to access profile reports for each state as well as a national summary.
- Demographic Trends in the 20th Century (PDF—3.32 MB)
- Printed Reports—Select PHC 1–4 to access printable reports of Census information for each State as well as the nation.
- Special Reports—View PDF reports providing in-depth analysis of Census 2000 population and housing topics, including geographic distribution, race, and ethnicity and immigration.
- The U.S. in International Context (PDF—519 KB)—Report on the United States in international context for the year 2000.

Other Useful Data and Statistics

- County and City Data Book—Find data about your city or county.
- E-Stats—Measuring the electronic economy.
- FTP—Another way to download Census data.
- Historical Census Data—Find data from censuses before 2000.
- State and Metropolitan Area Data Book—One way to find data for states and their metropolitan areas.
- Statistical Abstract—A source for data and statistics including some analysis on various demographic topics.
- USA Statistics in Brief—A brief summary of some key statistics for popular topics.
- World Population Rank by Country—A list of the countries of the world ranked by population.

(continued)

(continued)

Map Resources

- Census Atlas of the United States—Choose from PDF maps covering a variety of topics ranging from language and ancestry characteristics, housing patterns, and geographic distributions of the population. A print copy of the Census Atlas can be purchased at the Government Printing Office online bookstore.
- Census 2000 Geographic Products and Information—Your source for extracts of selected geographic and cartographic information from the Census Bureau's TIGER® (Topologically Integrated Geographic Encoding and Referencing) database. You can also view and work with Census 2000 maps, data files, and reference resources.
- Census Tract Outline Maps—Purchase plotted maps and related products.
- Gazetteer—Download 1990 and 2000 Census files with geo-codes, names, and other basic geographic attributes for places, counties, county subdivisions, and ZIP Code Tabulation Areas (ZCTAs).
- Geocoding—Maintained by the Federal Financial Institution's Examination Council, the Geocoding system enables you to enter a street address and get a Census Demographic Report or a Street Address Map. Geocoding is primarily intended to assist financial institutions covered by the Home Mortgage Disclosure Act (HMDA) and Community Reinvestment Act (CRA) to meet their reporting obligation.
- Geospatial One Stop—Electronic maps and other geographic data from multiple government sources in one web site.
- Landview—Map-viewing software tool for spatial database with data from the U.S. Census Bureau, the Environmental Protection Agency (EPA), the U.S. Geological Survey (USGS), and the National Oceanic and Atmospheric Administration (NOAA).
- TIGER—TIGER stands for Topologically Integrated Geographic Encoding and Referencing system. It is a Census Bureau computer database that contains all census-required map features and attributes for the United States and its possessions, plus the specifications, procedures, computer programs, and related input materials required to build and use it.

Other Census Bureau Resources

- Census Bureau Sales Catalog—Place an order with the Census, or request some of the free publications and releases.
- Census Calendar—Ongoing communications events for the Census and its customers.
- Genealogy Resources—A place to start looking for genealogical resources.
- News Releases—A list of news releases about important census topics and discoveries.
- RadioZone—Check out audio news and features for broadcast. You can listen to Profile America or our Spanish program Al Dia.
- State Data Centers—Find out what your state has done with Census data.
- U.S. Census Bureau Regional Offices—A guide including the locations of the U.S. Census Offices around the country.

(continued)

(continued)

Related Sites and Resources

- Census Information Centers—Census Information Centers serve as repositories of census data and reports, making census information and data available to the public and the communities they serve.
- Federal Depository Libraries—Federal Government publications and other information products are made available for free public use in Federal depository libraries throughout the United States.
- USA.gov—The U.S. government's official web portal.
- International Statistical Data—Links to international statistical agencies.

Source: U.S. Census Bureau. Last Revised: March 14, 2008.

Reasons for a person's tendency to consume goods and services extend beyond age, income, and education. Energy, self-confidence, intellectualism, novelty seeking, innovativeness, impulsiveness, leadership, and vanity play critical roles. These personality traits, in conjunction with key demographics, determine an individual's resources. Different levels of resources enhance or constrain a person's expression of his or her primary motivation.

Reading the following summary of an Innovator provides insight into one of the primary Target Customer profiles for Susan's Healthy Gourmet utilizing the VALS system (Figure 4.4).

Innovators are successful, sophisticated, take-charge people with high self-esteem. Because they have such abundant resources, they exhibit all three primary motivations in varying degrees. They are change leaders and are the most receptive to new ideas and technologies. Innovators are very active consumers, and their purchases reflect cultivated tastes for upscale niche products and services.

Image is important to innovators, not as evidence of status or power but as an expression of their taste, independence, and personality. Innovators are among the established and emerging leaders in business and government, yet they continue to seek challenges. Their lives are characterized by variety. Their possessions and recreation reflect a cultivated taste for the finer things in life.

Source: *http://www.sric-bi.com/VALS/innovators.shtml* (Accessed June 5, 2008).

Refer to Figure 4.5 and review the characteristic attitudes, behaviors, and media habits of both the Innovators, who are Susan's customers, and the Strivers, who are not. Both of these VALS segments define adult consumers who have "different attitudes and exhibit distinctive behavior and decision-making patterns." Susan's customer profile sharpens when reviewing the Innovators' behaviors, and this gives her some ideas for where she should market her services.

In conjunction with Equifax, Standard Rates and Data Services (SRDS) publishes *Market and Lifestyle Profiles,* available in most major business or college libraries. These profiles offer additional insight into Susan's Healthy Gourmet's customer. Indexed statistics allow you to compare customers in a target county to the overall marketplace and to contrast these figures with several different market areas. With 100 being the average market index throughout the United States, the SRDS *Market and Lifestyle Profiles* demonstrate

figure **4.4**

The VALS Segment Profiles

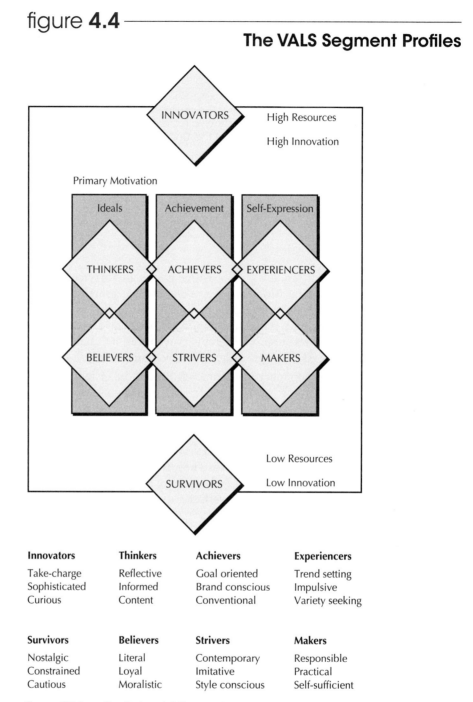

Innovators	Thinkers	Achievers	Experiencers
Take-charge	Reflective	Goal oriented	Trend setting
Sophisticated	Informed	Brand conscious	Impulsive
Curious	Content	Conventional	Variety seeking

Survivors	Believers	Strivers	Makers
Nostalgic	Literal	Contemporary	Responsible
Constrained	Loyal	Imitative	Practical
Cautious	Moralistic	Style conscious	Self-sufficient

Source: SRI Consulting Business Intelligence, *http://www.sric-bi.com/vals.*

once again that Orange County's high-income earners who travel extensively and participate in sports and gambling are Susan's primary target market.

Susan once briefly described her primary customers as follows:

- Sophisticated
- Knowledgeable and concerned about their health
- Age 30 to 60
- Baby boomers who are in excellent shape and interested in retaining their health

figure **4.5**

VALS—Characteristics, Attitudes, Behaviors, and Media

INNOVATORS
Characteristic Attitudes and Behaviors
Cross-country ski
Sail
Wrote something that has been published
Belong to a business club
Participate in environmental groups/causes
Practice yoga
Downhill ski
Go to museums
Backpack/hike
Actively worked for a political party/candidate
Buy the latest technology
Are interested in health and nutrition

Buy environmentally safe products
Believe that career is important
Believe that quality is more important than price
Shop at specialty stores
Are willing to pay more for brand/company reputation
Are skeptical of advertising
Are adventurous/fun loving

Travel to foreign countries (for business or pleasure)
Make contributions to public radio
Own an espresso/cappuccino maker
Use online banking services
Own a digital camera
Visit a national park
Drive a convertible
Own a multicomponent audio system
Drink imported wine
Have owned a home computer for 5+ years

Media
Atlantic Monthly
Business Week
Conde Nast Traveler
New York Times
Smithsonian
Wall Street Journal

The News Hour with Jim Lehrer
NOVA (PBS)
Wall Street Week
Washington Week in Review

STRIVERS
Characteristic Attitudes and Behaviors
Roller-skate
Play basketball
Play softball
Play video games
Play football
Go to movies once a week or more
Play volleyball
Play baseball
See movies on opening weekend
Collect sports trading cards

Are influenced by celebrity endorsements
Spend lots of time with friends
See job as "just a job," not as a career
Are influenced by opinions of peers
Aspire to "make it rich"
Find brand important
Often make impulse purchases

Drink malt liquor
Are heavy users of aftershave lotions and cologne
Drink energy drinks
Spend $200 or more on a video-game system
Are heavy users of mouthwash/dental rinse
Have recently purchased work boots
Visit a theme park
Drink beer
Own a compact car
Are heavy users of chewing gum

Media
Hotrod
Parenting
Penthouse
Rolling Stone
Seventeen
Vibe

Showtime at the Apollo
Jerry Springer
Passions
Ricki
WWF Smackdown

Source: This list derives from ongoing survey data collected by VALS and Mediamark Research SRI Consulting Business Intelligence, *http://www.sric-bi.com/vals.*

- Professionals, entrepreneurs, and others who work very long hours and are active physically
- Highly educated
- Expect the best
- Purchase products to save time and energy and thus require high-level service and consistency

In reviewing all of the information from the various sources both demographically and psychographically, we can see that Susan has a handle on

Action Step 25

Initial Customer Profile

1. Based on what you know to date, continue to profile your Target Customer using the following:

   - http://www.census.gov
   - http://www.claritas.com
   - http://www.easidemographics.com fttp://www.sric-bi.com/VALS
   - SRDS Lifestyle Market Analyst (if available in library)
   - Any additional databases that you can locate on the Internet or in the library.

2. For B2B businesses, first access your customers' NAISC codes. Use sources you have already discovered as well as the following to profile your B2B clients:

   - http://www.hoovers.com
   - http://www.dnb.com
   - http://www.edgar-online.com

   Also, search the library, association Web sites, and the Internet for directories that address your market. How large is the market in terms of numbers of customers? How large is the market in terms of potential sales? Who are the major players? List your top ten prospects.

   Focus on your Target Customer throughout the remainder of the chapter. As you recognize variables to add, or questions to be asked, jot them down. Action Step 27 entails further profiling.

her customers and their needs. Susan's Healthy Gourmet also reaches two secondary markets—those over age 70, whose children often purchase food for them, and dieters. Each segment has different needs, and each requires a different marketing and sales effort.

After being in business for 12 years and keeping records diligently, Susan now knows exactly who her target market is. But for those just starting a business, the previous resources provide a good head start toward defining Target Customers. Many more profiling systems are available online to use and purchase, we have only touched on a few to boost your search. By knowing your target market intimately, you will be far ahead of your competition. Continue to refine your profile as you work through the remainder of the Action Steps. Before continuing, be sure to complete Action Step 25.

PROFILING BUSINESS TO BUSINESS (B2B) CUSTOMERS

Business-to-business markets include a wide range of customers that include government agencies, educational facilities, nonprofit organizations, as well as many industrial customers. You will need to evaluate your customer based on demographics (size, geographic location), customer type, end-use application, and purchasing situation.

End-user profiling concentrates on how a product or service is used. Small firms often thrive in specific niches because larger firms may ignore small markets. Geographic profiling is used when customers are concentrated in a specific geographic area. Some examples include furniture makers in North Carolina, filmmakers in Vancouver, Canada, and biotechnology in San Diego. Such users have narrow and specific needs. If an industry leader is opening a plant in a different location, a new support business may do well, because there will be less competition in the new area. If you followed the mass immigration of businesses to Las Vegas, you would have been able to provide innumerable services to a growing industrial base.

Segmentation of business markets include the following:

- NAISC or SIC codes
- Sales revenue
- Number of employees
- End-use application
- Location
- Purchasing method (for example, low bid only or single sourcing)
- Credit risk
- Years in business
- Type of ownership (public, private, city, state, or federal government, nonprofit organizations)
- International versus U.S. sales
- Ability to reach decision maker
- Purchase decision: group or individual
- Economic and technological trends affecting industry
- Competitive nature of particular segments
- Barriers to entry into various segments

Use available secondary business information to help you:

- Check a firm's financial stability.
- Compare a firm's sales to its number of employees.

- Discover ownership of a firm or its subsidiaries.
- Locate specific companies.
- Search specific industries.
- Size up current and new markets by using multiple selection criteria.
- Search potential prospects or prospective employers in a targeted market.
- Identify decision makers so you can reach them directly.
- Identify and track competitors.

Chapter 5 contains information sources to track down business-to-business information. Hoover's and Dun and Bradstreet (D&B), both available online, are frequently used to locate B2B customers. An abbreviated sample listing from Hoover's appears in Figure 4.6. Also, throughout the text we have highlighted many government buyers who purchase billions of dollars of products and services from civilian firms.

In addition to the variables and information previously mentioned, personal traits of the individual buyers within each firm are important. Knowing the hobbies, activities, and lifestyles of the people to whom you are selling may be as important as the listed demographic and geographic variables of the firms themselves. Relationships tend to be long term in B2B markets, and your ability to break into new markets may depend on your ability to break long-term relationships. Do *not* underestimate how difficult this may be.

---
figure **4.6**

Hoover's Custom Report Builder: Apple, Inc.

The Basics
1 Infinite Loop
Cupertino, CA 95014 United States (Map)
Phone: 408-996-1010
Fax: 408-974-2113

http://www.apple.com
Computers are still an important part of its mix, but these days music-related products are at the top of Apple's playlist. The company scored a runaway hit with its digital music players (iPod) and online music store (iTunes). Apple's desktop and laptop computers—all of which feature its OS X operating system—include its Mac mini, iMac, and MacBook for the consumer and education markets, and more powerful Mac Pro and MacBook Pro for high-end consumers and professionals involved in design and publishing. Other products include mobile phones (iPhone), servers (Xserve), wireless networking equipment (Airport), and publishing and multimedia software. Its FileMaker subsidiary provides database software.

Key Information
DUNS Number 060704780
Doing Business As "Apple"
Company Type Public–NASDAQ (GS): AAPL
Location Type Headquarters
Year of Founding or Change in Control 1976
State of Incorporation CA

Key Numbers
Fiscal Year End September
Sales (mil.) $24,006.0
1-Year Sales Growth 24.3%

Net Income (mil.) $3,496.0
1-Year Net Income Growth 75.8%
Total Employees 21,600
Employees at This Location 2,000

Rankings/Stock Indexes
#103 in FORTUNE 500
S&P 500
#85 in FT Global 500

Officers and Employees
Key People
CEO and Director Steven P. (Steve) Jobs
COO Timothy D. (Tim) Cook
SVP and CFO Peter Oppenheimer
SVP, General Counsel, and Secretary Daniel Cooperman
SVP iPod Anthony (Tony) Fadell

Industry Information
First Research Industry Profiles New Extensive Industry Intelligence
Computer Manufacture

Hoover's Industries
Computer Hardware
Computer Peripherals
Computer Software
Consumer Products Manufacturers
Media
Retail

Primary SIC Code
3571: Electronic computers

Primary NAICS Code
334111: Electronic Computer Manufacturing

Source: Abbreviated courtesy of Hoovers, Inc., *http://www.hoovers.com.*

PRIMARY RESEARCH IS ABSOLUTELY NECESSARY

Secondary sources of demographic and psychographic information, especially media sources, may provide enough data to form a fairly accurate profile of your Target Customer. Chances are, though, that you will need to test your profile against reality. Field **interviews**, surveys, and observation are three primary tools that will provide you a more accurate profile of your Target Customer as you undertake primary research.

Interviews Planned conversations by phone, mail, face-to-face, or on the Internet with another person or group of persons for the purpose of eliciting specific information

FIELD INTERVIEWS

Sometimes people enter into small businesses because of personal circumstances rather than an initial grand desire. Often they have to learn new skills and learn them fast. Fortunately, entrepreneurs tend to be bright, creative, and hardworking people. Jen Liong is a good example. When Jen discovered that she would have to work for herself, she quickly began to research her Target Customers by conducting field interviews.

Baby Store?

It was no secret that Jen Liong was distressed when her husband was transferred. She could not blame him for wanting the transfer; she would have wanted it, too. But Jen had a terrific job as regional manager of a full-line baby furniture and bedding store chain, and to keep both job and husband, she would have to commute more than 150 miles, 5 days a week. After many conversations and much soul searching, Jen and her husband decided to move to a lovely town with affordable housing near her husband's new workplace.

She missed her store, and it was hard living on one salary when they had gotten used to two. She also missed the excitement of retailing and customer contact. When Jen started to look for work, she found that her reputation had preceded her. The two local baby store owners knew of the chain where she had worked and were pretty sure that the only reason she wanted to work for them was to get a feel for the area so that she could open a store of her own and compete with them. This gave Jen an idea—to go ahead and compete with them. Their fear gave her confidence!

One thing Jen had learned on her way up the managerial and sales ranks was that it pays to know your customer. So, in the mornings after sending her children off to school, Jen would drive to various baby stores within a 30-mile radius of her town, and when customers came out of the store, she would strike up conversations with them and conduct interviews.

Her enthusiasm must have helped—she liked people, especially babies, and it showed. Being a mother helped her understand other mothers. She always dressed up a bit and carried a clipboard. Jen asked obvious questions like:

- *What items did you buy?*
- *Was there anything you wanted and could not find?*
- *What do you like about this store?*
- *How close is this store to your home?*
- *Were the people helpful and courteous?*
- *How frequently do you shop here?*
- *At what other stores do you shop for baby items?*

Sometimes Jen parked in an alley to research the arrival and unloading of the delivery trucks. From experience she was able to estimate the store's purchases.

Jen developed a separate list of questions for pregnant women:

- *Have you had a baby shower?*
- *Which gifts did you like best?*
- *Which gifts seemed most useful?*
- *What things are you buying before your baby comes?*
- *What things are you waiting to buy?*
- *How are you going to decorate the baby's room?*
- *What do you really need the most?*
- *What services would be most helpful to you?*

After completing 30 time-consuming interviews, Jen had an abundance of information to make sound decisions concerning her Target Customer. She also knew the strengths and weaknesses of her competition. Many times entrepreneurs look only for their competitors' weaknesses, but an entrepreneur can learn just as much from their competitors' strengths. Never underestimate the power of those strengths and the time and energy that went into developing them. Capitalize on the strengths of your competitors and take advantage of their weaknesses.

OBSERVING TARGET CUSTOMERS

In addition to interviewing, Jen was involved in **observing** her customers. This is the least expensive but one of the most effective forms of market research. Put personal bias and intuition aside and truly listen to and observe your Target Customer. Take away all you know about your product or service and Target Customer, and observe how your customer truly behaves—remember that actions speak louder than words.

Jen Liong's Target Customers shared that they bought all their children's clothing at upscale stores, but on observation she realized that more than half of the kids were dressed in Target and Wal-Mart clothing. People often say one thing but do another. Also, people do not always know why they make the purchasing decisions they make unless they spend some time thinking about their actions. They might not even recognize a need, but when presented with a new product or service based on your observations, it may be just what they wanted. Jen also observed that the local stores focused on selling not only to mothers but also to the very large and lucrative market of doting grandmothers and aunts.

A small, ladies' specialty clothing store considered hiring a marketing consultant who offered to conduct a research study to help define their target market for $4,000. Another consultant proposed $1,000 to review the store files and help the store develop their target market profile. After the second consultant was hired, she focused her research on the top 100 customers. The list was shared with the store's top five salespeople during a three-hour meeting with the owner and consultant, at which a circle was drawn around the Target Customer; and the owner and salespeople knew from that point on who to put at the center of the dartboard. From that meeting, the buyers knew exactly who to buy for, and even the newsletter was reworked to meet the target market's needs and wants. The $3,000 saved was used to carry an additional line that the salespeople believed, based on what they had learned, would sell quickly.

Use curiosity as you observe and interview. Ask as many open-ended questions as possible. When Jen Liong wrote down her interview responses, she also made notes of the following information:

- Makes and years of cars the women drove
- Attitudes toward their children
- Clothing worn by the children and their moms

Observing Using "new eyes" to learn about Target Customers

Action Step 26

Interview and Observe Prospective Target Customers

Now that you have profiled your Target Customers using computer and media kit research, it is time for you to take a big step—to move from the world inside your head to the arena of the marketplace. It is time to rub elbows with the people who will be buying your product or service.

You know where your Target Customer hangs out, as well as his or her habits, income, lifestyle, personality, and buying patterns. You can guess this customer's dreams and aspirations. Now you are going to check out your assumptions directly by interviewing your potential Target Customers through additional research and observation.

1. First, observe your customer in the marketplace. Remember Jen Liong and the steps she took. Take notes as you simply observe.
2. Next, prepare for interviews. Develop questions in advance; most should be open ended and must call for more than just simple yes-or-no answers. Remember, the most important part of your research will be for you to keep an open mind. Your goal is to satisfy your customers' needs and you need to be open to *their* needs.
3. You may also conduct research by posting questions to newsgroups and social networks. Internet communities exemplify the free flow of information and you may find a very responsive group of people.

- Types and brands of strollers
- Children's snacks
- Hairstyles and grooming of the mothers and children
- Amount spent on their own children versus gifts for others

In addition, Jen decided to check out the local playgrounds and snoop around. She borrowed her friend's two children, and off she went to ask questions. When Jen was surrounded by children, women were very open.

Jen combined the information she gathered from *http://www.census.gov*, *Standard Rates and Data Services Lifestyle Market Analyst* (SRDS), and VALS with her observations, interviews, and secondary data. She was then able to focus in on her target market and make it the center of her dartboard.

Where can you spend some time observing your Target Customer, and what will you ask them? In Chapter 5, when we research competition, we will return to interviewing and observing. Here, we will use another skill—surveying—to reach a more refined picture of a Target Customer.

Surveys

When Patti Hale, a budding entrepreneur, decided that she was going to work for herself, she quickly began to research Target Customers. The methods she chose were observation, interviewing, and surveying. You can do the same with your primary marketing research. Action Step 26 and Patti Hale's experience in the following paragraphs will guide you in conducting research for your potential business.

Designing and Conducting a Survey

Patti Hale, a supervisor at a textile plant, decided to leave the plant and turn her love of food and people into a business: a restaurant. For some time, Patti had been developing her business skills. She had taken several courses in restaurant and bar management and an evening small-business course at a local college. In an attempt to gain a handle on her Target Customer, Patti read many studies on the dining habits of people in the Southeast. But how did these translate to her local market? Although the secondary research was very revealing, Patti could not risk her future on someone else's research and decided to do her own survey. She studied survey design and received advice from her professor, an experienced surveyor.

Patti considered surveying customers at Joe's Joint, one of the most popular eating spots in town. She often had a bite to eat there and got to know Joe, the owner, quite well. She told Joe about her plan to open a small restaurant some day and about how much she was learning in her small-business course. Patti convinced Joe to let her do a survey of his customers. After all, the price was right. Patti would do the survey free of charge and would give Joe the results—a classic win–win proposition.

Patti spent the next few weeks designing her survey method. How many customers should she survey? When should she do the survey? How should she conduct herself? There was so much to do. She launched a weeklong written survey of Joe's customers. To Joe's surprise, customers wanted to fill out the questionnaire. To Patti's surprise, she overheard Joe explaining to someone that he thought it was about time he learned a bit more about what the customer wanted. From her survey Patti determined that her target market saw no need or desire for additional restaurants in the town and in fact were actually cutting back on the amount they spent to eat out. This was a rude awakening for Patti. But at this point, she had only lost time and now could regroup and find another business idea, which might have more potential for profit.

MAKE CUSTOMER PROFILING A REFLEX

Profiling your customers will take time, energy, and diligent maintenance of sales records. As you learn more and more about your customers, predicting their needs will become easier. In addition, if you are fortunate, you will also uncover previously invisible customers who will emerge with needs that you have not anticipated. An alert entrepreneur will listen carefully to unexpected requests and be quick to respond to these opportunities, because a new market may be emerging. The following case is a typical example.

Invisible customer Surprise customer; usually a great find

Some people go into business for themselves because they cannot work for someone else. Some are mavericks who do not like to take orders. Others are dreamers who love their own ideas. Still others, like Fred Bowers, have a physical handicap that makes them prefer self-employment to a job with a large firm. Sometimes customers "come out of the woodwork," as Fred's experience illustrates.

Soccer City
Revealing "Invisible Customers"

Fred Bowers had planned to be a career Marine until he was injured in a fall from a training helicopter. He could still walk, painfully, but his military career was finished. With a medical discharge in his pocket, Fred looked around for work, but none was to be found that would accommodate his disability.

"I'd always loved soccer," Fred said. "I'd been a pretty fair player, and my coaching experience had given me a good understanding of kids and their parents. I thought there might be a place for a soccer specialty shop in our community, but before I went for financing, I spent several months checking it out."

Using the Internet, Fred found ten sporting-goods shops located within a 20-mile radius of his desired site. If he wished, for a small fee he could access customer profiles, credit ratings, and credit reports on each of his potential competitors by conducting a search at http://www.hoovers.com.

When Fred began profiling his Target Customers, he came up with two easy targets:

- *Primary target: male soccer players, age 6 to 17, and their parents*
- *Secondary target: female soccer players, age 6 to 17, and their parents*

He also gathered the following information:

- *Household income: $60,000 to $100,000 per year*
- *Level of parents' education: college degree*
- *Interests: sports, video games, computers, movies, and music*
- *Automobiles: SUVs and Vans*

Then Fred segmented the youngsters into three groups: members of school soccer teams, members of American Youth Soccer Organization (AYSO) teams, and members of club teams.

Because of Fred's knowledge of the game and helpful demeanor, his store prospered. Schools counted on him for an honest deal, and parents of players counted on his advice for equipment. "I had thought I'd just be selling products," Fred said. "What I was really doing was providing a service."

After being in business a year, a third market began to emerge. The customers in this third group were adults, mostly foreign-born, from countries such as Great Britain, Mexico, and Brazil. They had grown up playing soccer and loved the game. To them, it was a fiercely fought national sport they loved to play. These heretofore-invisible customers would drive 50 to 75 miles to Fred's store for equipment they could not find elsewhere. He agreed to sponsor several adult teams, and his business continued to grow.

The next year, the local Boys and Girls Club started an indoor soccer league for 1,200 kids. Fred offered to sponsor all of the team photos. Needless to say, his business grew by supplying special indoor-soccer shoes and knee and shin pads. Fred now supplied AYSO and boys' high school soccer in fall, indoor soccer in winter, girls' high school soccer in spring, and adult leagues that played primarily in spring and summer when fields were available.

"If I hadn't opened up, I wouldn't have known about the adult players. Now they make up at least 30 percent of my business. One day they weren't there; the next day they were. I like that. I like it a lot. It makes this whole adventure more interesting. Also, they really help with the cash flow, as the previous summers were awfully slow. In addition, keeping busy all year makes it much easier for me to be in the store day after day and to remain profitable."

VISUALIZING YOUR TARGET CUSTOMER

At this point, you have researched, surveyed, and observed your Target Customer. Now read how Louie Chen from Seattle was able to visualize his customer. Soon you will be able to do the same.

Louie Chen and His Dreams

Louie Chen, born in Seattle, grew up playing baseball but switched to tennis. This was a good choice because he became a professional and played on the tennis circuit for 3 years.

Worn down by constant travel, Louie Chen left the pro tour and returned to Seattle and a comfortable life as a stockbroker. He was a member of the chamber of commerce and several organizations for Asian Americans. Because of his tennis, Louie did a lot of business at the country club. Louie was looking around for a new opportunity when he met Jiangli Chang, a recent immigrant to America.

Jiangli Chang, a middle-aged tennis player with a terrific backhand, was part of the Hong Kong exodus. He was in business importing art from Japan and China. Jiangli expressed to Louie his difficulty in establishing a good banking relationship. Jiangli's problem started Louie Chen thinking. More and more Asians were coming to the Pacific Northwest. Recently, the Asian population in Washington had jumped 50 percent, from 215,000 to 350,000. With such growth, Louie Chen smelled opportunity. Louie enrolled in a local community college entrepreneurship course. His instructor was Grace Rigby, a marketing specialist, whose favorite tool was the Target Customer profile and collage.

"Profile your Target Customer. When you sleep, dream profiles. You'll have fun. You won't go wrong," Grace told him.

With Grace's help, Louie profiled his Target Customer. One of Grace's key teaching techniques was the Target Customer Collage.

"The collage combines all your data, interviews, surveys, and observations into a visual presentation," Grace said. "The idea is to clip pictures, statistics, phrases, and advertisements from magazines that represent your Target Customer. Then arrange all the pieces to form a collage. Hang the collage on the wall near your desk. When you find it difficult to write your Business Plan, focus on the collage. It should bring you right back into focus. Your sole purpose is to solve the needs and wants of your Target Customer."

Louie Chen's collage included the following pictures:

- *Six Asian men and women in business suits*
- *A private jet*
- *The Bank of Hong Kong*
- *Sushi*
- *An expensive leather briefcase and fine luggage*
- *Fine gold and diamond jewelry*
- *A laptop, Blackberry, and cellular phone*
- *An Asian man in shirtsleeves*
- *A man in a hardhat studying blueprints at a construction site*
- *An Asian man in golf gear teeing up at Pebble Beach*
- *Asian families traveling together*
- *Stock market tables*

The collage centered Louie on his Target Customer. Because he had an excellent credit history, a well-developed Business Plan, and a keen sense of his Target Customer, venture capitalists were eager to finance Louie's bank. Louie chose the name Shangzai American Bank of Credit (SABC) for his bank and located it in the international district adjacent to downtown Seattle.

Specializing in the Asian market, Louie hired greeters such as Maryann Wu, who was fluent in Mandarin Chinese and Korean and spoke enough Japanese to get by. Maryann was studying Thai as well. She shook hands with customers and then directed them to a manager who spoke their native language or was very familiar with their country of origin.

One day while sitting at his desk, Louie saw an Asian male in his early fifties in the lobby. He wore an expensive tailored suit, carried a briefcase, and looked just like one of the men in his original collage. Louie hurried out of his office and greeted the gentleman, Sam Song, who subsequently deposited $1 million in his new SABC account.

Louie never stopped focusing on his Target Customer collage and had been adding to it during the past year in business. In fact, it was hanging in his office. But now he knew the person he wanted to celebrate with was Grace Rigby. Without Grace's insistence on focusing and refining his target market, he knew SABC would not have been a success.

Sam Song would probably be classified as an Innovator on the VALS scale. Louie's Target Customer collage reflected business leaders with resources and deep interests in music and art. Louie found out later that one reason Sam Song immigrated to Seattle was for access to the Seattle Art Museum and the Pacific Northwest Ballet. You will notice that visiting museums ranks high on the Innovator's preferred activities lists. (See Figure 4.5.)

It is now time for you to complete your own Target Customer collage following the instructions in Action Step 27. Start to visualize your customer. Keep the picture of your Target Customer in the forefront as you move into evaluating your competition and promoting your product.

Action Step 27

Target Customer Collage

Gather up all the information from the past three action steps. It is time to visualize your data.

1. Develop a collage—a composite image of your Target Customer. Look through magazines or online and select at least 30 pictures, phrases, and possibly statistics that represent your Target Customer's lifestyle.

2. Make a list of your customers' favorite television shows, movies, restaurants, activities, stores, radio stations, music, Internet sites, magazines, and books. Attach it to the back of your collage.

Your collage should represent the demographics, geographics, and psychographics of your market. After you complete the collage, hang it up wherever you work on your Business Plan. Eat, sleep, and drink your Target Customer with the collage always in your line of sight as you prepare to hit the market with your product or service.

If you have a business-to-business product, complete your collage with NAISC/SIC codes, a list of ten best prospects, pictures of the types of people you will be selling to, their lifestyles, and so on. FOCUS! FOCUS! FOCUS!

SUMMARY

Before you open your doors, profile your Target Customer at least five times. After your doors are open, continue to gather data through surveys, interviews, sales information, Internet metrics, and observation. Refine the profile continually.

A profile combines demographic and geographic data (age, sex, income, education, residence, cultural roots, and so on) with psychographic insight (observations of lifestyle, buying habits, consumption patterns, attitudes, and so on). The magazines read by your B2B Target Customers will reveal a fairly well-drawn profile of your business customer.

Questions you need to answer through profiling your Target Customer are:

1. Who are my Target Customers?
2. How can I best reach them?
3. What need will my product or service fill? (For example, landscaping is not just mowing grass and trimming shrubs. Its major selling points are enhancing the appearance of property and providing free time for homeowners.)
4. Where and how can I communicate my message with a minimum of confusion?
5. What additional services do my Target Customers want?
6. What quality of service or product do my customers desire, and what are they willing to pay?
7. Who else is after my customers?
8. Why do my customers act the way they do?
9. How can I build a relationship with my customers?

THINK POINTS FOR SUCCESS

- The term *psychographics* is derived from *psyche* and *graphos,* the Greek words for "life," or "soul," and for "written." Thus psychographics is the charting of your customer's life, mind, soul, and spirit.
- Segmenting is discovering the piece of the pie you should focus on. As you go deeper into your research, you will discover that perhaps you could reach the blueberries in the pie, and if you go further, you will reach the seeds—your true Target Customer. In essence, your collage developed in Action Step 27 should represent your blueberry seed.

- You can save a lot of time and money by using market research that has been conducted by others.
- To discover your target market, use everything available: media kits, Internet metrics, demographic studies, lifestyle segmentations, and census data.
- Use NAISC or SIC codes to begin your research for B2B customers.
- Focus on your Target Customer.

KEY POINTS FROM ANOTHER VIEW

February 14, 2008

¡Hola, Surfers!
By Ellen McGirt

Every marketer, pollster, and advertiser knows this much about Hispanics living in the United States: They are deeply family oriented, and their families are big. So when Alicia Morga, founder and CEO of the Hispanic-focused online marketing firm Consorte

Media, first started working with ad agencies on home-financing campaigns, she was told to use cheery images of happy, home-owning families. Problem: "The pictures of the big, brown family turned out to be the lowest-performing creative among Hispanics," Morga says with a laugh. "By far." What worked instead were simple shots of well-kept homes with white fences and lush lawns. "It's aspirational," she explains. Who knew?

Anyone who bothered to think outside the *caja* would know—and Morga does. In less than two years, she and Consorte Media have changed the thinking on how to find Hispanic Web surfers in the United States and convert them into customers, replacing the stereotypes that often typify minority-targeted marketing with insights gleaned from rigorous data collection and analysis. And she has built a business that's already profitable, scored big-name clients including Best Buy and Monster.com, and completed two rounds of venture funding worth $10 million. Her secret: "Data works. There's too much of the anecdotal in this marketplace."

The Hispanic online market is already huge and getting huger quickly; half of the 44 million Hispanics in the United States are online, and according to the most recent data available from Forrester Media, PC ownership among Hispanics shot up 45% from October 2005 to January 2007.

The language barrier is obstacle enough for many marketers—the most infamous example is a Spanish-language version of the "Got Milk?" campaign, in which the mangled-in-translation tagline ended up meaning something akin to "lactation." But Morga emphasizes that the demo "is not monolithic": One-third of U.S. Hispanics are English-dominant, one-third speak primarily Spanish, and one-third are fully bilingual. And Forrester Media analyst Tamara Barber adds that "it's not just about language. It's about culture." U.S. Hispanics are incredibly diverse, hailing from more than two dozen countries—and that jumble of mores, traditions, and cultural quirks renders generalizations problematic.

"I don't ever pretend that I know what Hispanics are thinking or that I'm the target audience," says Morga, 35, a Mexican-American who grew up in L.A. and, as the eighth of eleven kids, does come from a big, brown family. A venture-capital and corporate-finance veteran who hails from the Carlyle Group by way of Hummer Winblad and Goldman Sachs, she got the entrepreneurial itch in 2005. As she surveyed the online-ad landscape, she saw no lead generators or ad networks for the Hispanic market. "I wanted to apply what I knew to a vertical I cared about," she says.

So Morga converted a closet at home into an office and built a business to satisfy her inner data junkie—every element of every campaign is tested and retested. She uses, among other techniques, the Taguchi method,

a type of web analysis originally developed to measure manufacturing efficiency. Her goal: to get the deepest, most comprehensive understanding of what Hispanic surfers do online. That knowledge informs the content sites that Consorte hosts, helps to deliver ads for publishers, and is the basis for custom lead-generation programs targeting Hispanic prospects in every category from loan applicant to job seeker.

Morga's methodology quickly won over clients such as Manuel Treto, CEO of BuenaMusica.com, a Latin music portal with 200,000 unique visitors a day. He'd worked with six ad networks, including Ad Jungle and Google, before finding Consorte, which he now uses exclusively. "Within two months, they were generating 25% of my revenue," he says. "They know my audience so well that they can bring a much different approach."

Big brands are also on board. Last spring, Best Buy approached Morga for help recruiting bilingual tech- and service-savvy employees in markets like Kansas City, which lack the labor pool of cities like L.A. that have larger Hispanic populations. Morga took Best Buy's existing job application and distilled it into a few key questions. Then she built a microsite, linked to Best Buy's main site that targeted job seekers. "It was up for about 45 days, and she iterated constantly along the way," says Jeff Weness, Best Buy's director of Hispanic initiatives. That process led to a thousands-long list of prospective employees and a "conversion rate significantly higher than on any other initiative we've done." Impressed, Best Buy selected Consorte as an ad partner for its Spanish-language site, which launched in November.

Now Morga is taking her business mobile and global. She plans to develop an emphasis on luxury advertising aimed at the affluent Hispanic traveler—"an overlooked market within an overlooked market," she says. She's also opening her first satellite office in her parents' native Mexico. It will be her first foray into Latin America, the kind of market Morga generally prefers—tons of online consumers (60 million, excluding Brazil), plenty of data to crunch, and few competitors. Her only real rivals there are two companies, Directaclick and Click Diario, both recently bought by News Corp's Punto Fox unit. "I will absolutely," she says, "be getting Rupert's attention."

http://www.fastcompany.com/magazine/123/hola-surfers. html (Accessed May 16, 2008).

- Define competition in terms of size, growth, profitability, innovation, market leaders, market losers, and potential competitors.
- Discover your Target Customer's touchpoints.
- Understand the value of positioning in relationship to competitors.
- Evaluate competitors using primary, secondary, and "new eyes" research.
- Develop skills to become the best marketplace detective you can be.

- Evaluate the competitive landscape broadly.
- Use a competitor matrix.
- Create uniqueness.
- Develop skills to become a lifelong scanner of the competitive landscape.
- Prosper in a rapidly changing competitive marketplace.

chapter 5

Reading and Beating the Competition
Finding Marketplace Gaps

Only a few years ago, the subject of business competition conjured up warlike terms such as "beat the competition," "disarm your competitor," "take a piece of their market," and so on. This market-sharing mentality assumed that when one went into business, one would take a piece of the action away from someone else. In an environment in which industries changed at a slow and predictable pace, the focus was on attacking the competition—after all, there was little change going on, and this strategy seemed to be the only way to drum up new business.

The knowledge-based economy, technology, and the new, informed consumer have changed the way businesses view competition. Learning from and dancing with your competition is what the new economy is all about. Create your own market niche and continually change and improve your product or service as the customer dictates. Today, competition is intense and constantly forces you to respond to market and industry changes.

In the previous chapters, we learned about trend spotting, opportunity selection, and Target Customer profiling. We focused your business toward industry growth segments and customer needs. This chapter explains how your perceived competition can help you further define your specific niche—and it all starts with the customer.

Debbee and Steve Pezman, founders of *Surfer's Journal*, a high-quality, photograph-rich quarterly journal targeted to surfers older than 30, are guided by the following principle: "Identify your Target Customer, and serve them with a 'plus' that is hard to copy." As the Pezmans review new opportunities, they proceed only if they can answer "yes" to the following questions: Is this a plus for our customer? Is this something our competitors will find difficult to copy?

As you read through Chapter 5, complete the Action Steps, and develop your business idea, continually ask the Pezmans' two questions to keep yourself on track and your customer in focus. Also, as noted by Roger Blackwell, speed of information and change make being an entrepreneur more challenging, because products transition through the product life cycle so quickly.

Roger D. Blackwell, independent consultant and professor of marketing at Ohio State University, shares that:

> There are too many companies chasing too few consumers, and the survivors are getting better and better at providing what consumers want. In the past many companies faced competition from great, average, and bad companies. But the bad and the average are being eliminated rapidly, and we are left with only top-notch companies that are more likely to strive to have what the consumer wants. That puts pressure on all the surviving corporations, whatever their size, to conduct precise and speedy market research, so they can offer products that match consumers' desires sooner than the competition.

Product cycles have shortened in part because new products and product improvements have come from countrywide chains. A good idea in one part of the country quickly rolls out across the landscape. Local companies no longer have the luxury of waiting years before their competitors come up with better ideas. Now, new products that have been tested elsewhere—including other countries—quickly become competitive with local products. Honda, for example, has cut conception-to-production time from years to a matter of months. Technological advances in product design and development also have greatly sped up the pace of new product offerings.

Source: Joshua D. Macht, "The New Market Research," *Inc.*, *http://www.inc.com/ magazine/19980701/964.html* (Accessed July 20, 2004). © 2004 Gruner + Jahr USA Publishing. First published in *Inc.* Magazine. Reprinted with permission.

WHO IS YOUR COMPETITION?

Think back to Chapter 3, where we talked about defining your business, not in terms of products, but in terms of benefits—not selling a book per se, but selling information, enjoyment, or pleasant memories. If your business were selling ice cream, old thinking would ask you to list as your competitors other ice cream vendors and manufacturers. In the new school of thought, your competition is anyone who does or could provide the same benefit. If the benefit for your Target Customer is an afternoon treat, then your potential competitor is anyone who provides those treats. Customers only have so many dollars, and everyone wants those dollars. Your customer could stop and buy flowers, specialty coffee drinks, yogurt, sweet rolls, fruit smoothies, or cookies. Other ice cream stores and yogurt stores in your area would be considered your primary or **direct competitors**, and the other businesses would be your **indirect competitors**. Never underestimate the power of your indirect competitors. When exploring your competition, define it as broadly as possible at the beginning, and then work through the industry to identify direct and indirect competitors. Your competition is not necessarily who you think it is, although your views are important. Your customers define the competition in terms of those who can best satisfy their needs.

Now we want to introduce you to a third kind of competitive threat known as **invisible competitors**; that is, businesses that have the capacity and desire to provide similar products, services, or benefits to your customer. In a borderless, virtual environment, where you can order goods from as near as your next-door neighbor or from a place whose name you can't even pronounce, this type of invisible competition has become a real threat. If your potential customers decide to finish their fence-building project on their own, in essence they have become your invisible competitor as well. In recessions, customers may choose not to spend money, and thus "lack of cash" becomes your invisible competition.

If you continue to scan the marketplace, you may also be able to identify future direct and indirect competitors who are forming on the horizon. As you enter into your business, keep in mind that scanning your competitors is part of your everyday business operation. We encourage you to define your competition as broadly as possible at the beginning, and then work through your industry to identify both direct and indirect competitors. Remember, your customers define the competition in terms of those who can best satisfy their needs.

As you work through this chapter and complete your research, keep files containing relevant information on each of your competitors; at some point, you will be able to develop an Elements of a Competitor Profile, as shown in Figure 5.1, for each of your major competitors. Each business will need to tweak the profile to fit specific needs and issues. Keep these files as up to date as possible.

Direct competitors Those companies or individuals that offer the same types of products or services, as perceived by your Target Customer

Indirect competitors Those companies or individuals that provide the same benefit, as perceived by your Target Customer

Invisible competitors People or businesses that have the capacity or desire to provide the same products, services, or benefits that you do

—————————————————————————————————————— figure **5.1**

Elements of a Competitor Profile

Elements of a Competitor Profile

A competitor profile will include data needed to effectively identify, classify, and track competitors and their behavior. You will be looking for points of comparison regarding your strengths and weaknesses versus theirs.

What follows is a comprehensive list of suggested data to consider. You may use this as a guideline or checklist, selecting only those elements that make sense for your particular business, industry, or competitive situation.

Company Identification:

Name—full legal name, informal or abbreviated versions, acronyms, logo. Identify any parent company or subsidiaries, both within the home country and globally

Access Information—address, office locations, Website, email, phone, fax, and so on

Company Structure—organizational structure and legal structure (proprietorship, partnership, corporation)

Ownership—owners, percentage of ownership and control, form of ownership (common stock, etc.), extent of involvement in company

History—background and track record

Corporate Culture—business philosophy, guiding beliefs

Is this a direct or indirect competitor? (This may vary for each of your product or service lines.)

Stature and Credibility of the Company:

Size—breadth and depth of resources of organization

Stability—length of time in business, or successful market presence

Reputation—ethical conduct (business practices, employee relations, customer relations), government or industry certification, community sponsorship

Credibility—market or industry recognition (honors, awards, references), record of effectiveness or success

Proprietary Assets:

Patents—any registered or pending copyrights, patents, or trade secrets

Proprietary attributes—trademarks, processes

Branding—recognized brand names or brand loyalty

Product Design/Services and Innovation:

Offering—product or service lines, features, and mix; customer support

Quality—perceived quality of products or services and support (from customer perspective)

Research and Development (R&D) Activities—anticipated new products or services (consider also new generations of existing products or services, complementary products or services, and replacement products or services). The R&D activities of suppliers and customers may also provide a glimpse of future prospects.

If you are introducing a new product, look out for potential competitors from other product or industry groups who may be planning to get into the same business.

Operations (Production/Service Capability):

Internal Resources and Capacity—staff, skills, equipment, facilities, communication technology. Consider status of staff (union vs non-, contract, shift, etc.), qualifications, experience; condition of equipment and facilities (obsolete vs. leading-edge); and staff communication and flexibility (telecommuting, remote access, etc.).

External Resources—subcontractors, strategic alliances, and so on.

Look out for competitive operating advantages, such as economies of scale (volume efficiencies), experience curve (learning curve advantages), low direct costs, or effective techniques.

Marketing and Sales Approach:

Sales—may be expressed as unit sales (number of product units sold) or dollar sales (sales revenue from units sold or services provided).

Market Share—a company's sales expressed as a percentage of total sales in the market. Although several definitions of market share are possible, the most readily available measure is of "overall market share." This is based on total industry sales, which are available from government or industry trade association sources.

Sales Force—internal versus external representation, size, recruitment and training, compensation

Sales Activities—process of identifying and qualifying sales prospects, number of sales calls per period, productivity of sales staff, average size of sale

(continued)

figure **5.1**

Elements of a Competitor Profile (continued)

Marketing Strategy and Pricing:

Target Markets—primary, secondary, market segments

Expansion Plans—growth objectives (market penetration) and strategy

Communication—promotion, advertising, public relations, Internet, publications, trade shows

Pricing—price levels, gross margins, discount structure (volume, prompt payment, etc.)

How does your product or service compare with others—from the perspective of the customer—on performance, price, and convenience?

Distribution:

Geographic Coverage—domestic, foreign, global

Distribution Channels—direct, agents, retail

Customer Support—product support, field service

Management Resources:

Key Decision Makers and Operating Staff—name, position, primary responsibilities, unique skills and experience, compensation

Board of Directors—name, position on board, background, extent of involvement with company

Planned Additions to Management Team—positions, primary responsibilities and authority, requisite skills and experience, recruitment process and timing of opportunities, compensation, and so on (available from recruitment ads and activities)

Finance:

Financial Resources—assets, liabilities, inventory, revenue, cost of goods sold, expenses, income, cash flow, profit margins, return on investment, new investment

Financial data is available from financial statements (included in annual reports or financial analyses). Financial statements comprise the balance sheet, earnings or income statement, retained earnings statement, and changes in financial position statement.

It may be difficult to find financial data on private companies. In this case, it may be useful to gather data on industry averages, which is often available from government sources.

Source: *http://www.ic.gc.ca/epic/site/dir-ect.nsf/en/h_uw00541e.html,* Industry Canada, (Accessed May 8, 2008).

COMPETITIVE INTELLIGENCE

Competitive intelligence The process of locating, acquiring, and using information about your competitors

To identify your direct, indirect, and invisible competitors, you are going to need to conduct competitive intelligence (CI). The Society of Competitive Intelligence Professionals (SCIP) defines **competitive intelligence** as the "process of ethically collecting, analyzing, and disseminating accurate, relevant, specific, timely, foresighted, and actionable intelligence regarding the implications for the business environment, competitors, and the organization itself. Intelligence is more than reading newspaper articles; it is about developing unique insight regarding issues within a firm's business environment. Note that the intelligence process generates insightful recommendations regarding *future* events for decision makers, rather than simply generating reports on the current competitive landscape. The process offers critical choices regarding future decisions that provide a desired competitive advantage."

Competitive intelligence is proactive, not reactive. Your major objective is to identify customer needs and opportunities as a result of your competitive intelligence. The objective is *not* to eliminate your competitors but to *learn* and *benefit* from them as you develop and improve your specific niche or position in the marketplace. The following are ten common goals of competitive intelligence:

1. Improve your product features and customer benefits.
2. Improve your customer service.
3. Find new ways to distribute your product or service.
4. Improve your advertising and promotions.
5. Develop more efficient production processes.
6. Reduce your reaction and delivery time.
7. Add value to your product or service.
8. Find new alliances and strategic partners.
9. Find new ways to grow your current product or service.
10. Develop new product or service opportunities.

Your competitive intelligence will require a well-researched understanding of your Target Customers, products, and current and future competition. One way to focus your research using information from your Target Customers is to develop a touchpoint analysis.

COMPETITIVE TOUCHPOINT ANALYSIS

As we have said before, people do not simply purchase products or services; they also buy what the products and services do for them. The customer's cry is, what's in it for me? How does your product make my life better, easier, more productive, and fun? How does it make me younger, sexier, or smarter? How does it reduce my costs and make me more profitable? To evaluate your competition, first you need to recognize what is of value to your customer.

Gather together a small group of your potential Target Customers for a "group think" on your competitors. Walk together through the entire experience your customers encounter with your competition. We like to call this process **competitive touchpoint analysis**. Each touchpoint represents a moment when the customer has contact with anything affiliated with the firm—advertising, products, Web site, public relations, receptionists, salespeople, or the building or store. When working with a restaurant owner, a list with over 100 touchpoints is possible.

Competitive touchpoint analysis
Review of each time customer has contact with company

Making a list of all the touchpoints allows you to focus on your competitors' strengths and weaknesses, as well your own. In addition, recognizing your competitors' strengths may indicate areas where you should not try to compete, or where competition will be very intense. List your touchpoints and rank their importance with your Target Customer. Then ask the following questions:

Where do openings exist? Can you successfully compete in those openings? What needs are not being met? What area could you capitalize on? Where do you see yourself being strong or weak? What images are your competitors projecting? What image will you project?

Recall Susan's Healthy Gourmet from Chapters 3 and 4. Let's walk through some possible touchpoints for Susan's customers. Keep in mind that many more touchpoints could be added to the following list:

- **Clicks on banner ad:** What is the quality of the banner advertisement? Is it professional? Is it directed to the right person? How many ads does the person probably see before responding?

Competitor matrix A grid used to get a clear picture of competitors' strengths, weaknesses, and other attributes

Distinctive competency Area of greatest strength in the marketplace

Action Step 28

Evaluating Customer Touchpoints

Investigate your customer's perception of the competition and what benefits are important to him or her. As you look for a niche in the marketplace, you must review your competitors' actions, services, and products. Take a moment now to review Susan's Healthy Gourmet's Customer Touchpoints.

Work with a group of your potential Target Customers, and walk through the experience of purchasing your competitors' products. Make a long list (at least 60 to 80 items) of the touchpoints for each time the customer comes in contact with any facet of the competitors' business. Each facet makes up the entire product—the jewel. The more you know about the jewel, the more you can make it shine.

1. After listing the touchpoints, ask Target Customers to select and rank their five most important touchpoints. As you review all your competitors' touchpoints, consider how you can equal or beat your competitors in these areas.

2. In what areas can you provide either real or perceived additional value for the customer?

You need to consider which facets are worth going head-to-head with, which are not worth dealing with, and in which areas you can outperform your competition. Keep your touchpoints handy; you will return to them in Chapters 6 and 7. When writing your Business Plan, capitalize on the touchpoints that make you stand out in the crowd.

- **Responds to advertisement:** How is the Website designed? How easy is it to navigate? How easy is it to determine costs and programs? If the potential client has diet issues, how easy is it to find information? If the information cannot be located, can a client contact Susan's Healthy Gourmet? Is there a phone contact? If so, is the person who answers pleasant? How long does the customer wait on hold for a salesperson? Is the on-hold music appropriate? Is the salesperson knowledgeable and helpful? If the customer asks a question, how quickly does he or she receive a response? Is the program explained clearly? Are the customer's concerns addressed fully?

- **Places order:** Is the order form easy to fill out online and understand? Is the form attractive? Is delivery clear? Are alternatives clearly spelled out? Is ordering online easy and quick? Is there a real person to call if the customer has problems ordering online?

- **Receives order:** Is the correct order received at the right time and place? Is the meal attractively presented? Are heating directions clear? How does the meal taste?

- **Calls to complain or change an order:** How are complaint calls or changed orders handled? How are problems resolved? How long is the customer placed on hold? Is it done politely? Is the problem solved in a timely fashion? Are follow-up calls made to ensure that the customer's problem has been rectified?

Discover the customer touchpoints in your business by completing Action Step 28. Later you will complete a **competitor matrix** to continue to evaluate your competitors. Once you have completed Chapters 6 and 7, return to Action Step 28 and refine your original answers.

To compete you need to stand out! Develop a **distinctive competency**. Own a niche. Success in business is not based merely on obtaining customers; true success is achieved by *retaining* customers. So as you seek out your competitors' strengths, look for those features that encourage customer loyalty by continually reviewing your touchpoints and exceeding your competitors' offerings. Remember to focus on the *benefits* your customers receive.

If you truly listened to your potential customers as you completed the previous Action Steps, you may already be on your way to developing a profitable market niche. Niches may make you rich, but to maintain a profitable business over the long run, it is more important to build a reputation. Through your research in Chapters 3 and 4, you should have a head start on defining and understanding your competition. This chapter enables you to dig even more deeply to develop a strategy and framework to compete as you put the pieces together from past Action Steps such as trend spotting, identifying your Target Customer, and doing market research.

SCOUTING THE COMPETITION

Competitive touchpoints are only one primary source of competitive intelligence and will need to constantly be redefined as you research the competitive landscape to further scout your direct, indirect, and invisible competitors. There are thousands of secondary sources from which you can gather information. One of the best online database resources we have found to begin your secondary search is Fuld & Company's Internet Intelligence Index, *http://www.fuld.com/fuld-bin/ f.wk?fuld.i3.home*, as shown in Figure 5.2. With links to over 600 intelligence-related Internet sites, you will be well on your way to gathering information and developing your competitive marketing strategy. An in-depth understanding of your industry and competitors allows you to better visualize the position of your company in the grand arena of the marketplace. Action Steps 29 and 30, which appear later in this chapter, will help you gain this understanding.

—— figure **5.2**

Internet Intelligence Index™

The Internet Intelligence Index is designed to help you gather information from a wide variety of public services in support of your competitive intelligence efforts. It contains links to over 600 intelligence-related Internet sites, covering everything from macroeconomic data to individual patent and stock quote information.

Search Engine Features Chart, from *http://www.searchenginesshowdown.com*

General Business Internet Resources

Alerting/Monitoring Services
Annual Reports
Associations
Benchmarking/Quality
Business/Economic Resources
Company Information
Competitor Intelligence
Corporate Filings and Public Records
Finding Experts
General Reference
Government Agencies
IPOs
Information Services
Job Listings
Knowledge Management Resources
Law and Legal Resources

Libraries
Market Research
News
Patents, Trademarks, and Intellectual Property
Phone Directories
Search Engines and Directories
Statistics
Trade Shows/Conferences
Usenet/Discussion Group

Industry Internet Resources

Advertising/Marketing
Aerospace/Defense
Agriculture
Apparel
Automotive
Chemicals
Computer Hardware and Software
Construction
Energy/Utilities
Engineering
Environment
Financial Services
Food and Beverages
General Industry Resources
Healthcare
Insurance
Law
Machinery and Heavy Equipment
Manufacturing

Mining/Minerals
Paint and Coatings Industry
Paper/Pulp
Pharmaceutical/Biotechnology
Plastics/Rubber
Publishing/Media
Retailing and Consumer Goods
Standards
Technology and Telecommunications
Trade
Travel and Transportation

International Internet Resources

Asia/Pacific Resources
Austria
British Resources
Business and Industry
Canadian Resources
Dutch Resources
French Resources
General Country Information
General European Resources
German Resources
Latin American Resources
Middle East Resources
Northern Irish Resources
Portuguese Resources
Russian Resources
Spanish Resources
Swedish Resources
Swiss Resources

Source: *http://www.fuld.com/fuld-bin/f.wk?fuld.i3.home,* (Accessed May 9, 2008)

Remember, work from your strengths: they are built on knowledge. Awareness of your competitors' strengths and weaknesses will increase your confidence. Then you can win. To analyze your competitors, use the following steps as you conduct primary and secondary research, which should lead you to your competition and eventually help you to find your competitive position.

Check Out the Competition

For anyone trying to grow a business, one of the first tasks is to map the competitive landscape. With a good understanding of the competition facing your company, you will be able to spot and exploit opportunities as they develop. These dozen points from All-Business should help you draw and refine your map, beginning with your earliest efforts to plan your new venture and continuing as long as you stay in business.

- **Be a customer.** Bring a notepad and pencil to competing establishments and ask a lot of questions. Testing a firm's ability to serve you will reveal much about their business. Do not just pretend to shop from competitors: Buy something. It is the only way to gain firsthand experience of the company's products and services.
- **Find out as much as you can about the people who run competing businesses.** Where did they go to school? Where have they worked? How long have they been in the business? What are their strengths and weaknesses? This information can help you anticipate your competition's moves. For example, a lifelong farmer may run an Indiana seed company very differently than will a young MBA.

- **Buy stock in your competitors.** If you are competing against a publicly traded firm, consider buying a few shares of its stock. That way, you will receive regular updates on the firm's financial results and business strategies.
- **Talk to your competitor's customers.** Why do they buy from your competitor? Is it because of the quality of the product or service, the price, the location, or the customer support? What do they dislike about the company? What else do they wish the competitors would provide?
- **Use the Internet.** Online services such as Dow Jones Factiva (*http://www.factiva.com*) allow you to search through thousands of publications for information about your competitors, especially if they include large companies. Searches are free, but you will have to pay a fee for articles on Dow Jones or for a monthly subscription.
- **Check public filings.** As an entrepreneur, you already know that companies must disclose information to government agencies. Such disclosures are required to undertake public offerings, receive building permits, and register for patents or trademarks. Many of those filings are public record and contain information about the company's goals, strategies, and technologies.
- **Get to know local librarians.** Many are virtuoso researchers and can save you a great deal of time and effort. Your library also will have local publications that may have information on competitors in your area.
- **Attend industry conferences and trade shows.** Your competitors' representatives will be pounding their chests about their firms' products or services. Take advantage of the opportunity to familiarize yourself with their product offerings and strategies and how they sell themselves.
- **Assess the competition's goals.** A competitor trying to increase its market share might lower prices, a firm attempting to increase profits may cut costs, and a business that wants to accelerate sales growth might kick off a marketing campaign. If you know your competitors' goals, you will be better able to anticipate their strategies.
- **Be aware of the potential for new competition.** These days, the competitive landscape can change faster than Internet stock valuations. A national chain may not have entered your region yet, but what if it does? Likewise, companies that do not currently compete with yours might shift their focus and pit themselves against your firm.
- **Don't delegate the job of keeping up with competitors.** You might appoint someone to work with you on the task, doing research and the like. But as the entrepreneur, you are in the best position to appreciate and act on information about your competitors.
- **Define the competitive landscape broadly.** Your competition includes anything that could draw customers away from your business. For example, movie theaters compete not only with other cinemas but also with restaurants, live music venues, theater, and even cable TV, video rentals, and video games.

Source: All Business, *http://www.allbusiness.com/articles/content/289.asp* (Accessed July 14, 2004).

Additional Secondary Research Sources

With the steps above in mind, it is now time to continue your secondary data research from previous chapters, but this time with the focus on your competitors. As in the past, we ask you to begin your research with secondary data through the Internet and library. The list of resources that follows, in addition to those previously presented, will assist you in your research. Performing secondary research first prepares and narrows your focus for primary data searching.

Library and Internet References for Companies and Industries

To determine if the firm is publicly owned or privately owned/closely held:

- Security and Exchange Commission's EDGAR database, *http://www.edgar-online.com*

For International Company Information:

- D&B Principal International Business
- European Wholesalers & Distributors Directory

- World Trade Center Association World Business Directory
- Dun's Latin America's Top 25,000
- World Trade Magazine

For parent companies and subsidiaries:

- Directory of Corporate Affiliations
- D&B's America's Corporate Families

- Who Owns Whom: North America
- Guide to American Directories
- American Corporate Families

For a company's type of business, executive officers, number of employees, and annual sales:

- Standard & Poor's Register of Corporations
- D&B's Million Dollar Directory
- Ward's Private Company Profiles
- Standard & Poor's Register of Corporations, Directors, & Executives
- Dun's Business Rankings
- Hoover's Billion Dollar Directory

For corporate background and financial data:

- Standard & Poor's Corporate Records
- Moody's Manuals
- Walker's Manual of Western Corporations
- Corporate Information, *http://www.corporate-information.com*

For company news:

- Predicasts F&S Index
- Business Periodicals Index
- Wall Street Journal Online, *http://www.wsj.com*
- PR Newswire, *http://www.prnewswire.com*

For specialized directories:

- Thomas Register of American Manufacturers
- Standard Directory of Advertising Agencies
- U.S.A. Oil Industry Directory
- World Aviation Directory
- Medical and Healthcare Marketplace Guide
- Standard Directory of Advertisers
- Thomson's Bank Directory

For company rankings:

- Annual issues of Fortune, Forbes, Business Week, include Fortune 500, Global 500, America's Most Admired Companies, and the 100 Best Companies to Work For

SECONDARY RESEARCH REPORTS

CI experts also suggest reviewing speeches, TV and radio programs, podcasts, vlogs, tradeshows, web sites, workshops, government documents and research, and any other information you can find. The importance of marketing research and CI is not the collection of the data but the processing of that data into information, analyzing the information so that it becomes knowledge, and then communicating that information to the decision makers. This process should be continual, encompassing all employees within your company.

Additional CI sources should include industry research reports, which can be purchased through three main resellers: *http://www.marketresearch.com, http://www.researchandmarkets.com,* and *http://www.alacrastore.com.*

These three sites each provide research from more than 400 leading national and international research firms. Figure 5.3 highlights an industry snapshot from Alacra Store, which covers industry overview, investment and market research, news, trade associations, and Web sites. With information at your fingertips, and free- and low-cost reports, you will find that many times, most of your secondary research has already been completed.

Also, MarketResearch.com's free online research specialists can guide you to available appropriate and relevant research to purchase. As we have said before, keeping in touch with your trade or professional associations is essential, as is attending special meetings, seminars, and trade shows. You should also access fee-based services, as discussed in Chapter 3.

Sources such as the Science and Technical Information Network at *http://stinet.dtic.mil* provide very detailed competitive information for a very low cost. College Internet sites will also lead you to researchers and programs in your area of expertise. Private database vendors are invaluable and necessary for anyone in a technical field.

Actively visiting online newsgroups, social networks, blogs, and your competitors' Websites will help you unearth competitive nuggets. Presentations and papers by managers and researchers can often be accessed directly through company Websites. Some researchers monitor company Website job postings and infer the direction a technical company may be headed by combing through job specifications.

figure **5.3**

Candy Industry Snapshot: Alacrastore.com

the
alacra™
Store

The Premium Business Information Source™   my purchases   🛒my cart   my account   help   logi

Search by   ▪ keyword   ▪ company   ▪ publisher   ▪ country   ▪ industry   Search ›

Industry Snapshot   **Candy Industry**

Candy Industry - Public Companies

Name	Ticker (Exchange)	Country	Market Cap (US $M)
Nestle SA	NESN (SWX Swiss Exchange)	Switzerland	176,789
Wrigley William Jr. Company	WWY (New York Stock Exchange)	United States	21,146
General Mills, Inc.	GIS (New York Stock Exchange)	United States	21,114
Cadbury plc	CBRY (London)	United Kingdom	16,949
Chocoladefabriken Lindt & Spruengli AG	LISN (SWX Swiss Exchange)	Switzerland	6,970
Kuala Lumpur Kepong Berhad	2445 (Malaysian Stock Exchange)	Malaysia	5,804
Grupo Nacional de Chocolates SA	CHOCOLATES (Colombian Stock Exchange)	Colombia	3,743
CSM NV	CSM (Euronext Amsterdam)	Netherlands	2,040
Premier Foods plc	PFD (London)	United Kingdom	1,749
Lotte Confectionery Company, Ltd.	04990 (Korea)	South Korea	1,661
Tootsie Roll Industries, Inc.	TR (New York Stock Exchange)	United States	1,477

View All »

Premium Content Results:

Credit & Investment Research (1 to 25 of 52)

Name	Publisher	Date	Price
Campbell Soup 3Q08 Tearsheet	CreditSights	Jun 11 2008	$150.00
Earnings Note: Ineos 1Q08 - Energy Sledgehammer	CreditSights	Jun 02 2008	$150.00
Earnings Note: Kraft 1Q08 - Margins Curdled by Input Costs	CreditSights	Apr 30 2008	$150.00
Campbell Soup 2Q08 Tearsheet	CreditSights	Apr 03 2008	$150.00
Earnings Note: Campbell Soup 2Q08 - Loaded For Price Hikes	CreditSights	Feb 19 2008	$150.00
Earnings Note: Kraft 4Q07 - Profits Thinly Sliced	CreditSights	Jan 31 2008	$150.00
Campbell Soup 1Q08 Tearsheet	CreditSights	Jan 17 2008	$150.00
2008 Euro Consumer Goods Outlook	CreditSights	Jan 07 2008	$150.00
Food & Beverage 3Q07 Review	CreditSights	Jan 06 2008	$150.00
Research Overview: As of December 17	CreditSights	Dec 17 2007	$150.00

Source: *http://www.alacrastore.com/industry-snapshot/Candy* (Accessed June 13, 2008).

Looking outward, CI forces one to consider legal and political changes and their potential ramifications on future products and services. In addition, you must also always be scanning the world environment for ideas and competition. Use the *CIA FactBook, World Competitiveness Yearbook, http://www.export. gov*, and other sources highlighted throughout the text to gather market intelligence and CI for your international business ventures. One way to keep competitive and to be able to sell internationally is to follow ISO standards (Global Village) as discussed on page 128.

A Fast Company article by Michael Tchong and Richard Watson offers a few additional tips and tactics for scanning the competitive landscape:

1. Be curious—and obsess—about everything.
2. Ask yourself why new things are happening, and leave no answer unquestioned.
3. Look for patterns. What are the links between new ideas, attitudes, and behavior?
4. Hang out at the edge of your market and watch what the upstart start-ups are doing.
5. Watch out for countertrends and their opportunities and challenges.
6. Remember that the biggest trends are always a confluence of smaller trends. Do not miss the macro because you are concentrating on the micro—and vice versa.
7. Keep it simple—start with what is individually true, and then look for the universal.

8. Do not confuse short-lived fads with major trends.

9. Use the history of products and markets as a guide to their future.

If you get all this right, there is good money to be made in second guessing the future. At the same time, good money can also be lost getting it wrong. And the really big money? Well, that does not come from following trends; it comes from people with original ideas who *create* trends, people with the courage to build something—and then see if anyone will come. For everyone else, being a fast follower is probably the next best option.

Source: Fast Company, *http://www.fastcompany.com/resources/innovation/ watson/071204.html* (Accessed July 14, 2004).

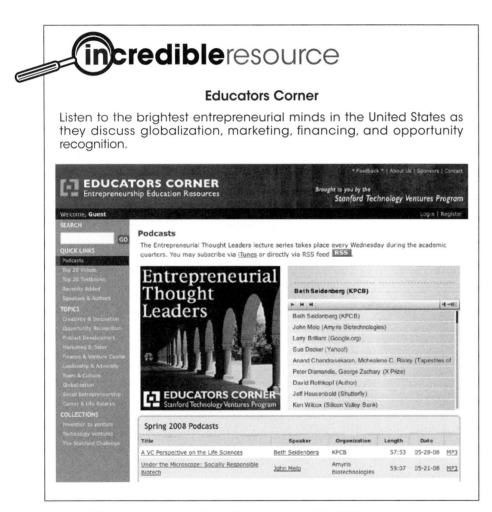

Source: *http://ecorner.stanford.edu* (Accessed June 11, 2008).

PRIMARY RESEARCH

Using Internet sources may turn up the most helpful future primary resource: access to the names and phone numbers of people involved in your industry and those who may have conducted research in your area. Now you have to be able to verify information and conduct interviews. You will be absolutely amazed at the incredible information people will share with you over the phone and through the Internet. Deal honestly with all of your contacts, and explain your reason for calling and requesting information; act responsibly and ethically.

Remember, when using the Internet, *you cannot believe everything you read*. Act with caution before proceeding on information based solely on your Internet research. Before proceeding, track down sources to verify the information. According to Jan P. Herring, a former employee of the CIA and current owner of Herring and Associates, "People's expectations about what they can find on the Internet are too high." He shared the following advice with Fast Company:

Counterintelligence Advice

The Best Things in Life Aren't Free.
Free information is usually secondary information, and the problem with secondary information is that everyone else has access to it. It doesn't give you an advantage. You won't gain an advantage over other people unless you spend more time and money than they do. That means subscribing to syndicated services and databases—and in some cases paying people to work those databases. But ultimately you want information that can't be found in any database.

Human Intelligence Beats Machine Intelligence.
Most information never gets written down—it's just floating in people's heads. The only way to access that information is to talk to people. That's why the most valuable network is the human network. If you find an interesting paper on the Internet, don't just download it—call the author after you read it. Attending conferences is still the best way to make connections and gather intelligence. You'll hear things that never make it onto the Internet. And remember: The best information on your competitors comes from your customers.

Group Intelligence Beats Individual Intelligence.
Tracking the competition is everyone's job. The more closely people work together, the better they do. For example, companies often send 15 or 20 people to a big trade show. But how often do those people bother to compare notes? Companies should do what's called "quarterbacking." At several points during the show, get into a huddle and ask: What have we learned? What else do we need to know? Eventually that quarterbacking mentality becomes an everyday thing.

Source: Gina Imperato, "Intelligence Tips," Fast Company, *http://www.fastcompany. com/magazine/14/intelligencetips.html* (Accessed July 20, 2004).

If you have completed the competitor touchpoints assignment and have conducted computer and library searches, it is time for you to become a snoop—as you are now armed with insight and prepared to ask questions. This is when your new eyes should come into full alert. If you are going to open a toy store, it is time to visit all the toy stores within a 60-mile radius of your home. Take a notebook and write down information on each toy store. If it is easier for you, take a tape recorder or iPhone and record your comments as you drive to the next store. Compile a list of customers' touchpoints, and rank each store on a scale of 1 to 10. In addition, make a list of anything else you think is vital for success in your selected industry, and rank accordingly. Become a paying customer at each store, and walk through the total buying experience. If your competitors have mailing lists, put your name on them. If they offer newsletters, sign up. The more you know about your competitors, the better informed, and thus the more competitive, you can be.

If your business or service is affordable, pay your friends and family members to purchase the products or services also. Then sit down with them and discuss their experiences as well as yours. The more feedback you have, the better.

For each business, develop a competitor worksheet; it will become a competitor profile (see Figure 5.1), which includes all the important touchpoints and the competitor's business name, owner, address, telephone, e-mail address, fax number, length of time in business, estimated market share, Target Customer profile, image, pricing structure, advertising, marketing, customer service, return policies, special order offerings, cleanliness, stocking, strengths, and weaknesses—adjust the list to fit your business. Take this part of your research seriously, because you are discovering your niche in the marketplace by evaluating your competitors.

Entrepreneurs frequently downplay their competitors. When you write your Business Plan, you will need to complete a thorough competitor section, explaining their strengths and weaknesses, and then you will need to convince your reader that your business can fill a niche left by these competitors. *Never underestimate the power of your competitors.*

Additional Snooping

You also may want to snoop with suppliers. They can and will provide great insight into your competitors and the big picture. Beware of and remember those suppliers who provide you with confidential information—they will provide the same information about you to your competitors in the future.

Attending trade shows and asking questions provides excellent market information. If you go with a friend or partner, you can split up so that you can cover the entire show, compare insights, and return to ask more detailed questions. And no one knows an industry better than the salespeople. The more of your competitors' salespeople you encounter, the more you will learn.

Half the battle of succeeding is learning to understand the obstacles and to be on top of developments—to take advantage of all opportunities. Never underestimate your Target Customers' loyalty, fickleness, or resistance to change. You must give them strong reasons to try your product and even stronger reasons to continue to use it.

Complete Action Step 29 to gain a foothold and improve your position on your customer's ladder.

Manufacturing and Scientific Competition

The following areas may also need to be addressed through your competitor research, especially if you are involved in a manufacturing or a scientific endeavor.

- Manufacturing facilities
- Distribution channels and facilities
- Patents
- Financial strength
- Profitability
- Ability to acquire expansion capitalization
- Cost of production
- Employees (skilled sales force, great engineers or software designers)
- Service reputation and availability
- Availability of spare parts
- Repair costs

Action Step 29

Scouting Competitors and Finding Your Position on the Competitive Ladder

1. Complete secondary research on competitors. Do not worry if your list of competitors gets too long. The more competitors you detect, the more you can learn.

2. Using your touchpoints and past research, develop a competitor review sheet for each competitor as you begin to build your competitor profiles, as shown in Figure 5.1.

3. Start snooping: Evaluate competitors and rate them from 1 to 10. If you can not move inside without blowing your mystery shopper disguise, send in a friend with your checklist, or make some cagey telephone calls. You can elicit valuable information from a phone-call survey prepared in advance. Interview everyone who will talk to you. Keep this Action Step handy; you will need it to complete Action Step 30.

GLOBAL VILLAGE

ISO in Brief

The International Organization for Standardization (ISO) develops International Standards over almost the entire range of technology. Its membership comprises the national standards of some 157 members in over 147 countries. ISO is a non-governmental organization, and the standards it develops are voluntary. However, a certain percentage of its standards—mainly those concerned with health, safety, or environmental aspects—have been adopted in some countries as part of their regulatory framework.

ISO standards are market-driven. They are developed by international consensus among experts drawn from the industrial, technical, or business sectors that have expressed the need for a particular standard. In addition, experts from government, regulatory authorities, testing bodies, academia, consumer groups, or other organizations with relevant knowledge may join them, or those who have expressed a direct interest in the standard under development.

Although ISO standards are voluntary, the fact that they are developed in response to market demand and based on consensus among the interested parties ensures widespread compliance. International Standards are increasingly important, especially for global communication, technology transfer, and international trade. According to the ISO organization, "businesses, customers, governments, trade officials, developing countries, consumers, and the planet" all benefit from standardization. ISO examples of the benefits such standards provide follow:

Standardization of screw threads helps to keep chairs, children's bicycles, and aircraft together and solves the **repair and maintenance** problems caused by a lack of standardization that were once a major headache for manufacturers and product users.

Standards establishing an international consensus on **terminology** make technology transfer easier and safer. They are an important stage in the advancement of new technologies and dissemination of innovation.

Without the standardized **dimensions** of freight containers, international trade would be slower and more expensive.

Without the standardization of **telephone and banking cards**, life would be more complicated.

A lack of standardization may even affect the **quality of life** itself: for **the disabled**, for example, when they are barred access to consumer products, public transport, and buildings because the dimensions of wheelchairs and entrances are not standardized.

Standardized symbols provide danger warnings and information across linguistic frontiers.

Consensus on grades of various materials gives a **common reference** for suppliers and clients in business dealings.

Agreement on a sufficient number of variations of a product to meet most current applications allows **economies of scale** with **cost benefits** for both producers and consumers. An example is the standardization of paper sizes.

Standardization of **performance or safety requirements** of diverse equipment makes sure that users' needs are met while allowing individual manufacturers the freedom to design their own solution on how to meet those needs.

Standardized **computer protocols** allow products from different vendors to "talk" to each other.

Standardized **documents** speed up the transit of goods, or identify sensitive or dangerous cargoes that may be handled by people speaking different languages.

Standardization of connections and interfaces of all types ensures the **compatibility** of equipment of diverse origins and the **interoperability** of different technologies.

(continued)

> Agreement on **test methods** allows meaningful comparisons of products and plays an important part in **controlling pollution**, whether by noise, vibration, or emissions.
>
> Safety standards for machinery **protect people** at work, at play, at sea, and at the dentist's.
>
> Without the international agreement contained in ISO standards on **metric quantities and units**, shipping and trade would be haphazard, science would be unscientific, and technological development would be handicapped.
>
> • For more examples of the many areas of life and work where ISO standards provide technical, economic and social benefits, visit *The ISO Café*.

Source: This text is reproduced from the ISO Web site of the International Organization for Standardization, ISO. More information on ISO can be obtained from any ISO members and from the Web site of ISO Central Secretariat at the following address: *http://www.iso.org*. Copyright remains with ISO.

Competition and Positioning

Michael Treacy presents the natural advantages small businesses have and shows how to capitalize on those advantages when competing with large companies. He distinguishes three value disciplines:

1. Operational excellence (e.g. Wal-Mart and Federal Express)
2. Product leadership (e.g. Intel)
3. Customer intimacy (e.g. Airborne Express and Nordstrom)

No company can excel in all three, so focus on a value that differs from your major competitors. A review of your customer touchpoints, competitor information, and completion of the competitor matrix at the end of the chapter will help you focus further on your distinctive competency in the marketplace.

Basically, competition is a game played out in customers' minds, where buying decisions are made. Inside customers' minds are many "ladders"— for products, services, sports figures, television programs, banks, and rental cars. To compete for a position at the top of one of these ladders, a business must first get a foothold and then wrestle with other businesses to improve its position. It is that simple.

Looking at competition from this perspective helps you focus on the mind of your Target Customer. The name of the competitive game is Change. It is the constant process of positioning your product or service to meet the changing needs of customers and markets. You will use your **positioning strategy** to distinguish yourself from your competitors and to create promotions that communicate that position to your Target Customers.

Positioning strategy The placement of a product in the customer's eye through pricing, promotion, product, and distribution

Another way to look at your competitors and situations is with a SWOT analysis that focuses on your strengths and weaknesses, as well as those of your competitors, in light of external opportunities and threats. By focusing on each of these areas, you will be able to develop a competitor matrix. You need to complete an internal analysis to discover the strengths and weaknesses of your own idea or firm. In addition, complete an external analysis of the threats and opportunities of the environment and your competitors. As you complete your analysis, you will be building your competitive advantages and positioning.

SWOT An abbreviation that refers to an analysis of internal strengths and weaknesses, and external opportunities and threats

Key Points from Another View at the end of this chapter provides an excellent example of how a small coffee store looked at its strengths and weaknesses when Starbucks came to town—and decided to fight rather than fold.

THE COMPETITION AND PRODUCT LIFE CYCLE

Like everything else in life and business, competition has a four-stage life cycle: embryo, growth, maturity, and decline. In this chapter, we examine these stages and look at ways you can use them to meet and beat your competition. Briefly, the four stages of the competition life cycle are as follows:

1. In the *embryonic* stage, the arena is empty. There is only you, your idea for a product or service, and a tiny core market. Being the first mover in a market does not ensure success.

2. As your industry *grows,* competitors smell money and attempt to penetrate the arena—to take up positions they hope will lead to profit. Curious Target Customers come from all directions. You have visions of great success.

3. As the industry *matures,* competition is fierce, and you are forced to steal customers to survive. Shelf velocity slows, production runs get longer, and prices begin to slide.

4. As the industry goes into *decline,* competition becomes desperate. Many businesses fail; weary competitors leave the arena.

Penetrate the arena Calculated thrust into the marketplace to secure market share

As discussed previously, competitive life cycles have greatly changed over the past few years. For example, a few years ago, the embryonic stage for a computer software package might have lasted as long as 2 or 3 years. The new economy has changed that. Today movement from one phase to another can occur at blinding speeds.

It is not unheard of for a product to go through one of these four cycles in a matter of months. In high-tech businesses, for example, a common rule of thumb is 3 to 6 months—that is, there are 3 to 6 months from the birth of an idea to product penetration. Beyond that, competitors have already entered the market, and the product begins to enter the maturity phase.

What all this means is that to survive, you must constantly be in touch with the market through CI, and you must always compete vigorously. Keep in mind that you will have no control over how fast the cycle moves, but you will have control over how you plan and react to changes. Figure 5.4 will help you understand the cyclical changes more clearly.

Where is your selected industry and segment on the competition life cycle? What does this mean to you if you are a start-up venture? What are the implications for your survival? When your industry enters maturity and decline, will you be ready with Plan B? Are you going to be a one-product wonder? The following information will help you gain a further understanding of each stage.

Competition Life Cycle

The Embryonic Stage

Excitement, naïve euphoria, thrust, clumsiness, a high failure rate, and much brainstorming mark the embryonic stage. Pricing is high and experimental. Sales volume is low because the market is very small, and production and marketing costs are high. You need to locate your core customer base and stress the benefits of your product. Educating the customer may be necessary and costly. Competition has not yet appeared. It is difficult to find distributors, and resellers demand huge gross margins. Profit is chancy and speculative. Shrewd entrepreneurs, however, can close their eyes and divine the presence of a core market. Keep trying! The writers of *Chicken Soup for the Soul* went to more than 30 publishers before they found the one that propelled their multimillion-dollar empire.

figure **5.4**

Product Life Cycle and Strategies

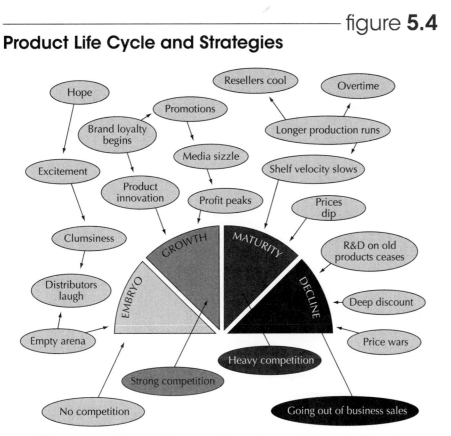

Different competitive strategies are needed at each stage of the product life cycle.

The Growth Stage

Product innovation, strong product acceptance, the beginnings of brand loyalty, promotion by media sizzle, and ballpark pricing mark the growth stage. Distribution becomes increasingly important. Resellers who laughed during the embryonic stage now clamor to distribute the product. Strong competitors, excited by the smell of money, enter the arena, as do new Target Customer groups. Profit percentages show signs of peaking.

The Mature Stage

Peak customer numbers mark the mature stage. Design concentrates on product differentiation instead of product improvement. Production runs get longer, so firms can take full advantage of capital equipment and experienced management. Resellers, sensing doom, cool on the product. Advertising investments increase in step with competition. Some firms go out of business. Prices are on a swift slide down, and competition is very heavy. At this stage, you should only enter the market if you have a unique twist on the product or truly provide a better product. But first ask yourself, "Can I realistically convey this message to my Target Customer?"

The Decline Stage

The decline stage is marked by extreme depression and desperation in the marketplace. A few firms still hang on. Research and development cease, promotion vanishes, and price wars continue. Opportunities may emerge for entrepreneurs in service and repair. Diehards fight for what remains of the core market. Resellers cannot be found; they have moved on to new products.

As you continue to research your competitors and your position, use Fuld's Strategic Organizer (Figure 5.5a), which looks at competition, marketing, strategy, costs, and benchmarking. Each of the 16 areas shown in Figure 5.5a lead to suggestions for additional intelligence, as shown in Figure 5.5b. Always seek to acquire information that will lead you to develop the best competitive strategy.

figure **5.5a** ─────────────────────────────────────

Fuld Intelligence Organizer

Source: *http://www.fuld.com/Tindex/IntelOrg.html* (Accessed June 11, 2008).

figure **5.5b** ─────────────────────────────────────

Intelligence You Will Need

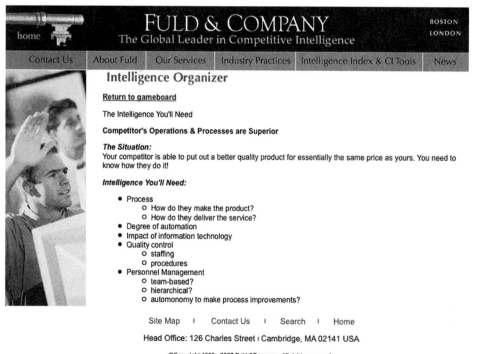

Source: *http://www.fuld.com/Tindex/IntelOrg/operat.html* (Accessed June 11, 2008).

COMPETITION AND POSITIONING IN A MATURE MARKET

Sometimes it becomes clear to a lone entrepreneur or a big business think tank that making a **change in the arena** can spell opportunity in a mature market. Although we have encouraged you to aim for growth markets and growth industries, that is not always possible or desirable. But competing in a mature market takes even more creativity. The change may be very small—a slight change in one aspect of the product or service—but the effect on the market can be very great indeed. The world of business—large and small—is filled with stories of such breakthroughs, and the common thread of these stories is the discovery of an **area of vulnerability** in the existing product or service. Entrepreneurs love to hear these stories, and it is no wonder: such stories contain lessons and inspiration. That is why we include several here as well as DLC Resources highlighted in the Passion box.

If you are in a mature industry, you will have to win customers away from competitors to survive. The name of the game is dictated first and foremost by your customers and second by your competitors. Continually learn from your competitors and customers to adjust your product or service to meet the needs and wants of the market. Guide your business back into growth segments, and thus create your own niche by using three major thrusts:

1. Beat the competition with superior service.
2. Create a new arena.
3. Create uniqueness by continually changing your product or service.

Beat 'em with Superior Service

Tire Pro

James Grenchik's father had died a year earlier, and James was left with the opportunity to carry on the family tire business. Because tires were lasting longer, he became quite concerned with the viability of his business. James tried price promotions and distress sales in an attempt to drive his competitors out of business, but these old techniques did not seem to work anymore, and profits declined.

In fact, every time James looked around, there seemed to be a new competitor setting up shop in his market. Costco became a major competitor as well. Discouraged, James finally decided that this was no way to do business or, for that matter, to live. He had two choices—get out of business or change. Before he went any further, he needed to analyze his competitors. He sat down with his employees and a few customers and developed a competitor matrix (see Figure 5.6; Action Step 30 will guide you in completing a competitive matrix for your business).

After months of soul-searching, family discussions, networking, brainstorming, and reviewing his matrix, James finally decided to change. Here's what James did:

1. *He created a partnership with two key groups. First, he sold 25 percent of his business to a major tire manufacturer and retailer that he knew was the best in the market. His major competitor would now be his partner.*

2. *James sold 24 percent of his business to his key employees. They had been with him a long time, and he knew they were hungry to own a piece of his pie. Now his best employees were also his partners.*

3. *He created uniqueness by changing his product through service add-ons. These new services were the result of cooperative brainstorming by everyone in the firm after completing a thorough analysis of*

Change in the arena Transform a product or service by adding a benefit that has immediate customer appeal

Area of vulnerability Competitor's soft underbelly or Achilles' heel—a weakness ready for you to exploit

Action Step 30

Construct a Competitor Matrix (Figure 5.6)

The purpose of Action Step 30 is to rank your competitors and to visualize the positioning of each in the marketplace. Whenever you unearth some hard data, compare it with industry averages. Keep looking for those areas of vulnerability.

Now that you have a good picture of your major competitors and your Target Customers' desired benefits, you are ready to complete a competitor matrix. Pull out Action Step 29.

1. List all of your major competitors on the vertical axis; list all of the important benefits to your Target Customers and vital elements for the operational success of your business in rank order on the horizontal axis.

2. Rank each competitor on a scale of 1 to 10 for each category, 10 being the best. Determine the total for each competitor. Next, place and rank your new venture on the matrix and rate yourself. Note that the competitive marketplace is imperfect. Sometimes a few miles or a few hundred miles can make a significant difference in how competitive a business must be. If a mature marketplace is saturated, keep exploring other areas.

You may find an underserved market that will welcome you instantly with healthy profit margins. By the time you have finished the Action Steps in this chapter, you will have an excellent overview of your competitors, and opportunities will be in your hands.

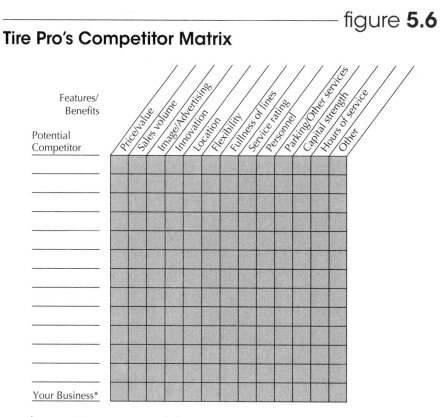

figure **5.6**

Tire Pro's Competitor Matrix

The competitive test matrix can help you evaluate your potential competitors. Use the features/benefits list as a guideline or checklist. Select or add those features/benefits that make sense for your particular business, industry, or competitive situation.

competitors' offerings. In addition, for 3 weeks each employee was to question each customer about additional services they might like to see Tire Pro offer. Tire Pro's implementation of customer suggestions and competitor intelligence follow:

a. Tire Pro now offers an installment plan for farmers who need tires early in the growing season when they experience cash flow problems. This action also created a new profitable arena—finance. With the financial clout of its new manufacturing partner, Tire Pro entered the finance business.

b. All customers are given free tire rotations every 6 months on their cars and trucks. At the same time, they get a free report card on potential trouble spots. This new service strategy has changed their product from just tires to "tires with a free rotation and inspection." Reminder postcards and emails are sent to each customer every 3 months, which keeps Tire Pro's name in front of their customers while providing a welcome service.

c. Customers who want a tire repaired can also pick up coffee and doughnuts, and they can logon to the Internet for the latest commodities and weather reports. A bulletin board for used farm equipment was installed in the waiting area, which is now filled with farm, business, and kids' magazines. Puzzles and coloring books were also added for the children. (One California car dealer now offers a putting green for its customers. This may not be the best marketing tool for South Dakota farmers, but it is just right for the Mercedes-driving entrepreneurs of Orange County, California.)

> d. *Everyone at Tire Pro now answers the phone with their first name and a pleasant hello, which is much easier now that they are making money again! The tire installers wear beepers and headsets so they can hear phone calls; as a result, distractions in the tire bays for both the employees and customers have been greatly reduced.*

*James and his new partners are now making money by providing the best products and services. But be aware that most of the adjustments they made involved labor or marketing expenses, which must be recouped through increased profit and sales. His **core product** is tires, but James is now also in the financing business. Tire Pro is now ready to open a second outlet. Changes in financing, personnel, service, and competitive techniques rescued Tire Pro from a declining sector and propelled it into a growth arena.*

Even if you start out in a growth market, one thing is certain: One day your market will enter a mature stage and eventually a declining one. You must adjust your product or service regularly to market changes, which may occur almost overnight.

Core product Item possessing perceived benefits that best fit customers' needs

Create a New Arena

Let us see how Jackson George, owner of Home Office Havens, successfully changed the arena by developing a niche for himself in a very mature construction market.

Media Room Havens

Positioning Your Business

Jackson George's family had been in the new-home construction business for 20 years. After a falling out with his family, Jackson knew he wanted to remain in the same type of business but wanted to specialize and find a niche for himself.

Many of his friends were looking for media rooms. At parties Jackson's friends complained that their family rooms were no longer ideal for their flat screen TVs and surround sound systems. There were never enough electrical outlets, family members complained of sound coming through the walls, and they wanted more privacy. In addition, they wanted custom-designed spaces to fit their individual needs.

Jackson kept listening and started scouting the area to see if anyone specialized in media rooms. He found firms specializing in bathrooms, closets, kitchens, family rooms, and home offices, but no one was in the media room market.

He sat down with five of his friends and brainstormed about media rooms. After about 5 hours, the information indicated to Jackson that his friends were willing to spend about $30,000 to $50,000 each for a customized media room. Jackson went into high gear, reading every magazine, contacting SohoOnline (http://www.soho.org), visiting furniture and high end equipment stores, and calling potential suppliers.

Jackson's best friend's sister, Susan Pollack, became his first customer. Susan agreed to show her media room to prospective customers for 3 months in exchange for additional lighting

To keep the competition at bay for a short time, Jackson limited his advertising and built his first three media room projects through word of mouth. Once he was established, Jackson developed his advertising and marketing with a professionally photographed portfolio of his projects. Because few competitors had developed expertise in working within the media room niche, Jackson was a tough competitor. Knowing the benefits his customers desired gave him the edge when competitors came knocking and bidding. On realizing 4 years later that he owned the market and had developed a viable concept, he contacted a franchise developer.

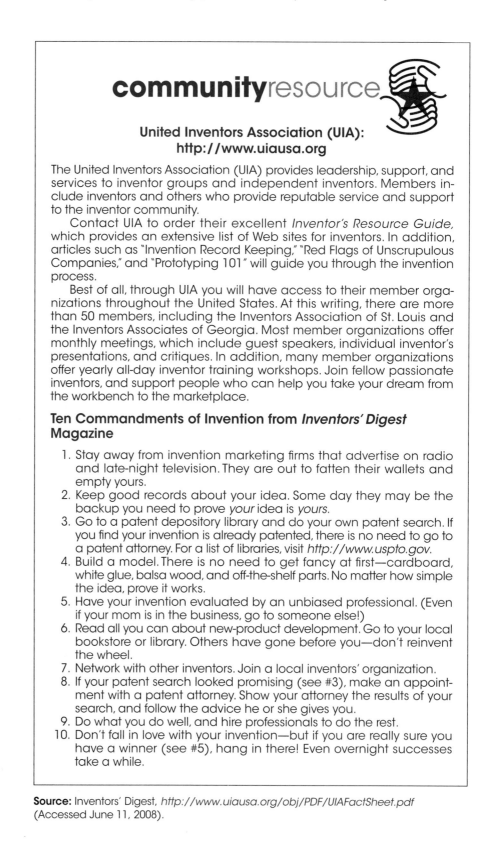

communityresource

United Inventors Association (UIA): http://www.uiausa.org

The United Inventors Association (UIA) provides leadership, support, and services to inventor groups and independent inventors. Members include inventors and others who provide reputable service and support to the inventor community.

Contact UIA to order their excellent *Inventor's Resource Guide*, which provides an extensive list of Web sites for inventors. In addition, articles such as "Invention Record Keeping," "Red Flags of Unscrupulous Companies," and "Prototyping 101" will guide you through the invention process.

Best of all, through UIA you will have access to their member organizations throughout the United States. At this writing, there are more than 50 members, including the Inventors Association of St. Louis and the Inventors Associates of Georgia. Most member organizations offer monthly meetings, which include guest speakers, individual inventor's presentations, and critiques. In addition, many member organizations offer yearly all-day inventor training workshops. Join fellow passionate inventors, and support people who can help you take your dream from the workbench to the marketplace.

Ten Commandments of Invention from *Inventors' Digest* Magazine

1. Stay away from invention marketing firms that advertise on radio and late-night television. They are out to fatten their wallets and empty yours.
2. Keep good records about your idea. Some day they may be the backup you need to prove *your* idea is *yours*.
3. Go to a patent depository library and do your own patent search. If you find your invention is already patented, there is no need to go to a patent attorney. For a list of libraries, visit *http://www.uspto.gov*.
4. Build a model. There is no need to get fancy at first—cardboard, white glue, balsa wood, and off-the-shelf parts. No matter how simple the idea, prove it works.
5. Have your invention evaluated by an unbiased professional. (Even if your mom is in the business, go to someone else!)
6. Read all you can about new-product development. Go to your local bookstore or library. Others have gone before you—don't reinvent the wheel.
7. Network with other inventors. Join a local inventors' organization.
8. If your patent search looked promising (see #3), make an appointment with a patent attorney. Show your attorney the results of your search, and follow the advice he or she gives you.
9. Do what you do well, and hire professionals to do the rest.
10. Don't fall in love with your invention—but if you are really sure you have a winner (see #5), hang in there! Even overnight successes take a while.

Source: Inventors' Digest, *http://www.uiausa.org/obj/PDF/UIAFactSheet.pdf* (Accessed June 11, 2008).

CREATE UNIQUENESS BY CONTINUALLY CHANGING YOUR PRODUCT OR SERVICE

Change is the most predictable element of competition. Thus, the entrepreneur needs to keep one eye on the market and the other eye on Plan B.

For three years, Tom Burns has been in Internet business, which allows him considerable freedom to be creative and many hours of free time to spend with his family. Before going into business for himself, Burns trained as an electrical engineer and spent 20 years in the aerospace industry.

Always Ready with Plan B

eBay Entrepreneur Tom Burns

Tom Burns has marketed and sold over 100 products during the past three years on eBay. He started out selling his own artwork and his friend's album cover collection. Feeling good about his success with these ventures, he opened up a store on eBay for his artwork. Although he was finding success, financially he knew he could make additional money on eBay, so he decided to sell products he found at his local Costco just to see what would happen. Well, what happened was he hit an unexpected goldmine! After buying products directly from Costco, he decided to contact the manufacturer and found out they would happily drop-ship the products for him which allowed him to have no capital tied up in inventory. Basically, he could just process eBay orders, which he did as he traveled the world, ducking into Internet cafes for an hour or two each day to answer emails and conduct business.

Plan B came whenever his products from Costco gained competition and were thus no longer profitable to sell. He needed to be able to cut those products and find new ones. Always knowing this was the game he would need to play made him continually search for new items. Finding items was not difficult, but finding those without heavy competition was hard. Tom persevered. He shopped frequently, and whenever he found potential products, he would research them on the Internet; and then before investing in any inventory, he would try out several products on eBay.

The key for Tom was to never fall in love with his products; he was willing to change whenever the need arose.

You Can Do It!

We have provided you with a number of studies about entrepreneurs who worked with and learned from competitors; they brought about significant changes in the marketplace. It is altogether possible that some day, we may be telling such a story about you. Yes, you can do it, too—but to start, you must do these things:

- Know what business you are in.
- Know your Target Customers.
- Know your competition.
- Know the benefits of your product or service.
- Develop strategies to capture and maintain your position.
- Give free rein to your creativity and your entrepreneurial spirit.

Surprise us! Surprise yourself! Action Step 30 will help you.

A "Green" Landscape Company Focused on Strong Relationships

Landscape companies, according to John Holbert, vice president of DLC Resources, Inc., are considered relatively unsophisticated, blue-collar enterprises.

"Usually, we're not recognized as being especially innovative in approach, or in use of advanced technology," he said. That's partly why the entire company is "extremely proud to be associated with the Spirit of Enterprise Award. It's a huge honor for us." DLC Resources, Inc. received the 2006 *Edward Jones Spirit of Enterprise Award.*

A commercial landscape company, DLC Resources currently works with 29 master-planned communities throughout the Phoenix metro area. The company works at establishing close ties with each home-owners' association and its residents.

"Other companies may have 300 contracts," Holbert said. But, he observed, "that often turns into a kind of revolving door. We believe that each community needs to be a good fit for us."

The company's founders, he said, began building a culture of com-munication from the very beginning, in 1989. "We know we need to have good relationships with our clients, our vendors, and our employees, and each is equally important to nurture."

The company takes a proactive approach to building solid relation-ships with their clients. "It's part of our culture. We want to be experts in the various kinds of landscaping in our communities—how we can best work together to maintain landscaping that works for them and our region—and that takes time."

"There are hundreds of [different] trees, thousands of plants," he ex-plained. "It takes an innovative approach with technology and creativity to manage the landscapes well, and it requires a partnership with the communities."

DLC Resources maps and tracks every critical tree, bush and plant-ing for every client landscape, using a database system linked to GIS technology.

This allows the company to quantify each client's landscape assets, calculate the value, design care programs attached to annual budgets, and track and record results. Practices can be tailored to specific needs within each landscape.

In striving to be environmentally responsible, the company works to develop water management programs that allow for sufficient water to keep landscapes healthy, while economizing on usage. They program watering, and rigorously track usage so that water is kept at "just right" levels for various plant varieties.

The company also replaces all two-cycle power equipment annually, thereby gaining additional efficiencies in fuel and emission reduction. They've recently downsized the company car fleet to Hondas, and now own three hybrids. They'll add more as other cars need to be replaced, Holbert said.

"We intend to be industry leaders in environmental awareness," he added.

Holbert said that it's critical for small businesses to "know what you're best at, stay focused, and remember your employees are your most important asset. You need to support them, mentor them, and provide good leadership. It pays huge dividends."

Source: *http://knowlege.wpcarey.asu.edu/article.cfm?articleid=1466,* (Accessed June 11, 2008).

SUMMARY

Now that you have identified your Target Customers and have evaluated your competition, it is time to ask yourself the questions we began the chapter with: Is this a plus for our customer? Is this something our competitors will find difficult to copy?

Customers do not change their habits easily, and businesses do not switch suppliers without extensive analysis. Unless you can offer something the others do not, your customer will not take a chance on purchasing your product or service, and you will struggle.

Competing on price alone is a very tough road. The big guy can almost always hold out longer than you and put you under more quickly than you could ever expect or believe. Review your touchpoints, your competitive research, and the interviews you have done with your prospective customers to determine how you will appear unique in their eyes during their experience with you and your product or service.

Conducting competitive market research, while essential for a start-up, should be an ongoing process for every business to ensure success. Your customer will tell you what he or she wants—if you will only *listen* and observe.

As you move on to Chapter 6, about promotion, and Chapter 7, about location, you should come back to this chapter as you consider additional areas of competitive strength you have discovered.

Today, products and services cycle through the four life-cycle stages rapidly. Being on top of your customers' needs and the competitive changes in the marketplace is more important than ever. Use computer research, constant evaluation of your competitors, and close contacts with customers, suppliers, and salespeople to stay on top of the curve. Learn from your customers and competitors, and let that knowledge help you guide your business into a growth market, where the action is.

THINK POINTS FOR SUCCESS

- Do it smarter.
- Do it faster.
- Do it with more style.
- Provide more features.
- Adjust your hours.
- Provide more service.
- Treat your Target Customers like family; consider their needs.
- Be unique.
- Change the arena through innovation.
- Know your niche.
- Keep your image in the prospect's mind.
- Disarm the competition by being better, faster, safer, or more user friendly.
- Remember that a new firm seldom can win a price war.
- Know that old habits are hard to break; give your Target Customer several reasons to switch over to you.
- Develop your own monopoly.
- Talk to your Target Customer constantly and truly listen.
- Thrive, don't just survive!

KEY POINTS FROM ANOTHER VIEW

Street Smarts: Taking On Starbucks.

How independents can hold their ground.
by Norm Brodsky

I've been doing what I love, helping small entrepreneurs who come to me for advice. One is a former New York City firefighter named Brian Kelly who has a coffee shop business, City Beans, with two stores in northern New Jersey, both located in office buildings. He opened the first in Newark in 1996, and it immediately attracted a following, turning cash flow positive and profitable within the first month. He later added soup and sandwiches to his menu and did even better. About a year ago, however, Brian received the kind of news that can strike terror in the heart of any independent coffee shop operator: Starbucks was coming.

He learned the coffee giant was sniffing around when the manager of his shop called to say that two guys from Starbucks (NASDAQ:SBUX) had shown up with a tape measure and walked through City Beans taking measurements. At the time, Brian's lease was expiring, but he thought he had already come to terms on a new one. When the landlord told him that Starbucks was putting in a bid, Brian had the good sense to refuse to renegotiate. Apparently, however, Starbucks insisted on terms the landlord found less attractive, because Brian wound up getting the lease anyway, causing him to breathe a sigh of relief.

Then he heard that Starbucks was moving into a large, empty retail space on the other side of the office building. At first, he felt a stab of panic and a flash of anger at the landlord, but he soon found out that Starbucks was coming at the invitation not of the building management but of a Hilton hotel located in the building. The shop would be in the hotel lobby.

Brian had only recently begun to make money on his second coffee shop, in Jersey City, which was in a new office building. Barely 20 percent of the office space had been occupied when he'd opened the store, and it had struggled for a year or more. Along the way, Brian had taken on a considerable amount of debt. He could wind up in trouble if the Newark store went under, which to him suddenly seemed a real possibility. He'd heard all the horror stories about companies like his being crushed when forced to go head-to-head with a national chain. Starbucks in particular had a reputation for aggressive marketing. "I'm not sure what I should do, if anything," he said. "Maybe I should just sit back and wait."

Sitting back and waiting is what a lot of small companies do when a giant moves in. They hope for the best and then react when the giant starts squeezing their margins and taking away market share. By then, it's too late. The outcome can be different, however, if owners capitalize on the advantages small companies have when competing with a giant. For one thing, they can establish close, personal, one-on-one bonds with customers that large companies can't match. Small companies can also outmaneuver giants. That's especially important if they're competing against a retail chain with a cookie-cutter approach to managing its stores. The managers have a formula they have to follow, and they're not allowed to deviate from it. So you can do things that they won't be able to respond to for months, if ever. You can also prepare for their arrival by taking steps to emphasize what makes your store different—and special. That's what I suggested Brian do. "You need to be preemptive," I said. "When is this store supposed to open?" He said he'd heard it would be up and running in December, which gave him four months to make and execute a plan. "Let's talk about your strengths," I said. "What can you do that Starbucks can't do—aside from offering a reasonably priced cup of coffee?"

Brian reminded me that City Beans was about to celebrate its tenth anniversary and had plans to do promotions thanking its customers. It already had a customer loyalty program–buy 11 cups, get one free—using magnetic cards that allowed it to track sales automatically and even offer electronic credits. To receive a card, customers gave City Beans some information about themselves, including their e-mail addresses. Brian thought that he and his partner, Jim Toscano, could expand the program and use the e-mail addresses to market directly to customers.

Brian also noted that he used a local coffee roaster. The coffee City Beans served was roasted every Thursday morning and delivered within 24 hours. As a result, he said, his coffee was fresher than Starbucks'. That would be worth promoting as well. At the same time, City Beans would be emphasizing its identity as a local business supporting other local businesses.

I pointed out that I happened to own, and be storing, several hundred Fire Department of New York lunch boxes left over from an earlier, ill-fated venture. They were taking up space in one of my warehouses. What if I gave them to Brian? He could use them in a promotion that told the City Beans story. Brian had known Jim [Toscano] since kindergarten. They'd grown up together and dreamed of starting their own business. Brian had joined the fire department, and Jim had become a professional drummer, but they hadn't given up their dream of becoming partners in a business. When coffee got hot, they decided to open City Beans as 50–50 partners, with Jim working inside and handling operations while Brian functioned as the CEO but continued to work as a fireman. (He retired from the department in June.) Finding a way to tell the story, I noted, would make the connection with customers that much more personal.

I had another suggestion. "No matter what you do," I told Brian, "Starbucks is going to take away a percentage of your business. It could be 5 percent, 10 percent, or 20 percent. Whatever it is, they're going to take it. So let's look for additional sources of income."

"We do a little catering when people come and ask us to do it," Brian responded. "Maybe we could do more."

"What are the gross margins like?" I asked.

"They're good."

"So that's a great idea. Why don't you put some real effort into signing up more catering customers. The extra money you make could help offset whatever you lose."

In the end, Brian and Jim decided to do all of the above. They would run a series of promotions to celebrate the tenth anniversary of City Beans, introducing a new one every few weeks. They would run specials on soup-and-sandwich combinations and generate a list of customers who wanted to receive daily e-mail announcements on the special of the day. They would expand the customer loyalty program and sign up as many new members as possible. When a new company moved into the office building, they would offer loyalty cards to all its employees, with a credit they could use to try City Beans for the first time. They also gave credits to existing members of the loyalty program in appreciation of their ongoing patronage. At Christmas, they sold the lunch boxes for the price of the sandwich inside and included a one-page history of the company. Meanwhile, they ramped up the catering business, taking advantage of contacts they already had at major corporations and big law firms throughout northern Jersey.

As it turned out, the Starbucks opening was delayed several months. When it did open, Brian saw a drop in sales. But many of his customers came back, and Brian talked to them about their experience at Starbucks. Some told him they'd been disappointed. The store had offered free iced coffee for a day, but the employees weren't as knowledgeable or as friendly as those at other Starbucks shops. Whatever anxiety Brian felt had melted away by the time he came to see me after competing directly with Starbucks for a couple of months. "You don't seem too worried," I said.

"I'm not," Brian said. "Our sales in the shop haven't dropped as much as I expected, and the additional catering business has made up the difference. I guess it also helps that it isn't a real Starbucks."

"What do you mean?" I asked.

"Well, it looks like a regular Starbucks, but I think it's actually a licensed operation. The people all wear Hilton name badges, and the service isn't up to Starbucks standards."

"That sounds like a bad move by Starbucks," I said. "They're cheapening the brand."

In any case, Brian isn't relaxing his guard. He and Jim are working on new signage for City Beans and looking for more effective ways to market their catering services. I wouldn't be surprised if the business picked up market share in the next year. It's almost enough to make you feel a little sorry for Starbucks. Well, not quite.

Norm Brodsky (*brodsky13@aol.com*) is a veteran entrepreneur whose six businesses include a three-time Inc. 500 company. His coauthor is Editor-at-Large Bo Burlingham.

chapter 6

Location and Distribution
Evaluating Alternatives

Two of the most important decisions an entrepreneur has to make are how to distribute products and where to locate the business. Previously these two decisions were easy, as most entrepreneurs selected one **channel of distribution** and one location. In today's business world, multichannel distribution and multilocation alternatives are the norm.

Today with the vast range of options for distribution, location, and promotion, these three variables are melding together and need to be looked at together more closely than ever. With multichannel distribution, we are also confronted with the issue of multichannel marketing and assuring that all are integrated to meet the needs and eyes of our Target Customers.

As we suggested previously, target market selection and competition need to be addressed together. We now suggest you read both Chapter 6 and 7 before beginning the Action Steps in this chapter. New avenues, which meld promotion and distribution—such as eBay and, to some extent, Alibaba.com (Global Resources)—continually develop, with new opportunities appearing each day; technology is unstoppable and unlimited.

As we look down the road—which is a superhighway—we ponder how promotion, distribution, and location will change if the mobile phone becomes our "remote control for life," as predicted by Rohit Talwar, founder of Fast Future. The thought of reaching people and offering products and services anytime, anyplace, or anywhere, becomes a reality. Your goal as an entrepreneur is to be ahead of the technological curve and to take advantage of the changes.

Channels of distribution Relationships involved in moving products to consumers or industrial users

incredibleresource

Entrepreneurship: A Flexible Route to Economic Independence for People with Disabilities

U.S. Department of Labor/Office of Disability Employment Policy
Benefits of Entrepreneurship

Many people with disabilities, particularly those in rural areas where jobs are often scarce, have already created opportunities for themselves through entrepreneurship. In fact, according to the U.S. Census Bureau, people with disabilities are nearly twice as likely to be self-employed as the general population, 14.7 percent compared to 8 percent. Some of the benefits these individuals enjoy include:

Independence and the opportunity to make their own business decisions

The ability to set their own pace and schedule

Reduction of transportation problems when a business is home based

Continued support from Social Security Disability Insurance (SSDI) or Supplemental Security Income (SSI), including health care, when income and assets are within these programs' requirements

(continued)

(continued)

Addressing Barriers to Self-Employment

People with disabilities often confront barriers when attempting to start entrepreneurial ventures. For example, they may not be able to access the capital needed to start a business, because they lack satisfactory credit or assets to use as collateral for a loan. Also, they may not have the information and resources they need to develop an effective Business Plan.

Increasingly, traditional public service providers, such as vocational rehabilitation (VR) professionals and workforce development professionals, are implementing strategies and establishing partnerships with other public and private sector organizations to advance entrepreneurship as an effective route to economic independence for their clients. Through creative thinking and leveraging of existing resources, they are helping break down these barriers. For example:

> The Social Security Administration's (SSA) Plan for Achieving Self-Support (PASS) program allows people with disabilities receiving SSI benefits to set aside money and resources to help achieve a particular work goal, including self-employment.

> The Ticket-to-Work program connects SSI and SSDI beneficiaries with Employment Networks (EN) for training and other support services needed to achieve their employment goals, including self-employment.

> More than 1,100 Small Business Development Centers (SBDC) offer free or low-cost counseling, training, and technical assistance to individuals seeking to start their own business in communities across the nation.

> Local One-Stop Career Centers funded through the U.S. Department of Labor's (DOL) Employment and Training Administration (ETA) assist people in training for and obtaining employment, including self-employment.

Success Story

Ann Morris Bliss, President, Ann Morris Enterprises, Inc.
In 1985, Ms. Morris Bliss developed a mail order catalogue company that sells a wide range of innovative products for people with vision loss. The company generates more than half a million dollars in revenue and over the years has employed a number of people, including individuals with disabilities. Ms. Morris Bliss is completely blind from a process that began from complications at birth.

Resources

Small Business and Self-Employment Service (SBSES)
1–800–526–7234 or 1–800–232–9675 (V/TTY)

SBSES is service from the U.S. Department of Labor's Office of Disability Employment Policy that provides advice and referrals to entrepreneurs with disabilities who are interested in starting their own business or exploring other self-employment options. The SBSES Web site includes links to other entrepreneurship sites, including the SBA and state VR programs.

Small Business Administration (SBA)
1–800–U-ASK-SBA (1–800–827–5722) (V); 1–704–344–6640 (TTY)

SBA sponsors a variety of programs and resources to assist entrepreneurs with disabilities start and grow their businesses, including the nationwide network of SBDCs that offer free or low-cost one-on-one counseling to help potential entrepreneurs with planning, financing, management, technology, government procurement, and other business-related areas.

Social Security Administration (SSA)
1–800–772–1213 (V); 1–800–325–0778 (TTY)

SSA provides information about disability cash-benefit programs, employment support programs, and where beneficiaries can get the services they need to successfully enter the workforce or self-employment.

Source: Adapted from *http://www.dol.gov/odep/pubs/misc/entrepre.htm* (Accessed May 24, 2008).

DISTRIBUTION

Figure 6.1 highlights the common distribution channels used for consumer goods and services, business goods and services, and electronic marketing. Today, one firm may offer products through multiple channels such as retail stores, online retailing, and private branding through wholesalers. Your goal is to determine which channels offer you the most profitable and sustainable business opportunities. Once your initial distribution channels have been established, you must be open to the constant channel changes and new possibilities.

Intermediaries (wholesalers, agents, brokers) perform many functions: sorting, financing, grading of products, transportation, risk taking, and possibly even financing. But one of the most important roles intermediaries perform is providing access to markets and customers. Knowledge is power, and listening to the suggestions intermediaries provide is essential for your success.

figure **6.1**

Distribution Channels

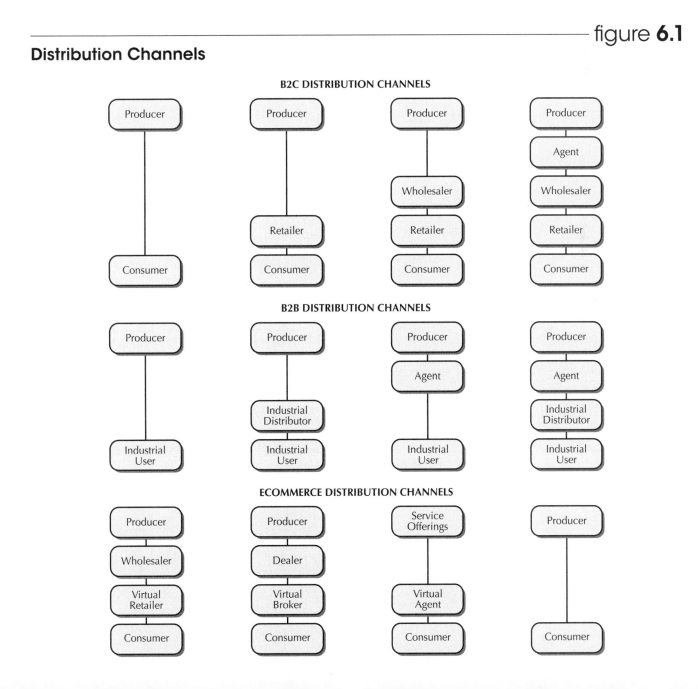

Buyers at Nature's Best, with years of experience and knowledge of customers and competitive products, work closely with their suppliers in perfecting packaging, sizing, and taste. Consider buyers one of the best sources of market research information you have.

The physical location you choose will be largely dependent on your distribution strategy and whether you are a B2B or B2C business. If your business will be distributing consumer goods, a home office and garage may work while B2C business may require a large warehouse and a bricks-and-mortar location to meet with customers.

Following in the footsteps of many businesses, such as Victoria's Secret, you might start with a catalog and end up with physical stores and an Internet site. So as you explore channels, understand that technology and the market may lead you down a different path than you first intended. Chapter 7 reviews additional distribution avenues, which meld with promotion.

Chapter 6 focuses on brick and mortar, manufacturing, and Internet locations, recognizing that many businesses will operate in a combination of locations to reach different market segments. If your business requires a bricks-and-mortar retail location, you will also need to consider the importance of leasing, which is covered toward the end of the chapter.

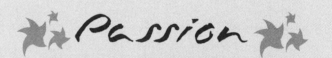

It Was a Woman's Raw, Bleeding Hands that Led Jock Brandis to Make a Promise

CNN Hero and Social Entrepreneur

In 2002, Brandis was helping a friend repair a water treatment system in a Mali, Africa, village. There, he encountered a woman whose hands were bleeding from shelling peanuts to support her family—and this was not uncommon.

In Africa alone, women spend 4 billion hours a year shelling peanuts by hand, according to the Peanut Collaborative Research Support Program.

"A sun-dried peanut is like a little rock. It's that hard," says Brandis. "Cracking the shells takes hours of effort for the village women who traditionally do the chore, and it often leaves their hands bloody."

Brandis promised the women in the village he would return in a year with a machine to speed the shelling. That turned out to be easier said than done.

"When I went back to America, it didn't exist," recalls Brandis.

So he started asking around.

"I didn't know much about peanuts, so I guess I did what any Canadian with a question about peanuts would do. I wrote Jimmy Carter," Brandis said.

Through former President Jimmy Carter's library, Brandis tracked down an expert who suggested he look at a sketch from a Bulgarian scientist. Brandis attempted to replicate the sketch, but it didn't work. Having tinkered and toiled with "gizmos" as a former gaffer in the film industry, Brandis set out to make a peanut sheller himself.

After fiddling, cranking, and grinding his way through a number of prototypes in his Wilmington, North Carolina, studio, Brandis developed a simple machine that could shell nuts up to 50 times faster than by hand. Designed with a simple, durable hand crank, the "universal nut sheller" could be built with $28 worth of materials.

(continued)

(*continued*)

To give this "gift to the world," Brandis joined forces with a group of former Peace Corps volunteers and cofounded the Full Belly Project in 2003, a nonprofit organization dedicated to designing and distributing technologies like the universal nut sheller. Brandis travels with others to developing countries to show local shellers how to use and make the machines themselves.

"It makes their work less tedious and increases productivity up to 50 times," says Brandis. "One machine will work for an entire village, so when we're talking about 100 machines, we're not talking about 100 families—we're talking about 100 villages."

Not only does Brandis refuse to patent the device, but designs for the shelling machine also are available online for anyone to download, assemble, duplicate, or improve upon, which Brandis encourages.

"One of the great things that happened is that when this machine went out, we started getting word back from all over the world saying, 'Oh, we don't use it for peanuts. We use it for shea, for jatropha, for coffee,'" he says. "It's now become much bigger than just being a peanut sheller."

The Full Belly Project works on four continents in 17 countries. Hundreds of machines are in use or being produced locally at minimal cost in the Philippines, Uganda, and Guatemala, resulting in health benefits and increased family incomes, according to the Full Belly Project.

"I get up in the morning and there's an e-mail from a total stranger and a picture," says Brandis. "It's a happy person standing beside their machine with a big grin. That's the [moment] I live for."

Source: *http://www.cnn.com/2008/LIVING/wayoflife/02/28/heroes.brandis/index.html* (Accessed May 22, 2008).

BRICKS-AND-MORTAR LOCATION FOR RETAIL AND SERVICE BUSINESSES

According to the old axiom, "location, location, location" is the key reason for retail business success. To some extent, and especially in bricks-and-mortar retail, this philosophy has a great deal of merit. In essence, if you will be selling on the Internet, "location, location, location" basically refers to appearing in the top five of a Google search. (For search engine optimization [SEO] information, see Key Points from Another View in Chapter 7.)

Search engine optimization (SEO) Boosting search engine ranking

If you are planning to rent a location for a number of years or purchase a building, site selection is critical, and most retail leases reflect this importance in their duration—usually 5 to 10 years—and complexity: 50 to 75 page leases are not unusual. In this chapter, we ask you to define the perfect location, then we lead you through the process of finding such a place for your business using primary and secondary research and, if necessary, negotiating a lease that will serve you well.

Lease A legal contract for occupancy

A cautionary note is in order, however: What you believe will be a good location is certainly relevant, but more important is what your Target Customer believes is a good location. You have to be able to climb inside your customer's mind to answer the question, What is the best location?

What Is the Perfect Location?

The perfect location differs for every enterprise. If you are in the house-cleaning business, you can work out of a van equipped with a cell phone. If you are in the mail-order business, you can work out of a "cocoon" or a post office box.

But if you are selling high-end furniture, a specific retail or Internet location may be best. Action Step 31 on p. 152 asks you to brainstorm the perfect location for your business, review now and complete upon reading the chapter one time through. As you continue your research throughout the next two chapters, continue to add your ideas to this Action Step and fully develop in your Business Plan.

A good location can make everything easier for a new retail business. A highly visible building that is easy for your customers to reach may save you advertising dollars. Once you have been discovered, and your customer base is well established, location may be less important. Nonetheless, for most retail firms, a good location is absolutely essential.

RETAIL LOCATION FILTER

Before you charge out to scout possible locations for your business, you need to decide what you really want from your location. This checklist will help you zero in on your ideal business location. Use a scale of 1 to 10, 10 being the most important, to rate the relative importance of each item on this list. When you finish scoring, go back and note any factor above 5—and focus the rest of your research on these factors. Although we focus our questions below on bricks-and-mortar retail, they can all be adjusted to fit an Internet location.

Target Customers

How far will your customers be willing to travel, and how much traffic will they put up with? If your business is located in Manhattan, your target-market radius may be a three-block radius; if you are located in a rural area, your customers may come from within a 120-mile radius. Will you need to travel to your clients or deliver products to your customers (flowers, dry cleaning, plumbing, pizza, etc.)? If so, how far can you travel and still make a profit? Will fax, e-mail, AIM, and video suffice to keep you in touch with clients?

Consider highway access, construction, and other potential obstacles that could make coming to your place of business inconvenient or unpleasant. Check out plans for potential road construction and closings. Visit city hall and attend city and county planning meetings. Read past meeting minutes as well. If you are in bricks-and-mortar retailing make sure you also look at the cities within your area that you compete with for customers.

Neighbor mix The industrial/commercial makeup of nearby businesses

Anchor tenant A business firm in a commercial area that attracts customers

Neighbor Mix

Who is next door? Who is down the street? Which nearby businesses target your customers? If you are considering a shopping center, who is the **anchor tenant** (the big department store or supermarket that acts as a magnet for the center)?

Competition

Do you want competitors miles away or right next door? Think about this one: If you are in the restaurant business, it can help to be on "restaurant row." (A good example of a working "competitor cluster" is San Diego's well-known Mile of Cars; having Nissans, Dodges, Chevrolets, Toyotas, and others all in one area cuts down customer driving time and allows for easy comparison shopping.) Does your competition have a strong hold on the market? Is there room for additional competitors?

Security, Safety, and Parking

How safe is the neighborhood? Is it as safe as a nursery at noon but an urban nightmare at midnight? Is there anything you can do to increase security? Are you willing to be the first in an area to try to turn it around? What can you do to mitigate any problems? Is adequate safe parking available? Is the area safe for your employees if they have to close late in the evening?

Labor Pool and Education

Who is working for you, and how far will they have to commute? Does your business require more help at certain peak periods of the year? How easy will it be to find that kind of help? Will you need skilled labor? If so, where is the nearest source of it? Is the site near a bus, train, or subway stop? Will you need trained technical employees? Is there a labor pool of trained engineers and scientists? Can you draw from the potential pool of part-timers, teens, seniors, and homemakers? Is affordable housing available for your employees? Are educational facilities nearby to provide employee training and also to provide research capabilities and experts in your field? How are the local schools rated? Do local colleges and universities offer entrepreneurial assistance?

Labor pool Qualified people who are available for employment near one's business location

Restrictions and Opportunities

What local rules (state, county, city, merchants' association) will affect your location? For example, what are the restrictions on signs, hours of business, wages, parking, deeds, zoning, covenants, and employee parking?

Restrictions City/county laws governing business locations

Services

What is included in the rent (security, trash pickup, sewage, maintenance) and who pays for those services that are not included? Are adequate fire and police protection available?

Costs

Costs include the purchase price if you are buying; otherwise, they are the rent or lease costs. We generally advise against buying property and starting a business at the same time, because it diverts precious energy and capital that you need. Also keep in mind taxes, insurance, utilities, improvements, and routine maintenance costs—you need to know who pays for what. Can you negotiate these expenses?

Ownership

If you are still planning to buy property, who will advise you on real estate matters? Consider a lease with an option to buy. A real estate attorney should review all contracts before signing.

Present and Past Tenants

What happened to the past tenants? What mistakes did they make, and how can you avoid those mistakes? If at all possible, contact present and past tenants and listen to what they have to say. Benefit from their experience.

Space

If you need to expand, can you do it there, or will you have to move to a new site? Moving is very expensive, so consider potential growth while evaluating your location decision.

History of the Property

How long has the landlord owned this property? Is it likely to be sold while you are a tenant? If the property is sold, what will happen to your business? What will happen to your tax obligations? What is the lease status of the other tenants? If the property goes on the market, do you want the first right to meet an offer?

Taxes

Property and business taxes can change from street to street. Also, try to find out if there are any plans for reassessment.

Approvals

Have you considered necessary approvals, such as those required from health officials, the fire marshal, the city planning office, and the liquor licensing board?

Physical Visibility

Does your business need to be seen? If so, is this location easily visible? Can you make alterations to increase visibility? Make sure current or future landscaping will not block signage.

Life-Cycle Stage of the Area

Is the site in an area that is embryonic (vacant lots, open space, emptiness), growing (high-rises, new schools, lots of construction), mature (building conversions, cracked streets, sluggish traffic), or declining (decrepit buildings, emptiness)? What will the area be like in 5 years? What do the municipal planners have in mind for the area? What is the quality of life? If the property is in a declining area, subsidies may be available for employee training or building rehabilitation. Can you take advantage of these?

Community Support

Is a strong entrepreneurial support community available? What local and state economic-development incentives exist for your location? Read the many articles published by *Inc.* and *Fast Company* that rate entrepreneur friendly communities. For retailers, Gainesville, Florida, and Boulder, Colorado, are two examples of cities that truly support their own, where residents will go out of their way to buy local from nonfranchise operations.

Image

Is the location consistent with your firm's image? How will nearby businesses affect your image? Is this an area where your customers would expect to find a business like yours? Look for a place that you can develop to reinforce a positive perception of your business for the customer. The Key Points Article

GLOBAL VILLAGE

Opportunities Unlimited

http://www.alibaba.com

Welcome to Alibaba.com! Join Free | Sign In | 💶 TradeManager | Help | 🔲 Translate this page

Alibaba.com®
Global trade starts here.™

| For Buyers | For Sellers | My Alibaba ▾ | Community | News |

Products | Selling Leads | Suppliers | Buyers | Trade Shows | 🔍 Try Our Attributes Search

[Select Country/Region] [Search] More search options

Popular Searches: car mp3 player, shoes, cement, handbags, cell phones, fashion T-shirts, plywood, fabric, jewellery, ATV 250CC

Browse by Category ▶

- Agriculture
- Apparel
- Automobile
- Business Services
- Chemicals
- Computer Hardware & Software
- Construction & Real Estate
- Electrical Equipment & Supplies
- Electronic Components & Supplies
- Energy
- Environment
- Excess Inventory
- Fashion Accessories
- Food & Beverage
- Furniture & Furnishings
- General Industrial Equipment
- General Mechanical Components
- Gifts & Crafts
- Hardware
- Health & Beauty
- Home Appliances
- Home & Garden
- Lights & Lighting
- Luggage, Bags & Cases
- Manufacturing & Processing Machinery
- Measurement & Analysis Instruments
- Minerals, Metals & Materials
- Office Supplies

Get FREE Promotion for your ECO-FRIENDLY PRODUCTS! **Apply Now**

Hot News ▸ Alibaba.com Launches New China TrustPass Product for Individuals

Trade with the World ▸ China ▸ India ▸ All Countries

Latest Buying Leads		Latest Selling Leads	
Dolls With Sticky...	24-Jun	Portable IPL mac...	23-Jun
Hamburger Patties	24-Jun	Polo shirt	23-Jun
5 Inquiries (Pill...	24-Jun	Selling Brand New...	23-Jun
Nylon Taslon Fabr...	24-Jun	T Shirt BASIC Rou...	23-Jun

◀ 123 ▶

SuperDeals | Raw Materials Promotion
19-25 June 2008

Lump Sulphur (99.9222% Purity)	Formoterol Fumarate (Brand Name:OM)	Pigment Blue (57: 1)
US$660-670 MOQ:12,000 Metric Ton	US$200-250 MOQ:100 g	US$9.5-9.7 MOQ:500 kgs
Bitumen 60 / 70	Khairtsc Mountain Of Dust Charcoal	Nickel Ore 1. 8% Reject Below 1. 7%
US$520-550 MOQ:1,000 Metric Ton	US$100-200 MOQ:18 t	US$43-46 MOQ:40,000 Metric Ton

▸ More ▸ List your products here

Buyer Seminars & Events

Home Textiles Sourcing Event Hosted by Alibaba.com

Alibaba.com members share their success stories in our Hong Kong outdoor campaign

Products and Suppliers through Trade Shows

Featured Trade Shows
Computex 2008 Taipei Speical
June 3-7, 2008
Computer Hardware & Software
Jun 03, 2008 - Jun 07, 2008
[Taiwan]
COMPUTEX TAIPEI
1 2 3 4 5 6 ▸ More

New Products! Top Suppliers! Join our 1st Online Trade Show now
600 Verified Suppliers, 41 industries, thousands of new products.

Join Free! New to Alibaba? Join Free Now!

| Display Your Products FREE | Post Your Purchase Requests FREE |

Take the effort out of sourcing!
Tell suppliers exactly what you need

Absolutely Free! No Sign in Required

TRUSTPASS™
查看简体中文介绍 查看繁體中文介绍

Trade with the Big Buyers

KCX International RT G.GUELDENPFENNIC

▸ View all our Big Buyers

Success Stories

With TrustPass, prospective clients are more confident in dealing with us

Mr. Mayank Goyal [India]

How do you earn hundreds of thousands of $s without spending a single cent?
The answer is Alibaba.com. It was a big challenge when I started selling on the Internet about 4 years ago. ...

▸ More

Who are the 2008 Global e-Business Champions?
▸ Vote now and decide!

ABAC **The 2nd APEC Business Advisory Council SME Summit** Hangzhou, China 2-3 August 2008

Fast Company recently named Alibaba.com one of the 50 most innovative companies in the world. "When Alibaba went public last November and raised a stunning $1.5 billion—the biggest Internet IPO since Google's—it also raised eyebrows around the world. But probably not those of founder Jack Ma, who back in 1999 recognized that China's 42 million small- and medium-size companies (the vast majority of business in the country) might create some opportunities for e-commerce. Alibaba provides a point-and-click system for suppliers to get online and connect with distributors and consumers all over the world. The Chinese version today boasts 16 million users, and the English version has 9 million."

Action Step 31

Fantasize Your Perfect Location

1. Sit down where you will not be disturbed and brainstorm the ideal location for your business. With pencil and paper or fingers on the keyboard, let yourself dream. Draw a mind map or use a list format.

   If your location is retail, start with your Target Customer. For example, if opening a candy or newspaper stand, you might want to locate in the center of New York's Grand Central Station, where tens of thousands of people pass by every hour. Or if you were opening an extremely upscale clothing boutique, you might visualize a location at Water Tower Place in Chicago.

   Once you have the general idea of the state, region, city, and neighborhood you want, using the information in this chapter and in Chapter 7, write down what other items would be important to you and your Target Customer. Writing down everything you dream will give you a starting point as you move out to explore the world.

2. If you are going to be an Internet-only business, you need to begin researching your options immediately. Review your options via Internet distribution channels from Figure 6.1. Start to investigate your options, various Web sites, costs, and methods used by each channel. Remember, many businesses will be looking at multiple channels. How will you integrate these channels to build synergy?

3. If you will need a manufacturing or distribution site, see pages 157–158.

4. If you are going to be home based, go directly to Action Step 32.

highlights Austin Taylor's excellent use of site selection as a marketing and promotion tool.

With this location filter in mind, complete Action Step 31. As you progress through the chapter, you will be refining your perfect location.

As you look toward a bricks-and-mortar location for your retail or service business, you will have many options that include the following retail centers: local neighborhood, downtown business district, shopping centers and malls, neighborhood or strip centers, community shopping centers, regional malls, and outlet and retail/entertainment centers.

ALTERNATIVE RETAIL LOCATIONS

Many interesting alternative retail locations exist today. These include a circuit for retailers who travel to colleges on a monthly basis, hawking their wares to college students. Another entrepreneur we highlight in this text owns five stores inside airports. Monthly arts and crafts fairs have offered many opportunities for artists to meet one-on-one with their customers; this way, they can tailor make the next fair's products. One local photographer we know not only talked with his customers during street art fairs, he also listened to them. When over 40 people in town had requested professional photography lessons, he knew he had another venue for his business. Thus, he now offers classes but only in the winter, when his fair business is closed down due to bad weather. These classes keep cash flowing all year long.

Swap Meets and Fairs

In many parts of the country, incredibly lucrative opportunities for retailing are provided through weekly or weekend swap meets. For example, Thursday night's street fair VillageFest in Palm Springs draws retailers from Arizona and New Mexico; San Luis Obispo, California, draws jewelry, food, and clothing dealers for weekly Farmer's Markets. In Southern California, many retailers and craftspeople net more than $75,000 a year working only two 12-hour days a week at the Orange County Marketplace Swap Meet (although additional hours are spent off-site ordering and preparing for the weekend). For many small retailers, starting at a swap meet provides an excellent way to test the market and pricing levels. In addition, swap meets and fairs offer incredible opportunities for seasonal businesses. One family runs a summer fair business, and all of the family members, including the parents and young adults, attend college full-time during the rest of the year.

Kiosks

An age-old form of retailing has made a comeback—the pushcart is now the "kiosk." Locating your retail business in a kiosk will make you part of an over $10 billion retailing venue, according to *Specialty Retail Report*, an industry-publication based in Boston (*http://www.specialtyretail.com*). Kiosks provide a low-risk environment in which to launch a specialty retail operation, with malls throughout the United States currently generating up to 10 percent of their income from kiosks. With a low cost of infrastructure, the ability to change product quickly, and the mall owners' desire to have unique and diverse products, a kiosk may be a retailing venue for you to explore. Testing the water for your products can be done inexpensively, and since you are mostly one-on-one with your customer, extensive one-on-one market research can be conducted during the selling process. Some large mall owners work directly with their kiosk tenants, advising and training in hopes the entrepreneurs will build successful businesses.

RETAIL AND SERVICE BUSINESS LOCATION INFORMATION

Retailers tend to stay in a location for awhile, because it is expensive to pack up, move, and reestablish a business. This is why location selection is a very important decision. You need to make sure you are in the heart of your target market or are able to reach your target market from your site. Where do you go for that information?

We discussed using the Census Bureau, city and county data, and independent research firms such as Claritas and Easy Analytic Software in Chapter 4 and 5. Most of the information covered in those chapters is also applicable to the location decision, and it should be reviewed and researched in more depth, for this chapter and the location portion of your Business Plan. We highlight several additional sources throughout the chapter to show how secondary information can assist you.

If you are selling primarily through e-mail, direct mail, or catalogs, review the information from Chapter 7 on advertising sources and mailing list procurement and from Chapter 4 on demographic and psychographic information to clearly focus on your Target Customer.

Targeting by Census Tract

Every 10 years the government gathers census data, which they make available online at *http://www.census.gov* or in print at Federal Depository Libraries. Chapter 4's Community Resource (see page 99) highlights how to use Census data. If you are locating your business in a rapidly growing or declining area, we again suggest you contact the fee-based information services discussed in Chapter 4 for updated information and projections.

STATS Indiana, at *http://www.stats.indiana.edu*, provides county and MSA (Metropolitan Statistical Area) information and rankings for the 3,141 U.S. counties. "These one-of-a-kind profiles provide a select compilation of demographic and economic indicators." This site compiles data from the Census; the Departments of Education, Health, and Workforce Development; and the U.S. Bureau of Economic Analysis, along with state tax and employment information.

For researching your retail or service location, you need data that provides a picture of the lifestyles of your Target Customers: population density, income, occupation, education, housing, and so on. In addition to census data, fee-for-service and software programs combine census and various other research data to provide a much more thorough and updated evaluation of your potential customer both demographically and psychographically. In many cases, the fee-for-service areas are overlaying census data, private research, and projections, along with psychographical profiles, to pinpoint potential customers and clients.

These geodemographic databases will be helpful also for locating business-to-business customers and for manufacturing or research site selection. Providers of the data assist clients in accessing the most relevant information required for location decision making. To explore site selection further, read *Business Geographics*, a magazine that focuses on the use of geographical information systems (GIS) and location intelligence (LI). You can also visit their Web site at *http://www.geoplace.com.*

For retail establishments, site-location ring studies are frequently conducted to evaluate 1-, 3-, and 5-mile rings around your potential site. Comparing sites using ring studies allows you to see which site would be best for your business. One location might cost twice as much in rent, but if it pulls in three times the Target Customers, the rent becomes a less important factor. See Figure 6.2 for a Three Ring Site selection from *http://www.easidemographics.com.*

figure **6.2**

EASI Demographics Three Ring Site Selection for Eugene, Oregon—Zip Code 97403

EASI Demographics on Demand
Updated Site Selection Reports & Analysis
Executive Summary
Location: EASI Northwest
Address: 2120 Summit Ave, Eugene, OR, 97403
Latitude: 44°: 02′: 14″
Longitude: -123°: 03′: 39″

Description	1 Miles	3 Miles	5 Miles
POPULATION BY YEAR			
Population (4/1/1990)	11,804	82,039	144,485
Population (4/1/2000)	10,358	88,117	162,736
Population (1/1/2007)	9,790	87,452	166,450
Population (1/1/2012)	9,478	87,615	169,961
Percent Growth (2007/2000)	-5.48	-0.75	2.28
Percent Forecast (2012/2007)	-3.19	0.19	2.11
HOUSEHOLDS BY YEAR			
Households (4/1/1990)	3,709	34,496	59,089
Households (4/1/2000)	3,632	38,159	68,498
Households (1/1/2007)	3,441	39,042	72,454
Households (1/1/2012)	3,335	39,916	75,668
Percent Growth (2007/2000)	-5.26	2.31	5.78
Percent Forecast (2012/2007)	-3.08	2.24	4.44
POPULATION CHARACTERISTICS			
Median Age	23.9	31.3	33.0
Male	4,997	43,501	82,092
Female	4,793	43,951	84,358
Density	2,159.0	2,946.9	2,397.4
Urban	9,580	86,458	164,239
Rural	210	994	2,211
HOUSEHOLD CHARACTERISTICS			
Households (1/1/2007)	3,441	39,042	72,454
Families	1,449	18,351	38,816
Non-Family Households	1,992	20,691	33,638
Housing, Owner Occupied	1,720	18,690	37,477
Housing, Renter Occupied	1,721	20,352	34,977
Average Size of Household	2.15	2.11	2.21
Median Age of Householder	41.4	45.0	46.0
Median Value Owner Occupied ($)	380,137	228,139	198,555
Median Rent ($)	1,041	883	895
Median Vehicles Per Household	2.1	2.0	2.1
HOUSING CHARACTERISTICS			
Housing, Units	3,634	40,976	75,937
Housing, Owner Occupied	1,720	18,690	37,477
Housing, Renter Occupied	1,721	20,352	34,977
Housing, Vacant	193	1,934	3,483

(continued)

—————————————————————— figure **6.2**

EASI Demographics Three Ring Site Selection
for Eugene, Oregon—Zip Code 97403 (continued)

POPULATION BY RACE			
White Alone	8,421	74,401	142,000
Black Alone	101	1,150	2,084
Asian Alone	635	4,163	6,797
Other	633	7,738	15,569
POPULATION BY ETHNICITY			
Hispanic	431	5,778	11,411
White Non-Hispanic	8,114	70,229	133,860
INCOME CHARACTERISTICS			
Total Household			
Income ($)	228,424,840	2,099,519,278	3,990,374,015
Median Household Income ($)	39,622	36,173	39,748
Average Household Income ($)	66,383	53,776	55,075
Per Capita Income ($)	23,332	24,008	23,973
RETAIL SALES			
Total Retail Sales			
(including Food Services) ($)	50,795	855,384	2,975,412
CONSUMER EXPENDITURES			
Total Consumer Expenditures ($000)	149,260.1	1,651,169.0	3,155,803.9
EMPLOYMENT BY PLACE OF BUSINESS			
Employees, Total (by Place of Work)	3,022	25,432	73,233
Establishments, Total (by Place of Work)	251	2,307	5,429
EASI QUALITY OF LIFE			
EASI Quality of Life Index (US Avg=100)	120	121	122
EASI Total Crime Index			
(US Avg=100; A=High)	85	81	73
EASI Weather Index (US Avg=100)	136	136	136
BLOCK GROUP COUNT	7	69	119

Footnotes: Easy Analytic Software, Inc. (EASI) is the source of all updated estimates. All other data are derived from the U.S. Census and other official government sources.
All estimates are as of 1/1/2007 unless otherwise stated.

Source: *http://www.cheapdemographics.com/samples/ExecutiveSummary3Rings.htm*
(Accessed May 28, 2008).

The spending patterns report in Figure 6.3, from *http://www.claritas.com*, focuses on Susan's Healthy Gourmet customers in Zip code 92625. Site selection data combined with additional data, such as the GeoVALS data and Roper's LifeMatrix (introduced in Chapter 4), will help to define your customer.

In Chapter 4 we presented the Claritas Prism NE customer groups for Susan's Healthy Gourmet customers. Following are the top three lifestyle groups for Zip code 46323, Hessville, an area of Hammond, Indiana, outside of Chicago. From the description of the groups below, it is obvious they would not be a part of Susan's target market; consider what products or services would sell well to these market segments:

Domestic Duos: Domestic Duos represent a middle-class mix of mainly over-55 singles and married couples living in older suburban homes. With their high-school educations and fixed incomes, segment residents maintain an easy-going lifestyle. Residents like to socialize by going bowling, seeing a play, meeting at the local fraternal order, or going out to eat.

Blue-Chip Blues: Blue-Chip Blues is known as a comfortable lifestyle for ethnically diverse, young, sprawling families with well-paying blue-collar jobs. The segment's aging neighborhoods feature compact, modestly

figure **6.3**

Claritas 2007–2012 Consumer Spending Patterns for Zip Code 92625

Annual Expenditures	Aggregate in 000's		Per Capita		Average Household		Market Index to USA*	
	2007	2012	2007	2012	2007	2012	2007	2012
Household Equipment:								
Total Household Textiles	7,334	8,513	598	688	1.249	1.438	207	197
Domestic Textiles	2,895	3,407	236	275	493	575	181	174
Window and Furniture Covers	4,439	5,106	362	413	756	862	228	217
Total Furniture	8,639	10,243	705	828	1,471	1,730	179	173
Bedroom Furniture	2,169	2,533	177	205	369	428	162	158
Living/Dining Room Furniture	3,967	4,516	324	365	675	763	187	180
Other Furniture	2,503	3,194	204	258	426	539	185	178
Major Appliances	2,680	3,051	219	247	456	515	134	130
Small Appliance/Houseware	8,217	9,423	670	762	1,399	1.592	204	196
Misc Household Equipment	4,451	5,192	363	420	758	877	144	139
Misc Personal Items:								
Personal Care Products and Services	8,422	9.801	687	792	1.434	1,655	137	136
Personal Expenses and Services	19,695	23,223	1,607	1,877	3,353	3 922	206	201
Smoking Products/Supplies	1,889	1,894	154	153	322	320	39	37
Miscellaneous Items:								
Total Education	19,580	24.711	1.597	1,997	3 333	4,173	216	210
Room and Board	1,524	1,494	124	121	259	252	242	230
Tuition/School Supplies	18,056	23,216	1.473	1.876	3.074	3,921	214	209
Pet Expenses	4,192	5,355	342	433	714	904	142	144
Day Care	2.898	3,341	236	270	493	564	160	154
Contributions (All)	31.570	30,947	2.575	2,501	5,374	5,227	294	264
Entertainment								
Sports and Recreation	16.344	19,576	1,333	1.582	2.782	3,306	186	180
TV, Radio and Sound Equipment	17.485	21,310	1.426	1.722	2.977	3,599	149	143
Reading Materials	5,855	6,166	478	498	997	1,041	187	182
Travel	20.452	23,607	1.668	1.908	3,482	3,987	222	212
Photographic Equipment	1,161	1.140	95	92	198	193	167	161
Other Miscellaneous Expenses:								
Housekeeping Supplies	2.642	3.100	216	251	450	524	124	123
Total Food away from Home	45361	53,031	3,701	4,286	7 722	8,956	151	147
Breakfast and Brunch	3,245	4.292	265	347	552	725	131	128
Dinner	14,267	14,916	1,164	1,205	2,429	2,519	166	162
Lunch	12,276	15,481	1,001	1,251	2,090	2,615	143	141
Snacks and Nonalcoholic Beverage	4,903	6,773	400	547	835	1,144	130	129
Catered Affairs	864	828	71	67	147	140	210	201
Food and Nonalcoholic Bevgs on Trips	9,805	10,741	800	868	1,669	1,814	158	155
Total Alcoholic Beverages	12,593	14,568	1.027	1,177	2,144	2,460	160	152
Alcoholic Beverages at Home	7,790	9,241	636	747	1,326	1,561	145	137
Alcoholic Beverages away from Home	4,803	5,326	392	430	818	900	193	187
Shelter and Related Expenses:								
Household Services	6,906	8,402	563	679	1,176	1,419	210	203
Household Repairs	10,632	11,557	867	934	1,810	1,952	155	148
Total Housing Expenses	8,628	10,091	704	816	1,469	1,704	118	119
Fuels and Utilities	720	738	59	60	123	125	72	74
Telephone Service	7,908	9,354	645	756	1,346	1,580	125	125

Claritas' Consumer Spending Patterns Report is derived from the Consumer Buying Power (CBP) database using information from the U.S. Bureau of Labor Statistics (BLS) Consumer Expenditure Survey (CE Survey).

The Annual Aggregate (in 000's) is used to obtain the Annual Per Capitas and the Average Household data by dividing the aggregate by the corresponding total household population and total households, respectively. The Market Index value is the ratio of the Annual Average Household Expenditure (AAHE) for the geography that this report is being produced, as compared to the "AAHE" for the U.S.A.

*Average USA market index equals 100.

Current Year Estimates and five year Projections are produced by Claritas.Inc.

Source: © Nielsen Claritas

priced homes surrounded by commercial centers that cater to child-filled households.

New Beginnings: Filled with young, single adults, New Beginnings is a magnet for adults in transition. Many of its residents are twenty-something singles and couples just starting out on their career paths—or starting over after recent divorces or company transfers. Ethnically diverse—with nearly half its residents Hispanic, Asian, or African-American—New Beginnings households tend to have the modest living standards typical of transient apartment dwellers.

Source: Mybestsegments.com, *http://www.yawyl.claritas.com* (Accessed May 22, 2008).

Once you are in business, continually monitor customer information and begin to develop your firm's customer. Determinations of pricing, merchandise mix, and new site selections will also be aided with careful profiling.

Josie Rietkerk, owner of Caterina's, found that although she runs gift and candy stores in six airport locations, the merchandise mix needs to be different in each store; the customer profile varies from airport to airport, although they are all within a 60-mile radius. In fact, she realized that if she had two stores located in different terminals within one of the larger airports, the merchandise mix would still vary, as some terminals serve international customers, others serve business customers on short-hop flights within the state, and still other terminals serve travelers on cross-country hauls.

Site location experts and associations develop various worksheets and analyses of locations and demographics. Many associations will approximate the population statistics you need within a certain radius to support a store location, including looking at where the nearest competitors may lie. If you are opening a business that is highly dependent on foot or car traffic, we suggest you hire an expert to assist you, as secondary data alone cannot provide you with all the information you need. An example would be if you were located in a place where most of your potential customers were accustomed to driving north to access retail establishments. You would need to recognize that your customer base would be highly limited unless your location was easily accessible to northbound drivers. Changing customer-buying and driving habits is difficult and attempted only if you have a lot of excess cash with which to entice people into your store with advertising and promotions.

Develop a location worksheet for your business based on the material at the beginning of the chapter, demographic and psychographic information of your customers, and additional expertise from site consultants. Before you begin, you might want to check with associations that represent your industry for their site location information as well.

LOCATION DECISION FOR MANUFACTURERS

If you are involved in manufacturing, your search for location will be focused on labor supply and energy availability costs, taxes, zoning restrictions, access to transportation corridors, and proximity to suppliers and customers. You will focus on the economy of the state, region, and city where you want to locate. Talk with state and local government officials and local Chambers of Commerce and economic development groups. Many of these groups will work with you to locate and develop a site. In addition, they may have knowledge of sites that you can rehab and thus reduce costs and possibly receive government incentives.

In fact, every state and local economic development office throughout the United States will be more than happy to send you vast amounts of data on their area. Tax incentives, job training, reduced-cost utilities, and infrastructure such as roads and utilities are just a few of the jewels counties and cities will dangle in front of you. Many low-income areas—including inner-city and rural locations—are anxious to lure new enterprises and offer incentives to employers willing to hire and train as few as five people.

Business incubator Home for emerging business

Many areas now offer **business incubators**, some of which specialize in manufacturing. In fact many are set up for manufacturing in certain areas, such as medical devices. Business incubators and Enterprise Zones are two alternatives that nonretail businesses should investigate.

Business Incubators

Incubators nurture young firms by helping them survive and thrive during the sometimes-difficult start-up period. More than 950 incubators provide trained, professional assistance in marketing, financing, and technical support. You will usually share office space, access to equipment, and storage or production areas. Generally, your firm will remain in an incubator for 2 to 3 years. Incubators are sponsored by academic institutions, government, economic development organizations, and for-profit entities. The 2008 NBIA Outstanding Incubator Client and the NBIA's 2008 Incubator of the Year are highlighted below.

Incubators—Survive and Thrive!

NBIA Outstanding 2008 Incubator Client: Technology Category
Millennial Media (45 employees) at Emerging Technology Centers, Baltimore, MD
Paul Palmieri and Chris Brandenburg, founders
http://www.millennialmedia.com

Less than two years after moving its headquarters to Baltimore's Emerging Technology Centers (ETCs), Millennial Media has become one of the nation's leading mobile advertising companies. And now, company officials have expanded the organization internationally. "There is tremendous growth opportunity for mobile advertising on a global basis, as evidenced by a rich and active mobile direct marketing industry, as well as surging demand from top brand advertisers," says Paul Palmieri, president and CEO of Millennial Media. "It's a natural progression to take our industry-leading networks and solutions global."

Incubator role: When Millennial Media joined ETC, the company had just four employees. Now, the firm employs 45 full-time workers. "From day one, the ETC staff has gone out of its way to accommodate us and not only help—but make it easy—to grow," Palmieri says. "They've made sure we're never without appropriate work space, with all the needed resources." In fact, ETC even vacated its own suite temporarily to make room. The incubator also has provided the firm with needed small business assistance and public relations support to encourage further expansion. With ETC's help, Millennial Media was named Maryland Incubator Company of the Year in May 2007.

NBIA's 2008 Incubator of the Year: Technology Category Winner
Environmental Business Cluster (EBC), San Jose, CA, established 1994
Jim Robbins, Executive Director
Incubator size: 24,000 square feet shared with Software Business Cluster (The leasable square footage at EBC fluctuates between 8,000 and 12,000 square feet, based upon client needs.)
Incubator clients: 25/ Incubator graduates: 120
http://www.environmentalcluster.org/Description.htm

Achievements: The slogan of Environmental Business Cluster is "Improving the environment one company at a time." And since 1994, EBC has been doing just that.

Because they believed there were too few promising, environmentally friendly products and technologies reaching the marketplace, a group of stakeholders—including Peninsula Conservation Center, Pacific Gas & Electric, Arthur Anderson, Gray Cary Ware & Freidenrich, Applied Materials, CitiBank, and Joint Venture Silicon Valley—formed EBC to assist early-stage companies developing clean and renewable energy products and other products that would have a positive impact on the environment.

Since its inception, the incubator has helped 145 companies commercialize environmental technology and create clean-tech jobs. In partnership with the city of San Jose and San Jose State University, EBC has become the largest private clean-energy commercialization center in the United States for start-up companies. "We have been instrumental in helping San Jose become the second-ranked 'CleanTech City' in the U.S. by SustainLane, an independent online media company," says EBC Executive Director Jim Robbins.

Source: *http://www.nbia.org,* The National Business Incubation Association (Accessed May 21, 2008).

communityresource

Incubate Your Baby for Success

To determine which incubators in your area might help drive your business to success, contact the National Business Incubation Association (NBIA), *http://www.nbia.org.* In selecting an incubator to serve your entrepreneurial needs, follow NBIA's tips below.

Tips for Finding the Right Incubator

Just as incubators screen prospective clients, so too should entrepreneurs screen prospective incubators. Here are some questions to ask when considering entering an incubation program.

Finding a Quality Program

Track record

- How well is the program performing?
- How long has the program been operating?
- Does it have any successful graduate companies, and if so, how long have they been in business independent of the incubator?
- What do other clients and graduates think of the program?

Graduation policy

- What is the program's graduation policy? (i.e., what are the incubator's exit criteria?)
- How flexible is the policy?
- How long, on average, have clients remained in the program?

Qualifications of manager and staff

- How long has the current staff been with the program?
- How much time does staff spend on site?
- Have they had any entrepreneurial successes of their own?
- Do they actively engage in professional development activities, or are they a member of a professional/trade association to keep them up to date on the latest in incubation best practices?

Finding the Right Match

Does the incubation program offer the services and contacts you need? What services do you need to make your venture successful? Business

(continued)

(continued)

Plan development, legal and accounting advice, marketing, Internet access, or specialized manufacturing facilities? Is access to a particular market critical? Then consider finding an incubator that specializes in that market. Special-focus incubators are programs that work with companies within a particular niche, such as gourmet foods, biotechnology, the arts, or software. Be sure the program offers what you need or can connect you to service providers who can meet those needs.

Do you meet the incubator's criteria? Find out the incubator's qualifications for accepting clients before applying. For example, some incubators expect prospective clients to have fully developed Business Plans, whereas others require a less-developed idea and offer Business Plan development assistance.

Is the program's fee structure right for you? Most for-profit incubators exchange space and services for an equity share in their client companies, whereas most nonprofits charge fees for space and services. If a large cash infusion and speed to market are essential for your business success, then giving up equity in your company in order to secure quick cash may be right for you. But if you believe you have the skills to raise your own funding (with some assistance), don't want to give up any equity in your venture, and are willing to build your company more slowly, then paying fees for services and space may be a better choice.

Source: National Business Incubation Organization, *http://nbia.org/resource_center/entrepreneurs_tips/index.php* (Accessed February 25, 2005). Reprinted with permission. Copyright © 2004 by the National Business Incubation Association.

Incubators provide a "home" to grow your business at a time when the support and expertise of others is essential to the launching of your business. Usually in the start-up phase, funds are not available to pay for expertise, nor is there background enough to know what services and professionals are available. Being surrounded by like-minded entrepreneurs is an incalculable benefit for budding entrepreneurs, because entrepreneurship can be a very lonely endeavor. In addition, an incubator often allows one to pay less than market rent, to receive discounted professional services, and to gain access to administrative support and professionals. Review the incubator information highlighted in the Community Resources above, and conduct research to determine if an incubator could be the right "home" for your venture.

Enterprise Communities and Rural Empowerment Zones

Certain areas of the United States, many in inner-city and rural communities, have been designated by the government as Enterprise Communities and Rural Empowerment Zones. Incentives are available to firms willing to locate in primarily economically depressed areas through these programs. To locate your state programs, visit *http://www.ezec.gov*.

Many firms have discovered ready and eager employees in these areas. In addition to finding employees, the financial incentives and generally lower rents can be of great benefit to a start-up firm. Each state offers various incentives; one example, the Iowa Enterprise Zone Program, is described below. In addition to state incentives, there may be local community incentives.

IOWA Enterprise Zones

Promoting Development in Economically Distressed Areas

Eligibility Requirements

- The business must make a minimum qualifying investment of $500,000 over a three-year period. Qualifying investment includes the cost of land, buildings, improvements to buildings, manufacturing machinery and equipment, and/or computer hardware.
- The business must create at least 10 full-time, project-related jobs over a three-year period and maintain them for an additional 10 years.
- The business must provide all full-time employees with a standard medical and dental insurance plan of which the business pays 80% of the premiums for employee-only coverage or provide a monetarily equivalent benefit package.
- The business must pay new employees a starting wage that is equal to or greater than 90% of the average county or regional wage, whichever is lower. (Check with IDED for the community's current wage requirement.)
- The business cannot be a retail establishment or a business whose entrance is limited by coverage charge or membership.
- The business cannot close or relocate its operation in one area of the state and relocate substantially the same operation in the Enterprise Zone.
- The local Enterprise Zone Commission and IDED must approve the business's application for Enterprise Zone program incentives prior to project initiation.
- Must meet wage thresholds requirements.

Tax Incentives

- A local property tax exemption of up to 100% of the value added to the property to a period not to exceed 10 years.
- Additional funding for training new employees. If applicable, these funds would be in addition to those authorized under the Iowa New Jobs Training Program.
- A refund of state sales, service, or use taxes paid to contractors or subcontractors during construction.
- For warehouse or distribution center projects, a refund of sales and use taxes paid on racks, shelving, and conveyor equipment.
- An investment tax credit of up to a maximum of 10% of the qualifying investment, amortized over 5 years. This tax credit is earned when the corresponding asset is placed in service and can be carried forward for up to seven additional years or until depleted, whichever occurs first.
- The State's refundable research activities credit may be doubled while the business is participating in the program for up to a maximum of 10 years.

Individual enterprise zones may have additional requirements. Contact the Iowa Department of Economic Development along with relevant organizations to determine eligibility. Businesses locating or expanding in an enterprise zone may apply for benefits by completing an application. Local enterprise zone commissions review applications and, upon approval, forward them to the Iowa Department of Economic Development for final approval.

Source: Adapted from *http://www.iowalifechanging.com/business/enterprise_zones. html* (Accessed May 23, 2008).

BEFORE YOU SIGN A LEASE

When you decide to rent a commercial location, the property owner's lawyer will draw up a lease document. Although its language is very specific, the terms spelled out are provisional; that is, the terms are proposed as a starting point for negotiation. Nothing you see in the contract is set in stone—unless you agree to it. Obviously, the terms proposed will favor the property owner.

Action Step 32

Seek Professional Help for Site Selection

Visit a commercial real estate office or online broker's site to gain information. Commercial real estate firms have access to planning reports and demographic information that will tell you a lot about growth in the community. If they are doing their job, they will also have information about major road plans and additional developments. Make an appointment to visit with a broker, prepare your questions, dress professionally, and explore your options.

Leave your checkbook at home!

Assume nothing when it comes to leases. Review the proposed lease seriously with your own real estate attorney, with others who have experience with leases, and possibly with some of the tenants if the property is located in a center or multiuse building.

Agents and Commercial Brokers

There is so much to know and analyze when making location decisions, and an *experienced* commercial real estate broker can save you time and money. He or she can guide you through the maze of what is available and advise you on leases, rents, taxes, terms, financing, zoning, and transportation options.

Selecting the right broker may be as simple as asking for recommendations from friends or businesspeople in your networking group. Brokers tend to specialize in retail, manufacturing, warehousing, or office space. When you call to request information about a particular property, you will be connected to the listing agent. If you like what you hear about the property but do not feel comfortable with that particular agent, do not be concerned. Usually, any agent or broker can show you any listed property; he or she does not have to be the listing agent. Keep in mind, however, if an agent shows you property and then you choose not to use that agent to complete the transaction, there may be problems.

Commercial brokers are paid primarily by the landlord or seller and earn their commissions only when a deal is final and money changes hands. Do not let yourself be rushed. Falling in love with a property before you know what is involved in the lease or purchase will definitely give the seller the edge in negotiations. Brokers affiliated with large commercial firms have extensive research departments at their disposal and should be able to help you with demographic data collection in addition to the material you have gathered on your own.

You can save an agent a lot of time if you have already defined your present and future needs. If you compare each site against your ideal location, you will probably have several workable alternatives. Typically, on-site leasing people have different objectives, because they are employees of the developer. They want to fill the building. Most developers of new and expanding facilities will also cooperate with commercial brokers. If your business requires leasing or purchasing a site, complete Action Step 32.

Anticipate the Unexpected

Bette Lindsay always had a soft spot for books, and when she finally chose a business, it was a bookstore in a shopping center. She had researched everything—trends, census data, newspapers, reports from real estate firms, suppliers—but she failed to anticipate an important potential pitfall, dependency on an anchor tenant.

> My husband and I researched small-business opportunities for almost two years, and my heart kept bringing me back to books. I've read voraciously since I was 7 years old, and I love a well-written story. So when a new shopping center was opening a mile from our home, I told my husband, "This is it."
>
> Everything looked perfect. They had a great anchor tenant coming in—a supermarket that would draw lots of traffic. The broker we'd been working with during most of our search showed us the demographics

of the area, which documented that we were smack in the middle of a well-educated market. According to statistics put out by the federal government, a bookstore needs a population of 27,000 people to support it. Our area had 62,000 people, and the closest bookstore was more than 5 miles away.

Everything else looked good, too. We had lots of parking. The neighboring entrepreneurs—three hardy pioneers like us—were serious about their businesses and excited about the center's growth and opportunities.

We wanted to be in for the Christmas season, because November and December are the peak months for bookstore sales, so we set a target date of mid-September. Construction work was still being done on the anchor tenant's building when we moved in, which concerned us.

We started off with an autograph party, and we ran some bestseller specials. Even though construction work from our anchor tenant blocked our access, we had a very good Christmas that year. We started the New Year feeling very optimistic.

One day in mid-January, construction work stopped on our anchor tenant's new building. The next day we read in the paper that the company had gone bankrupt.

*Well, the first thing I did was call the landlord. He was out of town, and his answering service referred me to a property management company. They said they knew nothing about what was happening and that all they do is collect the rent. January was slow. So were February and March. In April, two businesses in the center were forced to close down. The construction debris continued blocking customer access. It was a mess. In May I finally succeeded in getting in touch with the owner and tried to **renegotiate the lease**, but his story was sadder than mine.*

Renegotiate a lease Obtaining a new or modified contract for occupancy

Fourteen months after we moved in, a new anchor tenant finally opened! We hung in there, but we lost about $100,000 in sales—an expensive mistake that does not bear repeating.

How to Rewrite a Lease with Your Lawyer's Assistance

You live with a lease, and a landlord, for a long time. If you are successful in a retail business, your landlord may want a percentage of your gross sales receipts. If you are not successful, or if problems develop, you are going to need several Plan Bs and a location **escape hatch**. For example, your lease should protect your interests:

Escape hatch A provision to cancel or modify a lease if the landlord fails to meet the specified terms

- If the furnace or air-conditioning system breaks down
- If the parking lot needs sweeping or resurfacing
- If the anchor tenant goes under
- If the building is sold
- If half the other tenants move out

The possibility of such grief-producing eventualities needs to be dealt with in precise words and precise numbers in the lease.

Always negotiate reduced rent until the anchor tenant opens for business, and make the lease itself contingent on the anchor's leasing and opening. Also, you will want an escape clause stating that if and when the anchor tenant leaves, you may leave also. You also want to ensure that you are protected if the building is sold and that other tenants cannot disturb your business operations.

Rewrite a lease Alter the wording of a lease to make it protect your interests

Option to renew A guaranteed opportunity at the end of a lease to extend for another specific period of time

Cost-of-living cap An agreement that the rent from one year to another cannot be increased by more than the CPI for that period

Read the lease slowly and carefully. When you see something you do not understand or do not like, draw a line through it. Feel free to **rewrite the lease** if you need to. It is your lease, too. Always hire a real estate attorney to review and advise you before signing any lease. And make sure that the owner, or the leasing agent, indicates his or her agreement with your changes by initialing each one. Here is a checklist to start you on your rewrite:

1. Escape clause: If the building does not shape up, or the area goes into eclipse, you will want to get out fast. Be specific. Write something like "If three or more vacancies occur in the center, tenant may terminate lease."

2. Option to renew: Common leases today are for 5 years unless you are a major player, such as Pier 1, in which case the lease might be for 10 years. **Options to renew** are usually for 2 to 5 years. You should be planning for at least a 5-year run for retail. If you are afraid to sign for 5 years, rethink your commitment to your retail business.

3. Right to transfer: Circumstances might force you to sublet. In the real estate trade this is called "assigning your lease" Usually assigning requires landlord approval of the new tenant. Be sure the lease allows you to transfer your lease hassle-free if such circumstances arise.

4. Cost-of-living cap: Most leases allow the property owner to increase rents in step with inflation based on the Consumer Price Index (CPI). To protect yourself, insist on a cost-of-living cap so that your base rate does not increase faster than your landlord's costs. Try for half of the amount of the CPI increase; if the CPI rises 4 percent, your rate will go up only 2 percent. Such an agreement is fair because the owner's costs will not change much. Major tenants in your center will insist on a cap, so you should be able to negotiate one also. Proceed with confidence.

5. Percentage lease: Percentage leases are common in larger retail centers. They specify that the tenant is to pay a base rate plus a percentage of the gross sales; for example, $3 per square foot per month plus 5 percent of gross sales over $500,000 per year. It is important that you make realistic sales projections, because the natural break-even point—the maximum amount of gross sales before percentage rent kicks in—is negotiable. The percentage rate itself is also negotiable.

6. Floating rent scale: If you are a pioneer tenant of a shopping center, negotiate a payment scale based on occupancy. For example, you may specify that you will pay 50 percent of your lease payment when the center is 50 percent occupied, 70 percent when it is 70 percent occupied, and 100 percent when it is full. You cannot build traffic to the center all by yourself, and motivation is healthy for everyone, including landlords.

7. Start-up buffer: There is a good chance you will be on location fixing up, remodeling, and so on long before you open your doors and make your first sale. Make your landlord aware of this problem, and negotiate a long period of free rent. The argument: If your business is successful, the landlord who is taking a percentage will make more money. If your business does not do well or if it fails, the landlord will have to find a new tenant. You need breathing space. You have signed on for the long haul. By not squeezing you to death for cash, the landlord allows you to put more money into inventory, equipment, service, and atmosphere—the things that make a business successful.

8. Improvements: Unless you are extremely handy, you do not want to lease a place with nothing more than a cement floor and a capped-off cold-water pipe. With most retail sites, however, a plain vanilla shell with very

few tenant improvements is the norm. If the economy is slowing down or in a recession, tenant improvements will be easier to negotiate. Find space that does not require extensive and expensive remodeling if cash is tight. Do not go under before you get going.

9. Use clauses: Caterina's, an ice cream and candy store, had included the word *beverages* in the use clause, which the landlord approved. The landlord came back later to Caterina's owner and told her she could not sell smoothies or coffees. Fortunately, the owner showed the lease to the landlord and pointed out the word *beverages*, and no more was said. Additionally, the store owner had inserted into the lease that she would not sell "soft-serve yogurt." When she began to sell hard-packed yogurt, the landlord came calling. Again, she pulled out the lease. Wording your lease properly can mean the difference between success and failure.

10. Common Area Maintenance (CAM): Leases contain clauses that cover gardeners, building repairs, trash, and so on. Know these CAM charges before leasing; they can vary greatly. Make sure your CAM charges are based on your square footage. If a portion of the center is empty, be sure the landlord—not you—pays the CAM charges for the empty square footage.

11. Parking and storage: Determine before signing the lease how many parking spots for employees and customers you are assigned, or share in common with other tenants, and the amount of storage space available.

12. Option to purchase: Consider requesting that an option or right of first refusal to purchase the building be included, in case you want to purchase the building as your business grows.

13. Option for expansion: Include an option for right of first refusal for additional space that may become available, thus securing space for your business without requiring a costly move.

HOME OFFICE AND VIRTUAL BUSINESS ALTERNATIVES

What happens if you want to operate your business out of your home, car, or iPhone? First, congratulations! This is a growth market, and you just may be on the right track. In this updated version of the cottage industry, more and more of us will be working out of our homes and operating virtual businesses. All kinds of services and products are now provided by home-based businesses. Principal Technical Services operated out of a home, with the president and her son sharing his old room and three other full-time employees working out of their homes—and it was number 143 on *Inc.* magazine's top 500 companies. Staff meetings were held at the kitchen table.

Virtual business Firm without walls

Technology allows people to work within the home today in ways that were impossible even a few short years ago. With the growth in service- and knowledge-based industries, chances are good that one day, you will be operating some sort of business out of your home. In planning to set up your business at home, however, your location analysis is still important.

There are a number of critical location questions you are going to have to consider: Do local laws and my homeowner's association allow me to operate a home-based business? How do I balance my family and work life? How do I best set up an office within my home? Will I be able to maintain a professional appearance to my clients?

If you have a business that requires employees or customers to come to your site, your alternatives will be limited by parking spaces, neighbor issues,

ADAM By BRIAN BASSET

zoning laws, and physical space. Also, find out if delivery services will deliver and pick up at your home. They may be willing to deliver, but only to the door and not inside your home. This may pose a problem if you have large, heavy deliveries, or you cannot leave packages outside.

Home offices are an excellent place to start your business, and you will be joining over 25 million fellow home-based entrepreneurs. Some entrepreneurial ventures have been able to grow to multimillion-dollar businesses while based at home. Staying in your home still requires planning and discipline. Recommendations include hiring babysitters, arranging for back-up equipment, designing office space with comfortable furniture and adequate computer equipment and telephone lines, and planning your daily work schedule with breaks, so you do not become a hermit.

Dorothy Foltz-Gray, a professional writer, drives for coffee each morning to signify that her workday has begun. Casey Trout, a financial planner, has a routine of officially closing the office for the day at 5:00 PM by walking out the back door and walking in the front door.

You need to learn to manage your work time so that not *all* of your time becomes work time. The lure of the computer and work continue to pull on you, and it is sometimes 14 hours later when you realize you have not seen the light of day. We believe it helps if your office is not in the center of family activity, so that at the end of the day, you can close the door and join the world. Basements, garages, spare bedrooms, and even closets have become home offices. In fact, today there is a booming business in prefab office sheds, studios, and gazebos from companies like Summerwood Products (*http://www.summerwood.com*) to meet the needs of home-based entrepreneurs. If you can start in your home and stay as long as possible, you will certainly hold down costs. You must remember, however, that you are running a business that just happens to be run from your home.

The Internet, rising gasoline prices, corporate downsizing, early retirement, increases in two-income families—these factors, and single parents' and Generation Y's desire to strike out on their own and embrace technology, all have pushed the surge to home-based and virtual businesses. Although starting a business in your home is easy, it does not mean that you should not consider other alternatives in your decision. If your business requires storage, business deliveries, meeting food health and safety standards, hazardous materials, employees, and constant privacy, you will need to look to other locations or rectify these issues before starting. Also, consider how long you will be able to stay in your home as your business grows.

Review your homeowner's coverage with your insurance agent. If you have customers coming to your home, your present insurance may not be adequate, or it may not even be allowed in your community. Additional insurance requirements for home-based businesses are available in Chapter 12.

The following Internet sites will provide the answers to many of your questions about working at home:

SOHO, *http://www.soho.org*

Working Solo, *http://www.workingsolo.com*

Chief Home Officer.com, *http://www.chiefhomeofficer.com*

Entrepreneurial Parent, *http://www.en-parent.com*

Virtual businesses operate with cell phones, instant messaging, Internet-based meeting sites, Intranet's with calendars, meeting scheduling, and document sharing, all combined to provide the necessary technology. Some companies have hundreds of consultants working throughout the world, meeting at a central location once a month or less. Other businesses offer an office but expect only a certain percentage to be in at any one time. Again, you are building a business for *you*, so decide what will work best for you and your employees.

One unique virtual venture, FutureWork Institute, has a "core group of 20 consultants, but also maintains relationships with 80 on-call diversity experts." Founder Margaret Regan's four story townhouse has become the headquarters; she lives on the second and third floor, devotes the fourth floor to a twice-monthly meeting space, and the ground floor office is used to accommodate out-of-town employees. If you have always dreamed of a virtual business or working at home, complete Action Step 33.

INTERNET

As retail and business-to-business sites on the Internet continue to undergo vast changes, we believe you must explore the option of using the Internet as a channel of distribution and as a way to market your business or service. The Internet serves as a channel of distribution, but all of the functions that go into a successful business—marketing, pricing, advertising, and target marketing—are still required, and you must conduct the appropriate research.

Changes on the Net happen at warp speed, so instead of providing you with information that will soon be outdated, we recommend you seek e-commerce information online to access the most up-to-date information.

SUMMARY

Before making location decisions, reconsider your personal preferences and dreams, Target Customers, taxes, and available resources.

Channel decisions are among the most challenging you will make in establishing your business. In today's world, one needs to recognize that you will not make this decision once but many times as new channel opportunities continue to develop. As discussed earlier, the melding of location, distribution, and promotion of product and service occur constantly. The Key Points article highlights Austin Taylor, a California men's clothing retailer, whose location decision included an innovative way to meld the physical location with marketing.

In completing your research, use the information and resources through Chapters 4 through 7 in determining the best channels for your business. You will also need to access the current research information on Net metrics.

Action Step 33

Is a Home Business in Your Future?

Before starting a business in your home, answer the following questions: What are the benefits? What are the negatives? What is my distribution strategy? How will I reach my customers?

1. **List reasons to work at home.** Start with the obvious: low overhead, close to snacks, an easy commute, and familiar surroundings. If you have children and want to be near them, working at home is one solution. Keep listing.

2. **List the problems of working at home:** How do you handle interruptions? How do you show that you are serious? How do you focus amidst clutter? If you have clients, where do you see them? What is the zoning situation in your neighborhood? Keep listing.

3. **List solutions to the problems raised in number 2.** If you are being interrupted, you need to get tough. Set up a schedule, and post a notice: "Dad's working from 9 to 11. Lunch will be served at noon. If Dad does not work, there is no lunch!"

4. **Go technical. What will it cost you?** Consider expenses such as computers, scanners, printers, servers, and so on.

5. **Where will your workspace be?** Garage? Basement? Bedroom? Den? How can you keep it yours? What will it cost to make it usable, private, and productive space?

6. **Check out your home insurance.** (See Chapter 12) What does it cover? What additional coverage do you need, and what will it cost?

7. **Check out health insurance if needed.** If you did not do this earlier, now is the time! Can you qualify for insurance? If so, what will be the cost? (See Chapter 1.)

8. **Seek advice.** Talk with your family and friends who own home-based businesses. What are their concerns? What are your concerns? Work out as many issues now as you can.

Most of the Action Steps in this chapter can be applied and adjusted for Internet businesses. Hard and projected data not only will be appreciated by your lenders as they read and consider your Business Plan, but such data will also help you determine employee costs, housing patterns, retail sales, and the stability of the community.

Explore the opportunities of virtual businesses, various Internet locations, and incubators. Staying in your office or garage may help you conserve cash for many years, or possibly forever.

Some short journeys will help you recognize how extremely important the location decision is for bricks-and-mortar retail businesses. First, walk up and down the main business street of your town. Walk it on different days (weekends, weekdays), and at different times of the day (midmorning, noon, afternoon, and evening rush hour). Take notes on what you see happening. What stores are closing? What new stores are opening? Where is service good?

Now that you have walked the town, it is time to roam the Net and assess: Which sites are growing? Which sites are slowing down? What opportunities are there for you to capitalize on? The physical location decision is very important for bricks-and-mortar retailers, and for Internet entrepreneurs placement on a Google search is equally important to success.

We have focused this chapter primarily on retail businesses, but the process of site selection for manufacturing is fraught with more issues and complications. For a manufacturing business, the labor market, land costs, rent, ability to expand, taxes, and employee and legal issues play a major role in the location decision. Consider hiring experts to guide you in your decision making if the location decision will be costly to change.

After viewing and analyzing all of the data available, you may choose to locate your business based primarily on personal factors or passions, such as a desire to remain near your family; to be close to fly-fishing in the river near your home; to stay near your community and church or your children's schools; or to live near the beach or out in the middle of nowhere. Or you may have altruistic motives, such as wanting to create jobs in the inner city.

Remember, you are trying to not only grow a business, but also to build a life based on your dreams. Do them both with passion.

THINK POINTS FOR SUCCESS

- The irony of the search for a retail or business start-up location is that you may need the best retail site when you can least afford it.

- Take your time selecting a location. If you lose out on a hot site, keep looking. Do not give up; there are always more places. Compromising may be an extremely costly decision, and waiting for the right location may be worth it.

- Do not locate on a very busy street where traffic goes by too fast—potential customers will not see you and will keep on going.

- Begin with a regional analysis that will allow you to compare neighborhoods or areas.

- A site analysis should include everything that is unique

to a specific building or space. Many successful centers have some dead traffic areas. Hire a retail specialist for insight and recommendations.

- Who are your neighbors? Are they attracting your type of customers or clients? What will happen if they move or go out of business?

- Know the terms and buzz words and be aware that they may mean slightly different things in each contract or lease agreement.

- Everything is negotiable: rent, signage, improvement allowances, rates, maintenance. Do not be afraid to ask.

- Talk to former tenants; you may be amazed at what you learn.

- Never sign a lease without consulting an attorney who is experienced in lease negotiations.
- Be willing to seek out and pay for the advice of trained professionals.

- Coordinate your various distribution channels and make sure your image is consistent throughout the channels. When choosing several channels, you want to build synergy.

KEY POINTS FROM ANOTHER VIEW

Marketing Suitable for a Niche Clothier

When Ray Cohen, chief executive of Irvine-based Cardiac Science, wanted an unusual incentive prize for his top salesmen in 2002, he turned to his tailor. Austin Taylor, a custom men's clothier in Anaheim, had just launched a program for corporations to reward top male employees with a custom suit, shirt, and tie. Custom clothing is something most people won't buy for themselves, especially men, Cohen says. The $2,000 price tag was cheaper than for many sales incentives, and the payoff for the company was phenomenal.

"Winners were over-the-top thrilled to death," Cohen says. "They said it was the best gift they ever had. "And it's an investment for us, too, because whenever they have an important presentation, they wear the Austin Taylor suit. When you look good, you do well," he says.

Austin Taylor partners Dave Welch and Ron Viggiano realize that they cater to a small subset of all men, so they're always looking for the most effective ways to market to those clients. The corporate incentive program is just one of their approaches.

"We're not suit salesmen," Viggiano insists. "We make dressing well an experience."

During the first meeting with a client, Welch or Viggiano asks dozens of questions about the man's lifestyle, preferred look, and work environment. Then they take 45 measurements and fill out page after page of notes.

"An attorney might want an authoritarian look during opening arguments that doesn't make him look like a shark or a hired gun," Viggiano says. "We're to clothes what a financial adviser is to money."

Welch started Austin Taylor in his home in 1995. His first customer niche was professional hockey players, but they have dwindled to 5 percent of the business as Austin Taylor has marketed to corporate executives.

Viggiano, who used to have his own custom tailoring business in Laguna Beach, became a partner in 2000.

Most of their clients are busy, so the partners do 70 percent of their work away from their showroom office. They have done their work at client's homes or offices, the Admiral's Club at Los Angeles International Airport, or even in Cancun, Mexico.

For that reason, Austin Taylor doesn't really need an office. But the showroom next to the Catch restaurant across the street from Angel Stadium is another marketing tool.

If a client wants to see an Angels baseball game without getting stuck in parking lot traffic, he can use Austin Taylor's reserved parking spaces. One client who is a Boston Red Sox fan recently used the firm's back parking lot for a pregame tailgate party.

Rather than use the entire space for a shop, Welch created a back room with maroon walls, wood floors, and leather sofa, pool table, and wall-size entertainment center. Staffers can entertain clients there, or clients can use it for corporate parties that introduce the tailor to many potential clients.

Much of their new business comes from word of mouth. Before Cohen used the corporate incentive program, he bought an Austin Taylor wardrobe for himself and then referred the tailor to colleagues.

Buchanan Street Partners, a Newport Beach real estate investment bank, has brought Welch into the office to educate employees about dressing for maximum professional impact. Most of the firm's senior executives now use Austin Taylor services, says President Robert Brunswick.

"We are fiduciary partners for pension funds and high-wealth individuals, so we need to stay on the cutting edge of professionalism and fashion," Brunswick says. "Dave educates about the perceptions of one look versus another [such as] this is an East Coast look, that is inappropriate, don't let the dry cleaners iron your ties."

Welch says his personal crusade is to train business professionals that Orange County is not the land of shorts and flip-flops.

Some men have more fashion sense than others. For the latter, Welch and Viggiano have developed an individual, by-the-numbers wardrobe book. They assign a number to each suit, shirt, coat, pair of slacks, socks, and ties. Then they match the numbers to create outfits: wear suit No. 1 with shirt 5 and tie 17, for example.

"A lot of people don't want to think about [what to wear]. They just want to use the book," says Brunswick, who doesn't use the number system. "I find Dave's service and knowledge base superior to other [clothing] designers I've used."

Welch explains: "Most men buy a jacket here, pants there, and get a tie for Christmas. Or they fall into safety and always wear a white shirt and look like everyone else. We show them how to put everything together so people will say, "That's a great outfit. Where did you get it?" And they'll reply, 'Austin Taylor.' "

Source: Jan Norman, *Orange County Register*, June 14, 2004. Reprinted by permission of the *Orange County Register*, copyright 2004.

chapter 7

Marketing Promotions Overview
Connecting With and Engaging Customers

Promotion is the art and science of moving the image of your business to the forefront of a prospect's mind. The word *promotion* comes from the Latin verb *movere,* which means, "to advance, or to move forward." *Promotion* is an aggressive word, so learn to say it with passion!

Move your product into your customer's mind by connecting on multiple levels. By engaging them at each step in the buying process, you have the opportunity to retain them as customers and build trust and loyalty.

Now that you have visualized your customer with your collage and researched your competition and market niches, it is time to plan a promotional strategy that is tailored to fit your customer and your distribution strategy. Each business is unique, and you do not want to waste money on promotional schemes that will not work. For example, if your Target Customer is a college-educated, suburban female age 45 to 55 who earns more than $100,000, owns three cars, rides horseback 10 hours a week, and reads *Practical Horseman* and *Performance Horseman,* your best chance of reaching her is with **direct mail**. If, on the other hand, your Target Customers are male, age 18 to 25, with high-school educations and incomes under $30,000, you will achieve better results with Internet banner advertising or a Facebook promotion.

Direct mail An advertisement or sales pitch that is directed toward Target Customers

Developing a promotional plan requires five steps:

1. Determine your sales and marketing goals (e.g., sales of $750,000 for the year).
2. Develop strategies to achieve a goal (e.g., increase sales order size by 10 percent).
3. Create a specific promotional method for carrying out one or several of the strategies and have measurable objectives (e.g., mailer for special Christmas-shopping night with a goal of selling $20,000 worth of merchandise during the evening).
4. Detail and enact a program involving the specific promotion chosen following a predetermined budget (e.g., gold-embossed mailer sent to 300 best customers in November for special Christmas-shopping night with free cookies, pastries, cider, and gift-wrapping at a cost of $1,750).
5. Evaluate the effectiveness of your promotional vehicles (e.g., expected return of $20 in increased sales for every $1 spent on advertising and promotion) and adjust as needed.

Tie your promotional efforts into creating an overall image and presence consistent with your target market and business definition. Remember to stress customer benefits and your distinctive competency. Much of your marketing and promotion should be partially developed at this point through the past Action Steps, especially your customer touchpoints. At this point, you know the areas in which you can and must shine. The next step is to select and begin the promotion process that will tout your strengths.

Promotional mix All the elements that blend to maximize communication with your Target Customers

Any promotion or **promotional mix** that advances the image of your business is worth considering. Survey some of the more common and traditional means of promotion before you decide on your promotional strategy, and be sure you remain open to all options. With the rapid changes in the Internet new opportunities such as mobile advertising will occur at a rapid pace and you must keep up and integrate these into your promotional mix.

It is essential to keep an open mind as you brainstorm for strategies, examine **promotional campaigns**, and come to understand the importance of planning ahead. You will then be able to make wiser decisions on how to connect with the customer.

Technology allows you to grow closer and connect more intimately with your customers. However, in many ways, we are actually returning back to the old days, when one-to-one marketing meant the shop owner knew all of his customers and their buying patterns. They lived in the same community, so the owner understood the demographics of his customers; and they went to the same church, so the owner understood his customers' beliefs and underlying motives. Shop owners engaged their customers in conversation each day and completed marketing research naturally. But success was measured the same, in increased sales and loyalty of customers. Today's *buzz* was called *word-of-mouth*.

Today technology offers many more avenues to reach customers, promote products, and analyze buying habits. However, the goal remains the same: Know and serve your customer.

Coremetrics, a "leading provider of on-demand analytics and precision marketing solutions" shares this:

> The one constant is that technology will evolve, consumers will become more sophisticated and more empowered, and it will become increasingly important to know your visitors and customers at an individual level, and to build long-term, deep relationships with them. Personalization and relationship marketing are becoming more of a reality. To be successful, marketers need a robust behavioral analytics solution and a complete record of all visitor behavior—not a sampling of data, and certainly not simple statistics about click-throughs and page hits. Only with a customer-centric data asset will marketers be able to harness the power of the Internet and provide their visitors with a truly personal experience that optimizes their business goals.

> **Source:** *http://www.coremetrics.com/downloads/Coremetrics_web2.0_white_paper.pdf* (Accessed May 24, 2008).

Several concerns are critical to all promotional campaigns: What is appropriate for your Target Customer? What can you afford to spend? What are your own and others' prior experiences? Most importantly, what will give you the biggest bang for your buck? With online advertising growing at around 15 percent a year (see Figure 7.1), you will need to address this venue, as well as the many others we present in this chapter. Creativity, consistency, and repetition are the key elements to achieving a successful result.

PROMOTIONAL STRATEGIES

The Promotional Mix

The key to connecting with customers is to consider a wide variety of promotional strategies, select several, and work diligently to integrate them to put forth a consistent message to your Target Customer (Figure 7.2).

There are times when a firm will select one or more elements to reach one target market and other variables to reach another target market. There is a lot of trial and error in the beginning of most promotional campaigns, and as you learn more about your customers, you should continually revamp your promotional strategy. A closer look at many of these strategies

Promotional campaign A sales program designed to sell a specific product or service or to establish an image, benefit, and point

figure **7.1**

U.S. Online Advertising Spending, 2001–2011 (billions)

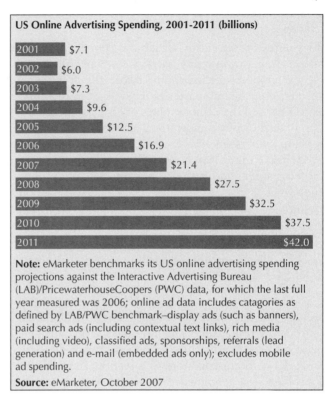

US Online Advertising Spending, 2001-2011 (billions)

2001	$7.1
2002	$6.0
2003	$7.3
2004	$9.6
2005	$12.5
2006	$16.9
2007	$21.4
2008	$27.5
2009	$32.5
2010	$37.5
2011	$42.0

Note: eMarketer benchmarks its US online advertising spending projections against the Interactive Advertising Bureau (LAB)/PricewaterhouseCoopers (PWC) data, for which the last full year measured was 2006; online ad data includes catagories as defined by LAB/PWC benchmark–display ads (such as banners), paid search ads (including contextual text links), rich media (including video), classified ads, sponsorships, referrals (lead generation) and e-mail (embedded ads only); excludes mobile ad spending.

Source: eMarketer, October 2007

follows. As you review the elements, please keep in mind the touchpoints from Chapter 5 and the gaps in the marketplace that you are trying to exploit. Remember, for each touchpoint, you have the opportunity to connect with your customer; many times, this will not be through traditional advertising but through building a relationship with your customer, which is the key to your success.

EXCEPTIONAL CUSTOMER SERVICE AS PROMOTION

Exceptional customer service provides your firm with three vital ingredients for growth: *relationships, reputation,* and *references.* As relationships build, people will spread your good name and provide you with qualified referrals.

Take the time and effort early on to learn everything you can about your Target Customers. The closer you are to your customers, the more likely you will be able to meet their needs. If you are passionate about your customers, you may be lucky enough to breed passionate customers who care about your success, such as TechSmith highlighted below. Customers who want to continue doing business with you will tell you how to improve, and they will provide constant feedback. Listen to these passionate customers, and encourage their participation in your business (see Passion Box, page 176). Out in the community or in your selected industry, they will be your unpaid—and quite possibly your strongest—salespeople. This is a sales force no amount of money can buy!

figure **7.2**

Connecting with Your Target Customer

Gaining a new customer costs five times more than retaining a customer. Do all you can to retain your customers, and practice continuous customer service improvement.

Remember, people are buying a solution to a problem and want an exceptional and memorable experience. Make the experience one they will want to share with friends and colleagues. You have studied your competitors and target markets extensively and should know what benefits and service levels are not only desired but also expected. Exceptional customer service increases the bottom line. Complete Action Step 34 by returning to Action Step 28 on touchpoints to determine how you can make each touchpoint a memorable and exceptional experience. You want your customers to shout your company name from the rooftops. Study premiere companies in customer service, such as Neiman Marcus and Nordstrom. If possible, implement the best of their service strategies into your business.

To be effective, everyone in the organization must practice exceptional customer service, and this service must be rewarded. It has to be a way of doing business at all times. Employees must know their responsibilities:

- Proactively serve the customer. ("How may I help you?")
- Display the power to act. ("How can I solve the problem?")
- Provide information. Educate and communicate with customers. ("No, we no longer sell Item B, but let me show you Item C, which we now carry, and how it compares favorably.")
- Be sociable and willing to help your customer at all times.

When developing your customer-service credo for your firm, consider what is most important to your customers, and honor that first. Remember that you cannot be everything to everyone, and be careful not to give away the store by offering more than you can provide profitably.

Action Step 34

Exceptional Service Through Touchpoints

Pull out Action Step 28 on customer touchpoints. With list in hand, brainstorm away and develop a way to make each touchpoint memorable for your Target Customer. In building exceptional customer service, you cannot just meet your customers' service needs—you must exceed them.

- If you are sending a package, what could you include to brighten their day?
- If you are serving them a fast-food meal, what could you do to make it quicker?
- If you are sending architectural drawings for review, how could you help them to better understand the drawings?
- If you own a candy store, what extra could you give each time a customer came in the door?

Some things you come up with will not be possible as a result of time or money constraints, but those that you can incorporate will be greatly appreciated by your customers, and you will be on your way to enjoying an exceptional business. Keep refining your touchpoints.

Ways to Win Referrals

Smart entrepreneurs have long worked to win referrals from happy customers, and some have found ways that don't require surveys.

Some entrepreneurs shower their biggest fans with material about their companies. Betsy Weber, 34, is a chief evangelist (yes, that's really her title) for TechSmith, based in Okemos, Michigan. The company (2007 revenues: $30 million) makes Camtasia Studio, a kind of VCR for your PC, capable of recording a sequence of screen shots. Weber spends her days scouring the net for people who have raved about TechSmith, perhaps on a blog or at a trade show. To those enthusiasts she sends packages that include a PowerPoint presentation about Camtasia Studio, T-shirts, one copy of the proprietary software (retail price: $300), and many 30-day trial versions. She follows up with a phone call. Says Weber: "I give them whatever they need so they can spread the word about us." Sales of Camtasia are up 41 percent so far this year.

Aaron Day, 32, founder of Tangerine Wellness, has turned one of his happy customers, Rockford Acromatic Products of Loves Park, Illinois, into a reliable rainmaker. Tangerine, based in Boston, offers weight-loss programs to the employees of big corporations. In 2006, Tangerine asked Rockford to provide testimonials about its service at various conferences. Since then Tangerine has signed up scores of customers in 26 states, and Rockford has played a role in about 10% of those deals, says Day.

Tangerine doesn't pay Rockford. So what's in it for that customer? The 60-year-old company makes parts for specialty vehicles, such as ATVs and motor homes. Many of the pitches are to Tangerine prospects that have the potential to become Rockford customers, too. "It's a win-win," says Day. Rockford executive Jim Knutson is just as enthusiastic. "It puts us on people's radar," he says.

Source: Adapted from *Get Customers to Sell for You,* Fortune Small Business, June, 2008. © Time Inc. All rights reserved.

Action Step 35

What Are Your Customers Worth? How Can You Remember Their Value?

1. Review the bookstore customer example.
2. Now it is time for you to determine the value of *your* customer. Determine approximately how much your customer will spend in one year at your business. Multiply that number by 5 or 10 years.
3. Now, design a creative and memorable way for you and your employees to remember that figure. Your firm is in business to make a profit. You need to convince your employees that the only reason they receive a paycheck is because customers return.

What Is Your Customer Worth?

Take a moment to determine how much your customer is worth (without inflation). If you own a bookstore, and your average customer purchases $25 in books a week, your customer is worth $1,300 (25 × 52) annually. If you plan on keeping that customer over the next 10 years, he or she now becomes a $13,000 customer.

Would you and your employees treat customers differently if you envisioned the figure $13,000 emblazoned on their foreheads? The answer for most of us is a resounding yes! Taking it further, what if that $13,000 customer brought in, on average, three new customers to your store. That customer is now a $52,000 customer.

The trick here is for everyone in your firm to realize the dollar value of each potential customer they serve. How can you get everyone to remember the $1,300, $13,000, and $52,000 figures? Put it on the terminal? Sales slips? Order forms? Paychecks? How about an employee prize of $1,300 to cover the cost of an iPhone for one year? Or if you are a bigger business, how about springing for a $13,000 one-year lease on a $52,000 Mercedes?

Action Step 35 asks you to determine the dollar value of your customer and think of creative ways to make that figure memorable to your employees.

GLOBAL VILLAGE

EXPORT.GOV
Helping U.S. Companies Export:

Register | Login

Search Export.gov

Advance Search

| Home | About Export.gov | Partner Agencies | Contact Us | Non-U.S. Companies |

Print | E-mail Page

Find Opportunities

▷ By Industry
▷ Market Research
▷ Trade Events
▷ Trade Leads

Find Solutions

▷ International Sales-Marketing
▷ International Finance
▷ International Logistics
▷ Regulations & Licenses
▷ Trade Data & Analysis
▷ Trade Problems

Contact Us

1-800 USA TRAD(E)

▷ Find a Local U.S. Office
▷ Find an Overseas Office

Main Topics

▷ Market Research Home
▷ Learn to Benefit from FTAs
▷ Webcasts on Exporting
▷ Country & Industry Webinars
▷ Order Custom Research
▷ Other Sources of Info

Step-by-Step Approach to Market Research

Step 1. Find Potential Markets

○ Obtain trade statistics that indicate which countries import your type(s) of products.

○ Perform a thorough review of the available market research reports in the country(ies) and industries in question to determine market openness, common practices, tariffs and taxes, distribution channels, and other important considerations.

○ Identify five to ten large and fast-growing markets for the firm's product(s). Analyze them over the past three to five years for market growth in good and bad times.

○ Identify some smaller but fast-emerging markets where there may be fewer competitors.

○ Target three to five of the most statistically promising markets for further assessment. Consult with U.S. Export Assistance Center near you.

Step 2. Assess Targeted Markets

○ Examine consumption and production of competitive products, as well as overall demographic and economic trends in the target country.

○ Ascertain the sources of competition, including the extent of domestic industry production and the major foreign countries the firm would compete against.

○ Analyze factors affecting marketing and use of the product in each market, such as end-user sectors, channels of distribution, cultural idiosyncrasies, and business practices.

○ Identify any foreign barriers (tariff or nontariff) for the product being imported into the country and identify any U.S. export controls.

○ Identify U.S. or foreign incentives to promote exporting of your product or service.

○ Determine whether your product is price competitive after you've figured in packaging, shipping, marketing, sales commissions, taxes & tariffs, and other associated costs. See "pricing considerations".

Step 3. Draw Conclusions

If the company is new to exporting, it is probably a good idea to target 2 or 3 markets initially. Your local Export Assistance Center can provide valuable insight into your "optimal" market opportunities.

Step 4. Test Demand

There are a number of low-cost on-line and off-line services that can help new exporters gauge foreign market interest and collect overseas inquiries:

○ Catalog Exhibitions

○ Commercial News USA

○ Foreign Partner Matching and Trade Lead Services

Source: *http://www.export.gov/mrktresearch/exp_mr_getting_started.asp* (Accessed May 27, 2008).

Additional Promotional Strategies

Paid Media Advertising   A surefire way to reach out is to advertise using radio, television, newspapers, magazines, the Internet, and trade journals. Advertising tickles the Target Customer's imagination. With a good ad and the right medium, you can reach right into your Target Customer's mind and create the desire to buy.

If you are targeting male consumers between the ages of 14 to 20, Internet advertising is one of the best mediums. If your market is major gamers, consider advertising on *http://www.ign.com*. For any paid advertising, you will need to be creative to cut through the clutter.

For magazine advertising, you will need to access the rate cards, which are listed on most publications' Web sites. In addition, you can find additional rate information in the *Standard Rates and Data Services* (SRDS) publications available in your library. Most entrepreneurs do not recognize the enormous cost for paid advertisements. We suggest you access the SRDS books, which cover radio and television advertising both, to get a handle on rates. The advertising rates for print and online newspapers and yellow pages are surprisingly high, but for many businesses, these are the most effective marketing tools to reach their target market.

Paid advertising has some obvious drawbacks: 1) it can be very expensive to create an effective ad, 2) **preferred placements** are reserved for the big spenders, and 3) costly repetition is usually essential for success.

Preferred placements The best locations within a publication, a store, or a Web site, or the best time slots on TV or radio

Advice: Be sure that a large percentage of the listeners, viewers, or readers are in one of your Target Customer groups; otherwise, your message will be wasted. Your practice with profiling in previous chapters should make you much wiser in selecting the proper media than the average entrepreneur. Many local publications have excellent in-house advertising managers who may help you develop ads and work on placement and timing. Some local cable stations have interns who will develop commercials for you for free or at a minimal cost.

Internet advertising requires constant diligence, as your options change rapidly. But one of the best parts of Web advertising comes from the tremendous tracking of sites and clicks through various metrics.

Stock photographs are available for print ads through stock photography agencies such as Hola Images, highlighted in Chapter 4. You describe what you want—for example, two clean-cut, in-love, Midwestern 18-year-olds on a movie date. The photo provider finds the photograph, and for a royalty payment, you are allowed to use it. Professional photographers supply the providers with hundreds of thousands of photographs, which they then categorize. Stock photography firms ply their trade on the Internet. The granddaddy site for stock photographs is *http://pro.corbis.com*. For a small fee, you may be able to select an incredible photo to catch your client's attention in a print ad or a mailing piece. Grabbing your client's attention is the first step; developing an interest, which is generally done with the words used in a print ad, is the second. Creating a desire is the third step, and the final step is when the customer takes action, and the cash register starts ringing. Profit, though, comes when they come back and purchase again and again.

Stock television and radio commercials are also available through firms that lease previously produced and successful local television commercials. For a fee, you lease the commercials for introduction into your local market—for example, a successful furniture commercial produced and aired in Spokane would have the firm's name replaced with your own and be shown in Topeka. Be sure the commercial you select is aimed at the Target Customers that you wish to reach. Contact *http://www.spotrunner.com* or *http://www.openad.net* to explore already produced commercials and to locate creative professionals.

If you use Spot Runner, you will be asked to:

1. Select an industry (i.e. personal care products)
2. Select a specific business (i.e. beauty salon)
3. Review and select stock ads of your choice
4. Choose your target market by age and gender
5. Select your region and cost
6. Choose your objective (e.g., generate awareness, limited time sale/promotional event, call to action/direct response)
7. Select starting date, campaign length, and weekly budget

The professionally produced ads are personalized with your company name, logo, telephone number, Web site address, slogan, and photo, and can cost as little as $499. In addition, further personalization can be purchased to include customizing additional text, voiceovers, and changing audio. Many small businesses purchase ads, which will run on local cable programming for as little as $300 a week. Spot Runner will assure the ads are run through the proper stations. The videos can also be purchased for use on Web sites in conjunction with TV ads or as stand-alone videos.

If you would like to research local cable advertising on your own, contact your stations first to determine the cost of advertising and to review any video production services they may offer to help you create original commercials. If you have a product that requires a lengthy demonstration to interest your customer, purchasing a 10- to 60-minute cable time slot may be an option. Today, many students have excellent video production equipment and years of video experience, and they might provide an option for inexpensive ad production. Please keep in mind that the ad itself is relatively inexpensive compared to the cost of media time. **Co-op advertising** dollars may assist you in reducing costs.

Ask for help, advice, and information from marketing departments of newspapers and radio and television stations. Be sure to check out circulation figures and analyze the costs of various media. Newspapers often offer targeted advertising in special supplements at reduced cost and are often appropriate for seasonal businesses, such as summer camps. The offers often include free editorial copy.

Co-op advertising A manufacturer's cosponsorship or contribution to a retailer's cost of advertising

Piggyback *A technique that allows one to coordinate a local ad campaign with the hoopla generated by national advertising*

P-O-P *"Point-of-Purchase"—a display that acts as a silent salesperson for a specific product*

Do not be afraid to **piggyback**. Let Madison Avenue build the market, then use your promotional mix to tell the Target Customer to buy at your place.

Consider classified ads in highly selective markets. Read publications on how to write effective classified ads. This is an art *and* a science. Considerable research has determined the most effective wording, size, colors, and so on. Hire an expert.

Point-of-Purchase Displays   A point-of-purchase (P-O-P) display encourages impulse purchases of last-minute items like paperbacks, pantyhose, candy, magazines, and flowers. A sharp P-O-P must perform all of the selling tasks for you, serving as a tireless silent salesperson, always on duty. A good P-O-P can be used for customer education. If your product is difficult to use, or the benefits are unclear to the Target Customer, the P-O-P will deliver your message. There are, however, problems with these displays: 1) you cannot use them to sell large items, because they crowd customers at the cash register; 2) merchants have limited floor, counter, and wall space available and do not always want to use it for P-O-Ps; and 3) the display must sell itself and the product. A tacky P-O-P turns prospective customers off instead of on.

Advice: Do weekly evaluations of all P-O-Ps. If this is your only distribution venue, hire professionals to design your P-O-P's.

Packaging   For P-O-P displays, packaging may be the only other method of marketing; but do not forget how important the packaging of any product is to your customers. Review your competitors' packaging by purchasing their products and checking out the cost and effectiveness of their packaging. What can you do better? What can you do more efficiently? What can you do more cost effectively? How could the packaging be made more attractive? Professionals in the packaging and distribution fields will be able to work with you on the proper sizing of packages and provide you with the benefits of their years of experience. One entrepreneur tried to sell her homemade sauces in 48-ounce jars, until one of her retail accounts suggested she sell them in 24-ounce jars and spiff up her packaging by including her start-up story on the label to distinguish herself in the marketplace. Sales of her gourmet sauces tripled when more accounts were willing to stock the smaller jars because they fit on the shelves much better.

Advice: Consider the following packaging points from a recent Guerilla Marketing Communiqué:

1. Environmental issues
2. Balancing function with appearance
3. Appropriateness for target market and position
4. Safety and ease in opening
5. Legal requirements for export markets
6. Ability to attach promotional material
7. Physical protection of product
8. Filling process required
9. Company's production capabilities to handle the packaging
10. Hygiene
11. Graphics and labeling
12. Convenience in opening and resealing
13. Effectiveness in delivering the product to the consumer
14. Acceptance by the distribution network
15. Package cost in relation to selling price

Source: Guerilla Marketing Communiqué, *http://www.gmarketing.com* (Accessed December 28, 2000). Jay Conrad Levinson, Father of Guerilla Marketing, Author, Guerilla Marketing series of books. Over 14 million sold in 41 languages. *http://www.guerillamarketingassociation.com.*

Catalogs　Catalogs are just right for isolated shoppers and shoppers in a hurry. Because we are so "time poor," more and more goods are now being purchased via catalogs in conjunction with a Web site. Customers shop at their convenience and do not worry about store hours, parking, or traffic. B2B and B2C customers can compare products and prices efficiently online, and thus pricing becomes a difficult variable to compete on.

Advice: If you attempt to print your own catalogs, be aware that several problems may occur: 1) the costs associated with design, artwork, photography, and mailing can be very expensive—especially if you attempt a four-color catalog; 2) your product may not show well in print; 3) the reader may not easily grasp the product's benefits; and 4) it takes time and extensive resources to develop a successful mail-order catalog business. If you are developing an Internet site to complement your catalog, make sure they are well coordinated. Catalogs can be considered another kind of silent salesperson, but one recent books-on-tape catalog retailer shared that each customer costs him $300 in marketing expenses. Thus, repeat business is essential for both print and on-line catalogs.

Catalog Houses　Catalog houses such as Lillian Vernon do not usually manufacture what they sell, so they are always looking for good products. Contact each of the catalog houses you feel are aimed at your Target Customer, and ask for details about their product submission process, which might also be available online at their Web site. Follow the process exactly. Products in catalogs are marked up (retailed) three to seven times what the catalog houses pay wholesale for them. Determine first if you can make a profit in dealing with these houses based on the products and prices in their current catalogs. Look into QVC-type programs as well. Television shopping networks search for items that they can sell in the tens of thousands. Their research is extensive, and they know what will move.

Advice: There are now many online catalogs as well, and one of these may also meet your needs. Let major catalog houses do your promotion, but make sure you can deliver if your product takes off. Ask for feedback from each catalog house to which you submit your **product description**. If your product does not fit their needs, they may help you locate a better fit. Their feedback will be invaluable, so *listen.* Such insight comes backed by years of experience and expertise.

Product description A list of features and benefits

Direct Mail　This promotional tool lets you aim your brochures and flyers where they will do the most good. Direct mail is very important for small business, because it can go to the heart of your target market; it is also used extensively in the B2B marketplace.

Direct mail advertising is a science. If you are going to write the content for direct mail pieces, read the Direct Marketing Association's material at *http://www.the-dma.org* before making the effort. Per customer, direct mail is very expensive. If, after reading the material, you want to hire a professional direct mail expert—which we suggest—consider asking him or her to write your piece for a percentage of sales. A terrific, experienced writer may achieve excellent results if he or she believes strongly in your product, and the two of you may hit a gold mine. The success of direct mail depends on your ability to narrowly define the target market and develop an appropriate direct mail campaign. If the market is too fragmented for you to do this, direct mail is not for you.

Advice: Stay up nights if you have to. Refine, refine, and refine again until your Target Customer becomes the blueberry seed discussed previously in Chapter 4. If your aim is off, you have wasted all of your money. Develop customer lists. Check out mail list vendors online who will offer you the right mail information one time to a selected list of you choice. Mail-list vendors work with you to select the proper mailing list, usually by combining many lists to arrive at your "blueberry."

Money-Back Guarantees   If you have not considered offering a guarantee as a form of promotion, consider it now. You can reach security-minded customers by emphasizing the no-risk features of your product. The problem is that you must back up your guarantee with time and money. An entrepreneur who purchased a kitchen remodeling business, and then found out that the former owners had treated several previous customers horrendously, decided to make good on their contracts. She won not only their loyalty but also the respect of everyone they told. It was an expensive and risky initial move, but it was money well spent. With the Internet, if you do not provide money-back guarantees and back them up, you will have a very difficult time selling online.

Advice: Figure 3 to 5 percent into your pricing to cover returned goods. If the product is fragile or easily misused—and people have been known to misuse just about everything—build in a higher figure. Be sure all employees understand and honor guarantees. One employee not abiding by your policy may have long-term adverse consequences. Remember that bad word-of-mouth always travels like wildfire!

Press release A news item written and sent to the media in an attempt to get cost-free advertising (free ink)

Free ink/free air Information about a business that is published or broadcast free of charge

Free Ink and Free Air   Reviews, features, interview shows, **press releases** (Figure 7.3), and newspaper columns cost nothing and are tremendously effective. **Free ink and free air** are both excellent promotional methods, as they establish your company in a believable way. Target Customers are likely to attach more credence to words that are not in the form of paid advertising and from third-party experts. You need to locate and convince a media person to believe your business is newsworthy. If you are lucky, your customers will spread the word via the Net.

Advice: Determine which media reaches your Target Customer, and contact the writers and reporters who cover your type of business. Often publications are seeking out new businesses and clever ideas. Every business is newsworthy in some way: Dig until you find something—news, charity, controversy, photo opportunities, or humor. Call, write, or fax with your entrepreneurial dream story. Also, consider utilizing one of the online press release sites such as *http://www.24-7pressrelease.com.* Make your press kit information visual—send accompanying photographs, videos, and podcasts that represent your principals, facility, and product or service in use. Follow the rules in Figure 7.3.

Personal Selling   It does not matter if you have never sold before; no one is a better salesperson than you. You *are* the business. It is your baby, and you will sell with more passion than anybody.

If you listen carefully, your Target Customers will tell you how to sell your product or service to them. That is why a good salesperson is an attentive listener, not a fast talker. Most customers love to talk with the owner of the business. Use that to your advantage.

Personal selling Client service calls made by an individual salesperson or business owner

Unfortunately, **personal selling** is expensive, especially if you have to pay others to do it, and it will boost your overhead unless you pay your salespeople on a commission-only basis. If you try to do it all yourself, you may not have the time and energy for other things that only you can do. In the beginning, some entrepreneurs do not have many options. One inventor worked all night in his shop, took a nap, and then changed clothes for 8 hours of selling on the road, only to return to his shop again at 5:00 PM to begin his design work. His firm is now valued at $40 million, and customers still love to see him in the field. Building and maintaining relationships is essential for any small business.

—— figure **7.3**

Small Business Advice and Great Tips for Writing a News Release

Being Newsworthy

For an announcement to be considered newsworthy, it must have a broad, general interest to the target audience and a strong news angle (e.g. material information, new development, drama, human interest, local angle, consequence, etc.). In addition, your release needs to be written in a journalistic rather than a marketing style. It should be objectively written, as though a reporter were writing the story for you. Most importantly, your release needs to inform people, *not* just sell them something.

Headline Formats

In most cases, your headline is the first thing an editor sees when reviewing your release. An effective headline can make the difference between an editor covering your story or hitting the delete button. To create an effective headline, consider the following points:

- Limit your headline to no more than one line. Many newsrooms have a limit on how many characters they can receive in a headline, and their systems are programmed to reject releases that exceed this limit.
- The headline should provide an editor with a tantalizing snapshot of what the news release is about. This is critical as many journalists view releases over their wire system by headline only, then pick and choose when they want to view the full text of the release.
- The headline should include the name of the company issuing the release.
- Do not include the terms "Company," "Incorporated," or "Limited" or their abbreviations unless they are necessary to clearly identify the organization, [such as] Tandy Corporation vs. Tandy Brands.
- Do not use exclamation points or dollar signs.
- Attribute all potentially critical, controversial, or judgmental statements.

Writing Style Requirements

Writing a professional and effective news release can be difficult. Here are a few guidelines to consider when crafting your release:

a. Get to the point quickly and back it up with quotes and evidence.

b. Use proper grammar and punctuation. Check for typos, and don't just rely on spell check!

c. Address *who, what, when, where, why,* and *how* in the news release.

d. Double check phone numbers and URLs.

e. Read your release aloud to see if it makes sense.

f. Include quotes to convey opinion or affiliation.

g. Don't forget to put your contact name, release date, dateline, Web site URL, and phone number in your release. Also make sure you are available for phone calls after sending the release out.

h. Your release should be written objectively, as if the writer has no affiliation with the company.

i. Do not use pronouns such as *I, we, us, our, your,* [and so on] except in direct quotes. Write in third person.

j. Do not use puffery statements or hype (i.e., we make the best widgets East of the Rockies), but do inform the reader of your status in your industry.

k. Always include standard boilerplate information about your company in the last paragraph. The headline for this section should read "About (insert your company's name here)."

Length Requirements

Your release should be concise and to the point. You should be able to convey your message in two pages or less. Releases that are less than 50 words in length tend to be advertisements and cannot be run as a news release.

Bullet Points

Yes, but sparingly.

Writing Tips for Multicultural Releases

If you're trying to target the Hispanic market, make sure to "Hispanicize"—adapt your release for this market. Incorporate appropriate market quotes, and have a spokesperson available who speaks fluent Spanish.

Remember news is news, so any news story can be related to multicultural markets.

Writing Tips for Feature Releases

If your news release does not contain breaking news, you may want to consider submitting your release as a feature distribution. Feature releases often get play in the Lifestyles or Living section of newspapers and are designed for verbatim pickup.

Source: *http://prtoolkit.prnewswire.com/index.php?s=20&item=67* (Accessed May 24, 2008).

Advice: Make everyone in your business a salesperson, including delivery and warehouse people, computer programmers, accountants, and clerical workers. Never underestimate the importance of the person who is hired to answer the telephone. Reinforce a positive attitude in all employees by reminding them that if nothing sells, they are out of a job; your valuable Target Customers need a lot of tender loving care.

Consider locating and hiring professional **sales reps** who will work on a percentage-of-sales basis. Keep cheerleading. Reps need encouragement too. Be sure to never get so big that you cannot personally go on some sales calls. If you lose touch with your customers, they may lose touch with you. Your goal as stated earlier is to make all your customers salespeople as well.

Increase your own visibility with your Target Customer and within the business community. Join local service and business organizations as well as trade associations. Consider writing a column for the local paper or a blog on your Web site.

Trade Shows   Trade shows display your product or service in a high-intensity environment to attendees who have a keen interest in your business area.

Sales reps Independent salespeople who sell a number of noncompeting but complementary products and services in a specific geographic area on a commission-only basis

communityresource

Take It Online

Virtual Trade Shows Take Care of Some Very Real Business

By Amanda C. Kooser | Entrepreneur Magazine - August 2007

Virtual trade shows, expos, and conventions are coming into their own. While event producers all insist that virtual shows won't replace real-world shows, there are some decided advantages to attending, hosting, or exhibiting at online events. Entrepreneurs save on the costs of travel, booth materials, and employees' lost productivity.

Robin Cowie, president of WorldwideBrands.com, a Maitland, Florida, wholesale and drop-ship resources provider, went from attending virtual B2B e-commerce trade show eComXpo to hosting a booth at the show. "We treat it like a normal convention," says Cowie, 35, whose company reached more than $3 million in sales last year. "We have three staff members dedicated to it. They're constantly chatting and exchanging information during the show, and I don't have to pay for travel."

Virtual trade shows have a lot in common with their physical counterparts. There are exhibit halls, educational seminars, booths manned by live staff, and networking lounges. Events run the gamut from business trade shows, consumer-oriented trade shows, job fairs, and corporate training to events that are open for up to a year. "We've built mechanisms to do very complex reporting and analytics for lead-qualification ranking," says Brent Arslaner, vice president of marketing at Unisfair, a virtual event solutions firm.

The cost savings and ease-of-use are compelling arguments for virtual events and for virtual online components to physical events. "Physical events are becoming much more tightly coupled with virtual events," says Arslaner. Already, these virtual trade shows and conventions are morphing into business communities—entrepreneurs are using them for ongoing networking and education.

Malcolm Lotzof, CEO of virtual event producer InXpo, says, "Online events are getting more cost-effective, faster and easier. It's just a force of nature."

Your appearance asserts your position in the industry. Research possible shows and attend several to determine which would be best for your firm. Trade show costs can be very expensive, if they are out of town and require travel costs, in addition to booth rental space and material. Furthermore, unless you are careful and study the layout, you could rent a space that is thin on **traffic**, and if you have not participated previously, you may not be offered a choice location.

Advice: Share booth space with another entrepreneur or with a complementary business. Conduct market research while you are promoting, and listen carefully to everyone. Study the trade show's floor plan, and try to position yourself in a high-traffic area. Have a plan, and most importantly set aside time for follow-up after the show.

Check to see if your industry sponsors a virtual trade show, such as those highlighted in the Community Resource box on page 184.

Industry Literature   Become a source of information in your industry by producing brochures, newsletters, handbooks, product documentation, annual reports, newspaper columns for the layperson, or even the "bible" for your industry. Become a recognized expert in your field. We believe this is one of the best promotional devices around, and with blogs, it is easy and inexpensive. If you are not handy with words, it can be an obstacle, but it is not an insurmountable one. Remember, expertise is admired and sought out by others. Newsletters keep your name in front of your customers frequently and can be snail-mailed or e-mailed.

Advice: If you put your thoughts down on paper, you are two steps ahead of the talkers. If your writing skills are not strong, hire a professional writer.

Working Visibility   Develop and maintain a presence. Make yourself stand out from your competitors. One pool-cleaning business owner required all his pool cleaners to wear spotless white laboratory coats on their routes. In addition, the business paid for the cleaners' trucks to be washed each week. Because of the employees' professional appearance, people felt safer with the firm's cleaners in their yards, and sales subsequently skyrocketed. In addition, many of the neighbors asked, "Who are those guys in the white coats?"

Many service firms display their presence as they work—they put signs on everything: their business, their trucks, and their work sites. Wherever they are busy, they let people know it. The drawback here is similar to one of the drawbacks with P-O-P displays: If the presence you maintain does not sell itself—if it is unattractive, or if it calls attention to an unappealing part of your business—you will lose rather than gain potential customers.

Advice: Exploit your public activities with signs that tell people who you are. Review your displays frequently. Make sure your clothing and signs tie into your overall promotional campaign; consistency is vital.

Traffic The number of potential buyers who pass by, view, or stop at a booth in a trade show; vehicles or pedestrians that move past a business site in the course of a normal day

Specialty Advertising/Promotional Products

Lesley Ronson Brown, a specialty advertising specialist for over 15 years, shares that specialty advertising, now known as *promotional products,* is a targeted, cost-efficient means of promoting a company's products or services. For the small business, this can be a very effective use of marketing dollars.

Promotional products break through communications clutter and leave a lasting impression. In addition to client marketing, many companies use promotional products for internal marketing to their employees via recognition and employee motivation programs.

Promotional products keep a company's name or message in the front of a customer's mind. They can be used as a thank-you, a trade-show traffic builder, a goodwill builder, a customer or employee loyalty reward, or a new product or service introduction tool.

The cost of promotional products ranges from pennies to several hundred dollars. When selecting an item, key considerations are budget, quantity needed, time frame, the audience receiving it, and, of course, the goal. What are you trying to achieve?

When used to build trade-show traffic, an item that involves the recipient can be effective at keeping a prospect at the booth, which allows time to qualify the prospect and generate interest in your products. An example is a stress-testing card, which requires the user to place his or her thumb on a stress indicator patch for 10 seconds. After completing the test, the person often shows the result and asks the trade-show staffer to take it, allowing even more time to build a relationship.

Preshow mailings also can be used to build traffic. An eyeglass case can be mailed with an invitation to stop by and pick up a free pair of sunglasses. Or a restaurant gift card can be mailed but activated only if the recipient brings it to the booth and perhaps fills out a short marketing questionnaire. Drawings for prizes and gifts can be used to develop a mailing list or to ask market research questions.

Sound-chip cards have proved an effective way to open doors or introduce new products and services. From a ringing phone to applause, these cards and their messages have impact, generate interest, and are helpful in contacting hard-to-reach prospects.

Continuity advertising programs can be developed in which several gifts are sent over time, often with a theme. A baseball theme campaign could include a stadium-seat cushion, baseball, cap, pennant, ticket-shaped key chain, bat-shaped pen, cap-shaped paperclip dispenser, sound-chip card that plays "Take Me Out to the Ball Game," and a package of peanuts.

PROMOTION IN CYBERSPACE

Can your customers find you on the Web? As many people use the Web or their iPhone to replace maps, phonebooks, catalogs, address books, newspapers, magazines, word-of-mouth recommendations and much more, a Web site and active involvement in Web marketing are vital.

Consider the following five key considerations for having a Web presence, as suggested by *www.entrepreneur.com*:

Visibility: With more and more consumers logging onto the Web to research products and services, if they are going to find your business, your business needs to be on the Web.

Reach: With a Web site, you are no longer limited to a customer base that is in physical proximity to your shop. Your place of business may be in Boston, but your customers can be in Bangkok.

Customer service: When customers can log on to your Web site and easily find the information they want—when they want it—their satisfaction increases.

Competition: A professional looking Web site can level the playing field for smaller companies trying to compete against larger enterprises. It's also a way to stay in the game; even if people can't find you on the Web, chances are they can find your competitors.

Credibility: When you can point customers, partners, even potential employees or investors to a Web site, it tells them you are a serious business.

Source: *http://www.entrepreneur.com/microsites/microsoftofficelive/ articles/192174.html* (Accessed May 27, 2008).

Promoting and locating on the web are much easier than many believe. The openness of the platform, the willingness of others to share information, and the competition between the major Web sites combine to offer excellent free advice everywhere and very low cost of entry to building Web sites and a presence on the net. For those interested in selling and promoting their products via eBay, attend the online workshops highlighted in Figure 7.4.

In addition to the workshops, online tutorials, and bimonthly town hall events, many eBay sellers are more than willing to assist potential sellers. One potential

figure 7.4

Online eBay Workshops

What to Sell? Research Can Help
Trusted Selling with Identity Confirmation
New International Site Visibility Listing Upgrade
How to Find Your Place in the Market: Niche Markets for eBay sellers
Tax Tips for the Family eBay Business
Understanding Safer Payment Requirements and eBay Item Holds
8 Ways to Differentiate Your Niche Business
A Good Foundation—the Basis for an eBay Business

Source: *http://pages.ebay.com/community/workshopcalendar/current.html* (Accessed May 27, 2008).

seller interested in unloading his hockey puck collection contacted an eBay seller near his home. They talked online for several days, and then the seller invited the collector over for two 3-hour "tips of the trade" one-on-one tutorials.

Due to the fact the Internet changes at warp speed, we are providing just the basics and encouraging you to keep abreast of changes and offerings that will help you better reach your target market. One of the most important elements in Web marketing is search engine optimization (SEO), which basically is the strategy to require the best ranking possible in the various search engines. This ranking is dependent on the best use of keywords and key phrases discussed in the Key Points from Another View article focusing on SEO.

Facebook, MySpace, YouTube, eBay, and others offer ever-evolving platforms for businesses in the Web 2.0 world, which, according to Coremetrics, "encompasses multiple trends and many different technologies. The technologies enable consumers to interact with your company and other consumers, participate in and influence discussions, and control their experience." Figure 7.5 provided by Coremetrics provides Web 2.0 at a Glance as of 2008. We suggest you explore all of these promotion elements along with the traditional elements.

Advice: Promote your Web site offline, as offline promotion can account for a major portion of first-time buyers. Try to make your Web site name easy to remember, and include the site on all advertising. Consider hiring professionals to design your Web site. Use stock photos and stock videos to enhance the professional appearance of your site. Design, of course, varies as to the target market; and if you have very different target markets, you should consider multiple sites. Web pages should be designed so that your customer has a reason to return.

As you prepare to complete Action Step 36, refer back to the touchpoints you created in Chapter 5. For each of those touchpoints, ask what promotional elements you can use to make each touchpoint a memorable moment. Austin Taylor, highlighted in the Key Points from Another View at the end of Chapter 6, provides one of the very best examples of a firm that utilizes its location and marketing effectively to reach its target market.

Earlier we said that if you fail to plan, you are planning to fail. When it comes to promotion, if you fail to plan, you are planning to keep your business a secret. One way to avoid keeping your business a secret is to brainstorm an ideal promotional campaign with no holds barred and no worries about costs. Action Step 36 helps you consider all of your creative ideas before discarding them as unrealistic. Save the ideas you come up with in Action Step 36, because you will use them later. We hope you will apply ingenious

Action Step 36

Brainstorm a Winning Promotional Campaign

Disregard all budgetary restraints. Pretend that money is no object. Close your eyes, sit back, and develop the ideal campaign for connecting with your Target Customers. It is okay to "get crazy" with this, because excellent, workable solutions often develop out of unrestrained thought.

- If your product or service needs a multimillion-dollar advertising promotion with endorsements by your favorite movie star, imagine that it is happening now.

- If you need a customer list created in marketing heaven, specify exactly what you need, and it is yours.

- If you are looking for the services of a first-class catalog house, just whisper the name three times and you are in business.

- If your business at its peak could use a thousand delivery trucks with smiling drivers who make your Target Customers feel terrific, write down "1000 smiling delivery people."

- If your product is small, brainstorm the perfect point-of-purchase device, perhaps one with slot machines whose money tubes are connected to your private bank vault. Watch the money roll in.

This chance to ignore costs will not come around again. (Reality is right around the corner.) But for now, have fun!

figure **7.5**

Winning in a Web 2.0 World: Metrics-Driven Success

Technology	Definition	Business Use	What Questions Do You Need to Answer?
User generated content			
Blogs	Websites where entries are made in journal style, displayed in a reverse chronological order, and often include a comment feature.	Build relationships with consumers.	• How do people get to my blog? • What do they do after visiting my blog? • Do blog visitors convert at a higher/lower rate than other visitors? • Who is adding content? • How often do they visit my blog? • How many unique visitors do I have?
User Reviews	Tool that enables site visitors to provide reviews of products, content and services.	Provide consumers peer product reviews. Establish site as resource for researching products.	• How many user reviews will a potential buyer read? • Do these reviews increase repeat visitor behavior? • Do the reviews draw new visitors to the site? • Do they see increase in unique visitors or sessions to product pages? • Do they increase conversion?
Wikis	A type of Web site that allows the visitors themselves to easily add, remove, and otherwise edit and change some available content, sometimes without the need for registration.	Allow individuals with special knowledge to contribute to data set.	• Is the content popular? • Does it affect conversions? • What visitor segment uses the wiki? • Who contributes to it? • Does it encourage more visitors to come to the site? • Does the contributed content get picked up by search engines and help pick up new audience?
Forums	A facility on Web for holding discussions.	Develop relationship with consumers.	• Is the content popular? • Does it affect conversions? • What visitor segment uses the wiki? • Who contributes to it? • Does it encourage more visitors to come to the site? • Does the contributed content get picked up by search engines and help pick up new audience?
New means of reaching consumers			
RSS	RSS delivers its information as an XML file, commonly called an RSS feed. Programs known as feed readers or aggregators can check a list of feeds on behalf of a user and display any updated articles that they find, giving the user a single place to aggregate information of their choosing.	Push time sensitive data (news, blog entries, and promotions) to consumers.	• How frequently are RSS feeds accessed? • Do the people who sign up for RSS feeds visit your site more often and for longer periods of time? • Do they browse content or products more deeply or visit that specific content or product and leave? • What is the impact on conversions? • How often is my feed viewed? • How many people are subscribed? • What is the growth rate of my subscribers? • Which content is most engaging to visitors?
Podcasts	A podcast is a multimedia file distributed over the Internet using syndication feeds, for playback on mobile devices and personal computers.	Provide value add, topical content in a manner easy to digest. Reach new audiences via podcast aggregators (e.g. iTunes),	• How many times was the podcast downloaded? • How many people came to my site as a result of the podcast? • What was the impact of podcast on conversions? • How long did people listen to the podcast?
Social Networks	A social network service is social software specifically focused on the building and verifying of online social networks for various purposes.	Identify and advertise to targeted groups of individuals.	• Are the social networking pages discussing my site/linking to my site? • How many visitors are coming to my site from social networks? • How do these visitors convert? • How many impressions, clicks and conversions are coming from my advertisements?
Comparison Shopping	A price comparison service (also known as shopping comparison or price engine) allows individuals to see lists of prices for specific products. Most price comparison services do not sell products themselves, but source prices from retailers from whom users can buy.	Reach a broader audience by placing your offerings on a comparison shopping engine.	• How many people come to your site from a comparison shopping engine? • What products/services most frequently generate these referrals? • What is the quality of referrals in terms of conversions?

(continued)

figure **7.5**

Winning in a Web 2.0 World *(continued)*

Technology	Definition	Business Use	What Questions Do You Need to Answer?
Richer, user defined experiences			
Video/ multimedia	Multimedia uses multiple forms of information processing (such as text, audio, graphics, animation, video) to inform or entertain the user audience.	Convey content that is in video format.	• How often was content accessed? • How long was it viewed? Was it viewed in its entirety? • What was the impact on conversions? • How much ad inventory do I have? • How many ads were viewed?
Ajax/Flash	Ajax makes web pages feel more responsive by exchanging small amounts of data with the server behind the scenes, so that the entire web page does not have to be reloaded each time the user makes a change. Flash is commonly used to create animation, advertisements, various web-page components, to integrate video into web pages, and more recently, to develop rich Internet applications.	Deliver more user friendly business applications that are easier to use, and provide visitors with a richer experience.	• How has Ajax/Flash improved the process? • What is the impact on my conversion rate? • Is the process completion rate higher?
Mobile web	The Web as accessed from mobile devices such as cell phones, PDAs, and other handheld gadgets connected to a public network.	Enable user to access content anywhere.	• What content is accessed via mobile devices?
Portals	A site on the Web that typically provides personalized capabilities to its visitors.	Provide a single place for visitors to aggregate content and create a personalized experience.	• What content or applications are accessed? • Where in the portal is the content/application being accessed?

Source: *http://www.scribd.com/doc/210493/Coremetrics-web2-0-white-paper* (Accessed June 3, 2008).

and cost-effective solutions to your promotional needs. Do not be afraid to put your passion for your business into your promotional ideas and campaigns. Creativity and passion can go a long way to promote your business.

As you have seen throughout this chapter, the entrepreneurs who succeed are the ones who have the best fix on their Target Customers and know how to wrangle all of their promotion options into a cohesive and consistent message. They are also the ones who understand the importance of market research, tracking, and evaluating their advertising expenses.

UNIQUE PROMOTIONAL STRATEGIES

As much as we may plan, the economy and circumstances may necessitate a change in our original path. However, true entrepreneurs know how to roll with the punches and accommodate change. While reading what these entrepreneurs have to say, you may discover your own unique creative winning ideas. Look for inspiration.

Peggy Sue's Dinner

Billboards

This January, when the owner of Peggy Sue's Dinner, located between Los Angeles and Las Vegas, realized that 2007 sales were flat at $3 million, Gabler rented a billboard just outside Sin City that costs him $1,600 more per month than his other locations. "Big casinos pay top dollar to advertise in that area. And here is ours, saying nothing more than our name and HUNGRY? 90 MILES," Gabler said. The result: In February, Peggy Sue's *sales jumped 12 percent despite traffic along the Interstate lagging by 5 percent compared with February 2006.*

Recently, the owners spent $40,000 on a 12-foot-tall King Kong and five liked-sized dinosaurs, hoping to capture some of the 40,000 cars and hungry passengers who pass by each day.

Garment District Guides

Free Ink

When my partner and I got the idea for guiding shoppers through the Los Angeles garment district, we thought it would be so exciting, we wouldn't have to do much except stop once a week to make bank deposits. Were we ever wrong!

We ran a good-sized ad in our local paper. We filled a couple of buses, but then our market ran out because those customers didn't need a return trip to Los Angeles for shopping on the bus. We had some flyers printed up and covered every car in every parking lot in our community. Two thousand flyers and sore feet netted us half a bus.

Then a feature story appeared in the "View" section of the Los Angeles Times about a tour to Hollywood and Beverly Hills. On an impulse, we called the reporter and told her about Garment District Guides.

It worked.

On the next trip, the reporter came along and brought a staff photographer. Two weeks later, our story was on the front page of the "View" section—a beautiful third of a page—and customers began calling us! Our local papers followed a month or so later with features about the service, and after we got bigger, a television reporter profiled us for one of the evening newsmagazines.

Now business is great. We haven't had to pay to advertise for 18 months. When times are slow, we increase our networking activities and try to book group trips. We also started targeting groups with special trips, such as the Back-to-School Bus, Santa's Sleigh, Spring Fling, and Mother–Daughter Specials. With each trip being unique, we continue to receive free press. When people ask me what kind of promotion I believe in, I tell them free ink!

We hope you found inspiration by reading about these entrepreneurs who—through planning, perseverance, or luck—found successful promotional strategies. You may not need King Kong, but you do need a well-organized promotional campaign and the ability to be flexible when required. Be sure to gather **customer files**. With good files, *information becomes knowledge and thus power.*

Customer files Lists of persons or firms that have already made purchases

SALES REPS AS CONNECTORS

Suppose you have a new product that has immediate sales potential across the country. How do you connect with the whole United States? Should you hire your younger brother to take care of it for you, or should you seek out a professional sales rep to act as a commissioned salesperson?

An army of trained professional sales reps awaits your call. However, all sales reps are not equal; select carefully. Exercise caution, because the reputation of your sales reps will become your reputation.

Interview potential buyers of your goods and ask them to recommend reps whom they consider the very best in their field and with whom they enjoy working with. When the same names surface several times, you will know whom to call. In addition, contact the rep associations listed in this chapter for recommendations.

Trade associations, shows, and journals also provide information on rep associations. Reps attend trade shows to discover new products to carry; so if you have a booth, try to reach reps at your show. Also, aggressive reps will contact you if you have a hot product.

To determine the prevailing practices for commissions, territories, and termination agreements for your selected industry, contact the associations listed here. Hire reps based on their knowledge of the industry, established customer base, and ability to sell to your customers effectively and efficiently. You are in essence paying the reps for immediate access to the market. Ask yourself how long it would take, and how much it would cost you, to set up a sales force to have similar characteristics to the independent sales rep organizations. Another option might be to use your own sales force for certain markets and independent sales reps for other market niches.

Reps must sell because they work solely on commission; you are assured of a fairly aggressive, experienced sales team to promote your product or service. Reps allow you risk-free exploration of new markets as well.

Ask the reps:

- How many salespeople are in your firm?
- What is your background and experience?
- What geographic territories do you cover?
- What complementary lines do you represent?
- What ideas do you have for trade show presentations?
- Would you work with us on a regional rollout while we prepare for national coverage?
- May I participate in sales meetings and help train the reps on my product line?
- What sales call reports can I expect?
- What performance guarantees do you offer?
- What results have you achieved for similar companies?

Provide all the encouragement and support to your reps that you can; never stop being a cheerleader. Insist on sales reports. Keep informed on what is going on in the field; pack your bags, and make calls with the reps. Write monthly sales letters and encourage feedback from both your reps and their customers. Feedback helps you to evaluate your product line and your reps. Provide your reps with materials such as brochures, testimonials, and samples. In addition, conduct any training necessary for your product. Also, be willing to share information you gather on recent sales and competition, and encourage sales reps to share information about their calls and responses from potential customers.

Sales Rep Resources

Manufacturer Representative Associations
Manufacturers Agents National Association
http://www.MANAonline.org
Electronics Representatives Association International
http://www.era.org

To locate sales representatives in foreign countries, call the embassy or consulate for each country and speak to a trade expert. The Department of Commerce and resources cited throughout the chapters also provide trade information and contacts.

NETWORKING GROUPS

Another source of promotional power is networking groups, which carry the image of your business to a support group. Orange County networking consultant Susan Linn defines the term broadly: "Networking is using your contacts to get what you want. Commonly, networking is used to refer to group situations in which business people can interact. It's a current buzzword for the age-old principle 'It's not what you know but who you know.'"

Networking gives you confidence and allows you to pass on helpful information to people who are not directly competing with you—and to receive feedback and support. Being around others dreaming the same dream provides a place where you can ask for advice in a nonthreatening environment.

Networking for Success and Survival

When Dorothy and Dan Gray decided to go into business, they looked around for more than a year. Dorothy had some training in graphics, and Dan was good with numbers. They finally decided on a franchised printing business. They paid a flat fee and agreed to pay the franchisor a percentage of their gross. The franchisor provided assistance and a well-developed business plan.

What they did not tell Dorothy and Dan about was networking.

When you are in the printing business, providing extreme customer service is how to forge ahead. They knew they had to promote their image and tried everything—brochures, leaflets, flyers, and half-page display ads in the local newspapers. But the business did not start rolling in until Dorothy joined her first networking group.

It was a Business Networking International (BNI) club, and the membership varied: a real estate broker, an insurance agent, the president of a small bank, the owner of a coffee service, a printer, a sign manufacturer, the owner of a chain of service stations, a sporting goods storeowner, a travel agent, a small manufacturer, and a contractor.

Several of the members told Dorothy that in previous years they had spent $30,000 in advertising, and since joining BNI, they were able to drop all paid advertising. This was very encouraging.

At the required breakfast meetings held once a week, members were asked to bring at least one referral for another club member. Several members brought three to four referrals each week. Dorothy and Dan generated more business from the club than from all other promotional efforts combined.

⊙ **incredible**resource

John F. Baugh Center For Entrepreneurship at Baylor University: Innovation Evaluation Program

Over 1,500 products have been scrutinized for potential market success by a team of evaluators with extensive business backgrounds and experience at Baylor University. If you have a product (not including medicine, toys, games, or foods), evaluators will review your product, and within 4 to 6 weeks, they will forward a thorough evaluation of the market potential for your product.

(continued)

(*continued*)

For a nominal fee of $150, which covers administrative costs, an un-biased team analyzes the commercial potential of an inventor's new product or idea through the knowledge of in-house experts in marketing, manufacturing, finance, and other fields. The invention or idea is evaluated according to more than 30 different criteria:

- Legality
- Safety
- Environmental impact
- Societal impact
- Functional feasibility
- Production feasibility
- Stage of development
- Investment costs
- Payback period
- Profitability
- Marketing research
- Research and development
- Potential market
- Potential sales
- Trend of demand
- Stability of demand
- Product life cycle
- Legal protection
- Competitiveness in marketplace
- Customer learning requirements
- Customer needs satisfied
- Dependence on complementary products
- Visibility of advantages
- Promotional requirements
- Distribution requirements
- Service needs
- Appearance
- Function
- Durability
- Price
- Competition (existing)
- Competition (new)

The statistical analysis is relatively Simple and Follows three separate evaluations:

The Critical Value Score (CVS) is based on five criteria that must be passed in order for the product to be considered for future activities. This score must be very high; in the 80 percent plus range.

The Aggregate Value Score (AVS) of the 33 criteria is the overall total. It should be relatively high; in the 60 percent plus range.

The Estimate of Success (EOS) should be in the 60 percent plus range in order for the product to receive additional consideration.

In order for a product to be considered as a serious candidate for the marketplace, it should score highly on all of the three evaluations.

The program provides the inventor objective data on the product's strengths and weaknesses, which may be used to determine the likelihood of commercial success before committing capital to fully develop and market the product. A good score could help secure a development loan by increasing credibility with banks and by encouraging an inventor to pursue the invention with a business plan and patent. A low score could warn an inventor to reconsider any further investment.

Source: *http://www.baylor.edu/business/entrepreneur/index.php?id=24007* (Accessed May 24, 2008).

Why You Should Network

You have probably been networking all your life. In school you networked for information about teachers and courses. When you moved into a new community, you networked for information about doctors, dentists, car services, babysitters, and bargains—all the details that make up daily life. On the job, you networked your way to sales leads, brainstormed your way to better design, or got in a huddle with some fellow manager or co-workers to solve problems.

Core groups Clusters of influential, key individuals who share a common area of interest

As an entrepreneur, you can network your way to a surprising number of new customer connections, which can spell success. Develop your networks and build **core groups** of people within them. Some networks grow naturally from the loose association of people you already know, and because you are at the center of the net, it has to help you.

Networking Organizations

The bottom line for networking is that people do business with people they know and are most comfortable with. So get out there and meet people who can help develop your business. When others spread the word about you, it is like having your own private, unpaid sales force working for you! This does not just happen. Joining a networking organization is not enough. You must decide to become an active member of the organization. Take a position of leadership. Meet and spend time with everyone you can. Do things for others. Make networking a way of life. Be sure you have your elevator speech from Action Step 23 down pat, because you will have many chances to present it. Before you join an organization, ask yourself:

- What is the purpose of this organization?
- What type of people do I enjoy being with, and are they part of this group?
- Do I want to make a political or social statement with this involvement?
- Am I participating solely for business purposes?
- How can my involvement in this network help promote my business?

Most organizations will allow you to attend at least one meeting free with no obligation to join. We suggest you attend various organizational meetings to determine which groups best fit your personal and business needs, as well as those whose members are most likely to be in contact with your target market.

What type of networking groups are out there?

Trade organizations focus on a particular industry and provide an opportunity to share primarily with your peers. They are an excellent place to make contacts to find suppliers, attorneys, accountants, and so on. Involvement at the local level can lead to positions at the national level, which will widen your exposure further.

Sales-leads clubs such as the one Dan and Dorothy belonged to, generally meet weekly for breakfast, lunch, or dinner to share leads. One national group is BNI, online at *http://www.bni.com*.

Political clubs also provide excellent opportunities to expose your business widely; but if you are a local retail business, tread lightly.

Women's organizations such as the American Association of University Women (AAUW), Women in Communications (WICI), and the National Association of Women Business Owners (NAWBO) focus on social issues, trade, or business efforts.

Chambers of commerce are excellent sources of local business contacts. One does not have to live or work in a city to join and participate in many chambers of commerce.

Local social and community groups offer the power of community participation to reach a local customer. Many mortgage brokers and real estate agents have found that participation in the local PTA has paid off handsomely by increasing their client pool. Visit many groups, join several, and participate heavily in a few that will have the best payoff for you.

During a recession, one marketing consultant, Nancy Hopp, continued to network heavily in six organizations. At one point, she was donating 20 to

30 hours of her time just to keep busy. As the recession wound down and the good times started to roll, her business skyrocketed. Her community contacts were back in business, and so was she! Nancy has never advertised and has relied totally on word-of-mouth and community contacts for customers. Networking does not cost anything but time, and it can yield incredible results for those willing to develop relationships.

ATTACH PRICE TAGS TO YOUR PROMOTIONAL STRATEGIES

You have reviewed the importance of networking, customer service, and an integrated promotional campaign. It is time to develop your ideas into a promotional strategy. Remember, you can hire an ad agency to create great advertisements that bring in customers, but only excellent customer service and products will bring them back and make your business profitable over time.

Time now to make decisions about your promotional mix. Look at the ideal promotional strategies you came up with in Action Step 36, pick the top four or five elements you can realistically carry out and integrate into a cohesive promotional campaign, and then determine the cost of each. Action Step 37 walks you through this process. Continue to focus your promotions on the Target Customer from your collage.

Do not be discouraged if cost knocks out part of your ideal promotional mix. That is why we filled Chapter 7 with so many inexpensive promotional ideas. And in the meantime, you have brainstormed the best possible promotional effort for your business.

When bankers review business plans, they will definitely want to know how and at what cost you are going to reach your customers. A well-thought-out marketing and promotion plan will demonstrate to your reader that you have done your homework and recognize the costs involved in promoting your product or service.

SUMMARY

Positioning your business in the prospect's mind and keeping it there takes a concerted, constant effort. Anything that will advance the image of your business is worth considering. Survey the whole range of promotional strategies available, and then choose the promotional mix that best targets your customer with the funds you have available. Potential strategies include paid media advertising, free ink and free air, personal selling, trade shows, industry literature, networking, and exceptional customer service. Present a consistent message and keep the message simple and clear for the clients. Synergies should develop among all your activities.

With technology, new and innovative promotion opportunities will occur frequently, and you will need to be aware of these changes and evaluate their value to your business.

Focusing on the touchpoints will show you areas and niches where you can best your competitors and focus your promotions. Small companies have the advantage of being able to respond to their customers' needs immediately, which gives them great strength, so take advantage of your speed.

Make every member of your organization understand the importance of their job in the relationship between the customer and the company. If all your employees act as salespeople, you will have dramatically increased the size of your sales force, and your clients will notice the difference.

Action Step 37

Attach a Price Tag to Each Item of Your Promotional Package

What will your customer connection cost? To get some idea, go back to Action Step 36, list the top four or five connections you want with your customers, and then research the cost of each. Let us imagine that you have chosen the following promotional mix:

Website: Determine the cost to develop a Web site and the costs to promote it.

Direct mail: Find mail-list brokers online and contact them. Discuss your business and the markets you want to reach. Ask for recommendations on appropriate mailing lists and strategy tips. Discuss costs.

Press releases: Visit marketing departments of local newspapers for information on targeting their readers. Use this to refine your release. Catch the reader's attention, and keep the message simple. Be sure to wield the five *W*s of journalism: *who, what, where, when,* and *why,* along with the noble H, *how.* Use Figure 7.3 to write a press release.

Personal selling: Budget time and money for sales staff, sales reps, or yourself to reach customers personally. If you plan on being the main salesperson for your firm, find networking opportunities and start building contacts. Allocate part of your salary and expenses as a promotional cost. If you are going to use sales reps, locate and determine their cost.

Determine the cost of any other promotional ideas you have developed including adwords, banner ads, and Web sites. Once you know the cost of each item of your promotional package, decide which you can afford. Always consider the message you want your Target Customer to receive, and how you can make each touchpoint moment memorable.

We also recommend that you seek creative solutions to the problem of small-business promoting. New businesses can take creative license and stretch the limits early on in getting their businesses off the ground. If you are not creative, hire people who are to help you stand out from the crowd. A coordinated marketing plan focused on Target Customers is essential for long-term success.

THINK POINTS FOR SUCCESS

- Be unique with your promotions. Instead of Christmas cards, send Groundhog's Day or St. Patrick's Day cards.
- Stand in your Target Customers' shoes. Refer back to your Target Customer collage to keep the customer in the center.
- Maintain a presence.
- A world in transition means opportunities for entrepreneurs.
- To launch your mailing lists, give away something. In return, potential customers will give you their names and addresses.
- Create excitement—excitement sells. Rent a Santa, a dancing robot, or a hot-air balloon.
- Remember to promote the benefits of your product or service. People buy solutions. How will what you offer make their lives better? How will it make them happier? How will it save them time?
- People also buy experiences. Make them memorable! Make them want to come back for more. Make them want to send their friends and family.

- Keeping a customer is far cheaper than finding a new one. Make the customer happy. When problems occur, ask the customer how you can solve them.
- Make customer service a passion.
- Passionate customers become walking billboards. Their desire for you to succeed will make you better. Strive for "raving fans."
- When you think you have it made, do not let your guard down—keep connecting with your customer. You will never be so big that you can afford to disconnect.
- Take the time to connect with customers who do not return. Be brave, and give them a call and find out why they are no longer your customers.
- *Listen* to your customers.

Remember these words: Creativity! Creativity! Creativity!

KEY POINTS FROM ANOTHER VIEW

Search Engine Optimization

Most effective search engine optimization (SEO) tactics have one thing in common: keywords. By anticipating the search terms used by customers and incorporating them into a Web site, marketers can boost their site's natural search engine ranking, which is vital to Internet marketing.

Obtaining a desirable search engine ranking requires good information about the keywords and keyword phrases related to your Web site's industry or topic. A good place to start is to examine the keyword density of pages on the Web site.

Keyword density is measured by the number of times a word appears on a page divided by the number of words on a page. Keyword density is used by search engines to help determine the rank of a Web site for a given keyword.

One of the best ways to determine the keyword density of terms on your Web site is to create a keyword cloud.

A keyword cloud is a visual representation of a Web page based on the way a search engine sees it. To generate your own keyword cloud, try one these free tools:

- Icon Interactive's Keyword Cloud Tool generates a keyword cloud. (*http://www.iconinteractive.com/ tools/wordcloud/*)
- SEO Tools generates a keyword cloud that includes phrases. (*http://www.seochat.com/seo-tools/ keyword-cloud*)

In a keyword cloud, some of the keywords that appear in your cloud are in larger fonts and some are in smaller fonts. The keywords in larger fonts have a higher "keyword density." This means that they occur more frequently in that Web site. Popular search terms should be the largest words in your site's keyword cloud.

It's important to incorporate popular keywords and key phrases into your site so potential customers using those words will find your site on search engines. The addition of newly popular and highly relevant keywords will improve the ranking of your site in natural search engine results. To find keywords you may be overlooking, try these free tools:

- Icon Interactive's Keyword Suggestion Tool helps find keywords related to the words you enter and displays the popularity of the term. (*http://www.iconinteractive.com/tools/*)
- Adapt Keyword-Finder Beta emails you a report of alternative keywords related to those you enter. (*http://keywordfinder.adapt.com*)
- Google Trends can be used to explore and compare the volume of queries over time, by city, regions, languages [and so on]. (*http://www.google.com/trends*)

Based on what you learn, you can rewrite pages to include popular and effective key phrases throughout your site. Place keywords in the page title, headings, metatags, comment fields, "alt" tags, URL link text, and throughout the body of your Web pages where a keyword or phrase is appropriate.

The trick is to improve density and placement of important keywords and key phrases throughout the site without negatively affecting the content. Keywords need to be as specific as possible to each page. This ensures that people who find the site through search engines won't be disappointed with the content they find.

Google and other search engines reward sites linked from other popular and reputable sites. Sites linking to your site should have an equivalent or higher page rank. Text for incoming links should include keywords and phrases.

Incoming links that contain keywords within the text of a link are also viewed as more relevant than links without keywords. Links that use phrases like "click here" or "learn more" are less relevant. And text links that only contain a company's name aren't relevant for keyword searches that leave out the name.

SEO is not about being highly ranked for every possible keyword or getting incoming links from every possible Web site. It's about being highly ranked for the right keywords and linked from the right kind of Web sites.

For more information about search engine optimization, see our discussions on:

- Link Popularity
- Sitemap XML Feeds
- Selecting an SEO Vendor

TIP: Work Smart

Search engine optimization isn't based on keywords alone. Importance is also a factor. "Important, high-quality sites receive a higher PageRank," according to Google, which uses its PageRank system to determine the best sites to display in natural search engine results.

"Google goes far beyond the number of times a term appears on a page and examines all aspects of the page's content (and the content of the pages linking to it) to determine if it's a good match for your query." An easy way to measure a site's PageRank is to visit a site like *checkpagerank.net*.

Source: *http://www.toolkit.com/small_business_guide/sbg.aspx?nid=P13_4000* (Accessed May 27, 2008).

chapter 8

Start-Up Concerns and Financial Projections
Researching and Preparing Numbers

We urge you in Chapter 8 to move beyond your start-up plans and venture out into the uncertain financial future. Throughout the past chapters, you have been gathering information on marketing and location costs, target markets, and competition; and if you have not already run numbers, as suggested earlier, it is now time to change your focus from the creative side of entrepreneurship to the financial side—the side that keeps you afloat.

This chapter will help you to avoid running out of money, estimate your start-up costs, and prepare you for capital searching by developing the financial projections required by lenders. Numbers work is time consuming and frustrating, but without it you are sure to fail. Many entrepreneurs put all their passion into selecting a site and developing a marketing plan, but unless you watch your finances passionately, all your other plans may never come to fruition. Use the measuring devices we present, and continue to revise projections as you acquire additional information.

CHART YOUR BUSINESS FUTURE WITH NUMBERS

Your first step is to ask questions about the financial state of your business. What will your start-up costs run? Which months will be strong in your particular business? Which will be weak? What are your projected gross sales estimates for the first year? The second? The third? What is the potential profit? Can you project cash flow? Necessary bank loans and lines of credit? Vendor credit? How many employees will you need, and how much will they cost? Will freight costs affect your profit? Will shipping revenue increase your profit? Can you add people to the team who will bring in cash infusions? What will your cash picture look like when your start-up dollars are spread over a full year?

How fast will your business grow? How will rapid growth affect your cash picture? Have any of your life experiences prepared you for handling money in business? What steps should you take to prepare yourself for handling your business's finances?

Generally, there are five areas you need to consider as you plunge into the numbers of financial management: start-up costs, pricing, seasonality scenarios, sales projections, and what-if scenarios with income, expenses, cash flow, and financial ratios. To conduct your research in these areas, there are many online and secondary resources to help you. One of the best is BizStats.com, highlighted on page 212.

Most bankers use the ratio studies published by the Risk Management Association. Every lending officer has a current copy, as do most business libraries. This publication, considered the bible for statement analysis, covers more than 190,000 businesses in 680 industries. Also at your library, or available at a nominal cost, is *Dun & Bradstreet Business Information Systems*. This annual publication provides key ratios on more than 100 businesses. The U.S. Small Business Administration has key ratio reports for several industries. BizStats.com, which we feature as an Incredible Resource, also provides a treasure trove of financial data. Trade associations often provide the most comprehensive work on financial ratios and expected revenue and expenses and should be contacted immediately.

Start-Up Costs

It is important to determine your costs before proceeding. For some businesses, start-up costs will be minor; for others, major expenses are involved. A service business may be up and going with only $2,000 in expenses, whereas a retail store may incur more than $300,000 in start-up expenses. Manufacturing firms can incur start-up costs of more than $30 million. Any money saved during start-up will help cash flow later, so begin asking the following questions: What can you buy used? What are the advantages of leasing versus buying? How can you conserve cash?

Pricing

As for pricing, you will need to determine if your firm is going to attract clients or customers with low-cost pricing, if you will try to be in the middle of the road, or if you will try to attract the top tier of clients by offering premium services or products at premium pricing. The hardest part of pricing is making sure you have included *all* the costs involved in providing a product or service to customers. Volatility in pricing for commodities and changes in the economy also present challenges for most entrepreneurs.

Seasonality Scenarios

Most businesses experience peaks and valleys. What will be your best and worst months? How will you manage cash flow? How will you deal with employee scheduling?

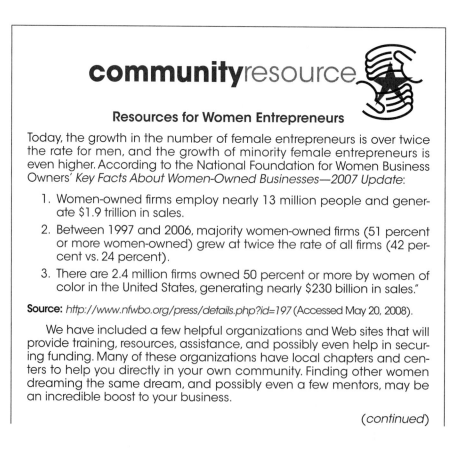

community resource

Resources for Women Entrepreneurs

Today, the growth in the number of female entrepreneurs is over twice the rate for men, and the growth of minority female entrepreneurs is even higher. According to the National Foundation for Women Business Owners' *Key Facts About Women-Owned Businesses—2007 Update*:

1. Women-owned firms employ nearly 13 million people and generate $1.9 trillion in sales.
2. Between 1997 and 2006, majority women-owned firms (51 percent or more women-owned) grew at twice the rate of all firms (42 percent vs. 24 percent).
3. There are 2.4 million firms owned 50 percent or more by women of color in the United States, generating nearly $230 billion in sales."

Source: *http://www.nfwbo.org/press/details.php?id=197* (Accessed May 20, 2008).

We have included a few helpful organizations and Web sites that will provide training, resources, assistance, and possibly even help in securing funding. Many of these organizations have local chapters and centers to help you directly in your own community. Finding other women dreaming the same dream, and possibly even a few mentors, may be an incredible boost to your business.

(continued)

(continued)

- National Association of Women Business Owners (NAWBO), *http://www.nawbo.org*
- Center for Women's Business Research, *http://www.nfwbo.org*
- Organization of Women in International Trade (OWIT), *http://www.owit.org*
- Association of Women's Business Centers, *http://www.awbc.biz*
- Count Me In, *http://www.countmein.org*
- eWomennetwork, *http://www.ewomennetwork.com*
- Ladies Who Launch, *http://www.ladieswholaunch.com*
- Resources for Women Entrepreneurs, *http://www.score.org/women_resources.html*

Sales Projections and What-If Scenarios

Before you jump into a business, you need to determine how much income and profit it will generate in a given period of time to determine if you should proceed. By conducting extensive research and completing the Action Steps throughout this text, you should be able to make reasonable projections.

In projecting your what-if scenarios, you need to project the very worst case scenario, a realistic one, as well as the one you dream of. When using a spreadsheet, you should look at various elements such as sales, cost of goods sold, rent, salaries, and so on, and complete a first-year forecast. Lenders will request monthly projections for the first year and yearly projections for the next 3 to 5 years. If you are not willing to project your business out 3 to 5 years, you should rethink whether you should be in business.

Projected Income Statements and Cash Flow

Your research to date should help you develop projected profit and loss statements, also known as *income statements*. An income statement is unique to each individual company, and expenses are dependent on the area, clients, salaries, and so on. Costs vary greatly throughout the country, so when doing comparisons with others, make sure you are in the same geographical area. All expenses should be justified and supported through notes to your income and cash-flow statements.

For many businesses, there is no time lag between delivering goods and receipt of payment. For others, a time lag of 15 to 60 days may exist. And some businesses, such as bed and breakfasts, collect cash up front. Find out what your selected industry standard is, and develop your projected cash flow accordingly. You will need to expend cash for labor, taxes, rent, utilities, inventory, and other expenses. If your business is to stay afloat in the interim, you have to know where every dollar is going. You must make arrangements for financial infusions long before the money is required.

Balance Sheet

A balance sheet shows a scale with assets on the left side and liabilities and owner's equity on the right side. For many start-ups, the balance sheet will contain few assets, but as the business grows, the balance sheet becomes an important tool to gauge the financial health of your organization.

Break-Even Analysis

In simple terms, a break-even analysis shows you the point where you will pay your bills; after that point, you will begin to realize a profit from additional sales. If you complete a break-even analysis that clearly shows that you will need to reach sales of $500,000 in the second year of business, you can then use what-if scenarios, spreadsheets, and other information to determine if that sales figure is realistic in light of the competition, location, product, and economy.

Financial Ratios

Published ratios from your associations and others can help guide you in developing your projected statements. Lenders will evaluate and compare your financial ratios to others in your selected industry and regional area and their lending decisions will be based on how you stack up.

START-UP COSTS AND CONCERNS

When successful entrepreneurs are interviewed and asked what surprises they had not anticipated when they started, they usually list quite a few. In almost every case, though, they respond that it cost more and took longer than they had anticipated. Start the planning process and make the best estimates you can so that you are not caught off guard.

To begin, we have provided a Start-Up Concerns and Cost Worksheet, Figure 8.1, which is a generic worksheet. You will need to add and subtract items from the worksheet to fit your business operation. As you complete your Business Plan in Chapter 15, you should return to this list to make sure you have dealt with all of the concerns on your final list. In fact, as you work through the remainder of the chapters, keep Figure 8.1 and Figure 8.2, the Start-Up Requirements Worksheet, nearby and add to them as concerns and costs arise. Many of the items on the list are discussed in detail in later chapters.

Action Steps 38 and 39 will help you anticipate potential surprises and costs, such as those that befell Ginny Henshaw.

Unexpected Costs

The reason I decided to start a day-care center was because I really loved children, and my experience as a preschool teacher and camp administrator led me to believe I could do it. I talked it over with my family, and they said they would help out if I got in over my head. If only they had known!

I think we planned things pretty well. We found a good location—smack in the middle of a neighborhood of young families with an average of 2.3 children. We worked hard, but it was fun, and it made us feel a part of something important. We spent many hours making sure we complied with the laws and regulations required of day-care centers.

About 3 weeks before our opening, we called the light and power people to ask them to turn on the lights. "Sure thing," they said. "Just send us a check for $3,000, and the lights will be on."

figure **8.1**

Start-Up Concerns and Costs Worksheet

I. Taxi Squad (people who can assist you)
  A. Lawyer
  B. Banker
  C. Accountant/bookkeeper
  D. Insurance agent
  E. Commercial real estate agent
  F. Mentor
  G. Consultants
  H. Suppliers
  I. Chamber of commerce
  J. SBA, SCORE
  K. Partners, board members
II. Organization
  A. Federal ID number
  B. DBA ("doing business as," fictitious business name)
  C. Partnership agreement
  D. Corporate bylaws
  E. Employees
  F. State ID number
III. Licenses, Permits
  A. Business license
  B. Resale permit
  C. Department of health
  D. Beer, wine, liquor
  E. Fire inspection permit
  F. Other
IV. Location
  A. Lease review (lawyer)
  B. First and last month's rent (rent payments during improvements may be negotiable)
  C. Security deposit
  D. Leasehold improvements (negotiate with landlord)
    1. Signage
    2. Lighting
    3. Electrical/plumbing
    4. Flooring
    5. Construction
  E. Insurance
  F. Security system
  G. Utilities, deposits, estimated monthly costs
    1. Electric
    2. Gas
    3. Water
    4. Phone installation
    5. Internet services
  H. Other
V. Auto
  A. Auto/Truck(s)
    1. New/used
    2. Lease/purchase
  B. Insurance
  C. Maintenance, repairs
VI. Equipment
  A. Office
  B. Retail space
  C. Warehouse
  D. Manufacturing area
  E. Kitchen
  F. Dining area
  G. Communication (fax/phone/Internet)
  H. Computer hardware and software
VII. Furniture
  A. Tables
  B. Chairs
  C. Desks
  D. File cabinets
  E. Workbenches
  F. Equipment
    1. Storage cabinets
    2. Display cases
    3. Refrigeration
    4. Computer
    5. Shelving/storage
    6. Safe
    7. Other
VIII. Insurance
  A. Liability
  B. Workers compensation
  C. Key man
  D. Health
  E. Business
  F. Auto
  G. Fire
  H. Other
IX. Office Supplies
  A. Business cards
  B. Letterhead
  C. Other
X. Inventory (What are the minimum/maximum average inventory requirements needed on hand to do business on your first day?)
XI. Advertising and Promotion
  A. Business cards
  B. Fliers/brochures
  C. Displays
  D. Ad layouts
  E. Media costs (newspaper, radio, other)
  F. Web site development
  G. Other
XII. Banking
  A. Checking account
  B. Savings/money market account
  C. Credit
    1. Credit cards
    2. Personal lines of credit
    3. Loans
    4. Credit from suppliers/vendors
    5. Merchant services
XIII. Employees
  A. Application/employment forms completed
  B. Training program
  C. Tax forms
  D. Payroll services

figure **8.2**

Financial Start-Up Requirements Worksheet

Initial Expenses
Legal
Office supplies
Office equipment
Brochures/design/letterhead, business cards, etc.
Web site development
Utility deposits and installation
Rent deposits
Licenses
Cell phones/pagers
Banking set-up fees
Computer
Software
Insurance
Construction costs
Installation of fixtures and equipment
Phone and fax systems, Internet servers/routers
Other _____

Total Initial Expenses

Monthly Money Reserves
Salary of owner-manager
All other salaries and wages
Payroll taxes
Rent
Advertising/promotion
Freight
Utilities
Operating supplies
Telephone/cell phones
Internet
Insurance
Car/truck payments
Maintenance and repairs
Taxes
Travel/equipment
Banking charges
Legal and professional fees
Other _____
Other _____

Total Monthly Expenses

Start-up Inventory

Other Expenses
Signage
Fixtures
Equipment
Other _____
Other _____

Total Other Expenses

Total Start-Up Costs

(Total initial expenses + [Total monthly expenses × 3 to 6 months] +
Start-up inventory + Other expenses)

Long-Term or Fixed Assets
Land
Plant
Equipment
Other _____
Other _____

Total Long-Term or Fixed Assets

Total Start-Up Requirements

"What?" I asked. "Did you say $3,000?" We had around $10,000 in the kitty, but that was earmarked for emergencies.

"That's right. You're a new commercial customer with a good credit rating. That's the reason the figure's so low. For your tonnage," they said, "it's right on the money."

"Tonnage? What tonnage?"

"Your air conditioner," they said. "You have a 5-ton unit on your roof. Figure you run it for a month, that's $1,100. The other $400 is for lights and gas."

"But we're not planning to run it!" I said. "The breeze here is terrific. We don't need the air conditioner."

"Sorry, ma'am. Our policy is pretty clear. As I said, sometimes we get 3 months' deposit, but for your business, we'll only require the two. Is there anything else I can help you with today?"

"No," I said. "Nothing."

If you exceed your budgeted start-up costs, your first year may be very difficult. Think of every way you can save: buy used, borrow, barter, or beg. Conserve cash at all times. One owner of five successful businesses worth more than $5 million demands his staff check the local library before purchasing any book. *Cash is king!* Especially at the beginning, do not squander cash. Norm Brodsky in the Key Points article at the end of the chapter reinforces the concept of cash as king.

BOOTSTRAPPING

It is no secret that start-ups are expensive, and those first few months can be a make-it-or-break-it time for the entrepreneur. When you are out of money, you are out of business! This is definitely the time to care passionately about each and every dollar that comes in and goes out of your business. Guard each dollar jealously so you can make your dollars work efficiently. If you work the dollars you do have, you will not have to shake the money tree so hard to find additional dollars.

Tips to Conserve

1. Ask your customers for **cash deposits** when they place orders.
2. Persuade vendors to give you more **trade credit** or **dating** and more time to pay.
3. Lease your equipment. Investigate purchasing used equipment.
4. Run a lean operation; do not waste anything.
5. Work out of your home if you can for as long as you can.
6. Get your landlord to make **on-site improvements** and finance the cost over the term of the lease.
7. Keep track of everything. Try to resell whatever waste or byproducts you have in your business.
8. Take markdowns quickly on **dead goods**. If they do not sell at markdown, dump or donate them. Turn merchandise.
9. Use as little commercial space as you can.
10. If your customers do not visit your business facility, it does not have to be highly visible or attractive.

Action Step 38

Attach Price Tags to Starting Your Business

Sit down at your desk and look around with new eyes.

1. List the items on your desk. Include pencils, paper, telephone, computer, fax, business cards, calendar, and so on. List the desk itself, the lamp, chair, bookcase, filing cabinet, and coffee machine. Now go through the drawers, writing down every item you use to make your work run easier and smoother.
2. List your expenditures for things you cannot see, some of which you might take for granted. These include such things as insurance, rent, utilities, taxes, legal and accounting services, and so on. (Chapter 12 covers insurance in depth.)
3. Beside each tangible item and each intangible expense, write down how much it will cost.
4. Use the Start-up Worksheets (Figure 8.1 and Figure 8.2) to serve as guides as you develop your start-up costs. If you have located more specific worksheets for your particular business; you should use those to complete this Action Step.

As you gather more information, you will be able to refine the numbers on the worksheets. By the time you reach Chapter 15, you will be able to produce an accurate representation of start-up requirements for your Business Plan.

Cash deposits Funds paid in advance of delivery

Trade credit or Dating A vendor's extension of the payment term into the near future

On-site improvements Modifications to real estate to accommodate the special needs of the business

Dead goods Merchandise no longer in demand

Action Step 39

Preparing for Surprises

Take time to brainstorm a list of surprises that could cost you money or time and thus threaten the survival of your business. Use our checklists to help you get started.

1. Talk to business owners in your industry. Ask them to tell you how they handled unfortunate surprises. Once you select a site, ask your fellow business neighbors about their experiences and surprises you may face in your location.

2. Talk to vendors, suppliers, customers, and insurance brokers. Ask. Probe.

3. When you finish your list, put a checkmark beside each item that may incur additional costs, and then try to estimate what those potential costs may be. How will you cover unforeseen expenses? How much money should you put aside for unexpected events?

Continue to revise these lists as you gather information. When you reach Chapter 15, the information will help you in writing your final Business Plan.

Liquid cash Funds that are immediately available, usually held in checking or other accounts

Entrepreneurial guru A wise person on the sidelines who can help you with advice and counsel

11. When you have to borrow money, shop around. The most expensive cash is the cash you never planned for.

12. Make sure your liquid cash is earning interest.

13. Add employees carefully.

14. Open a line of credit and establish a credit card for the business if at all possible.

15. Make "conserve cash" your firm's mantra.

Norm Brodsky, veteran entrepreneur and *Inc.* columnist advises:

Entrepreneurs usually put the blame of failure on lack of capital. But more often, the problem is how they use the capital they have. Forget about image. Forget about making a splash. Forget about everything except getting your capital to last until you do not need it anymore. You do not have to give up your dreams. Dreams are important. Just wait until you can afford them.

Source: *Inc.*, December 1995, p. 27, *http://www.inc.com/magazine/19951201/2505. html* (Accessed July 21, 2004).

Seeking Financial Advice and Support

There are a boatload of surprises awaiting every entrepreneur who enters the marketplace. We talked about Plan B, formulating your strategy, checking and double-checking your market, and peering into the future to see what lies ahead. There is another angle to planning; it is called *seeking advice*.

Think for a moment about where you are right now on your road to the marketplace. You are halfway through this book. You have analyzed your skills and needs and have probed your past and surveyed your friends. You have discovered what success means to you, and you have plotted trends and found your industry segment. You have profiled your Target Customer, studied the demographics, and developed a promotional campaign. You have examined the competition and used your new eyes to find a dynamite location. Now you need to locate several **entrepreneurial gurus** for financial advice.

Where might you find a financial business guru? What about your accountant? What about the real estate broker who helped you with your search for a location? What about your business insurance specialist, your lawyer, your distributors, and your competitors? What about your SCORE counselor?

Use your network to help locate financial advisors. Show them your list of potential surprises and financial projections and ask for their advice. Ask them for their ideas about what other surprises might also be in store for you.

PRICING YOUR PRODUCT OR SERVICE

In principle, the price you charge for your product or service must be acceptable to you and to your customer. From your customers' perspective, an acceptable price depends on competitive alternatives for your product or service in addition to the perceived value. As for you, your price can be based on any number of pricing considerations. But it is fairly safe to say that ultimately, you will be trying to maximize sales revenue and profits.

New businesses often make the mistake of charging either too little or too much for their product or service. To help you avoid making one of these mistakes, we outline four pricing methods. But use caution: The process of setting

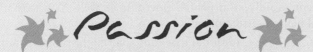

Opportunities for Passionate Scientists

Scientists Without Borders, a new global initiative conceived by the New York Academy of Sciences (NYAS) and the United Nations Millennium Project, today unveiled a Web site and database designed to match needs and resources among individuals and organizations working to improve quality of life in the developing world.

"Scientists Without Borders is a pioneering initiative that will link and mobilize institutions and people who apply science to improve lives and livelihoods in developing countries," said NYAS President Ellis Rubinstein, who chairs the Scientists Without Borders Advisory Council. "Whether exploring low-cost green energy technologies, improving strategies for sustainable agriculture, or developing tools to prevent and treat disease, science builds knowledge that advances global efforts to enhance health and prosperity."

Scientists Without Borders' first project is a Web site whose cornerstone is a simple yet powerful database that will link institutions and individuals across boundaries. Through a collection of structured and easily navigated profiles, the database provides registered users with a platform for addressing gaps and sharing knowledge, resources, needs, and expertise—allowing individuals and organizations to collaborate more effectively.

"Across the globe, groundbreaking science-based activities have the potential to transform the lives of people and communities," said Dr. Jeffrey Sachs, Special Advisor to the United Nations on the Millennium Development Goals and Director of the Earth Institute at Columbia University. "Scientists Without Borders will bring them together across organizations, disciplines, and distances to match needs with resources and benefit the world's poorest citizens."

To date, nearly 400 experts, 80 projects, and 150 organizations from across the globe have completed profiles. The database captures key data from scientific institutions, projects, and individual researchers, and gives other users access to this information. New members enter their details and those of their projects. An easy-to-use interface and comprehensive search tool allows individuals and organizations to quickly locate potential partners, match needs with resources, and discover who is doing what where.

"Scientists Without Borders offers tremendous new opportunities for international scientific collaboration—but to succeed, we need more individuals and organizations to sign up, submit profiles, and log on," said Rubinstein. "While Scientists Without Borders has received generous financial support from a range of companies and institutions, we call on international donors to help us maintain and expand our efforts."

The initiative offers a low-bandwidth version of the Web site and is developing mobile communication tools to give potential users access to the database even in areas with limited internet connectivity.

"Developing nations often suffer from lack of communication and insufficient technical resources, impeding effective scientific collaboration," said Dr. Mohamed H.A. Hassan, Executive Director of the Academy of Sciences for the Developing World. "By giving us a forum to share knowledge, needs, and resources, Scientists Without Borders will give us the power to collaborate more effectively."

Source: *http://www.nyas.org/about/newsDetails.asp?newsID=245* (Accessed June 23, 2008).

Markup A percentage of your cost of sales that is added to the cost to determine selling price

a price can become quite complicated and technical, and in many industries, changes occur rapidly, and profits fluctuate as well. You may need to seek professional help in setting prices.

Retail stores have traditional **markups** that might range from two to four times the cost of the product. Direct mail and catalogs may have markups of four to seven times the product cost. To price your products correctly so that you are able to realize a profit, you need to recognize *all* of the costs involved in delivering your product or service. Figure 8.3, Pricing Considerations, provides information on the elements involved in pricing electrical services.

Supply, demand, and your target market will ultimately determine the pricing of your products. Be careful not to price your product too low; customers may think it is cheap and will not buy. There are two fools in regard to pricing: one prices too high, and one prices too low. Recognize that some items are price-sensitive and some are not. You will be able to increase your margins on those products and services that have little price sensitivity.

Market research and analysis of your competitors' pricing and offerings should provide you with a starting point. In addition to the competition your product or service faces, you should also assess the customer service demanded by consumers. Both of these areas were covered in the Action Steps in Chapter 5. As mentioned previously, price is one of the most difficult elements to compete on and still realize a profit. No matter how well you plan your pricing, you need to be flexible and make adjustments quickly if necessary.

As you price your products or services, include a percentage for bad debts; if you are in retailing, also price in 3 to 5 percent for employee and customer

figure **8.3**

Pricing Considerations for an Electrical Contractor (sample from the back of a local contractor's bill)

Insurance (workers compensation, health, liability, theft, property, etc.)	Training and Retraining	Licensing	Trucks (maintenance, gas, repairs, insurance, licensing)

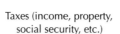

Electrical Equipment and Supplies	Taxes (income, property, social security, etc.)	Advertising	Tools and Supplies

Rent and Utilities	Administrative Costs (scheduling and billing, ordering, stocking supplies)	Salaries and Benefits	Business Expenses (accountant, legal, computers)

theft—a fact of life. In many businesses, theft from outsiders is even a larger issue. Professional thieves have targeted high-tech manufacturers that produce commodity products. After stealing the products, they are relabeled and dumped into the marketplace, where prices fall rapidly. Thus, we suggest you stay vigilant on any theft activities within your industry. Also, contact associations for estimated loss percentages, and heed their advice on loss prevention.

Common Pricing Methods

1. Competitor-Based Pricing

In Chapter 5, we asked you to review your competitor touchpoint analysis and state the prices of your products or services relative to your customers' perception of the competition. In fact, we were asking you to calculate your price relative to the market. We wanted you to find out what prices were acceptable to your potential customers given their possible choices and competitive options. Many new business owners begin their pricing strategy by first determining what prices or price range the target market will accept relative to the competition. This is often referred to as competitor-based pricing and is sometimes referred to as market-based pricing.

Competitor-based pricing or **Market-based pricing** Setting a price range whose main focus is competitor pricing

The price of your product or service depends on your competitors' prices, but you will also have to figure out your costs. If the market price cannot cover your costs, then your business is going to lose money. And naturally, you want to make sure that the price you charge is enough to yield a profit. This leads us to a second approach, called cost-plus pricing or profit-based pricing.

Cost-plus pricing or **Profit-based pricing** Setting a price that covers all costs plus a profit

2. Cost-Plus Pricing

One of the most common errors novice business owners make is pricing based solely on the costs to produce the product or service. And many entrepreneurs do not figure out all the costs involved in providing their services. Thus, Figure 8.3 lists out all the costs involved in offering electrical contract services and Action Step 40 will ask you to do the same. If you set your price based solely on cost, your business will not make any profit. The price you charge must also take into consideration your profit expectations. After all, you do not want to sell your service or product at the price you paid for it. There are different methods for calculating price to take profit into account. A simple and common formula for estimating price per unit follows:

Selling price = total cost per unit + estimated dollar profit per unit

Your costs for producing a particular product or supplying a particular service will include three broad costing groups: 1) direct material costs, or your cost of supplies; 2) direct cost of labor for producing your product or service; and 3) overhead, or fixed expenses, which are indirect costs such as rent and advertising.

Your estimated profit will depend on a number of factors: the type of product or service, the market demand, your costs, and so on. If available, rely on your primary and secondary research, such as industry averages for your type of business.

Using cost-plus pricing provides an established floor price for your product or service in many industries. This is the minimum price that you can accept to meet your profit targets. Second, the price you will be able to charge will be determined by the demand for your product or service, as well as by your competition.

Keystone pricing or **Industry-norm pricing** Setting a price that depends on generally accepted industry standards

3. Industry Norm or Keystone Pricing

Some types of businesses charge prices according to certain generally accepted or industry standards. This is called keystone pricing or industry-norm pricing. Two examples of this approach might be setting the price at triple the cost of goods sold or two times the labor costs.

The concept of markups might also help you determine your price. A markup is a percentage of your cost of sales that you add to the cost to determine your selling price. Note that you do not include overhead costs in your mark-up calculation; include only your costs for materials and supplies. For example, if the selling price is $3 and the cost is $2, the markup is calculated as follows:

$$\text{Markup} = (\text{price} - \text{cost})/\text{cost}$$
$$= (\$3 - \$2)/\$2$$
$$= 1/2$$
$$= .50, \text{ or } 50 \text{ percent}$$

Markups are calculated in some cases as a percentage of costs and in others as a percentage of the selling price. In the above example, the 50 percent markup was calculated as a percentage of cost. If we had calculated the markup as a percentage of selling price, then the markup would be 33 percent, or ($3 − $2)/$3.

If you know what the standard or industry markup is for your product or service, then you can estimate a selling price. For example, if you are selling greeting cards, and you know that the industry markup on the selling price is 50 percent, then you can determine your selling price. Your final price will ultimately depend on direct and indirect costs, the competition and the market demand.

4. Premium Pricing

Premium pricing Setting the highest price target consumers will pay for a product or service given their needs, values, and the competitive options

Premium pricing means setting the highest price target consumers will pay for a product or service given their needs and values and the competitive options. Your ultimate goal or strategy is to try to focus on a specific market segment, then create uniqueness and differentiate your product or service in the eyes of the customer. Some pricing analysts refer to premium pricing as the highest price the market will bear. This differentiation strategy will make your product or service more inelastic and less sensitive to price changes. If your product or service is inelastic, it means that your customers, on average, will be willing to buy your product or service even if your prices are on the high side relative to those of your competitors—because your customer values the fact that your product is different. But remember, you must also be able to see to it that this ceiling or premium price more than covers your costs and yields the desired profit. Premium pricing is sometimes used in the introductory phase of products and services that are unique, and thus buyers are willing to pay extra for early acquisition.

Other Pricing Methods   These four broad methods are not the only options available. For example, common pricing strategies used mainly by larger firms include:

Penetration pricing Setting the initial or introductory price artificially low to capture sales

Price skimming Pricing high to attract customers who buy the newest items and want to be trend setters

- **Penetration pricing**—setting the initial or introductory price artificially low to capture sales
- **Price skimming**—setting prices high initially to appeal to consumers who are not price sensitive, then lowering prices as competitors enter the market

Pricing Strategies

Depending on your business idea, you might need additional information and guidance than that provided above. Also, many businesses operate in highly volatile pricing environments, where you must be constantly aware of the major price fluctuations caused by commodity price changes and shifts in supply and demand. Those who are selling on the Internet will find a myriad of pricing strategies, because competitors' prices are clearly evident and can be researched by both you and your customers. Some online vendors change their prices daily or in real time to reflect competitors' prices.

The price you charge for your product or service will depend on a number of factors, including costs of production, market considerations, competitive forces, geography, size of business, product, service distribution channel, and economy. We suggest that you begin your pricing analysis by first considering the premium price strategy, then follow up by making sure that this price will cover your costs and lead to a profit. Many small business owners think they should start out with low prices to attract customers, but in most cases, this is a mistake. In general, small businesses should not aim to sell products or services at the lowest market price. Strategies such as penetration and price skimming are approaches that should be reserved for large firms, such as Coca-Cola and Wal-Mart, who want to increase their market share and dominate the market. In developing a pricing strategy, be flexible and expect changes to occur frequently and often rapidly. Pricing comparison via the Net has changed pricing strategies dramatically.

Pat Watt of Ikebana Designs shared how difficult it is to price her unique flower arrangements, because wholesale market prices fluctuate daily depending on the weather, season, and supply. With changes in the economy, Harrison Remodelers reported, "It was like they shut off the valve" as business slowed in light of the mortgage meltdown and subsequent downturn in the economy. Complete Action Step 40 now and consider how you will deal with recessionary and inflationary pressures.

SEASONALITY SCENARIOS

For some businesses, sales will remain fairly steady from month to month. However, most businesses, especially those in retail, experience seasonal variations. From your discussions with others, you should be able to gain a handle on possible variations and work the numbers into your sales and cash-flow projections. For the bookstore Know It All, it was fairly easy to determine inventory requirements based on the information provided by the American Booksellers Association. But to determine seasonal adjustments in sales, the owners sought out several bookstore owners in nearby towns to help determine monthly profit and loss and cash-flow projections based on monthly sales variations. One local bookstore owner shared the following sales breakdown.

Monthly Sales Breakdown for Retail Bookstore

January (6.5 percent)
"January is an anticlimax to Christmas, but it is still busy because of gift certificates and exchanges. I run some good specials at the end of January, prior to taking yearly inventory. Even though sales are slowing down, I have to order new titles because publishers (our suppliers) are giving me advance notice of their spring lists."

February (4.5 percent) and March (5 percent)
"Very quiet. I take inventory, weed out stuff that didn't sell, send it back, and usually feel bad when I see the restocking fees. I meet publishers' reps who are out on the road pushing new titles. On March 15, I have an Ides-of-March sale. Next year I'm planning a St. Patrick's Day tie-in."

Action Step 40
Discovering Costs and Developing a Fair Price

1. Review Action Steps 28, 29, and 30. If you have learned further information, revise your answers and utilize them in developing your pricing strategy.

2. Read trade magazines, and then talk with business owners, association representatives, distributors, your competitors, and possibly even other owners in similar lines of business to make a list—such as the one in Figure 8.3—to encompass all of the many costs you will incur to get the product or service to your client. Most entrepreneurs will not recognize all of the costs involved and will therefore price their products or services below cost. As a result, they will not make a profit.

3. Once you have made the list of the costs and activities, take the time and energy to determine the actual expenses involved with each. BizStats.com (see Incredible Resource) may be of benefit in your research.

4. Price your product using the primary pricing method utilized in your industry.

5. How do you want your product or service to be seen from the customer's viewpoint compared to your competitors? Business Plan readers will be interested in how you developed your pricing strategy from a numbers and a research standpoint. Justify your reasoning with facts and figures.

6. Discuss any of the major pricing issues your firm will need to deal with.

7. Continue to add relevant pricing information to this Action Step as you work through the rest of the chapters.

8. Complete a break-even analysis once you have completed the chapter (see Figure 8.9).

incredibleresource

BizStats.com

Your business needs to present reasonable sales and financial projections. If you have the back-up data to support each of your numbers, lenders will feel more comfortable that you have done your homework, and you also should feel more comfortable going forth with a business that can support your projections.

Locating financial statistics and ratios to benchmark your projections on can sometimes prove difficult, but one site, *http://BizStats.com*, may lead you directly to the numbers you are seeking. If you want to find out sales per square foot, retail sales per store, safest and riskiest small businesses, sizes of various industries and markets, restaurant benchmarks, and much more, log on to BizStats. Examples of their online statistics follow:

A) Industry Profitability: Sole Proprietorships (U.S. National Averages)

What does the average small business owner get to keep from each dollar of sales? The following table reports most recently available national averages for profitability as a percentage of total revenue for sole proprietorships. Since sole proprietors do not pay a salary to themselves, costs do not reflect the value of owner labor. Since an owner becomes increasingly reliant on employees as a business grows, the following results should be viewed in the context of the overall size of the business. For example, small proprietorships with no employees besides the owner will report zero payroll costs and a higher net income percentage than a larger business with several employees.

Retail Trade	All Proprietorships	Proprietorships with Net Income Only	Percentage of Proprietorships with Net Income
Motor vehicle and parts dealers	4.3%	6.4%	65.8%
Furniture and home furnishing stores	7.2%	13.1%	66.7%
Electronic and appliance stores	9.2%	12.3%	66.8%
Building materials and garden supplies	7.0%	10.4%	78.1%
Food and beverage stores	4.2%	6.0%	72.9%
Health and personal care stores	12.1%	15.7%	49.5%
Gasoline stations	2.2%	3.3%	62.9%
Clothing and accessories stores	9.6%	13.6%	59.5%
Sporting goods, hobby, book, and music stores	4.5%	12.3%	55.0%
General merchandise stores	8.4%	10.2%	80.9%
Miscellaneous store retailers	6.5%	13.4%	50.7%
Nonstore retailers	11.0%	23.6%	48.8%

Source: *http://bizstats.com/spprofitscurrent.htm* (Accessed February 28, 2005).

B) Sole Proprietor Annual Average Sales, Income, and Expenses: Heavy and Civil Engineering Construction

Sales	100.0%
Inventory (% of Sales)	12.34%
Cost of Sales	45.29%
COS-Labor Portion	5.23%
Gross Profit	54.71%
Salary-Wages	3.38%
Contract Labor-Commisions	2.71%
Rent	1.57%
Taxes	1.01%
Interest paid	1.54%
Amort. & Dep.	5.88%
Advertising	0.39%
Benefits-Pension	0.19%
Insurance (nonhealth)	2.11%
Home Office Expense	0.36%
Other SG&A Exp. SEE DETAIL >>	15.35%
Total Expenses	34.49%
Net Profit	20.24%
Total Direct Labor & NP	31.56%

http://www.bizstats.com/reports/sp.asp?industry=Heavy+and+civil+engineering+construction&var=&profType=income&coding=4.0400

(continued)

(continued)

C) Corporation Average Balance Sheet: Industrial Machinery

Cash	16.91%	Accounts Payable	8.33%
Receivables	17.42%	Loans Notes Payable	3.22%
Inventory	10.69%	Other Current Liabilities	10.69%
Other Current Assets	4.46%	Total Current Liabilities	22.24%
Total Current Assets	49.48%	Other Long-Term Liabilities	20.66%
Fixed Assets	24.77%	Total Liabilities	42.9%
Other Non-Current Assets	25.74%	Net Worth	57.10%
Total Assets	100.00%	Total Liabilities Net Worth	100.00%

http://www.bizstats.com/reports/corp.asp?industry=iindustrial+machinery&profType=balance&var=&coding=33.3.200

D) S-Corp Annual Financial Ratios: Gasoline Stations

Return on Sales (%)	1.68	Current Ratio	1.63
Return on Assets (%)	10.92	Inventory Turnover (x)	58.63
Return on Net Worth (%)	38.11	Assets:Sales (%)	0.15
Quick Ratio	0.94	Tot Liabilities:Net Worth (x)	2.49

http://www.bizstats.com/reports/scorp.asp?industry=Gasoline+stations&profType=ratios&var=&coding=7.0700

April (5 percent)
"Still slow. We get a slight jump in sales after the tenth, mostly because spring vacations give people time to read."

May (8 percent) and June (8 percent)
"Two holidays—Mother's Day and Father's Day—plus weddings and graduations give us our second-busiest season. Art books and gift editions do well, as well as encyclopedias and how-to's."

July (6 percent) and August (7 percent)
"We're not in a tourist area, and summers for us are slow. We sell mostly easy-to-read paperbacks and lots of landscaping books. Our minds, though, are on ordering books for Christmas."

September (9 percent)
"Back-to-school purchases. We're interviewing people for Christmas jobs and making last-minute purchases of gift items."

October (10 percent) and November (12 percent)
"The start of the busy season. Customers sense it, and we can feel the momentum. The rush is just around the corner. We usually hire more sales help at this time."

December (19 percent)
"The crush. Our computer does a great job of tracking sales. It is different every year, but with 2 years of great data gathering behind me, I am getting a feel for what really happens. And that helps us plan ahead for the next year."

After the first year of business, seasonal sales forecasting will become easier. Keep very careful records the first year so that you will know how your own peaks and valleys correlate with the seasonality of your selected industry. Most businesses are seasonal, and you will need to develop strong control systems to manage your financial resources. Begin to identify alternative sources of credit, and find ways to collect cash from customers so that you will be able to handle cash flow changes.

One dentist found his business could vary as much as 30 percent per month. People bring their children in during the summer months for checkups,

Action Step 41

Complete Seasonality Scenario and a Projected Profit and Loss (Income) Statement

1. Write a seasonality scenario for a typical year in your business. You can do part of the scenario with new eyes—just look around at obvious forces such as weather, holidays, buying patterns, etc.—and relate these to the life-cycle stage of your product, location, and competition. You will need to glean other information from business owners and from trade associations.

2. Now answer the following: When does your selected industry collect money? Before the sale? During? After? Long after? When will you have to pay for your inventory? What is the shortest time lag you can see between the time you pay for inventory and the time you receive money (payment, hard dollars) for the sale of that inventory? What is the longest time lag? When will you declare a lag a bad debt? If you are in manufacturing and have to alter, reshape, or rebuild raw materials into a product, what kind of time lag will there be?

3. Generate monthly numbers for the year:
   a. Using data from trade associations and small-business owners, forecast your sales for the year.
   b. Figure your cost of goods sold and subtract that figure from sales. This gives you your gross profit.
   c. Add up all expenses and subtract them from gross profit. Note in your income statement how you arrived at each figure. This gives you the net profit before taxes.
   d. Subtract taxes. (Uncle Sam uses what we might call "old eyes." You will be taxed on paper profit, so you have to build in this figure.) The figure you arrive at is your net profit after taxes for the year.

and many insurance companies' dental allowances need to be utilized by the end of June or December, thus causing a large increase in business during those two months and the summer. Contact your association and competitors to determine how your firm's sales may be subject to monthly changes; complete a seasonality scenario now, and use it as you complete your projected income statement in Action Step 41.

ECONOMIC CYCLES

If you are in business for more than a few years, you will begin to recognize the economic cycles of not only your specific business but those of the broader economy as well. When an economic slowdown hit in 2008, many firms were caught by the severe downdraft in sales and subsequent profits. Many new firms that had not saved for that proverbial "rainy day" were caught scrambling.

> Ed Horton, Matt Kuchinsky and Kevin Ryan, CPAs and partners in the accounting firm Citrin Cooperman & Company, offer their accounting tips in case of a downturn:
>
> **Keep an even closer eye on your budget and receivables.** "Review expenses, sales, margins, cash flow, and other indicators so that you can make informed decisions in an economy that can be shifting relatively quickly," Horton says. Also watch receivables: "They can be an indicator of how hard your clients are being hit with a downturn," Kuchinsky says.
>
> **Get tough on collecting payments.** Part of watching receivables is ensuring you have a healthy cash flow. "This includes reviewing and revising your processes for collecting payment and getting more aggressive with reminders, phone calls, and offering payment by credit card," Kuchinsky says. That last item, he says, is worth the 1.5 percent processing fee to keep the cash flowing into your business.
>
> **Negotiate with vendors.** "Many vendors will provide a discount for payment up front," Ryan says. "Others will provide discounts to loyal and longtime customers. Request an extension of credit with them so that your business can pay invoices in 60 days, and not 30."

Source: "Surviving a Slow Economy," *www.entrepreneur.com/article/printthis/191936.html* (Accessed June 20, 2008).

Recessionary periods can bring even the most successful businesses to their knees when customers do not pay. Reliance on only a few customers can make this happen even quicker. If at all possible, try not to be dependent on only a few clients. One distributor recently lost $84,000 on one account when the accountant did not review and check the credit card order. Many well-run businesses fail in recessionary times, and we again remind entrepreneurs not to take such failures personally. One formerly very successful entrepreneur shared that he paid cash for his Rolls Royce and just two years later would have been happy and lucky to drive a compact sedan.

SALES PROJECTIONS AND WHAT-IF SCENARIOS

Research is the key. The financial community wants to make sure that you spend time researching your projections, because sales drive everything else.

GLOBAL VILLAGE

globalEDGE Center for International Business Education and Research

Michigan State University's globalEDGE may be one of the best international business Web sites online. If you are considering exporting, the Country Insights section provides statistical, government, economy, and corporate information, as well as the most up-to-date information about the country. Links to sources within the country are also readily available to extend your research. In addition, a library of free online courses is available and can be accessed and completed as needed. Courses include the following:

Doing Business in Brazil, Japan, Latin America, Africa, and the European Union

Legal Systems of the World

Analyzing a Company's Ability to Export

Export Costing

Ethics

International Negotiations

General international business resource area links to trade information, marketing research, news, periodicals, and other reference materials at *http://globaledge.msu.edu*.

Action Step 41

(*continued*)

If you do not have Excel, go online to the many calculators and complete your income statements, start-up costs, and cash-flow projections. Also, as you continue your research, make specific notes to back up any figures or projections in your Business Plan. Remember that the notes section of your financial plans will be analyzed in depth by bankers and investors.

You also want to minimize surprises—even "good surprises" can wreak havoc with a well-thought-out plan if, for example, you receive ten times the orders you expected and simply do not yet have the resources to deal with them.

You have already conducted an industry overview. You may have identified total sales internationally, nationally, statewide, and in your service area. After factoring industry and local growth, determine which part of the market you can reasonably expect to penetrate in the first, second, and third years.

For your Business Plan, attach any appropriate printed data to your market research section in the appendix to prove and support your sales numbers. Fine-tune these numbers by showing your own research and including notes from industry experts that support your assumptions on projected sales. Every number you present in your Business Plan should have back-up support and be justified. When you list your competitors, estimate their market share and the part of their market that you have targeted. Projections are well-documented estimates. A third party's estimate will hold a great deal of weight for your reader, so quote as many sources as you can to support your numbers.

Lucy's projections in Figure 8.4 are based on past retail experience and research. Advertising expenses in this example are low due to the unique airport location. Rent is 22 percent of gross sales—with minimal marketing costs and a captive market, this expense is understandable. Salaries and payroll expenses are included. The owner, who will take a salary, will manage the store. If she did not take a salary, she would be putting in "sweat equity." Pay attention to

figure 8.4

Lucy's Income and Expense Projections for Various Sales Levels

Upscale Specialty Women's Boutique

Category	$50,000/mo Amount	% of Gross	$60,000/mo Amount	% of Gross	$70,000/mo Amount	% of Gross	$80,000/mo Amount	% of Gross	$90,000/mo Amount	% of Gross
Gross Sales	$600,000.00		$720,000.00		$1,080,000.00		$384,000.00		$388,800.00	
Cost of Goods	$240,000.00	40%	$288,000.00	40%	$336,000.00	40%	$384,000.00	40%	$388,800.00	36%
Gross Profit	$360,000.00	60%	$432,000.00	60%	$504,000.00	60%	$576,000.00	60%	$691,200.00	64%
Operating Expenses:										
*Salaries/Benefits/Payroll Taxes	$108,000.00	18.0%	$129,600.00	18.0%	$151,200.00	18.0%	$172,800.00	18.0%	$194,400.00	18.0%
Telephone/Pagers	$900.00		$900.00		$900.00		$900.00		$900.00	
Maintenance/Cleaning/Supplies	$600.00	0.1%	$720.00	0.1%	$840.00	0.1%	$960.00	0.1%	$1,080.00	0.1%
Insurance including Worker's Comp	$24,000.00	4.0%	$24,480.00	3.4%	$25,200.00	3.0%	$26,880.00	2.8%	$29,160.00	2.7%
**Advertising	$3,200.00	0.5%	$3,440.00	0.5%	$3,680.00	0.4%	$3,920.00	0.4%	$4,160.00	0.4%
Internet/Computer Services	$900.00		$900.00		$900.00					
***Rent	$132,000.00	22.0%	$158,400.00	22.0%	$184,800.00	22.0%	$211,200.00	22.0%	$237,600.00	22.0%
General and Administration	$60,000.00	10.0%	$72,000.00	10.0%	$84,000.00	10.0%	$96,000.00	10.0%	$108,000.00	10.0%
Operating Supplies	$4,200.00	0.7%	$5,040.00	0.7%	$5,880.00	0.7%	$6,720.00	0.7%	$7,560.00	0.7%
Banking/Merchant Services	$7,200.00	1.2%	$8,640.00	1.2%	$10,080.00	1.2%	$11,520.00	1.2%	$12,960.00	1.2%
Store Displays	$1,800.00		$1,800.00		$1,800.00		$2,880.00		$3,240.00	
Other Misc. Expenses	$1,800.00	0.3%	$2,160.00	0.3%	$2,520.00	0.3%	$2,880.00	0.3%	$3,240.00	0.3%
Total Expenses	$344,600.00	56.8%	$408,080.00	56.7%	$471,800.00	55.7%	$536,480.00	55.5%	$601,760.00	55.7%
Net Income Before Taxes	$15,400.00	2.6%	$23,920.00	3.3%	$32,200.00	3.8%	$39,520.00	4.1%	$89,440.00	8.3%

*Salaries include owner salary.
**Advertising minimal due to airport location.
***Rent based on 22% of gross sales.

the way notes have been added to Lucy's projections to explain the figures. Be sure you do the same on your projections, and be able to support and defend the notes to lenders and investors.

When projecting sales, you may want to consider doing high, low, and medium sales projections. This will allow you to make plans for your expenses and revenues based on various scenarios. With Lucy's' sales projections in hand, the owner could now begin to look at what-if scenarios. What if salaries increased by 10 percent? What if rent could be reduced by 2 percent? What if workers' compensation and other insurance increased by 3 percent? What if cost of goods sold increased by 5 percent due to increased freight charges?

During your research, you have discovered many potential financial surprises, and playing these out on paper may give you some idea of the financial impact changes and surprises could have on your bottom line.

INCOME STATEMENT AND CASH-FLOW PROJECTIONS

An income statement (Figure 8.5) tells you on paper when you are going to make a profit. Figure 8.6 graphically represents a cash-flow diagram and shows infusions of capital, sales, and the outflows of cash as well. A cash-flow projection (Figure 8.7) tells whether you can pay bills and when you will need cash infusions to keep going. Both of these projections are essential to the survival of your business. Some worksheets include both on one statement. For your Business Plan, you will be required to present monthly income statements for the first year and yearly statements for the next 3 to 4 years. Cash-flow statements may also be required on the same basis.

Income statements (see Figure 8.5) track revenue and expenses but do not tell the whole story. Even a documentary movie can only be shot from one angle at a time. Action Step 41 leads you through a monthly projected income statement. In addition, be sure to include projected cash-flow scenarios in your Business Plan.

It is nice to watch paper profits, but you must also be alert to what is happening to real cash. Figure 8.6 shows the typical pattern of cash flows.

Projections involve more than just sales. You also need to project the turnaround time for collections and other time lags so you can have a feel for the way cash will flow through your business. You need to discover all expense categories involved with your business to be able to make proper projections. Forecasting your income and cash flow is like projecting a moving picture of your business. If you are careful in how you prepare your numbers, that movie will be reasonably accurate.

Cash-flow projections are a tool used to help you control money. The lifeblood of any business is cash flow, and many businesses are profitable but fail because of cash-flow problems. Without completing pro forma cash flows, entrepreneurs can easily underestimate their cash needs and fail early on. *Inc.* magazine columnist Philip Campbell provides the following hard and fast cash-flow rules:

figure **8.5**

Casey's Auto Restoration Monthly Income Statement

Profit and Loss YTD Comparison

	July	% of Income	August	% of Income	September	% of Income
Ordinary Income/Expense						
Income						
EPA Fees	37.54	0.2%	29.50	0.1%	41.50	0.1%
Labor	12,952.70	51.9%	13,474.10	42.9%	19,135.60	51.8%
Paint and Materials	2,312.00	9.3%	2,871.20	9.2%	3,820.80	10.3%
Parts	8,405.35	33.7%	12,729.12	40.6%	12,259.07	33.2%
Storage and Towing Fees	386.00	1.5%	558.00	1.8%	0.00	0.0%
Sublet Labor	842.00	3.4%	1,717.00	5.5%	1,669.60	4.5%
Total Income	24,935.59	100.0%	31,378.92	100.0%	36,926.57	100.0%
Expense						
Advertising	231.00	0.9%	20.00	0.1%	125.00	0.3%
Automobile Expense	88.74	0.4%	141.45	0.5%	88.92	0.2%
Bad Debts	0.00	0.0%	0.00	0.0%	199.16	0.5%
Bank Service Charges	73.85	0.3%	82.68	0.3%	82.28	0.2%
Cost of Sales						
Paint	1,826.36	7.3%	1,731.68	5.5%	1,317.84	3.6%
Parts	9,248.52	37.1%	10,133.31	32.3%	4,557.14	12.3%
Sublet	3,743.69	15.0%	4,949.78	15.8%	5,280.50	14.3%
Towing	361.00	1.4%	30.00	0.1%	376.00	1.0%
Total Cost of Sales	15,179.57	60.9%	16,844.77	53.7%	11,531.48	31.2%
DMV Renewal	0.00	0.0%	0.00	0.0%	0.00	0.0%
Dues and Subscriptions	0.00	0.0%	0.00	0.0%	88.70	0.2%
Equipment Lease	0.00	0.0%	700.00	2.2%	420.00	1.1%
Insurance						
Fire	130.00	0.5%	130.00	0.4%	0.00	0.0%
Health	0.00	0.0%	0.00	0.0%	0.00	0.0%
Liability Insurance	210.00	0.8%	0.00	0.0%	0.00	0.0%
Other	0.00	0.0%	130.00	0.4%	0.00	0.0%
Total Insurance	340.00	1.4%	260.00	0.8%	0.00	0.0%
Interest Expense						
Finance Charge	0.00	0.0%	0.00	0.0%	0.00	0.0%
Other	0.00	0.0%	717.81	2.3%	125.00	0.3%
Total Interest Expense	0.00	0.0%	717.81	2.3%	125.00	0.3%
Licenses and Permits	0.00	0.0%	0.00	0.0%	290.00	0.8%
Miscellaneous	0.00	0.0%	0.00	0.0%	0.00	0.0%
Office Supplies	293.83	1.2%	123.86	0.4%	238.72	0.6%
Payroll Expenses	3,056.88	12.3%	2,971.14	9.5%	2,712.78	7.3%
Professional Fees						
Accounting	0.00	0.0%	0.00	0.0%	0.00	0.0%
Environmental	0.00	0.0%	0.00	0.0%	0.00	0.0%
Total Professional Fees	0.00	0.0%	0.00	0.0%	0.00	0.0%
Rent	2,625.00	10.5%	3,245.00	10.3%	5,260.00	14.2%
Repairs						
Equipment Repairs	0.00	0.0%	0.00	0.0%	0.00	0.0%
Total Repairs	0.00	0.0%	0.00	0.0%	0.00	0.0%
Supplies						
Office	42.52	0.2%	45.40	0.1%	59.00	0.2%
Shop	484.56	1.9%	500.57	1.6%	550.02	1.5%
Tools	0.00	0.0%	0.00	0.0%	0.00	0.0%
Total Supplies	527.08	2.1%	545.97	1.7%	609.02	1.6%
Taxes						
Property	1,048.30	4.2%	32.14	0.1%	877.20	2.4%
Total Taxes	1,048.30	4.2%	32.14	0.1%	877.20	2.4%
Telephone	0.00	0.0%	549.43	1.8%	118.02	0.3%
Utilities						
Cable	43.19	0.2%	43.19	0.1%	43.19	0.1%
Gas and Electric	343.99	1.4%	310.70	1.0%	312.19	0.8%
Trash	140.53	0.6%	101.62	0.3%	0.00	0.0%
Water	53.95	0.2%	51.39	0.2%	54.19	0.1%
Total Utilities	581.66	2.3%	506.90	1.6%	409.57	1.1%
Total Expense	24,045.91	96.4%	26,741.15	85.2%	23,175.85	62.8%
Net Ordinary Income	889.68	3.6%	4,637.77	14.8%	13,750.72	37.2%
Other Income/Expense						
Other Income						
Interest Income	0.82	0.0%	1.40	0.0%	0.91	0.0%
Total Other Income	0.82	0.0%	1.40	0.0%	0.91	0.0%
Net Other Income	0.82	0.0%	1.40	0.0%	0.91	0.0%
Net Income Before Taxes	890.50	3.6%	4,639.17	14.8%	13,751.63	37.2%

October	% of Income	November	% of Income	December	% of Income	Jan.-Dec.	% of Income
26.46	0.1%	27.70	0.1%	32.50	0.1%	358.82	0.1%
11,543.70	50.2%	10,817.10	57.9%	20,062.41	39.6%	164,322.43	46.0%
2,710.20	11.8%	2,451.50	13.1%	3,847.35	7.6%	35,018.95	9.8%
7,589.52	33.0%	5,102.55	27.3%	23,705.18	46.8%	141,726.85	39.7%
283.00	1.1%	0.00	0.0%	252.00	0.5%	2,490.00	0.7%
879.00	3.8%	273.00	1.5%	2,781.78	5.5%	13,170.12	3.7%
23,011.88	100.0%	18,671.85	100.0%	50,681.22	100.0%	357,087.17	100.0%
0.00	0.0%	60.00	0.3%	0.00	0.0%	496.00	0.1%
125.90	0.5%	166.27	0.9%	174.72	0.3%	910.46	0.3%
0.00	0.0%	0.00	0.0%	757.68	1.5%	984.84	0.3%
119.81	0.5%	119.92	0.6%	77.15	0.2%	1,466.37	0.4%
1,067.88	4.6%	1,881.73	10.1%	2,016.98	4.0%	21,094.92	5.9%
5,052.40	22.0%	8,428.09	45.1%	9,096.16	17.9%	107,068.30	30.0%
3,387.50	14.7%	6,504.95	34.8%	6,461.69	12.7%	58,992.54	16.5%
252.00	1.1%	0.00	0.0%	271.00	0.5%	1,718.00	0.5%
9,759.78	42.4%	16,814.77	90.1%	17,845.83	35.2%	188,873.76	52.9%
0.00	0.0%	0.00	0.0%	0.00	0.0%	49.00	0.0%
0.00	0.0%	80.00	0.4%	0.00	0.0%	257.40	0.1%
0.00	0.0%	0.00	0.0%	0.00	0.0%	6,020.00	1.7%
0.00	0.0%	0.00	0.0%	0.00	0.0%	260.00	0.1%
0.00	0.0%	69.00	0.4%	0.00	0.0%	256.00	0.1%
0.00	0.0%	253.00	1.4%	0.00	0.0%	673.00	0.2%
0.00	0.0%	0.00	0.0%	0.00	0.0%	130.00	0.0%
0.00	0.0%	322.00	1.7%	0.00	0.0%	1,319.00	0.4%
0.00	0.0%	325.12	1.7%	110.46	0.2%	1,015.59	0.3%
0.00	0.0%	0.00	0.0%	0.00	0.0%	842.81	0.2%
0.00	0.0%	325.12	1.7%	110.46	0.2%	1,858.40	0.5%
0.00	0.0%	0.00	0.0%	478.54	0.9%	1,584.25	0.4%
0.00	0.0%	0.00	0.0%	1,000.00	2.0%	1,000.00	0.3%
41.20	0.2%	152.33	0.8%	37.00	0.1%	2,932.67	0.8%
2,841.96	12.3%	3,200.20	17.1%	2,712.78	5.4%	33,332.39	9.3%
0.00	0.0%	0.00	0.0%	0.00	0.0%	350.00	0.1%
0.00	0.0%	0.00	0.0%	0.00	0.0%	204.01	0.1%
0.00	0.0%	0.00	0.0%	0.00	0.0%	554.01	0.2%
0.00	0.0%	2,755.00	14.8%	5,384.50	10.6%	33,811.15	9.5%
0.00	0.0%	0.00	0.0%	0.00	0.0%	340.00	0.1%
0.00	0.0%	0.00	0.0%	0.00	0.0%	340.00	0.1%
0.00	0.0%	73.80	0.4%	152.97	0.3%	531.73	0.1%
718.20	3.1%	428.31	2.3%	115.29	0.2%	6,555.32	1.8%
0.00	0.0%	0.00	0.0%	0.00	0.0%	52.10	0.0%
718.20	3.1%	502.11	2.7%	268.26	0.5%	7,139.15	2.0%
0.00	0.0%	0.00	0.0%	0.00	0.0%	1,957.64	0.5%
0.00	0.0%	0.00	0.0%	0.00	0.0	1,957.64	0.5%
282.78	1.2%	272.34	1.5%	359.32	0.7%	3,669.02	1.0%
43.19	0.2%	43.19	0.2%	43.19	0.1%	414.38	0.1%
100.11	0.4%	297.42	1.6%	292.97	0.6%	3,215.74	0.9%
203.24	0.9%	101.62	0.5%	101.62	0.2%	1,273.41	0.4%
57.27	0.2%	0.00	0.0%	112.26	0.2%	462.90	0.1%
403.81	1.8%	442.23	2.4%	550.04	1.1%	5,366.43	1.5%
14,293.44	62.1%	25,212.29	135.0%	29,756.28	58.7%	293,921.94	82.3%
8,718.44	37.9%	-6,540.44	-35.0%	20,924.94	41.3%	63,165.23	17.7%
0.33	0.0%	0.66	0.0%	1.40	0.0%	9.94	0.0%
0.33	0.0%	0.66	0.0%	1.40	0.0%	9.94	0.0%
0.33	0.0%	0.66	0.0%	1.40	0.0%	9.94	0.0%
8,718.77	37.9%	-6,539.78	-35.0%	20,926.34	41.3%	63,175.17	17.7%

figure **8.6**

Cash Flow

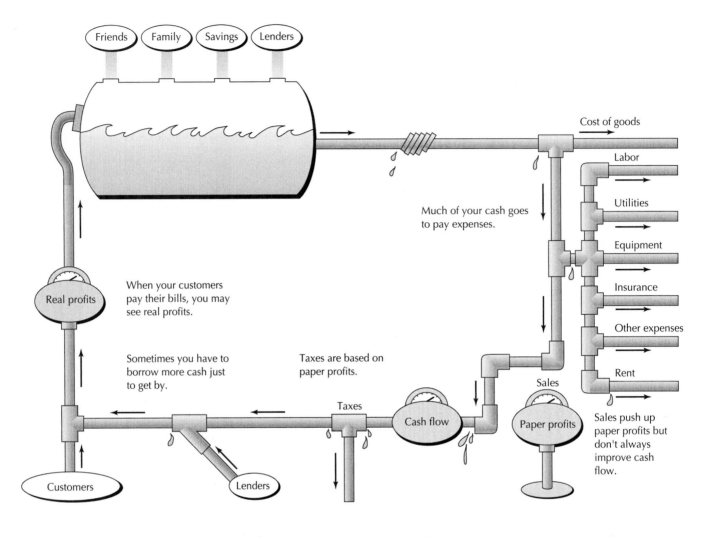

Friends Family Savings Lenders

Cost of goods

Labor

Utilities

Equipment

Insurance

Other expenses

Rent

Much of your cash goes to pay expenses.

Real profits

When your customers pay their bills, you may see real profits.

Sometimes you have to borrow more cash just to get by.

Taxes are based on paper profits.

Taxes

Cash flow

Sales

Paper profits

Sales push up paper profits but don't always improve cash flow.

Customers

Lenders

Ten Absolutely Must-Follow Cash-Flow Rules

1. Never Run Out of Cash.
Running out of cash is the definition of failure in business. Make the commitment to do what it takes so it does not happen to you.

2. Cash Is King.
It's important to recognize that cash is what keeps your business alive. Manage it with the care and attention it deserves. It's very unforgiving if you don't.

Remember, Cash Is King, because No Cash = No Business.

3. Know the Cash Balance Right Now.
What is your cash balance right now? It's absolutely critical that you know exactly what your cash balance is. Even the most intelligent and experienced person will fail if they are making business decisions using inaccurate or incomplete cash balances. That is the reason why business failures are not limited to amateurs or people new to the business world.

4. Do Today's Work Today.
The key to keeping an accurate cash balance in your accounting system is to do today's work today. When you do this, you will have the numbers you need—when you need them.

5. Either You Do the Work or Have Someone Else Do It.
Here is a simple rule to follow to make sure you have an accurate cash balance on your books: You do the work or have someone else do it. Those are the only two

figure **8.7**

R & J Enterprises' Statement of Cash Flow

For the Years Ended December 31, 2008, 2007, 2006

	2008	2007	2006
Cash Flows from Operating Activities:			
Cash Received from Customers	$1,665,361	$1,260,814	$782,750
Cash Paid to Suppliers and Employees	(1,374,758)	(1,059,580)	(659,112)
Interest Received	1,213	1,620	0
Income Taxes Paid	(6,050)	(1,500)	(800)
Interest Paid	(41,867)	(21,122)	(10,898)
Net Cash Provided by Operating Activities	243,899	180,232	111,940
Cash Flows from Investing Activities:			
Purchases of Property, Plant, and Equipment	(102,341)	(323,899)	(41,492)
Vehicle Lease Deposit	0	473	0
Purchase of South River Location	(21,400)	0	0
Small Business Administration Loan Costs	0	(5,577)	0
Net Cash Provided Used in Investing Activities	(123,741)	(329,003)	(41,492)
Cash Flows from Financing Activities:			
Bank of America Line of Credit	0	51,928	0
Payments on Bank of America Line of Credit	(569)	0	(3,523)
Loans from Members	0	100,000	0
Payments on Loans from Members	(20,032)	(14,595)	0
Loan for South River Location	10,000	0	0
Payments on Loan for South River Location	(4,350)	0	0
Small Business Administration Loans	0	100,000	0
Payments on Small Business Administration Loans	(34,399)	(19,666)	(17,470)
Equipment Lease Financing	42,518	40,516	15,741
Payments on Equipment Leases	(15,863)	(13,565)	(2,328)
Contributions by Members	31,400	69,100	37,023
Distributions to Members	(113,566)	(159,331)	(115,137)
Net Cash Provided by Financing Activities	(104,861)	154,387	(85,694)
Net Increase (Decrease) in Cash and Cash Equivalent	15,297	5,616	(15,246)
Cash and Cash Equivalents at Beginning of Year	31,317	25,701	40,947
Cash and Cash Equivalents at End of Year	$46,614	$31,317	$25,701
Reconciliation of Net Income to Net Cash Provided by Operating Activities:			
Net Income	$139,565	$95,362	$75,882
Adjustments to Reconcile Net Income to Net Cash Provided by Operating Activities:			
Depreciation and Amortization	79,282	54,682	33,535
(Increase) Decrease in Inventory	5,688	(48,863)	(2,096)
Decrease in Interest Receivable	0	0	1,698
(Increase) in Deposits	(9,990)	(650)	(3,789)
(Increase) in Prepaid Interest	(4,563)	(11,891)	(2,298)
Increase in Accounts Payable	28,375	79,263	6,903
Increase in Wages Payable	2,979	6,404	497
Increase in Accrued Taxes Payable	2,563	5,925	1,608
Net Cash Provided by Operating Activities	$243,899	$180,232	$111,940

choices you have. The work must be done. It's like mowing the lawn. You can't just ignore it. Someone has to do it. That means either you do it or have someone else do it.

6. Don't Manage From the Bank Balance.

The bank balance and the cash balance are two different animals. Rarely will the two ever be the same. Don't make the mistake of confusing them. It's futile (and frustrating) to attempt to manage your cash flow using the bank balance. It's a prescription for failure. You reconcile your bank balance. You don't manage from it.

7. Know What You Expect the Cash Balance to Be Six Months From Now.

What do you expect your cash balance to be six months from now? This one question will transform the way you manage your business. This question really gets to the heart of whether you are managing your business or whether your business is managing you.

8. Cash-Flow Problems Don't "Just Happen."

You would be shocked and amazed at the number of businesses that fail because the owner did not see a cash flow problem in time to do something about it. The key is to always be able to answer the question, what do I expect my cash balance to be six months from now?

9. You Absolutely Positively Must Have Cash-Flow Projections.

Cash flow projections are the key to making wise and profitable business decisions. They give you the answer to the all-important question from Rule # 7. It's impossible to run your business properly without them.

10. Eliminate Your Cash Flow Worries So You Are Free to Do What You Do Best—Take Care of Customers and Make More Money.

This is the real key to your success in business. The reason you have to make sure you have the cash flow of your business under control is so you are free to focus all your time and talents where you can make the most difference in your business.

When you have your cash flow under control, you are free from worry, doubt, and concern. You have the cash flow information you need to make sure that everything you do each day in your business is clearly focused on making your business better.

You have the information you need to measure your progress using the amount of cash you generate (and keep) for yourself and your business as your ultimate financial measurement.

Source: *http://www.inc.com/resources/finance/articles/20040901/10rules.html* (Accessed March 28, 2008).

Review Lucy's, Casey's, and R&J Enterprises' (Figure 8.7) projections. What would you recommend to these entrepreneurs? Could the owners increase sales dramatically to improve cash flow and income? To increase cash flow, look beyond the initial product or service and extend your facilities and products.

Are you willing to put in sweat equity? Are your projections realistic? Will you be able to forgo taking a salary for a few months if serious cash-flow problems occur? When you have completed your projections, show the results to an expert, and ask if they look accurate. It is better to know the truth now, while you are working on paper; paper truth is a lot easier than reality on the pocketbook.

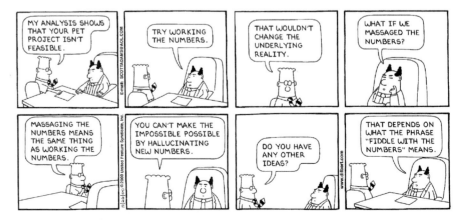

Source: Dilbert reprinted by permission of United Features Syndicate, Inc.

figure **8.8**

Casey's Auto Restoration's Balance Sheet

As of December 31, 2008
Assets
  Current Assets
    Cash 5,000
    Accounts Receivable $10,000
      Less: Allowance for bad debts of $300
        Net Accounts Receivable 9,700
    Inventory 40,000
    Prepaid Expenses 1,000
      Total Current Assets 55,700
  Fixed Assets
    Land 50,000
    Buildings and Equipment .... $600,000 (at cost)
      Less Accumulated Depreciation of $300,000 ...... (300,000)
    Notes Receivable 1,000
    Other Assets 4,000
      Total Fixed Assets 355,000
Total Assets **$410,700**
Liabilities
  Current Liabilities
    Accounts Payable 5,000
    Accrued Expenses 2,000
    Note Payable—Equipment 30,000
      Total Current Liabilities $37,000
  Long-Term Liabilities
    Building Loan 270,000
      Total Long-Term Liabilities 270,000
Total Liabilities **$307,000**
Equity
  Owner's Equity $103,700
Total Liabilities and Equity **$410,700**

BALANCE SHEET

A financial snapshot of your business is called a **balance sheet**. It is a picture of what your business owns and owes. Three categories make up a balance sheet: *assets* (anything of monetary value your business owns) minus *liabilities* (money owed to creditors) equals *net worth* (owner's equity).

Figure 8.8, Casey's Auto Restoration's Balance Sheet, shows his current financial picture. As your business continues to prosper, the net worth should increase substantially. Any of these numbers that is not in sync with industry standards should be addressed in footnotes on the balance sheet. Thus if a business has high **accounts receivables**, but the owner knows the major account will be paid within 20 days, and payment is late due to flooding and loss of records, it should be noted.

Balance sheet Financial snapshot of assets, liabilities, and equity

Account receivable Money owed to a firm

BREAK-EVEN ANALYSIS

Knowing a few key numbers can help you avoid painful surprises. If you know your estimated costs (variable and fixed) and gross sales, you can use a break-even formula that will tell when you will start making money. A break-even analysis is particularly useful at 1) start-up time, 2) when you have completed your income and expense projections, and 3) when you are considering launching a new product or service (Figure 8.9).

figure **8.9**

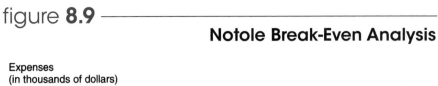

Notole Break-Even Analysis

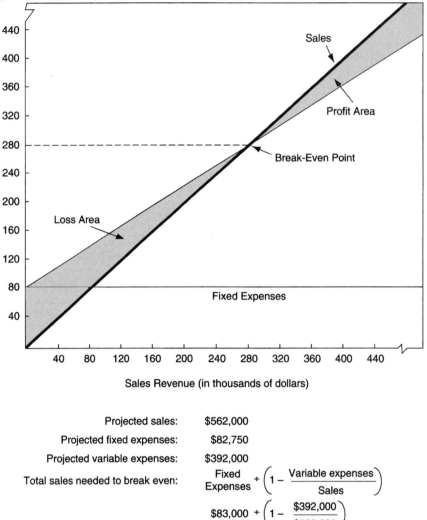

Projected sales:	$562,000	
Projected fixed expenses:	$82,750	
Projected variable expenses:	$392,000	
Total sales needed to break even:	$\text{Fixed Expenses} + \left(1 - \dfrac{\text{Variable expenses}}{\text{Sales}}\right)$	
	$\$83,000 + \left(1 - \dfrac{\$392,000}{\$562,000}\right)$	
	$\$83,000 + (1 - .6975)$	
	$\$83,000 \div .3025$	
	$274,380	
Break-even range:	$270,000 to $280,000	

Notole Figures Surprise Owners

A small manufacturing company was completing a plan for its second year of operation. Its first-year sales were $177,000, and a sales breakdown for the last 3 months of their first year looked like this:

October	*$15,000*
November	*24,000*
December	*29,000*
Total	*$68,000*

The owners took a look at the numbers and called in a consultant to help. The consultant gathered information from sales reps, owners, and customers, and then projected that sales for the second year would be a whopping $562,000. The owners reacted with disbelief.

"You're crazy," they said. "That is more than three times what we did last year."

The consultant smiled. "Didn't you tell me you were going to add three new products, and new reps in March, June, and September?"

"Yes, but—"

"And what about those big promotions you've got planned?"

"Well, sure, we've planned some promotions, but that doesn't get us anywhere near three times last year."

"All right," the consultant said. "Can you do $275,000?"

The owners got into a huddle. Based on the fourth quarter, they were sure they could stay even, and four times $68,000 (the fourth-quarter sales) was $272,000. They knew they had to do better than last year.

"Sure, no problem. We can do $275,000."

"All right," said the consultant, rolling out his break-even chart. "I've just projected $562,000 in sales for the year. To break even, you only need about $275,000."

"Hey," the owners said, "we're projecting $90,000 the first quarter."

"I'm glad you're thinking my way," the consultant said. "Because if you do not believe you can reach a goal, you will never get there."

"Just tell us what to do," the owners said.

Based on a careful cash-flow analysis, the consultant determined that the company would need to borrow money. The owners knew their business—industry trends, product line, competitors, sales, and promotion plans—but what banker would believe such growth? The key to getting the loan would be to convince the banker that the company could do better than break even. The consultant prepared a break-even chart on the $562,000 sales figure (see Figure 8.9). Note in the chart that after $280,000 in sales, the firm will have passed its break-even point and will be earning a profit.

Their banker granted the loan, realizing the company could pass the break-even point with room to spare. The key, as is usual in business, was a combination of numbers and human confidence.

LEAVING A PAPER TRAIL AND SOFTWARE APPLICATIONS

If you are a typical entrepreneur, you are not real big on details, and you are very busy; nonetheless, you know it is important to keep good records. A good starting point is to download *Starting a Business and Keeping Records*, IRS Publication 583, from *http://www.irs.gov/pub/irs-pdf/p583.pdf*. Your records need to be thorough and complete so that your accountant can take full advantage of all tax deductions and complete your tax records and financial statements.

Many beginning entrepreneurs commingle their business accounts with their personal accounts. This is bad business practice and is frowned upon by the IRS. An accounting software package, separate checking accounts, and your own efforts will alleviate this problem.

Be sure to track expenses thoroughly, and keep all receipts for as long as your accountant tells you to. Limit any petty cash expenditures so that you know where the money is flowing.

At the very start of the process of opening your business, purchase a computer and track your financial activity using one of the major accounting programs provided by Quicken, Peachtree, or Microsoft Money. These programs will 1) track your expenses and income, 2) help you reconcile your bank accounts, 3) help you manage payroll and invoices, 4) help you manage inventory, 5) help you manage customer reports, and 6) help you develop proposals. In addition, all financial statements required by lenders will be at your fingertips at all times. Also with good up-to-date records at hand, you will be able to substantiate your asking price if you decide to sell.

When preparing cash-flow and income statements, software allows you to play with what-if scenarios easily. With these scenarios on hand, meet with your accountant and financial advisor to gather feedback. In addition, costing out your products and services and determining pricing will be much easier with software that allows you to see alternatives side by side for easy comparison. Also, if you are in a volatile commodity-pricing situation, having ready access to pricing scenarios is a must.

Your software should include word processing, spreadsheet, database management, accounting and bookkeeping, and desktop publishing programs. Many of these programs can be purchased in an integrated office suite. In addition, you may want to purchase software recommended by your association that is already adapted to your particular industry needs. Or, you can choose to hire a software consultant to customize an off-the-shelf package to meet your needs. If you operate your business solely on the Internet, additional specialized and custom software is available for managing and tracking. As your firm grows, additional productivity software may be required.

Even with accounting software, consider hiring a bookkeeper familiar with your software to assist you. Expect to hire a bookkeeper for 8 to 20 hours a month for a small business with revenue of less than $750,000. Please note that even if bookkeepers and accountants manage your firm's accounts, *you* remain responsible for the money flowing through your firm. If you have little knowledge of numbers, enroll in a basic accounting class so that you can follow the cash flow and understand the financial statements.

FINANCIAL RATIOS

Calculating a few simple ratios will help you analyze how your venture compares with other businesses in your selected industry. Lenders use ratios as measuring devices to determine the risks associated with lending. Again, use biostats to determine industry ratios. To the entrepreneur, ratios are control tools for maintaining financial efficiency.

Current Ratio

Does the business have enough money to meet current debt? Have you anticipated a safety margin for losses resulting from uncollectible funds owed to the business? Most start-up ventures are undercapitalized. The current ratio is computed from the balance sheet. Divide current assets by current liabilities. If current assets are $200,000 and current liabilities are $100,000, you have a current ratio of 2. Many lenders see this as a minimum, and they like to see that you have at least twice as much invested as you owe. The current ratio is the most widely used method to determine the financial health of a business.

Quick (Liquidity) Ratio

The quick ratio tells you if you have cash on hand or assets that can be converted into cash quickly to pay your debts. The more liquidity, the better. An untapped credit line will help beef up your liquidity.

Return on Investment

Return on investment (ROI) is the favorite tool of investors and venture capitalists. This ratio shows the return expressed as a percentage of their financial investment. Investors and entrepreneurs want the highest return, or profit, for the least amount of money invested. Additional financial ratios are shown in Figure 8.10.

figure **8.10**

Financial Ratios

Ratio Name	How to Calculate	What It Means in Dollars and Cents
Balance Sheet Ratios		
Current	$\dfrac{\text{Current Assets}}{\text{Current Liabilities}}$	Measures solvency: the number of dollars in current assets for every $1 in current liabilities *Example:* A current ratio of 1.76 means that for every $1 of current liabilities, the firm has $1.76 in current assets with which to pay it.
Quick	$\dfrac{\text{Cash + Accounts Receivable}}{\text{Current Liabilities}}$	Measures liquidity: the number of dollars in cash and accounts receivable for each $1 in current liabilities *Example:* A quick ratio of 1.14 means that for every $1 of current liabilities, the firm has $1.14 in cash and accounts receivable with which to pay it.
Cash	$\dfrac{\text{Cash}}{\text{Current Liabilities}}$	Measures liquidity more strictly: the number of dollars in cash for every $1 in current liabilities *Example:* A cash ratio of 0.17 means that for every $1 of current liabilities, the firm has $0.17 in cash with which to pay it.
Debt-to-worth	$\dfrac{\text{Total Liabilities}}{\text{Net Worth}}$	Measures financial risk: the number of dollars of debt owed for every $1 in net worth *Example:* A debt-to-worth ratio of 1.05 means that for every $1 of net worth the owners have invested, the firms owes $1.05 of debt to its creditors.
Income Statement Ratios		
Gross margin	$\dfrac{\text{Gross Margin}}{\text{Sales}}$	Measures profitability at the gross profit level: the number of dollars of gross margin produced for every $1 of sales *Example:* A gross margin ratio of 34.4% means that for every $1 of sales, the firm produces 34.4 cents of gross margin.
Net margin	$\dfrac{\text{Net Profit before Tax}}{\text{Sales}}$	Measures profitability at the net profit level: the number of dollars of net profit produced for every $1 of sales *Example:* A net margin ratio of 2.9% means that for very $1 of sales, the firm produces 2.9 cents of net margin.
Overall Efficiency Ratios		
Sales-to-assets	$\dfrac{\text{Sales}}{\text{Total Assets}}$	Measures the efficiency of total assets in generating sales: the number of dollars in sales produced for every $1 invested in total assets *Example:* A sales-to-assets ratio of 2.35 means that for every $1 dollar invested in total assets, the firm generates $2.35 in sales.

figure **8.10**

Financial Ratios (continued)

Ratio Name	How to Calculate	What It Means in Dollars and Cents
Return on assets	$\dfrac{\text{Net Profit before Tax}}{\text{Total Assets}}$	Measures the efficiency of total assets in generating net profit: the number of dollars in net profit produced for every $1 invested in total assets *Example:* A return on assets ratio of 7.1% means that for every $1 invested in assets, the firm is generating 7.1 cents in net profit before tax.
Return on investment	$\dfrac{\text{Net Profit before Tax}}{\text{Net Worth}}$	Measures the efficiency of net worth in generating net profit: the number of dollars in net profit produced for every $1 invested in net worth *Example:* A return on investment ratio of 16.1% means that for very $1 invested in net worth, the firm is generating 16.1 cents in net profit before tax.
Specific Efficiency Ratios		
Inventory turnover	$\dfrac{\text{Cost of Goods Sold}}{\text{Inventory}}$	Measures the rate at which inventory is being used on an annual basis *Example:* An inventory turnover ratio of 9.81 means that the average dollar volume of inventory is used up almost ten times during the fiscal year.
Inventory turn-days	$\dfrac{360}{\text{Inventory Turnover}}$	Converts the inventory turnover ratio into an average "days inventory on hand" figure *Example:* An inventory turn-days ratio of 37 means that the firm keeps an average of 37 days of inventory on hand throughout the year.
Accounts receivable turnover	$\dfrac{\text{Sales}}{\text{Accounts Receivable}}$	Measures the rate at which accounts receivable are being collected on an annual basis *Example:* An accounts receivable turnover ratio of 8.00 means that the average dollar volume of accounts receivable are collected eight times during the year.
Average collection period	$\dfrac{360}{\text{Accounts Receivable Turnover}}$	Converts the accounts receivable turnover ratio into the average number of days the firm must wait for its accounts receivable to be paid *Example:* An average collection period ratio of 45 means that it takes the firm 45 days on average to collect its receivables.
Accounts payable turnover	$\dfrac{\text{Cost of Goods Sold}}{\text{Accounts Payable}}$	Measure the rate at which accounts payable are being paid on an annual basis. *Example:* An accounts payable turnover ratio of 12.04 means that the average dollar volume of accounts payable are paid about 123 a year.
Average payment period	$\dfrac{360}{\text{Accounts Payable Turnover}}$	Converts the accounts payable turnover ratio into the average number of days a firm takes to pay its accounts payable. *Example:* An accounts payable turnover ratio of 30 means that it takes the firm 30 days on average to pay its bills.

Source: *From Entrepreneurship* 4th edition by Kuratko. Copyright 1998. Reprinted with permission of South-Western, a division of Thomson Learning: www.thomsonrights.com, Fax 800 730-2215.

SUMMARY

Not surprisingly, many entrepreneurs find it difficult to project numbers for their businesses. There are several explanations for this:

- They are action people who are in a hurry; they do not think they have time to sit down and make projections.
- They are creative; their strengths are greater in the innovation area than in the justification area.
- They tend to think in visual terms rather than in terms of numbers or words.
- They believe they cannot fail.

Business is a numbers game, and despite an entrepreneur's feelings about numbers and projections, survival in the marketplace depends on having the right numbers in the right color of ink. This chapter, and your past and future research, should smooth the way for you to work with the numbers you need to move forward.

The point behind projecting numbers is to make the numbers as realistic as possible. You need to relate each projection to your specific business and to industry standards and then to *document* them in your Business Plan. The case studies and examples in this chapter will help you make your projections believable to your banker and to yourself. That is the key. Your numbers may seem reasonable to you, but you must make them seem reasonable to others as well. You make them believable by keeping them realistic and by documenting them properly.

What you do not need during the start-up phase is expensive surprises that knock you and your business for a loop. Before opening your doors, anticipate as many potential unpleasant surprises as possible, and have a plan of action for each one of them. For example, what will you do if:

- Your anchor tenant leaves?
- Your Web site is ineffective?
- The customer who accounts for 75 percent of your business declares bankruptcy?

Expecting and *planning for* the unknown may make the difference between the success or failure of your business. Looking at the future will help you eliminate some surprises, and it may even cause you to question whether you are truly ready to take the plunge. Remember: no one can anticipate everything, and your start-up will cost more than you expected and take longer than you planned.

THINK POINTS FOR SUCCESS

- It is cheaper and easier to make mistakes on a spreadsheet before you go into business.
- When you visit your banker to ask for money, make sure you know how much you are going to need for the long run.
- Projecting will help control the variables of your business—numbers, employees, promotion mix, product mix, and the peaks and valleys of seasonality.

- Purchase accounting software on day one.
- Cash flow is king.
- Walk away if the business is not going to work financially. There will always be other opportunities.

KEY POINTS FROM ANOTHER VIEW

Deciding to Grow—Street Smarts

When a business is successful, it's only natural to want to expand it, but be careful: bigger isn't always better.

I've often noted that failure is a great teacher. When you fail in business, you can look back, see what you did wrong, and learn the appropriate lesson.

Success is another matter. It's often difficult, if not impossible, to figure out why a particular business

concept clicks. You may be able to list a number of important factors, but you still won't necessarily know exactly what combination of them came together at the right moment and in the right proportions to make the business take off.

That's worth bearing in mind when you're deciding how you're going to take your business to the next level in sales. If you don't really know what's driving your success, you have to be careful about the strategy you adopt.

There's a risk, after all, that you may accidentally undermine whatever made your company successful in the first place.

Consider a friend of mine who owns one of the hottest little stores around these days. For purposes of the column, I'll call him Seymour and his store Hot Pants. It's a tiny shop—about 1250 square feet—located in a suburban strip mall; it specializes in jeans and casual clothing, mainly for young women and teenage girls. From that one location, Seymour racks up several million dollars a year in sales, giving him one of the highest sales-per-square-foot figures in his segment of the retail clothing industry.

For Seymour, the shop has been a dream come true. A self-taught businessman, he'd had several previous ventures that did well enough, but none of them took off the way Hot Pants did following its launch in 1994. His plan, he says, is to grow the business and sell it in 5 years or so. Toward that end, he's opened a second Hot Pants, in a town about 60 miles away from the first store. He also has a discount store, where he sells his old and discontinued inventory.

A couple of months ago, I got a call from Seymour, who said he had to see me. A big opportunity had come along, and he wanted my advice.

It turned out that the space next to the original Hot Pants was becoming vacant. Seymour wanted to lease it, knock down the wall, and double the size of his store. He figured he could generate between $1 million and $2 million in additional sales pretty much overnight. What did I think?

Now, you have to understand that Hot Pants is a very crowded place. On most days there are lines at the registers and the dressing rooms. Somehow, Seymour has managed to generate tremendous buzz among middle-class girls a certain age—say, 13 to 18 years old—and large numbers of them show up on a regular basis, not only to shop but to socialize with their friends.

That's good for the buzz, but Seymour thought he was losing a significant amount of business from customers who didn't want to wait in line or deal with the crowds. He figured he could solve the problem by expanding.

I was skeptical. For one thing, I wasn't sure he could make enough additional profit to justify the investment. "What does the landlord want?" I asked. Seymour said the landlord wanted him to give up his old lease and sign a new one for the combined space at the current market rate. Because rates have increased since he signed his original lease, he'd wind up paying about 25 percent more on his old space in addition to the rent for the new space. He'd also have to put up "key money"—a sort of signing bonus for the landlord. Then there was the cost of fixing up the new space, carrying additional inventory, and hiring more staff.

"You have to look at the effect on your margins," I said. Seymour agreed. Seymour went through the numbers. It quickly became clear that he'd need more than $1 million in additional sales just to break even on his investment.

And could he, in fact, count on getting those sales? I had my doubts. A specialty-clothing store is not a restaurant. When a would-be diner walks out of restaurant because the wait is too long, that sale is probably lost. Why? Because it almost always goes to a competitor. I wasn't convinced, however, that the same thing happened when Seymour's customers decided against waiting. When you have a hot store, people come partly because they want to say they bought from you. They're looking for prestige and merchandise. My guess was most Hot Pants' customers who left because of the crowds would simply return when the store was less busy.

In that case, I pointed out, Seymour was losing few if any sales because of overcrowding. He'd saturated his marketplace. Everybody who wanted to shop at Hot Pants already did. "Well, then, maybe I'll bring in new lines," Seymour said "like for young guys."

That's what I was afraid of. To justify his investment, Seymour might be tempted to change his concept. "You're talking about a whole new business," I said. "You could be jeopardizing what you already have. Maybe the girls want to be alone."

The truth is, Seymour doesn't know why his business is so successful, nor do I. It could be the music he plays or the quality of his staff or the store's name or his own personality. Most likely, it's some combination of those things and a dozen other factors—perhaps even the lack of space. The kids may like being jammed together. They may not mind waiting in line to use a dressing room. All Seymour knows for sure is that right now he's blowing away all the standard projections for a business of his type, size, and location. His sales are two and a half times the amount anyone would have predicted for a jeans store in a strip mall with limited foot traffic.

You can't explain that kind of success. You can only recognize it, respect it, and handle it with care. Seymour's most valuable asset is the brand he's created; by doubling the size of his store, he's taking a chance that he'll inadvertently devalue the brand. It's a risk that, in my view at least, is way out of proportion to the potential reward.

I'm not saying that Seymour shouldn't grow his business. He already has a second Hot Pants up and running. It hasn't yet matched the performance of the first store, but it probably just needs time.

So what should Seymour do? I urged him to think about starting a third Hot Pants. I suggested he choose a location near enough to the original store that local kids would have heard the buzz but far enough away that they wouldn't already be regular customers. If the new store did well, Seymour would have a proven concept that he could sell in 5 years to someone interested in taking it national. If the spin-off failed, well, at least he wouldn't have damaged his core business.

But Seymour wasn't looking for that type of advice. He mainly wanted to know whether I thought he was crazy to double the size of the original Hot Pants. "Do you think I'll go out of business?" he asked. "No," I said, "but I think you'll hurt yourself."

Seymour didn't care—or maybe he simply disagreed. In any case he plans to go ahead with his expansion, and that may be the right decision for him personally even if it's wrong for the business. It's much easier to expand an existing store than to start a new one. It's also less expensive. Seymour already works 6 to 7 days a week, putting in long hours, and he's a guy who likes to have a direct control of operations. So he may be happier with a larger main store than with a third smaller one. I'm just afraid he'll lose some of the value he's worked so hard to build. This is one time I hope I'm wrong.

Source: Norm Brodsky, "Deciding to Grow," *Inc.* Magazine, March 2001, *http://www.inc.com/magazine/20010301/ 22055.html* (Accessed March 28, 2008).

chapter 9

Shaking the Money Tree
Locating Hard Cash

Would it sound too easy if we told you to go out and simply shake a money tree to secure financing for your business? Yes! And you know it will *not* be that easy. First you must become familiar with the world of money. Then you must learn to tell the forest from the trees. And finally you must find the right branches (see Figure 9.1). Once you have accomplished these things, you might be surprised at how money turns up when you shake the right branch.

figure **9.1**

Shaking the Money Tree

Looking for Money: Hawkins Case Study—Surgery Shunt

The Prototype

Don Hawkins started his career as a model maker in a large medical manufacturing firm. Don had talent and was envied and admired because he usually got the models routinely right the first time.

Margo Mckay, a product manager at Don's firm, often sought out Don when she needed help on a glitch that slowed production. One day, over a cup of coffee, Margo confided to Don that she had a microsurgeon friend looking for a special design for a wound drainage device of 5 millimeters.

It took Don four days to comb through the medical literature on microsurgery. It took him five weeks to develop the prototype. Margo and Don went to the president of their company to present the prototype. Two weeks later the president shared that the firm did not believe there was a large enough market for the product for the firm to support it.

Don and Margo started to investigate the market further over the next two months and believed there truly was a market for such a product. They decided to quit their jobs and put together a venture team.

The Team

In the next few weeks, they recruited Bob Bernstein, a production supervisor, and Nancy Jones, the best salesperson in the company. Before they got too deep into dreams and celebrations, Margo warned the group they would need cash. To get cash, they needed investors. To get investors, they needed a Business Plan.

To keep the weak spots to a minimum and to maximize their strengths, all four members of the venture team enrolled in a college course titled "The Weekend Entrepreneur: Writing Your Business Plan." By organizing their ideas and capitalizing on their expertise, in six weeks their Business Plan was ready to present to investors. Their numbers showed they would need $2,000,000 in start-up capital to make it through the first 18 months.

The Money

Each partner had to come up with $500,000, a quarter of the first-year's seed money. Margo refinanced her houses. Don tapped his Uncle Marvin, who was worth several million. Nancy found two investors, a couple of go-getter doctors, with $250,000 each. Bob borrowed from his credit union and cashed in two life insurance policies.

Their destination was a small warehouse. The rent was cheap, the security great. The microsurgery trade show was 62 days away. For a piece of the corporate pie, a shrewd attorney waived his fee for doing the patent work. With the patent pending in hand, production began on Don's prototype.

The first trade show they attended proved to be a goldmine. On opening day, their booth was swamped. By the end of the first day, orders for the device exceeded their first-year sales forecast.

The Niche

Their niche truly was microsurgery, and they continued over the next three years to develop new products. In their third year, Don discovered the solution to a problem that had confounded two generations of optical surgeons. To get approval would take two to three years and with such a long lag time between production and sales, developmental costs would hurt the firm, maybe even take it under.

Then their CPA introduced them to Dream Funds, a venture capital group in Minneapolis. This was Dream Funds' deal: In return for

60 percent of the company's stock, Dream Funds would deposit $20 million in the company's bank account. Although they didn't want to lose control of the company, the financial opportunity for all was too good to pass up.

BEFORE COMMITTING MONEY

Don and his colleagues put up their *own money first*. Committing your own nickel is essential for *all* entrepreneurs. Lenders and investors will make sure you have committed your own resources before they will commit theirs. You have already completed Action Step 3 from Chapter 1, which asked you to complete a budget and a personal financial statement, and the Action Steps in Chapter 8, which asked you to determine your start-up costs, cash-flow requirements, and break-even point. So you now know the amount you need to start and the amount you have to do it with. Now, it is time to reconcile and determine how to fund the difference.

The vast majority of ventures are self-financed in the start-up stage, so first you must consider your own risk tolerance, your credit history, and the availability of your own cash.

What Is Your Risk Tolerance?

How much are you willing to risk? $10,000? $20,000? $200,000? $2,000,000? Are you willing to go deeply in debt for your venture? Are you willing to work as hard as one sushi vendor, who worked for more than 7 years—and spent millions of dollars—before he hit on a successful way to flash-freeze his product?

Are you willing to give up a successful career with benefits for the unknown? If you lose your house, will you be devastated, or will you pick yourself back up and start again like a true entrepreneur? One Hilton Head Island contractor was a millionaire at age 22 and lost it, a millionaire again at age 28 and lost it, and a millionaire again at 35. Is this a roller coaster you are willing to ride?

Remember, you must also consider the risk tolerance of the members of your family and any persons you partner with. If additional capital is needed down the road, will you and your partners be able to provide equal shares? If not, will that be a problem as the percentage of the amount invested changes?

CREDIT REPORTING AGENCIES: WHAT DO THEY KNOW ABOUT YOU?

Loan officers will look first at your credit report. If it does not pass, you are sunk at the bank! Take action to determine your credit history. Approximately 25 to 40 percent of all credit reports have one or more problems, and it is your responsibility to clear these problems up before searching for capital.

Credit reporting agencies keep track of your financial moves—the good, the bad, and the ugly—including bill paying, credit (requested and denied), loans, liens, and legal judgments. Information is retained for 7 years, and bankruptcies stay on the records for 10 years.

Credit inquiries from potential lenders will show up on a credit report. Unfortunately, many TItimes lenders request credit information without your authority, and only by obtaining a copy of your credit report will you discover these requests.

Be warned: What might appear minor to you, such as one missed or late payment, may not appear minor to potential lenders. *Never* miss a house payment! Making a house payment 30 days late will drop your credit score dramatically. If you have unpaid medical bills, try to avoid letting them go to collections. Doing so may end up saving you thousands in higher interest rates that you would later be charged. No outside agency can guarantee that incorrect items can be removed from your credit reports. Thus, tread carefully with firms who make such guarantees.

Most entrepreneurs will depend on their own credit histories as they reach out for money. Thus it is essential that your credit report be perfectly clean. Mistakes are very common, so check with each of the three separate credit bureaus 3 to 6 months before you anticipate needing money; if there is a problem, you will have time to take the necessary steps to correct it. The trend for using Fair Issue Credit Organization (FICO) scores to determine small-business loan eligibility continues to grow, so you need to make every effort to see to it that your score is as high as possible. Review the following key factors from *http://www.Bankrate.com*, and determine what steps you need to take immediately to improve your credit score.

Key Factors of Your Credit Score

1. **How you pay your bills** (35 percent of the score): The most important factor is how you have paid your bills in the past, placing the most emphasis on recent activity. Paying all your bills on time is good. Paying them late on a consistent basis is bad. Having accounts that were sent to collections is worse. Declaring bankruptcy is the worst.

2. **Amount of money you owe and the amount of available credit** (30 percent): The second most important area is your outstanding debt—how much money you owe on credit cards, car loans, mortgages, home equity lines, and so on. Also considered is the total amount of credit you have available. If you have ten credit cards, each with a $10,000 credit limit, that is $100,000 of available credit. Statistically, people who have a lot of credit available tend to use it, which makes them less attractive credit risks. "Carrying a lot of debt doesn't necessarily mean you'll have a lower score," Watts says. "It doesn't hurt as much as carrying close to the maximum. People who consistently max out their balances are perceived as riskier. People who never use their credit don't have a track history. People with the highest scores use credit sparingly and keep their balances low."

3. **Length of credit history** (15 percent): The third factor is the length of your credit history. The longer you have had credit—particularly if it is with the same credit issuers—the more points you get.

4. **Mix of credit** (10 percent): The best scores will have a mix of both revolving credit, such as credit cards, and installment credit, such as mortgages and car loans. "Statistically, consumers with a richer variety of experiences are better credit risks," Watts says. "They know how to handle money."

5. **New credit applications** (10 percent): The final category is your interest in new credit—how many credit applications you are filling out. The model compensates for people who are rate shopping for the best mortgage or car loan rates. The only time shopping really hurts your score, Watts says, is when you have previous recent credit stumbles, such as late payments or bills sent to collections.

Source: Bankrate, Inc., N. Palm Beach, FL, 2004.

According to Fair Isaac, a credit scoring developer, 40 percent of the public will have a FICO score over 749. The recently enacted Fair and Accurate Credit Transactions Act provides consumers the right to request one free credit report through the website *www.annualcreditreport.com*, which contains scores and reports from each of the following three major credit report agencies:

- Equifax—*http://www.equifax.com*
- Experian—*http://www.experian.com*
- Trans Union Corporation—*http://www.transunion.com*

Cautionary Steps

Reviewing your personal financial statement from Action Step 3 in Chapter 1, and the start-up costs from Chapter 8, it is now time to ask how much money you are able to commit. Are you able to sell any of your assets? Take a second or a third mortgage on your house? Refinance your car? Sell your baseball card collection? Take a loan from your 401K?

Reviewing your budget from Action Step 3, how much do you need to live on each month? How much extra in your budget can you commit to the venture? Are you willing to change your lifestyle? Are you willing to rent? Share an apartment? Live in your parents' home? Are you willing to go without health care and disability benefits? (If you have answered yes to that last one, you might want to rethink). Can you dine out less? Buy a cheaper car?

What sacrifices are you willing to make for your dream? Can you obtain a part-time job to help support your dream? Can you hang on to your present job and start your new venture part-time? Do you need to find a partner who has some cash? Can you start in your basement? Living room? Garage?

Once you know the start-up costs and your available cash, determine next how much unsecured credit you have to draw upon. This will give you a general picture of how the financial world rates you at this time. Once taken, this step can help you determine if there are any untapped sources of funds or fallbacks and emergency sources for your business or personal expenses. Use Table 9.1 and your last credit card statements to determine your available credit. If your credit cards have very low limits, now may be the time to raise those limits before you open your business or quit your job. You may need to call or write to several businesses for limit information if it is not clearly stated on your bills.

When you have filled in the amounts for each of your credit accounts, add them up. Surprised? Few people are aware of how much credit they really have. However, before you tell your boss what to do with your job, there are a few additional concerns you might want to address. For example:

1. Order complete medical checkups for your entire family. You might also ask to read through your medical files to make sure there are not any statements that might preclude you from obtaining health insurance in the future. Examples might include possible problems with drinking or drugs. In addition, preexisting conditions such as high blood pressure, skin cancer, and even negative biopsies can be major roadblocks to securing affordable health insurance (see Chapter 12).

2. Check out the costs and possibility of continuing your present health insurance or purchasing new insurance. If you are unable to qualify for a private insurance plan, a group plan might be available through a business trade association or possibly through a state program. Look into

table **9.1**

Your Current Untapped Financial Sources

Source	Limit	Available
Retail Stores		
Sears		
Target		
Others		
Oil Companies		
Exxon		
Shell		
Texaco		
Others		
Bank Credit Cards		
American Express		
Visa		
MasterCard		
Discover Card		
Others		
Personal Lines of Credit		
Bank		
Savings and Loan		
Credit Union		
Others		
Home Equity		
Total Credit		

high deductible plans. Many entrepreneurs find they need one member of their family to continue working for a company that provides family coverage.

3. Apply for additional credit cards or increased limits. Check with *http://www.bankrate.com* for cards with the best terms. Use cards only for business expenses. Pay bills as they come due with company checks. Banks do not care who writes the check, as long as it clears. In addition, it will give you good documentation for your bookkeeper and the IRS. Plus, you will have some additional credit for your business. You may need it!

Line of credit An unsecured lending limit

Four Cs Capacity, collateral, character, and capital

4. Consider applying for a personal line of credit. Usually, depending on the Four Cs of credit (your capital, character, capacity, and collateral), you can obtain anywhere from $5,000 to $50,000 of unsecured credit at very attractive rates. If you have a personal line of credit, you are in a much more flexible position for your new business. If you need it to finance the new business, credit is available. If not, it can be the security blanket that will be there for you if unexpected expenses should pop up—and they will.

5. Explore the possibility of a home-equity loan or home-equity line of credit.

6. Check into borrowing from your 401(K) plan, although CPA David Wasserstrum, partner in charge of executive compensation and employee benefits at Weiser LLC, refers to 401 (K) plans as "the lender of last resort." The maximum you can borrow is $50,000 or 50 percent of the vested balance, whichever is less. If you default on your 401 (K) loan payments, the money borrowed will be treated as a distribution and taxed as ordinary income.

With regard to points 3, 4, and 5, bankers are much more relaxed about extending credit to a "steady citizen"—a person with steady employment income. In addition, you would be making arrangements for the money when you did not need it, and bankers tend to like lending money to those who have no real need for it.

Do not quit your job until you have finished your Business Plan and checked with your banker. You need to have enough money to withstand setbacks. And do not be surprised when your business does not support you, right away anyway, in the manner to which you have become accustomed or would like to be.

Your Bottom Line

You are not risking your own capital and providing sweat equity for *just* an immediate paycheck or return. You are building your business's potential. If you only consider the income from the first year or two, you will not be able to justify risking your capital or working 12- to 14-hour days. You must look ahead 3 to 5 years. Money is a strong motivating factor; just thinking about it should keep your business on the success track. Additional thoughts to consider as you explore the bottom line for starting and building your business follow:

- **Income stream:** What can you count on from your business? Salary? Profit? Benefits? Company car? Insurance? Travel? Retirement fund? What can you count on in the first year? The second year? Subsequent years?
- **Profit from sale of business:** What is the potential profit if the business is sold? What could you make if you took the company public via a stock offering? What will you leave to your children?
- **Profit life cycle:** How long will it take for your business to move from start-up to a profit position? Many businesses take 2 to 3 years to show a profit. What happens to your investment if you project profit-making status to be 3 to 5 years down the road?
- **The rule:** *Your business should provide you with two sources of financial return: an income stream and growing equity. If you have income without equity, you are just replacing your former income. If you have equity without income, you could starve to death.*

SHAKING THE MOST FRUITFUL BRANCHES FIRST

Shaking the money tree takes effort for most entrepreneurs. Although many outside financial resources are available, they *all* come with strings attached. Control of the business, family and friends' emotions, your risk tolerance, and taxes are all issues that should play a part in determining which branches of the money tree you can and should shake. Sitting down with a knowledgeable small-business accountant or attorney will give you great insight. Although there are many funding opportunities available to entrepreneurs, more than 90 percent of start-up capital comes from self-financing, friends, and family—which means banks provide less than 10 percent of start-up capital.

If you bootstrap your company as we suggest, you may find yourself on *Inc.'s* annual listing of the 500 fastest-growing businesses in the country. Almost half of the businesses on the list started in the home, and a recent overall list had an average start-up cost of only $20,000! It does not always take large amounts of capital to launch your business, but it will take enormous amounts of risk taking, time, energy, and passion.

SELF-FINANCING

Your Money and Your Credit

We have discussed several ways to tap into your financial resources. Many individuals are unable to tap home equity, retirement, stock, or bond funds; therefore credit cards may come to the rescue. For many entrepreneurs, credit cards become the standard way of accessing capital to keep the doors open and the fires burning. More than 30 percent of entrepreneurs use credit cards routinely in their businesses to help with cash flow. However, it is *always* safer to use cold hard cash to start and support your business, if possible, before depending on credit cards.

Many of the larger credit card companies, such as American Express, *http://www.americanexpress.com*, court small-business owners. Unfortunately, many of the small-business credit cards, which provide excellent recordkeeping, are available only to businesses with a two-year track record. When selecting cards, consider the following:

- **Payment dates.** If you have several cards with varying closing and payment dates, you may be able to manage your cash flow creatively by using the cards in tandem.
- **Annual Percentage Rate (APR).** Check your newspaper or Bank Rate Monitor (*http://www.bankrate.com*) for the lowest current credit card rates. If you have a card and are paying too high of an APR, call the credit card company and request that they lower the rate. Yes, this can work!
- **Annual fees.**
- **Maximum credit limits.** Call your current credit card issuers and request an increase in your credit line. Many times all it takes is a phone call.
- **Additional fees.** Make sure any "extras" you receive with the card are worth paying for.
- **Grace periods.** This is extremely important if you are using the card to manage cash flow.
- **Mileage points or other incentives.** Determine if these are worth the potential costs.
- **Late fees.** *Never* incur late fees. In the past, credit card companies did not balk if you were up to 30 days late. Today, a payment that is one day late may incur high late fees, will show up on your credit report, and can possibly increase your interest rate by up to 50 percent!

Judicious use of credit cards can be a lifesaver for many entrepreneurs. They help track your expenses and help to build a financial history. But unless you realize that the credit card bills need to be paid on time, and that there are spending limits, you may find yourself in over your head—and your business underwater. Be sure to read all inserts with your credit card statements, because extra fees and changes in the credit terms may occur; it is your responsibility to be aware of these changes. In addition, if you are using credit cards, make sure to include in your Business Plan repayment of this debt, along with interest charges. Keep your personal and business cards separate.

Credit Cards—Know the Risk

Using credit cards is a very risky way to finance your company. You have the huge bill to face every month, instead of several smaller ones that can be juggled. Once you max out, you cannot pay your other bills anymore, and the interest payments on carrying a balance can make a grown entrepreneur cry. Also, funding businesses with credit cards violates the consumer cardholder agreement, although it is a standard practice for thousands of company owners.

For more information, visit *http://www.inc.com/incmagazine/archives/02980501.html*.

FAMILY AND FRIENDS

For many entrepreneurs, heading to Mom and Pop is the second branch they shake, after looking at their own financial contributions. If you plan on making it your next stop, think again. According to many experts, parents may be the largest single source of start-up capital in the United States, but having a banking relationship with your parents is fraught with potential problems. Before continuing further, ask yourself, "Is money for this venture worth damaging or losing my relationship with my parents?" At the moment, you may just be thinking about speeding ahead with your venture, and all you can see is success; the reality is, however, you could fail. If you do, you might not be able to pay your parents back in a timely fashion—or ever.

Consider your parents' emotional ties to money. Especially if your parents or grandparents are in their eighties and lived through the Depression, for many money means security. If you borrow money, they may never truly feel secure until you have completely paid it back. Also, if you take a trip to Paris while you still owe them money, will you feel guilty? Will you feel guilty if you purchase a new car? Will you truly be secure in expanding your business if you are not secure in your lending relationships? If you are borrowing money from friends or family, be sure that the loss of that money will not affect the lenders' future or lifestyle. Borrowing Grandma's last $50,000 is not fair to Grandma.

In addition to borrowing money directly from parents, you may consider asking them to cosign loans. Remember, that legally obligates them to the debt and will impact their financial transactions and borrowing capabilities. Also, your parents, friends, or relatives may be more willing to loan you money if you put up your house, car, or jewelry as collateral.

Remain at your job and save for another year before striking out on your own, rather than risking the capital of those you love. Mixing money and personal relationships is never easy, and with family and friends it tends to be even more emotional and volatile. Long-running family issues come into play, and sibling relationships may also be harmed. There are unseen and unknown issues for both parties. How will you deal with them? If your folks get sick, will you be able to pay back the loan? If your dad and mom want to be part of the business to oversee their investment, how will you feel?

If you are still willing to borrow from friends and family after reviewing potential issues and problems, here are a few things you can do to alleviate some of the difficulties.

- Put everything in writing.
- Make it a business loan, not a personal loan. Have loan papers drawn up. State the amount, payments, duration of loan, interest rate, payment date, collateral, and late-payment penalties.
- A provision in the loan may be included for repayment in case of emergencies. This will alleviate much of the stress and concern for both parties.
- Discuss thoroughly with your lenders the company's goals. Make sure they understand that the money will be needed for a certain length of time. If the business starts to be profitable, it will still require their cash infusions for working capital.
- Discuss your fears for potential problems, and encourage lenders to discuss their issues as well. Putting feelings and concerns out on the table early may stem future problems.

To alleviate these issues, Virgin Money, *http://www.virginmoney.com*, now manages business loans between friends and family. Borrowers and lenders determine the loan amount, payment schedule, interest rates, and whether the loan is secured or not. Virgin Money assists in developing the necessary paperwork and services the loan with automated electronic payments at a very low cost.

Borrowing from friends and family can be done successfully. But it is hard work and takes exceptional people with good relationships who have no axes to grind. *Tread lightly and carefully. Friends and family cannot be bought or replaced.*

Friends and family are the most likely sources of additional financing, but person-to-person online lending networks among strangers can provide an alternative lending source for small loans, usually less than $25,000. Sites such as *http://www.prosper.com*, *https://us.zopa.com*, *http://www.gobignetwork.com*, *http://www.fundinguniverse.com*, *http://www.raisecapital.com*, and *http://www.lendingclub.com* offer online lender–borrower "matchmaking" services.

BANKS

Although most new ventures begin with an entrepreneur's own capital and the capital of friends and family, a small number of entrepreneurs are able to tap into traditional bank financing. If you have other sources of income and collateral—such as home equity, stocks, or bonds—you may be able to borrow against your assets for funding. Although banks are in the business of lending money, they also have a responsibility to their depositors. Therefore bankers tend to choose the safest deals. They want to help businesses expand, but they have to be picky. Banks can help you in many areas, but they are neither investors nor venture capitalists, so do not expect them to take risks. Your chances to receive a bank loan increase substantially after being in business several years, when you can demonstrate to the bank that yours is a viable business by providing them with past sales records and tax returns.

A small, local community bank, where the chief loan officer may be a part owner, may be an excellent choice for small business banking. You are hunting for a permanent relationship, not merely a place to park your money, and you are more likely to find it in a small community bank. Contact the Independent Community Bankers Association at *http://www.icba.org* to access the names of more than 5,000 community banks. Also, network with your attorney, accountant, suppliers, and customers to find a good bank officer referral. Bear in mind though that your business could outgrow a small bank and that

incredibleresource

ACCION: Capital Available for Struggling Entrepreneurs

ACCION USA's mission is to make access to credit a permanent resource to low- and moderate-income small-business owners in the United States. By providing small or "micro" loans to men and women who have been shut out of the traditional banking sector, ACCION helps build their businesses and increase their incomes.

ACCION sees business credit as a resource that can help narrow the income gap and provide economic opportunity, thereby stabilizing and strengthening communities and economies. At the heart of this vision is the recognition that microlending institutions must be financially sustainable, not perennially dependent on donations or government aid. For this reason, ACCION's microlending programs seek to become financially self-sufficient.

ACCION USA's lending methodology is character-based. "Unlike traditional lenders, we don't make loans based on credit history or collateral alone. Instead, we focus on a potential borrower's initiative and desire to succeed, knowledge of his or her business and market, as well as on references from customers and neighbors."

ACCION USA was named as Fast Company's 2004 Social Capitalist of the year. The story of Deborah Taylor below illustrates how a small amount of capital made a big difference in one entrepreneur's ability to expand her dream business.

Deborah Taylor learned how to make delicious jellies and jams in her own kitchen, perfecting her recipes over the years. Given as gifts, these "spreadable fruits" helped brighten the days for her friends and family. Deborah rented a kitchen in the dynamic Boston neighborhood of Jamaica Plain and started selling her jellies and jams at farmers' markets across Massachusetts—while still working her day job as a freelance graphic designer. When she heard of ACCION USA, Deborah knew a small-business loan would make a big difference to her fledgling business.

Initial loan fuels business growth. Deborah's first ACCION USA business loan helped her expand her presence at farmers' markets, buy more jars, rent a tent, and improve the labels on her jars. "ACCION helped me think about my business in ways I hadn't before," recalls Deborah. "I wanted a partner to help me grow my business. ACCION loans bring me the funding I need."

Continuing the commitment with multiple loans. Aided by multiple loans from ACCION USA, Deborah's business has grown quickly. She recently added a line of kosher jellies, jams, and fruit spreads. And she hopes to own her own kitchen soon.

The impact of ACCION USA's small business loans is clear to Deborah. "ACCION is a godsend for people who need a leg up to get started in business," she concludes.

For information on ACCION microloans, ranging from $500 to $25,000 with repayment periods of 1 to 60 months, contact the national headquarters at ACCION USA, 56 Roland Street, Suite 300, Boston, MA 02129, Phone: (866) 245-0783, e-mail: *info//www.accionusa.org*, or visit ACCION online at *http://www.accionusa.org*.

Source: *http://www.accionusa.org/site/c.lvKVL9MUIsG/b.1415343/k.8DC9/ACCION_USA_Spreads_Small_Business_Financing_to_Jelly_Maker.htm* (Accessed April 4, 2008).

some firms need support services, such as import–export assistance, that only a large bank can offer.

Several large banks, such as Chase and Bank of America, provide assistance to fledgling businesses with big plans. Also, creative leasing programs may be available through these larger banks.

BOTTOM LINERS

"One last question: Have you begged for a loan before?"

Microlending programs, which generally refer to business loans of less than $35,000, are available through various banks and economic development programs. These small loans give new hope to entrepreneurs. According to Small Business Administration (SBA) research, more than 500 banks and organizations participate in microlending programs, providing billions of dollars in start-up and working capital funds for entrepreneurs. For further information on microlending, see the Incredible Resource that highlights Accion.

Lenders' Expectations

In general, lenders tend to not make start-up loans without home equity or stocks to secure the loan. And even when they do, they expect:

1. A very solid Business Plan with good projections and supporting data—numbers are king. Bankers use the RMA's *Statement Studies: Annual Financial Ratio Benchmarks* and *Industry Default Probabilities and Cash-Flow Measures* published by the Risk Management Association, previously discussed in Chapter 8. Make sure your numbers are in line with the firms in these annual statement studies and provide support data for any that deviate. Bankers live and breathe numbers, and so must you when you present your Business Plan.
2. Experience in managing a business, preferably in the same industry.
3. Background in the industry—the longer and broader the better.
4. Enough other assets for the borrower to live on while the business is growing—typically 6 to 12 months.
5. Your personal financial commitment to be a major part of the financing.
6. Possibly a cosigner who guarantees your loan.
7. A second salary in the family.
8. Generally at least 2 to 3 years of successful operation. Once again, unsecured bank lending is rare for start-ups without collateral.
9. Income statements that demonstrate you are willing to take a reasonable salary, or no salary, in the beginning.
10. A detailed explanation of what you are going to do with the funds.
11. A compelling product or service with strong management.
12. Capacity to repay the loan in a timely fashion.
13. A solid business or social relationship with the potential borrower.

Unsecured bank loans or lines of credit may not be available to an entrepreneur even after 3 to 5 years of successful business operations. Your personal assets and your business assets are therefore intertwined for a long time, whether you like it or not.

Strategies for Working with Your Banker

Bankers may lead you to money sources you may have not considered, and they may provide a gateway to the world of money. Seek your banker's advice on pulling your Business Plan together. If you ask for your banker's input, he or she may have a harder time refusing financial assistance later on.

In the SBA section that follows, a paperwork checklist is provided for SBA loans. A similar checklist will be required by most lending institutions.

Bring your banker into your **information loop**, and involve him or her in your business idea. Stop thinking about a banker as someone who will lend you an umbrella only on a sunny day; that may be true today, but it may not be true in the long run. You would not lend money to a stranger, so make sure your banker knows exactly what you are up to.

> **Information loop** A network of people who need to be kept informed about your business

Lure a banker to **your turf** if you have a retail or manufacturing operation. Say, "It's difficult to explain to you exactly what my shop is like. Why not come out for a look? We could have lunch. How's Thursday around noon?" On your own turf, you will be at ease and in a stronger position.

> **Your turf** One's place of business or the place one feels most comfortable

Comparison shop for money just as you would shop for any major purchase. The deals could surprise you. But like any major purchase, price is only one factor to consider.

Questions for Your Banker

What are your lending limits?
What is the loan approval process and who makes the final decisions on loans?
What experience does your bank have working with businesses in my industry?
Could you recommend a highly qualified lawyer? Bookkeeper? Accountant? Computer consultant? Advertising consultant? Patent attorney?
Are you interested in writing equipment leases?
What kind of terms do you give on accounts receivable financing?
Does your bank offer businesses Visa and MasterCard accounts? If so, what credit limit would be available?
What handling charge would I have to pay on credit card receipts?
What interest can I earn on my business checking account?
Do you have a merchants' or commercial window?
Do you have a night depository?
If you cannot lend me money, can you direct me to people who might be interested in doing so?
Do you make SBA-guaranteed loans?
If I open up a business checking account here, what else can you do for me?
What specifically will you be looking for in my Business Plan?

> **Equipment lease** Long-term arrangement with a bank or leasing company for renting capital equipment

> **SBA-guaranteed loans** Loans in which up to 90 percent of borrowed funds are insured by the federal government

---

Make Your Banker a Member of Your Team

A helpful banker can be an entrepreneur's best friend and a member of his or her auxiliary management team. Business growth demands money from external sources, and the more successful you become, the more likely you will need a close banking relationship to help you finance prosperity. If you grow more than 25 percent a year, you will most likely need financing help. Manufacturers often fall into financial trouble very fast, but even service firms have to wait for their customers to make payments.

Small Business Development Centers (SBDCs)

Federal funds are awarded to state universities and economic development agencies to establish Small Business Development Centers (SBDCs) at universities, chambers of commerce, and community colleges. These 63 centers, with almost 1,100 service locations, provide assistance in marketing, finance, and management to entrepreneurs. To access the SBDC sites in your area, click on *http://www.asbdc-us.org*. These programs will not fund your venture, but they will provide assistance and prepare you to seek funding.

Specialty programs exist within each state to meet the changing needs of each state's economy and to exploit the assets of each area. For example, New York offers the Veterans' Business Outreach Program, Manufacturing and Defense Development Center, Self-Employment Assistance Program, and the International Business Program. To address the needs of entrepreneurs in Florida, the SBDCs offer the following:

Business Technology Commercialization (BTC) Program

The BTC was established to serve as a commercialization catalyst by the FSBDCN [Florida Small Business Development Center Network] in 2003, providing support for the rapid commercialization of innovative products and processes, systems integration, productivity, and quality improvements by small and medium-sized enterprises (SMEs) engaged in R&D or manufacturing in Florida. The BTC assists in locating sources of venture capital, angel investors, and other alternative financing.

Defense Economic Transition Assistance (DETA) Program

The DETA Program was established in 2002 as a special program of the FSBDCN, hosted by the University of West Florida. The program is funded by the SBA and provides management and technical transition assistance to targeted defense-dependent businesses and individuals.

Office of International Programs

The Office of International Programs coordinates a statewide program designed to advance the global competitiveness of small business through preparation, education, and consultation.

Procurement and Technical Assistance Center (PTAC) Program

Established in 1985 as a special program of the FSBDCN, hosted by the University of West Florida, the PTAC Program is funded through federal and state agencies to provide assistance to Florida firms interested in doing business with the government. Federal matching funds are provided by the Defense Logistics Agency.

Brady Built Technologies, highlighted in Key Points from Another View, successfully used SBDC assistance to grow their business in Kentucky. Check out your state's SDBC programs. In addition, if you have specific needs that are not met by a program in your state, contact other state programs to see how they can assist you. Free SBDC counseling may prove to be more helpful than you could ever imagine. One of the best reasons to use these centers is to access the contacts they have developed through the years with government agencies, bankers, suppliers, and possibly even your potential customers.

Source of Florida SBDC information: *http://www.floridasbdc.com/SpecialPrograms/ SpecialPrograms.asp* (Accessed April 4, 2008).

Bankers are more willing to help if they understand your needs and know you are trying to anticipate them.

Start to develop a relationship with your local bank by completing Action Step 42, Befriend a Banker. If you have tapped out your own resources, investigated borrowing from friends and family, made a few bank inquiries, and there is still not enough in the money pot, it is time to shake a few other branches.

SBA PROGRAMS

Many people find out about SBA loan programs through their local bank referrals, Small Business Development Centers (SBDCs) (see Community Resource), and Service Core of Retired Executives (SCORE) offices. In 2007, SBDCs served over 600,000 clients and SCORE provided over 330,000 clients with advice and developed 29 online training modules. During 2007, more than 5,600 commercial and nonbank lenders made over 100,000 SBA-guaranteed $14.3 billion in small-business loans. Although direct loans are available, they are scarce; thus the SBA is primarily a guarantor of loans made by commercial and nonbank lenders.

The guarantee is between the SBA and the lending institution. If the business goes under, the government repays a major portion of the loan. Real estate loans are a major component of the SBA loan portfolio, because they are collateralized and more secure than other loans. Banks, lending in cooperation with the SBA, want to see at least a 20 to 30 percent commitment of personal funds before they loan money. Your local SBA office will provide you with a list of major SBA-guaranteed lenders in your area. Use the most experienced ones to cut through government red tape.

Several major SBA programs, their functions, and customer information provided by the SBA are highlighted below. If you plan to export, the information highlighted in the Global Village box will lead you to a vast array of resources. For further details and for the latest information on SBA programs, log on to *http://www.sba.gov/financing*.

Action Step 42
Befriend a Banker

Money creates its own world. There are several doorways into that world, and your banker sits at the threshold of one of them.

Start with a familiar place, the bank where you have your checking account. Make an appointment to talk to the chief officer (president, vice president, or branch manager). Use Questions for Your Banker on page 245 as a guide. If you are happy with your banker's answers, talk over the possibility of opening a business account for your business. If you have money tucked away in life insurance, or in a money-market fund somewhere, ask about the bank's money-market accounts. Check out business checking and bank fees, and compare them to other banks.

If you have specific lending needs such as exporting or leasing, seek out lenders who offer such services.

SBA Program Snapshots

The SBA offers numerous loan programs to assist small businesses. It is important to note, however, that the SBA is primarily a guarantor of loans made by private and other institutions.

PROGRAM: Basic 7(a) Loan Guaranty
FUNCTION: Serves as the SBA's primary business loan program to help qualified small businesses obtain financing when they might not be eligible for business loans through normal lending channels. It is also the agency's most flexible business loan program, since financing under this program can be guaranteed for a variety of general business purposes.

Loan proceeds can be used for most sound business purposes, including working capital, machinery and equipment, furniture and fixtures, land and building (including purchase, renovation, and new construction), leasehold improvements, and debt refinancing (under special conditions). Loan maturity is up to 10 years for working capital and generally up to 25 years for fixed assets.

CUSTOMER: Start-up and existing small businesses, commercial lending institutions

DELIVERED THROUGH: Commercial lending institution

SBA offers multiple variations of the basic 7(a) loan program to accommodate targeted needs.

PROGRAM: Certified Development Company (CDC), a 504 Loan Program
FUNCTION: Provides long-term, fixed-rate financing to small businesses to acquire real estate or machinery or equipment for expansion or modernization. Typically a 504 project includes a loan secured from a private-sector lender with a senior lien, a loan secured from a CDC (funded by a 100 percent SBA-guaranteed debenture) with a junior lien covering up to 40 percent of the total cost, and a contribution of at least 10 percent equity from the borrower.
    CUSTOMER: Small businesses requiring "brick and mortar" financing
    DELIVERED THROUGH: Certified development companies (private, nonprofit corporations set up to contribute to the economic development of their communities or regions)

PROGRAM: Microloan, a 7(m) Loan Program
FUNCTION: Provides short-term loans of up to $35,000 to small businesses and not-for-profit child-care centers for working capital or the purchase of inventory, supplies, furniture, fixtures, machinery and/or equipment. Proceeds cannot be used to pay existing debts or to purchase real estate. The SBA makes or guarantees a loan to an intermediary, who in turn makes the microloan to the applicant. These organizations also provide management and technical assistance. The loans are not guaranteed by the SBA. The microloan program is available in selected locations in most states.
    CUSTOMER: Small businesses and not-for-profit child-care centers needing small-scale financing and technical assistance for start-up or expansion
    DELIVERED THROUGH: Specially designated intermediary lenders (nonprofit organizations with experience in lending and in technical assistance)

PROGRAM: Loan Prequalificationt
FUNCTION: Allows business applicants to have their loan applications for $250,000 or less analyzed and potentially sanctioned by the SBA before they are taken to lenders for consideration. The program focuses on the applicant's character, credit, experience, and reliability rather than assets. An SBA-designated intermediary works with the business owner to review and strengthen the loan application. The review is based on key financial ratios, credit and business history, and the loan-request terms. The program is administered by the SBA's Office of Field Operations and SBA district offices.
    CUSTOMER: Designated small businesses
    DELIVERED THROUGH: Intermediaries operating in specific geographic areas

Source: *http://www.sba.gov/services/financialassistance/sbaloantopics/snapshot/index.html* (Accessed April 4, 2008).

In addition to the programs already discussed, two other major avenues of assistance may be of value to you, especially if you need equity capital or are involved in developing products.

- Small Business Investment Companies (SBICs) are private lenders licensed by the SBA to provide equity capital to small businesses. The recipients may give up some ownership, but not necessarily control, in exchange for the funds. Offering both debt and equity financing, the SBICs expect to recoup their investment in 5 to 7 years. In addition, according to New Markets Venture Capital (NMVC), their program has been developed to "promote economic development and the creation of wealth and job opportunities in low-income geographic areas and among individuals living in such areas." Access *http://www.sba.gov/aboutsba/sbaprograms/inv/index.html* and *http://www.sba.gov/aboutsba/sbaprograms/inv/nmvc/INV_NMVC_INDEX.html* for further program information.

- The Small Business Innovation Research (SBIR) program provides direct funding for development efforts. The SBIR offers an opportunity to develop innovative ideas that meet the research needs of the federal government, while opening the door to future commercialization. For further information, log on to *http://www.sba.gov/sbir* and access the *Handbook for SBIR Proposal Preparation*. See Chapter 3 for additional SBIR information.

SBA/Bank Financing Checklist

The following checklist for SBA/bank-financing applicants gives a fair idea of the *major* paperwork required for applying for a loan. The SBA's Application for a Business Loan, Form SBA-4, is included in Appendix C. Additional forms are available on the Web and at local SBA offices. For further information, contact the SBA Answer Desk at (800) UASK-SBA (827-5722) or visit *http://www.sba.gov*.

Checklist of required papers to be obtained from applicants for SBA/Bank Financing

1. Application for Loan: SBA form 4, 4I
2. Statement of Personal History: SBA form 912
3. Personal Financial Statement: SBA form 413
4. Detailed, current (within 90 days of application), signed balance sheet, profit and loss statements, and last 3 fiscal years' supplementary schedules required on current financial statements.
5. Detailed one-year projection of income and finances (please attach written explanation as to how you expect to achieve).
6. A list of names and addresses of any subsidiaries and affiliates, including concerns in which the applicant holds a controlling—but not necessarily a majority—interest and other concerns that may be affiliated by stock ownership, franchise, proposed merger, or otherwise with the applicant.
7. Certificate of doing business (if a corporation, stamp corporate seal on SBA form 4 section 12).
8. By law, the agency may not guarantee a loan if a business can obtain funds on reasonable terms from a bank or other private source. A borrower therefore must first seek private financing.

   A company must be independently owned and operated, not dominant in its field, and must meet certain standards of size in terms of employees or annual receipts. Loans cannot be made to speculative businesses, newspapers, or businesses engaged in gambling.

   Applicants for loans must also agree to comply with the SBA regulation that there will be no discrimination in employment or services to the public based on race, color, religion, national origin, gender, or marital status.
9. Signed business federal income tax returns for previous 3 years.
10. Signed personal federal income tax returns of principals for previous 3 years.
11. Personal resume, including business experience of each principal.
12. Brief history of the business and its problems: Include an explanation of why the SBA loan is needed and how it will help the business.
13. Copy of the business lease or a note from the landlord giving terms of the proposed lease.
14. For purchase of an existing business:
    a. Current balance sheet and profit and loss statement of business to be purchased.
    b. Previous 2 years federal income tax returns of the business.
    c. Proposed bill of sale including terms of sale.
    d. Asking price with schedules of:
       1. Inventory
       2. Machinery and equipment
       3. Furniture and fixtures

Source: Adapted from *http://www.sba.gov/idc/groups/public/documents/sba_homepage/forms_sba_disaster_reg6.txt* (Accessed June 25, 2008).

STATE PROGRAMS AND LOCAL DEVELOPMENT AUTHORITIES

Contact your local SBA office for a copy of *The State and Small Business: A Directory of Programs and Activities*. Local development authorities can be extremely flexible in their financing programs and are very helpful and interested in securing financing for growing businesses. Throughout the text we have highlighted many additional funding programs in the Incredible Resource and Community Resource boxes (for example, the SBDC information in this chapter's Community Resource on page 246 and in the Key Points from Another View on page 259).

Over 1,000 Community Development Financial Institutions (CDFI) serve economically distressed communities by providing credit, capital, and financial services that are often unavailable from mainstream financial institutions. CDFIs provide funding for individuals and communities outside the mainstream—financially, socially, and geographically. Their goal is to promote job creation, affordable housing, and financial literacy. CDFIs are affiliated with community development banks, credit unions, loan funds, and venture funds.

CDFIs are willing to loan to borrowers with less than pristine credit who are willing to accept advice and support from the institutions. In areas where good jobs are scarce, such as depressed or rural areas, funding may be available for $150,000 to $500,000. Locate your area CDFI institution at *http://www.cdfi.org*.

VENDOR FINANCING

An often-overlooked technique for reducing your capital requirements is to probe your vendors, major suppliers, for the best prices and terms available. Professional buyers and purchasing agents may ask their vendors to fill out an information sheet that forces them to write down the terms and conditions of their sales plans. This is a good idea for you as well.

A small business must buy professionally, and a **vendor statement** will help you do just that. With this form, your vendors' verbal promises become written promises. How well you buy is as important as how well you sell, because every dollar you save by buying right drops directly to the bottom line. To compete in your arena, you need best terms and prices available. The vendor statement will help you negotiate the best.

Personalize your vendor statements by placing your business name at the top. Then list the information you desire and provide blanks for the vendors to fill in. The following list provides the basics for a vendor statement:

1. Vendor's contact information
2. Sales rep's contact information
3. Amount of minimum purchase
4. Existence of quantity discounts (how much and what the requirements are to earn them)
5. Availability of dating or extended payment terms
6. Advertising/promotion allowances
7. Policies on returns for defective goods, including who pays the freight
8. Delivery times
9. Assistance (technical, sales, etc.)

Vendor statement A personally designed form that allows you to negotiate with each vendor from a position of informed strength

10. Product literature available

11. Point-of-purchase material provided

12. Support for grand opening, such as if the supplier will donate products or provide other support

13. Nearest other dealer handling this particular line

14. Special services the sales rep can provide

15. Credit card purchases

16. Vendor's signature, the date, and the agreement that you will be notified of any changes to the above immediately

Remember, the information the vendor writes on this statement is the starting point for negotiations. You should be able to negotiate more favorable terms with some vendors because they want your business. Revise your application form as you learn from experience how vendors can help you. If you are a new business, you will most likely be required to *personally* guarantee payment of your purchases in writing or only receive COD shipments.

If you are a new account, flash them your Business Plan. Then flash them your vendor form. Show them you are going to be a very important customer soon. Now it is time to prepare your own vendor statement form with Action Step 43.

ANGELS

While Janice was sharing her concept and Business Plan for a firm that specialized in home health care for the chronically ill and disabled with her best friend Sally, Sally's mother, Carol, popped in and said, "That sounds like a great idea. Tell me more." After a few hours, the "Angel Carol" invested $100,000 for a 20 percent share of the business. In addition, Carol offered to have dinner meetings once a week and provide business counseling. Her 30 years in various health care management positions made her a great mentor for Janice's home health care agency.

Angels may just appear, but such appearances should not be counted on. Thus, you will need to search out potential investors. The first step is to tell all your friends and family about your business idea and ask them if they have any possible contacts for you. Your research and their contacts may unearth potential investors. Always follow up with *anyone* who expresses an interest. Research shows that a business angel interested in your venture very often lives within 10 miles of you.

Angels come in many different sizes and types—from the small investor who just came into money to the professional investor who wants to help others follow their passion. Most angels like to invest in companies where they have knowledge and experience in the industry. It is hoped that your angel will not only support the financial part of your business but will also offer contacts and experience; in the end, such assistance may be far more important to your success than investment capital.

Specific industries and some communities offer angel networks, some of which offer a matchmaking process for investors and entrepreneurs. Private or college-sponsored investors' forums are offered where individuals are given 10 to 15 minutes to present their idea to potential investors. Forums are an excellent place to sell your idea, receive feedback, and possibly secure financing. SBA research reports that 250,000 angels provide more than $20 billion

Action Step 43

Designing a Vendor Statement Form

One of the best ways to save money is to ask for help from your vendors or suppliers. To do that, you will need to create your own special form that specifies the terms to be negotiated.

Be firm. Be pleasant. Be tough. Personalize this form by placing the name of your business at the top. Prepare your list of necessary information using the list of 16 suggestions provided. The vendor form provides talking points. Most vendors hold something back; design your form to help you learn what those things are, and get the best deal for your business.

Before negotiating, determine the standard terms offered in the industry. During negotiations, use a lot of open-ended questions like, "What else can you do for me?" Remember, vendors will ask you for detailed information. Also, dating and credit may be very limited for new accounts.

COD Paid in full upon delivery

annually to 300,000 new and expanding businesses each year. Your chance of finding an angel may be better than you thought!

Individual angel investors are now joining forces to form investor groups throughout the country that focus investments on a local or regional basis, as well as choosing to select specific industries on which to focus. The Kaufman Foundation, in association with the Angel Capital Association (ACA), has sought to gather together 200 investor groups throughout Canada and the United States. Access to these groups can be found through ACA's *http://angelcapitalassociation.org* Web site.

Information from one investor group highlighted on the ACA Web site, the Maine Angels at *http://www.maineangels.org*, follows:

> Maine Angels was founded in 2003 to enhance regional economic development by providing a cooperative mechanism for qualified investors to collaboratively locate, investigate, and make investments in promising early-stage companies. Maine Angels collective investments in companies typically range from $50,000 to $250,000 in most deals. In addition to providing financial capital, where appropriate Maine Angels members also provide intellectual capital to portfolio companies and the entrepreneurs who run them. Investments in companies based in Maine typically are eligible for Maine's Seed Capital Tax Credit Program administered by the Financial Authority of Maine (FAME).
>
> Maine Angels continues to grow its membership and its investment portfolio, aiming to remain the premier angel investment group in Maine. As of January, 2008, Maine Angels consists of 36 members who collectively have invested more than $2 million in 16 promising early stage companies. Naturally, Maine Angels focuses on companies based in Maine, but will consider—and has participated in—opportunities throughout the region and elsewhere, at times in collaboration with other angel or venture groups. Maine Angels members make individual investment decisions; no legal entity acts on behalf of Maine Angels investors. Maine Angels is an independent, non-governmental organization. Maine Angels members include current and former C-level executives, founders of successful companies, and experienced financial and technical professionals from a variety of industries. The group generally meets on the fourth Friday of each month to review investment opportunities. Many Maine Angels members are interested in actively mentoring the companies in which they invest, and this is encouraged.

Access sites referenced in this chapter to locate the angel groups in your area, then link to several and read through their Web sites to determine if any of these groups might be willing and able to finance your dream. Many of these groups offer training and workshops for entrepreneurs in addition to providing funds. Can you transfer the passion you have for your business to angel investors? Review the information on your elevator pitch from Chapter 3, and continue to refine it, now with financial data—your pitch will need to be very persuasive as you try to entice angel investors or venture capitalists.

VENTURE CAPITAL FIRMS

With venture capital firms, we enter the world of high rollers and high flyers. Unlike banks, which lend money that is secured, usually by real estate, venture capitalists do not lend money; they buy a piece of the business. They gamble

GLOBAL VILLAGE

Export Express Program

<u>How to Apply</u>

Interested businesses should contact their existing lender to determine if they are an SBA Express lender. Lenders that participate in SBA's Express program are also able to make Export Express Loans. Application is made directly to the lender. The lenders use their own application material in addition to SBA's Borrower Information Form. Lenders approve the request and then submit a limited amount of eligibility information to SBA's National Loan Processing Center. The SBA provides a response within 24 hours.

<u>SBA's Role in Export Express Financing</u>

The SBA has placed a priority on helping small business exporters. 70% of all U.S. exporters have 20 or fewer employees. Most banks in the U.S. do not lend against export orders, export receivables or letters of credit. SBA provides lenders with up to an 85% guaranty on export loans as a credit enhancement, so that participating banks will make export loans that make the necessary export financing available.

<u>Eligible Businesses</u>

SBA Export Express loans are available to businesses that meet the normal requirements for an SBA business loan guaranty. Financing is available for manufacturers, wholesalers, export trading companies and service exporters. Loan applicants must demonstrate that the loan proceeds will enable them to enter a new export market or expand an existing export market. Applicants must have been in business, though not necessarily in exporting, for at least 12 months.

<u>Loan Amount</u>

The maximum Export Express line of credit/loan amount is $250,000. Participating banks receive an 85% SBA guaranty on loan amounts up to $150,000 and 75% on loan amounts between $150,000 - $250,000.

<u>Interest Rate</u>

The SBA does not establish or subsidize interest rates on loans. Interest rates are negotiated between the borrower and the lender, but may never exceed SBA interest rate caps. Rates can either be fixed or variable, and are tied to the prime rate as published in The Wall Street Journal.

<u>Collateral</u>

Lenders follow collateral policies and procedures that the lender has established for its non-SBA guaranteed loans.

<u>Export Financing</u>

The SBA Export Express program provides exporters and lenders a streamlined method to obtain SBA backed financing for loans and lines of credit up to $250,000. Lenders use their own credit decision process and loan documentation; exporters get access to their funds faster. The SBA provides an expedited eligibility review and provides a response in less than 24 hours.

<u>Key Benefits</u>

SBA Export Express helps small businesses develop or expand their export markets. Loan proceeds may be used to finance any export development activity, including:

(continued)

(continued)

> Standby Letters of Credit when required as a bid bond, performance bond or advance payment guarantee
> Participation in a foreign trade show
> Translation of product brochures or catalogues for use in overseas markets
> General lines of credit for export purposes
> Service contracts from buyers located outside the United States
> Transaction-specific financing needs associated with completing actual export orders
> Purchase of real estate and equipment to be used in the production of goods or services for export
> Provide term loans and other financing to enable small business concerns, including export trading companies and export management companies, to develop foreign markets
> Acquire, construct, renovate, modernize, improve or expand productive facilities or equipment to be used in the United States in the production of goods or services for export

How to Apply

Interested businesses should contact their existing lender to determine if they are an SBA Express lender. Lenders that participate in SBA's Express program are also able to make Export Express Loans. Application is made directly to the lender. The lenders use their own application material in addition to SBA's Borrower Information Form. Lenders approve the request and then submit a limited amount of eligibility information to SBA's National Loan Processing Center. The SBA provides a response within 24 hours.

Source: *http://www.sba.gov/services/financialassistance/SpecialPurposeLoans/ exportexpress/index.html* (Accessed April 5, 2008).

on the business's rapid growth, hoping to reap a 300 to 500 percent return on their investment within 3 to 5 years. Venture capitalists provided more than $29.4 billion to entrepreneurs in 2007. The payoff for most venture-capital firms occurs when the company interests enough investors in an initial public offering (IPO) of common stock, or when the company they are invested in is purchased by another business. When the business goes public or is sold, the venture capitalists take out their original investment and, it is hoped, a substantial profit.

Go public Firm sells stock to raise capital

Venture capitalists vary, but most prefer to enter the financial picture at the second stage of a firm's development—when the business has proven its potential and needs a large infusion of cash to support growth. Currently, they tend to prefer high-tech concepts in embryonic industries with high growth potential. The funders look for compelling ideas backed by a strong, experienced team. Credibility of your financial projections and a validation of your research are essential to gain credibility with venture capitalists.

Venture capitalists come in many forms. For example, there are family firms (Rockefeller), industrial firms (GE), banks, and other firms (insurance companies, finance companies). Some venture-capitalist firms target specific industries such as health care, biotechnology, the Internet, software, and telecommunications. One example is SAIL Venture Partners, headquartered in Costa Mesa, California, which specializes in finding firms in the energy/clean-tech sector that are "doing good while doing well." Managing partner Alan Sellers shares, "In our case, we look for global, multibillion-dollar markets. You have to be able to grow the product throughout the world profitably. Those kinds of markets aren't entirely easy to find, but you don't need a huge percentage of the market to succeed. If we get 5 percent of it, we're doing really well." An overview of one company in SAIL'S portfolio follows:

WATERHEALTH INTERNATIONAL

Water contamination affects up to 2 billion people and, and according to some sources, at least one million die every year because of it. With bold new technology, Lake Forest, CA based WaterHealth International intends to do something about that, not only saving lives but also permitting economic growth in the impoverished Third World. The technology utilizes an ultraviolet light source suspended in air to inactivate a wide array of microorganisms.

"We have rapidly growing operations in India and the Philippines, and we're starting to do some things in Africa," says Dr. Tralance Addy, the company's president and CEO.

Source: OCMetro, May 10, 2007.

The *Directory of Venture Capital & Private Equity Firms 2008*, available in most large public libraries, provides names, addresses, and desired investments of venture-capital firms. Also, local newspapers and business magazines frequently compile names of local and regional venture capitalists. Use these sources and others online to determine which firms are interested in your selected industry and to determine the firms' minimum and maximum investment levels.

For additional financing options, visit Idea Café's superb "Financing Your Business" Web site, *http://www.businessownersideacafe.com/financing/index.php*. You might discover venture funds such as those unearthed by Evergreen Lodge, highlighted on page 257.

The following additional Web sites provide excellent listings of venture capitalists—*http://www.vfinance.com* and *http://www.ncva.org*. Also, vFinance provides a questionnaire shown in Figure 9.2, for people who would like to know if they are ready for venture-capital funding. Take time to review the questions to determine if venture capital is in your future.

After thoroughly reviewing all your financing options, it is time to test the waters with Action Step 44.

--- figure **9.2**

Are You Ready for Venture Capital?

1. **What is the current development stage of your business venture? Choose only one.**
   - o **Idea:** Conceptual product without revenues/customers/employees
   - o **Start-up:** Prototype product with preliminary sales
   - o **Growth:** New product—minimum revenues
   - o **Expansion:** Established product with customers—close to break even
   - o **Mature:** Established—operating at a profit

2. **What is the value added by your product or service? Please compare to direct and indirect competitors in your industry.**
   - o Similar product to others
   - o Product offers new features not available elsewhere
   - o Radically new product and service with overwhelming advantages
   - o Product with 20% to 50% cost-benefit advantage
   - o Product with greater than 50% cost-benefit advantage

3. **How developed is your relationship with customers? Pick the best one.**
   - o None yet
   - o Some identified
   - o Signed letters of intent
   - o Current test customers
   - o Paying customers
   - o Established repeat customers

4. **What are your "trailing revenues"? (i.e., sales for the past 12 months)?**
   - o None
   - o Less than $100,000
   - o Between $100,000 to $1M
   - o Over $1M
   - o Over $5M

5. **What are your expected revenues four years from now?**
   - o Less than $1M per year
   - o Over $1M but less than $10M per year
   - o Over $10M but less than $100M per year
   - o Over $100M but less than $500M per year
   - o Over $500M

(continued)

figure **9.2**

Are You Ready for Venture Capital? (*continued*)

6. What is your expected market share in your industry in 4 years?
o   Do not know
o   Less than 20%
o   Between 20% and 40%
o   Between 40% and 70%
o   Over 70%

7. How large are your target market and industry? Note that you should be very specific. (For example, selling peanuts at the circus puts you in a very small market, not in the multibillion-dollar food or entertainment industry). Base your answers on the preceding two questions, or revise your answers from above.
o   Less than $10 M per year
o   Over $10M but less than $100M per year
o   Over $100M but less than $500M per year
o   Over $500M but less than $1B per year
o   Over $1B

8. What is the current state of competition in your industry?
o   Unidentified competitors
o   Many small competitors
o   Several large competitors dominate the industry
o   One or two large competitors dominate the industry

9. What is your relative size versus your competitors?
o   Similar size/advantage over others
o   One of the first movers into the industry
o   Best network and alliances with exclusive contracts
o   First Place: Currently larger by 10% to 49% over next competitor
o   First Place: Currently the largest by 50% over next competitor

10. What intellectual property does your venture currently have?
o   None
o   Trademarks and copyrights
o   Process patents
o   Patent-pending technology
o   Patented technology (granted)
o   Patented technology implemented in product
o   Patented technology with royalty stream

11. Is your key executive team (CEO/CFO/Marketing/ CIO/Ops) on board?
o   Founders only—top spots pending funding
o   CEO and others currently on a part-time basis
o   CEO and others have full-time commitment
o   CEO and others have worked on venture for over 1 year full-time

12. Has top management had previous successes?
o   None . . . yet!
o   With previous employers
o   Small-business success
o   IPO or company sold for more than $10M but less than $100M
o   Company sold for more than $100M
o   IPO taken to market for more than $100M

13. How much money has management committed to the venture so far (pure capital, without any in-kind or labor costs)?
o   None
o   Less than $10,000
o   Between $10,000 and $100,000
o   Between $100,000 and $500,000
o   Over $500,000

14. What are the most likely exit scenarios for tyour investors (i.e., how will they get their money back in 5 years)?
o   Have not thought about it
o   Interest payment
o   Dividends
o   Sale to management
o   Sale to strategic buyers
o   IPO

15. What detail exists for your financial statements?
o   None written yet
o   Basic income statement only
o   Detailed income statement, balance sheet, and cash flows
o   Complete set of statements reviewed by accountant
o   Complete set of statements audited by accountant

16. How developed is your marketing plan?
o   None written yet
o   Promotion, pricing, and distribution addressed
o   The above, plus branding and image
o   Test-marketed branding and marketing

17. How much market research have you done for new or follow-on products?
o   None
o   Industry literature
o   Surveys
o   Focus groups
o   Market tests with selected customers
o   Functioning product with multiple customers

18. How does your Business Plan address inherent risks?
o   Best-case scenario is realistic
o   Worst-case scenarios are outlined
o   Multiple scenarios are considered and planned
o   Measures to counter risk are identified
o   Measures to counter risk are implemented

19. How detailed is your Business Plan document?
o   None written yet
o   Executive summary of about four pages
o   Business Plan written by CEO, about 20 pages
o   Total business and operational plan, ready to implement
o   Professionally written and edited plan

20. How much venture capital are you seeking right now?
o   Less than $200,000
o   Between $200,000 and $1M
o   Between $1M and $5M
o   Over $5M

Source: *http://www.vfinance.com* (Accessed July 22, 2004).

✦ *Passion* ✦

The Resort that Serves its Staff

Entrepreneurs turn around a rustic lodge—and the lives of the needy youth they employ

Evergreen Lodge (*http://www.evergreenlodge.com*) in Groveland, California, near Yosemite National Park, is a rare phenomenon: a business that has achieved its dual mission of giving back to society and earning a profit. While building its thriving internship program, Evergreen Lodge achieved about $3.5 million in sales for 2005 and should exceed $4 million for 2006.

The founders—marketing executive Lee Zimmerman, 42; his Stanford Business School roommate, Brian Anderluh, 39, a former Internet executive; and Dan Braun, 38, who runs a mountain-climbing tour business—made their first distribution to investors in the spring of 2006. They are considering buying other properties, such as a hotel, where they can add similar internship programs. Tom LaTour, former chairman and CEO of Kimpton Hotels & Restaurants in San Francisco, recently joined their board and is helping plan their next steps.

Early on, the company's founders discovered from their business contacts that helping underprivileged kids opened up little-known sources of start-up money that are not available to many small businesses. These pools included grants and venture capital set aside for community development and equity capital from investors with social goals.

Zimmerman attributes the company's success in fundraising to its unique business model and "our tenacity and relentlessness in tapping the ill-defined capital market for such ventures."

By avoiding conventional, more costly sources of financing, such as traditional venture capital—which would be hard for new entrepreneurs in the hospitality industry to obtain, in any case—they insulated themselves from outside pressures to scale back the internship program in the early days when money was tight.

Running the program costs about $150,000 annually, because the lodge employs a full-time manager for the youth program, provides an outdoor recreation program for the interns, and subsidizes housing for both the staff and interns. "Companies like this one have to strike a balance between their social goals and their financial return," says Rick Aubry, a lecturer in social entrepreneurship at the Stanford Graduate School of Business. "The successful ones are the exception rather than the rule."

The internship program has also helped lure committed employees to the out-of-the-way lodge's 60-member, full-time team. "We have been able to attract fantastic staff whose priorities are aligned with ours and who have the kind of compassionate personality that is a good fit for our industry," says Zimmerman.

With the internship program established, the founders plan to start emphasizing it in marketing materials that they will place in the cabins this spring to draw visitors who want to help young people. "It will differentiate us from competitors," says Zimmerman.

Teaming up with Braun, who runs a successful mountain-climbing business, Zimmerman and Anderluh bought a family-run guest lodge for wilderness travelers for $1.25 million in 2001. They envisioned offering internships that would train needy 18- to 24-year-olds in skills including cooking, housekeeping, maintenance, and carpentry. The lodge would provide social services, such as

Action Step 44
Prepare to Meet Your Lenders

Know who your potential lenders are and why they should want to help you.

Part A. List potential lenders and investors. Begin with family and friends and move on to business acquaintances and colleagues. Do not forget to include institutional lenders.

Part B. Now list reasons why lenders should want to invest in your business. What inducements are you offering potential investors? The following chapters will discuss the legal form of your business and you will need to ask yourself if incorporation would encourage additional investment.

Part C. Test your proposed presentation to bankers with your colleagues. Explain that this is just a test, and that you would like their honest feedback on your presentation and the business itself. Watch their reactions, and listen carefully to all their questions and objections. Take the time to write down thorough answers to each of their questions and objections, Send an email to your colleagues with your responses. Ask them to review your responses and ask if they have any additional questions or thoughts, Are there any questions or objections still remaining? If so, take time now to find the answers, as your investors may ask the same questions. Be prepared.

Part D. Time to go out and meet with lenders and shake another branch of the money tree. Good luck!

(continued)

(continued)

career-planning sessions, while giving interns a chance to hike, bike, and kayak.

To buy and renovate the lodge with 50 new cabins, the three partners raised a total of $10 million, taking out loans and obtaining equity investments from a variety of public and private sources. Although upgrading the resort was difficult (contractors had to haul supplies to build the cabins through remote woods), achieving the company's social goals was tougher.

The first summer, in 2002, the lodge recruited six interns from social-service groups and the Job Corps. The founders decided generally not to include those who lacked work experience or needed costly medical treatment for problems such as drug addiction. It would be too expensive to add the necessary staff and resources. They paid the interns $7.50 to $8.50 an hour.

Not every hire worked out. For starters, the partners had not realized just how foreign the lodge might seem to recruits, many of whom had never been out of an urban area. Two of the six interns left before their four-month internships ended because they missed city life.

Determined to attract career-oriented candidates, the partners contacted more vocational-training agencies the following year and fine-tuned their job descriptions. They also learned to be firmer with interns who showed up late for work, firing them if necessary. To retain recruits, they teamed each intern with a specific staff member and had supervisors meet with them regularly. They also extended internships for those who needed extra help.

So far, 40 youths have completed the internship program, which now includes about 20 recruits a year. Many graduates have won full-time jobs. After his recent internship, Roy Edwards, 24, of Richmond, California, found a position in maintenance at the Tony Lambourne Hotel on San Francisco's Nob Hill. "I'd probably never have gotten this job otherwise," he says.

Source: Adapted from Ann Field, *http://money.cnn.com/magazines/fsb/ fsb_archive/2006/12/01/8395129/index.htm* (Accessed February 26, 2008). © 2008 Time Inc. All rights reserved.

SUMMARY

Few start-up firms have access to venture-capital markets, bank financing, vendor credit, or angels at the beginning. The majority of ventures start from the bottom up—bootstrapping their venture and using capital from friends and family.

Keep excellent financial records. When investors come calling, you will be prepared with the documents they want to see. Cultivate your relationship with your banker while you are growing your business.

Be prepared to put in sweat equity for at least the first few years. Learn how to conserve capital and manage debt and accounts receivables. If you are fulfilling your customers' needs and keeping your nose to the grindstone, your day will come.

Money creates its own world. It has its own customs, rituals, and rules. Before you start asking people for money for your business, research the world of money. Read *Barrons, Fast Company, Forbes, Fortune, Business Week,* and the *Wall Street Journal*. Find someone who knows more about money than you do. Ask questions. Listen. As you continue to work on your Business Plan, remember what lenders are looking for:

- Capacity and time frame of repayment
- Character and commitment of borrower
- Strong idea with identifiable target market in a growing market
- Collateral
- Background and experience of management team

THINK POINTS FOR SUCCESS

- Your banker may be a doorway to the world of money. Use that door.
- Conserving capital is essential in the beginning and prudent at all times.
- Take as little capital out of your business as possible.
- In dealing with bankers and vendors, use lots of open-ended questions, such as "What other steps do you think I need to take to improve my Business Plan?"
- Become operational as fast as you can.
- Aim for your break-even point and strong cash flow as soon as possible.

KEY POINTS FROM ANOTHER VIEW

Brady Built Technologies
Lebanon, Kentucky
www.bradybuiltinc.com

In 2000, Joe Brady knew there was room in the marketplace for another metal fabricating business in Central Kentucky. In his job in the industry, he consistently saw mid-size companies being overlooked or turned away. He just wasn't sure how to capitalize on this niche opportunity. The local banker suggested that Joe and his wife, Carla, utilize the SBDC to determine the feasibility of opening a metal fabrication business in a building located next to their home. The relationship between the Bradys and the SBDC began at their kitchen table, when Patricia Krausman met with them to assist with the feasibility analysis of the idea and put together a proposal for funding. Throughout the life of their business, they have continued to rely upon the services of the SBDC for management assistance in growth planning and financing.

After just one year in operation, the Bradys again looked to the SBDC for assistance with securing funding for an expansion and guidance on assessing their growth challenges related to cash flow. Patricia helped them gather data, analyze their historical financials, and assess cash flow problems. By creating financials and a growth plan for the bank, they realized their first expansion for the business.

Two years later, Brady Built Technologies completely outgrew the facilities located next to their home. They decided it was time to move operations into a larger, more suitable industrial setting. Again, they contacted Patricia Krausman for assistance with their need to move and expand the operations. She helped gather the data for the loan proposal, assessed expenses related to their building, identified appropriate funding sources, and connected them with those agencies. She ensured that they were able to acquire the funding necessary to move forward with their project.

The Bradys continued to work with Patricia as they designed their new facility, decided on a location, purchased additional equipment, and hired new employees. By the spring of 2006, and after 6 years of counseling with Patricia Krausman, Brady Built Technologies moved to their new, 18,000-square-foot facility, which allowed them to realize their growth potential and meet true market demand.

Patricia Krausman's assistance helped build the business from the ground up to its current success. Throughout the life of the business, she has served as an advisor and management consultant to ensure their growth and success. She helped them create documents and gather financial data imperative to the financing of start-up and expansion. Additionally, she helped them understand and manage their cash flow by creating spreadsheets and introducing them to QuickBooks.

Because the Bradys sought funding from local economic development agencies and were looking to acquire land for their facility, the expansion became a community affair. Patricia, who has worked extensively with economic and community leaders in their area, helped facilitate the communication between the Bradys and the community officials they needed to work with. By identifying appropriate funding resources and bringing everyone to the table, she was able to leverage traditional bank funding with job creation and economic impact program dollars.

As a result of those efforts, Brady Built Technologies currently employs 27 employees at their 18,000 square foot facility in Lebanon, Kentucky. Sales have grown from under $100,000 during their first year to $1.5 million in 2006. They are projecting sales to exceed $2.3 million in 2007. This is substantial economic impact—especially in Lebanon, a town of 5,500 people.

Brady Built Technologies was the third place winner of the ASBDC and Bank of America 2007 Small Business Client Success Competition.

Source: *http://www.asbdc-us.org/2007_Success_Kentucky.html* (Accessed April 4, 2008).

- Understand the importance and necessity of professional legal advice from the start.
- Decide which legal form is best for your business.
- Explore the good, the bad, and the ugly of partnerships.
- Review the advantages of forming a limited liability company.
- Explore nonprofit opportunities.
- Understand legal escape routes.

- Protect your business with a buy–sell agreement.
- Review patent protection.
- Understand copyright laws.
- Take action to protect your trademark or service mark.
- License your invention.
- Review rules for advertising within safe, legal limits.
- Explore family business issues.

chapter 10

Legal Concerns
Staying Out of Court

In your interviews of successful entrepreneurs, you have probably run across the four main legal forms for small business: sole proprietorship, partnership, corporation, and limited liability company. Which is the right form for you? It is common, although not always advisable, for an entrepreneur to start out as a sole proprietorship or a partnership and then to **incorporate** later. But after you explore the options that follow, you may decide to protect yourself early on.

Incorporate Form an artificial, immortal business entity

IT PAYS TO LOOK AHEAD

How will you exit a partnership? What liabilities could occur, and are your personal assets sheltered? Is your insurance in place? Are you aware of taxes due? Who is your lawyer?

Imagine that you are in a great business with a partner you trust and respect. When should you incorporate or sign a partnership agreement? Perhaps sooner than you think. That's what Phil Johnson would tell you now.

Sail Away

The Power Sailor was my idea. My partner, Steve Savitch, said it would break us, and I should have listened to him. We'd been friends for at least a dozen years and we'd been partners—Savitch and Johnson, Software Consultants—for the past three. This year we were each going to clear more than $200,000.

I had this idea that we could buy a boat for the partnership; write off the down payment as an expense, and do our company image a world of good.

"Image, Steve," I said. "Image."

"Uh-oh," Steve said. "Here we go with the immeasurable intangibles."

"It's not intangible when you think about those prospects coming from Chicago next week," I said. "A cruise to Captiva Island should soften them up, don't you think?"

The first payment wasn't due for a month, and when Steve and I took the boat out with our wives, I felt like a prince of the sea. We'd pulled off a smooth deal, and I patted myself on the back every time I thought about the write-offs.

Our boat, Sunbiz, boosted business, just like I'd thought it would. We closed the Chicago deal and were busy on a couple of other deals that looked promising. We made the first payment with no trouble, and when Steve countersigned the check, he admitted he was beginning to like the boat.

For a couple of weeks, Steve took his laptop and slept on the Sunbiz. I didn't recognize this early sign. We took the Sunbiz out one weekend with four prospects from St. Louis, and Steve seemed preoccupied. I closed the deal on Sunday, 15 minutes before putting them on the plane for home. But when I called Steve's house to tell him the good news, his wife, Mary, told me he was still at the boat.

Monday, Steve didn't come to work until almost noon. He looked tired, but he handed me his projections and we got on with planning our strategy for the next couple of months.

"Anything wrong, partner?" I asked. "You seem a little far-off today."

"Sorry," Steve said. He was never one to admit to having problems. "My mind wandered a bit there. Where were we?"

Write-offs Legitimate business deductions accepted by the IRS

Countersigning A situation in which two or more signatures are required before action can occur

On Thursday, Steve still didn't make it to work after missing Wednesday. I called his house in the morning. No answer. I thought of driving down to the dock to check the boat, but didn't. When I arrived at the dock with clients around 4:30 that afternoon, there was no Sunbiz. Someone on the next dock said Steve had taken off early that morning.

Then Joey, the guy who pumps gas, came up waving a gas bill for $800—one I'd thought Steve had paid. And the bad news didn't end there. The next day, a fellow who sells radar equipment called me with a $2,000 bill.

I was in shock. There I stood, with two clients in deck shoes and shorts.

My cell phone rang. It was Mary, Steve's wife. She read me Steve's goodbye letter—he was off to explore the world with his new love.

Now my stomach was really hurting. My partner Steve was gone and I was going to have to cover all his business debts, including the payment on the Sunbiz. Terrific!

The problem was that Steve and I had never seen the need for having anything in writing. We were both men of good faith. We had each pulled our weight in the business, and we had balanced each other's skills.

Now that Steve was gone, I felt lost, angry, and betrayed. For the first time in 22 years of business, I made an appointment to talk to a lawyer. He just shook his head.

Last week, when I was closing the business down and preparing to return to work for my old boss, I received a postcard from Steve, from Tahiti. "Sorry, Phil," it read. "Didn't mean to run out on you. It was the only way I could handle it. These things happen. Your partner, Steve."

HIRE AN EXPERIENCED ATTORNEY FIRST

If you do not want to end up left high and dry like Phil Johnson, start your search for a good, experienced small-business attorney now. Attorneys can help you:

- Create the right business structure for a partnership or a corporation—a structure that gives the protection, tax treatment, and flexibility you will need.
- Review advertising and marketing materials to ensure no state or federal laws are violated.
- Organize your human resources department to keep you outside the courtroom; hiring and firing employees is problematic to say the least—improper handling of even one employee can cost you your business.
- Research and protect you in regard to **product liability**.
- Review all contracts and agreements before you sign.
- Protect intellectual property through proper use and development of **trademarks**, **servicemarks**, **copyrights**, and **patents**.
- License your product.
- Handle collections and **bankruptcy** problems.
- Plan your **exit strategy**.
- Write partnership agreements and **buy–sell agreements**.

Network with your contacts to secure a lawyer with experience in your. Many laws are state specific, so you also need someone well versed in your

Product liability Legal exposure if a customer becomes ill or sustains injury or property damage because of a faulty product

Trademark A word, phrase, logo, design, or anything used to identify goods or services and differentiate them from competitors

Servicemark Used to protect services offered

Copyright Protects the expression of an idea

Patent Right to make, sell, offer for sale or use an invention

Bankruptcy Legal and financial process if a debtor's financial obligations are greater than his or her assets

Exit strategy A plan to disengage from business at a future point in time

Buy-sell agreement An advance contractual agreement that determines how a business is to be valued if one or more partners buys out another

Action Step 45

Interview Lawyers

1. Network your business contacts for the names of three to five attorneys with experience in forming small business corporations and partnerships. Concentrate on those with experience in your industry.
2. Contact the state bar association and review information on each attorney.
3. Contact the most promising candidates and set up appointments to interview prospective lawyers. The first thing to look for is someone you can get along with. Then look for experience in the world of small business. A hot trial lawyer may have a lot of charisma, but you want a nuts-and-bolts, experienced, small-business or entrepreneur specialist who can save you time, pain, and money.
4. During your meeting, discuss fees and costs for such things as drawing up a complex partnership, a buy-sell agreement, or the cost of setting up a corporation. Record any pertinent information. Note: legal fees are not an area you want to scrimp on.
5. A good lawyer will offer perspectives that will be helpful in the formation of your business. You may have to search for awhile, and it will cost you, but there is no substitute for good legal help. After your interviews, review your impressions of each attorney, and determine which one you would like to hire.

Retainer fee An agreement to secure the services of an attorney for a fixed fee for a given period of time or for a specific legal problem

state's laws. This is not the time to save money by using your niece who just passed the bar examination. Large law firms may prove very advantageous for rapidly growing biotechnology, environmental, and manufacturing firms, all of which often have specific legal issues. Expertise is vital for initial and continued success in these types of businesses, and thus they require the resources of a large firm.

If you are dealing with intellectual property or international customers and manufacturers, read the Incredible Resource and Global Village information on pages 287 and 280; they provide many educational sources that will lead you to legal professionals handling these complex issues.

Another important role an attorney plays is to provide you entrée into his or her contacts throughout an industry and to bankers, investors, advertising agencies, and accountants. No amount of money can buy you such ready access.

Business litigators are attorneys who primarily handle lawsuits. Initially, you are more likely to be looking for a transactional attorney whose specialty is handling corporate and contract matters. If you are dealing in an industry or an area known for litigation, then having a firm that covers both litigation and transaction would be preferable. Before hiring an attorney, contact your state bar to make sure the person is in good standing.

You need to have a good attorney, accountant, financial planner, banker, and insurance agent on your team. Their support and expertise can keep you on track, out of jail, and protected from unforeseen circumstances. Develop an attorney–client relationship before an employee or customer sues you or your partner leaves for Tahiti. Preventive legal fees are far less costly than clean-up fees if you are sued.

After you have networked to find several lawyers, contact each of them to set up a half-hour consultation. Prepare for your meetings by listing several questions you have about your business as well as questions about financial issues. You are looking for someone you are comfortable with and someone who understands the needs of your business. The attorney–client privilege covers your meetings, so be honest and share relevant information. If you are organized, you will be able to gather a great deal of information in a short time. Select someone with a reputation for integrity and experience in your industry. Complete Action Step 45.

Understanding How Lawyers Operate and Reducing Your Legal Costs

Lawyers either charge by the hour for services they render or they work on a retainer fee based on prepaid hours. Or you may have access to a prepaid legal plan in which you receive a variety of services for a flat annual fee. In addition, in the high-tech sector, some lawyers are willing to work for stock options. Legal fees range from $150 to more than $750 an hour. Specialized attorneys, such as patent or copyright experts, may have even higher hourly charges.

To benefit from each appointment with your lawyer, arm yourself first with basic legal research you conduct using the library or Internet. This will cut down the time you spend with the lawyer and may reduce your fees. As suggested throughout the text, using online legal resources and books does *not* eliminate the need for—and should *never* be used as a substitute for—professional legal advice from your attorney. Legal online sources *do* provide an excellent starting point for gathering information and beginning your initial research. In addition, many of the sites provide guidelines on selecting legal counsel, which may be of great service—especially if you need to locate a specialized attorney, such as a trademark specialist.

The following sites, in addition to many others provided throughout the text, offer excellent preliminary information:

http://www.lawsource.com/also—American Law Source Online is a compilation of links to online sources of legal information for the United States.

http://www.findlaw.com—Findlaw includes basic legal information concerning contracts, employment, and patents.

http://www.ilrg.com—Internet Legal Resource Group links to over 4,000 Web sites and is an excellent source of legal forms.

http://www.patentpending.com—American Patent and Trademark Law Center provides access to basic patent and trademark information.

http://www.law.cornell.edu—Legal Information Institute provides access to constitutions, codes, court opinions, statutes, enterprise law, etc.

http://www.nolo.com—Nolo provides free information and an incredible list of legal workbooks and manuals to assist you.

http://www.morebusiness.com—More Business offers excellent articles offering advice concerning legal, marketing, and technology issues.

Again, these and other sites provide excellent advice, but *always* use experienced legal counsel when conducting business.

CHOOSING BUSINESS LEGAL FORMS

You can open a sole proprietorship with a minimum of hassle. You might need only a city license, a resale license, and perhaps a Doing Business As (DBA) statement or a Fictitious Business Name Statement, though the name of this form may be different in various states. It is also advisable to obtain an employer's identification number (EIN) from the federal government (see Appendix C).

Fictitious Business Name Statement An accurate and easy-to-find record of the responsible party who is conducting business

The legal paperwork for a partnership is sometimes as simple as that for a sole proprietorship, if all parties agree on basic concepts. You can form a partnership with a handshake and dissolve it without a partnership agreement, and if you are very lucky it might work. But, we strongly urge you to hire a lawyer to prepare a partnership agreement that will protect you from trouble. Do not be left high and dry like Phil. Less than 10 percent of the small businesses in the United States are partnerships; select your partners wisely and carefully.

A limited liability company (LLC) may be ideal for closely held firms. It offers limited personal liability protection to all owners, termed members, and is treated like a partnership or Subchapter S corporation on members' individual tax returns. This avoids the double taxation of income (tax on business profits and individual income) and is usually less costly to form than a corporation. An LLC operating agreement must be filed with the state (see Figure 10.1).

Subchapter S corporation Legal entity that may provide positive tax treatment for small business

Forming a corporation takes the most paperwork but gives you more flexibility and a shield that may protect you in case your business harms someone. Table 10.1 summarizes the major business entities.

WHICH BUSINESS ENTITY IS BEST FOR YOU?

Only you, your lawyer, and your business and tax advisors together can decide what form your business should take based on your present situation, the possibilities within your business, and the future you desire. Discuss the following with your advisors before making the determination:

- International exposure
- Tax implications

- Liability issues
- Litigiousness of customers, employees, and businesses in your state
- Plans for business growth
- Family structure and involvement in the business
- Relationship with potential partners
- Capital requirements
- Exit strategy
- Employment issues

Spend time and money consulting with your financial team to determine what is best for you early on, because there are many pitfalls, and change can be costly. Let your team provide guidance and help you avoid major errors.

The legal form of your business is just that—a form, a shape. To your customers, the particular form you choose may not be obvious; but to you, the right shape is absolutely essential. You want your business to be rock-solid, stable, and protected—and you want to be able to change its form if the first choice does not work.

Beyond the mental images we have of these forms of ownership, there are business realities—and various amounts of paperwork—that you should know about. Table 10.1 summarizes the differences among the various forms.

Sole Proprietorships

Most small businesses begin as sole proprietorships. If you start a business on your own without partners, you are a sole proprietor *unless* you form an LLC or corporation. If this form is your choice, the paperwork will be relatively easy. Check with your local city offices to determine which licenses will be needed. If you are a service business, you may be required to purchase a license to do business in each city in which you operate. In some cities, inspectors visit work sites to ensure that all businesses are in compliance. Procure your required licenses—fines are considerably more expensive than licenses.

You will also need to discuss tax requirements with your accountant, insurance matters with an insurance representative, and legal issues with an attorney before you open your doors. If you are conducting a business in a name other than your own, the Uniform Commercial Code (UCC) requires that you publish notice in your community newspaper to notify customers and creditors of who owns the business. Corporations may be exempt. Contact your newspaper for the DBA forms, fill out the forms, and send a check—usually for less than $100—to the newspaper to complete the process. Normally, this must be done prior to opening your bank account.

Partnerships

A partnership, as many find out too late, is only an accounting entity. It does not shield you from trouble. It will not make your business immortal or continuous, and it is taxed in the same way as a sole proprietorship. One advantage of a partnership is that it allows the financial and moral support of teammates.

A partnership is made up of at least two parties. There can be more, but the more partners a business has, the trickier the decisions become. Think of a ship with a dozen captains—who will chart the ship's course?

table **10.1**

S Corp., C Corp., or No Corp., Choice of Business Entities—A Comparison

Applicable Factor *Formation*	Sole Proprietor	Partnership	Limited Liability Company*	S Corporation	C Corporation
Method	None	Partnership agreement	Articles of Organization filed in state recognizing LLCs	Articles of Incorporation Must meet criteria to file as S Corp	Articles of Incorporation
Owner Eligibility Number of Owners	One	Two or more for limited partnership; one or more general and one or more limited for general partnership	No limit	35	No limit
Type of Owners	Individual	No limitation	No limitation	Individuals and certain trusts	No limitation
Affiliate Limits	No limitation	No limitation	No limitation	No subsidiaries	No limitation
Capital Structure	No stock	No limitations (multiple classes)	No limitation	Only one class of stock	No limitations (multiple classes permitted)
Liability	Unlimited	General partners jointly and severally liable. Limited partners are generally limited to capital contributions.	Limited to member's capital contribution	Limited to shareholders' contributions	Limited to shareholder's capital contributions
Operational Phase Tax Year	Calendar year	Generally calendar year	Generally calendar year	Generally calendar year	Generally any year permitted (limit for personal service corporation)
Tax on Income	Individual level	Owner level	Member level	Owner level	Corporate level
Allocation of Income/ Deductions	N/A	Permitted if substantial economic effect	Permitted if substantial economic effect	Not permitted (except through debt/equity structure)	Not permitted (except through multiple equity structure)
Character of Income/ Deductions	Flow-through to individual	Flow-through to partners	Flow-through to members	Flow-through to shareholders	No flow-through to shareholders

*Some states (New York, for example) use the term LLP—Limited Liability Partnership.

In a limited partnership composed of two or more limited partners and one general partner, the general partner assumes both the managerial duties and the downside risk. A limited partner's liability is restricted to the amount of his or her original investment, as long as he or she has had no role in management decisions. *Do not enter into such a partnership without legal advice.* You can form a partnership with a handshake and dissolve it without one; however, it is not advisable to proceed with any partnership, including those with family members or friends, without the benefit of legal counsel.

communityresource

Family Businesses—Who Can Help?

A wealth of information and assistance is available in your community for your family business venture through family business centers and consultants, which can be found through the Family Firm Institute's site, *http://www.ffi.org.* The Institute provides listings internationally and nationally by state and includes private business counselors, accounting firms, lawyers, and therapists who deal with entrepreneurs in family businesses. In addition, listings of most of the family business centers available at colleges throughout the nation are included.

Consulting, coaching, seminars, research, legal advice, and roundtables for family entrepreneurs are available at many family business centers for reasonable fees. Following are two of the best centers in the country according to *Fortune Small Business* magazine:

Cox Family Enterprise Center
    Coles College of Business, Kennesaw State University

The Center provides research, newsletters, consultations, and sponsorship of the Georgia Family Business of the Year Award Banquet. In addition, Kennesaw offers an Executive MBA for Families in Business. The Center offers a forum that provides knowledge and experience on topics most crucial to family business success and survival. It focuses on the strategies used by real family firms to take advantage of opportunities and overcome challenges. Additionally, the forum provides efficient access to leading expertise in accounting, banking, insurance, law, financial management, business strategy, human resources, succession planning, and family dynamics. Moreover, the forum provides a relaxed environment where important family business issues can be openly addressed, and it encourages the exchange of ideas and information among family business owners and leading experts.

Source: *http://www.kennesaw.edu/fec* (Accessed February 28, 2008).

Loyola University of Chicago Family Business Center
    For ten years, the Family Business Center (FBC) has served over 100 family businesses of varying sizes, industries, and complexity. Today, the needs of FBC members continue to push the frontier of family enterprise research to new levels. Our innovative programs provide the opportunity for our members to share knowledge and cultivate synergies with one another. After a decade of nurturing family enterprises, FBC endeavors to become the premier research and learning center for family-owned businesses in the United States.

Source: *http://www.luc.edu/fbc* (Accessed February 28, 2008).

Family Business Review (quarterly) follows the issues surrounding family businesses, which present their own set of relationship and business challenges. We suggest you seek out others who have trod the same path for their expertise, experience, and support. Participate in monthly forums with others, and seek out professionals experienced in dealing with family enterprises. The Key Points from Another View at the end of this chapter provides additional information on how to keep your family business healthy.

A partnership is somewhat of a paradox. In a legal sense, the partnership does not do much for you; but as many partners admit, there are sound psychological and financial reasons for going into business with someone else.

What are some of those reasons? Say you have analyzed your personal skills, and realize you need balance in a couple of critical areas. For example, you may be an engineer who can come up with 20 original ideas a day, but you could not sell ice in Florida in the summer. Or perhaps you do not have much money, so you need a partner who can supply your new business with capital. Or maybe you get along with people and love to sell, and you need to team up with an inventor or manufacturer who can supply you with products to sell. Many successful business owners could never have started or succeeded in business without a partner.

Before committing to a partnership, realize that friendship alone will not resolve business problems. All involved partners need to decide exactly what each brings to the table and then decide if what is brought is worth the complications of a partnership. There will be many unspoken fears and needs for all involved parties. Keeping the lines of communication open is essential for survival.

Business counselors run a lucrative business trying to work out the problems of warring partners. To reduce problems, do your research before starting a partnership, and talk continually to keep the partnership successful. You must trust your partners and have confidence in their decisions. A partnership is like a marriage but without the love, and you most likely will spend more time each week with your business partner than your marriage partner. During tough times in a marriage, factors such as duty, commitment, and children may hold the partnership together. What will hold your business together during the rocky times? Following are concerns that should be discussed with your potential partners.

Questions for Partner Discussion

- **Management and control:** Who will make the final decisions on both small and large issues? Who will have control and responsibility for each area of the business? In one partnership, the owners take turns each year, trading off being the president and final decision maker.

- **Dispute resolution:** How will disputes between the partners be resolved? Will you use mediation or arbitration if you reach a stalemate?

- **Financial contributions:** How much will each partner contribute? It is necessary to determine not only initial contributions but also possible future contributions. An initial 50–50 partnership may turn into a 75–25 partnership if capital needs arise. How will each of you deal with this change? If one partner supplies the risk capital and others supply the management, how will profits be divided? How will profits and responsibilities change if the financial commitments change?

- **Time contributions:** How much time will each partner commit? Are these contributions considered equal? If you commit 20 hours and the other partners commit 40, will profit distributions reflect this variance?

- **Demise of the partnership:** If the partnership is to be dissolved, how will the ending be dealt with? What is the buyout procedure? How will the valuation of the business be determined in the event of a partner's death or disability or the sale of the business? What steps should you take to protect the business and its transfer?

- **New partners:** Can new partners be added? If so, what will be the process for accepting additional partners? How many partners are you willing to take on? Do current partners have veto power over the addition of a new partner?

- **Participation of family members as employees and their input into the business:** See Key Points from Another View at the end of the chapter for additional information.

- **Ethics:** Review the ethics material in Chapter 12. Answer the ethics questionnaires separately, and then sit down with your partners and discuss your answers. Better to discover ethical differences now than in the courtroom later.

On the surface, partnerships make a lot of sense. Two or more entrepreneurs face the unknown together and pool their skills. They can raise more capital than one person could alone. But forming a good partnership can be more difficult and challenging than forming a good marriage.

After the previous questions are answered, you may be ready to review sample partnership agreements that can be found on the Net for further discussions with your partners. These should serve as a starting point and are *not* meant to become your partnership agreement, as each state's statutes vary. Reviewing the issues in this chapter, the ethical issues in Chapter 12, and the sample agreements will give you a fair idea of what you should be discussing with your attorney and partners. Also, return to the Action Steps in Chapter 1 to make sure you and your partners are dreaming the same dream and consult your attorney before signing any agreement.

Corporations

In general, we think most owners of small businesses fail to incorporate because they do not see the signals their businesses are giving them. Ask yourself if there is any chance that your employees, customers, or suppliers might sue you. The truth is that for almost all firms, a great deal of risk for lawsuits exists; therefore incorporating as an LLC, Subchapter S corporation, or a standard C corporation should be seriously considered.

Employees driving your vehicles, customers being harmed in some way by a product or service—in ways you would never believe or consider—and customers or employees slipping and falling are just a few of the potential litigious situations that may occur. Consider the following reasons for incorporation:

1. **You limit your liability:** A corporation acts as a shield between you and the world. If your business fails, your creditors cannot come after your house, your condo, your car, your firstborn, or your hard-won collectibles—provided you have done it right. And that is the key. To keep your corporate shield up, make sure you: 1) hold scheduled board of directors' meetings, 2) keep up the minutes book, and 3) act as if you are an employee of the corporation.

   The fact is almost all entrepreneurs use most of their personal assets as collateral for their business loans, so the limited liability provided by a corporation may only limit your risk of personal financial loss. Ask your attorney how to reduce personal liability issues within your firm's operations. Safety precautions, disclaimers on products, having your employees covered by very high liability policies on their own cars, and proper hiring and firing methods are just a few ways to reduce risk.

2. **To change your tax picture:** Discuss with your CPA how passive and active income will be handled, as well as retained earnings for each type of corporation. Consult the current IRS schedules, and ask a CPA for advice.

3. **To upgrade your image:** What does the word *corporation* mean to you? IBM? Intel? Wal-Mart? GM? Let us look at that word. It comes from the Latin *corpus*, which means "body." To *incorporate* means to make, form, or shape into a body. Looked at from that angle, *incorporating* starts to sound creative. As a corporation, you may enjoy more prestige, attract better employees, and have more clout in the world.

4. **To have the opportunity to channel some heavy expenses:** Medical and insurance premiums and FICA payments become business expenses.

5. **To guarantee continuity:** If one owner goes to Australia, dies, or becomes ill, the corporation keeps on chugging because you have gone through a lot of red tape and planning to set it up that way.

6. **To offer internal incentives:** When you want to reward special employees or retain your best ones, you can offer stock or a promotion—for example, a vice presidency—in addition to, or in place of, pay raises. Becoming a corporate officer carries its own special excitement, and this gives you flexibility.

According to *http://www.Nolo.com*, a C corporation may be advised over an LLC if the following factors exist:

1. You expect to have multiple investors in your business, or you plan to raise money from the public.

2. You want to set up a single-member LLC, but you live in a state that requires two or more members.

3. You would like to provide extensive fringe benefits to owner–employees.

4. You want to entice or keep key employees by offering stock options and stock bonus incentives.

5. Your accountant has reviewed the issue of self-employment taxes and weighs in on the decision.

Limited Liability Companies

Most states have recently allowed LLCs as an acceptable form of business. This entity limits liability but does not limit the number of investors; it also allows profits to be distributed in a manner other than in proportion to investors' capital contribution as a "pass-through" tax entity. It is expected that LLCs will be the entity of choice for closely held businesses in the near future, because they are designed to provide the tax flexibility and ownership of partnerships with the limited liability features of corporations.

The operating agreement sets out the company's membership and operational rules. In addition, the agreement states how members' profits and losses are shared. LLCs provide the pass-through tax treatment that has been available to partnerships and Subchapter S corporations. The required documentation, known as *articles of organization*, is less detailed than articles of incorporation and usually less costly. See Figure 10.1 for a sample state registration application for articles of organization.

The articles of organization contain an "operating agreement" that resembles a partnership agreement. LLC members may manage the business themselves or delegate such authority to active managers.

Most state statutes require that identifying information such as "limited liability company" or "LLC" appear in the name of the company to notify others of the limited liability enjoyed by the organization. The IRS taxes such organizations at the individual rate. Be careful: if an LLC is not properly structured, it will be taxed as a corporation.

LLCs generally will not be appropriate for existing corporations or businesses that raise, or want to raise, capital through the public or venture-capital markets. If you are considering converting to an LLC, be aware there may be significant tax consequences. It is vital that you consult competent tax, legal, and accounting advisors. A few states allow LLPs (Limited Liability Partnerships), which contain liability exceptions for certain professional service firms such as for doctors, architects, engineers, and so on. Check the laws in your state.

figure **10.1** ──

Illinois Limited Liability Company Act

Print	**Reset**

Form LLC-5.5

April 2007

Secretary of State Jesse White
Department of Business Services
Limited Liability Division
501 S. Second St., Rm. 351
Springfield, IL 62756
217-524-8008
www.cyberdriveillinois.com

Payment must be made by certified check, cashier's check, Illinois attorney's check, C.P.A.'s check or money order payable to Secretary of State.

Illinois
Limited Liability Company Act
Articles of Organization

SUBMIT IN DUPLICATE
Must be typewritten.

This space for use by Secretary of State.

Filing Fee: $500
Approved:

FILE #

This space for use by Secretary of State.

1.   Limited Liability Company Name: _____

   _____
   The LLC name must contain the words Limited Liability Company, L.L.C. or LLC and cannot contain the terms Corporation, Corp., Incorporated, Inc., Ltd., Co., Limited Partnership or L.P.

2.   Address of Principal Place of Business where records of the company will be kept: (P.O. Box alone or c/o is unacceptable.) _____

   _____

3.   Articles of Organization effective on: (check one)
   ❏   the filing date
   ❏   a later date (not to exceed 60 days after the filing date): _____
                                                                                           Month, Day, Year

4.   Registered Agent's Name and Registered Office Address:

   Registered Agent: _____
                            First Name   Middle Initial   Last Name

   Registered Office: _____
   (P.O. Box alone or   Number   Street   Suite #
   c/o is unacceptable.)

                            _____
                            City   ZIP Code   County

5.   Purpose(s) for which the Limited Liability Company is organized: (If more space is needed, attach additional sheets of this size.)

   "The transaction of any or all lawful business for which Limited Liability Companies may be organized under this Act."

6.   Latest date, if any, upon which the company is to dissolve: _____
   (Leave blank if duration is perpetual.)   Month, Day, Year

Printed by authority of the State of Illinois. April 2008 — 5M — LLC-4.12

(continued)

figure **10.1**

Illinois Limited Liability Company Act *(continued)*

LLC-5.5

7. **(OPTIONAL)** Other provisions for the regulation of the internal affairs of the Company: (If more space is needed, attach additional sheets of this size.)

8. The Limited Liability Company: (Check either a or b below.)
   a. ❑ is managed by the **manager(s)** (List names and business addresses.)

   b. ❑ has management vested in the **member(s)** (List names and addresses.)

9. **Name and Address of Organizer(s)**
   I affirm, under penalties of perjury, having authority to sign hereto, that these Articles of Organization are to the best of my knowledge and belief, true, correct and complete.

   Dated ______________________ , __________
   Month & Day Year

1. ______________________ Signature
   ______________________ Name (type or print)
   ______________________ Name if a Corporation or other Entity, and Title of Signer

1. ______________________ Number Street
   ______________________ City/Town
   ______________________ State ZIP Code

2. ______________________ Signature
   ______________________ Name (type or print)
   ______________________ Name if a Corporation or other Entity, and Title of Signer

2. ______________________ Number Street
   ______________________ City/Town
   ______________________ State ZIP Code

Signatures must be in black ink on an original document. Carbon copy, photocopy or rubber stamp signatures may only be used on conformed copies.

Printed by authority of the State of Illinois. April 2008 — 5M — LLC-4.12

Source: *http://www.cyberdriveillinois.com/publications/pdf_publications/llc55.pdf* (Accessed February 28, 2008).

Subchapter S Corporations

In addition to LLCs and the standard C corporations, there are Subchapter S corporations, which are semicorporate bodies that limit an owner's liability while still allowing a pass-through of business losses to the personal income statements of the owners, founders, and others. Subchapter S refers to the section of the IRS code that describes the way the corporation will be taxed.

The number of stockholders is limited to 35. The IRS has specific time requirements for filing, and some states do not recognize the tax aspects of the Subchapter S category, so verify your state laws. In a Subchapter S corporation, you cannot have any corporate stockholders, partnership stockholders, or trusts as investors. For this reason, most S corporations lose their S status when venture-capital firms invest.

Subchapter S corporations are required to supply stockholders with a "K-1" tax report by April 15 of each year and you must follow a calendar tax year with few exceptions. S corporation status can be dropped if you find there are tax advantages to being a regular corporation, but timing is important. Consult your tax attorney.

Nonprofit Corporations

Many social entrepreneurs today are interested in reaching out to solve social, health, and environmental problems through profit and nonprofit organizations. A nonprofit operates and is formed much in the same way as a corporation with limited liability for the trustees, officers, and members and possessing unlimited life. You must apply to the state for nonprofit status and to the IRS for approval of your tax-exempt status by completing IRS Form 1023 or IRS Form 1024 and following the sometimes lengthy process. Use an attorney to help you complete your paperwork; each state requires different forms and agency approvals. Your state may have a separate state office designed to help nonprofit organizations. If so, seek their help early on.

Two excellent sites for you to review are *http://www.idealist.org* and the Nonprofit Boot Camp Online provided by *http://www.craigslistfoundation. org*. Both are excellent resources; Idealist links you to most of the federal and state resources you will need to access to develop a nonprofit organization. Throughout the text, we have highlighted many other sources that can help you fulfill your dream of making the world a better place, as well as highlighting many social entrepreneurs operating as profits and nonprofits.

Technically your organization will be defined as a 501(c)(3) public charity or a 501(c)(4) social welfare organization. According to Idealist, you will need to take the following steps in addition to the ones above:

1) Apply for an Employer Identification Number (EIN) SS-4; this is outlined in Appendix C.
2) Set up postal service at *http://www.usps.com/tools/calculatepostage/ nonprofitpostagerates.htm*.
3) Organize and plan to build charter documents using *http://www.idealist. org/en/faqcat/5–5*.

Remember, you will still be required to pay insurance, social security, unemployment, and any other taxes required the same as any other organization. Nonprofit organizations should follow through with most of the text's Action Steps, changing them to fit the nonprofit's situation.

LEGAL AND PERSONAL ISSUES FOR FAMILIES AND COUPLES

Although many entrepreneurs do not see the need for formal, written legal agreements between family members—be they spouses, children, or siblings—we cannot emphasize enough the need for such documents. There are those rare partnerships between family members that never experience a problem, but rare is not common. Protect yourself, your business, and your relationships. You may want to meet with family business consultants, legal advisors, and accountants to develop and plan your personal, business, tax, and financial affairs. As your business grows, relationships change; as family members join or leave the organization, you will need to return to your advisors.

For further information on family business structure and success, read the Key Points from Another View article at the end of this chapter. Also, the Community Resource on page 268 can lead you to a family business center or consultant. If you are forming a business with your spouse, the following article may provide additional insight for you.

For Couples Working Together, Setting Ground Rules Is a Must

By Carol Sorgen

You married your beloved for better or for worse, in sickness and in health, for richer or for poorer.

But for profit or for loss? If you're in business together, that's about the size of it.

Take David and Sharon Nevins, for instance.

David Nevins credits much of Owings Mills-based Nevins and Associates' success to his wife. Sharon Nevins joined the 10-year-old public relations, marketing, advertising, and customer service firm 2 years ago and started the company's advertising division.

But David Nevins, whose firm had capitalized local billings of $6 million last year, admits the partnership—the business one—isn't necessarily a "forever" thing. "It's advantageous now, but we have no long-term plans," he says.

That's not because the two don't work well together. They do, and it's because they've established certain rules that they follow, he says.

Having individual lines of authority is essential for a successful business partnership, say family business experts.

"You need a clear definition of responsibility," says William Ross Adams, president of Baltimore's Baker-Meekins Company, financial advisers to owners of family and private businesses.

That advice is echoed by Harsha Desai, professor of management and director of the Loyola Center for Closely Held Firms at Loyola College.

"A couple has to have different areas of expertise, so you don't run into each other's area," Desai says. "One of you has to be a boss. You can take turns—one is boss for six months, then the other one is—but someone has to defer to someone else. One person has to have the final decision-making responsibility."

Leaving Some Room

One tip Nevins offers other married business partners is to give each other space—literally.

"Sharon has an office down the hall. Other than the times we meet with a client together, she runs her division, and we don't see that much of each other. If we were in the same room, or meeting together all the time, that would be too much of a good thing," he says.

Another policy both Nevins and Susana V. Ptak, co-owner of Gascoyne Laboratories, recommend is leaving work at the office.

Ptak, who co-owns the Baltimore environmental testing lab with husband Francis, agrees: "Two things have helped us not to kill each other," she says, laughing. "One is that we don't do the same thing (Francis is a chemist and handles the analytic end of the company; Susana takes care of the business side), and the other is that we don't talk business at home. In the car, yes, but once we're actually at home, we just talk family stuff.

"Don't confuse your business with your family," Ptak continues. "If you do, you'll go berserk."

Handling Conflict

To make the business work, a couple must recognize that the company has specific needs, says Patrick O. Ring, Baker-Meekins' managing director. "Make a plan, examine your goals, and build in some mechanism to achieve those goals and to resolve conflicts."

Certain overriding issues need to be addressed. "What makes sense for the business? How is the business going to grow? In which direction is it going to grow? How can you make it grow?" Ring adds.

"You need to talk explicitly about such issues," says Desai. "You can't wait until a crisis occurs to make a decision."

In times of conflict, keep the argument between yourselves. "Don't put the employee, or the business itself, in the middle," Adams advises.

"It's important to be fair to your workers," agrees Susana Ptak, whose lab has 61 employees. "Be careful that your employees see you and your spouse as a united front."

Of course, not all partnerships work out as successfully as the Nevins' and the Ptaks'. Sometimes couples get divorces, just as sometimes business partnerships fail. "That's an eventuality couples should be prepared for," says Adams.

He recommends that spouses make an agreement at the beginning that one partner can buy out the other in case of divorce. Without an agreement, you could spend time and money in litigation.

"Life's too short to spend all that energy on disputes," he says.

While arguments are bound to crop up, whether in a marriage or a business partnership, they don't have to destroy either relationship.

"Money breeds all sorts of snarling snakes," Adams says, "but you can work out your problems. It just requires discipline and a willingness not to let a disagreement destroy a marriage—or a business"

Source: *http://www.fambiz.com* (Accessed February 28, 2008).

PROTECT YOURSELF WITH CONTINGENCY PLANS

If you do not use a good lawyer to help structure your business, you probably will not have a plan to handle unforeseen events that may take you by surprise and cost you dearly. Work with your lawyer, accountant, and banker to prepare for contingencies.

Contingencies Steps taken to protect one against unforeseen future events

Many small business owners ignore the need for buy–sell agreements or for having a will drawn up or purchasing life insurance to protect the business. They put it off, believing nothing bad could happen to them.

When forming your partnership, one of the major contingencies to consider is the dissolution of the partnership. Partnerships can end as a result of death, illness, divorce, lack of interest, financial or philosophical differences, or desire for a change in lifestyle. Protect your business, yourself, and your loved ones.

Dissolution of a partnership The separation of partners, an eventuality that needs to be prepared for with intricate planning and much thought

In case of death, these agreements are often funded by "key man" life insurance policies on the owners so that if one dies, the business or other owners can collect the life insurance policy's proceeds and use those funds to buy out the deceased's interest in the business.

For dissolving the partnership under other circumstances, your buy–sell agreement should indicate who will evaluate the business, how payment will be made by the remaining partners, and over what time period. As your business grows and changes, you will want to reevaluate your agreement. When partners split up, and most eventually do, a buy–sell agreement may keep the dissolution out of court. Think of it as a prenuptial agreement.

Legal fees to draw up a buy–sell agreement and key-man insurance premiums are probably two of the best financial investments you and your partners will ever make. No buy–sell agreement should ever be undertaken without advice of legal and financial counsel. Although sample buy–sell agreements are available online, use them for preliminary assistance only. Most of these are state based, so you need to make sure you are reviewing one that complies with your state laws.

Passion

Bacteria Beware: MIT Student Invents Knockout Punch for Antibiotic Resistance

Timothy Lu Awarded $30,000 Lemelson-MIT Student Prize for Inventiveness

Cambridge, Mass. (February 27, 2008) – MIT graduate student and synthetic biologist Timothy Lu is passionate about tackling problems that pose threats to human health. His current mission: to destroy antibiotic-resistant bacteria.

Today, the 27-year-old M.D. candidate and Ph.D. in the Harvard-MIT Division of Health Sciences and Technology received the prestigious $30,000 Lemelson-MIT Student Prize for inventing processes that promise to combat bacterial infections by enhancing the effectiveness of antibiotics at killing bacteria and helping to eradicate biofilm, bacterial layers that resist antimicrobial treatment and breed on surfaces, such as those of medical, industrial, and food processing equipment.

Bacterial infections can lead to severe health issues. The Centers for Disease Control and Prevention estimates that the antibiotic-resistant bacterium MRSA, or methicillin-resistant *Staphylococcus aureus*, causes approximately 94,000 infections and contributes to 19,000 deaths annually in the United States through contact that can occur in a variety of locations, including schools, hospitals, and homes. Bacteria can also infect food, including spinach and beef, and may damage industrial equipment.

Lu explained that fewer pharmaceutical companies are inventing new antibiotics due to long development times, high failure rates, and high costs. According to the Tufts Center for the Study of Drug Development, the cost to develop a new drug is $930 million (based on the value of the dollar in 2006). These factors, coupled with a decline in the number of prescriptions authorized for antibiotics, constrain profits. "Antibiotic-resistant bacteria are also becoming more prevalent," Lu noted. "My inventions enable the rapid design and production of inexpensive antibacterial agents that can break through the defenses of antibiotic-resistant bacteria and bacterial biofilms."

According to Lu, his engineered enzymatically-active bacteriophage could be initially applied in food processing settings to kill food-borne bacteria, such as the *Escherichia coli (E. coli)* that contaminates spinach and causes severe illness when ingested. In line with these hopes, there is evidence that U.S. regulatory authorities are warming up to the therapeutic use of bacteriophage. For example, in 2006, the U.S. Food and Drug Administration approved the first U.S. treatment for Listeria contamination of processed meats using natural bacteriophage.

Lu added that enzymatically-active bacteriophage could also benefit industry by being used to treat infected pipes and reduce corrosion.

Inherited Inventiveness

Born in Stanford, California, and raised in Yorktown Heights, New York, and Taiwan, Lu credits his inventiveness to his father, Nicky, an engineer and entrepreneur who helped develop modern semiconductor memories with IBM and the integrated circuits industry in Taiwan. Lu recalls spending time at his father's office during his formative years, where he reviewed plans and designs for new integrated circuits.

"I inherited my interest in invention and entrepreneurship from my father," Lu said. "It was very inspiring to see the amount of effort my father and his team put into their work and their joy and elation when they achieved success."

(continued)

(*continued*)

"Tim is one of the young stars in the emerging field of synthetic biology," said his advisor, J. J. Collins, professor of biomedical engineering at Boston University. "I am confident he will develop into a leading clinical investigator and innovator."

"Tim demonstrates the type of ambitious and inventive thinking the $30,000 Lemelson-MIT Student Prize was established to recognize," said Josh Schuler, executive director of the Lemelson-MIT Program, which provides the annual award. "What is truly impressive about Tim's approaches is the breadth of his applications. Not only does his work have potential in health care, but also in protecting the general public through safer food processing and prevention of industrial biofouling. Harmful bacteria everywhere should be afraid."

Source: Adapted from *http://web.mit.edu/invent/n-pressreleases/n-press-08SP.html* (Accessed February 28, 2008).

PATENTS, TRADEMARKS, AND COPYRIGHTS

Patents, trademarks, and copyrights are important elements of your business. Without protecting them, you may lose your business, your ideas may be stolen, or your products may be copied.

THE FOLLOWING 2008 MATERIAL ON PATENTS, TRADEMARKS, AND COPYRIGHTS IS PUBLISHED BY PERMISSION FROM THE COPYRIGHT HOLDER: KNOBBE, MARTENS, OLSON, AND BEAR, LLP. BECAUSE INTELLECTUAL PROPERTY LAWS ARE SUBJECT TO CHANGE, CONSULT WITH YOUR INTELLECTUAL PROPERTY COUNSEL RATHER THAN RELYING ON THIS MATERIAL ALONE FOR LEGAL ADVICE.

Ten Things You Should Know to Protect Your Inventions

1. **What Is a Patent?**

   A patent is a right granted to inventors by the government to exclude others from making, selling, offering for sale, using, or importing an invention. The U.S. Government has issued over 7,000,000 patents during the past 200 years. These patents cover many types of inventions and discoveries, including machines, compositions of matter, methods, computer software, plants, microorganisms, and designs. Three types of patents are available in the United States.

   The first, called a utility patent, covers useful inventions and discoveries, which are defined in the claims of the patent. Generally, a utility patent expires 20 years from the day a regular patent application is filed for the invention. In addition to the claims, a utility patent includes a written description of the invention and also often includes drawings. A second type of patent, called a design patent, covers nonfunctional, ornamental designs shown in the drawings of the design patent. This type of patent expires 14 years from the date it issues. The third type of patent gives the owner the right to exclude others from asexually reproducing a patented plant, or from selling or using an asexually reproduced patented plant. Plants that are sexually reproduced, *i.e.*, through seeds, can be protected under the Plant Variety Protection Act.

2. **How Do I Obtain a Patent?**

   To obtain a utility patent, the invention defined in the patent claims must be new and nonobvious to a person of ordinary skill in the field of the invention. Many patents are combinations of previously existing parts combined in a new, nonobvious way to achieve improved results. A design patent requires a new, nonfunctional, ornamental design which is non-obvious to an ordinary designer in the field of the invention. In all cases, the initial evaluation and patentability decision will be made by an examiner at the U. S. Patent and Trademark Office. Only the first and original inventor(s) may obtain a valid patent. Thus, you cannot obtain a patent in the U.S. for an invention you saw overseas, because you are not the first or the original inventor. Similarly, someone who sees your invention cannot obtain a valid patent on it because that person is not the first or original inventor. Someone else could, however, improve your invention and then patent the improvement. It typically takes a year or more after filing the U.S. application before the examiner sends the initial evaluation of patentability.

3. **What Is a Patentability Search?**

When a U.S. patent application is filed, the Patent Office will conduct a search of prior patents from both the United States and foreign countries, and may also search for prior non-patent references. Inventors can have a similar patentability search conducted in order to better evaluate the cost and probability of obtaining patent protection for their invention. Evaluation of patentability search results is complex, requiring not only an understanding of the pertinent technology, but also of patent law. The U.S. Patent Office tests and authorizes persons with appropriate technical backgrounds to file and prosecute patent matters before the Patent Office. You should consider contacting a registered patent attorney authorized to practice before the U.S. Patent and Trademark Office to assist with your evaluation.

4. **What Is a Patent Notice?**

A product or accompanying literature is typically marked with a patent notice such as "Patent 5,000,000" or "Pat. No. 5,000,000" when the product, or the method used to produce the product, is patented. Marking the patent number on patented products is ordinarily required to collect damages from potential infringers. The term "Patent Pending" means a patent has been applied for, but has not yet issued.

5. **When Must I Apply for a Patent?**

If two different inventors were to apply for a patent for the same invention, every country except the United States would award a patent to the first inventor to file. Conversely, the United States would award a patent to the party who invented first. However, there is legislation pending in Congress to change the law in the United States to be consistent with the "first to file" system prevalent outside the United States. In any event, an application for a patent must be filed in the United States within one year of the first date that the invention is (1) disclosed in a printed publication; (2) publicly used; or (3) offered for sale. A patent in the United States is only valid in this country. In most foreign countries, a patent application must be filed before any public disclosure is made anywhere in the world. The rules for determining when an invention is publicly disclosed, used or offered for sale are complex, and you should seek the advice of a patent lawyer if you have a question in this regard. By treaty with most, but not all, foreign countries, if a U.S. application is filed before any public disclosure is made, a foreign patent application may be filed up to one year after the U.S. filing date. Thus, if a U.S. patent application is filed before any public disclosure of the invention, the option to pursue foreign patent rights in many foreign countries is preserved for one year. Filing a U.S. patent application after a public disclosure, however, usually prevents filing in most foreign countries.

U.S. patent laws also provide for an informal and less expensive filing, called a "provisional patent application," to preserve patent rights for 12 months. It also extends the term of the patent for one year. The provisional application is not examined and lapses after 12 months. Accordingly, a regular patent application must be filed within those 12 months in order to claim the benefit of the provisional application's filing date. Likewise, foreign applications generally must be filed within those 12 months.

6. Is There a Worldwide Patent?

There is no single, worldwide patent. Each country has different patent laws and, therefore, rights provided by a patent are enforceable only in the country or countries issuing the patent. For example, a U.S. patent can prevent an infringing product that is made overseas from being sold in the United States, but will not generally prevent the product from being sold in a foreign country. There are several international treaties that enable most of the initial steps in the patenting process to be consolidated for many countries, provided there was no public disclosure before the U.S. application was filed. Ultimately, however, the patent application must be filed in each country where a patent is sought and translated into an official

GLOBAL VILLAGE

International Intellectual Property Laws

Legal details are a concern to a growing number of U.S. exporters because of the increasing technological and informational content of products and services. Before conducting business abroad, familiarize yourself with the appropriate patent, trademark, copyright, and licensing laws of the country in question. Use the Internet for your initial search, and then work directly with international intellectual property attorneys. There are a number of ways of protecting your product in a foreign market, and each has its own merits according to circumstance and country.

Patent laws vary from country to country, and a few countries do not have patent laws. Consider selling patent rights or granting licenses in a foreign market. To track down information on international intellectual property laws, use the following sources:

http://www.wipo.int—the World Intellectual Property Organization tracks worldwide changes and development of intellectual property and also provides access to various databases of international intellectual property.

http://www.asil.org/resource/ip1.html—the American Society of International Law's excellent online resource guide includes research strategies, primary and secondary sources, recommended link sites, blogs, organizations, electronic newsletters, and discussion lists.

http://www.law.cornell.edu/world—the Cornell University Law School Legal Information Institute offers a comprehensive collection of world legal materials.

http://www.glin.gov.search.action—the Global Legal Information Network (GLIN) provides a searchable database of laws, regulations, and other complementary legal sources.

http://www.llrx.com—Legal and Technology Resources for Professionals lets you search for information on international competitive intelligence and foreign and comparative law.

language of each such country. The Patent Cooperation Treaty allows the additional cost of translating and filing in each foreign country to be delayed for up to 30 months from the U.S. filing date. During this 30-month period, it is often possible to test the market for the product and better judge the potential benefits of pursuing foreign patent protection.

7. **Does a Patent Guarantee My Right to Sell My Product?**

A U.S. patent gives its owner the right to exclude others from practicing the patented invention for the duration of the patent. However, it does not actually give the owner the right to make, use, or sell the patented invention. It is thus possible to have an improved and patented product that infringes a prior patent. For example, one person obtains a patent for a chair. Later, a second person obtains a patent for a rocking chair. The first person may be able to stop the second person from selling the rocking chair if the rocking chair incorporates claimed subject matter of the original chair. In such a case, the second person's rocking chair infringes the first person's patent.

8. **What Is an Infringement Study?**

An infringement study determines whether an unexpired patent has claims that might encompass a product or method that is being made, used, offered for sale, or sold without authorization by the patent owner. If it is determined that a product or method may infringe someone else's patent, the design may be altered to avoid infringement, or a license may be negotiated with the patent owner. Infringement studies require an in-depth understanding of both the applicable patent law and the pertinent technology. Accordingly, you should consider contacting an experienced patent lawyer for such infringement studies.

If a defendant is found guilty of willfully infringing another's U.S. patent, the court can treble the damage award and require the payment of the patent owner's attorneys' fees. Thus, questions of patent infringement should not be taken lightly. A written opinion from a competent patent counsel that provides a well-reasoned basis that the patent is either invalid or not infringed, can provide a defense to a charge of willful infringement, even if a court ultimately does not agree with the arguments in the opinion.

9. **Are Patents Worth the Costs?**

Although recent judicial decisions, pending legislation, and proposed Patent Office rule changes may make it more difficult to obtain and enforce patents in the United States, patents remain extremely valuable to most technology companies. A well-crafted patent portfolio can attract investment dollars and provide a substantial competitive advantage. Patents can be used to exclude competitors from a company's core technology, block competitors from improving their own technologies or innovating within the company's commercial market, and discourage competitors from asserting their patents against the company. Patents can also provide substantial value through licensing revenue and through enhanced negotiation leverage. For example, Texas Instruments, Inc. is reported to have received $600 million dollars in patent income. Polaroid's lawsuit against Eastman Kodak shut down Kodak's entire instant-camera facility, and the damages awarded totalled nearly a billion dollars. Thus, patents are worth the investment to most patent owners. On the other hand, those accused of patent infringement should take prompt steps to minimize their exposure.

10. **Where Can I Get More Information on Patents?**

Additional information on patents may be obtained from the U.S. Patent and Trademark Office in Washington, D.C. Patents are accessible over the

Internet from the U.S. Patent Office and other private companies. The U.S. Patent and Trademark Office website (*www.uspto.gov*) contains information on more than 7,000,000 issued U.S. patents.

To contact a patent lawyer or learn more about Knobbe Martens, visit *www.kmob.com*.

Ten Things You Should Know to Protect Your Product and Business Names

1. **What Is a Trademark?**

   A trademark is usually a brand name for a product. It can be a word, phrase, logo, design, or virtually anything that is used to identify the source of the product and distinguish it from competitors' products. More than one trademark may be used in connection with a product, for example, YAMAHA® and WAVERUNNER® are both trademarks for personal watercraft. A trademark represents the goodwill and reputation of a product and its source. Its owner has the right to prevent others from trading on that goodwill by using the same or a similar trademark on the same or similar products in a way that is likely to cause confusion as to the source, origin, or sponsorship of the products.

   A service mark is like a trademark, except it is used to identify and distinguish services rather than products.

   The terms "trademark" or "mark" are often used interchangeably to refer to either a trademark or service mark.

2. **How Should a Mark Be Used?**

   Trademarks must be used properly to maintain their value. Marks should be used as adjectives, and not as nouns or verbs. For example, when referring to your WAVERUNNER® brand personal watercraft, do not say that you "bought a WAVERUNNER®" or that you "want to go wave running." To prevent loss of trademark or service mark rights, the generic name for the product should appear after the mark, and the mark should appear visually different from the surrounding text. Use different type size, type style, color, or quotation marks for the trademark or service mark, as in OAKLEY® sunglasses, APPLE® computers, or CARL'S JR.® restaurant services. You may also use an asterisk (*) after a mark where the asterisk refers to a footnote explaining the ownership of a mark.

   If a mark is not used correctly, the exclusive right to use it may be lost. For example, trademark rights can be lost if the mark becomes the generic name for the product. Kerosene, escalator, and nylon were once trademarks, but are now generic names. Because competitors need to be able to describe their products, no one can own the exclusive right to use generic terms.

   If a mark is registered with the U.S. Patent and Trademark Office, the federal registration symbol ® should be used next to the mark. If the mark is not federally registered, the letters ™ may be used to indicate a trademark, or ℠ to indicate a service mark.

3. **What Is a Trade Name?**

   A trade name is the name of a business. Unlike trademarks, a trade name can be used as a noun. It need not be followed by generic terms.

   It is permissible to use all or a portion of a trade name as a trademark or service mark. "Ocean Pacific Apparel Corporation" is a trade name. OCEAN PACIFIC® is a trademark when used on clothing, and may be a service mark when properly used with surfing competitions.

4. **Does My Incorporation or Fictitious Business Name Statement Give Me the Right to Use My Business Name?**

Most businesses form a corporation or file a fictitious business name statement. Neither the certificate of incorporation nor the fictitious business name statement gives a business the right to use a trade name which is likely to cause confusion with a trade name, trademark, or service mark that was previously used by someone else in the same area of trade.

The state or county agencies that issue the certificates of incorporation and fictitious business name statements do not perform searches sufficient to ensure that one's use would not infringe another's prior rights.

A court's determination of trademark infringement will override any fictitious business name statement or any certificate of incorporation. Further, the legal test that the courts apply to determine the right to use trade names, trademarks, or service marks does not require that the names or marks be identical; it requires only enough similarity to cause a likelihood of confusion. Thus, neither of these filings means that you have the right to use your name in the advertising, promotion, or sale of goods or services.

5. **Must Trademarks Be Registered?**

There is no requirement to register your mark, but there are many advantages to doing so. A federally registered mark is presumed to be a valid mark and the registrant is presumed to have the exclusive right to use the trademark throughout the United States on the goods or services listed in the registration. A registered mark will also be revealed in searches conducted by other businesses in their effort to avoid selecting marks that may conflict with those of others. In addition, only federally registered trademarks or service marks may use the ® symbol.

After five years, the registration may become incontestable, which significantly limits the grounds on which competitors can attack the registration. An application for a federal registration may be filed before a mark is used in commerce, assuming the applicant has a good faith intent to use the mark. Actual use must begin, however, prior to the issuance of a registration.

Marks may also be registered in each of the 50 states. The advantages of a state registration vary according to the laws of each state. Most states require that you use a mark on goods or services before applying the registration. A California trademark registration, for example, is usually faster, cheaper, and less difficult to obtain than a federal registration. It also allows its owner to sue infringers under several California statutes that offer advantages not available under federal law. A California trademark registration, however, has no force outside of the state.

6. **What Is a Trademark Search?**

There are a number of professional search services that may be used to help ensure that your mark or trade name does not conflict with the rights of another business. The goal of such searches is to avoid spending time, effort, and money promoting a product name or business name, only to find out that it conflicts with someone else's rights.

These searches are typically performed through trademark lawyers who evaluate the search report to determine if there is an actual or potential conflict with another name or mark. This evaluation depends upon the consideration of numerous legal factors and case law decisions.

7. **Is My Product's Shape or Packaging Protectable?**

The non-functional features of a product's shape or packaging (its "trade dress") may be protectable if they are sufficiently distinctive to identify the owner of the trade dress. Product shapes are being protected with ever-increasing frequency. For example, the appearance of a "C" clamp, a Ruger's 22 caliber pistol, a fingernail polish bottle, and the red border and format of TIME® magazine have all been protected against look-alike competitive products.

To help achieve this type of protection, non-functional and distinctive product features or packaging should be selected. These features should then be promoted through "image" advertising or "look for" advertising so that customers recognize the product shape or packaging and associate it with a single source.

8. Can I Register My Trade Dress?

If your trade dress is non-functional and is either inherently distinctive or has acquired customer recognition from sufficient promotion of the protectable features, it may be registered as a trademark. For example, the shape of the WEBER® barbecue grill and the clear tip of a SHAKESPEARE® fishing rod have been registered with the U.S. Patent and Trademark Office.

9. What About Protection in Foreign Countries?

Trademark owners who have not registered their marks in foreign countries may find that the mark has been appropriated by a third party who was the first to register in that country. Many foreign countries regard the first to register in that country as the owner of the mark, even if it is a pirate who saw the mark in the United States and appropriated it. This pirate may even be a trusted foreign distributor of the U.S. trademark owner.

Foreign pirates may be able to prevent the original U.S. trademark owner from using or registering the mark in one or more foreign countries. In some cases it may be possible to recover the mark, but the U.S. owner may face expensive litigation or exorbitant demands from the pirate.

If a U.S. product is sold overseas, care must be taken to ensure the U.S. federal registration symbol ® is not used unless the mark is registered in the foreign country where the product is being sold. Some countries have both civil and criminal penalties for using the ® symbol with a mark not registered in that country. Improper use of the ® symbol may also make the mark unenforceable in some countries.

10. Where May I Get Information on Protecting Product and Business Names?

Information on trademarks may be obtained from the Trademark Unit of your Secretary of State's Office. Information on federal registrations may be obtained from the U.S. Patent and Trademark Office at *www.uspto.gov*.

The assistance of a lawyer experienced in trademark matters can help avoid problems before they arise. To contact a trademark lawyer or learn more about Knobbe Martens, visit *www.kmob.com*.

Ten Things You Should Know To Protect Your Artwork, Ads, Writings, And Software

1. What Is a Copyright?

Copyright protection exists in any original "expression" of an idea that is fixed in any physical medium such as paper, electronic discs, or tapes. Copyrights cover such diverse things as art, music, technical and architectural drawings, books, computer programs, and advertisements. Copyrights protect only the expression of an idea, not the idea itself; they do not protect facts, short phrases, or slogans.

Because copyright protection requires originality, it bars others from copying copyrighted work to create substantially similar works. It is possible, however, for two very similar works to be independently created, with each author owning a separate copyright. For example, if two strangers stand next to each other and each take a photograph of the same scene, each would own a copyright in his or her respective photograph.

2. **What Protection Does a Copyright Give?**
Copyright protection encompasses a bundle of exclusive rights that include: (1) the right to reproduce the work; (2) the right to make derivative works; (3) the right to distribute copies by sale, lease, or rental; (4) the right to publicly perform certain works such as plays or audiovisual works; and (5) the right to publicly display certain works such as pictorial or sculptural works.

Compilations of actual data, like names or part numbers, may be copyrightable, but the protection is limited to such things as the selection and arrangement of the information. Facts by themselves cannot be protected by copyright, even if considerable time and expense went into compiling the facts. In appropriate cases, trade secret protection may be available for the factual information.

Copyrights may be licensed or transferred together or separately. For example, an author may grant a book company the rights to reproduce a book, may grant a movie studio the rights to make a movie derived from the book, and may grant foreign distribution rights to other companies.

3. **Are Websites Copyrightable?**
A website may embody numerous works protectable by copyrights. For example, protected works may include individual graphic images within web pages, textual content of web pages or the visual appearance of entire web pages. Copyrights may also protect certain selections or arrangements of data or images embodied in a website, such as a library of thumb-nail graphical images of Caribbean fish, or a database of recipes to prepare an authentic southwestern dish.

Other copyrightable subject matter includes original sequences of computer instructions that: (1) format web page content; (2) hyperlink to other web pages; (3) prompt users for input; (4) respond to user input; and/or (5) carry out other related processes. Examples may include sequences of markup language (e.g. HTML) instructions, CGI scripts, or JAVA modules.

Authors who create copyrighted works available for downloading via the Internet should be careful to use appropriate notice. If they do not, an implied license to do more than simply download the work for viewing may be granted. To limit the scope of an implied license, a copyright owner should include an express limitation in addition to a standard copyright notice. For example, if the copyright owner intends that the work be viewed only, then the owner may wish to include the following notice: "The recipient may only view this work. No other right or license is granted."

As with any other copyrightable subject matter, website-related works can only receive copyright protection if they are original works of authorship, embodying, or fixing the independent expression of the author or authors. Generally, copyright protection arises automatically upon fixing such expression in a tangible medium such as computer memory. While copyright protection is automatic and does not require copyright notice, the owner of copyrights related to a website may further discourage copying by including a copyright notice on protected features.

4. **How Long Does a Copyright Last?**

   U.S. copyright protection for works created after January 1, 1978 will last for the life of the author plus 70 years after his or her death. If the work was created for an employer by an employee within the scope of his or her employment, the copyright protection will last for 95 years from the date of first publication, or 120 years from the date of creation, whichever is shorter.

   If a U.S. work was created before January 1, 1978, the copyright can last for a total of 95 years, assuming that the owner has not inadvertently forfeited his or her work to the public domain by not using appropriate notice or filing the necessary renewals in a timely manner. Determining precisely when the term of the copyright ends and who owns any renewal rights, are complex matters for which legal advice should be sought.

5. **If I Use Only 10%, Can I Use Copyrighted Works?**

   If the portion taken is the heart of the copyrighted work or from a widely recognized portion of the work, then infringement can exist even though less than 10 percent of the copyrighted work is taken. The test for copyright infringement is whether the accused work is copied from and "substantially similar" to the copyrighted work. While the copyright statute provides "fair use" guidelines, these are evaluated case-by-case. Thus, there is no single "rule" or fixed amount regarding the portion of a work which one must change in order to avoid infringement. If you have concerns about specific situations, you should consult with an experienced copyright lawyer.

6. **Must Copyrights Be Registered?**

   Under current law, a copyright need not be registered until a U.S. citizen wants to file a copyright infringement lawsuit. Early registration, however, offers the copyright holder some significant advantages. For example, if a work is registered before an infringement commences, the infringer may be liable for statutory damages up to $150,000 for each copyright that is infringed, and may also have to pay the attorney's fees incurred by the copyright owner in the lawsuit. It is advisable to register within three months of publication in order to claim the maximum remedies under the Copyright Act.

7. **Do I Need a Copyright Notice?**

   For U.S. works first published after March 1, 1989, a copyright notice is not necessary to maintain copyright protection. Using a copyright notice, however, makes it difficult for other people to claim that they are "innocent" infringers who were misled by the absence of a copyright notice. For U.S. works first published between 1978 and 1989, the omission of a copyright notice from published works could result in the loss of copyright protection unless certain steps were taken in a timely manner. For U.S. works first published before 1978, omission of a copyright notice from published works usually resulted in the loss of any copyright protection.

   A copyright notice consists of the copyright symbol ©, the year a work is first published, and the name of the copyright owner, (e.g. © 2008 Knobbe Martens Olson & Bear LLP). If a sound recording is copyrighted, use ℗ with the first publication date and owner. If the copyrighted material is revised, add the year of the revision to the copyright notice. It is also advisable to add "All Rights Reserved."

8. **Do I Own the Copyrights I Pay Others to Create?**

   You probably do not own the copyright material you pay independent contractors to prepare, unless you have a written agreement transferring the ownership of any copyrights.

Source: Courtesy of the Lemelson-MIT Program, *http://web.mit.edu/invent/h-main.html* (Accessed February 28, 2008).

While a business usually owns the copyrights in works created by full-time employees within the scope of their employment, the business has only limited rights to use copyrightable works created by independent contractors. Ownership of works created by employees, but not in their normal course of employment, varies with the facts of each case. Also, certain types of copyrightable works are entitled to "moral rights" protection, which must be considered at the time of any transfer of copyrights.

Ownership issues are often complex. An experienced copyright lawyer should be consulted on such issues.

9. Do Foreign Countries Protect Copyrights?

The United States has long been a member of the Universal Copyright Convention, through which copyright protection may be obtained in many foreign countries. In 1988, the U.S. joined the Berne Convention through which copyright protection may be obtained in the vast majority of foreign countries.

Obtaining and enforcing copyrights in foreign countries requires compliance with the laws and treaties of each individual country. A lawyer knowledgeable in copyright law should be consulted about any specific needs.

10. Where Can I Get More Information On Copyrights?
Information on copyright registrations may be obtained from the Register of Copyrights, Library of Congress, in Washington, D.C. at *www.copyright.gov*. To contact a copyright lawyer or learn more about Knobbe Martens, visit *www.kmob.com*.

Source: Knobbe, Martens, Olson and Bear, LLP. Use of company names and trademarks is solely for the purpose of examples, and does not imply sponsorship, affiliation, or endorsement by respective trademark owners. © 2008 Knobbe Martens Olson & Bear LLP. All rights reserved.

LICENSING YOUR PRODUCT

Those inventors who choose not to produce and manufacture their products may elect to sign a product licensing deal with a firm that has the financial, production, and marketing resources to bring the product to market. Many times inventors do not have the time or desire to take the product to market, or the time is ripe for the product, but it will take too much time to arrange for financing and manufacturing if they undertake the idea themselves. Also, many engineers and scientists are more interested in inventing than running a business. The Incredible Resource on page 287 guides you to a very thorough online Inventor's Handbook produced by the famous Lemelson-MIT program, which also goes into product licensing in depth. Securing a license for your product takes a great deal of work and most likely will entail hiring others who can assist you in your efforts; less than 10 percent of entrepreneurs seeking licensing are successful.

The Passion Box on page 277 that highlights Timothy Lu, the winner of the Lemelson-MIT Student Prize for Inventiveness, details an invention that will probably be licensed to a manufacturer.

The Sloan brothers of Startup Nation share that before taking on a new product and paying a licensing fee, "Companies will evaluate such criteria as customer feedback, retail price points, unit costs to manufacture, competitive landscape, manufacturing feasibility, and market opportunity." Their licensing tips follow.

Ten Tips for Landing a Product-Licensing Deal

By the Sloan Brothers
Here are some things we learned along the way about trying to land a product licensing deal.

1. **Know Your Stuff.** First and foremost, to have any chance of licensing your invention, you must *know your stuff*. You have to become an expert in the field in which your invention applies. You should be able to rattle off who the competition is, what the potential market size is, what the projected demand for your product is, and why your product is the best to meet and satisfy that market demand.

2. **Know the Downside.** While it is important to be passionate about your idea, it's also important to be sober. Your credibility will be assessed by potential licensees

partly based on whether you present a realistic analysis of the risks the licensee will have to deal with—things like product failure, the potential for slower-than-expected customer adoption, etc.

3. **Present like a Pro.** Information you present to potential licensees should be provided in written form and in a PowerPoint presentation. The information should include market research data, competitive analysis information, patent status, and extent of coverage. It helps to provide a letter from your patent attorney summarizing the initial search results and any other pertinent opinions relating to the extent and value of the patent coverage awarded to you. Also include your product specifications, drawings, prototypes—even if they demonstrate only what the product looks like without the actual functionality. Add to this presentation your production cost estimates, testimonials you've collected, and any and all other materials that help demonstrate the potential your invention has in the marketplace.

4. **Get it Protected.** Big corporations usually have intellectual property or licensing departments specifically set up to handle and manage the inflow of product licensing opportunities. Most of these offices will not accept any submission of a licensing opportunity for which a patent has not yet been issued. And many will not sign a confidentiality agreement, while many others will require that only their own agreement be signed. In some cases, companies might be willing to sign your confidentiality agreement, but only rarely.

5. **Submit Smart!** Work closely with your intellectual property attorney when submitting an idea to a potential licensee to ensure that your idea is adequately protected. Never sign a confidentiality agreement without first having an attorney review it. And never turn over materials to a company without your attorney giving you the green light. It may be dangerous unless you have adequate patent protection in place or a confidentiality agreement that your attorney deems sufficient to protect your intellectual property.

6. **Analyze Your Targeted Licensee.** Always do research on the company you're targeting prior to pitching to them. Check to see if the potential licensee has the manufacturing and distribution capability you need already in place. If they do, their risk is mitigated to a substantial degree, and they will be much more likely to seriously consider the opportunity. Believe it or not, though, you may have to educate them on how your product can fit into their existing lines of business.

7. **Don't Reinvent Procedures.** It's important to follow the established protocol of a licensee when submitting your idea for consideration. If you attempt to bend the rules, your submission can be stopped dead in its tracks before ever being given consideration. If a targeted licensee has a licensing office, always start there to get a case file started at the company's licensing office, and attend to their confidentiality procedures.

8. **Find a Champion.** Once you have clearance from the company to present your idea, always try to find a champion from within the company who gets excited about your idea and works to "pull" the idea into the company rather than you simply attempting to "push" the idea onto the company.

9. **"No" Is an Opportunity.** Remember, it's always safer for the company to say *no* to an idea than it is to say *yes*. The key is to be able to overcome the likely onslaught of negative responses the company will undoubtedly throw your way. It's imperative—even in the midst of a *no*—that instead of hanging up or walking out in defeat, you ask to understand specifically *why*. If someone says *no* to you, that's a perfect opportunity to learn. Immediately ask *why*. What are the concerns? Are they insurmountable? What could be done to address the concerns? You'll use what you learn to create a *yes* next time around.

10. **Multiple Baskets.** As the old saying goes, don't put all your eggs in one basket. Relying on a single potential licensee just adds more risk to a challenge that already has plenty of inherent risk. It's smart to approach more than one potential licensee to increase your odds for success. Further, playing multiple bidders off of each other can actually put some well-needed leverage on your side of the negotiating table by bringing out the competitive nature of the potential licensees. Ultimately, if you generate serious interest—and your aim is to license your invention to just one licensee—be sure you know when to stop playing competitors against each other. The moment you select your licensee, you'll have to begin building good faith with them, and you don't want bad blood to tarnish how they perceive you, and work with you, in the long run.

Bottom Line

While obtaining a license from a third party to produce and sell your product is very challenging, it can be done. And if you properly prepare and equip yourself for the challenge, you have a shot at the dream of landing that product-licensing deal and collecting royalties while the licensee does all the work and takes all of the risk.

Source: Adapted from *http://www.startupnation.com/NET_ROOT/print_template/ PrintContent.aspx?content_id=878* (Accessed February 28, 2008).

ADVERTISING WITHIN THE RULES

Beware of the many state and federal laws that oversee advertising, because misleading or deceptive ads may land your business in a courtroom. Legal counsel should review *all* advertisements, mailers, Web sites, and Internet material. The Federal Trade Commission (FTC) may take action in the event that your competitors or customers allege unlawful advertising. Review the information on advertising at *http://www.ftc.gov*. Other regulatory agencies such as the Federal Deposit Insurance Corporation, NASDAQ, state corporation commissions, and state consumer-protection agencies may also investigate, levy fines, and suspend business activity. State consumer-protection laws may also provide consumers with the right to sue for deceptive advertising.

As Internet advertising, podcasting, YouTube, pop-up ads, and so on grow daily, and new media options continue to develop, the government is having a tough time regulating these options. It will be your responsibility to keep up on any legal changes within these areas. According to *http://www.Nolo.com*, a leading source of legal self-help books, the following rules will help keep your traditional ads within safe, legal limits.

Seven Rules for Legal Advertising

Rule 1: Be Accurate

Make sure your ads are factually correct. Don't show a picture of this year's model of a product if what you're selling is last year's model, even if they look almost the same. Be truthful about what consumers can expect from your product. Don't say ABC pills will cure headaches if the pills offer only temporary pain relief. Don't claim a rug shampooer is a wizard at removing all kinds of stains when there are some it won't budge.

"Waterproof" or "fireproof" means just that—not water resistant or fire resistant under some circumstances. The term *polar*, when describing winter gear, suggests that it will keep people warm in extreme cold, not just in temperatures near freezing.

Rule 2: Get Permission

Does your ad feature someone's picture or endorsement? Does it quote material written by someone not on your staff or employed by your advertising agency? Does it use the name of a national organization such as the Boy Scouts or Red Cross? If so, secure written permission.

Under U.S. copyright law, the "fair use" doctrine allows limited quotations from copyrighted works without authorization from the copyright owner. In some circumstances, this doctrine provides legal justification for the widespread practice of quoting from favorable reviews in ads for books, movies, and plays—and even vacuum cleaners. However, with the exception of brief quotes from product or service reviews, you should always seek permission to quote protected material. For more on the fair use doctrine, and many other aspects of copyright law and practice, see *The Copyright Handbook: What Every Writer Needs to Know*, by Stephen Fishman (Nolo Press, 2006).

Rule 3: Treat Competitors Fairly

Don't knock the goods, services, or reputation of others by giving false or misleading information. If you compare your goods and services with those of other companies, check your information to make sure that every statement in your ad is accurate. Then check again.

Rule 4: Have Sufficient Quantities on Hand

When you advertise goods for sale, make every effort to have enough on hand to supply the expected demand. If you don't think you're able, state in your ad that quantities are limited. You may even want to state the number of units on hand. State law may require merchants to stock an advertised product in quantities large enough to meet reasonably expected demand, unless the ad states that stock is limited. California, for example, has such a law. In other states, merchants may have to give a rain check if they run out of advertised goods in certain circumstances. Make sure you know what your state requires.

Rule 5: Watch Out for the Word "Free"

If you say that goods or services are "free" or "without charge," be sure there are no unstated terms or conditions that qualify the offer. If there are any limits, state them clearly and conspicuously. Let's assume that you offer a free paintbrush to anyone who buys a can of paint for $8.95, and that you describe the kind of brush. Because you're disclosing the terms and conditions of your offer, you're in good shape so far. But there are pitfalls to avoid.

- If the $8.95 is more than you usually charge for this kind of paint, the brush clearly isn't free.
- Don't reduce the quality of the paint that the customer must purchase or the quantity of any services (such as free delivery) that you normally provide. If you provide a lesser product or service, you're exacting a hidden cost for the brush.
- Disclose any other terms, conditions, or limitations.

Rule 6: Be Careful When You Describe Sales and Savings

You should be absolutely truthful in all claims about pricing. The most common pitfall is making doctored price comparisons with other merchants or with your own "regular" prices.

Rule 7: Observe Limitations on Offers of Credit

Don't advertise that you offer easy credit unless it's true. You don't offer easy credit if:

- You don't extend credit to people who have a poor credit rating.
- You offer credit to people with marginal or poor credit ratings, but you require a higher down payment or shorter repayment period than is ordinarily required for creditworthy people.
- You offer credit to high-risk customers, but once all the fine print is deciphered, the true cost of credit you charge exceeds the average charged by others in your retail market.
- You offer credit to high-risk customers at favorable terms but employ draconian (although legal) collection practices against buyers who fall behind.

If you advertise specific credit terms, you must provide all relevant details, including the down payment, the terms of repayment, and the annual interest rate.

Source: Reprinted with permission from the publisher, Nolo, copyright 2000. Available at *http://www.inc.com* (Accessed February 28, 2008).

SUMMARY

Determining your legal form of business should be undertaken with the advice of your attorney, accountant, and business advisor. As your firm grows and changes, reassess your decision with your legal and financial team, but know that changes to the business form can be difficult and costly.

Partnerships can be a rocky road, so you should evaluate your need for a partner and your choice of partner thoroughly. Do *not* enter into *any* partnership without legal assistance.

Protecting yourself through copyrights, trademarks, and patents requires the assistance of intellectual property counsel. Legal issues are significant and have many nuances and complications. Thus, never skimp on finding the best legal advice available. As for the information gleaned from the Internet, buyer beware.

THINK POINTS FOR SUCCESS

- We only remember what we want to. Get *everything* in writing.
- If your business is small and you like it that way, keep it simple—like your hobby. But still take steps to protect yourself.
- Most growth businesses need outside infusions of cash. Your business structure may hinder or enhance your ability to reach out for money.
- Do not pay Uncle Sam more than you have to, but make sure you pay what is due. Have your accountant structure your business according to your needs.

- Tax planning is an essential element of operating a successful business.
- Even if you incorporate, a banker may still want a personal guarantee for loans, and this guarantee may be in place for years to come.
- The increasing incidence of lawsuits should encourage most businesses to consider incorporating.

KEY POINTS FROM ANOTHER VIEW

12 Keys to Family Business Success
By the Sloan Brothers

Family members start a major portion of new businesses launched in the U.S. every year. Brothers come to mind, of course.

Whatever the family ties, however, starting a business with a spouse, parents, siblings, children, or other family members presents unique challenges over and above the usual problems a start-up faces. That's why **only one in three family businesses survives to the next generation.**

In the start-up stage, the dangers can be especially acute. Family members sometimes join the excitement of a business start-up without a clear idea of their role once the business is underway. If family is involved in your start-up venture, you should be clear up front about compensation, exit plans, and other details before they become a problem.

We've given this a great deal of personal reflection and come up with 12 essentials for striking the right balance when starting a family business.

12 Essentials for Striking the Right Balance in a Family Business.

Set some boundaries. It's easy for family members involved in a business to talk shop 24/7. But mixing business, personal, and home life will eventually produce a volatile brew. Limit business discussions outside of the office. That's not always possible, but at least save them for an appropriate time—not at a family wedding or funeral, for example.

Establish clear and regular methods of communication. Problems and differences of opinion are inevitable. Maybe you see them already. Consider weekly meetings to assess progress, air any differences, and resolve disputes.

Divide roles and responsibilities. While various family members may be qualified for similar tasks, duties should be divvied up to avoid conflicts. Big decisions can be made together, but a debate over each little move will bog the family business down.

Treat it like a business. A common pitfall in a family business is placing too much emphasis on "family" and not enough on "business." The characteristics of a healthy business may not always be compatible with family harmony, so be ready to face those situations when they arise.

Recognize the advantages of family ownership. Family-owned businesses offer unique benefits. One is access to human capital in the form of other family members. This can be a key to survival, as family members can provide low-cost or no-cost labor or emergency loans. Firms run by trusted family members can also avoid special accounting systems, policy manuals, and legal documents.

Treat family members fairly. While some experts advise against hiring family members at all, that sacrifices one of the great benefits of a family business. Countless small companies would never have survived without the hard work and energy of dedicated family members. Qualified family members can be a great asset to your business.

But avoid favoritism. Pay scales, promotions, work schedules, criticism, and praise should be evenhanded between family and nonfamily employees. Don't set standards higher or lower for family members than for others.

Put business relationships in writing. It's easy for family members to be drawn into a business start-up without a plan for what they will get out of the business relationship. To avoid hard feelings or miscommunication, put something in writing that defines compensation, ownership shares, duties, and other matters.

Don't provide "sympathy" jobs for family members. Avoid becoming the employer of last resort for your kids, cousins, or other family members. Employment should be based on what skills or knowledge they can bring to the business.

Draw clear management lines. Family members who often have a present or presumed future ownership stake in the business have a tendency to reprimand employees who don't report to them. This leads to resentment by employees.

Seek outside advice. The decision-making process for growing a family business can sometimes be too closed. Fresh ideas and creative thinking can get lost in the tangled web of family relationships. Seeking guidance from outside advisors who are not affiliated with any family members can be a good way to give the business a reality check.

Develop a succession plan. A family business without a formal succession plan is asking for trouble. The plan should spell out the details of how and when the torch will be passed to a younger generation. It needs to be a financially sound plan for the business, as well as for retiring family members. Outside professional advice to draw up a plan is essential.

Require outside experience first. If your children will be joining the business, make sure they get at least 3 to 5 years business experience elsewhere first, preferably in an unrelated industry. This will give them valuable perspective on how the business world works outside of a family setting.

Our Bottom Line:

It's hard enough launching a company without the added pitfalls and potential baggage of family relationships. But family businesses have some great advantages over others—mainly a dedicated pool of people ready to stand behind your effort. If your start-up is a family business, you'll need to take extra steps to avoid burnout, ensure on-the-job harmony, and attract advice from business experts outside the family circle.

Source: *http://www.starupnation.com/articles/1109/1/AT_12-Keys-to-Family-Startup-Success.asp* (Accessed February 28, 2008).

- Accept that you cannot do everything well.
- Write a profile of the founding team.
- Understand the importance of balance to the survival of your business.
- Explore new ways of putting together a team, including the virtual organization.
- Look back and see if you know anyone who could work with you in this venture.
- Review using independent contractors.
- Explore hiring practices and legal issues.
- Understand the true cost of an employee.
- Discover the importance of following the law to avoid sexual harassment lawsuits.
- Determine the importance and cost of workers' compensation insurance.
- Review employee leasing.
- Locate a mentor to help guide you.
- Use a personality profile system to identify who you are and the types of people you need for a balanced team.

chapter 11

Build, Maintain, and Thrive with a Winning Team
Teaming with Passion and Following the Law

Building a winning team can be one of the most enjoyable tasks you face, but it will be challenging. Now is the time for *you* to build the team of *your* dreams. To do so, first look at yourself objectively, and then build a team that will fulfill your business, psychological, and financial needs to be a successful entrepreneur. Chapter 11 will show you various ways to build a winning and strong team.

Create a team of people who have a common purpose and specific goals. In a small venture, it is important to share the rewards of success with your team players. Remember, each employee in a small business plays a significant role in its success. As the leader of your company, you must represent and live by the mission you have set forth for your firm. One of your primary responsibilities will be to inspire your employees with your passionate behavior. Strive to consistently communicate your vision to all members of your team. The Key Points' article delineates specific traits to look for in entrepreneurial employees.

It is fun being an entrepreneur. You are on your own, doing your own thing, running your own show. And one of the toughest things you have to admit is that you cannot perform all business tasks with the same success. Once you know where you need help, today's options for finding assistance are vast.

In this chapter, we touch on how to build a team, and we stress the importance of internal understanding for a stronger team. Balance, proportion, the right people, and the right personalities are equally important in building a winning team. Figure 11.1 provides seven steps to help you build a thriving entrepreneurial organization that will lead to success and profitability.

---

figure **11.1**

Seven Keys to Shaping the Entrepreneurial Organization

According to Michie P. Slaughter, chairman of the Kauffman Center for Entrepreneurial Leadership, "The entrepreneurial organization may look like any other firm. Yet it thrives on an attitude toward growth that exists only when a team spirit is fostered among the associates and with the suppliers and customers of the firm." Shaping the entrepreneurial organization is not a difficult process when growth, strongly supported by the founders and the top management team, is well planned and constantly reinforced.

The seven keys to shaping an entrepreneurial organization are:

1. Hire self-motivated people.
2. Help others to be successful.
3. Create clarity in the organization—clarification of purpose, direction, structure, and measurement.
4. Determine and communicate your own values and philosophies.
5. Provide appropriate reward systems.
6. Create an experimental learning attitude.
7. Celebrate your victories.

Source: *http://www.kauffman.org/signatureseries/resources/AAP_Seven_Keys.pdf* (Accessed March 13, 2008).

THE FOUNDING TEAM

Anyone reading your Business Plan will be most impressed by a founding team with industry-related experience, complementary skills, and a record of achievement. Investors want you to learn on *your* dime and time, not theirs. They will be evaluating your background in depth, so you will need to prove to investors that your team has the experience, ability, and pedigree to ensure success. Information about the founding team is the most-read and often the first-read section of any Business Plan.

The following management team examples are not full-blown résumés but brief biographies that demonstrate that the founders understand what they are doing. Vendors, bankers, and investors believe past success is the greatest indication of future success.

Manufacturing Team

Bill Jones and Lee Gray spent more than 11 years in the fitness business, Bill as a product designer and Lee as a sales representative. Bill developed and patented the FastBike, an exercise bicycle that burns energy faster than a stair climber, and he has sold more than 10,000 units. Lee has been in the top 10 percent of Acme Exercise Equipment's sales force for the past 4 years and has been personally responsible for more than $8 million in sales.

Bill has hired Lee to be vice president of sales. A recently retired manufacturing manager of Sport Tech, Ed Riggs, has been hired to serve as vice president of manufacturing. Ed has an operations management degree from Purdue University and managed a light assembly manufacturing plant for more than 20 years. He also teaches quality control management classes part-time at two universities. Jan Wilkes, a retired CPA with manufacturing experience, has agreed to serve as CFO on a part-time basis.

Restaurant Team

Dorothy Foltz won many prestigious awards as executive chef of the Daniel Gray Hotel, and she is well known in the community. As one of the founders of Éclair, she will work full-time and serve as president. Ms. Foltz is certified as a master pastry chef and trained in Paris at the Culinary Institute. She will supervise the kitchen and own a majority interest in the limited liability company. Leslie Perk was, until December, a training manager for the French Connection restaurant chain. Ms. Perk will act as general manager under the direction of Ms. Foltz. Pat Watter is a minority investor. Ms. Watter intends to retain her position as food and beverage manager of Crooked Stick Country Club but will be available as needed to monitor inventory and accounting activities.

Virtual Team

Nancy Hipp, a graphic artist from Indianapolis, will develop the Internet site for a children's bookstore, Annie Gale's. Cindy Barn, who recently retired from a New York management position in publishing, will serve as the fulfillment manager for all Internet orders. She will continue living in New York. Three teachers—Pat Tran in Arizona, Peggy Galt in Florida, and Troy Ball in Iowa—will answer all customer inquiries and review all new books. Fran Shue and Amy Peters, both children's librarians, will pen book descriptions and review books from their homes in the Northwest.

No matter how you begin your business, at some point you will find yourself needing the assistance of others. The previous examples illustrate solutions found to round out a team. As you look to fulfill your business needs, remember to search for people who will balance your skills and personality.

In one firm, the owner had poor customer-relation skills; he scared off all but the hardiest customers and employees. His brother realized that the business was headed for disaster. Taking a chance, he approached his brother. They agreed that the front office and customers should be off limits for him. Several months later, the business was back on track, and the employees and customers were relieved and happier.

Do what you do best and hire the rest!

Next, we will discuss various ways to acquire the help you need to grow your business without hiring full or part-time employees.

THE VIRTUAL ORGANIZATION AND OUTSOURCING

Virtual organizations and outsourcing have not only become buzzwords, they are reality for millions of small businesses today. The advancements in technology and the ease of communication through cell phones, the Internet, and video conferencing allow entrepreneurs to compete with larger firms without sacrificing scale, speed, or agility. Virtual organizations are like forming an all-star team to exploit a market opportunity.

Let us examine how the old motion picture studios used to work. They owned real estate, studios, and equipment; they had performers under contract; and they owned many other fixed assets with which they cranked out movies, both good and bad. Most of the old movie studio giants have gone the way of the dinosaurs.

In their place today are project teams of highly creative people, hired just in time to make a great picture, who will disband after the project until the next opportunity presents itself. They rent everything they need, and each aspect of the film is outsourced to specialists.

An advertising agency may consist of a solo entrepreneur who presents his client with an idea. Once the idea is approved, the entrepreneur assembles freelance graphic designers, copywriters, photographers, models, performers, and media experts to produce the promotion package. The virtual advertising agency has little overhead and can bring together the best talent, which will provide the client with a high-quality campaign at a lower cost.

Suppose you have an idea for a new widget. You develop a prototype, demonstrate it at a trade show, and take orders. Do you build a factory and hire workers? Or may outsourcing be your answer? By using NAISC codes and industry sources, you can locate assemblers, packagers, box makers, food mixers, toolmakers, public warehouses, sales agents, and whatever else when the need arises.

One printer discovered that her sales ability far exceeded her desire to produce printed materials, so she redefined herself as a "printer's broker" and used her knowledge to select from a wide variety of printers available for the most appropriate product. She sold her own small shop to an employee and increased her income several times over by providing assistance to customers who knew little about printing. Her virtual organization had just-in-time access to more than 100 experienced and specialized printers.

With continued corporate downsizing come mushrooming opportunities for alert "virtual organization" entrepreneurs. The benefits include:

- Having access to the skills and experience of proven experts in their field
- Paying only for services needed
- Obtaining variable production quantities
- Gaining higher reliability

Action Step 46

Consider a Virtual Organization and Consider Outsourcing

1. Make a list of people or firms who might assist your efforts on an as-needed basis either as employees, independent contractors, or consultants. To keep your overhead to an absolute minimum, ask and shop around; look for those people and businesses who share your vision. Make adjustments to your list as you continue to explore.
2. If you will be outsourcing design, graphics, accounting, human resources, manufacturing, or order fulfillment, it is now time to research prospective sources and also to explore costs. Chapter 8 asked you to look at your start-up and operating costs, and you may have conducted your outsourcing research at that time. If not, now is the time!
3. Explore joint ventures.
4. Explore strategic alliances.

GLOBAL VILLAGE

www.export911.com
Portal to the World of Exporting and Importing

To learn more about exporting and importing one of the best free resources on the net is Export 911 (*http://www.export911.com*). The site will direct you to specific information on the business of exporting covering such topics as letters of credit, bar codes, export labeling, product inspections, export cargo insurance, and so on.

The site's thousands of links are broken down into the following areas:

Gateways to Global Markets
Export Department
Purchasing Department
Shipping Department
Production Department
Administration Department
Product Coding

- Achieving better quality and consistency
- Having lower internal developmental costs
- Locating a customer who is presold
- Maintaining flexibility to instantly address new market opportunities
- Lower benefit and worker compensation costs
- Lower recruiting and training costs

With the above benefits in mind, the virtual organization needs to be extremely customer-driven and opportunity-focused. Performance standards are critical and there must be agreement and a shared vision among all the participants.

The virtual organization might exist for weeks or years—and then, when the opportunity has been fully exploited, it might disband quickly. Develop an exit plan when you develop a virtual organization, so you know where you are headed. Action Step 46 will help you explore the virtual organization alternative.

PARTNERSHIPS

Consider as partners those firms with special capabilities that will share your risk in bringing a product or service to market. For example, if you have a new product, a team that includes retailers or end users could solve a lot of your marketing problems. Businesses usually form partnerships or associations in two fundamental ways: as a joint venture or a strategic alliance.

A **joint venture** is usually a goal-oriented cooperation among two or more businesses. It involves the creation of a separate organization owned and controlled jointly by the parties. The joint venture usually has its own management, employees, production systems, and so on. Cooperation is limited to defined areas and often to a predetermined time frame. For a sample joint venture contract, link to *http://www.ilrg.com/forms/jointventure.html*.

A **strategic alliance** is a goal-oriented cooperative effort among two or more businesses based on formal agreements and a Business Plan. In contrast

Joint venture Partnership formed for a specific undertaking resulting in the formation of a new legal entity

Strategic alliance Partnership formed between companies to create a competitive advantage

to a joint venture, however, it usually does not involve the establishment of a separate new organization. The objective of a strategic alliance is to improve the competitiveness and capabilities of the individual members by using the strengths of the team. Depending on the need, the network may be organized in a variety of forms with regard to function, structure, and organization.

INDEPENDENT CONTRACTORS

Many people misunderstand the rules for independent contractors. If you tell a worker when to start and stop work, and if you supply tools or office equipment, you *may* have an employee. On the other hand, if the work assignment is task-driven, if the worker sets his or her own hours, if you pay by the job and not by the hour, and if most of the work takes place away from your office using the worker's resources, then you *may* have an independent contractor relationship.

You *may* save money if your workers are independent contractors—no Social Security, Medicare, workers' compensation insurance, health insurance, retirement benefits, paid holidays, vacations, sick days, and so on. Most employers can locate workers who will work without mandated benefits—but sooner or later they will get hurt, apply for unemployment, or attempt to collect Social Security benefits. When they do, the government may come back to the employer with high fines and penalties. *Review independent contractor rules with a CPA and your attorney, because the rules are rigid.* In addition, independent contractor status receives a high level of state and IRS scrutiny. An abbreviated version of IRS Publication 15-A (Figure 11.2) provides further information.

If you choose to pay a person as an independent contractor, understand that if the person becomes disgruntled and you have not followed the IRS rules, you may find yourself investigated. Also, if your competitors feel you have an unfair

figure **11.2**

Employee or Independent Contractor?

(Excerpted from IRS Publication 15-A)
An employer must generally withhold federal income taxes, withhold and pay social security and Medicare taxes, and pay unemployment tax on wages paid to an employee. An employer does not generally have to withhold or pay any taxes on payments to independent contractors.

Common-Law Rules
To determine whether an individual is an employee or an independent contractor under the common law, the relationship of the worker and the business must be examined. In any employee–independent contractor determination, all information that provides evidence of the degree of control and the degree of independence must be considered. Facts that provide evidence of the degree of control and independence fall into three categories: behavioral control, financial control, and the type of relationship of the parties. These facts are discussed below.

Behavioral control. Facts that show whether the business has a right to direct and control how the worker does the task for which the worker is hired include the type and degree of:

Instructions that the business gives to the worker. An employee is generally subject to the business' instructions

about when, where, and how to work. All of the following are examples of types of instructions about how to do work.

- When and where to do the work.
- What tools or equipment to use.
- What workers to hire or to assist with the work.
- Where to purchase supplies and services.
- What work must be performed by a specified individual.
- What order or sequence to follow.

The amount of instruction needed varies among different jobs. Even if no instructions are given, sufficient behavioral control may exist if the employer has the right to control how the work results are achieved. A business may lack the knowledge to instruct some highly specialized professionals; in other cases, the task may require little or no instruction. The key consideration is whether the business has retained the right to control the details of a worker's performance or instead has given up that right.

Training that the business gives to the worker. An employee may be trained to perform services in a particular manner. Independent contractors ordinarily use their own methods.

(continued)

figure 11.2

Employee or Independent Contractor? *(continued)*

Financial control. Facts that show whether the business has a right to control the business aspects of the worker's job include:

The extent to which the worker has unreimbursed business expenses. Independent contractors are more likely to have unreimbursed expenses than are employees. Fixed ongoing costs that are incurred regardless of whether work is currently being performed are especially important. However, employees may also incur unreimbursed expenses in connection with the services that they perform for their business.

The extent of the worker's investment. An independent contractor often has a significant investment in the facilities he or she uses in performing services for someone else. However, a significant investment is not necessary for independent contractor status.

The extent to which the worker makes his or her services available to the relevant market. An independent contractor is generally free to seek out business opportunities. Independent contractors often advertise, maintain a visible business location, and are available to work in the relevant market.

How the business pays the worker. An employee is generally guaranteed a regular wage amount for an hourly, weekly, or other period of time. This usually indicates that a worker is an employee, even when the wage or salary is supplemented by a commission. An independent contractor is usually paid by a flat fee for the job. However, it is common in some professions, such as law, to pay independent contractors hourly.

The extent to which the worker can realize a profit or loss. An independent contractor can make a profit or loss.

Type of relationship. Facts that show the parties' type of relationship include:

Written contracts describing the relationship the parties intended to create.

Whether or not the business provides the worker with employee-type benefits, such as insurance, a pension plan, vacation pay, or sick pay.

The permanency of the relationship. If you engage a worker with the expectation that the relationship will continue indefinitely, rather than for a specific project or period, this is generally considered evidence that your intent was to create an employer–employee relationship.

The extent to which services performed by the worker are a key aspect of the regular business of the company. If a worker provides services that are a key aspect of your regular business activity, it is more likely that you will have the right to direct and control his or her activities. For example, if a law firm hires an attorney, it is likely that it will present the attorney's work as its own and would have the right to control or direct that work. This would indicate an employer–employee relationship.

IRS help. If you want the IRS to determine whether or not a worker is an employee, file Form SS-8, Determination of Worker Status for Purposes of Federal Employment Taxes and Income Tax Withholding, with the IRS.

Misclassification of Employees

Consequences of treating an employee as an independent contractor. If you classify an employee as an independent contractor and you have no reasonable basis for doing so, you may be held liable for employment taxes for that worker (the relief provisions, discussed below, will not apply). See Internal Revenue Code section 3509 for more information.

Relief provisions. If you have a reasonable basis for not treating a worker as an employee, you may be relieved from having to pay employment taxes for that worker. To get this relief, you must file all required federal information returns on a basis consistent with your treatment of the worker. You (or your predecessor) must not have treated any worker holding a substantially similar position as an employee for any periods beginning after 1977.

Technical service specialists. This relief provision does not apply for a technical services specialist you provide to another business under an arrangement between you and the other business. A technical service specialist is an engineer, designer, drafter, computer programmer, systems analyst, or other similarly skilled worker engaged in a similar line of work. This limit on the application of the rule does not affect the determination of whether such workers are employees under the common-law rules. The common-law rules control whether the specialist is treated as an employee or an independent contractor. However, if you directly contract with a technical service specialist to provide services for your business and not for another business, you may still be entitled to the relief provision.

Source: *http://www.irs.gov* (Accessed March 14, 2008).

advantage by treating those working for you as independent contractors, they may turn you in. Be aware that state employment laws may differ from federal rules.

EMPLOYEE LEASING

Consider employee leasing as a way to reduce administrative costs, paperwork hassles, legal issues, and costly benefits. Not unlike leasing physical property, in this instance you will be leasing people—employees—whose leasing organization handles payroll and most, if not all, of the human resources functions.

The leasing firm will help you stay in compliance with the myriad of federal, state, and local employment laws. California and federal labor codes run more than 460 pages, so keeping in compliance is a full-time job. For your protection, we suggest you only use a leasing organization that possesses a strong track record and a sound financial background. Many new ventures are unable to offer employees health insurance benefits and retirement programs and thus lose out on top employees. Due to economies of scale, large leasing firms are able to provide these benefits to your leased employees. The National Association of Professional Employer Organizations, *http://www.napeo.org*, provides further information on employee leasing.

Employee leasing may appear to cost more initially, but it does allow for additional benefits. For example:

- Background screening checks are completed by the leasing organization.
- Termination issues are eliminated. If the person does not fit the position, you can send him or her back to the leasing organization.
- Turnover is reduced.
- Hiring costs such as advertising, interviewing time, reference checks, turnover, and so on are eliminated.

THE FIRST EMPLOYEES

When to hire your first full-time employee is a question often asked. You may require full-time employees immediately, but many small firms do well using part-time or temporary workers or independent contractors until the owners have a strong feel for what needs to be done and who is best suited to do the job. Some firms never hire full-time employees and always choose to use part-timers, as illustrated in the example of Charlene Webb.

A Team of Part-Timers

Charlene Webb has built a winning team of part-time employees. After she sold her gourmet cookware shop, she opened a women's specialty clothing store. The shop is small—about 2,000 square feet—and it is located in a small shopping center in an upscale community of about 60,000 people.

Charlene discovered that her ideal employees were local women who were active in community life and who preferred to work only one day a week. Monday's saleswoman is a golfer whose country-club friends come in to visit and buy from her on her day of work. Tuesday the tennis player is on, and her friends have followed her to the store. Wednesday, a sailing instructor and officer of the largest sailing club in the area; Thursday, a leader of hospital volunteers; Friday, a well-known PTA member; and Saturday, an attorney's wife. All of the women know fashion and have a lot of energy. They never tire from the routine, and they are excellent customers and employees. Also, they serve as walking store models at all times.

Charlene demonstrates in her stores how a well-connected group of part-time employees can surpass full-timers. But for most businesses, that will not be the case; for them, full-time commitment and loyalty will be part of the hiring goals and future growth.

If you require someone with a high level of technical skills, or a person who will take your organization to the next level, you may need to provide an extra carrot, depending on the economy and industry. Talented workers may prefer the entrepreneurial adventure to big business bureaucracy, and they may work for less if they share your vision and passion for entrepreneurship and a future financial payoff.

As you continue to add people, you must understand that competence is not the only criterion to consider. You are assembling a venture team that wants to see growth and prosperity as much as you do. It is impossible to grow and expand until you have people who are not only capable but also motivated to ensure success. The Key Points article at the end of the chapter provides an additional excellent discussion of desirable characteristics for entrepreneurial employees.

The quest for new employees begins with a written job description. You may not find a perfect fit, so do not fence yourself in with too many specifications. Define the duties to be performed and the skills needed to perform them. A small business cannot afford a misfit or an unproductive person.

If past experience is not critical when hiring, look into hiring graduating students from vocational, trade, and professional schools. Local colleges and high schools also have placement offices. Also, inexperienced employees can sometimes be found through programs offered through social agencies that might subsidize the training of workers, as shown in the Passion box in Chapter 9. Check out public and private employment agencies. In addition, temporary agencies may be able to locate short-term help. Hiring through a temporary agency allows you to check out the person before actually hiring him or her for full-time employment. Many business owners hire from agencies to reduce the paperwork and liability of hiring workers directly.

Monster.com and Craigslist.com may also be recruiting sources for you. If you require someone highly educated and skilled in a very specific area, you may also need to use a professional recruiter. Also, many job posting sites on the Internet target specific markets and may also prove helpful. National associations often allow job postings and listings on their Internet sites as well.

If you are just starting out, you may want to network your way through your contacts. E-mail job descriptions to your friends and associates, and see if any of them will act as recruiters for you. Keep in mind, though, that firing someone recommended by a friend or family member might prove difficult, and one of the most important requirements of a small business is the ability to let go of an employee as soon as possible if he or she is not working out.

What *is* critical in hiring is your effort to make sure you have investigated the applicants to the best of your ability within legal parameters. Unfortunately, firing employees can trigger lawsuits—and justified or not, they can cost you an incredible sum of money and time. Be sure you have a qualified and experienced attorney on call at all times to assist you with employment law issues.

Be prepared: you *will* have employee turnover in the beginning. Either they will quit or you will decide to terminate their employment. Restaurants and retail stores should overhire for the opening months.

You should develop personnel policies to cover hiring, firing, and managing your employees. If you provide an offer letter to an employee, list compensation based on a weekly or monthly basis so as not to imply a long-term commitment. It might be best not to provide an offer letter at all; in some instances, it may imply a contract. You want to maintain that the relationship is "at will," meaning that you can fire the employee whenever you want. Your policies need to be reviewed so that they do not compromise the "at will" status. Check your state laws to determine if you are an "at will" state.

Additionally, if you are a firm with competition and privacy concerns, contact your lawyer to discuss drafting noncompete and confidentiality agreements. In high-tech industries, these agreements are commonplace.

One source that allows you to develop policies using online software is located at *http://www.hrtools.com*. Remember, any form you take from the Internet should be reviewed by your attorney for compliance with state and federal laws.

Due to potential problems inherent in the hiring and employment process, we recommend firms such as ADP or Paychex to assist you in managing required legal paperwork and payroll. Such firms also provide you with legal updates and will make sure you are in compliance with the vast state and federal laws. Upon reading only one of ADP's newsletters, you will know immediately that it would be impossible for you to be able to keep up with the legal changes affecting the employer–employee relationship. Employment law has become a very difficult road for most employers to travel, and we advise that you *never* do it alone. The cost of this type of service is minimal, and the service will also help you avoid penalties for missed filing dates and potential filing errors.

Adhering to the law, acting with good intentions, and using ADP or Paychex should enable you to avoid most legal employment issues. Please review Figure 11.3 for additional tips for avoiding legal troubles.

---

figure **11.3**

Tips for Avoiding Legal Trouble with Employees

By Attorneys Amy DelPo and Lisa Guerin
You can't afford to ignore or mishandle employment problems. A botched employment situation can cost you millions of dollars if it turns into a lawsuit. Protect yourself using these commonsense tips:

1. **Treat your workers with respect.** Workers who are deprived of dignity, who are humiliated, or who are treated in ways that are just plain mean are more likely to look for some revenge through the legal system—and juries are more likely to sympathize with them. For example, if you march fired workers off the premises under armed guard, publicize an employee's personal problems, or shame a worker in public for poor performance, you can expect trouble.

2. **Communicate with your workers.** Adopt an open-door policy and put it into practice. This will help you find out about workplace problems early on, when you can nip them in the bud. And it will show your employees that you value their opinions, an important component of positive employee relations.

3. **Be consistent.** Apply the same standards of performance and conduct to all of your employees. Workers quickly sour on a boss who plays favorites or punishes scapegoats. Successful discrimination lawsuits start when you treat workers in the same situation differently.

4. **Give regular evaluations.** Performance evaluations are your early warning system regarding employment problems—and your proof that you acted reasonably, in case you end up in court. (In the worst cases, evaluations can be valuable proof in a lawsuit, illustrating that you put a poor performer on notice and gave him a chance to improve.) In the best situations, they can turn a poor performer into a valued worker. You can find detailed information about giving performance evaluations in *Dealing With Problem Employees: A Legal Guide*, by Amy DelPo and Lisa Guerin (Nolo).

5. **Make job-related decisions.** Every workplace decision made should be guided by job-related criteria—not by a worker's race or gender and not by a worker's personal life or your personal biases. Make sure that your personnel decisions are business-related, make economic sense, and will keep you out of lawsuits for discrimination, violation of privacy, and wrongful termination.

6. **Don't punish the messenger.** Employers get in trouble when they discipline whistleblowers or workers who complain of harassment, discrimination, or unsafe working conditions. Take action to deal with the problem itself, not with the employee who brought the problem to your attention.

(continued)

figure 11.3

Tips for Avoiding Legal Trouble with Employees (continued)

7. **Adopt sound policies and follow them.** An employee handbook is an indispensable workplace tool that can help you communicate with your employees, manage your workforce, and protect your business from lawsuits. But once you adopt policies, you have to follow them. If you bend the rules, your workers won't take them seriously. Some courts have found that employers who don't follow the policies set out in their employee handbook or personnel manual might be on the hook for breach of contract. You can find detailed information about giving performance evaluations in *Create Your Own Employee Handbook: A Legal & Practical Guide*, by Amy DelPo and Lisa Guerin (Nolo).

8. **Keep good records.** If a worker sues you, you'll have to not only remember and explain what happened, but also prove that your version of the story is accurate. To make your best case, keep careful records of every major employment decision or event for each

worker—including evaluations, disciplinary warnings, and reasons for firing.

9. **Take action when necessary.** Once an employment problem comes to your attention, resist the temptation to hide your head in the sand. Take action quickly, before it turns into a real mess.

10. **Be discreet.** Loose lips about employee problems are a sure-fire way to bring the law down upon your head. An employee could sue you for defamation or could haul you into court for causing her emotional distress, for creating a work environment that is hostile toward her, or for poisoning prospective employers against her. The stakes are high, so protect yourself by giving information on a need-to-know basis only. You can find more information on employee privacy rights and other workplace issues in *Everyday Employment Law: The Basics*, by Amy DelPo and Lisa Guerin (Nolo).

Source: Reprinted with permission from the publisher, Nolo, Copyright 2004, *http://www.nolo.com* (Accessed March 14, 2008).

INTERVIEW *AND* STAY OUT OF COURT

Interviewing can be considered an art, but the questions you ask must not only be insightful—they must keep you out of court. Consider the questions discussed in the following section, and review Table 11.1, before conducting your first interviews.

Ask the Right Questions

Use open-ended questions to start the applicant talking, but avoid too much small talk; you may inadvertently ask an illegal question, such as, "Grenchik—that's an interesting last name. What nationality is it?" A question of this type might be construed by the applicant as national-origin discrimination.

table 11.1

Lawful and Unlawful Inquiries

The following chart provides examples of ways that you can receive the information you need without running afoul of anti-discrimination laws.

Subject	Lawful Inquiry	Unlawful Inquiry
Age	Are you 18 years of age or older? (to determine if the applicant is legally old enough to perform the job)	How old are you?
Marital status	Is your spouse employed by this employer? (if your company has a nepotism policy)	Are you married?
Citizenship	Are you legally authorized to work in the United States on a full-time basis?	Are you a native-born citizen of the United States? Where are you from?
Disability	These [provide applicant with list] are the essential functions of the job. How would you perform them?	Do you have any physical disabilities that would prevent you from doing this job?
Drug and alcohol use	Do you currently use illegal drugs?	Have you ever been addicted to drugs?

Source: Reprinted with permission from the publisher, Nolo, Copyright 2004, *http://www.nolo.com* (Accessed March 14, 2008).

Develop a list of questions appropriate to the position you want to fill based on the job description and responsibilities you have defined. To avoid any charges of discrimination, ask each applicant the same questions. Any written application form should be reviewed by your attorney to make sure it is also not discriminatory. The following sample questions will help you begin to prepare your own list of interview questions:

1. How did you prepare for this meeting?
2. What are some of the obstacles you have overcome on previous jobs?
3. How have you worked independently on the job in the past?
4. What gives you satisfaction in a job?
5. What have been your most memorable work experiences?
6. What do you expect from an employer?
7. Have you ever organized an event? Explain.
8. What did you like and dislike about your last job?
9. How do you handle change and uncertainty?
10. Give an example of when you were a team player in your last position.
11. What do you do best at work?
12. When I call your last two employers, what are they going to tell me?
13. What type of challenges do you like best?
14. Describe a problem in your last job and how you resolved it.
15. How best can a boss support you?

During your interviews, make sure you have uninterrupted time to put the applicant at ease and to be able to listen thoroughly to comments and answer questions. Take notes throughout the process, and encourage the applicant to ask questions. Make your purpose for the interview clear, and explain the interview and hiring process, including time frames and reference and background checks.

At the end of the interview, review your notes and your thoughts. Ask yourself the following questions: 1) Is this person able and willing to do the job? 2) Is this person someone I can manage? 3) Will I and the other team members enjoy working with this individual? 4) How will my customers view this prospect?

Action Step 47 asks you to determine what additional questions you would add to those above to fit your particular job specifications, industry, and work situation. To determine how responsible applicants are, and how well they take instructions, one retailer requires all applicants to bring their picture ID and Social Security card to the first interview. She explains to the applicants that unless they bring these two items, she will not interview them when they arrive. Approximately 40 percent of the applicants forget one or both items and thus do not receive an interview or a job.

At the end of the interview, and after you have selected several potential employees, investigate their past with reference checks through their previous employers. Depending on the area of the country you live in, this may be easy—or it may prove *very* difficult.

Checking References

If you have any doubts about the importance of checking references, review ADP's 2008 Screening Index report covering almost 6 million job applicants (Figure 11.4).

Action Step 47

Interview Questions

1. First, review Table 11.1 to understand what questions are lawful and unlawful.
2. Review the list of interview questions in the text and the Key Points article in this chapter. Next, determine how you can legally adjust these questions to fit job specifications, your industry, and the work situations of your future employees.
3. Make a list of the questions based on the above and all the additional information throughout the chapter.
4. Prepare a short, 3- to 5-minute introduction to your firm, the specific job, and the job's requirements to present to prospective employees.
5. What steps will you take to share your passion for the business with employees?

figure **11.4**

2008 Background Screening Statistics

Total completed background checks performed by ADP Screening and Selection Services in the 2007 calendar year: 5,757,648

10% of the total completed background checks contained a record

Criminal Records
Total Completed: 1,777,076

6% had a criminal record in the last seven years

Credit Records
Total Completed: 243,063

44% had credit records showing a judgment, lien or bankruptcy, or had been reported to a collection agency

Workers' Compensation Claims Records
Total Completed: 58,712

8% had a previous workers' compensation claim

Driving Records
Total Completed: 498,167

36% had one or more violations or convictions on their driving record
5% had four or more violations or convictions on their driving record
2% had one or more drug or alcohol violations on their driving record in the last seven years
1% had one or more "at fault" accidents on their driving record in the past three years
10% had one or more suspension, revocation or withdrawal of their driver's license within the last seven years
4% had a driver's license that was currently invalid, suspended, revoked or expired

Reference Verifications
Total Completed: 453,320

45% of employment, education and/or credential reference checks revealed a difference of information between what the applicant provided and the source reported
5% of the information differences were received with negative information from the source in regard to the applicant

Background Screening Statistics by Industry

What are the hiring risks associated with specific industries? View the chart below to find out.

TYPE OF CHECK	Manufacturing	Healthcare	Hospitality	Construction	Retail	Auto Dealer	Business Services	Transportation
Criminal	7%	3%	6%	9%	8%	7%	5%	4%
Credit	42%	48%	58%	54%	55%	56%	40%	40%
Workers' Compensation	9%	6%	9%	8%	8%	8%	4%	6%
Driving (one + violations)	35%	29%	39%	40%	43%	42%	36%	34%
Driving (four + violations)	5%	4%	6%	7%	8%	9%	5%	4%
Reference (info difference)	57%	54%	57%	49%	53%	56%	54%	41%
Reference (negative info)	7%	4%	14%	5%	9%	10%	3%	5%

Background Screening Statistics by Employer Size

Listed below are background screening results for three common size ranges.

	NUMBER OF EMPLOYESS		
TYPE OF CHECK	1-49 Employees	50-999 Employees	1000+ Employees
Criminal	4%	7%	5%
Credit	41%	48%	44%
Workers' Compensation	11%	8%	6%
Driving (one + violations)	40%	37%	34%
Driving (four + violations)	7%	6%	5%
Reference (info difference)	37%	41%	43%
Reference (negative info)	4%	6%	5%

Know the whole story behind every candidate.

SCREENING INDEX 2008

Source: *http://www.screeningandselection.adp.com/resources/screeningIndex.html* (Accessed August 27, 2008).

Professional payroll service firms will perform reference checks, which can save you time, money, and paperwork and ensure your compliance with the law. The following points underscore the importance of reference checks:

1. A 2004 study by the Washington D.C. Employment Policy Foundation states that the "average turnover costs reached $13,355 per full-time private-sector worker."

2. Hiring an illegal alien can result in fines of $250 to $10,000, according to the Immigration and Naturalization Services.

3. Losses from employee theft cost U.S. retailers almost $20 billion in 2006, while shoplifting cost retailers $13.3 billion, according to the National Retail Security Survey.

4. An average settlement of $550,000, and jury awards of up to $3.35 million, for security negligence again reinforces the need for careful hiring and the importance of monitoring employees.

Because of potential libel lawsuits, employers are very reluctant to provide information about past employees, thus making it necessary to investigate the backgrounds of potential employees in other ways.

For employment screening services, review the services of *http://www.hireright.com* and *http://www.adp.com,* along with others. HireRight's services include searching the National Criminal Database, felony and misdemeanor searches, terrorist watchlist, address history, SSN validation, National Sex Offender list, motor vehicles check, and previous employment verification for around $100 per screening with a two-day turnaround. Before conducting employment screening or using any screening services, we suggest you consult with your attorney. Review Figure 11.5 to further understand the legalities surrounding background checks, and recognize the importance of using professionals to conduct the inquiries.

If the driving record of a prospective employee shows four moving violations in the last year would you reconsider? If the person has relocated ten times in the past 7 years would you reconsider? If he or she has lied about a degree would you reconsider? Not considering these factors can cost you a great deal, so spend the money to hire correctly, and firing will be less frequent and less costly.

Many employers may also want to perform drug and blood tests. However, the laws regarding testing are complicated and sometimes confusing. If you are considering testing, contact your attorney for legal advice; making a mistake in this area could prove *very* expensive. Industry associations may also provide information on hiring and screening practices.

WHAT DO EMPLOYEES REALLY COST?

If you plan on hiring employees, consider *all* the costs associated with hiring, training, and retaining employees.

- Ad placements (possibly very expensive)
- Recruiting and hiring
- Salary
- Employment taxes—Social Security, unemployment, and Medicare
- Worker's compensation insurance

figure **11.5**

Running Background Checks on Job Applicants

You must respect a job applicant's privacy rights when conducting a background check.

When making a hiring decision, you might need a bit more information than an applicant provides. After all, some folks give false or incomplete information on employment applications. And workers probably don't want you to know certain facts about their past that might disqualify them from getting a job. Generally, it's good policy to do a little checking before you make a job offer.

However, you do not have an unfettered right to dig into applicants' personal affairs. Workers have a right to privacy in certain personal matters, a right they can enforce by suing you if you pry too deeply. How can you avoid crossing this line? Here are a few tips:

- **Make sure your inquiries are related to the job.** If you decide to do a background check, stick to information that is relevant to the job for which you are considering the worker. For example, if you are hiring a security guard who will carry a weapon and be responsible for large amounts of cash, you might reasonably check for past criminal convictions. If you are hiring a seasonal farm worker, however, a criminal background check is probably unnecessary.

- **Ask for consent.** You are on safest legal ground if you ask the applicant, in writing, to consent to your background check. Explain clearly what you plan to check and how you will gather information. This gives applicants a chance to take themselves out of the running if there are things they don't want you to know. It also prevents applicants from later claiming that you unfairly invaded their privacy. If an applicant refuses to consent to a reasonable request for information, you may legally decide not to hire the worker on that basis.

- **Be reasonable.** Employers can get into legal trouble if they engage in overkill. You will not need to perform an extensive background check on every applicant. Even if you decide to check, you probably won't need to get into extensive detail for every position. If you find yourself questioning neighbors, ordering credit checks, and performing exhaustive searches of public records every time you hire a clerk or counterperson, you need to scale it back.

In addition to these general considerations, specific rules apply to certain types of information:

- **School records.** Under federal law and the law of some states, educational records—including transcripts, recommendations, and financial information—are confidential. Because of these laws, most schools will not release records without the consent of the student. And some schools will only release records directly to the student.

- **Credit reports.** Under the Fair Credit Reporting Act, or FCRA (15 U.S.C. §1681), employers must get an employee's written consent before seeking that employee's credit report. Many employers routinely include a request for such consent in their employment applications. If you decide not to hire or promote someone based on information in the credit report, you must provide a copy of the report and let the applicant know of his or her right to challenge the report under the FCRA. Some states have more stringent rules limiting the use of credit reports.

- **Bankruptcies.** Federal law prohibits employers from discriminating against applicants because they have filed for bankruptcy. This means you cannot decide not to hire someone simply because he or she has declared bankruptcy in the past.

- **Criminal records.** The law varies from state to state on whether, and to what extent, a private employer may consider an applicant's criminal history in making hiring decisions. Some states prohibit employers from asking about arrests, convictions that occurred well in the past, juvenile crimes, or sealed records. Some states allow employers to consider convictions only if the crimes are relevant to the job. And some states allow employers to consider criminal history only for certain positions: nurses, child care workers, private detectives, and other jobs requiring licenses, for example. Because of these variations, you should consult with a lawyer or do further legal research on the law of your state before digging into an applicant's criminal past.

- **Workers' compensation records.** An employer may consider information contained in the public record from a workers' compensation appeal in making a job decision only if the applicant's injury might interfere with his or her ability to perform required duties.

- **Other medical records.** Under the Americans with Disabilities Act, or ADA (42 U.S.C. §12101 and following), employers may inquire only about an applicant's ability to perform specific job duties; they may not request an employee's medical records. An employer may not make a job decision—on hiring or promotion, for example—based on an employee's disability, as long as the employee can do the job with or without a reasonable accommodation. Some states also have laws protecting the confidentiality of medical records.

- **Records of military service.** Members and former members of the armed forces have a right to privacy in their service records. These records may be released only under limited circumstances, and consent is generally required. However, the military may disclose name, rank, salary, duty assignments, awards, and duty status without the member's consent.

- **Driving records.** An employer should check the driving record of any employee whose job will require large amounts of driving (delivery persons or bus drivers, for example). These records are available, sometimes for a small fee, from the state's motor vehicles department.

For more information on background checks, see *The Manager's Legal Handbook*, by Lisa Guerin and Amy DelPo (Nolo).

- Benefits—health, retirement, dental, vacation, sick leave
- Space, furniture, equipment
- Additional management time
- Any additional perks you might offer—child care, car allowance, and so on
- Training

Each employee will cost you 130 to 200 percent of his or her salary due to the above costs. Employees in an entrepreneurial venture need to pull *more* than their own weight, so choose wisely. To keep abreast of salaries and wages, use salary comparison information from the following Internet sites:

http://www.salary.com
http://www.salaryexpert.com
http://www.payscale.com
http://www.vault.com

To gain the most accurate information on actual wage and salary rates, contact similar employers in your area, review area want ads, and search on-line listings. Also, local unions and trade associations may prove to be valuable sources of compensation data.

LABOR LAW COMPLIANCE

Ignorance is not an acceptable defense if you are charged with breaking labor laws, as shown in Figure 11.6. Check with all government agencies to be sure that you do not overlook any legal requirements. The penalties for failure to comply may be very stiff, and some firms have lost their businesses because of noncompliance. Again, do not enter this realm without professional assistance. Contact the following federal organizations to learn about your legal responsibilities:

- Occupational Safety and Health Administration (OSHA), *http://www.osha.gov*
- Equal Employment Opportunity Commission (EEOC), *http://www.eeoc.gov*
- Department of Labor, *http://www.dol.gov*
- Internal Revenue Service (IRS), *http://www.irs.gov*
- U.S. Department of Justice, Americans with Disabilities, *http://www.ada.gov/business.htm*
- U.S. Citizenship and Immigration Service, *http://uscis.gov/*

In addition to the federal offices, you will need to contact your state offices for further employment law information. State laws supersede federal laws if they are stricter than the federal laws. You will need to obtain a federal employment identification number by filing IRS Form SS-4 (see Appendix C), and then register with your state's employment department for payment of unemployment taxes. In addition, you or your accountant must file IRS Form 940-EZ or IRS Form 940 to report your federal unemployment tax each year.

Also, check to see that all employees are able to work legally in the United States, and have each one fill out an Employment Eligibility Verification form (I-9 in Appendix C) as well as IRS Form W-4, Withholding Allowance Certificate. The U.S. Citizenship and Immigration Services has developed an online E-Verify system to establish employment eligibility for new hires.

—— figure **11.6**

Major Laws of the Department of Labor

The Department of Labor (DOL) administers and enforces more than 180 federal laws. This brief summary is intended to acquaint you with the major labor laws and not to offer a detailed exposition. For authoritative information on these laws, you should consult the statutes and regulations themselves.

Wages and Hours
The Fair Labor Standards Act (FLSA) prescribes standards for wages and overtime pay, which affect most private and public employment. The act is administered by the Wage and Hour Division of the Employment Standards Administration (ESA). It requires employers to pay covered employees who are not otherwise exempt at least the federal minimum wage and overtime pay at one-and-one-half times the regular rate of pay. For nonagricultural operations, it restricts the hours that children under age 16 can work and forbids the employment of children under age 18 in certain jobs deemed too dangerous. For agricultural operations, it prohibits the employment of children under age 16 during school hours and in certain jobs deemed too dangerous.

The Wage and Hour Division also enforces the labor standards provisions of the Immigration and Nationality Act that apply to aliens authorized to work in the United States under certain nonimmigrant visa programs (H-1B, H-1B1, H-1C, H2A).

Workplace Safety and Health
The Occupational Safety and Health (OSH) Act is administered by the Occupational Safety and Health Administration (OSHA). Safety and health conditions in most private industries are regulated by OSHA or OSHA-approved state programs, which also cover public-sector employers. Employers covered by the OSH Act must comply with the regulations and the safety and health standards promulgated by OSHA. Employers also have a general duty under the OSH Act to provide their employees with work and a workplace free from recognized, serious hazards. OSHA enforces the act through workplace inspections and investigations. Compliance assistance and other cooperative programs are also available.

Employee Benefit Security
The Employee Retirement Income Security Act (ERISA) regulates employers who offer pension or welfare benefit plans for their employees. Title I of ERISA is administered by the Employee Benefits Security Administration (EBSA), formerly the Pension and Welfare Benefits Administration, and imposes a wide range of fiduciary, disclosure, and reporting requirements on fiduciaries of pension and welfare benefit plans and on others having dealings with these plans. These provisions preempt many similar state laws. Under Title IV, certain employers and plan administrators must fund an insurance system to protect certain kinds of retirement benefits, with premiums paid to the federal government's Pension Benefit Guaranty Corporation (PBGC). EBSA also administers reporting requirements for continuation of health care provisions required under the Comprehensive Omnibus Budget Reconciliation Act of 1985 (COBRA) and the health care portability requirements on group plans under the Health Insurance Portability and Accountability Act (HIPAA).

Unions and Their Members
The Labor-Management Reporting and Disclosure Act of 1959 (also known as the Landrum–Griffin Act) deals with the relationship between a union and its members. It protects union funds and promotes union democracy by requiring labor organizations to file annual financial reports; by requiring union officials, employers, and labor consultants to file reports regarding certain labor relations practices; and by establishing standards for the election of union officers. The act is administered by the Office of Labor-Management Standards (OLMS), which is part of ESA.

Employee Protection
Most labor and public safety laws and many environmental laws mandate whistleblower protections for employees who complain about violations of the law by their employers. Remedies can include job reinstatement and payment of back wages. OSHA enforces the whistleblower protections in most laws.

Selected information on the E-Verify system from *http://www.uscis.gov* follows:

Why E-Verify?

E-Verify is a free, Internet-based system that allows employers to confirm the legal working status of new hires in seconds. With one click, E-Verify can match your new hire's Social Security Number and other Form I-9 information.

E-Verify reduces unauthorized employment, minimizes verification-related discrimination, is quick and non-burdensome to employers, and protects civil liberties and employee privacy.

Initial verification returns results within 3 to 5 seconds.

Know the requirements for complying with the Americans with Disabilities Act before undertaking your tenant improvements and before conducting any interviews or hiring, by reviewing *http://www.ada.gov*. If you are not clear on the legal requirements, remember: ignorance is not bliss—you are still required to adhere to all the laws.

Be aware of overtime and employment laws and especially those laws pertaining to employment of anyone under 18. Post a copy of the labor laws conspicuously, where everyone can read them. If you have even *one* non–English-speaking employee, also post the laws in that employee's language. Go to *http://www.dol.gov/compliance/topics/posters.htm* to locate the federal posters that you must by law display in your workplace. Also, adhere to your state's poster requirements as well.

In addition to complying with state and federal labor laws, you must also comply with all federal and state tax laws. See Chapter 12 for a brief review of employee taxes. *Hire a payroll services company to prepare payroll and to ensure compliance with all employment and tax laws.* As stated previously, the cost of these services is a fraction of the cost of the time it would take you to become an expert on labor law or the cost of fines for noncompliance. An approximate cost for monthly services would be about $120 for a firm with five employees.

In addition to complying with the above laws and regulations, two additional major issues face most employers today: sexual harassment lawsuits and increasing workers compensation costs.

Sexual Harassment

Small businesses are not immune from sexual harassment issues and lawsuits. Federal, state, and local laws and ordinances may apply to your growing firm. To limit your firm's exposure, communicate and educate your workforce about what constitutes sexual harassment after reviewing the information at the EEOC site, *http://www.eeoc.gov/types/sexual_harassment.html*. In addition, your firm must make clear to all employees that sexual harassment will not be accepted or tolerated at any time amongst the employees or in their interactions with customers and suppliers. It is imperative that sexual harassment issues are dealt with consistently and fairly within your firm.

According to the EEOC, sexual harassment can occur in a variety of circumstances, including but not limited to the following:

- The victim as well as the harasser may be a woman or a man. The victim does not have to be of the opposite sex.
- The harasser can be the victim's supervisor, an agent of the employer, a supervisor in another area, a co-worker, or a nonemployee.
- The victim does not have to be the person harassed but could be anyone affected by the offensive conduct.
- Unlawful sexual harassment may occur without economic injury to or discharge of the victim.
- The harasser's conduct must be unwelcome.

Prevention is the best tool to eliminate sexual harassment in the workplace. Employers are encouraged to take steps necessary to prevent sexual harassment from occurring. They should clearly communicate to employees that sexual harassment will not be tolerated. They can do so by providing sexual harassment training to their employees and by establishing an effective complaint or grievance process and taking immediate and appropriate action when an employee complains.

Source: U.S. Equal Employment Opportunity Commission, *http://www.eeoc.gov/types/sexual_harassment.html* (Accessed March 14, 2008).

To help guard against sexual harassment liability, outline a written policy to include 1) the reporting process, 2) the investigation process, and 3) disciplinary actions. In addition, disseminate your firm's sexual-harassment policy to all employees, and document that they have received the policy. Hire outside presenters so employees feel more comfortable in their discussions. Also, third-party intervention may help to avoid misinterpretations of comments during the training.

Take all complaints seriously. If you need to investigate a sexual-harassment complaint, consider hiring a third party. The cost of sexual-harassment lawsuits can sink any entrepreneur, so beware and prepare.

Workers' Compensation Laws

Each state develops its own worker compensation requirements and statutes. Access your state's workers' comp laws through your state department of labor's Web site. Workers' comp insurance is primarily obtained through commercial insurance carriers.

Depending on your state's statutes, workers' comp insurance may cover medical care, temporary and permanent disability, vocational rehabilitation services, and death benefits for on-the-job injuries or occupational illnesses. Fault is generally not considered in determining whether the worker qualifies for benefits.

Insurance rates are based on previous claims and the industry you are in. When doing expense projections, one of the largest costs many businesses have is employees' salaries, and the cost of benefits and workers comp in some cases will almost equal the salary expense. To reduce workers comp claims and insurance increases, keep your employees safe on the job. Your insurance is based on one of the 700 occupational codes used by insurers and is calculated as a percentage of each $100 in payroll. In some states, mental and emotional stress workers comp claims are growing rapidly. The following article provides information.

How to Comply with Workers' Comp Laws

**Determine if Your Small Business Really Needs It—
and Then Start Doing Some Research**

By Larry Rosenfeld

Employers need to make certain they are complying with their state's workers' compensation act. While workers' compensation is not truly "insurance," every state has an act with laws that provide for compensation for loss resulting from injuries received at work. Although each state's workers' compensation laws are different and constantly changing, the general purpose of these laws is to afford workers a right to relief for injuries received on the job. Depending on the state, workers' compensation laws can be either compulsory or elective. Under elective laws, an employer may choose to accept or reject the act, but if he rejects it, he loses certain defenses if a worker is injured on the job. Therefore, most states require employers to accept its provisions and provide the benefits specified therein.

It's worth noting that every state's workers' compensation act provides that minors are covered. In fact, the acts in some states even provide that if a minor is illegally employed, and that minor is injured on the job, he will receive additional compensation.

With respect to the issue of whether a worker is hired as an independent contractor or an employee, each state's workers' compensation law is different with respect to how these categories are treated. Some states require all workers to be covered under their workers' compensation programs, regardless of whether or not they are employees or independent contractors. Other states, on the other hand, only require employees to be covered. It is noteworthy that if an independent contractor were injured on the job in a state where he is not covered by workers' compensation, he would not be limited in the type of civil action he could file against the employer arising out of that injury. In states where independent contractors are covered by workers' compensation laws, the contractor is limited to the remedies provided under those laws. Accordingly, employers need to research their state's laws to determine who in fact is covered and what is required of them to comply.

Employers need to be particularly cautious not to incorrectly classify a worker as an independent contractor, as the liability for doing so can be significant. The workers' compensation statutes in some states also provide specific guidance with respect to what is necessary to establish independent contractor status.

In sum, because each state has its own workers' compensation act, employers must look to their state's statute to determine what is required in order for them to be in compliance.

Note: The information in this column is provided by the author, not entrepreneur.com. all answers are general in nature, not legal advice and not warranted or guaranteed. readers are cautioned not to rely on this information. because laws change over time and in different jurisdictions, it is imperative that you consult an attorney in your area regarding legal matters and an accountant regarding tax matters.

Larry Rosenfeld is co-chair of the national labor and employment practice of the law firm Greenberg Traurig LLP. A frequent writer and lecturer on employment law topics, Rosenfeld is experienced in the areas of federal laws pertaining to employment issues, EEOC, ADA, termination matters, employment liability, and the Fair Labor Standards Act.

Source: Entrepreneur.com, *http://www.entrepreneur.com/humanresources/employmentlaw/article52082.html* (Accessed March 18, 2008).

TEAM MEMBERS

Action Step 48 uses the idea of balance to scout potential team members. If you are able to imagine how each candidate will work in your new venture, you are well on your way to building a winning team.

Building a dream, working 60 to 80 hours a week, spending more time together than with your family: this may be the reality of a new-venture team. How do you keep the employer–employee relationship strong and healthy? It is one of the toughest parts of the job for many an entrepreneur. To understand the potential pitfalls, and to explore ways to avoid problems, review the following advice.

Boss vs. Buddy

It is human nature to want people to like you, but separating the roles of boss and buddy can help head off management headaches. That does not mean you need to chuck compassion when you become a manager. Warmth and openness are valuable elements of an effective working relationship. Nor do you need to an adopt an aloof attitude that says, "I'm above all the grunt work that I hired you to do." Workshop contributor Karen Bankston points out that new companies especially are finding that nonhierarchical structures in which managers and employees work together can be productive and morale boosting.

Action Step 48

Brainstorm Your Ideal Team

What do you need to win at the game of small business? Money, of course, and energy—tremendous energy. (You have that, or you would not have read this far.) You also need footwork, a terrific idea, intensity, the ability to concentrate, a sense of industry and thrift, curiosity and tenacity, and the ability to be organized.

And you need people: people to support your effort, people to balance your skills, people to take up the slack, people to help you with tasks you find distasteful or do not understand. People help your passion become reality.

1. Analyze yourself first. What do you like to do? What are you good at? What do you hate to do? What does your business need that you cannot provide yourself? Who can fill those needs? Start building your ideal team.

2. After you have taken the time to do some research into your own personality, especially your strengths and weaknesses (refer back to the Action Steps you have already completed), you will begin to get a feel for what kind of help you need in your venture. Is there anyone out there who can balance your skills? Now that you have the idea of balance firmly in mind, network your vendors and your competitors for potential team members. Whenever you meet someone new, keep asking yourself: "How could this person fit into my new business?"

3. Keep looking for your future team with new eyes. Make a list of all potential team members, the role they could play, and their strengths and weaknesses. What will it take to have them join your team?

"Those issues are separate from treating people differently based on how well you get along with them," contends Susan Stites, a human resources consultant with Management Allegories in Madison, Wisconsin.

The two foremost risks of befriending employees are the potential conflict of interest and discomfort level in giving friends job performance feedback and the perception of unfairness.

The latter pitfall surfaces regularly when a work group plans after-hours outings or social gatherings around activities some employees are not interested in or cannot join in. For instance, some employees may have family commitments that limit their spare time.

"A common lament is, 'I have kids to go home to. I can't go out and party,'" Stites notes. "Those people always feel left out the day after everyone else goes out on the town. It can be very demoralizing."

Stites recalls a management retreat she attended several years ago that included a morning on the golf course. "I was the only one there who didn't golf, and I felt really closed out the next day from all the in-jokes that came out of that golf game."

Thus a good rule of thumb is to plan social activities that everyone enjoys at a time when everyone can attend.

Another issue is the interplay of personalities in the workplace. Effective managers need to get along with people with varied approaches to life and work. Stites cites the example of companies that suffer when the presidents "hire themselves." They end up with a staff that supports their strengths—and magnifies their weaknesses.

"A manager needs to be a role model in accepting diversity in work and thinking styles and in capitalizing on that diversity," she suggests. Building on everyone's strengths is a foolproof recipe for success and for turning personality differences into complementary assets.

To learn more about personalities in the workplace, Stites suggests that managers look into seminars on personality profiling by Myers-Briggs, Social Styles, and DISC. They can be expensive, but they are well worth the money, even for managers in small companies.

"Coach" and "mentor" may be better titles than "friend" to strive for when you become a boss. "There's been a lot of recent emphasis on those terms," Stites adds, "but I think good business leaders—even back in the twenties when everything was autocratic—have always been good mentors."

Source: Adapted from Karen Bankston, published on NFIB online, *http://www.nfib. com/object/1583908.html* (Accessed March 17, 2008).

Rounding Out the Personalities of Your Team

If you are an entrepreneur, you like to move fast. You want quick answers and quick action. You have studied the marketplace and found your market niche. You did not think you would need much of a team, but now you are growing so quickly that you have to do some team building. You want to move fast, so you need a key to human behavior. You want people who can help you, not harm you, because every person counts in small business. A test—called an *assessment instrument* in the training field—might help you locate the key that unlocks the door behind which your team awaits.

We would like to point out that the search for the key to human behavior is not a recent phenomenon. In the earliest civilizations, astrologers and stargazers tried to explain human behavior based on the four elements: earth, air, fire, and water. In the fourth century BCE, Hippocrates, who gave us the Hippocratic Oath, kept the four-part framework developed by the astrologers but changed the labels to choleric, phlegmatic, sanguine, and melancholic.

Today, we find behaviorists renaming the quadrants again, some calling them driver, expressive, amiable, and analytical and others using controller,

community resource

Global Entrepreneurship Week

For one week, millions of young people around the world will join a growing movement to generate new ideas and seek better ways of doing things. Over 60 countries and 70 organizations are coming together to host Global Entrepreneurship Week, a global initiative to inspire young people to embrace innovation, imagination, and creativity. To think big. To turn their ideas into reality. To make their mark.

While it may be global in scope, at its heart the Week remains a local initiative driven by community-based activities. Founded by the Kauffman Foundation and the Make Your Mark campaign, Global Entrepreneurship Week/USA will inspire and inform young people through these activities—online and face-to-face—helping them explore their potential as self-starters and innovators. The Week will harness the energy of social networking and connect people—students, educators, entrepreneurs, business leaders, employees, non-profit leaders, government officials, and others—who are taking action to catalyze an entrepreneurial society.

Global Entrepreneurship Week/USA will weave into the fabric of everyday life, engaging young people in school, at home, on the Web, and at work. Through this initiative, the next generation of entrepreneurs will emerge–acquiring the knowledge, skills, networks, and values needed to grow innovative, sustainable enterprises with a positive impact on their lives and the lives of those around them.

Log on to *www.unleashingideas.org* to take part in the activities in your community and to connect with other budding entrepreneurs around the world.

Source: *http://www.unleashingideas.org/* (Accessed July 2, 2008).

organizer, analyzer, and persuader. Our advice is to leave name calling to the experts and to get help building your team. If you are an entrepreneur, there is a good chance you are either a dominant driver–controller or an expressive inducer–persuader. In either case, you are busy leading and charging, so you need help with details and organization. Find a simple test, take it yourself, and use it to help build your team. Before using any test, check with your attorney to determine if the test is legal as a screening, evaluation, or training device. Access these sources for help:

1. The counseling–testing center of your local community college or university
2. The Internet under "human resource training"

3. *http://www.keirsey.com* for an abbreviated Myers-Briggs Inventory Test

4. *http://www.onlinediscprofile.com* for access to DISC personality testing

5. *http://www.strengthsfinder.com* for access to information on strengths testing

These Web sites lead you to free and low-cost personality testing that can help you understand yourself better and discern the areas in which you need balance in building your team.

Read how Alaska Wilderness Adventures, highlighted in the Passion box, built their team. According to Winning Workplaces,

> There are at least eight specific ways in which being a good place to work contributes to increased profitability and growth: 1) improved customer service and loyalty, 2) higher productivity, 3) the ability to attract top talent, 4) decreased turnover, 5) decreased absenteeism, 6) decreased risk of adversarial labor-management relationships, 7) decreased risk of employment litigation, and 8) decreased health care costs.

Source: *www.winningworkplaces.org/consultingandtraining/business_case.php* (Accessed March 8, 2008).

Now it is your turn. Complete Action Steps 48 and 49 and build your team with passion.

Find Mentors

In addition to being a mentor and coach to your employees, if you are starting up a business for the first time, there is a good chance *you* may need mentors—fellow entrepreneurs who provide advice and encouragement. Perhaps you have mentors already. If not, how can you find such help? First, network with your friends, co-workers, and business associates. Tell them that you are looking for successful business owners with good track records. The perfect mentor would be one with experience in your particular market segment. Second, join your local chamber of commerce and one or more civic clubs if appropriate. If not, consider joining professional associations where you can make contacts. Third, keep your new eyes peeled for a mentor appearing on the horizon. If your community has a chapter of Service Corps of Retired Executives (SCORE), contact them to see if you can find a match.

In addition to the traditional routes for finding mentors, the Internet has opened up additional avenues for you to find like-minded individuals who share your dreams, as well as possible mentors. The Incredible Resource in this chapter highlights an individual who became a mentor after being mentored by the same organization, Micromentor.org.

Many entrepreneurs have become bloggers, and you may find a community, and mentors, at various sites. In addition, *https://www.ideacrossing.org* and *http://www.businessownersideacafe.com* offer opportunities to locate mentors. New mentoring opportunities continue to develop online, so stay abreast of new sites.

Once you have located several candidates, develop a set of questions and arrange a meeting or write an e-mail; you want to pick the brains

Action Step 49

Who's in Charge?

Time to Impress Your Business Plan Reader

Investors and vendors are often more interested in the founders than in the Business Plan itself. Experience in the same type of business, and former business experience or ownership, are powerful positive components of the plan. You will need to focus on past responsibility and authority. Present the balance and diversity of your founding team.

Several paragraphs in the Business Plan may be sufficient for each key founder. If experience is lacking, discuss consultants or committed strategic partners who will bring balance to the management team and contribute experience and special skills. You may also want to include an organizational chart in your Business Plan's appendix.

If at this time you do not have your team in place, write bios and résumés of your dream team and supporters.

1. Write short, strong bios for each member of your team to include in your Business Plan.
2. Write complete résumés for each major member of your team. These will later be added to the appendix of your Business Plan.
3. If you are rounding out your team with major support from consultants or strategic partners, write up several paragraphs explaining their roles.

Passion

Passion for Employees
Winning Workplaces 2007: Alaska Wildland Adventures

Alaska Wildland Adventures, with 2006 revenues revenues of over $4 million, was selected as one of 15 Top Small Workplaces of 2007 by the *Wall Street Journal* and Winning Workplaces. Discover other successful small businesses at *http://www.winningworkplaces.com*.

Hanging onto talented employees is a continuing struggle for many small businesses. Without ample opportunities to move up, good employees inevitably move on.

Alaska Wildland Adventures—a Girdwood, Alaska, tour operator with 11 year-round and 76 seasonal employees—seems to have found a way around that problem. The average tenure of current year-round employees is 7½ years, and eight were promoted from other roles within the company.

General manager Kyle Kelley originally started in 1997 as an Alaskan safari driver during a summer internship. The company later promoted him to natural history guide, then safari manager, then program director, and then operations manager, before Kelley assumed his current role in 2006. "They'd always rather hire from someone in our entry-level pool and train them up than hire an outsider who's already trained," says Kelley.

This upward flow through the company means employees acquire a holistic understanding of how the business functions, so they can assume one anothers' jobs on short notice, says Heather Dudick, marketing director. Because the company is so small, all employees chip in on mundane tasks such as stuffing envelopes, licking stamps, and answering phones. But that coziness also means the company accommodates each employees' personal goals and will custom fit jobs and schedules to their needs.

"People can sort of carve out their niche and build on their individual talents," Ms. Dudick says. Former receptionist Jackie Collins, 26, showed skill in handling customer inquiries and was encouraged by managers to do some marketing work by handing out promotional materials to local businesses. Ms. Collins was so successful that the company created a half-receptionist, half-marketing job for her. She was recently promoted to full-time marketing assistant.

Judges were impressed with the camaraderie and loyalty among Alaska Wildland's employees, and how they all seemed to enjoy coming to work. In 2005, when the company needed to install plumbing at a company-owned lodge, many employees lent a hand digging trenches. "The fact that both customers and employees come back is unbelievable," says Colleen Barrett, president of Southwest Airlines and one of the judges.

Beyond job growth, the company tries to give employees ample time for fun and adventure—a main driver for joining the travel industry. Most year-round employees get 15 paid vacation days, 12 holidays, and "sprinkle days," when only a few employees need to come to work. Employees can also make use of the two company-owned lodges, along with complimentary fishing trips and rafting trips.

Company owner and president Kirk Hoessle also practices open-book management; employees get yearly briefings from him on the company's financial results. And each year the company donates 10 percent of its pretax earnings to nonprofit Alaska conservation groups.

(in)credibleresource

MicroMentor

Sturdy McKee came to MicroMentor as a small business owner looking for a mentor, and the timely and targeted help that he found helped him to steer his small business to success. Now, just 2 years after he first sought help, Sturdy has returned to MicroMentor as a mentor: "My life changed drastically when we were able to move from the stress of kind of breaking even for several years to profitability. Moving the business to profitability changed a lot of things in my business and my life, and I hope to help other people to do that. I want to help people figure out how to plan and make their businesses viable."

Sturdy McKee decided to start his own business when he got laid off. The hospital where he had been working as a physical therapist downsized, and Sturdy received a pink slip. After a frustrating job search, Sturdy sat down with his wife and had a conversation about what it would take to start his own business.

There were a lot of challenges to getting started. Sturdy had no formal business training, and banks were refusing to finance his planned expansion. Then Sturdy found MicroMentor. He was matched with a U.K. accountant who did not transfer her accountant's license when she moved to the United States with her husband, and had decided to volunteer instead. Sturdy's mentor helped him make sense of his balance sheets, cash-flow statements, and profit and loss statements and also helped him identify areas in need of improvement. "She reinforced our opinions that we were a healthy company and that we were viable, even though we were unable to secure funding from a bank. [It] gave us the confidence to fund our own growth from our own profits."

Now, just seven years after opening its doors, Sturdy's physical therapy company has seven branches and over 20 employees. But still to this day, Sturdy's greatest success happens when he can help people recover from their injuries and get back to work and return to playing sports.

MicroMentor, *www.micromentor.org*, helps microentrepreneurs gain access to markets and increase revenue and profitability by offering online, time-convenient mentoring. By merging Internet technology with personalized mentoring, MicroMentor is dedicated to the proposition that low-income microentrepreneurs are crucial to the economic and social well-being of our communities.

MicroMentor focuses on microbusinesses with less than five employees and start-up financing of less than $35,000.

Source: MicroMentor, *http://www.micromentor.org* (Accessed March 17, 2008). Reproduced with permission of the author.

of all the candidates. Here are some things to consider when selecting a mentor:

Do you feel comfortable with this person?

Can you trust him or her?

Is he or she easy to communicate with?

Does he or she have experience and contacts that can help your new business?

Will he or she consider mentoring for at least 6 months?

Keep in close contact with your mentor as you develop and grow your business. Maintain contact by keeping in touch at least once a month. Your mentors may be able to help you establish banking connections and vendor–supplier relationships. A good mentor can be invaluable for checking your leases, contracts, and marketing materials, but most importantly, providing moral support.

SUMMARY

An entrepreneur's venture team often goes beyond bankers, lawyers, and accountants. A single-person entrepreneur today may never need to hire an employee to prosper, as many of today's successful firms use strategic partners, outsourcing, and strategic alliances for almost everything.

But if you grow beyond current capacity and need to hire employees, hire wisely, train carefully, and encourage always. Remember, very few employees will ever have the "fire in the belly" for your business as you do. If you expect them to believe in your dream as much as you do, you may be very disappointed. Remember, this is "your baby," and unless you are willing to share the financial successes, your employees are not likely to share the same passion for your dream.

Consider the total costs of hiring full-time employees. Review your options for hiring part-time employees, independent contractors, leased employees, as well as full-time employees. Build the best team you can under current constraints.

You have the right and responsibility to build a culture for your firm and employees. What kind of environment do you want to provide for your employees? Strict and by the book? Easy going and free flowing? Open door? Jeans and t-shirts? Three-piece suits? Employees who can rise from inside the firm? Hiring from outside? Offering the best benefits around? Child-friendly policies? Hiring cheap?

You wanted your own business. Now you must passionately build the environment you want to work in with the type of people you enjoy working with.

THINK POINTS FOR SUCCESS

- People tend to "hire themselves." How many more like you can your business take?
- A winning team may lurk in your network.
- Look to your competitors and vendors for team members.
- Your company is *people*.
- Balance the people on your team.
- Have each team member write objectives for his or her responsibilities within the business. Set up your own internal system of management by objectives.
- You cannot grow until you have the right people.
- When you hire the wrong person, terminate them as soon as your realize the error. Start over.

- How much of your team can be part-timers and moonlighters?
- Consider a virtual organization.
- Consider independent contractors.
- Consider employee leasing.
- Find a mentor.
- Control workers' compensation costs.
- Follow all employee federal and state laws, and hire professionals to keep you in compliance.
- Educate and train employees to recognize and eliminate sexual harassment and discrimination from the workplace.
- Build your team with passionate employees.

KEY POINTS FROM ANOTHER VIEW

Seven Characteristics of Highly Effective Entrepreneurial Employees

By Joe Hadzima with George Pilla

Fast-growing entrepreneurial organizations need employees who regularly demonstrate entrepreneurial characteristics and work habits. Management of entrepreneurial companies must work diligently to recognize, identify, and attract this type of employee during the recruitment process to ensure a steady stream of the people with the "Right Stuff" to fuel growth of the venture.

Employees come in all shapes and sizes with all sorts of different skills and quirks. Their outlook and approach has been tempered by past experiences, good or bad. In the relatively short period that you have to do hiring, you have to cut through the prospective employee's résumé and verbal statements and figure out if he or she has the "Right Stuff." This is really important, because just as "a bad apple will spoil the barrel," an employee with the "Wrong Stuff" will drag your whole effort down. It would be one thing if a Wrong Stuff employee simply didn't contribute, but it is worse than that—he usually sucks up scarce management time, creates diversions for Right Stuff employees—you get the picture.

So what are the characteristics of highly effective "Right Stuff" entrepreneurial employees? Here are a few to keep in mind as you interview potential new hires; you probably can think of others.

ABILITY TO DEAL WITH RISK

An entrepreneur has to operate effectively in an environment filled with risk. The Right Stuff employee can deal with risk and uncertainty. He or she is able to make progress toward goals and is able to make decisions when lacking one or several critical resources or data.

RESULTS ORIENTED

The Right Stuff employee is results oriented—he or she takes control to get the task done. He or she is a "can do" person who demonstrates common sense in decisions and actions and is able to cut through and resolve problems that divert others. His or her business judgment is sound and becomes stronger with each experience, decision, or recommendation. While supervisors and managers may disagree with her ultimate recommendation, they usually agree that the presented alternatives are reasonable for the situation at hand.

ENERGY

The Right Stuff employee has high levels of enthusiasm and energy; he or she consistently generates output that is higher than could be reasonably expected. He or she is fully committed to the organization, its goals, and overall success. Not only does he or she desire to make a contribution to results, he or she needs to see the results of contributions quickly, not measured in years! He or she will seek out an organization that solicits and acts on his or her ideas, gives credit where credit is due, and points out errors and poor decisions quickly and clearly. He or she performs effectively with limited supervision and is able to self-motivate and set priorities with minimal guidance.

GROWTH POTENTIAL

The Right Stuff employee's reach exceeds her or his grasp today. Today's Right Stuff employee is often next year's supervisor and a department manager soon thereafter. She or he is willing to accept much higher levels of responsibility than is the norm for the position, title, experience level, or salary. She or he acts as a strong role model, trains and coaches others, and soon begins to assume supervisory responsibilities, again much earlier than would be expected in a normal corporate environment.

TEAM PLAYER

The Right Stuff employee is a true team player; she or he recognizes how her or his role contributes to the overall effort and success of the organization. She or he accepts accountability and ownership for the area of responsibility and expects others on the team to do the same. She or he also recognizes the roles and contributions of others and applauds their efforts sincerely.

MULTITASKING ABILITY

The Right Stuff employee is flexible to accept new duties, assignments, and responsibilities. He or she can perform more than one role until the incremental duties and functions assumed can be assigned to co-workers in newly defined roles. He or she is also willing to dig in and do grunt work tasks that eventually will be performed by lower-level employees.

IMPROVEMENT ORIENTED

The Right Stuff employee is more than willing to challenge, in a constructive way, existing procedures and systems; to her or him, the status quo is temporary. She or he suggests changes and improvements frequently and encourages others to do so also.

Right Stuff employees are easier to manage in some ways but require a higher level of management involvement in others. Ordinary (average) employees will not produce extraordinary results over time; Right Stuff employees will generally produce extraordinary results consistently over time. Unfortunately, unless properly motivated, managed, and rewarded, Right Stuff employees could perform at lower levels and only produce ordinary results. So what makes a Right Stuff manager?

First of all, the Right Stuff manager must have the characteristics of the Right Stuff employee. Beyond that she or he must have the basic skill set of sound business judgment, practical hands-on experience, general management skills, and common sense. She or he must be committed to and contribute to the organization's vision and mission and must convey this commitment in multiple ways: written, verbal, and by actions. She or he needs an awareness, understanding, and interest in the technology trends that affect the venture and its customers.

Externally, the Right Stuff manager must be able to identify and build creative strategic relationships, especially for partnering opportunities in areas of limited resources. Internally, he or she must effectively produce and manage change as the organization evolves, gaining enthusiastic support for change and improvements from the Right Stuff employees in the ranks.

So when you interview each new employee or manager, look beyond the mere facts of the résumé and ask yourself: Is this a "Right Stuff" person? You are most likely interviewing the person because of the résumé. Now is the time to put the résumé aside and focus on the "Right Questions."

Source: MIT Enterprise Forum, *http://enterpriseforum.mit.edu/ mindshare/startingup/seven-characteristics.html* (Accessed March 14, 2008).

- Understand the importance of protecting your assets through insurance.
- Explore insurance needs for your specific business.
- Investigate and initiate loss-prevention strategies for both internal and external crimes.
- Recognize the need to file all tax forms in a timely manner.
- Understand the importance of tax planning—not just tax filing.

- Prepare for your exit at the beginning.
- Recognize that ethical behavior is required of the owner before ethical behavior can be expected of the employees.
- Understand the daily ethical dilemmas entrepreneurs face.
- Learn the seven steps to better decisions.

chapter 12

Protecting Your "Baby" and Yourself

Insurance, Taxes, and Ethics; Reducing Employee and Cyber Crime; and Preparing Your Exit Strategy

You will work incredibly hard to start and grow your business, but you also must take steps to *protect* the business that has become your "baby." Using insurance wisely, paying taxes as required, negotiating effectively, protecting your firm from computer security breaches, and following ethical principles will keep your business on track for success. The Internal Revenue Service (IRS), lawyers, and computer hackers are formidable foes. Be prepared!

In addition, you need to plan for the future by planning for the finish. In other words, when you begin your business, you need to plan for how you will exit your business. When reviewing your exit strategy, we will ask you to return to the questions in Chapter 1, which asked you to assess your reasons for starting a business.

Protecting your business also includes short- and long-term financial planning, and we cannot emphasize enough the need for a team of financial and insurance advisors, legal counsel, and accountants. In the Action Steps, we ask you to take steps to protect your "baby" and yourself.

INSURANCE AND MANAGING RISK

Can I forgo insurance? If not, what type of insurance should I carry? How much coverage should I have? First consider:

- The size of any potential loss
- The probability of loss
- The resources available to meet a loss if one occurs
- The probability of lawsuits (some industries and areas are heavily targeted)

Can you eliminate all risks? That is doubtful. Can you reduce risk? Yes, but you also *must* assume risk.

How do you decide whether a particular risk should be transferred to an insurance company or assumed? Calculate the maximum potential loss that might result. If the loss would force your company into bankruptcy or cause serious financial damage, *recognize the risk and purchase insurance to help protect your assets.*

Losses that occur with predictable frequency, such as shoplifting and bad debts, can usually be absorbed by the business and are often budgeted as part of the normal costs of doing business; the cost of the loss is incorporated into the price. Where probability of loss is high, a more effective method of controlling the loss is to adopt appropriate precautionary measures and purchase better than adequate insurance. The key to purchasing insurance, and all risk management, is this: *Do not risk more than you can tolerate losing.*

Insurance Planning

First consider all of the insurable risks faced by your business. In general, the following risks can be covered by insurance if you have followed the law:

- Personal injury to employees and the general public. Some retail stores have become targets for slip-and-fall claims.
- Certain businesses have higher personal injury claims and require additional protection.

Passion for Employees

Rachel Hubka Proves "Doing Right" Pays Off

Rachel Hubka has no illusions about the many accolades she has received for her business achievements and innovative employee programs. She is convinced that her success in transforming people into conscientious workers with self-esteem, a strong work ethic, a sense of pride, and an intense desire to excel is simply an expected outcome of her belief in the people themselves. Besides, she'll tell you: it's just good business!

Rachel's Bus Company is a metaphor for all that is good about people who combine social conscience with sound management practices. Rachel Hubka "walks the talk" with the people who work for her, and she has located her business in one of Chicago's poorest inner-city neighborhoods: "I needed reliable part-time drivers, and I wanted to tap a neglected labor pool," she says.

She hires disadvantaged workers from the community; gives new drivers comprehensive training, professional pride, and an incentive program; then guides them into positions of increasing responsibility. She has formed partnerships with local schools to teach her employees computer skills and help her drivers earn their GEDs. Her motivational program teaches her employees pride and confidence in their appearance and capabilities—qualities that do not come easily on the street.

An amazing transformation usually takes place: Her staff members become role models within the community. They catch her entrepreneurial spirit, and she is right there with support. When one of her employees developed a software program to handle her charter business, she helped him through the hurdles of starting his own consulting business, and then became his first client.

And doing well really is a good business. Rachel's Bus Company has grown into a $5 million enterprise in little more than a decade. She has built a team of committed drivers, a supportive staff, and a solid reputation for service, safety, and professionalism.

Her success is a tribute to her strong personal commitment to Chicago's schoolchildren, her love affair with people, and her dedication to the advancement of all her employees.

Source: *Wise Women, Success Strategies for Women Entrepreneurs*, Bank One, 2001. A brochure.

- Legal action stemming from hiring, firing, sexual discrimination, libel, slander and so on.
- Loss to the business caused by the death or disability of key employees or the owner—an essential coverage needed to protect your business.
- Loss or damage of property—including merchandise, supplies, fixtures, and building. A standard fire insurance policy pays the policyholder only for those losses directly caused by fire. Make sure when dealing with your insurance agent that you understand your policy thoroughly.
- Loss of income resulting from interruption of business caused by damage to the firm's operating assets (storms, natural disasters, electrical blackouts).

Other indirect losses, known as *consequential losses,* may be even more harmful to your company's welfare. You can protect yourself against these losses by obtaining business-interruption insurance. Consequential losses include the following:

- Extra expenses of obtaining temporary quarters
- Loss of rental income on buildings damaged or destroyed by fire, if you are a landlord
- Loss of facility use
- Continuing expenses after a fire—salaries, rents paid in advance, interest obligations, and so on
- Loss of customer base

Do not fail to provide safe equipment and working conditions. Hire competent employees and warn employees of any existing danger. In every state an employer must insure against potential workers' compensation claims. However, employee coverage and the extent of the employer's liability vary from state to state. The cost of workers' compensation varies greatly by occupation and risk involved, and it can cost up to 42 cents on every dollar you pay your employees. Ask your insurance company if they have any loss-prevention services, and use them to the fullest extent. If your employees speak several different languages, you are responsible for making sure *everyone* thoroughly understands the safety rules.

General liability covers most kinds of nonemployee bodily injury except that caused by automobiles and professional malpractice. In some cases this coverage may even extend to trespassers. As a business owner, you may also be liable for bodily injuries to customers, pedestrians, delivery people, and other outsiders—even in instances in which you have exercised "reasonable care." In highly litigious states, you may need substantial liability coverage to protect your business.

Vehicle use is a major source of liability claims. Under the "doctrine of agency," a business can be liable for injuries and property damage caused by employees operating their own or someone else's vehicle while on company business. The company may have some protection under the employee's liability policy, but the limits are probably inadequate. If it is customary or convenient for employees to use their own vehicle while on company business (e.g., salespeople on the road or covering a route), you should purchase nonownership liability insurance. The best form of general liability insurance for a small business consists of a comprehensive general liability policy combined with a comprehensive auto liability policy and a standard workers' compensation policy.

One retail storeowner discovered that merchandise she transported in her van from store to store was not covered while she was in transit. An additional rider had to be added to her policy to provide insurance protection. Sitting down and going through various scenarios with your insurance agent is one of the best ways to make sure you are protecting *all* areas of your business. Finding an insurance broker who is familiar with your line of business is very important; such experience and knowledge may help to insure you are covered properly.

Types of Coverage

Although you can purchase insurance to cover almost any risk, most business owners most commonly protect themselves with the following types of coverage, but additional insurance needs are listed in Figure 12.1.

1. **Fire and general property insurance:** protects against fire loss, vandalism, hail, and wind damage.
2. **Consequential loss insurance:** covers loss of earnings or extra expenses when business is interrupted because of fire or other catastrophe (see also item 4 following).
3. **Public liability insurance:** covers injury to the public, such as customer or pedestrian injury claims.
4. **Business-interruption insurance:** coverage in case the business is unable to continue as before.
5. **Crime insurance:** protects against losses resulting from burglary, robbery, and so forth. Fidelity bonds provide coverage from employee theft.
6. **Malpractice insurance:** covers against claims from clients who suffer damages as a result of services that you perform.

figure **12.1**

Insurance Information Institute Checklist

LIABILITY
- ☐ Comprehensive General
  - ☐ Premises/Operations
  - ☐ Products/Completed Operations
  - ☐ Owners & Contractors Protective
  - ☐ Contractual – Blanket
  - ☐ Contractual – Schedule
  - ☐ Personal Injury
  - ☐ Advertising Injury
  - ☐ Medical Payments
  - ☐ Broad Form Property Damage
  - ☐ Watercraft
  - ☐ Liquor Liability
  - ☐ Incidental Medical Malpractice
  - ☐ Fire Legal Liability
  - ☐ Employees as Insured
  - ☐ Extended Bodily Injury
  - ☐ New Organizations Insured
  - ☐ Pollution and Clean-Up
  - ☐ Limited Worldwide Products
- ☐ Workers Compensation
- ☐ Aircraft
- ☐ Owned Automobiles
- ☐ Leases or Hired Automobiles
- ☐ Drive Other Car
- ☐ Auto Medical
- ☐ Bailee Liability
- ☐ Directors & Officers' Liability
- ☐ Employment Practices Liability
- ☐ Professional Liability
- ☐ Railroad Protective Liability
- ☐ Signs
  - ☐ Pavements/Underground Property
- ☐ Glass
- ☐ Contamination/Pollution Clean-up and Removal
- ☐ Debris Removal
- ☐ Functional Replacement Cost
- ☐ Vacancy Permit
- ☐ Satellite Dishes

BUILDINGS
- ☐ Basic Causes of Loss
- ☐ Broad Causes of Loss
- ☐ Special Causes of Loss
- ☐ Coinsurance
- ☐ Earthquake
- ☐ Flood
- ☐ All Risk DIC (Difference in Conditions or Gap Filter Coverage)
- ☐ Replacement Cost
- ☐ Inflation Guard
- ☐ Agreed Value
- ☐ Building Ordinance
- ☐ Outdoor Property
- ☐ Signs/Glass
- ☐ Pavements/Underground Property
- ☐ Contamination/Pollution Clean-Up and Removal
- ☐ Debris Removal
- ☐ Functional Replacement Cost
- ☐ Vacancy Permit
- ☐ Satellite Dishes

BUSINESS INCOME
- ☐ Business Income
  - ☐ Loss of Earnings
  - ☐ Continuing Expenses
- ☐ Extra Expenses
- ☐ Dependent Properties
- ☐ Extended Property of Indemnity
- ☐ Payroll Limitation/Exclusion
- ☐ Tuition and Fees
- ☐ Building Ordinances

BOILER AND MACHINERY
- ☐ Boiler Machinery
- ☐ Business Income
- ☐ Outage

BUSINESS PERSONAL PROPERTY
- ☐ Basic Causes of Loss
- ☐ Broad Causes of Loss
- ☐ Special Causes of Loss
- ☐ Earthquake
- ☐ Flood
- ☐ Value Reporting Form
- ☐ Replacement Cost
- ☐ Peak Seasonal Form
- ☐ Improvements and Betterments
- ☐ Manufacturer's Selling Price
- ☐ Valuable Papers/Records
- ☐ Accounts Receivable
- ☐ Crops
- ☐ Animals
- ☐ Auto Physical Damage
- ☐ Aircraft Physical Damage
- ☐ Marine Hull Damage
- ☐ Transported Property
- ☐ Equipment Floater
- ☐ Salesperson's Floater
- ☐ Installation Floater
- ☐ Processing Floater
- ☐ Parcel Post
- ☐ Computers
- ☐ Other High Value Property
- ☐ Coinsurance

MANAGEMENT PROTECTION
- ☐ Life
  - ☐ Key Person
  - ☐ Proprietor
  - ☐ Partnership
  - ☐ Corporation
- ☐ Business Continuation
- ☐ Retirement Continuation
- ☐ Retirement Benefits
- ☐ Personal Auto Liability
- ☐ Offers' and Directors' E&O
- ☐ Split Dollar
- ☐ Deferred Compensation
- ☐ Disability Buyouts
- ☐ Overhead Insurance

HUMAN FAILURE
- ☐ Employee Dishonesty
  - ☐ Blanket
  - ☐ Schedule
- ☐ Money and Securities
- ☐ Other Property
- ☐ Forgery and Alteration
- ☐ Computer Fraud
- ☐ Extortion
- ☐ Innkeepers
- ☐ Lessees of Safe Deposit Boxes
  - ☐ Safe Depository
- ☐ Securities Deposited with Others
- ☐ Public Employees Fund
- ☐ Financial Institutions Bond

EMPLOYEE PROTECTION
- ☐ Group Life
- ☐ Group Disability
- ☐ Major Medical
- ☐ Accidental Death and Dismemberment
- ☐ Hospitalization—Surgical
- ☐ Pension
- ☐ Profit Sharing
- ☐ Keogh
- ☐ ESOP
- ☐ Dental
- ☐ Vision Care
- ☐ Legal Expenses
- ☐ SEPPs (Substantially Equal Periodic Payments)

7. **Errors and omissions insurance:** covers against claims from customers who suffer injury or loss because of errors you made, things you should have done but failed to do, or warnings you failed to supply.

8. **Employment practices liability insurance (EPLI):** covers against claims from employees for employment practices related to sexual harassment, wrongful discharge, discrimination, breach of contract, libel, and so on.

9. **Key-man insurance:** covers the death, dismemberment, or physical disability of owners or key employees. Check with a CPA to determine how this insurance should be paid, because death of the "key man" may impact taxes.

10. **Product liability insurance:** covers injury to the public resulting from customer use or misuse of a product.

11. **Disability insurance:** covers owners and employees against disability and usually allows for payments to continue during rehabilitation. Disability for an owner is a much greater risk than death, but few owners insure themselves adequately against such risk.

12. **Health insurance for employees:** check with state and federal laws to determine what coverage is required.

13. **Workers' compensation insurance:** protects employees if they are injured on the job (see Ch. 11 and *www.iii.org/smallbusiness/workers*).

14. **Extra equipment insurance:** covers specialized equipment not covered in standard policies.

15. **Directors' and officers' liability insurance:** if company stock is held by outside investors, directors and officers should be protected from liability.

16. **Other:** see Checklist (Figure 12.1).

According to the Insurance Information Institute, *http://www.iii.org*, about 40 percent of small-business owners carry no insurance at all because of cash concerns. If you cannot afford minimal insurance coverage, rethink your Business Plan and delay starting your business until you *can* afford adequate coverage. One mishap or incident can destroy everything you have worked for. Do not let this happen to you.

In addition to contacting independent insurance brokers, we suggest you first contact trade or business associations in your field to determine if they offer insurance for their members. In addition to insurance, they may have recommendations on how to reduce and prevent losses. Their experience and knowledge of your industry and its risks can assist you in determining which risks you need to insure for and which risks you need to assume. Also, their familiarity with various state issues may also prove useful to you. Obtaining reasonably priced health insurance is a challenge for small businesses, and associations may be able to assist with this crucial element of insurance planning.

Home-based and e-commerce businesses should not overlook the need for insurance. Thus, you will find the Insurance Information Institute's recommendations for e-commerce businesses in Figure 12.2. Additional industry-specific insurance needs can be found at the Insurance Information Institute Web site.

With the Insurance Checklist for Business Owners (Figure 12.1) in hand, and with the knowledge you have gained from your insurance research, it is time to sit down with your insurance broker or association representative to determine your insurance needs and costs while completing Action Step 50.

Action Step 50

Protect Your Venture

1. Network your way to a business insurance salesperson or association.

2. Read information online from your association and from various insurance Web sites that focus on your industry. Make a list of questions.

3. Determine your Business Plan with your broker and review the insurance checklist in Figure 12.1.

4. Discover the cost of insuring your business for the first year, and also discuss how your insurance needs may change as you grow.

figure 12.2

Insurance Information Institute: Insurance for E-Commerce

INTERNET BUSINESS

If your business promotes or markets its products or services over the Internet, there are unique property and liability risks. For example, you are vulnerable to major loss exposures from malicious attacks, loss of service or theft of customer information from your database.

As use of the Internet has grown, insurers have worked to develop products that address the insurance needs of businesses that engage in e-commerce. This is an area of rapid evolution in the insurance industry.

For the majority of small businesses, the most efficient and cost effective way to obtain e-commerce-related coverage is with a Businessowners Policy (BOP), preferably one that is specifically tailored to your type of business. These policies roll a number of different types of coverage into one insurance contract. Though marketed under a variety of names, the policies typically have provisions similar to the property insurance and liability insurance sections of the BOP, with the option to add various other coverages that you may need.

PROPERTY INSURANCE

In addition to insuring your real and personal property and providing other coverage, the BOP includes as part of the basic policy two types of e-commerce-related property coverages. Computer Operations Interruption Coverage pays for business income lost and extra expenses incurred as a result of many computer problems. Electronic Data Loss Coverage pays the cost to replace or restore electronic data destroyed or damaged as the result of causes of loss named in the policy. These include a computer virus or harmful code. For

more coverage, there are several endorsements you can choose to add to your BOP. You should discuss your needs with your agent.

LIABILITY INSURANCE

E-commerce creates liability risks. One is that a breach of your system may cause private information to be compromised. You can add the Electronic Data Liability Endorsement to your BOP to cover liability resulting from loss of electronic data that is caused by an "electronic data incident."

Another is the risk that someone could accuse you of libel, slander or advertising injury because of something published on your Web site. The BOP would provide coverage to defend you and pay any damages for which you are legally liable, up to the policy limit.

While these coverages help protect your e-commerce endeavor, there are events that would not be covered. For example, the Electronic Data Liability Endorsement, defines an "electronic data incident" as an "accident, negligent act, error or omission" that results in loss of electronic data. If the data loss is from some other cause—such as theft—there is no coverage. Insurers are working to develop products that will fill in this and other gaps in e-commerce insurance coverage.

WORKERS COMPENSATION

States have varying rules about when an employer must provide workers compensation insurance. If you have three or more employees, you should check with your state department of workers compensation to see if you are required to provide workers comp insurance.

Source: Insurance Information Institute, *www.iii.org*

EMPLOYEE CRIME: BE PREPARED— TAKE PREVENTATIVE STEPS

According to the U.S. Chamber of Commerce, 30 percent of small-business failures can be attributed to employee theft—a sobering statistic, no doubt, for any entrepreneur. You must be prepared and take preventative steps not to be in this 30 percent. Seeing your hard work and money go down a rat hole because of employee theft is enough to crush even the hardiest entrepreneur. You must be knowledgeable of both internal crime and external crime and prepare for both. Your trade organization may be helpful in providing you with loss-prevention information pertinent to your industry. In addition, large insurers offer specialists to work with industry-specific issues. Potential issues you will face include the following:

- Credit card fraud
- Check deception
- Shoplifting
- Computer terminal vulnerability, with employees shortchanging customers

- Cash mishandling
- Bookkeeping theft
- Fraudulent refunds
- Counterfeit money
- Fitting room theft
- Burglary
- Robbery
- Bomb threats
- Theft of items from stockroom, layaway, and displays

- Computer fraud
- Sabotage
- Theft of private information
- Manipulation of time card data
- Illegal use of company time
- Fraudulent expense reports
- Sweethearting (discounts for family and friends)
- Theft of trade secrets
- Theft of intellectual property

We seldom meet an entrepreneur who has not experienced one or more of these problems. Take action promptly when any of these take place in your firm, and make it known throughout your firm that none of these actions will be tolerated. Do not look the other way or believe crime cannot occur in your organization. Keep your eyes and ears wide open. Explain to your employees the financial consequences of shoplifting and employee theft. One retail storeowner recently wrote the following letter to her employees regarding merchandise theft:

> Theft in our store is a serious problem. For each $2 candy bar we sell, we pay 10 percent of our gross sales (20 cents) to our landlord. The cost of the candy bar is 86 cents, and we have a 10 percent (20 cents) additional overhead on gross sales. Thus our costs are $1.26. This means that we need to sell three $2 candy bars (with a net profit at 74 cents each) to cover the loss of just one candy bar. Please keep your eyes on our customers. In addition, please understand that the employee policies regarding free food and sweethearting are there to protect our business and your job.

As that owner has discovered, theft cannot be tolerated. It must be guarded against constantly and dealt with immediately. Talk with others who run similar businesses to find out the ways employees have stolen from them and what tactics they used to reduce theft within their own stores. Many associations offer training, workshops, or consultants to help you deal with employee theft. Take advantage of these programs before your employees take advantage of you. If in retailing, watch employees; if an employee rapidly switches to another display screen or appears to hide the screen as you come by, this may serve as a warning to you. Also, look for employees who claim printed register tapes are jamming or becoming torn constantly, causing them to lose track of transactions. Watch for cashiers who seem to have excessively long lines or lingering customers. Also, keep an eye on customers who always insist on a certain cashier or wait around until their chosen cashier is available. If employees are responsible for closing at night alone, make sure a closing routine is written down and followed by each employee. Be vigilant; your success may depend on it.

One restaurant manager we know of always insisted on closing out the register every night, never took a vacation, and never missed closing. Everyone was thrilled, including the owners, to have such a conscientious employee; that is, until they realized he did these things because he was stealing. In fact the owner of the restaurant shared, "We think he stole more than $110,000 in two years. We trusted him like he was our own son and thought he loved the restaurant as much as my wife and I. But we found out what he really loved was the cash drawer!"

Preemployment testing, background checks, drug testing, mystery shoppers, awareness training, and employee hotline programs can reduce, but not eliminate, retail theft. In addition, surveillance technology and well-designed point-of-sale software can limit theft. Shifting managers around to different stores and to different shifts can serve as another deterrent.

Make sure your business establishes a code of conduct that new employees sign and review. According to O'Brien and Associates, loss prevention consultants based in Ontario, Canada, "The code of conduct should clearly state that the taking of merchandise or cash without payment or management authorization—or helping others to do so—are violations that may result in disciplinary action up to and including termination of employment and possibly criminal charges."

CYBER CONCERNS

As an entrepreneur, you must be ever vigilant to protect employee and customer data. To ensure that all data within your firm is kept private and secure, hire professionals to help protect your business by installing appropriate software and providing training to your employees. Costs to secure data are minimal compared to the losses that could occur if customer data is comprised or money is transferred illegally.

Cyber crooks aim for unsuspecting and unprotected small businesses, and they change their tactics frequently. Thus, your firm requires an expert, not only to set up a secure system, but also to constantly review and make changes to thwart the crooks who come from within your company and those who hack into your system from the outside. Review the Cyber Security Issues for Entrepreneurs, Figure 12.3, along with Table 12.1, What We're Worrying About, and log on to the United States Computer Emerging Readiness Team's site at *http://www.us-cert.gov/cas/tips* Web site to familiarize yourself with the vast array of potential cyber problems.

figure **12.3**

Cyber Security Issues for Entrepreneurs

General information
- Why is Cyber Security a Problem?
- Guidelines for Publishing Information Online
- Understanding Internet Service Providers (ISPs)

General security
- Choosing and Protecting Passwords
- Understanding Anti-Virus Software
- Understanding Firewalls
- Coordinating Virus and Spyware Defense
- Debunking Some Common Myths
- Good Security Habits
- Safeguarding Your Data
- Real-World Warnings Keep You Safe Online
- Keeping Children Safe Online

Attacks and threats
- Dealing with Cyberbullies
- Understanding Hidden Threats: Corrupted Software Files
- Understanding Hidden Threats: Rootkits and Botnets
- Preventing and Responding to Identity Theft
- Recovering from Viruses, Worms, and Trojan Horses

- Recognizing and Avoiding Spyware
- Avoiding Social Engineering and Phishing Attacks
- Understanding Denial-of-Service Attacks
- Identifying Hoaxes and Urban Legends
- Avoiding the Pitfalls of Online Trading

Email and communication
- Understanding Your Computer: Email Clients
- Using Caution with Email Attachments
- Reducing Spam
- Benefits and Risks of Free Email Services
- Benefits of Blind Carbon Copy (BCC)
- Understanding Digital Signatures
- Using Instant Messaging and Chat Rooms Safely
- Staying Safe on Social Network Sites

Mobile devices
- Protecting Portable Devices: Physical Security
- Protecting Portable Devices: Data Security
- Securing Wireless Networks
- Cybersecurity for Electronic Devices
- Defending Cell Phones and PDAs Against Attack

(continued)

— figure **12.3**

Cyber Security Issues for Entrepreneurs (*continued*)

Privacy
- How Anonymous Are You?
- Protecting Your Privacy
- Understanding Encryption
- Effectively Erasing Files
- Supplementing Passwords

Safe browsing
- Understanding Your Computer: Web Browsers
- Evaluating Your Web Browser's Security Settings
- Shopping Safely Online
- Browsing Safely: Understanding Active Content and Cookies

- Understanding Web Site Certificates
- Understanding Internationalized Domain Names
- Understanding Bluetooth Technology
- Avoiding Copyright Infringement

Software and applications
- Understanding Patches
- Understanding Voice over Internet Protocol (VoIP)
- Risks of File-Sharing Technology
- Reviewing End-User License Agreements
- Understanding Your Computer: Operating Systems

Source: *Inc.* by Dan Briody. Copyright 2007 by Mansueto Ventures LLC. Reproduced with permission of Mansueto Ventures LLC in the format Textbook via Copyright Clearance Center.

— table **12.1**

What We're Worrying About

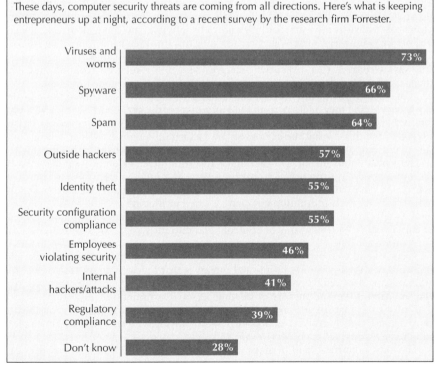

These days, computer security threats are coming from all directions. Here's what is keeping entrepreneurs up at night, according to a recent survey by the research firm Forrester.

Viruses and worms	73%
Spyware	66%
Spam	64%
Outside hackers	57%
Identity theft	55%
Security configuration compliance	55%
Employees violating security	46%
Internal hackers/attacks	41%
Regulatory compliance	39%
Don't know	28%

Source: Keep Out the Cybercrooks Who Have a New Target: You, *Inc.* magazine, March, 2007.

To find a security technology expert to help protect your firm, log on to *http://www.giac.org* to locate professionals who possess a Global Information Assurance Certification, or *https://www.isc2.org* to find Certified Information Systems Security Professionals. Also, never stop reading up on your industry Web sites for current cyber problems and the solutions others have found.

Build a "culture of security" amongst your employees, and spread that sense of security to your customers as well. "Business owners are legally required to protect customer and employee personal information and can face significant state and/or Federal fines if they're found to be noncompliant and privacy is compromised," according to Oliver Brew, vice president of technology media and telecommunications underwriting for Hiscox, a specialty insurer offering privacy protection policies.

The National Federation of Independent Business (NFIB) provides additional cyber security advice to avoid data breaches.

Protecting Your Small Business Against Data Theft

Experts suggest:

Establishing secure policies. Require that data contained in laptop computers must always, without fail, be encrypted (full-disk rather than just file) and the laptops password protected. This goes for desktop computers also.

Require that all sensitive documents be shredded, and hold these in locked containers until they are, says Brew. Assign specific employees to handle the destruction, and verify and record that this has taken place. Establish appropriate checks and balances like assigning employees to oversee those who have access to, or who handle, sensitive information.

Look at areas where your business is vulnerable and create policies or procedures to address these weaknesses (for example, do your employees unfailingly check credit card signatures or look to see if the driver's license photo matches the person standing in front of them?). And then train and monitor your employees on these routines.

Staying current with technology. Know the technologies that can make you vulnerable to a breach. For example, says McDowall, desktop computers—even those loaded up with firewalls, antivirus programs, and spyware—can still be at risk, in particular from keylogger programs. These programs, designed to read keystrokes, are secretly deposited on computers, and the information transmitted back to the hackers. According to McDowall, 85% or more of these programs are getting past antivirus software. And it's easy to be infected. You can pick up a keylogger program by visiting legitimate Web sites, accessing links, or even by downloading MP3s.

Keylogger programs affect even those who encrypt their stored and transmitted data, says George Waller, executive vice president of StrikeForce Technologies. The company, based in Edison, N.J., develops products for preventing identity theft.

"One reason why identity theft is the fastest-growing crime is that even though sites may be secure, and they might encrypt their information, the keyloggers have found a way to record keystrokes coming from the keyboard to the browsers. These keystrokes are not encrypted, and this is what the keyloggers are picking up," explains Waller, whose company offers technology that will encrypt keystrokes from the keyboard to the browser.

Get smart about hiring. Do criminal background checks on all would-be hires. Make it a policy to drug test. Employees represent a huge vulnerability to business owners and their customers, says Johnny May, president of Security Resources Unlimited, an identity theft prevention company located in Bloomfield Hills, Mich. He says that ID theft occuring in the workplace due to disgruntled, exiting, or plain old dishonest employees is "spiraling out of control" and currently represents a greater threat than outside hackers.

"People tend to focus on external threats, like hackers, spyware, or stolen credit cards, but what's so scary about internal threats is that they can go on for a long time without being detected," says May, also sounding the alarm about temporary workers who come in for the sole purpose of stealing personal information.

And it's not just intentional employee theft that small-business owners need to guard against; poorly trained, unaccountable employees who consequently mishandle data pose a risk as well, says McDowall.

The most important, and perhaps most effective, thing small-business owners can do is to take the risk of ID theft seriously and to remain vigilant.

"Remember," says Brew, "Just because you have a lock on the door, doesn't mean your information is secure."

Source: *http://www.nfib.com/object/IO_36313.html* (Accessed February 26, 2008).

THE TAX MAN COMETH

What are the laws when it comes to taxes? What forms do I have to fill out? If I am audited, how can I protect myself? These are just a few of the questions answered in IRS Publications 334 and 583, "Tax Guide for Small Business" and "Starting a Business and Keeping Records." For twice-yearly tax updates, forms, and business tax advice, CD Publication 3207 is published by the IRS and is available for $25 by calling 1-877-233-6767.

Table 12.2 lists the most common tax forms businesses are required by law to file. Schedule C and Schedule C-EZ for sole proprietors are provided in Appendix C.

If you will be conducting commerce throughout the world, refer to the excellent international tax and business guides for over 50 countries at this link on Deloitte's Web site, *http://www.deloitte.com/dtt/section_node/ 0,1042,sid%3D11410,00.html*. Germany's information from Deloitte's site is highlighted in the Incredible Resource on page 334.

In the United States, you will at least be responsible for corporate or personal income taxes, employment taxes, sales taxes, and property taxes. If you have employees, you will need to file an Application for Employer Identification Number, Form SS-4 (found in Appendix C).

Some of these taxes apply only to the employer, some are levied on employees, and some apply to both employer and employees. Federal employment taxes include federal income tax withholding, Social Security and

table 12.2

Which IRS Forms Must I File?

IF you are a . . .	THEN you may be liable for . . .	Use Form . . .
Sole proprietor	Income tax	1040 and Schedule C[1] or C–EZ (Schedule F[1] for farm business)
	Self-employment tax	1040 and Schedule SE
	Estimated tax	1040–ES
	Employment taxes:	
	• Social security and Medicare taxes and income tax withholding	941 (943 for farm employees)
	• Federal unemployment (FUTA) tax	940 or 940–EZ
	• Depositing employment taxes	8109[2]
	Excise taxes	See *Excise Taxes*
Partnership	Annual return of income	1065
	Employment taxes	Same as sole proprietor
	Excise taxes	See *Excise Taxes*
Partner in a partnership (individual)	Income tax	1040 and Schedule E[3]
	Self-employment tax	1040 and Schedule SE
	Estimated tax	1040–ES
Corporation or S corporation	Income tax	1120 or 1120–A (corporation)[3] 1120S (S corporation)[3]
	Estimated tax	1120–W (corporation only) and 8109[2]
	Employment taxes	Same as sole proprietor
	Excise taxes	See *Excise Taxes*
S corporation shareholder	Income tax	1040 and Schedule E[3]
	Estimated tax	1040–ES

[1] File a separate schedule for each business.
[2] Do not use if you deposit taxes electronically.
[3] Various other schedules may be needed.

Note: *Estimated tax.* Generally, you must pay taxes on income, including self-employment tax, by making regular payments of estimated tax during the year.

Sole proprietors, partners, and S corporation shareholders. You generally have to make estimated tax payments if you expect to owe tax of $1,000 or more when you file your return. Use Form 1040-ES, Estimated Tax for Individuals, to figure and pay your estimated tax. For more information, see Publication 505, Tax Withholding and Estimated Tax.

Corporations. You generally have to make estimated tax payments for your corporation if you expect it to owe tax of $500 or more when you file the return. Use Form 1120-W, Estimated Tax for Corporations, to figure the estimated tax. You must deposit the payments as explained on page 8 under "Depositing Taxes." For more information, see Publication 542.

Source: Internal Revenue Service, *http://www.irs.gov/publications/p583/ar02.html#dOe577* (Accessed February 26, 2008).

Medicare taxes, and Federal Unemployment (FUTA) Tax. Many employees do not realize the significant impact taxes play in operating a business. Thus some firms, such as IRMCO (see Key Points from Another View), allow employees access to financial information through an open-book management system.

In addition to federal taxes, you will also be responsible for state, county, and local taxes. State and federal rules do not always mesh, so be sure you understand both systems. An *experienced* CPA who specializes in your selected industry will be able to keep you on track with what is acceptable practice to the IRS. The IRS offers additional help for business

(in)credibleresource

Deloitte.

International Tax   January 2008

Germany *Highlights*

Currency: Euro (EUR)

Foreign Exchange Control: No restrictions are imposed on the import or export of capital; however, the local Landeszentralbank must be notified if a transfer involves more than EUR 50,000.

Accounting principles/financial statements: German Commercial GAAP/IFRS. Financial statements must be prepared annually.

Principal business entities:

These are the joint stock company (AG), limited liability company (GmbH), general and limited partnership, sole proprietorship and branch of a foreign corporation.

Corporate taxation:

Residence – A corporation is resident if it maintains its registered office (as determined by its articles of incorporation) or central place of management in Germany.

Basis – Residents are taxed on worldwide income; nonresidents are taxed only on German-source income. Branches are taxed the same as subsidiaries.

Taxable income – Corporation tax is imposed on a company's profits, which consists of business/trading income, passive income and capital gains. Business expenses may be deducted in computing taxable income.

Taxation of dividends – Dividends received by a German resident corporation (from both resident and foreign corporations) are 95% tax exempt. The remaining 5% represents nondeductible business expenses and is added back to taxable income.

Capital gains – Capital gains derived from the sale of a domestic or foreign corporate subsidiary are 95% tax-exempt.

Losses – Losses may be carried back 1 year and carried forward indefinitely. However,

minimum taxation applies: losses may be offset against profits up to EUR 1 million without restriction, but only 60% of income exceeding EUR 1 million may be offset against loss carryforwards. From 1 January 2008, a direct or indirect ownership change of more than 25%/50% to one shareholder results in a partial/complete forfeiture of all tax loss carryforwards. No exception applies for intragroup transfers.

Rate – The corporate rate is 15% as from FY 2008. The municipal trade tax typically ranges between 14% and 17%. The effective corporate rate (including the solidarity surcharge and trade tax) typically ranges between 30% and 33%.

Surtax – A solidarity surcharge of 5.5% is levied on the income tax or corporate income tax.

Alternative minimum tax – No

Foreign tax credit – Foreign tax paid may be credited against German tax that relates to the foreign income. Typically, Germany applies the exemption system.

Participation exemption – See under "Taxation of dividends".

Holding company regime – No

Incentives – Various incentive programs are available, e.g. for the purchase or production of movable assets in Eastern Germany and for founders of new business.

Withholding tax:

Dividends – A statutory rate of 20% (21.1%, including the solidarity surcharge (25% (26.375%) as from 2009)) applies, with a possible 40% refund for nonresident corporations, giving rise to an effective rate of 15.825%. No tax is levied on dividends qualifying under the EC parent-subsidiary directive.

Interest – Generally no withholding tax is levied on interest, except for interest on deposits with German banks/financial institutions (30%) and certain hybrid instruments.

Royalties – As from FY 2008, the withholding tax on royalties is 15% (15.825%, including the solidarity surcharge) paid to nonresident corporations (0% if the royalties qualify under the EC interest and royalties directive). The rate is 20% (21.1%, including the solidarity surcharge) if paid to nonresidents that are not in the form of a corporation.

Branch remittance tax – No

Other taxes on corporations:

Capital duty – No

Payroll tax – No, but employers are obliged to withhold wage tax on a monthly basis from an employee's income and remit it to the tax authorities.

Real property tax – Tax is levied by the municipality in which the real estate is located. The rate is 0.35% of the tax value of the property, multiplied by a municipal coefficient.

Social security – Employers are required to bear 50% of the wage-related social security contributions (health, nursing care, unemployment and pension insurance).

Stamp duty – No

Transfer tax – A real estate transfer tax of 3.5% (Berlin 4.5%) of the sales price/value of transferred real estate is levied.

Other – Shipping companies may apply for lump sum tonnage taxation in certain cases.

Anti-avoidance rules:

Transfer pricing – Business dealings between related persons must be in according with transactions that would have been agreed upon by independent third parties dealing at arm's length, whereby the

Audit.Tax.Consulting.Financial Advisory.

Source: *http://www.deloitte.com/dtt/cda/doc/content/dtt_tax_highlight_germany_123107.pdf* (Accessed April 14, 2008).

owners on their Web site, providing specialized tax information by industry through their Audit Technique Guides. See the Community Resource on page 336 for the IRS's restaurant information. To determine if there is a specialized Web site for your industry, go to *http://www.irs.gov/businesses/ small/industries/index.html.*

The best thing you can do for your business is to keep excellent records of *all* transactions. A candy manufacturer was recently audited, and the audit took one day instead of the usual three—the result of excellent record keeping and no problems! The IRS and your accountant will tell you exactly what is required and expected.

While preparation is essential, your CPA can be of great assistance to you in *tax planning.* Owning a business offers many entrepreneurs the opportunity to shield income with excellent retirement planning options; if undertaken legally and properly, these can be of great advantage. Waiting until your taxes are prepared is often too late. Keep your accountant abreast of any major business changes, and *make your accountant part of your planning team.*

Income Taxes

If you owe less than $1,000 in federal tax for the year, or if you paid no income taxes last year, you *may* not need to pay estimated taxes. But the majority of business owners will be required to pay estimated income and self-employment taxes on April 15, June 15, September 15, and January 15 of the following year. In most states, you will also be required to send estimated payments. See the IRS Web site for help calculating your tax payments. If calculations are not done properly, and you pay too little, you will be responsible for penalties.

Excellent additional tax information can be found at *http://www.turbotax. com,* which links to Quicken accounting products; *http://www.hrblock.com*; and *http://www.toolkit.com.*

Self-Employment Taxes

A tough tax for many sole proprietors to absorb is the self-employment tax. As of 2008, the self-employment tax rate on net income was 15.3 percent. This includes 12.4 percent for Social Security (old-age, survivors, and disability insurance) and 2.9 percent for Medicare (hospital insurance). The 2008 rate is 15.3 percent of the first $102,000 of income and 2.9 percent on anything above that amount. To calculate your tax, use Schedule SE in Appendix C or the most updated Schedule SE online at *http://www.irs.gov.* For some relief, one-half of the self-employment tax is deductible from your gross income.

Employment Taxes

Keeping up with employee taxes and laws is a headache for most employers. As recommended in Chapter 11, use a payroll service. Some employers pay their employees cash in an illegal attempt to save on taxes and worker's compensation. If an employee gets injured, the deception will be discovered, and fines are heavy. In addition, if an angry employee calls the IRS to report you, the IRS *will call* you! Another possibility is that a competitor might report you to the IRS for suspected tax evasion. Tax laws and regulations are a burden, but they are *not* to be avoided or taken lightly at any time.

If you have employees, be sure to order Form 940, Employer's Annual Federal Unemployment Tax Return and Publication 15, Circular E, the Employer's Tax Guide. According to the IRS, "The term, 'employment taxes' describes several federal, state, and local taxes that employers have the responsibility to manage." As an employer, you must remit half of your employees' Social Security and Medicare taxes, unemployment taxes (which are only the responsibility of the employer), and possible state disability taxes.

Sales Taxes

For sales tax and resale numbers, contact your State Board of Equalization. Some states tax both products and services, others tax products only.

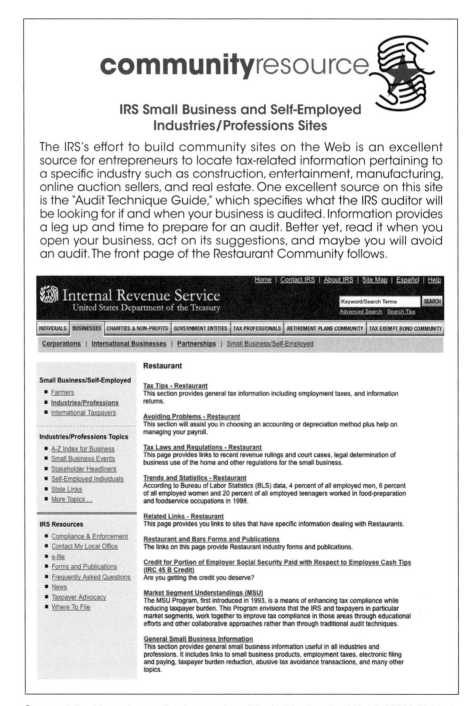

Source: *http://www.irs.gov/businesses/small/industries/content/0,,id=98720,00.html* (Accessed February 25, 2008).

Each state's list of products that are exempt varies, and also when and how you submit your taxes vary as well. Check with state offices where your business operates to determine requirements.

Many small-business owners attempt to avoid reporting sales taxes for cash transactions. This is not a wise idea; the IRS has many ways to determine your true sales figures. For example, they might look at the number of disposable cups you purchased and thereby determine how much coffee you sold; or they may review your water and electric bills to estimate how many loads your laundromat washed and dried. Do not forget to remit your collected sales tax.

If you are starting up, try to make realistic quarterly estimates. If projections are too high, you will be required to post a higher **bond** to get a resale number and permit. Use the numbers you found in your research for Chapters 8 and 9.

Bond Guarantee of payment

Final Tax Thoughts

Fines for violations of tax laws are considerable. Once you have been audited, your chances of being audited again increase. Realize most everyone is audited at some time or another. So be prepared with excellent recordkeeping, a payroll service firm to support you, and an experienced accountant to represent you. In addition, excellent records from the start will provide a paper trail for potential lenders, partners, suppliers, and potential buyers of your business. Complete Part 1 and 2 of Action Step 51 after reviewing tax information from this chapter, IRS publications, and past chapters.

EXIT STRATEGY

Return to the first five Action Steps in Chapter 1 and your notebook and review your answers. Have your answers changed since you began your adventure? If so, revise the answers and proceed. Business Plans usually include a section referred to as the "Exit Strategy." Your exit should be based on the reasons and purposes for which you started the business. Some entrepreneurs pursue a small business to create long-term capital appreciation. For others, they dream of leaving a successful, viable business to their children. Other entrepreneurs hope to work 30 hours a week, pull as much cash out of the business as possible, and close it down in 10 years to retire. To protect your business along with your personal and financial goals, you need to discuss your potential exit strategy with your legal and tax-planning team; they need to be aware of your desires early on in the formation of your business.

The legal form of your business may have a significant impact on tax consequences in the immediate term, as well as for the potential sale or transfer. If your exit strategy changes at any time, you need to contact your legal and tax-planning team again to review your options. We suggest you assess your exit strategy at the end of each year, and consider valuing your business yearly as well. Your options may also change over the years with the economy, technology, employees, and possibly even legal changes, which might affect the viability of your business. As these changes happen or are foreseen, communication with your team is absolutely essential. Structural differences in your business and tax planning may impact your financial gain when selling your business. After working hard for many years, few of us would want to leave any money on the table at the end.

Action Step 51

1. Review the tax material provided in this and past chapters. Make a list of all tax forms you will need and print them out. Read through the IRS's *Small Business Tax Guide.* Make a list of any questions you might have.
2. Contact the IRS or your accountant to find the answers to the questions discovered in point 1 above.
3. Review Action Steps 1 through 5 in Chapter 1 and make the appropriate changes to your original plans based on what you have learned in this chapter.
4. Begin to develop your formal exit strategy, which will be included in your final Business Plan.

Your final reward for developing a successful business will take a great deal of planning, which should not be overlooked as you deal with the daily effort required to run a business. You must also protect your business from other unforeseen exits such as death, disability, and divorce. Planning for the eventuality of any of these is absolutely essential. Your tax, legal, and insurance advisors must play a major role in protecting you and your firm.

Potential exit strategies include the following:

- Selling all or a portion of the business
- Having a going-out-of-business sale (liquidating)
- Handing down the business to family members (either slowly or all at once)
- Franchising your business
- Selling to employees through an Employee Stock Ownership Plan (ESOP)
- Merging with another firm or being acquired
- Being bought out by partners in the business
- Taking the company public

For owners who would like to share their business with their employees, they should consider an Employee Stock Ownership Plan (ESOP), which makes the employees of a company owners of stock in that company. ESOP's provide tax advantages to employees and the business owner, and they can provide an excellent corporate finance strategy, a retirement strategy, and an exit strategy. For further information, contact the ESOP Association at *http://www.esop.org*. If you follow this option, locating an ESOP specialist is key.

Investopedia.com adds that "employee stock ownership plans can be used to keep plan participants focused on company performance and share price appreciation. By giving plan participants an interest in seeing that the company's stock performs well, these plans are believed to encourage participants to do what's best for shareholders, since the participants themselves are shareholders."

According to Jennifer Lawton, senior vice president of consulting and technology at Interliant Inc., "There is plenty to fear about continuing to work in entrepreneurial nirvana with no consideration of its end or change. The reality is that unless you define that end or change, your business may change in a way that was not in your plan." Lawton suggests you consider the following words of wisdom:

1. **Know why you're in the business** and what is most important to you. Know this in parallel tracks—the personal and the professional—and also know where the two can merge.
2. **Educate yourself through listening, reading, and interacting** to know what others strive for, both in like-minded and not-so-like-minded businesses.
3. **Communicate your goals and intentions,** include people in them, and enlist support.
4. **Understand that your exit strategy may be that you will never leave,** or alternatively, that you will sell high and retire early.
5. **Do what's right for you.**

Source: Jennifer Lawton, "Exit Strategies: What's Yours?" *http://www.inc.com/articles/1997/09/20234.html* (Accessed February 25, 2008).

If you are seeking investment capital, your investors will want to know your personal financial goals and anticipated time frames. Venture capitalists and angel investors are looking at investing for usually 3 to 5 years. In addition to your personal and financial goals, a realistic exit plan should consider your needs—both personal and financial—particular industry, competitive environment, management needs, and business life cycle.

GLOBAL VILLAGE

Business Ethics in a Global Marketplace

NFIB.com 05/16/2005

When it comes to business, the world is shrinking—the global marketplace is becoming more accessible with each day and every transaction. Although business has brought people together, culture has kept us different.

When dealing in business with people of other cultures, it is important to keep differences, whatever they may be, in mind and at ease. It's important to understand that the global marketplace is a diverse one, and that your potential clients may have different perspectives on ethics and proper behavior than those to which you are accustomed.

Find Common Ground

Remember that the second you step into the global marketplace, you need to be in a global state of mind. Leave behind traditional American jargon and opt for general, direct, and courteous ways of communicating thoughts, feelings, and ideas.

Don't speak the language? Find someone who does. When it comes to translating, take no shortcuts. It is important that you and your client have a clear understanding of what you are discussing.

Also, research the country and the culture of those with whom you will be working. It is important that you know the boundaries when it comes to asking personal questions. What you think is polite chitchat could actually be an offensive question to someone else.

Be Accommodating

Broadening your marketplace broadens your workday. If you're working with someone who is halfway around the globe, "nine to five" won't always cut it. Be prepared to put in the occasional late and odd hours to make sure that everything is running smoothly 24/7.

Not only should you be available when someone needs you, but also so should any company information. Be sure that your employees and partners around the world have access to the information they need in the language they need. Also, make sure there is someone they can contact, should they need additional support. Remember, toll-free numbers don't work outside of North America, so your co-workers in other countries will need a direct-dial number.

Keep It Legal

When dealing in business on a global level, some of the basic rules still apply: play it straight. Under the Foreign Corrupt Practices Act (FCPA), it is illegal for any individual, firm, or anyone in connection with the firm to pay, offer to pay, or bribe in any fashion foreign government officials to obtain or retain business. One exception to this act is "grease payments," where firms will pay lower-level government officials to secure routine government actions.

Getting into the global marketplace is a challenging, but extremely rewarding, endeavor if you do it right. Just be sure that you're informed and ready to take on the responsibilities involved, and you'll find the global marketplace is a great place for your business to be.

Source: *http://www.nfib.com/object/IO_22263.html* (Accessed February 26, 2008).

Action Step 52

Assess Ethical Positions and Design Code of Conduct

1. Respond to questions in Ethical Issues for Entrepreneurs (Figure 12.4).
2. Next, have potential partners—including family members—complete the questionnaire as well. Then sit together over a cup of coffee and discuss your answers.
3. Do you see any potential problems? If so, how will you work the problems out?
4. Are your potential partners people you want to be in business with?
5. Discuss the Ethical Principles for Entrepreneurs in Figure 12.5. Which areas do you and your potential partners agree and disagree on?
6. How will you solve your differences with your partners when you disagree on an issue from an ethical standpoint?
7. Review Figure 12.6. How would your ethical decision making change if you followed these steps?
8. Develop your firm's code of conduct. Use the Center for the Study of Ethics in the Professions at the Illinois Institute of Technology's Web site at *http://ethics.iit.edu/codes/coe.html* to help you complete this Action Step. Excellent resources and sample codes are available through the Center's Web site to assist you. Remember, you have the chance to design the business and workplace of your dreams; setting ethical standards is one step on the ladder to success.

According to Tom Richman, business journalist, when he looked at the exit strategy for his potential business venture:

I was forced to think about myself as an entrepreneur the way a venture capitalist thinks about his money: How much will I have to invest, and over what time period, before I can get out with a decent return? Only in my case, I was the capital, and the exit strategy we worked out suggested I'd have to invest a lot more of myself, and for a good many more years than I thought I could. So I decided to get out before I got in. Creating an exit strategy helps one visualize not just the start and bailout points for a nascent enterprise but also the distance and journey between them.

Source: *The Exit Strategy: Cashing Out and Other Premeditated Escapes,* Tom Richman, *Inc.* magazine, May 1999. Copyright © 2004 Gruner & Jahr USA Publishing. All rights reserved.

Understand when developing your exit strategy that you are developing the road map for your business, but this road map must be a flexible one, because opportunities widen and narrow. Also, partners and employee relationships may change over the years, and you may change your mind on how you want to grow and eventually divest yourself from the business. In answering the exit strategy questions, you are brought back to your original goals for opening a business. Always work to maintain control of your entrepreneurial dreams along with your financial and personal goals. After reviewing your early Action Steps, complete Parts 3 and 4 of Action Step 51.

ETHICS

You will be confronted with many ethical issues in running your business, and how you react will set the tone for your employees and the future of your company. Figure 12.4 lists potential ethical issues and dilemmas entrepreneurs

figure 12.4

Ethical Issues for Entrepreneurs

How important is each of the following to you?

4 = Very important, 3 = Important, 2 = Not very important, 1 = Not important

1. _____ Expecting a "full day's work for a full day's pay" work ethic.

2. _____ Not allowing petty theft (i.e., supplies, telephone, photocopying, etc.)

3. _____ Not cheating on expense accounts.

4. _____ Not allowing employee acceptance of gifts or favors from vendors.

5. _____ Not distorting or falsifying internal reports.

6. _____ Not allowing cheating or overreaching on benefits (sick days, insurance, etc.)

7. _____ Sexual or racial non-discrimination in hiring, promotion, or pay.

8. _____ Invasion of employee privacy.

9. _____ Providing safe and healthy working conditions.

10. _____ Providing honest, fair, and timely work appraisals.

11. _____ Not recruiting for employee's replacement without telling employee being replaced.

12. _____ Not allowing strategies or technical justifications to deny employees' earned benefits.

13. _____ Dealing fairly with employee complaints.

14. _____ Having fair expectation of paid staff.

15. _____ Providing adequate compensation.

16. _____ Providing adequate recognition, appreciation, or other psychic rewards to staff.

17. _____ Promoting "healthy" competition among employees.

18. _____ Promoting "good" communication.

19. _____ Promoting mutual support and teamsmanship.

20. _____ Fair product pricing.

21. _____ Commitment to honest and truthful marketing and advertising.

22. _____ Providing and ensuring safe and healthy products.

23. _____ Fair handling of customer complaints.

24. _____ Providing truthful tax reports and financial statements.

25. _____ Protecting the environment.

26. _____ Avoidance of bribes, payoffs, or "grease" to union or public officials.

27. _____ Doing business in countries with inhumane or anti-American policies.

28. _____ Community involvement and philanthropy.

Source: Josephson Institute of Ethics, Los Angeles, CA.

face, many of which have been discussed in the text. Review these issues on your own to determine where you stand. If you have partners, ask them to review the issues and then meet to discuss your thoughts. Knowing what your partners truly believe and where they stand ethically can prevent potential problems for your business. Complete Action Step 52 to determine where possible conflicts may lie regarding ethical issues amongst your partners.

Another additional ethical dilemma for many entrepreneurs is navigating the ethical differences among various countries. One entrepreneur pulled out of Latvia when what was required for him to continue operating was not in congruence with the ethical standards he had set forth for his corporation. Review the Global Village box on page 339 for further information.

We have included an entrepreneur's code of ethical principles (Figure 12.5), which serves as a guide to the difficult issues that may be encountered while operating a business. Knowing where you stand and what you believe can

---

figure **12.5**

Ethical Principles for Entrepreneurs

Ethical values, translated into active language, establish standards or rules describing the kinds of behavior an ethical entrepreneur should and should not engage in. The following list of principles incorporates the characteristics and values that most people associate with ethical behavior. Ethical decision-making systematically considers these principles.

1. **HONESTY.** Ethical entrepreneurs are honest and truthful in all their dealings and they do not deliberately mislead or deceive others by misrepresentations, overstatements, partial truths, selective omissions, or any other means.

2. **INTEGRITY.** Ethical entrepreneurs demonstrate personal integrity and the courage of their convictions by doing what they think is right even when there is great pressure to do otherwise; they are principled, honorable, and upright; they will fight for their beliefs. They will not sacrifice principle for expediency or be hypocritical or unscrupulous.

3. **PROMISE-KEEPING AND TRUSTWORTHINESS.** Ethical entrepreneurs are worthy of trust, they are candid and forthcoming in supplying relevant information and correcting misapprehensions of fact, and they make every reasonable effort to fulfill the letter and spirit of their promises and commitments. They do not interpret agreements in an unreasonably technical or legalistic manner in order to rationalize noncompliance or create justifications for escaping their commitments.

4. **LOYALTY.** Ethical entrepreneurs are worthy of trust, demonstrate fidelity and loyalty to persons and institutions by friendship in adversity, and display support and devotion to duty; they do not use or disclose information learned in confidence for personal advantage. They safeguard the ability to make independent professional judgments by scrupulously avoiding undue influences and conflicts of interest. They are loyal to their employees and colleagues. They respect the proprietary information of their former employer, and refuse to engage in any activities that take undue advantage of their previous position.

5. **FAIRNESS.** Ethical entrepreneurs are fair and just in all dealings; they do not exercise power arbitrarily, and do not use overreaching nor indecent means to gain or maintain any advantage nor take undue advantage of another's mistakes or difficulties. Fair persons manifest a commitment to justice, the equal treatment of individuals, and tolerance for and acceptance of diversity and are open-minded; they are willing to admit they are wrong and, where appropriate, change their positions and beliefs.

6. **CONCERN FOR OTHERS.** Ethical entrepreneurs are caring, compassionate, benevolent, and kind; they live the Golden Rule, help those in need, and seek to accomplish their business objectives in a manner that causes the least harm and the greatest positive good.

7. **RESPECT FOR OTHERS.** Ethical entrepreneurs demonstrate respect for the human dignity, autonomy, privacy, rights, and interests of all those who have a stake in their decisions; they are courteous and treat all people with equal respect and dignity regardless of sex, race, or national origin.

8. **LAW ABIDING.** Ethical entrepreneurs abide by laws, rules, and regulations relating to their business activities.

9. **COMMITMENT TO EXCELLENCE.** Ethical entrepreneurs pursue excellence in performing their duties, are well informed and prepared, and constantly endeavor to increase their proficiency in all areas of responsibility.

(continued)

figure **12.5**

Ethical Principles for Entrepreneurs (continued)

10. **LEADERSHIP.** Ethical entrepreneurs are conscious of the responsibilities and opportunities of their position of leadership and seek to be positive ethical role models by their own conduct and by helping to create an environment in which principled reasoning and ethical decision making are highly prized.

11. **REPUTATION AND MORALE.** Ethical entrepreneurs seek to protect and build the company's good reputation and the morale of it's employees by engaging in no conduct that might undermine respect and by taking whatever actions are necessary to correct or prevent inappropriate conduct of others.

12. **ACCOUNTABILITY.** Ethical entrepreneurs acknowledge and accept personal accountability for the ethical quality of their decisions and omissions to themselves, their colleagues, their companies, and their communities.

Source: *Ethical Obligations and Opportunities in Business: Ethical Decision Making in the Trenches,* Josephson Institute of Ethics, Los Angeles, CA.

make the hard decisions much easier. Guidelines such as those presented in Figure 12.4 and the Josephson Institute's Seven-Step Path to Better Decisions (Figure 12.6) assist individuals to act in the best interest of others. Several online sites, such as *http://www.inc.com,* provide sample codes of ethics that might help you in developing your own company code of ethics. Your code sets the tone for your business and becomes part of the culture of how you treat your employees, customers, competitors, and suppliers. When your employees wonder whether something is right or wrong, they will have a guide to help them decide.

figure **12.6**

The Seven-Step Path to Better Decisions

1. Stop and Think
One of the most important steps to better decisions is the oldest advice in the world: think ahead. To do so, it's necessary to first stop the momentum of events long enough to permit calm analysis. This may require discipline, but it is a powerful tonic against poor choices.

The well-worn formula to count to ten when angry and to a hundred when very angry is a simple technique designed to prevent foolish and impulsive behavior. But we are just as apt to make foolish decisions when we are under the strain of powerful desires or fatigue, when we are in a hurry or under pressure, and when we are ignorant of important facts.

Just as we teach our children to look both ways before they cross the street, we can and should instill the habit of looking ahead before they make any decision.

Stopping to think provides several benefits. It prevents rash decisions. It prepares us for more thoughtful discernment. And it can allow us to mobilize our discipline.

2. Clarify Goals
Before you choose, clarify your short- and long-term aims. Determine which of your many wants and don't-wants affected by the decision are the most important. The big danger is that decisions that fulfill immediate wants and needs can prevent the achievement of our more important life goals.

3. Determine Facts
Be sure you have adequate information to support an intelligent choice. You can't make good decisions if you don't know the facts.

To determine the facts, first resolve what you know and then what you need to know. Be prepared to get additional information and to verify assumptions and other uncertain information.

Once we begin to be more careful about facts, we often find that there are different versions of them and disagreements about their meaning. In these situations, part of making sound decisions involves making good judgments as to who and what to believe.

Here are some guidelines:
- Consider the reliability and credibility of the people providing the facts.
- Consider the basis of the supposed facts. If the person giving you the information says he or she personally heard or saw something, evaluate that person in terms of honesty, accuracy, and memory.
- Remember that assumptions, gossip, and hearsay are not the same as facts.

(continued)

─── figure **12.6**

The Seven-Step Path to Better Decisions *(continued)*

- Consider all perspectives, but be careful to consider whether the source of the information has values different than yours or has a personal interest that could affect perception of the facts.
- Where possible seek out the opinions of people whose judgment and character you respect, but be careful to distinguish the well-grounded opinions of well-informed people from casual speculation, conjecture, and guesswork.
- Finally, evaluate the information you have in terms of completeness and reliability, so you have a sense of the certainty and fallibility of your decisions.

4. Develop Options

Now that you know what you want to achieve and have made your best judgment as to the relevant facts, make a list of options, a set of actions you can take to accomplish your goals. If it's an especially important decision, talk to someone you trust, so you can broaden your perspective and think of new choices. If you can think of only one or two choices, you're probably not thinking hard enough.

5. Consider Consequences

Two techniques help reveal the potential consequences.
- *"Pillar-ize" your options.* Filter your choices through each of the Six Pillars of Character: trustworthiness, respect, responsibility, fairness, caring, and citizenship. Will the action violate any of the core ethical principles? For instance, does it involve lying or breaking a promise; is it disrespectful to anyone; is it irresponsible, unfair, or uncaring; or does it involve breaking laws or rules? Eliminate unethical options.
- *Identify the stakeholders and how the decision is likely to affect them.* Consider your choices from the point of view of the major stakeholders. Identify whom the decision will help and hurt.

6. Choose

It's time to make your decision. If the choice is not immediately clear, see if any of the following strategies help:
- *Talk to people whose judgment you respect.* Seek out friends and mentors, but remember, once you've gathered opinions and advice, the ultimate responsibility is still yours.
- *What would the most ethical person you know do?* Think of the person you know or know of (in real life or fiction) who has the strongest character and best ethical judgment. Then ask yourself: what would that person do in your situation? Think of that person as your decision-making role model, and try to behave the way he or she would. Many Christians wear a small bracelet with the letters WWJD standing for the question "What would Jesus do?" Whether you are Christian or not, the idea of referencing a role model can be a useful one. You could translate the question into: "What would God want me to do?" "What would Buddha or Mother Teresa do?" "What would Gandhi do?" "What would the most virtuous person in the world do?"
- *What would you do if you were sure everyone would know?* If everyone found out about your decision, would you be proud and comfortable? Choices that only look good if no one knows are always bad choices. Good choices make us worthy of admiration and build good reputations. It's been said that character is *revealed* by how we behave when we think no one is looking and *strengthened* when we act as if everyone is looking.
- *Golden Rule: do unto others as you would have them do unto you.* The Golden Rule is one of the oldest and best guides to ethical decision making. If we treat people the way we want to be treated, we are likely to live up to the Six Pillars of Character. We don't want to be lied to or have promises broken, so we should be honest and keep our promises to others. We want others to treat us with respect, so we should treat others respectfully.

7. Monitor and Modify

Since most hard decisions use imperfect information and "best effort" predictions, some of them will inevitably be wrong. Ethical decision makers monitor the effects of their choices. If they are not producing the intended results, or are causing additional unintended and undesirable results, they reassess the situation and make new decisions.

Source: Michael Josephson, *Making Ethical Decisions,* Josephson Institute of Ethics, *http://www.josephsoninstitute.org,* Los Angeles, CA, 2002.

SUMMARY

Protect your business, yourself, and your employees by insuring against losses, paying taxes on time, and acting ethically. It is not worth taking unnecessary or unethical risks after all the effort you have taken to create "your baby."

Determine your insurance needs early and pay to protect your business and personal investment. Work with an experienced agent in your selected industry who is qualified as a business insurance broker.

Work with your accountant (CPA) and payroll service to be sure you are complying with *all* federal, state, and local tax laws. Tax planning is an important element in the financial success, longevity, and exit strategy of your business. Your accountant and financial advisors not only will keep you in compliance with the laws, they will help you plan for the future. An experienced financial business advisor must be part of any entrepreneurial team.

Protect your business from internal and external crime. Take all feasible loss-prevention measures and insure as needed. Establish a code of conduct for your firm and discuss it openly and frequently with your employees.

Plan your exit strategy early on, because it will guide you throughout your venture. Your exit strategy may well determine the form of business you should undertake (corporation, LLC, or sole proprietorship).

Act ethically and responsibly; your actions will set the example for your employees and customers.

THINK POINTS FOR SUCCESS

- Protect your investment with insurance.
- Reduce the risk of employee theft and crime with loss-prevention strategies.
- Find and hire an expert accountant and financial advisor.
- Pay taxes on time.
- Keep impeccable, organized records. They will help you survive an audit and enhance your ability to sell your business.
- Keep personal and business funds separate.
- Plan your exit strategy.
- Follow the golden rule.

KEY POINTS FROM ANOTHER VIEW

Open-Book Management

The path to a winning workplace can begin in an unusual way. For Evanston, Illinois-based manufacturing company, IRMCO, it started in the mid-1980s, when owner and CEO William O. Jeffery III was suffering from terminal cancer. Jeffery committed his final years to making IRMCO a better place for his employees and its products better for its industrial customers. He replaced the oil and animal-fat–based lubricants IRMCO had made for decades with more environmentally friendly, water-based products.

As Jeffery overhauled his company's product line, he also reshaped the way management dealt with employees. "He got extra focused on people," recalls his son and IRMCO's current CEO, William C. "Jeff" Jeffery, who runs the 22-employee company with his brother, Bradley. A key first step was to put in place what is now commonly referred to as "open book" management, in which all financial details, except payroll, are shared with employees on a regular basis.

Opening the books, especially with an employee profit-sharing plan in place, clears away any workers' feelings that the company is a piggybank for the owners. "Employees can see what is available for my brother and me to take out," says Jeff, who represents the fourth generation of family owners. "When they see during tough times that we aren't taking money out, they understand that we are all in this together. It helps create goodwill," Jeff says. General manager Jennifer Kalas, who worked at two other industrial companies before IRMCO, also notices something different. "People are aware of what's going on, the budget, where the money is being spent," she says. "People take ownership."

The culture of openness, trust, and cooperation has evolved under the Jeffery brothers through other programs. The brothers use the metaphor of the wolf pack— "the only perfect team in nature," says Jeff—to build teamwork and information sharing. Monthly "wolf pack" meetings with all employees provide a forum for business updates, question answering, and nominations for the "lone wolf" award for exceptional work. At the end of each quarter, the winner is drawn from a hat and presented with $250 of "wolf dough" that must be spent on some kind of celebration.

The teamwork idea extends to intradepartmental cross training, where a red book of job tasks and responsibilities is provided to—and is expected to be understood by—all employees. This flexibility has been an important asset in allowing IRMCO to operate through the good times and bad. As general manager, Kalas points out, "In the good times, we don't have to add more people, so that in the bad times, we don't have to lay them off."

In fact, times have been rough at IRMCO for more than a year as the company is heavily dependent upon auto industry suppliers, which have been hit hard by the economy. IRMCO has adapted, however, supported by the undercurrent of employee–management goodwill.

The company has even managed to make money without having to resort to layoffs or the elimination of core programs. However, there is always a give and take. A salary freeze is in effect, and an open-ended tuition reimbursement program, which employees took advantage of to further their education and leave, has since been replaced. Now, IRMCO applies for state job-training grants to fund half of the tuition costs and is targeting specific skill improvements. Thus, the company is aligning itself more closely with the interests of its employees. Other programs have remained intact, such as a $250 wellness bonus for demonstrated improvement of mind or body.

While many of his customers are "getting crushed," Jeff leaves no doubt that there is a clear line connecting his company's relative success and its legacy of trust and support. "We are nimble and creative, with smart people communicating and working together." Sounds like a howl from a wolf pack.

Source: ©2006 Winning Workplaces, *http://www. winningworkplaces.org* (Accessed March 3, 2008).

chapter 13

Buying a Business
Maneuvering Through the Pitfalls

So far you have been exploring starting your own business from the ground up but another doorway, purchasing a business, may offer you a better option. In this chapter you will learn several ways to evaluate businesses for sale. Although our focus in this chapter is on ongoing independent operations, many of the tactics can be applied to evaluating franchise opportunities as well. However, Chapter 14 focuses specifically on franchising and multilevel marketing. Purchasing the right business or franchise requires careful effort and a tremendous amount of skepticism at all times.

When you buy an ongoing business, you are buying an income stream from a proven business. You may also be buying a inventory, a location, good will, and an agreement that the seller will not compete with you. When you buy a new franchise, you are primarily buying the right to use a name. You may also be buying a training program, a Business Plan, advertising assistance, lease negotiation assistance, and purchasing advantages.

Enough emphasis cannot possibly be given to warn you of the traps that are inherent in purchasing a business. Thus informed, experienced advisors familiar with your industry are essential, and no purchase should be undertaken without extreme due diligence and legal representation.

As you begin your search for a franchise or business to purchase, make sure that you do not fall in love with a "deal" but rather fall in love with a business that will fulfill your needs and desires. Return to the beginning Action Steps in Chapter 1, where you explored your interests, strengths, weaknesses, and your "Inc. plan." Review your thoughts. You will be expending a great deal of your time, money, energy, and emotion, so choose wisely based on intuition and factual information. Trust your instincts, research, and follow your passion.

Investigate each deal thoroughly and completely. Focus on finding the right opportunity first and the right price second. Spend time searching for an opportunity that fits you. Will this be something you will enjoy doing day in and day out? Can you see yourself at work each day, improving the business? Are the customers the type of people you want to interact with? Are the employees the type of individuals you want to supervise and work with? Does this look like fun? Are you passionate about the business?

Make sure the business opportunity will be able to show a profit and a return on your investment. If you purchase an ongoing business, someone else has already taken the risk and high cost of starting a business from scratch. Your goal is not to pay too much for their risk taking. We caution you to not buy a business and then completely revamp it. It is very easy and egotistical for an entrepreneur to think he or she can do much better than the previous owner. But you purchased the business because it was profitable, and it was profitable because of the systems and products in place at the time of purchase. Do not discount them.

By now you are far enough along on your quest to sense the atmosphere of the marketplace, and it is time to explore businesses for sale. Talking to sellers is just one more step toward expanding your entrepreneurship education. Have fun, but leave your checkbook at home.

WHY PURCHASE A BUSINESS?

The overwhelming reason for buying an ongoing business is money, primarily the ongoing income stream. *If* you do your research, and *if* you strike a good deal, you may start making money the day you take over an ongoing business. Because most start-ups plug along for months—on average 2 years—before showing a profit, it is smart to consider this doorway to business ownership. Other items to consider when buying an existing business may include the following:

1. If you find a "hungry seller," you should be able to negotiate good terms. You might be able to buy into a business for very little up-front cash and negotiate seller financing. See Key Points From Another View at the end of the chapter for seller financing specifics.

2. Fixtures and equipment will be negotiable. Be sure the equipment is in good working condition and that it has been well maintained. Ask to see service records and have fixtures and equipment appraised.

3. Training and support may be available through the seller and can sometimes be negotiated. If the seller is financing, he or she will have a stake in your success. Many banks like to see some seller financing, because they believe it secures the seller's interest and thus the bank's interest. You may request that the owner continue to work in the business for a short time to help you adjust and to serve as a bridge with the customers.

4. An established customer base should be in place. You will need to determine how loyal the customers are and whether there is good will or ill will. If the customer base is not strong or loyal, consider this fact appropriately in your price negotiations. If business has recently been souring, good will may be difficult to quantify. Assess the cost and possibility of rebuilding customer loyalty. Also, make sure the business is not dependent on only a few customers or clients.

5. Relationships with suppliers and distributors are in place. Make sure you spend time talking to them to determine the status of the relationship. They will provide great insight into the owner's business. Also, ascertain if there are any special agreements between the owner and the suppliers and distributors that are based on friendships, which may not continue when you purchase the business.

6. The location may be excellent and not easily duplicated. Determine if the lease can be reassigned to you. Have your attorney review the lease and determine if the owner of the building has other goals for the location. Make sure you conduct due diligence to determine if there are any planned changes for the shopping areas, community, environmental restrictions, roads, and so on that may affect the continued success of the current location.

7. Employees may possess specialized knowledge that benefit the business immensely. In high-technology industries, purchasing businesses for

GLOBAL VILLAGE

Test Your Export Quotient

	YES	NO
1. Are you entrepreneurial?	☐	☐
2. Do you have a reliable, service-oriented character?	☐	☐
3. Are you a natural networker who builds and maintains relationships?	☐	☐
4. Do you see yourself as highly organized and research oriented?	☐	☐
5. Have you a sense of mission?	☐	☐
6. Do you possess good communication skills?	☐	☐
7. Is a sales, marketing, or distribution background featured in your résumé?	☐	☐
8. Do you excel in finance and business-related subjects?	☐	☐
9. Do you pride yourself on your strong negotiating skills?	☐	☐
10. Are you experienced in handling complex documentation?	☐	☐
11. Are you an avid follower of global politics?	☐	☐
12. Do you have the ability to speak and write more than one language?	☐	☐
13. Are you sensitive to different cultures?	☐	☐
14. Do you consider yourself able to adopt ideas easily, even under pressure?	☐	☐
15. Are you well traveled or curious about other cultures?	☐	☐
Total (award 1 point for every "yes"):		

Evaluating Your Score

1–6: Although you have acquired some skills related to exporting, you need further assessment to find out if you are suited to this field.

7–10: You show a keen interest in the subject. However, you should consider increasing your knowledge, language, and technical trading skills training.

11–15: You have a high rating in the critical factors that make companies and individuals successful in the exciting field of global trade.

Source: Excerpt from *Global Entrepreneurship Skills,* Module 1, p. 206. Copyright Forum for International Trade Training. Used with permission.

brainpower is common practice. You will have no guarantee, though, that the employees and their expertise will remain—you must consider the possibility that key employees may leave and compete.

8. Existing licenses and permits may be difficult to replicate. Check with your attorney or licensing agencies to determine the availability and process of transferring licenses and permits before proceeding with any purchase.

9. You will be able to see actual financial data and tax-reporting forms. Investigate! Assume they have two sets of books and ask to see both; some firms have three sets. Be skeptical of all reported numbers in any cash-only business.

10. An inside look into the business operation will determine if using advanced technology could increase operational effectiveness and thus profits. Throughout the book we have asked you to explore all business areas where increased efficiency or cost reduction or a change in marketing or distribution strategies could increase sales and profit. Keep these potential changes in mind at all times as you examine businesses for sale.

11. Completing your due diligence will reduce but not eliminate uncertainties when purchasing a business.

HOW TO BUY AND HOW NOT TO BUY

Smart buyers scrutinize everything about a business with a microscope, computer analyses, and sage advice from business gurus. They do not plunge into a business for emotional reasons. For example, you may have eaten lunch around the corner at Millie's with your pals for years, and when the place goes up for sale, nostalgia may make you want to write out a check for it on the spot. That would be a wrong reason to buy.

In purchasing an ongoing business, you will need to use the expertise of experienced **business brokers**, accountants, small-business attorneys, and business appraisers. As when searching for all professionals, use your eyes and ears to search out the best. References are important for each part of your team and should be checked thoroughly. Not only do you want someone who is trustworthy and experienced, you also want to use advisors who have experience in the particular industry or area where you are purchasing a business. Contact several references and ask them how their advisors aided their decision making. Also, ask what the advisors did poorly and what questions they wished they would have asked up front. If utilizing trained, experienced, and honest brokers, the advisors' fees and commissions should be considered minimal when compared to their invaluable expertise.

FranNet and VR Business Brokers are two of the largest franchised business brokerage firms in the United States. In addition, many independent brokers will serve your needs. Business brokers have helped thousands of individuals realize their dreams and reach their financial goals. A business broker's expertise can be invaluable in your search. Always remember, though, that brokers work for the seller, and that is where their allegiance lies. Try not to sign exclusive agreements with brokers.

Locate an attorney with expertise in business-sale transactions and an accountant who thoroughly understands the tax implications involved in the transfer of a business. A good accountant with tax expertise may be able to turn up some interesting legal loopholes that will benefit both buyer and seller. Experienced *industry* accountants will also know where owners hide their problems and where there may be potential for additional profits.

Keep in mind; every business in the country is for sale at some time. Deals are like planes. If you miss one, another one will be along soon.

Good buys are always available to the informed and careful buyer, but they may be difficult to discover. Seeking the right business to buy is much like an employment search: the best deals are seldom advertised. In contrast, the worst business opportunities are advertised widely, usually in the classified sections of newspapers. When you see several advertisements for a particular type of business, you know where the unhappy businesspeople are.

Running your own advertisement may be a good idea. This was true for one man, who ran the following advertisement in the business section (not the classifieds) of a large-circulation Midwestern newspaper:

Business broker A real estate professional who specializes in representing people who want to sell their businesses

Tired of golfing and tennis. Ready to build and manage again. Sold successful business at 35. Desire to buy manufacturing business with more than 6 million dollars in annual sales. Email H.G. at newbusinessfartooyoungtoretire@gmail.com.

H.G. received more than 100 replies and said reading the proposals was one of the most educational and entertaining experiences he has ever had. After researching several of these companies, he joined the legions of people who seek to purchase an established business who never close on their dream.

Spread the Word

Once you are ready to look for a business to purchase, you will need to learn what is for sale. Informing everyone you know that you are a potential buyer will bring in leads. The following tips will also help:

1. Inform your friends, family members, club members, church friends, and anyone else you associate with.
2. Contact everyone you can in your chosen industry—manufacturers, resellers, agents, dealers, trade associations, and so on; let them know you are looking.
3. Ask your network of bankers, attorneys, CPAs, and community leaders to help you in your search.
4. Advertise your desires in trade journals and answer ads which have been posted. In addition, trade associations may rent their member lists; you can use them to send query letters to their members or post online.
5. Send letters or emails of inquiry to potential sellers you have identified (see Action Step 53).
6. Knock on doors. You may be surprised!
7. Network your way to the best business brokers in your area or industry.
8. Talk with firms that deal in mergers and acquisitions.
9. Do not allow yourself to be rushed; time is your ally, and the deals will get better.
10. Check out businesses you would like to operate and buy. Ask the owners if they would consider selling.
11. Look for owners who want to retire or sell due to partnership disagreements, illness, retirement, boredom, or divorce.
12. Look for businesses that are not doing well that you believe your expertise and energy could improve. Make sure the business is not in a shrinking marketplace.
13. Check out businesses with a great product but possibly poor marketing or a poor location. Would a new location or a great marketing campaign help the business take off? If it is a manufactured product, could reducing the costs of production by moving the facility reduce costs enough to make the business profitable?
14. Visit *http://www.BizBuySell.com* (see Figure 13.1 on page 356) and other sites on the Internet which list businesses for sale.
15. Review classifieds in your local and city papers as well as the *Wall Street Journal* and industry magazines.
16. Evaluate whether new technology can increase production, sales, and so on and subsequently profit.
17. Use Internet blogs and social networking sites judiciously to spread the word and look for opportunities. Buyer beware!

Use Action Step 53 to spread the word and discover opportunities.

Action Step 53

Spread the Word

1. If appropriate, send an email to your friends, family, and colleagues, expressing your desire to purchase a business. Lay out your parameters and ask the recipients to forward your email to anyone they think might be of service to you in your search.
2. From the list on this page, select three or four avenues to locate businesses for sale in your industry or area.
3. Locate three businesses and interview the owners.
4. Summarize your thoughts after each visit.

It is best to learn of businesses for sale by networking, but you may find the most eager sellers advertising in the classified section of your local newspaper or through online listings.

Leave your checkbook at home when you visit. This action step will cost you practically nothing. Your goal at this point is to explore opportunities.

INVESTIGATE THE BUSINESS FROM THE OUTSIDE

Once you have located promising opportunities, check them out by playing marketplace detective. This section suggests some techniques that will make you feel like a super spy. After investigating each business from the outside, you will be ready to move inside, review the books, and talk to the owners in an attempt to learn the *real* reasons they are selling. Unfortunately, Ben and Sally Raymundo did not look deep enough and learned about fraud the hard way.

A Story from the Suburbs

Ben and Sally Raymundo bought a women's sportswear store, GeeGees, in a thriving suburban community about two miles from a regional shopping mall. They learned too late that the seller had a more profitable store in another part of the county whose store's records were used to misrepresent the store they bought. Here are the particulars:

1. *The seller moved the computerized register from the higher-volume store to the store she wanted to sell so that the store's sales were greatly inflated.*
2. *The price was fixed at inventory plus $20,000 for* **good will***. This seemed a bargain for a store whose cash register records showed it was grossing $600,000 per year at a 50 percent average gross margin.*
3. *Ben and Sally paid full wholesale value ($100,000) for goods that had been shipped there from the other store, which they did not realize. The "dead goods" were already shopworn and out of date and eventually had to be marked down to less than $20,000.*
4. *Ben and Sally assumed the remainder of an iron-clad lease at $5000 per month, and the landlord made them sign a personal guarantee that pledged their home as security on the lease.*
5. *The location proved to be a dead foot-traffic location in a marginally successful center.*

Fortunately, Ben had kept his regular job. Sally worked at selling off the unwanted inventory and replaced it with more salable stock hoping to survive. They spent $36,000 for advertising during the 12 months they stayed in business. It was another year before the landlord found a new tenant and Ben and Sally could get out of the lease. GeeGee's was a tough and very expensive mistake for Ben and Sally.

Good will An invisible commodity used by sellers to increase the asking price for a business; often it's worth the price.

Learn from Others' Mistakes and Keep Digging

What could Ben and Sally have done to avoid this fiasco? Many things. They could have asked the mall merchants how well the shopping center was doing. They could have spent some time observing the store and the shopping mall before they committed. Parking in front of the store and counting customers and packages would have been beneficial. Checking out the inventory in person would have also helped. They also could have insisted that Sally be allowed to work in the store prior to or during the escrow period, with a clause that would have allowed them to bail out.

Ben and Sally were honest, hardworking people who took the seller at face value—a huge mistake! A talk with suppliers might have uncovered the seller's fraud. They are now suing. The CPA and attorney they have *now* hired could have really helped them *before* they purchased the business. Hiring experts after the fact usually proves expensive, because it puts them on the defense rather than on the offense. The chances of any financial recovery through legal means is slim for Ben and Sally.

Some sellers do not count the value of their own time and money as costs of doing business. This makes the firm show an inflated return on investment (ROI). Suppose a firm earns $100,000 per year and has an inventory of $250,000. This could be a poor investment if the seller, his spouse, and their two children work a total of 200 hours per week and if a $250,000 investment could earn 4 percent or more per year in high-yield bonds. If the business you are considering is a retail business, have friends visit the store at different hours throughout the day to assess how many people are actually working. For many families who run a business that has become their life, honestly assessing the time they devote to the business can be very difficult; your research will provide you with accurate data on which to base your purchasing decision.

Look at each deal from the viewpoint of what it would cost to hire a competent manager and help at market wage rates. In this case, let us suppose you had to pay $50,000 a year for a manager, $30,000 a year for an assistant, and $40,000 a year for two hourly employees. You will have spent $120,000 and lost the opportunity to earn another 5 percent on your investment. Yes, this would be a no-brainer, but a lot of businesses with even less going for them are bought every day.

It is time now to venture out and investigate a business on your own. Remember what you have learned from Ben and Sally's bad experience, and take along your new eyes and your camera. You will be surprised how much there is to see. Action Step 54 tells you how to do it.

Know When You Need Outside Help

We have already discussed the need for a team of small business gurus to help you realize your dream of small-business ownership. When you evaluate a small business for purchase, however, you may need a special kind of outside help. If you have any lingering doubts about the business you are researching, you may need the perspective of someone who is more objective than one of your team players. If you are not the Sherlock Holmes type yourself, hire someone who is. You may have to put your dream on hold as a result of this kind of investigation, but you will save money in the long run.

Georgia Webster had some doubts about the business she and her husband were considering. See what you can learn from the Websters' experiences.

Saved by a Bulldozer

Fred and I graduated from college in 2006, we both loved sports and were college-athletes, so with our parents financial backing we decided to look around for a sporting goods store to buy.

We found the perfect store to buy; The Sports Factory, located a block from a complex of tennis courts, three blocks from a new Pilates and yoga studio, and a quarter mile from a park where volleyball, softball, and soccer tournaments are held every month.

A friend of ours, an accountant, checked over the books. He said they looked perfect. "Great profit and loss statement," he said, "and accounting ratios you wouldn't believe for this business. If you arrive at the right terms, you could clear $40K every quarter, and that's only the beginning. This guy doesn't even advertise."

We learned from the owner that he wanted to sell the store because he was tired of it—the long hours, being tied down, and so on. He'd been at it for a dozen years and he wanted to start enjoying life. We contacted, Harry Henkel, a local entrepreneurship professor, and asked his advice. He offered to spend about 2–3 hours investigating for $400.

Action Step 54

Study a Business from the Outside

Studying a business from the outside will tell you whether you should go inside and probe more deeply. Adjust the five steps below for manufacturing, service, or Internet businesses.

1. **Make sure the business fits into the framework of your industry overview.** You want a business that is in the sunrise phase, not the sunset phase, of the life cycle.

2. **Diagram the area.** What is the location, and how does the area fit into the city and county planning for the future? What is the life-cycle stage of the community? Where is the traffic flow? Is there good access? How far will your Target Customers have to travel to get there? Is parking adequate? Is the parking lot a drop-off point for carpoolers? What is the employee pool of the area?

3. **If the business is a retail business, take photographs of the exterior.** Analyze them carefully. Is the building in good repair? What are the customers wearing, driving, and buying? What can you deduce about their lifestyle? Take photographs on different days and at different times of day.

4. **Talk with and analyze neighbors.** What do the neighboring businesses know about the business for sale? Will their businesses help draw Target Customers to your business? Do you want to be close to competitors—Restaurant Row, Mile of Cars, and other such successful business areas—or do you want to be miles away? Could a competitor move in next door the day after you move in? Ask the tenants about their leases, but understand that each lease can vary.

5. **Interview customers.** What do they like about the store? Is the service good? What changes would they recommend? What services or

(continued)

Action Step 54

(continued)

products would they like to see added? Where else do they go for similar products or services?

6. **Check with local authorities.** What are the plans for this location? What is the local municipality planning to do with sewers, roads, and signage? Are there any new proposals for building permits? If you do not think this is important, read about Georgia's experience in the next section.

Two days later, Harry our marketplace detective called and said he had some news, "I talked to a bulldozer driver working across the street from the Sports Factory today and he told me the property is being developed into a seven-store retail complex, and one of the stores is going to be a discount sporting goods store."

I asked him if the owner knew, and if maybe that's why he's so "tired."

"Yes, I believe so," Harry said. "I double-checked at the city planning office, and the building permit was issued 6 weeks ago." And he paused again.

Georgia and Fred Webster came very close to buying the right business at the wrong time. The outsider's perspective and detective work helped them avoid making a terrible mistake. As valuable as these outside perspectives are, however, you have to have an inside look to truly get a feel for the business you are investigating.

INVESTIGATE THE BUSINESS FROM THE INSIDE

Once you have learned all you can from the outside, it is time to cross the threshold for a look at the inside. This is an important, time-consuming process, but it is an important milestone in your quest.

There are two ways to get inside the business: either contact the owner yourself or receive assistance from a business broker. Professional brokers have access to many listings and may be the only way you will be allowed into many businesses for sale. Locate brokers in the Yellow Pages under *Business Brokers*, newspaper classifieds, industry sources or through networking.

Contact brokers to learn of listings in your area of interest, and meet with several to find a good fit. Be prepared for disappointment as you explore businesses for sale; 90 to 95 percent of people looking for a business for sale never purchase one. You will probably look at a great many businesses before you find anything close to your requirements. Nevertheless, you will learn and benefit from the experience.

Dealing with Brokers

Business brokers are active in most communities and industries, and they play an important role in matching up sellers with buyers. Their level of competency ranges from specialists who know as much about fast-food franchises as Taco Bell to part-timers who know so little about business that they will only waste your time. A good broker can save you time and can be very helpful in playing a third-party role in negotiations.

Fiduciary Legal relationship between two or more parties with loyalty and trust

A broker has a **fiduciary** responsibility to represent the seller and is not paid unless he or she sells something. Typically, the broker's commission is around 10 percent for businesses less than one million dollars, but the percentage is much less on large deals, and everything is open to negotiation. You may prefer a buyer's broker; although they are rare, their first responsibility is to you—but the seller will still pay the commission.

Some sellers list with brokers because they do not want it generally known—to their customers, employees, or competitors—that they want to sell their business. Others who list with brokers, however, do so out of desperation because they have already tried to sell their business to everyone they know.

Spending time with a skilled broker can be a fascinating educational experience. If you want a particular type of business, and you are able to examine a half-dozen that are on the market, you may end up with a better grasp of the overall business situation than the current owners. Network your business contacts to locate a competent broker. Ask brokers for referrals from their former clients. Quiz them on their business knowledge: Can they explain a cash-flow forecast, an **earn-out,** or the **bulk sales law?** And as we have said so many times before, leave your checkbook at home. Do not let anyone rush you. A good business broker will provide several services, and those that follow give you an idea of what to expect.

Matching Buyers and Sellers   If you are a buyer, a business broker will interview you thoroughly to determine your needs, desires, personal and financial goals, and limitations. From your responses and your broker's knowledge of the market, opportunities will be presented to you that best suit your interests, desired lifestyle, abilities, and financial resources. Sharing your Chapter 1 Action Steps with your broker would be an excellent start.

Determining Fair Market Value   Professional business brokers develop strong working relationships with various business, land, commercial, and equipment appraisers who can assist in determining the fair market value of an ongoing business. Their contacts with attorneys and accountants are invaluable. Remember at all times you are paying for and benefiting from your broker's expertise and contacts.

Facilitating the Negotiating Process   Buying a business is an emotionally charged process; you are making a lifestyle decision, as well as making a long-term major financial investment. You will therefore benefit greatly from an experienced third party serving as a go-between. A broker understands the motives behind each party and thus keeps the process moving forward.

Untangling Red Tape   Assistance in acquiring necessary permits and licenses, as well as help with locating financing and reputable escrow companies, are all part of the responsibilities of a professional broker.

The BizBuySell Web site, affiliated with the *Wall Street Journal,* database of businesses for sale can be searched by state, county, business category, and asking price in addition to home-based business and those that are relocatable. Figure 13.1 highlights a recent search on BizBuySell for Indiana manufacturing businesses priced from $1,000,000 to $5,000,000 appears in Figure 13.1.

Below are broker listings from BizBuySell for a manufacturer, a retailer, and an Internet business.

Earn out The seller agrees to accept a portion of his payment for the business from the business's future earnings

Bulk sales law Uniform Commercial Code governs transfer of goods from seller to single buyer

---

Samples of Business Brokers' Listings from www.BizBuySell.com

Medical & Surgical Instrument and Prototype I

Fort Wayne, Indiana, Indiana (Allen County)

Mfg.—Measuring & Analyzing Instr. | Mfg.—Miscellaneous Manufacturing

Asking Price $2,700,000	Inventory $100,000 (Approximate)*
Gross Income $1,302,613	Real Estate $600,000*
Cash Flow $436,864	Year Established 1976
FF&E $750,000*	Employees 8

* included in the asking price

It is rare for a unique business like this to find its way to the marketplace. The sellers have established a solid foundation in the medical industry. They seek an aggressive new owner to take this business to the next level and beyond. It is important to understand that this is a "model shop" environment, building prototypes of surgical instruments that are used primarily in the implementation and retrieval of orthopedic devices, but is not limited to such. The prototypes eventually become small product runs, anywhere

figure **13.1**

Business for Sale on BizBuySell.com

8 Businesses found

location: IN
options: **Price from 1000000, Price to 5000000**
categories: **Manufacturing Businesses**

Listings by Email   Sign up to receive new for-sale listings by email for free.

| Established Businesses | Franchises | Asset Sales | Start-Up Businesses | Real Estate |

Refine your results   Enter city or keyword   go ▶   or Start a New Search

FEATURED BROKER   More Indiana brokers
Houston D Jones Jr   THE HOUSTON GROUP, INC.

Houston has over 20 years of experience in the Restaurant industry from actually owning and operations of his own to designing , building and brokering some of Louisville areas finest restaurants. Houston has a well rounded knowledge of the area and industry to match potential buyers or enterpenuers concepts for sale. Our only focus is restaurants and your sucess.

Established Businesses for Sale	Asking	Cash Flow	Location
Commercial Bakery	$4,000,000	Undisclosed	Indianapolis, IN
Flexible Packaging Mfg. - Plastic Bag converting and...	$3,300,000	$663,000	IN
Successful Commercial & Business Printing Service	$1,200,000	$250,000	South Cent..., IN
Highly Profitable Publishing Business	$1,295,000	$533,224	Central In..., IN
Highly Profitable Contract Manufacturing / Machine Shop	$1,300,000	$725,000	Northern I..., IN
Surgical Instrument Manufacturer Enjoying Banner Yea...	$2,700,000	$441,311	Fort Wayne..., IN
Industrial Painting Company	$1,200,000	$391,000	Fort Wayne, IN
Custom Plastic Injection Molder - Automotive	$4,500,000	$1,250,000	IN

Source: *http://www.BizBuySell.com* (Accessed January 29, 2008).

from a few dozen per month to hundreds or thousands of very specific instruments, fixtures, and devices. Many of the products repeat themselves periodically as short runs, while the stream of new prototypes and modifications to existing products is perpetual. The company not only supports the traditional medical industry, but also the veterinary industry and even some dental. This company is located in Northern Indiana.

Facilities: This medical instrument manufacturer is housed in an FDA-compliant facility. The building is approximately 10,000 s.f. and is strategically placed on a 4-acre parcel in an industrial park. The equipment inside includes machinery ranging from simple Bridgeport machines and workstations to more complex wire EDMs and CNCs. It is all arranged in a "model shop" environment.

Competition: Since 1976, this company has met the demands of the medical industry with optimum quality and has secured the trust and dependability of a loyal base of customers. This company's "niche" is its desire to manufacture very small quantities at acceptable, premium prices, while maintaining a high degree of confidentiality. Whereas the competition becomes quickly disinterested because they do not understand the value in small runs.

Growth/Expansion: Growth possibilities are endless because new medical devices are constantly being developed and introduced. The aging U.S. population, as well as the high rate of obesity at younger ages and the rapid growth in the veterinary industry, are all causing this market to escalate. Current ownership just keeps a finger on the pulse of the industry and does not aggressively market its products at this time. This creates a distinct advantage for the buyer who can build upon the current base and increase the sales volume rapidly.

Financing: Buyer required to have substantial investment equity and liquidity.

Support/Training: Ownership is dedicated to ensuring a smooth transition. Will stay on board, with an employment contract, for as long as needed, up to 5 years or more.

Reason Selling: Preparation for eventual retirement in the next 5 years.

Fairhope Alabama Contemporary Boutique

Fairhope, Alabama (Baldwin County)

Retail—Apparel & Accessory Stores | Retail—Home Furniture & Furnishings

Asking Price	$135,000	Inventory	$56,000*
Gross Income	$322,970	Real Estate	
Cash Flow	$36,758	Year Established	N/A
FF&E	$24,000*	Employees	N/A

* included in the asking price

Hurry so you can accompany the owner to market on February 14 to preview and order the fall lines! This very attractive boutique is in downtown Fairhope, Alabama, a picturesque town on Mobile Bay near the white sands of the Gulf of Mexico. The exclusive lines of contemporary ladies clothing and apparel appeal to young ladies from 21 to 39. Most of the lines are rarely seen, and they have a line of privately branded clothing. They have an excellent Web site. Sales were $322,970 in just its first full year. The store is profitable, and the purchase price includes $56,000 of current fashion inventory. The fixtures are great, there is an excellent point-of-sale system, and the location is one of the most attractive in town. The store is on the main walking part of downtown, easily accessible to both the growing local customer base as well as the many guests and visitors to the city. The owner will train and even accompany the new owner to market in both Atlanta and New York. There are three great employees that would be a wonderful asset for the new owner. There is a highly recommended business manager who would also be available for the new owner who may desire continuing support.

The Internet Ergonomic Superstore for products, services, and more

San Diego, California (San Diego County) (relocatable)

Internet – Consumer Services (B2C) | Internet – Business Services (B2B)

Asking Price $850,000	Inventory
Gross Income $450,000	Real Estate
Cash Flow Not Disclosed	Year Established 2000
FF&E N/A	Employees 3

Ergoboy.com was conceived in 2000 with the idea that ergonomics should extend into all aspects of our daily life. Our mission at Ergoboy.com is to promote and advance an awareness of ergonomic principles and products. We offer ideas and information that improve efficiency and comfort and encourage prevention. We are committed to bringing the latest information and cutting-edge products that will improve the efficiency and safety of life today and for the future. Ergoboy.com, the Internet Ergonomic Superstore and low-price leader, offers its customers hundreds of ergonomic products in a range of categories including computer users, office and industrial, home, driving, kids, elderly, disabled, travelers, sports, communication, students, musicians, pets, as well as ergonomic services and more. Individuals and businesses can shop quickly and easily at Ergoboy.com 24 hours a day, 7 days a week. This company holds top rankings on search engines for the most competitive commercial and informational search terms in its market. Site generates 100% of traffic through natural and paid search-engine results and destination visitorship. Site performs no advertising or marketing of any kind. Company carries hundreds of products and represents over 25 leading suppliers in the ergonomic and innovative products industry. All product is drop shipped and company carries no inventory. This site is rapidly growing, both in terms of traffic and sales. Please reply for more information to contact an agent of the company.

Facilities: Ergoboy.com Web site with over 1000 Web pages.

Competition: Leading source of online ergonomic products and services as well as information.

Growth/Expansion: During the first 5 years of business, sales grew by 300% annually.

Support/Training: Training in all aspects of company operations is provided.

Brokers have provided the information in these listings. BizBuySell has no stake in the sale of these businesses, has not independently verified any of such information, and assumes no responsibility for its accuracy or completeness. Read the disclaimer at *http://bizbuysell.com/legal.htm* before responding to any ad.

Source: *http://www.BizBuySell.com* (Accessed January 29, 2008).

HOW TO LOOK AT THE INSIDE OF A BUSINESS

Once you have wedged your foot in the door and have established yourself as a potential buyer, you will be able to study the inner workings of the business. Take full advantage of this opportunity, and do not stop until you have investigated the business thoroughly and *all* your questions are answered.

Does the thought of walking into someone's business for the purpose of snooping around, looking at the books, and asking the owner probing questions still fill you with anxiety and make you nervous? It should not. Sellers expect

Action Step 55

Study a Business from the Inside

Looking at a business from the inside enables you to determine its real worth and to see what it would be like to own it. In the past Action Steps you have been exploring but now you are ready to look inside and look at hard data.

Make an appointment—or have a business broker arrange it—to take a serious inside look at the business or businesses you think you might want to buy. Before you go, review everything we have explained in this chapter, and make a list of detailed questions. Do not allow anyone to rush you.

Leave the checkbook at home; this fun is free.

prospective buyers who are seriously looking for a business to buy to do those things. After reading this next section, you will be ready for Action Step 55, investigating a business close up.

Study the Financial History

What you need to learn from the financial history is where the money comes from and where it goes. Ask to see all financial records, preferably audited ones, for at least the past 5 years, and take your time studying them. Hire an accountant with *industry experience* to review the records. Your aim in buying an ongoing business is to step into an income stream. The financial records give a picture of how fast the stream is flowing and where there might be dams along the way.

Before allowing you to review financial documents, most sellers and brokers will screen and qualify you as a potential buyer. They want to make sure only buyers with the financial ability to purchase are shown company financial data. You will be required to present your personal financial data to the seller or broker. In addition, signing a nondisclosure agreement assures the seller that you will not talk to employees, suppliers, or customers until an appropriate, agreed-upon time. You will also be prohibited from disclosing any information about the business to others except your advisors, who also must not disclose any information. You may also be requested to sign a non-piracy agreement, which prevents you from pirating the business's system, products, or ideas.

Review cash-flow statements, profit and loss statements, accounts receivables, and payables. If the seller has a stack of accounts receivable a foot high, remember that, in general:

- After 3 months, the value of a current account's dollar will have shrunk to 90 cents.
- After 6 months, it will be worth 50 cents.
- After a year, it will be worth 30 cents or less, depending on the industry.

Review every receipt you can find. If a fast-food owner tells you he sells 900 hamburgers per week, ask to see the receipts from the suppliers. If none are offered, ask permission to contact the suppliers for records of shipment. Make him prove to you what he has bought from suppliers so you can accurately measure sales. If the seller will not cooperate, run—do not walk—away; the seller is hiding something. You can use this technique with any firm that is buying and marking up material or merchandise.

Evaluate closely any personal expenses that are being charged to the business. This allows you to get a clearer picture of the firm's true profits. Your accountant will help you with this.

It is also a good idea to review canceled checks, income tax returns (preferably for the past 5 years), and the amount of salary the seller has been paying himself or herself. If your seller was stingy with his or her own salary, decide whether you could live on that amount. Look for items that the seller may have purchased for his home and run through the business.

Many cash businesses will be very difficult to evaluate. Owners many times skim cash off the top and do not report it to the IRS. Beware of cash-only businesses.

If the seller brags that she does not pay her taxes, ask yourself if you can trust her. If she is willing to lie to the IRS, which can land her in jail, she will more than likely be willing to lie to you.

Make sure the owner has not been paying his employees in cash. If he is, employee costs will be underestimated. Explore whether family members are working in the business and not getting paid. If so, projected employee costs will need to be revised. Many owners also underestimate the number of hours they personally work. If you will be hiring a manager to run the business, you may need to hire a full-time manager and an assistant to cover the number of hours the owner alone has been willing to devote to the business.

The following provides a list of items you need to review with the owner, your accountant, your attorney, and business broker before finalizing your purchase of any business. Depending on the industry, additional items will need to be evaluated as suggested by your team of experts. Following the steps we have outlined in Chapter 13 may take you several weeks or months. Do not skip any steps in your haste to purchase a business.

Due Diligence: Items for Review

Accounting services contract

Accounts payable records (if not being paid within 30 days, be on alert)

Accounts receivable records (aging?)

Advertising agreements with media companies (usually not assumable)

Agreements (franchise, other)

Appraisals (equipment, land, buildings)

Bank account statements including deposit receipts, checking-account statements with canceled checks

Community relationships and support

Contributions and dues records

Copyrights, trademarks, patents

Corporate minutes book

Credit-card company agreements

Creditworthiness of customers

Customer agreements (wholesale)

Employment contracts (oral or written) and evaluation of their individual roles with clients or customers

Equipment lease agreements (check to see if assumable; if they are—which is rare— what will it take to assume these?)

Equipment suppliers list

Financial statements for past 3 years, profit and loss statement, balance sheet

Industry relationships and reputation

Insurance policies, including property, liability, medical, business interruption (beware of potential large increases)

Inventory list (current or out of date?)

Labor union problems

Leasehold agreements and options to renew

Legislation or pending legislation that might affect the business

Licenses and fees

Liens

Maintenance records, receipts, and agreements

Noncompete agreements

Number of customers and percentage of sales

Payroll records

Personal and financial affairs of sellers (private investigators provide services)

Personnel policies including vacation, sick leave, maternity, commissions, deferred compensation, pensions, stock options, and profit sharing

Recipes

Records of litigation and notice of litigation pending against the business or anyone associated with the business

Roles and responsibilities of owners and top employees

Supplier agreements and contracts

Taxes, including personal property, municipal, sales, and employment taxes, along with IRS returns

Travel and entertainment details

Utility bills, including telephone (consider possible utility changes that might adversely affect business—i.e., skyrocketing electric costs)

Warranties, invoices, titles, encumbrances, operating instructions, manuals

Web sites and agreements with advertisers

Word of mouth (evaluating good will and ill will)

Zoning (potential changes)

Evaluate Tangible Assets

Inventory Items carried in stock

If the numbers initially look good, move on to assess the value of everything you can touch, specifically real estate, equipment and fixtures, and **inventory**. Pay advisors and consultants to guide you in assessing the assets.

1. **Real estate:** Order an outside professional appraisal of the building and the land. Review deeds, titles, liens, and title insurance, and have them reviewed by your attorney. Have property inspected.

2. **Equipment and fixtures:** Remember, these are used. You can arrive at a good idea of current market values by asking equipment dealers and reading want ads. Scour your area for the best deals, because you do not want to tie up too much capital in equipment that is outmoded or about to come apart. Suppliers and brokers have lots of leads on used equipment, so check with them. If you are not an expert in the equipment field, seek help from someone who is. Expensive used equipment will need to be appraised by an equipment specialist.

3. **Inventory:** Count the inventory yourself, and make sure the boxes are packed with what you think they are. Make certain you specify the exact contents of shelves and cabinets in the purchase agreement. Do not be careless and write in something vague like: "All shelves are to be filled." Specify what goes on the shelves. Once you have made your count, contact suppliers to learn the current prices. If you find merchandise that is damaged, out of date, out of style, soiled, worn, or not ready to sell as is, do not pay full or even half price for it. *Negotiate.* This is salvage merchandise, and it should have a salvage price tag.

4. **Lease/Location:** How important is location to success? Parking? Walk-in or drive-by traffic? Transportation? Signage? Storage space? Expansion capabilities? Are there deferred maintenance costs?

Talk to Insiders   There is no substitute for inside information. Every detective takes it seriously.

1. **Suppliers:** Will suppliers agree to keep supplying you? Are there past difficulties between seller and suppliers that you would inherit as the new owner? Are there alternative suppliers available? Remember, you are initially dependent on your suppliers and the relationships which currently exist.

2. **Employees:** Identify key employees early. In small business, success may rest on the shoulders of one or two people, and you do not want them to walk out the day you sign papers. Usually business owners will forbid you to talk with employees until the sale is finalized. You must honor this request no matter how difficult it may make your decision. If and when you are able to talk with the employees, consider all they have to share with you. Consider that you may need to provide incentives to keep key employees. Include those incentives when evaluating the final terms of the sale.

3. **Competitors:** Identify major competitors and interview them to learn what goes on from their perspective. Expect some bias, but watch for a pattern to develop. Are there price wars? What sets apart each competitor? What sets your opportunity apart? (Review Chapter 5 for competitor research clues.)

4. **Customers:** Who are the major customers? What percentage of sales is generated from the major players? Is their loyalty to the business or to the owner?

Analyze the Seller's Motives

People have many reasons for selling their business. Some of these reasons favor the buyer, and others favor the seller. The following reasons may favor the buyer:

1. Retirement
2. Too busy to manage—seller has other investments
3. Divorce, family problems
4. Disgruntled partners
5. Expanded too fast—out of cash
6. Poor management
7. Burned out, lost interest
8. Ill health
9. Change in lifestyle
10. Wants new challenge
11. Owner incapable of embracing new technology

Beware of the following reasons for sellers wishing to exit their businesses:

1. Local economy in a decline
2. Specific industry declining
3. Intense competition
4. High insurance costs
5. Increasing litigation and costs
6. Skyrocketing rents
7. Technological obsolescence
8. Problems with suppliers
9. High–crime-rate location
10. Lease not being renewed
11. Location in decline
12. Potential laws changing the business landscape
13. Employment issues (potential lawsuits, changes in employment law, and attrition of best employees)

EXAMINING THE ASKING PRICE

Many owners view selling their firm as they would view selling their homes; that is, they are emotionally attached to the business and therefore overvalue its worth. Pride also plays a role: they want to brag about how much they sold out for. If you run into irrational and emotional owners, walk away or turn to your professional team to intervene and develop a fair agreement. In addition to reviewing all past records, you need to assess the future financial outlook for the business, the economy, and the industry. Remember you are buying the future not the past. Take the time to write a complete Business Plan based on the Action Steps throughout the text before you purchase a business.

Now that you have looked inside and outside of the business, reviewed the firm's past history, and looked to future potential, you and the seller must agree on a price that is beneficial to both of you. In this section, we provide you with several ways to value businesses, and we guide you to online information and professionals who can help you. As noted earlier, price is only one element in the negotiations; we encourage you to look at all the issues. The Incredible Resource on pages 363 to 365 leads to an excellent online cash requirements worksheet and a pricing worksheet. After you have completed your research, completing the worksheets will provide information to use in your negotiations.

Rule-of-Thumb Pricing

We will discuss many ways to determine price, but one of the easiest ones is rule-of-thumb pricing, which gives you an idea—a ballpark price—to work with. Still, you need to realize that the motive of the seller, the business, and future potential play a major role in valuation. General rule-of-thumb pricing, provided below by BizBuySell.com, serves as an illustration.

INNS/BED AND BREAKFASTS
Rule of Thumb:

- $50,000–100,000 per guest room
- 3 times net operating income + $20,000–40,000 for aesthetics and task benefits plus value of real estate and furnishings

Pricing Tips and Information

Income is usually $5,000 to $10,000 per guest room depending on location. Business evolved from stagecoach stops to about 20,000 B&Bs and inns today. Usually an antique house and furnishings, most have private baths now. Operating expense can range from $3,000 to $10,000 per room, depending on occupancy and size of building. What is the comparative value of the underlying real estate? What will the bottom-line return be?

Investment plus a lifestyle business. Cast a wide net when reviewing the rack rates of other lodging properties to establish pricing policies.

Debt service shouldn't exceed 40% of gross room income. I pay attention to building maintenance, marketing, and business records. The better these items are, the more positively I can value the property with business.

FLORISTS
Rule of Thumb:

- 34% of annual gross sales + inventory
- $1.7 \times$ SDC (owner's cash flow) + inventory

incredible resource

Interactive Pricing Worksheet on BizBuySell.com

Overview of Business Pricing Method

The method used for our pricing calculations is a very basic model that is most appropriate for small privately held businesses. It is not a valuation method, but a simple way of calculating an approximate price for a small business. It is a good starting point in which to begin negotiations.

    It is based on calculating the earning power of the business to arrive at the goodwill factor of the business. This is then added to the fixed assets, the inventory and the furniture, fixtures and equipment (FF&E). This total is the basic price of the business.

    Remember, a seller may ask for more than this basic rule of thumb price, and the buyer may want to pay less.

Section 1: Adjusted Income and Expense Worksheet

Income (latest 12 months)

Sales	$_____
Other Income	$_____

Adjustments to Income. If there are any subtractions from the stated income such as a one-time income item, enter both a note describing the adjustment(s) as well as the dollar amount to be subtracted.

_____ $_____

Total Income	**$0**
Cost of Goods Sold	$_____
Total Gross Profit	**$0**

Expenses (latest 12 months)

Owner's Salary	$_____
Other Payroll	$_____
Outside Labor	$_____
Payroll Taxes	$_____
Employee benefits (including medical and life insurance)	$_____
Utilities	$_____
Telephone	$_____
Insurance (business only)	$_____
Rent	$_____
Travel and entertainment	$_____
Auto	$_____
Auto expenses (gas, insurance, etc.)	$_____
Legal and Accounting	$_____
Depreciation	$_____
Interest	$_____
Advertising	$_____
Dues and subscriptions	$_____
Bad debt expense	$_____
Supplies	$_____
Miscellaneous expenses	$_____

Total Expenses	**$0**
Net Profit Before Taxes	**$0**

Adjustments to Expenses. Most methods used to arrive at a fair selling price are based on a reconstruction of the business's profit and loss statement. This process goes by several different names—normalizing the statements or adding back to the statements. What these adjustments do show is the true earning power or cash flow of the business. By adding all of the non-essential items not necessary to operate the business and the non-cash items plus the net profit, a more realistic cash flow for the business can be depicted. If the business shows a loss, then the cash flow is the add-backs less the loss. Items to consider are:

Owner's salary	$_____
Travel and entertainment	$_____
Contributions to retirement and/or medical insurance programs	$_____
Auto	$_____
Auto expenses (gas, insurance, etc.)	$_____
Depreciation	$_____
Interest expense	$_____
Any other non-applicable expenses (note below)	

_____ $_____

Total Adjustments	**$0**
Total Discretionary Cash Flow	**$0**

(continued)

(continued)

Section 2: Assets Worksheet

1) Inventory The inventory is priced at seller's cost and included in the price you will calculate. This means that the seller must provide an estimate of the inventory for pricing purposes. It also means that that the full price will fluctuate as the inventory increases or decreases. It should be noted whether the suggested selling price includes the inventory and, if so, how much. The actual value of the inventory will be determined at the time of closing. If the inventory is of significant value it is recommended that an inventory service be used (consult your local yellow pages).

Inventory at Cost	$_____

2) Furniture, Fixtures and Equipment (FF&E) The value of the FF&E is also included in the price you will calculate. It is assumed that the value of the FF&E is the actual replacement value. If you need a rough "rule of thumb" for calculating the replacement value of the FF&E, take the FF&E depreciated value and multiply it by 150%.

Approximate Replacement Value of FF&E	$_____
3) Discretionary Cash Flow (From Section 1)	$0
Basic Rule of Thumb Approximate Selling Price (Cash Flow + Asset Value)	$0

Section 3: Business Comparables

Use the multipliers developed in the for-sale or sold comps section of the pricing Report, or use multipliers from your own analysis. These multipliers will then be used with the gross income and estimated cash flow from Section 1 above to develop two estimated asking prices.

Gross Income Multiplier	$ 0.00
Cash Flow Multiplier	$ 0.00
Last 12 Months Gross Income (From Section 1)	$0
Selling Price Gross Income Rule of Thumb	$0
Discretionary Cash Flow (From Section 1)	$0
Selling Price Cash Flow Rule of Thumb	$0

Summary: Basic Selling Price Rules of Thumb

Based on all the factors contained in this Pricing Worksheet, the business under consideration has an estimated selling price within the range of the various "Rules of Thumb" developed above and summarized below:

Basic Rule of Thumb (Approximate Selling Price) (Cash Flow + Asset Value)	$0
Gross Income Multiplier Rule of Thumb (Gross Income Multiplier [0.00] × Gross Income)	$0
Cash Flow Multiplier Rule of Thumb (Cash Flow Multiplier [0.00] × Cash Flow)	$0

Interactive Cash Requirements Worksheet on BizBuySell.com

Section 1: Initial Cash

Total Cash Down Payment	$_____
Inventory (if not included in purchase price)	$_____
Other	$_____

Section 2: Existing Encumbrances
Non-cash, to be assumed

Existing Seller Loans	$_____
Equipment Loan	$_____
Other	$_____

Section 3: Seller Financing

Non-cash, new loan created to be owed to seller	$_____

Section 4: Closing Costs

Attorney or escrow fees	$_____
Inventory service	$_____
Insurance prorations	$_____
Reimbursement of lease deposits	$_____
Miscellaneous prorations	$_____
Other	$_____

(continued)

(continued)

Section 5: Startup Costs

Utility deposits	$_____
Liquor license fees	$_____
Business license permits	$_____
Insurance costs	$_____
Taxes, bonds, etc.	$_____
Legal & accounting	$_____
Workman's compensation	$_____
Prorations or other closing costs (not included in Section 4)	$_____
Other	$_____

Source: *http://www.BizBuySell.com* (Accessed January 29, 2008).

Pricing Tips and Information

These stores are usually sold for depreciated price of fixtures and equipment plus dry inventory and one-half year's net "recasted" profit before taxes. Another industry standard is 25% of the annual gross sales, plus F&E and inventory at cost. Floral stores are usually small, space is not a problem, and rent should never run over 3% of gross sales; 7% (triple net) would be more realistic for a retail store.

Annually, Americans spend about $7.5 billion on cut flowers, which works out to be about $28 per person. Roses make up about a quarter of these sales. (Society of American Florists)

Sometimes rule-of-thumb pricing is more difficult to determine, as with rapidly expanding Internet and technology businesses, although purchasing and evaluating online businesses is facilitated by the fact that all transactions are usually conducted via PayPal and credit cards. In addition, repeat sales, visits, and marketing efforts are usually tracked by the owner and are easily accessible. If you are purchasing an Internet business, utilize an appraiser and broker who are experienced in evaluating online businesses and who understand the intricacies of source codes, Webmasters, Internet metrics, search engine optimization, programming, passwords, e-mail lists, and online credit card processing.

Online Sources of Sales and Transactional Data

Online private-firm resources provide excellent financial information on businesses that have been sold and those currently for sale. Most of these databases can be searched by company size, location, sales, income, number of employees, and selling price. In addition, many of these databases provide information on individual transactions.

Table 13.1 on page 366 illustrates BizComp's compilation of data on printing businesses sold throughout the central United States. To determine comparisons for your area and selected industry, logon to *http://BizComps.com*, where reports can be purchased for less than $150.

Another source for pricing reports and evaluation reports can be found at *http://BizBuySell.com* for a reasonable fee. Figure 13.2a contains a BizBuySell evaluation report for retail home furnishing stores that are currently for sale and 13.2b contains those retail home furnishing stores that have sold. Please note that the average multipliers for the firms for sale are substantially higher than the multipliers for those firms that *have* sold.

table **13.1**

All Food Product Distributors Sold in BIZCOMPS Data Base

EXHIBIT #34-All Food Product Distributors in Data Base

Asking PR (000)	SIC #	Bus Type	SALES W/INV (000)	SDE (000)	SDE/ SALES	SALE DATE	PR(000) W/INV	SALE/ %DOWN	SALE/ TERMS	INV/ SALES	SALE/ SDE	FF&E (000)	RENT/ AMT (000)	RENT/ SALES	DAYS ON MKT	AREA
1500	5141	Distr-Food Products	4,359	303	0.07	1/6/05	1250	100%	N/A	0.29	4.1	200	N/A	3%	999	Maryland
450	5141	Distr-Food Products	1,687	205	0.12	9/3/04	450	100%	N/A	0.27	2.2	20	30	0.9%	558	Georgia
2555	5141	Distr-Food Products	4,787	610	0.13	11/20/03	2263	100%	N/A	0.47	3.7	458	46	1.7%	526	Georgia
555	5141	Distr-Food Products	2,592	168	0.06	11/7/03	480	28%	4Yrs @8%	0.19	2.9	280	185	N/A	119	Florida
709	5141	Mfg/Distr-Food Products	400	104	0.26	10/31/03	409	75%	2Yrs @6%	1.02	3.9	29	30	N/A	150	Los Angeles, CA
1300	5141	Distr-Food Products	3,701	337	0.09	10/9/03	964	100%	N/A	0.26	2.9	407	63	1.7%	356	Florida
675	5141	Distr-Food Products	1,201	212	0.18	8/27/03	675	59%	5Yrs@7%	0.56	3.2	50	40	1.4%	127	Florida
600	5141	Whsle-Detr Products	1,380	204	0.15	3/30/03	500	100%	N/A	0.36	2.5	20	N/A	0.9%	60	Los Angeles, CA
700	5141	Distr-Food Products	2,786	650	0.23	2/10/03	700	35%	2Yrs@7%	0.25	1.1	26	310	0.7%	31	Georgia
750	5141	Distr-Food Products	1,500	257	0.17	1/2/03	750	80%	10Yrs @6.5%	0.50	2.9	40	2	5%	540	Colorado
395	5141	Distr-Import Food Products	1,535	142	0.09	9/1/02	350	100%	N/A	0.23	2.5	26	175	N/A	365	Fresno, CA
600	5141	Distr-Food Products	1,371	187	0.14	8/26/02	425	31%	10 Yrs @ 8.5%	0.31	2.3	100	125	3.5%	200	Florida
484	5141	Distr-Food Products	2,661	206	0.08	10/22/01	484	100%	N/A	0.18	2.3	33	185	2.2%	68	Colorado
602	5141	Distr-Frozen Food	638	209	0.33	8/15/01	462	36%	5Yrs@10%	0.72	2.2	12	128	1.1%	225	Florida
3845	5141	Distr-Dry Food Products	10,500	830	0.08	4/30/01	2645	100%	N/A	0.25	3.2	500	970	N/A	184	Florida
650	5141	Distr-Prepared Meals	2,444	187	0.08	3/23/00	500	100%	N/A	0.20	2.7	100	232	2.3%	55	Southeast Florida
475	5141	Distr-Food Products	2,094	266	0.13	10/6/98	430	100%	N/A	0.21	1.6	0	67	N/A	107	West Central
875	5141	Distr-Food Products	6,500	337	0.05	5/31/97	865	40%	7Yrs@9%	0.13	2.6	250	100	N/A	N/A	Inland Empire, CA
800	5141	Distr-Frozen Food	819	293	0.36	8/27/02	781	51%	5Yrs@8%	0.95	2.7	50	500	1.6%	191	Florida

All Food Product Distributors in Data Base For
An Average of 81% of Asking Price
Median = .27

Average Sale Price Divided By Gross Sales
= .39 (i.e: Sale Price Was 39% of gross Sales)
Median = .27

Average Sale Price Divided By SDE 2.7
(i.e: Sale Price Was 2.7 Times SDE)

Source: Jack Sanders, BIZCOMPS 2006, National Industrial Edition. Additional Information can be found in at www.Bizcomps.com Jack Sanders 702-454-0072.

figure **13.2a**

BizBuySell.com
Valuation Report for Businesses for Sale

FOR-SALE COMPARABLES ANALYSIS
Prepared for:
Business Category: Retail—Home Furniture & Furnishings
Location of Business: All US States

GROSS INCOME ANALYSIS

No. of businesses in Gross Income Analysis	572
Average Asking Price	$452,024
Average Gross Income	$819,240
Average Gross Income Multiplier	.55
Median Gross Income Multiplier	.51

CASH FLOW ANALYSIS

No. of businesses in Cash Flow Analysis	515
Average Asking Price	$477,683
Average Cash Flow	$148,787
Average Cash Flow Multiplier	3.21
Median Cash Flow Multiplier	2.50

Source: *http://www.bizbuysell.com/cgi-bin/xcomps4* (Accessed Februaury 6, 2008).

Excellent individual transaction reports, such as the one shown in Table 13.2, can be purchased through *http://www.bvmarketdata.com*. This particular report from Pratt's Stats provides the financial details and transactional information for the sale of Quality Care Solutions, a software firm.

Firstresearch.com offers excellent industry profiles that cover the competitive landscape, products, operations, technology, sales, marketing, finance, regulation, regional and international issues, human resources, recent developments, business challenges, trends, opportunities, and potential questions for business owners. If you were considering purchasing a business, but you had little knowledge of the industry—something we would not recommended— such a report would be an excellent starting point for you. If you are familiar with the industry, you will be sure to learn additional information. In addition, the reports, which can be purchased online for $129, cover financial ratios, balance sheet, and income statements for over 200 industries.

The Incredible Resource on pages 363–365 provides two excellent workshets on pricing and cash requirements, which are interactive online at BizBuySell.com. The cash requirement worksheet will allow you to work with different purchase scenarios to determine your cash requirements for the initial purchase and start-up phase of the business you are purchasing. You need to be careful to be sure enough cash is on hand for day-to-day operations after initial cash and start-up needs are funded. Remember, as discussed previously, positive cash flow is what keeps you afloat. In addition to rule of thumb pricing, businesses are evaluated in a wide variety of methods such as those that follow.

Valuation Methodologies

Strictly speaking, a company's fair market value is the price at which the business would change hands between a willing buyer and a willing seller when neither is under any compulsion to buy or sell and both parties have knowledge of relevant facts. This is a somewhat circuitous statement, because it begs the question, how do buyers and sellers arrive at this value?

figure **13.2b**

BizBuySell.com Valuation Report for Businesses Sold

SOLD COMPARABLES ANALYSIS
Prepared for:
Business Category: Retail—Home Furniture & Furnishings
Location of Business: All US States

GROSS INCOME ANALYSIS

No. of businesses in Gross Income Analysis	361
Average Sold-For Price	$343,662
Average Gross Income	$924,887
Average Gross Income Multiplier	.37
Median Gross Income Multiplier	.35

CASH FLOW ANALYSIS

No. of businesses in Cash Flow analysis	354
Average Sold-For Price	$349,560
Average Cash Flow	$145,602
Average Cash Flow Multiplier	2.40
Median Cash Flow Multiplier	2.00

SOLD-FOR/ASKING PRICE ANALYSIS

No. of businesses in Asking/Sold-For Price Analysis	361
Average Asking Price	$402,142
Average Sold-For Price	$343,662
Sold-For Price as a Percentage of Asking Price	85%

ABOUT THESE REPORTS [13.2a and 13.2b]
These comparables analysis reports give snapshots of the current businesses for sale and those sold in the BizBuySell database created and maintained by business brokers that are members of BizBuySell.com/BrokerWorks.

Each comparables report contains both dollar averages as well as average and median multipliers. For comparable asking prices, we suggest you use the median multiplier numbers as the averages may include numbers that are significantly outside the normal range.

The numbers contained in this comparables report have not been verified by BizBuySell or any professional business broker or appraiser, so if you use them, you use them at your own risk. They can serve as a "ballpark" starting point, and can provide an approximation of what a particular business might be offered and sold at—but they do not replace a professional valuation.

This information is for your business use only and cannot be reproduced, copied or used for any commercial purpose other than your internal office use or direct one-on-one presentations to a client of, or advisor to, your business and cannot be distributed, made available or promoted in any form whatsoever to groups of individuals without the prior written permission of BizBuySell.com, Inc.

Source: *http://www.bizbuysell.com/cgi-bin/xcomps5* (Accessed Febrauary 6, 2008).

Arriving at the transaction price requires that a value be placed on the company for sale. The process of arriving at this value should include a detailed, comprehensive analysis that takes into account a range of factors, including the past, present, and—most important—the future earnings and prospects of the company.

Valuing a business is not an exact science. The valuation process involves comparing several different approaches and selecting the best method, or a combination of methods, based on the analyst's knowledge and experience. Practitioners use several different methods to value businesses. Among these are:

1. Asset-based valuation
2. Comparable transactions analysis
3. Comparable public company method
4. Discounted cash flow

— table **13.2**

Pratt's Stats Transaction Report

Pratt's Stats® Transaction Report   Prepared: 1/18/2008 12:13:24 PM (PST)

Seller Details

Company Name:	Quality Care Solutions, Inc.
Business Description:	Software and Information Technology Solutions for the Healthcare Payer Industry
SIC:	7372 Prepackaged Software
NAICS:	511210 Software Publishers
Sale Location:	United States
Years in Business:	N/A Number Employees: N/A

Source Data

Public Buyer Name:	TRIZETTO GROUP INC
8-K Date:	1/16/2007
8-K/A Date:	3/27/2007
Other Filing Type:	N/A
Other Filing Date:	N/A
CIK Code:	0001092458

Income Data

Data is "Latest Full Year" Reported	Yes
Data is Restated (see Notes for any explanation)	No
Income Statement Date	12/31/2005
Net Sales	$48,100,000
COGS	$19,423,000
Gross Profit	$28,677,000
Yearly Rent	$1,037,000
Owner's Compensation	N/A
Other Operating Expenses	N/A
Noncash Charges	$1,779,000
Total Operating Expenses	$22,744,000
Operating Profit	$5,933,000
Interest Expenses	$152,000
EBT	$5,822,000
Taxes	$0
Net Income	$7,937,000

Asset Data

Data is Latest Reported	Yes
Data is "Purchase Price Allocation agreed upon by Buyer and Seller"	No
Balance Sheet Date	9/30/2006
Cash Equivalents	$11,372,000
Trade Receivables	$5,681,000
Inventory	$0
Other Current Assets	$3,823,000
Total Current Assets	$20,876,000
Fixed Assets	$2,714,000
Real Estate	$0
Intangibles	$1,605,000
Other Noncurrent Assets	$907,000
Total Assets	$26,102,000
Long-term Liabilities	$1,073,000
Total Liabilities	$21,243,000
Stockholder's Equity	$4,859,000

Transaction Data

Date Sale Initiated:	N/A
Date of Sale:	1/10/2007
Asking Price:	N/A
Market Value of Invested Capital*:	$148,200,000
Debt Assumed:	$1,000,000
Employment Agreement Value:	N/A
Noncompete Value:	N/A
Amount of Down Payment:	$147,200,000
Stock or Asset Sale:	Stock
Company Type:	C Corporation
Was there an Employment/Consulting Agreement?	No
Was there an Assumed Lease in the sale?	No
Was there a Renewal Option with the Lease?	No

*Includes noncompete value and interest-bearing debt; excludes real estate, employment/consulting agreement values, and all contingent payments.

Additional Transaction Information

Was there a Note in the consideration paid? No   Was there a personal guarantee on the Note? No

Terms:

Consideration: Cash in the amount of $147,200,000 and the assumption of the seller's debt in the amount of $1,000,000. In addition to the purchase price of $147,200,000, there was a $5,000,000 holdback (dependent on working capital) and a potential contingent payment of $7,000,000 based upon license and software maintenance revenues for the year of 2007. In addition, the Buyer incurred acquisition costs in the amount of $5,200,000.

Assumed Lease (Months): 55

Noncompete Length (Months): N/A   Terms of Lease: Future minimum lease payments total $4,617,000 through July 2010

Employment/Consulting Agreement Description: Noncompete Description: N/A

Additional Notes:

EBT includes interest income of $41,000. Net Income includes a tax benefit of $2,115,000.

Allocation of the Purchase Price (allocates cash paid, holdback, and acquisition costs): Tangible assets $24,600,000, Goodwill $91,400,000, Customer relationships $39,900,000, Trade name $900,000, Core technology $9,500,000, Existing technology $6,700,000, Total assets acquired $173,000,000, Liabilities assumed ($15,600,000), Net assets acquired $157,400,000.

Quality Care Solutions, Inc. (QCSI) (the "Company") is a Nevada Corporation that develops, markets and licenses health insurance claims reimbursement, health insurance benefits administration, integrated care management and consumer-driven health care solutions throughout the United States primarily under term licenses. The Company's software products manage the interaction between payors (i.e., insurance companies, managed care organizations, government agencies, self-insured employers, third-party administrators, providers who maintain financial responsibility for healthcare claims and other enterprises that implement health plans and pay the majority of healthcare expenses), providers (i.e., physicians, dentists, medical and dental practice groups, laboratories, hospitals and other organizations that deliver care and services), and patients. This is performed by automating significant portions of the claims, benefit administration and enrollment processes such as analyzing a patient's healthcare plan and related coverage to determine patient eligibility for healthcare benefits, calculating the payor's and patient's responsibility for the claim, authorizing referrals to other providers, and providing products to assist with consumer directed health insurance enrollment and administration.

Valuation Multiples

MVIC/Net Sales	3.08
MVIC/Gross Profit	5.17
MVIC/EBITDA	19.22
MVIC/EBIT	24.98
MVIC/Discretionary Earnings	N/A
MVIC/Book Value of Invested Capital	24.98

Profitability Ratios

Net Profit Margin	0.17
Operating Profit Margin	0.17
Gross Profit Margin	0.60
Return on Assets	0.30
Return on Equity	1.63

Leverage Ratios

Fixed Charge Coverage	53.22
Long-Term Debt to Assets	0.04
Long-Term Debt to Equity	0.22

Earnings

EBITDA	$7,712,000
Discretionary Earnings	N/A

Liquidity Ratios

Current Ratio	1.04
Quick Ratio	1.04

Activity Ratios

Total Asset Turnover	1.84
Fixed Asset Turnover	17.72
Inventory Turnover	N/A

N/A = Not Available

Source: *http://www.bvmarketdata* (Accessed Febrauary 6, 2008).

In applying these methods to determine the value of a business, one or more of the following factors are generally reviewed and analyzed:

1. The nature of the business and its operating history
2. The industry and economic outlook
3. The book value and financial condition of the company
4. The company's earnings and dividend-paying capacity
5. The value of the company's tangible and intangible assets
6. Market prices of public companies engaged in similar lines of business
7. Transaction prices of other private companies engaged in similar lines of business

Throughout the valuation process, it is important that the purpose of the valuation be kept in mind. A valuation can serve many purposes, but if the aim is to sell the business, then the valuation should objectively determine the fair market value of the business. This objective market valuation should also take into account the synergies and fit that the business may have with potential buyers. In addition to valuing a business for an impending sale, a business valuation can also be required for legal proceedings, estate planning, shareholder disputes, and capital raising.

Source: USBX, *http://www.usbx.com* (Accessed May 1, 2001).

Business-Valuation Analysts

In his 2003 *Inc.* magazine article, "What's Your Company Worth Now?" Randall Lane shared this: "There are two senior certifications for which you should look when hiring an appraiser, although not every qualified firm will have them. The ASA (American Society of Appraisers) gives out an ASA (Accredited Senior Appraiser), which requires courses, exams, 5 years of experience, and peer review of reports. The IBA (Institute of Business Appraisers) certifies its CBA (Certified Business Appraiser) in much the same way. Strong recommendations from an expert's savvy, satisfied customers are better than any certificate."

Valuation professionals may have experience as Certified Public Accountants (CPAs) and in completing business evaluations for either the private or public sector. Their backgrounds will include accounting, tax law, auditing, finance, insurance, economics, and investments. Their coursework and experience may also include valuation theory, practical application, and litigation support that allows them to prepare a comprehensive analysis and competent valuation.

The analysts will determine which is the most appropriate methodology to value a specific business, taking into account the financials as well as industry comparisons and economic, business, and market risks. To find a qualified appraiser, contact either of the above associations. A good appraiser's fee will be well earned, as his evaluation will be based on facts and figures rather than emotion, keeping you and the seller grounded.

PROTECT YOURSELF

Evaluate each business opportunity by the criteria we present in this chapter. When you find one you think is personally and financially right for you, and have completed due diligence, pricing and terms will become the next issue. Your goal is the lowest possible price with the best possible terms. Start low; you can then negotiate up if necessary.

When asked to put down a deposit, place the money in an escrow account, and include a stipulation in your offer that says the contract is subject to your inspection and subject to approval of all financial records and all aspects of the business. Include an escape hatch so that you can get your deposit back—and back out of the deal—if things are not as represented.

One of the best things you can do to protect yourself is to work in the business for a few weeks before signing papers with the option to back out if you have a change of heart. One prospective entrepreneur, Sondra Nyugen, fell in love with a retail photography business. Her business advisor suggested she work in the business for free for several weeks to explore the business further. She discussed the arrangement with the seller. While reluctant, the seller gave in.

After 3 weeks, Sondra knew that working with fussy children, crabby parents, and stressed teenagers brought her little joy. This was not the business for her. She continued on her search and recently purchased an established tutoring franchise after working there free for 4 weeks.

communityresource

Federal Contract Opportunities

FED BIZ OPPS (Federal Business Opportunities)

https://www.fbo.gov (877) 472-3779

FedBizOpps.gov is the single government point-of-entry (GPE) for Federal government procurement opportunities over $25,000. Government buyers are able to publicize their business opportunities by posting information directly to FedBizOpps via the Internet. "Through one portal, commercial vendors seeking federal markets for their products and services can post, search, monitor, and retrieve opportunities solicited by the entire federal contracting community."

For assistance in selling to the government, procurement center representatives are available for each region of the country. Sample listings for representatives and their responsibilities follow:

TPCR—Traditional Procurement Center Representative: TPCRs increase the small-business share of federal procurement awards by initiating small business set-asides, reserving procurements for competition among small business firms, providing small business sources to federal buying activities, and counseling small firms.

BPCR—Breakout Procurement Center Representative: BPCRs advocate for the breakout of items for full and open competition to effect savings to the federal government.

CMR—Commercial Marketing Representatives: CMRs identify, develop, and market small businesses to large prime contractors and assist small businesses in identifying and obtaining subcontracts.

A sample listing of a procurement representative and her needs, accessed from *http://www.sba.gov/idc/groups/public/documents/va_do_files/va_fedagencylist.pdf* follows:

Karen Hosaflook
U.S. Forest Service
North River Ranger District
401 Oakwood Drive
Harrisonburg, VA 22801
540–432–0187 Fax: 540–432–1917

Purchases: Timber/timber cutting supplies, equipment and supplies to maintain recreation areas, trees, wildlife-related supplies and equipment, A/E and landscaping services, road maintenance, and pesticide services and equipment.

Federal opportunities are limitless. Seminars, workshops, Web sites, procurement specialists, and consultants are waiting to enlist your business as a federal contractor or subcontractor. Reach out!

Obtain a Noncompete Covenant

Once you buy a business, you do not want the seller to set up the same type of business across the street or elsewhere online. Customers are hard to come by, and you do not want to pay for them only to have them spirited away by a cagey seller. So secure an agreement, in writing, that the seller will not set up in competition with you—or work for a competitor, or help a friend or relative set up a competitive business—for the next 5 years. An attorney should make sure all loopholes are closed.

Be sure to specify the exact amount you are paying for the noncompete covenant to assure the IRS will treat it properly.

Determine Whether Bulk Sales Escrow Is Required

You need to determine if creditors will tie up the inventory you are purchasing. If they will, the instrument you will use to cut those strings is a bulk sales transfer, a process that will transfer the goods from the seller to you through a qualified third party. In most states, bulk sales transfer is specified under a series of regulations known as the *Uniform Commercial Code (UCC)*.

Escrow company A neutral third party who holds deposits and deeds until all agreed-upon conditions are met

Bulk sales escrow An examination process intended to protect buyers from unknown liabilities

If there are no claims by creditors, the transfer of inventory should go smoothly. If there are claims, you will want to be protected by law. Either consult an attorney who has experience in making bulk sales transfers, or arrange for an escrow company to act as the neutral party in the transfer. The quickest way to find an escrow company is to look in the Yellow Pages under *Escrow*. A better way is to ask your banker, broker, or CPA to recommend one. Try to find one who specializes in bulk sales escrows. If you do not transfer the company through a bulk sales transfer, protect yourself by holding funds to pay for unknown debts that might be lurking.

Tax Issues

In structuring a business-purchase transaction, both the buyer and seller need to consider accounting and tax implications. As these can vary depending on the type of business and the specific tax issues faced by those businesses, an experienced business tax accountant should be at your side throughout the transaction. Also, an experienced accountant will discover how the business may have legally or illegally reported income in the past and thus help and protect you in the transaction. Your accountant may uncover possible value within the business that is not being realized due to improper accounting or tax planning.

During the purchase transaction, what may be best for one party may not be best for the other from an accounting and tax standpoint. Thus negotiation and compromise will be necessary to arrive at a fair transaction for both parties. The goal for both parties should be to legally minimize the total taxes paid both during the transaction and in the future. Expertise and cooperation are necessary.

The timing of the transaction may impact the seller's tax situation, and you may need to compromise on that issue as well. In some cases, the seller's accountant may suggest structuring the transaction so payments are made over time to delay the taxable gain. The value added to any purchase transaction through the structuring of the tax implications for both sides may be substantial.

Negotiate the Value of Good Will

If the firm has a strong customer base with deeply ingrained purchasing habits, this has value. It takes time for any start-up to build a client base, and the wait for profitability can be costly.

Some firms have built up a great deal of **ill will**—customers who have vowed never to trade with them again and suppliers who won't sell to the business. A large proportion of the businesses on the market have this problem. If the amount of ill will is great, the business will have little value; it may be that *any* price would be too high. Ill will is very difficult, and sometimes impossible, to turn into good will. Do *not* assume you can change ill will to good will. It might not happen regardless of your efforts.

Ill will All the negative feelings about a business; the opposite of good will

A smart seller will ask you to pay something for good will. Thus you will need to play detective and find out *how much* good will there is and *where* it is. For example, consider the seller who has extended credit loosely. Customers are responding, but there is no cash in the bank. If you were to continue that policy and keep granting easy credit, you would be sacrificing your source of cash flow. Or maybe the seller is one of those very special people who is loved by everyone and will take that good will with him or her—like a halo—when he or she walks out the door.

You must negotiate. Suppose the asking price for the business you would like to buy is $200,000 and that its tangible assets (equipment, inventory, and so on) are worth $125,000. In other words, the seller is trying to charge you $75,000 for good will. Before you negotiate, do the following:

1. Compare the good will you are being asked to buy to the good will of similar businesses on the market.
2. Figure out how long it will take you to pay that amount. Remember, good will is intangible; you will be unhappy if it takes you years to pay for it. Even the most cheerful good will comes out of profit.
3. Estimate how much you could make if you invested that $75,000 in T-bills.
4. Consider the time it would take you to attain the same profitability if you were to start a similar business from scratch.

This gives you a context in which to judge the seller's assessment of the value of good will, and you can use the hard data you have generated to negotiate a realistic—and no doubt, more favorable—price. Another caveat: talk with your accountant before negotiating a price; he or she will discuss with you the tax implications involved with good will.

THE DECISION TO PURCHASE

Too many people purchase businesses emotionally. They buy a business as if it were a home, a car, or a suit. They are drawn to businesses that they think will enhance their image and impress their friends and relatives. Physically attractive businesses are often the worst investments, because image-conscious buyers allow sellers to charge an unreasonable price. The "ugly" or "invisible" business often provides the best return on time and investment.

Others view buying a business as buying a *job;* they look at the business as their new employer. Unfortunately, many buyers with this attitude lack the experience to make a good choice and often invest their life savings in ventures that demand 70 to 80 hours per week to operate and that often pay them less than their 40-hour-a-week jobs did.

If you think you are ready to make your decision, do not do it just yet. First, read the checklist that follows for important details you might have overlooked. Even if you *know* you have found your dream business, complete this checklist and the due diligence list before you sign the papers.

The Final Before-You-Buy List

How long do you plan to own this business?

How do you plan to exit this business?

How old is this business? Can you sketch its history?

Is this business in the embryonic stage? The growth stage? The mature stage? The decline stage?

Has your accountant reviewed the books and made sales projections for you?

How long will it take for this business to show a *complete* recovery on your investment?

What reasons does the owner give for selling? Have you investigated the business thoroughly?

Will the owner let you see bank deposit records? (If not, why not?)

Have you calculated utility costs for the first 3 to 5 years? (With increasing rates, this can be a huge surprise.)

What does a review of tax records tell you?

What is the compensation and benefits plan for employees? What are the employees' expectations? What is the expected employee retention?

What is the seller's salary? Is it low or high?

Are there any unpaid employees?

Have you interviewed your prospective landlord?

Have you made spot checks on the currency of the customer list?

Who are the top 20 customers? The top 50?

Is the seller locked into fewer than four major customers who control the business?

Are you buying inventory? If so, how much is the seller asking?

Have you checked the value of the inventory with vendors?

Have you checked the value of the equipment against the price of used equipment from another source?

Does your seller owe money to creditors? If so, who are they?

Has your attorney checked for liens on the seller's equipment and property?

Do maintenance contracts exist on the equipment you are buying? Can you assume those contracts?

Has your attorney reviewed all information and documents and answered all of your questions?

Have you determined how best to structure the purchase and business for tax purposes?

Are you able to obtain adequate insurance coverage at an affordable rate?

Are there any pending or potential product liability issues?

Have you checked to determine if there are any potential environmental issues with hazardous waste, the Clean Air Act, or new or pending legislation that might affect the business?

Has your attorney or escrow company gone through bulk sales escrow?

Is there any pending litigation?

Are you purchasing all brand names, patents, logos, trademarks, and so on that you need?

Has the seller signed a noncompete covenant, and has your attorney reviewed it?

Will the key lines of supply stay intact when you take over?

Will the key employees stay?

Is the seller leaving because of stiff competition?

Are you paying for good will but taking delivery of ill will?

Are you getting the best terms possible?

Are you buying an income stream?

Are you passionate about the business?

PREPARE FOR NEGOTIATIONS

Let us say you know you are ready to buy. You have raised money, the numbers say you cannot lose, and you are ready to start negotiating. If you are an experienced entrepreneur, you already know how to negotiate. If not, read up on negotiating, and take an experienced business negotiator with you. Your appraisals, research, and broker's expertise should all be brought to the negotiating table.

First, when it comes time to talk meaningful numbers, the most important area to concentrate on is *terms,* not asking price. Favorable terms will give you the cash flow you need to survive the first years and then move from survival into success. Unfavorable terms may torpedo your chances for success, even when the total asking price is well below market value.

Second, when the seller brings up the subject of good will, be ready for it. Good will is a "slippery" commodity; it can make the asking price soar. It is only natural for the seller to attempt to get as much as possible for good will. Because you know this ahead of time, do your homework, and go in primed to deal. Action Step 56 will help you do this.

In negotiating the purchase price, you will have worked with your accountant, attorney, and banker to determine what steps are best taken to insure the best tax breaks, continuity of the business, cash flow, and ability to continue to grow the business.

★ *Passion* ★

Parents and Kids Want to Sell Goods that Do Some Good

For decades, children have hawked candy and cookie dough to friends and family to help fund extracurricular activities and school playgrounds. Now a handful of entrepreneurs have set out to change that paradigm, offering ecologically friendly products for kids and parents to sell for school fund-raisers. From recycled wrapping paper to fair-trade coffee, the business owners are pitching the products as viable fund-raising alternatives for schools.

To date, Greenraising, a firm whose catalog features such products as recycled gift-wrap paper and reusable water bottles, has helped about 500 schools and nonprofits raise money, says Lisa Olson, who founded the Agoura Hills, Calif., company last year. The company asks schools or nonprofits to distribute its catalog, from which customers then buy directly. For an item that costs, say, $20, Greenraising keeps $12 and returns $8 to the school or nonprofit.

Some eco-friendly fund-raisers have come to another realization as well: It's the parents who are taking on more of the fund raising—largely because of fears about their kids' safety—and they'd rather buy and sell products that they want to use themselves.

Action Step 56

Probe the Depths of Good Will and Ill Will

1. How many products have you vowed never to use again? How many places of business have you vowed never to patronize again? Why?

2. Make a list of the products and services you will not buy or use again. Next to each item, write the reason. Did it make you sick? Did it offend your sensibilities? Was the service awful?

3. After you have completed your list, ask your friends what their positive and negative feelings are about the businesses they patronize. Take notes.

4. Study the two lists you made. What are the common components of ill will? How long does ill will last? Is there a remedy for it, or is a business plagued by ill will cursed forever?

5. Turn your attention to the business you want to buy. Learn as much as you can about the good will and ill will that exist toward the business. Spend as much time as you can with current and past customers, exploring their feelings toward the business. Have fun with this step, but take it seriously—and think about the nature of ill will when your seller starts asking you to pay for good will.

(continued)

(continued)

Green Students Fundraising Ltd., a Toronto-based company, began by selling energy-efficient compact fluorescent light bulbs. But as more mainstream retailers began offering them, Mr. Berman says, the company wasn't able to compete on cost and knew it had to diversify. So, the company started selling stainless-steel water bottles, which got a lift from the recent outcry against bisphenol A, a chemical commonly found in plastic water bottles.

Lots of families also buy coffee, which is something that led eco-minded schools to contact Chris Treter, co-founder of Higher Grounds Trading Co., a fair-trade coffee roaster in Traverse City, Mich. Fair-trade coffee is a concept begun a few years ago by small producers that wanted to show consumers their coffee is produced under conditions beneficial to workers and the environment. Schools looking to incorporate lessons about the environment and labor standards will call and ask if they can purchase the coffee for a fund-raiser, Mr. Treter says.

One challenge these companies face is coming up with products that parents and friends will purchase year after year. Both Greenraising and Green Students say they plan to periodically change the items in their catalogs to keep them fresh.

Source: Adapted from Simona Covel, "Businesses Help School Fundraisers Go Green," *Wall Street Journal*, 21 July 2008. Copyright 2008 by Dow Jones & Company, Inc. Reproduced with permission of Dow Jones & Company, Inc. in the format Tradebook via Copyright Clearance Center.

SUMMARY

There are two good reasons to explore businesses for sale: You will learn a lot by exploring the marketplace, and you might find a gem—a business that will make money right from the start. If you do purchase an ongoing business, remember the reasons you have purchased it: ongoing income stream, name, location, product selection, and so on. You have paid good money for an ongoing business—stick with the formula you have purchased until it proves you wrong. Many people who purchase a retail outlet or online store immediately change store design and product offerings only to fail miserably and wonder why. The customer base one has paid dearly for no longer wants to shop in the "new store"; they were happy with the old, and that *is* why they *were* loyal customers.

Trained and experienced attorneys, accountants, and bankers are necessary for you to complete a business purchase transaction. Sellers are tied emotionally to their business, and you are tied emotionally to your dream. You need impartial third parties to keep the sale on a rational basis. Accountants will be able to evaluate financial statements to determine where the owners are hiding money, bad debts, employee theft, and countless other problems, which you might never discover on your own.

One of the most important formulas for you to consider in evaluating any business is the return on your effort (ROE):

$$ROE = \text{hours spent} \times \text{the value of your time per hour}$$

Be sure to purchase a business that meets your income needs. If you pay too much, there may not be enough left to pay yourself an adequate salary or to invest in new equipment. If this happens, you will sour on the business early, and you may not be willing to put in the effort required for success.

You should be willing to pay a higher price for a firm with above-average growth potential than one that is declining. In fact, you should not buy a declining business unless you believe you can purchase it cheaply, turn it around quickly, or dispose of its assets at a profit.

Keep your checkbook at home as you initially explore. Make sure, once you have entered into any negotiations, that you do not sign *anything* without your attorney's review. If at all possible, work in the business before signing a final purchase agreement. Buy a business that fits your personal and financial needs and goals. Do not fall in love with a business—fall in love with the profits that business will provide. Finally, follow your passions.

THINK POINTS FOR SUCCESS

- Stick to what you know.
- Do not buy a business you know nothing about. If you are so inclined, research the industry thoroughly and work in the business before purchasing.
- If your seller looks absolutely honest, check him or her out anyway. Private detectives can run a thorough background check for very little money—a wise investment.
- Worry less about price; work harder on terms.
- Most good businesses are sold behind the scenes, before they reach the open market.
- Make sure you are there when the physical inventory takes place. Look in those boxes yourself.

- Get everything in writing. Be specific. Do not sign anything without understanding every word, and get your attorney's approval.
- Buying a corporation is tricky. Have an experienced corporate attorney assist you.
- Be ready to hold your own through the negotiation process, but do not nitpick. Look at the whole picture.
- Do not let a seller or broker rush you.
- Consider the cost involved in starting from scratch versus buying a business.
- Income stream is vital. Be sure it is there and that your loan payments will not take it all away from you.

KEY POINTS FROM ANOTHER VIEW

Seller Financing Basics: A primer for buyers and sellers

by Glen Cooper, CBA

Most small business sales are financed, at least in part, by the sellers themselves. Offering seller financing puts the seller in a stronger position to get a better price and a faster sale.

Buyers nearly always need seller financing. Their advisors strongly recommend it. Seller financing acts like a bond for performance to assure that the seller will live up to the promises made to the buyer during the sales process. Seller financing is seen by most buyers as an indication that the seller has faith in the future of the business.

Buyers can expect, however, that sellers who offer seller financing must also act a lot like a bank! A buyer can expect to be asked to secure the loan and sign a personal guaranty.

What Is Seller Financing?

Sellers of small businesses usually allow the buyer to pay some of the purchase price of the business in the form of a promissory note. This is what is known as *seller financing*.

Seller financing is particularly common when the business is large enough to make a cash sale difficult for the buyer (over $100,000) but too small for the mid-market venture capitalists (under $5 million). Seller financing is also common when the business, for any number of reasons, does not appeal to traditional lenders.

A rule of thumb is that sellers will typically finance from one third to two thirds of the sale price. Many do more than that. It all depends on the situation; each transaction is unique. The interest rate of the seller note is typically at or below bank prime rates. The term of the seller note is usually similar to that of a bank.

For a service business that sells for $500,000, for example, the transaction might be structured as $150,000 down from the buyer and $350,000 in seller financing. The seller note might run for 5 to 7 years and carry an interest rate of 8% to 10%. Monthly payments are the norm and usually start 30 days from the date of sale unless the payment schedule must be modified to allow for the seasonality of the business revenues. The seller note would also usually have a longer term if real estate were being financed.

When a seller offers seller financing, the price the buyer can afford to pay goes up as the amount of the down payment required by the seller goes down.

Why Would a Seller Offer Financing?

Sellers are nearly always reluctant to offer seller financing. Like all of us, they fear the unknown. Despite the advantages of playing bank, it is an uncomfortable role for them. They usually come around to seller financing only after some effort has been made to persuade them.

A seller's first encounter with this issue might be with the business broker. In many cases, but not all, the business broker will bring up the issue. Most business brokers agree that sellers need to offer seller financing, but not all are willing to discuss the issue at the beginning of the listing. When the buyer is unknown, the seller's fear of seller financing is greatest. Some brokers prefer to wait until the buyer prospect is known before suggesting the amount and terms of seller financing.

Offering seller financing up front, however, can attract buyers and speed up the business sale. This is the major issue that usually persuades a seller to offer some type of financing.

Seller financing is seen by buyer prospects as comforting proof that the seller is not afraid of the future of the business. Buyers are more likely to believe a seller's optimistic view of the business's future when seller financing is offered. Some buyers can't or won't look at businesses for sale unless seller financing is a possibility. The more buyer prospects that look at a business, the better the chance a seller has to get an acceptable offer. A seller can also get a better price for a business that has financing in place. As in nearly all buying situations, buyers are often focused on achieving a purchase on terms that allow them to buy with as little 'cash in' as possible, even if the long-run costs are higher.

Seller financing can also lead to a speedier sale. If the seller plays bank, then the deal gets done more quickly. Applying for a bank loan takes a long time for some buyers, and the rejection rate for new acquisition loans is very high—sometimes as much as 80%! Banks also move much slower than sellers, even when they do approve a loan. A seller is much more likely to grant a loan request, approve a transaction, and close it as fast as the attorney can get the agreements prepared. Banks take anywhere from 30 to 120 days to approve and close a loan. There is also the possibility that the bankers will give the buyer negative feedback about the business, so that the buyer backs out.

A seller may also see tax advantages and profitability in seller financing, but these alone are not usually compelling reasons to offer seller financing. Capital gains from a small business sale can be reported in installments if seller financing is in place. This stretches out the capital gains tax into future years. Charging interest is also profitable. Sellers, however, are usually not as worried about tax liabilities as they should be until after the sale has taken place. They also usually believe they can get better interest rates from investments than from seller notes.

Why Should a Buyer Ask for Seller Financing?

Buying a business without seller financing is like buying a home without a homeowner's warranty. The seller note is a bond for performance. This is the major reason a buyer ought to ask for seller financing.

Beyond that, sellers have a strong motive to maintain the business good will if they have a remaining stake in its future ability to pay back the seller note. Without such an interest, sellers may choose to question the new owner's skills and integrity. After a sale takes place, the seller and buyer frequently disagree about the future of the business. This disagreement is a natural outgrowth of their different positions and can become serious. If a seller note is in place, the seller has a motive to temper any irritation caused by the buyer with forbearance.

Even with a noncompete agreement in place with the seller, the fact that the business owes the seller a major amount of money may change the nature of the seller's attitude. Instead of being indifferent or quarrelsome, a seller who is still owed money is more likely to be solicitous and genuinely helpful.

How Is Seller Financing Usually Secured?

Seller financing can be as creative as sellers and buyers want to make it. Most sellers, however, like to add security provisions in as many forms as possible. This can encompass personal guarantees as well as specific collateral, stock pledges, life and disability insurance policies, and even restrictions on how the business is run.

The most common requirement is for a personal guaranty by the buyer and the buyer's spouse. Sellers expect this. If a buyer objects, sellers immediately question their seriousness. A personal guaranty is not a specific lien on any particular buyer asset but is the guaranty that the buyer is placing all assets at risk as needed to satisfy the loan. If the seller note payments are not made, the seller has to proceed with the long process of formal foreclosure. But to satisfy the foreclosure, the seller will have access to all buyer assets. The spouse's signature is required to prevent the transfer of assets to the spouse's name to dilute the buyer's net worth.

Specific collateral is the other common source of security. If no bank financing is involved, the seller wants a first mortgage on any real estate and first security agreements on all personal property involved in the sale. Sometimes, the seller will require that the buyer offer additional security in the form of additional mortgages and security agreements on real and personal property that the buyer owns. If a bank is involved, the seller must usually settle for second place in the line of secured creditors behind the bank.

A third type of security is the "stock pledge." The buyer is required to form a corporation and give the seller the rights to "vote the stock" in case of seller note default. This allows the seller a speedier solution than foreclosure. If the terms of the seller note are not met, the seller can vote to require that payments be made and can even vote to replace management of the business. This threat is usually enough to guarantee seller note payments are not missed.

Life and disability insurance policies on key members of the buyer's new management team are less frequently used methods of adding security to a seller-financed transaction. Term life insurance is available at rates that are relatively low, so this is most common. Disability insurance is used less often because it is more expensive. The seller will typically want the business to pay for these policies up to the amount of the seller note. These policies stay in effect until the seller note is paid.

Restrictions on how the business is run are sometimes added. These restrictions can be in the form of requiring that the new owner preserve certain account or employment relationships, that certain operating ratios of the business are maintained, that the new owner's pay is limited, or that other important operating benchmarks are met until the seller note is paid. Most sellers won't use this form of adding to their own security as a creditor. They usually readily identify with buyer objections to any controls placed on the new business owner.

How Can Both Buyer and Seller Benefit?

If you are a buyer or seller and this all seems a bit intimidating to you, take heart! It's just as intimidating for the other party! Don't lose sight of the fact that this is just a normal transaction between two parties who must each benefit if a deal is to be struck.

Buyers are just looking for a fair chance to buy a job and a reasonable return on investment. They usually have modest goals about what they need to earn for the job they are buying. They are usually fair about how they define what they need to receive as a return on investment for the business risks they are assuming.

Sellers are mostly just ordinary people who once bought or started a business and now want to sell it. They want to get the most they can, but they have learned to be practical. They are usually persuaded by fairness and reasonableness. If not that, then they are at least eventually persuaded by the reality of what's possible.

If you are a buyer, seller financing can offer you better terms and a friendlier lender. You will be able to buy the business quicker because you won't have to wait a month for the bank's loan committee to meet. There are no loan processing or guarantee fees and, usually, no invasive lender controls or audits.

If you are a seller, I would advise an early commitment to seller financing. It will save you a lot of time. You'll get a better price because you'll see more buyer prospects. There are many more buyers who can afford to take a chance when the admission price is reasonable.

Seller financing, properly understood and employed, can really benefit both buyer and seller.

Source: *http://www.bizbuysell.com/guide/b_finance_2.htm* (Accessed January 26, 2008).

- Learn how your daily life is influenced by the franchise system.
- Explore franchising as an alternative doorway into business ownership.
- Gain an overview of how the franchise system works.
- Evaluate the pros and cons of being a franchisee.
- Develop techniques for examining franchises.
- Understand what you need to look for in the franchise disclosure document.
- Understand risk–reward factors in "ground floor" opportunities.
- Learn why a franchise may not be for you and why some people should consider franchising as the preferred doorway.
- Recognize the advantages of owning multiple franchises.
- Understand why the true entrepreneur is always the franchisor.
- Explore multilevel marketing.

chapter 14

Investigating Franchising
Reading Between the Lines

Your walk-through of opportunities in small business is almost finished. Decision time approaches. If you seriously considered franchising from the beginning, you may have begun your journey through the Action Steps with a franchise in mind.

If not, and you now want to explore franchising, you can begin to apply those insights already gained to franchising operations. You have spent months gathering data and talking to people in small business. You have spent time exploring businesses that are up for sale and talking to sellers. If you want to write a Business Plan now, you could sit down and do it. But before you do that, however, there is one other doorway to explore: a franchised business.

FRANCHISING'S REACH

Did you scarf down an Egg McMuffin on your way to work? Did your kids lead you to Burger King or Taco Bell for dinner last night? On your way from Tacoma to Taos, did you stop at a Perkins for pancakes? When you bought your last piece of real estate, did you happen to check out properties with a Prudential agent?

When was your last trip to a 7-Eleven store? What do you think of the advertisements for Kinko's, the instant printer? If you want a business of your own but do not feel strong enough to strike out on your own without some support, check out a Play It Again sports equipment franchise, a Sylvan educational **franchise**, or any other franchise of your choice.

Franchise Authorization granted by a manufacturer or distributor to sell its products or services

If you had money from an early retirement buyout package, a minimum of $72,000 in liquid assets, one year's living expenses, and a minimum $300,000 net worth, would you purchase an Alphagraphics franchise? Would you search the marketplace for an existing El Pollo Loco outlet that still had some legs? Or would you opt for a clever business such as Takeout Taxi, which delivers gourmet meals to upscale diners at home?

Whether or not you personally patronize franchises—although it is almost impossible not to, with the franchise market including burgers, real estate, construction, Internet businesses, distributors, printing, tax preparation, equipment rental, travel agencies, soft drinks, and used cars, to name a few—the franchising game is big.

According to estimates from the International Franchising Association (IFA), there are more than 3,000 **franchisors** in the United States, representing over 230 lines of businesses with 900,000 **franchisees**. An additional 300 new firms offered franchises during the past year. A study prepared by PricewaterhouseCoopers on behalf of the International Franchise Association Educational Foundation showed, "The total impact of franchising was to provide 21 million jobs and $660.9 billion of payroll in 2005." View the growth of franchising's economic impact in Figure 14.1.

Franchisor A firm that sells the right to do business under its name to another for a fee but continues to control the business

Franchisee An individual who, for a fee, is licensed to operate a business under the franchisor's rules and directives

Although franchising is growing rapidly, Scott Shane, economics and entrepreneurship professor at Case Western Reserve University in Cleveland, issues words of caution: "Twenty years from their start, less than 20 percent of the franchisers will still be around," and "In fact, of the more than 200 new franchise systems established in the United States each year, 25 percent don't even make it to their first anniversary." Franchises offer wonderful opportunities, but they should be evaluated as fully as any other business opportunity. Before you begin your search for a franchise we think it is important to first ask yourself if franchising is the right fit for you.

figure **14.1**

Franchising Impact 2001–2005

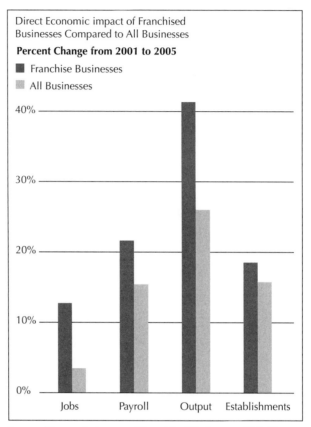

Direct Economic impact of Franchised
Businesses Compared to All Businesses

Percent Change from 2001 to 2005

■ Franchise Businesses
■ All Businesses

Source: "Economic Impact of Franchised Businesses: Vol. 2"
Pricewaterhouse Coopers, March 2008. *http://www.franchise.org/
Franchise-News-Detail.aspx/id=38358* (Accessed April 20, 2008).

EXPLORING THE THIRD DOORWAY

As the third doorway to business, franchising offers entrepreneurs ready access
to an opportunity with business and marketing plans already in place. With personnel, advertising, and purchasing systems, the franchise entrepreneur needs
primarily to execute the franchisor's plan and systems. Follow the steps throughout this chapter to discover if the third doorway is the right one for you.

If you think you might enjoy being a franchisee, take the next step and look
at opportunities, and evaluate them based on your answers to the Action Steps in
Chapter 1 and to the many others that we suggest throughout this chapter. It will
take a great deal of time and energy, but do not compromise. Look for an opportunity that is the right match for your talents, goals, financial needs, and passions.

Take the quiz, "Is Franchising for Me?" at *http://www.sba.gov/idc/groups/
public/documents/sba_homepage/serv_sbp_isfforme.pdf*. If you search the net,
you will find many more franchise quizzes online and many on franchise-broker
Web sites who want desperately to sell you franchises. Keep your answers
from Chapter 1, along with your answers to the online quizzes, in the forefront as you explore franchising.

Next, review your financial goals. If you have decided you need to net $60K
per year, then focus only on franchises where that is at least the average. Do

incredible resource

SBA Franchising Information and IFA Introduction to Franchising Course

To explore franchising further on the Internet, follow the links below at *http://www.sba.gov/smallbusinessplanner/start/buyafranchise/index.html* to a wealth of free, unbiased information.

Business franchising offers many opportunities. This form of ownership has helped many entrepreneurs get started in business and succeed.

Franchising Overview Get a general description of franchising.

Consumer Guide to Buying a Franchise Learn how to examine and buy an existing franchise.

Franchising Strategy Learn to research your perspective franchise and examine its possible problems.

Associations and Forums The American Franchisee Association (AFA) is a national trade association of franchisees and dealers with over 7,000 members.

Buying a Franchise FAQs Find answers to questions frequently asked when buying a franchise.

Franchising FAQs Find answers to commonly asked questions about franchising.

Guides and Instructions for Buying a Franchise Get help on successfully purchasing an existing franchise.

Contact your local SCORE and SBA offices to determine if they have formal workshops on franchising. Many of these are excellent, as they present both the franchisor and franchisee perspectives. Also, the International Franchise Association at *http://www.ifa-university.com/home* offers a free online "Franchising Basics" course to encourage people to explore the franchise door. The course covers how franchising works, what questions you should ask when considering a franchise, what laws and regulations apply to franchising, companies and types of businesses available in franchises, pros and cons of franchising, the variety of franchising forms, and additional information resources.

not make the assumption that you will make a great deal more than the average franchise. You will also need to determine your net worth and the amount of investment capital you have available before you begin your search, as many franchisors will pre-qualify you before sharing financial information.

Surfing for Franchising Basics

The Internet has volumes of material on franchising, but *user beware:* most of the sites are developed by firms selling franchises, thus their information and advice can be biased. The steps that follow walk you through various Web sites along with those in the Incredible and Community Resources, which can help you assess if this is a doorwary you want to explore further. If it is, the information and sites will help you develop the questions to ask as you explore franchisors and their opportunities.

1. **FAQs:** Start with answers to frequently asked questions, which may include, What kind of franchises are available? Is financing available? Who provides the location? Do I need professional help?

Action Step 57

Exploring the Web

Take a couple of hours to check out the general franchising Web sites throughout this chapter and others you locate on your own.

1. Take an online quiz at Franchise Help, *http://www.franchisehelp.com/franchise/quiz/publicquiz.cfm*. What are your results? Do you agree or disagree with the results?

2. Jump start your search with these sites: *http://www.franchisee.org, http://www.aafd.org, http://www.franchisetimes.com, http://www.franchise411.com,* and *http://franchises.about.com.* Which of these sites did you find most helpful? Why?

3. Check out articles on the top 50 franchises, low-cost franchises, or whatever else interests you. What franchises are hot? What franchises are growing the fastest? Do not get lost: Keep a list of the good ideas gleaned from your reading. This is your time to explore franchising.

4. Explore the sites in the Incredible Resource box.

5. Reach out to franchisees through the sites listed in the Community Resource box.

FDD (Franchise Disclosure Document) Franchise information outlining 23 tightly defined areas required by the FTC to be disclosed to prospective franchisees before any fees are paid or contracts signed

Action Step 58

Franchise Information Packet

Using the insights gained from searching out franchises on the Internet, in magazines, or from a franchise directory, your next step is to request information from selected franchisors.

At this point, you are the prospective buyer. You have the funds, the drive, and the will to succeed. The franchisor has a product to sell, which will be represented by the franchise information packet.

1. Call or e-mail to request several packets from franchisors of your choice. Although many are available online, some franchisors choose to prequalify potential buyers before sending information packets. Take time to study: compare Subway to Blimpie's, Home Instead to Visiting Angels, and so on.

2. When you have examined the online packets, write a page or two summarizing what you have learned. You can also download the Franchise Comparison Worksheet at *http://www.entrepreneur. com/uploadedfiles/images/ formnet/frn1.doc*. Focus on the need, the uniqueness, and the advantages of the franchise format. Advantages should include economies of scale in advertising and bulk buying, the established goodwill of the name, the franchise track record, and the reputation of the franchisor.

3. Start to formulate questions for the franchisor and franchisees.

2. **Terminology and getting started:** If you are new to franchising, you would be smart to acquire some of its specialized vocabulary. Check out the glossary of terms on one of the major sties. One of the key terms you will need to know is **Franchise Disclosure Document (FDD)**, formerly known as a *Uniform Franchise Offering Circular (UFOC)*, a disclosure document provided by the franchisor to the prospective franchisee. Appendix C contains an FDD outline. If you reach this step later on in your search and receive an FDD, consult an attorney who specializes in franchising to help you review the document. Also read "A Consumer Guide to Buying a Franchise," an excellent primer, which may be found online at *http:// www.ftc.gov/bcp/edu/pubs/consumer/invest/inv05.shtm*.

3. **Searching the world:** For a super-positive view of franchising in the world, check out the Web site for the IFA at *http://www.franchise.org*. The IFA offers a multitude of services to members for only $100 a year.

4. **A click away, opportunities abound:** You can spend weeks viewing all the sites, including *http://www.franchisee.org*, *http://www.aafd.org*, *http://www. franchisetimes.com*, *http://www.franchise411.com*, and *http://franchises. about.com*. Visit pages such "Low Investment 150" and "International 200"

5. **Litigious Gloom:** The wonderful world of franchising is not all rosy sunsets and profits made easy. A dour U.S. government Web site at *http:// www.ftc.gov* leads you to case summaries involving franchisors and creative business developers who landed in court for attempting to sell opportunities that either did not exist or were misrepresented. Franchising is a very litigious business. Attorneys get rich over the problems associated with deceptive or irresponsible franchising. People who buy franchises have to do things *exactly* the way they are laid out in the franchise agreement; they cannot deviate from the system. When people *do* try to deviate from the system, they often end up in court. Franchise agreements are airtight and favor the franchisor.

After reading for several hours, using the Web sites noted in this chapter as a starting point, locate several franchises that interest you. Visit their Web pages and explore their franchise opportunities. In addition, determine their major competitors, and explore their competitor's Web sites as well. In the past, you had to request a franchise information packet, but most of the franchisors' Web pages include most of the information you will need to conduct preliminary research. Complete Action Steps 57 and 58 now.

Another good way to learn about franchising in a short time is to attend a franchise exposition. You can learn when and where they are to be held in your area by watching for announcements in major newspapers or checking Web sites such as *http://www.franchisehelp.com*. If a franchise exposition is available in your area, complete Action Step 59. If you are adventurous, consider looking abroad for a franchise opportunity. The Global Village box on page 385 illustrates international franchise expos that you can attend.

Keep your checkbook at home, because this is not the time to make any commitments. Up-front franchise fees are very profitable for franchisors, and an incredibly hungry and aggressive force of franchise salespeople can part you from your money quite easily. They know that many people looking for franchises are eagerly awaiting the lift-off of their dreams, and thus many people are vulnerable. Do not be one of them!

Another way to explore a particular franchisor would be to attend the franchisor's annual convention. Contact the franchisor to determine the date of the next state, regional, or annual convention. If they will not allow you to attend because you are not an owner, consider planting yourself in the lobby of the convention hotel and asking questions of every franchisee you meet.

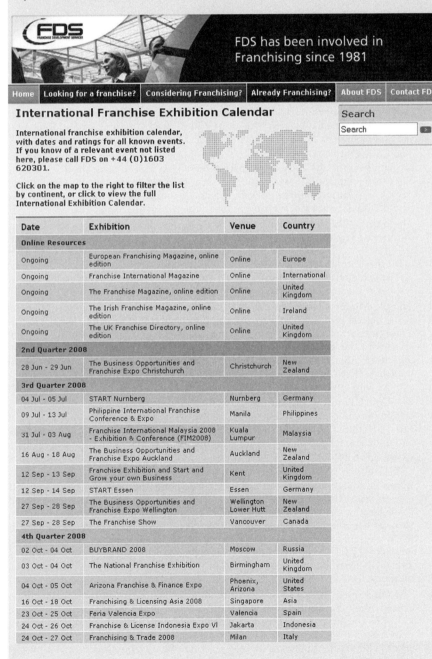

GLOBAL VILLAGE

A Franchise Overseas?

Suppose you like to travel, you speak several languages, and you want to explore business opportunities abroad; suppose you also want to determine if there might be an overseas franchisor looking for U.S. representation. If you latch onto a successful franchise that is already up and running, your chances for success are better. You can attend one of the many international exhibitions throughout the world, as shown in the calendar below, and you can log on to one of the many international franchise magazines. If your dreams can stretch across the oceans, opportunities abound.

FDS has been involved in Franchising since 1981

| Home | Looking for a franchise? | Considering Franchising? | Already Franchising? | About FDS | Contact FDS |

International Franchise Exhibition Calendar

International franchise exhibition calendar, with dates and ratings for all known events. If you know of a relevant event not listed here, please call FDS on +44 (0)1603 620301.

Click on the map to the right to filter the list by continent, or click to view the full International Exhibition Calendar.

Search

Date	Exhibition	Venue	Country
Online Resources			
Ongoing	European Franchising Magazine, online edition	Online	Europe
Ongoing	Franchise International Magazine	Online	International
Ongoing	The Franchise Magazine, online edition	Online	United Kingdom
Ongoing	The Irish Franchise Magazine, online edition	Online	Ireland
Ongoing	The UK Franchise Directory, online edition	Online	United Kingdom
2nd Quarter 2008			
28 Jun - 29 Jun	The Business Opportunities and Franchise Expo Christchurch	Christchurch	New Zealand
3rd Quarter 2008			
04 Jul - 05 Jul	START Nurnberg	Nurnberg	Germany
09 Jul - 13 Jul	Philippine International Franchise Conference & Expo	Manila	Philippines
31 Jul - 03 Aug	Franchise International Malaysia 2008 - Exhibition & Conference (FIM2008)	Kuala Lumpur	Malaysia
16 Aug - 18 Aug	The Business Opportunities and Franchise Expo Auckland	Auckland	New Zealand
12 Sep - 13 Sep	Franchise Exhibition and Start and Grow your own Business	Kent	United Kingdom
12 Sep - 14 Sep	START Essen	Essen	Germany
27 Sep - 28 Sep	The Business Opportunities and Franchise Expo Wellington	Wellington Lower Hutt	New Zealand
27 Sep - 28 Sep	The Franchise Show	Vancouver	Canada
4th Quarter 2008			
02 Oct - 04 Oct	BUYBRAND 2008	Moscow	Russia
03 Oct - 04 Oct	The National Franchise Exhibition	Birmingham	United Kingdom
04 Oct - 05 Oct	Arizona Franchise & Finance Expo	Phoenix, Arizona	United States
16 Oct - 18 Oct	Franchising & Licensing Asia 2008	Singapore	Asia
23 Oct - 25 Oct	Feria Valencia Expo	Valencia	Spain
24 Oct - 26 Oct	Franchise & License Indonesia Expo VI	Jakarta	Indonesia
24 Oct - 27 Oct	Franchising & Trade 2008	Milan	Italy

Source: *http://www.fdsfranchise.com/franchise-exhibition-calendar* (Accessed February 18, 2008).

Action Step 59

Visit a Franchise Exposition

Most major cities have at least one franchise show a year.

1. Go to *http://www.tsnn.com* to determine if an expo will be in your area anytime soon. If one is available, attend the expo and talk with the exhibitors. Learn what you can from their sales presentations, and attend any free workshops.

2. Collect literature and select several franchises that seem worth a second look. When you come home, go online to see if there are any blogs, references, or success stories regarding your chosen franchise. Compose a brief summary of your findings, and present it to your colleagues. Have your colleagues evaluate the franchise along with you.

   Remember, it is usually the small and new franchisors that exhibit at the shows, and their salespeople work on commission. Do not allow yourself to be persuaded; you are there to observe and evaluate, you are probably not yet ready to buy. Leave your checkbook or debit card at home.

BEWARE OF SCAMS

Unfortunately, many scammers and schemers ply their wares to unsuspecting dreamers. We cannot emphasize enough the importance of conducting due diligence and using an experienced franchise attorney throughout the purchasing process. In addition, follow your gut.

> ## The Top 10 Warning Signs of a Shady Franchise or Business Opportunity

If you're in the market to buy a business, protect yourself by being on the lookout for these ten warning signs of a franchise or business opportunity scam.

1. **The Rented Rolls-Royce Syndrome:** The overdressed, jewelry-laden sales representative works hard to impress you with the appearance of success. These people reek of money—and you hope, quite naturally, that it will rub off on you. (Motto: "Don't you want to be like me?") Antidote: Check the financial statements in the Franchise Disclosure Document; they're required to be audited.

2. **The Hustle:** Giveaway sales pitches: "Territories are going fast!" "Act now or you'll be shut out!" "I'm leaving town on Monday afternoon, so make your decision now." They make you feel that you'd be a worthless, indecisive dreamer not to take immediate action. (Motto: "Wimps need not apply.") Antidote: Take your time, and recognize The Hustle for the crude closing technique that it is.

3. **The Cash-Only Transaction:** An obvious clue that companies are running their programs on the fly: They want cash so there's no way to trace them and so you can't stop payment if things crash and burn. (Motto: "In God we trust; all others pay cash.") Antidote: Insist on writing a check—made out to the company, not to an individual. Better yet, walk away.

4. **The Boast:** "Our dealers are pulling in six figures. We're not interested in small thinkers. If you think big, you can join the ranks of the really big money earners in our system. The sky's the limit." And this was in answer to your straightforward question about the names of purchasers in your area. (Motto: "We never met an exaggeration we didn't like.") Antidote: Write your Business Plan and make it realistic. Don't try to be a big thinker—just a smart one.

5. **The Big-Money Claim:** Most state authorities point to exaggerated profit claims as the biggest problem in business opportunity and franchise sales. "Earn $10,000 a month in your spare time" sounds great, doesn't it? (Motto: "We can sling the zeros with the best of 'em.") If it's a franchise, any statement about earnings—regarding others in the system or your potential earnings—must appear in the Franchise Disclosure Document. Antidote: Read the FDD and find five franchise owners who have attained the earnings claimed.

6. **The Couch Potato's Dream:** "Make money in your spare time . . . This business can be operated on the phone while you're at the beach . . . Two hours a week earns $10,000 a month." (Motto: "Why not be lazy and rich?") Understand this and understand it now: The only easy money in a deal like this one will be made by the seller. Antidote: Get off the couch, and roll up your sleeves for some honest and rewarding work.

7. **Location, Location, Location:** Buyers are frequently disappointed by promises of services from third-party location hunters. "We'll place these pistachio dispensers in prime locations in your town." (Motto: "I've got ten sweet locations that are going to make you rich.") Turns out all the best locations are taken, and the bar owners will not insure the machines against damage by their inebriated patrons. Next thing you know, your dining room table is loaded with pistachio dispensers—and your kids don't even like pistachios. Antidote: Get in the car and check for available locations.

8. **The Disclosure Dance:** "Disclosure? Well, we're, uh, exempt from disclosure because we're, uh, not a public corporation. Yeah, that's it." (Motto: "Trust me, kid.") No business-format franchisor, with very rare exception, is exempt from delivering a disclosure document at your first serious sales meeting or at least 14 days before the sale takes place. Antidote: "Disclosure: Don't let your money leave your pocket without it."

9. **The Registration Ruse:** You check out the franchisor with state authorities, and they respond, "Who?" (Motto: "Registration? We don't need no stinking registration!")

Franchisors are required to register in 15 states; in Florida, Nebraska, and Texas, franchisors may file for exemption. Antidote: If you are in a franchise-registration state and the company is not registered, find out why. (Some companies are legitimately exempt.)

10. **The Thinly Capitalized Franchisor:** This franchisor dances lightly around the issue of its available capital. (Motto: "Don't you worry about all that bean-counter hocus-pocus. We don't.") Antidote: Take the FDD to your accountant, and learn what resources the franchisor has to back up its contractual obligations. If its capitalization is too thin or it has a negative net worth, it's not necessarily a scam, but the investment is riskier.

Source: Adapted from Andrew A. Caffey, "The Top 10 Warning Signs of a Shady Franchise or Business Opportunity", *http://www.entrepreneur.com* (Accessed January 29, 2008). Andrew A. Caffey is a practicing franchise attorney in the Washington, D.C., area, an internationally recognized specialist in franchise and business opportunity, and former general counsel of the International Franchise Association. Reprinted with permission from *Entrepreneur* Magazine, January, 2001

Now that you know how to research the world of franchising, protect yourself from scams, consider the two overwhelming reasons for buying a franchise: to benefit from name recognition and for brand loyalty. Consumers grow to trust brand-name products and services. Look at the items you purchase: Do you drink Coca-Cola? The Coca-Cola headquarters are in Atlanta, but the beverage is bottled by regional franchisees. Do you buy gas at Exxon or Mobil? They are franchises, too.

Franchised products and services are predictable and reliable. Many consumers go out of their way to do business with franchisors, and this customer loyalty may be worth paying for. You need to assess whether paying for the fees associated with a franchise will leave you with enough profit despite the customer loyalty. Also, consider the advertising fees required by the franchise agreement to keep that branding alive and well. Sales bring dollars, but profits keep you alive.

WHAT THE FRANCHISEE MAY RECEIVE

Let us examine what you can expect when you purchase a franchise from a franchisor—that is, when you become a franchisee. During your investigation of franchise opportunities, research each of these questions as part of your due diligence; the answers will vary greatly among franchisors.

Potential franchisees will be provided a Franchise Disclosure Document (FDD) that includes information on many issues. It includes contact information for present and past franchisees in the system. Many potential franchisees have found it difficult to contact past franchisees; with the revised FDD document, it will be easier to contact at least five to ten past franchisees to discuss their franchise experience. In addition, the new rules require franchisors to list organizations that have formed to represent franchisees.

New rules force franchisors to disclose litigation against franchisees relating to the franchise relationship within the past fiscal year. Disclosures must be updated within 120 days of the franchisor's fiscal year end.

Unfortunately, franchisors will not be required to disclose the names of their franchise sales brokers, though "gag clauses" signed by franchisees during the past 3 fiscal years *will* need to be disclosed. Earnings claims remain optional in the document.

If you purchase a franchise, each of the following areas should be explored fully with the franchisor and current and past franchisees. Again, we stress that you also need to compare and contrast the offerings of competing franchisors.

Online Franchising Communities

The online franchise sites and blogs highlighted below can provide excellent information, and many times very honest feedback, from franchisees. But when searching these sites, be forewarned: *buyer beware applies.* Many unhappy franchisees have axes to grind and attempt to do so on several sites. Also, brokers who do not always represent both sides of the franchising coin sponsor many online sites and blogs. For additional information on franchise brokers, read the Key Points from Another View on page 406.

http://www.BlueMauMau.org
http://franchisepundit.com
http://www.thefranchiseking.typepad.com
http://www.franchiselawblog.com

If you do not find what you need with the resources above, Google the franchise of your choice and find franchisee blogs. Also, try Facebook and YouTube.

1. **Brand-name recognition.** If you ask the right questions and pick the right franchise, the marketing boost you receive from the name of your franchise will be worth the cost. This is truly a major portion of your up-front fees and you should be convinced you are getting what you pay for.

2. **Immediate, brand-loyal customers.** Determine if the franchisor has been operating in good faith and providing good products and services, Competition today is much stiffer and customers tend to be much less brand-loyal.

3. **Support.** Corporate support services may include site selection, employee training, inventory control, vendor connections, a corporate-produced Business Plan, and more. Never underestimate the importance of associating with other franchisees. They will often mentor and guide you, and you will have people to benchmark your numbers with. Many franchisees band together and form independent associations in addition to the formal franchisor networks that exist. We cannot stress enough the importance of talking to franchisees.

4. **Training.** The franchisor will teach you the business, in anywhere from 2 days to 4 weeks, and may offer additional training as needed. Training may come at additional cost, so determine what is covered; be sure to inquire about training, materials, housing, airfare, and meals. Also, determine if there is ongoing training and if so, at what cost.

5. **Money.** The franchisor may also provide direct financing or assistance in locating financing. Some franchises have relationships with large lenders, making financing readily available for qualified buyers. Even if the franchisor offers financing, review other financing alternatives to determine which will be best for you.

6. **Planning.** You are buying a proven Business Plan, although if you are purchasing a franchise start-up, this may not be the case. You are buying a system, so make sure the system is in place and is proven. We suggest you complete your own Business Plan, whether purchasing a new or existing franchise, utilizing many of the Action Steps within this text.

7. **Bargains**. Collective buying power may bring economies of scale in purchasing goods, services, and promotion. One complaint of franchisees is that franchisors do not always pass these savings down.

8. **Psychological handholding and field visits from the franchisor**. Be sure to inquire, because support offered varies greatly among franchisors and even within areas. Spend time exploring this issue extensively with current and past franchisees. Too many visits can be overwhelming and make you feel like you are constantly under watch and too few visits provide scant assistance.

9. **Assistance in site selection and layout and design**. Large franchisors spend millions on research in these areas. Also, they may provide help in negotiating leases and purchases and their years of expertise and experience may prove invaluable.

10. **Standardized and pretested products**. Hopefully, your franchisor pretests all of the products and services they offer to you. In addition, you want to look for franchisors who contantly are abreast of changes and react promptly by offering new services or products to a changing market.

11. **Promotional materials**. Web sites, mailings, advertisements, flyers, store displays, and so on are often offered. Discuss with your franchisor the cost and requirements of purchasing such materials.

12. **Area or master franchises**. These offer you the opportunity to purchase an area and the responsibility to build the area with additional franchisees. Many entrepreneurs with strong sales and managerial skills have found riches with area franchises, You may also want to investigate if current franchisees are offered new opportunities first.

13. **Assistance of a store-opening specialist**. An experienced team of specialists may help effectively launch your business franchise with a grand opening event.

14. **Operations manuals**. Ask to review these to see if they cover the material you will need. They can be minimal to extensive. If you are paying for expertise, the operations manuals should provide that expertise and hopefully help you operate an efficient business.

15. **Sales and marketing assistance**. If you are purchasing a service franchise, make sure the franchisor has developed a marketing system for prospecting for clients, sales presentations, and closing methods.

16. **National or regional advertising with single-message strategy**. Continuity of message is essential. Franchisors who flip-flop with message lose customers, and your success may depend on national advertising. Confused customers will fly the coop.

17. **Territory protection**. You will be offered a certain territory or area in which to operate. Some franchisors do not offer protection and others provide only limited protection.

18. **Software packages**. Integrated accounting, financial, personnel, marketing, and operating software may be available, free or a fee. Check with the franchisor to determine who will update and service these packages and at what cost.

Area or master franchise Business arrangement in which a franchisor sells the rights of an area or territory to a franchisee, who is normally required to sell or establish and service a specified number of franchises in its area within a specified time period

In addition to the areas you need to explore above, Figure 14.2 offers a very detailed list of questions to ask current and past franchisees. Recognize that although the FDD of each franchisor spells out in detail what the franchisee receives and what is expected and legally required of the franchisee and franchisor, spending time with franchises will tell you the truth and the interpretation of the details. By law, you must receive a copy of the FDD 14 days before you are asked to sign any contract or before any money changes hands. Please note that the contract you sign is a *long-term commitment* and should be addressed

figure **14.2**

Talk to Franchisees Before You Join the Club!

By Jim Coen for http://franchisepundit.com

Suggested Questions for Franchisees:

- How has the franchisor responded to your calls for support about business operations or any other general questions you may have had?
- Do you feel the franchisor cares about your success and is willing to help you as needed?
- How would you describe your overall franchisor/franchisee relationship?
- Did you receive assistance in site selection, lease negotiations, build-out and permit processes, or any other areas unique to the opening of the business?
- What happens in a typical day?
- What will go wrong?
- How long did it take for you to realize a return on investment?
- What are your approximate earnings, and are they in line with your expectations?
- Did the franchisor adequately estimate the amount of operating cash that you needed?
- Was the training the franchisor provided thorough, and did it sufficiently prepare you to run this business?
- Were there any hidden fees or unexpected costs?
- Is your territory big enough to hit your goals?
- Are there restrictions on the products you sell and use in your business?
- Are you required to use designated vendors?
- Does the franchisor advertise as much as it said it would?
- What type of business experience, education, and skills did you possess before buying this franchise?
- Why did you select this particular franchise system over others in the same type of business?
- Did the training only cover the operating system, or did the training prepare you to compete with other businesses providing similar products or services?
- Did you encounter any problems with the franchisor, the site, or establishing your business, and how did the franchisor respond to problems?
- What are your sales patterns like? Are they seasonal? If so, what do you do to make ends meet in the off-season?
- Are there expansion opportunities for additional franchise ownership in this system?
- Knowing what you know now, would you make this investment again?
- What are your thoughts on this industry, the products, and/or services available, and what trends do you see happening for the future?
- Do you have any issues or concerns with the franchise agreement? Were there any clauses that stuck out over others that may impact your relationship with the franchisor?
- Has the franchisor responded to any of your ideas about improving the franchise system?
- Are there any other franchisees or former franchisees you recommend I contact?

Questions to Ask Former Franchisees:

- Why did you leave the franchise system?
- Did the franchisor cooperate in helping you sell your franchise?
- If there was a termination or non-renewal, did the franchisor explain why and provide a reasonable opportunity for you to cure the problem?
- Would you consider buying a franchise from a different franchisor?

Source: Jim Coen, *http://franchisepundit.com/index.php/2007/05/16/talk-to-franchisees-before-you-join-the-club* (Accessed April 2, 2008).

as such and thus not signed before extensive investigation and review by an experienced franchise attorney.

WHAT THE FRANCHISOR RECEIVES

Franchisors earn money in several ways:

Franchise fee One-time, up-front fee paid to a franchisor

1. Franchisors collect a one-time, up-front, nonrefundable initial **franchise fee** for the rights to use their name and system. This fee may range from $3,000 for a small service firm to more than $1.5 million for a well-established name, such as that of a hotel, auto dealership, or major restaurant. The franchise fee, paid upon signing the franchise agreement, usually covers 5 to 10 years. If any additional fee is due for subsequent renewal periods, it will be stated in the franchise agreement.

2. **Royalty fees**, which range from 2 to 15 percent of gross sales, are collected. Average royalty fees are 3 to 6 percent.

3. Additional advertising and promotion fees of 2 to 5 percent of annual gross sales will be directed primarily to national advertising, although a lesser amount may be allotted to local or regional advertising. Even if your franchise is not profitable, you *will* still be paying all of these fees.

4. Franchisors profit on items they sell to franchisees.

5. Franchisors make additional money through the sale of training materials, computer systems, and fees for training classes.

Read through Item 11 of the franchisor's FDD to understand what you are paying for, and talk to franchisees to make sure the franchisor is delivering on their promises. Franchisors may not pass on the volume rebates they receive from suppliers to their franchisees.

Some of the fees *may* be open to negotiation—especially with a new franchisor. For example, it might be possible to delay the royalty fee for 6 months or until the franchise is profitable. It is always a good idea to ask for concessions and for those concessions always to be made in writing. Advice from your attorney and accountant can provide back-up data to reinforce your negotiating points. Determining potential earnings when purchasing a franchise is challenging, so we suggest you review Figure 14.3 and dig as deep and as long as it takes to assure yourself that the franchise you want to purchase will support your financial goals.

Royalty fee Ongoing obligation to pay a franchisor a percentage of gross sales; may or may not include advertising fee

---

figure **14.3**

Earnings Potential: Evaluate in Depth

You may want to know how much money you can make if you invest in a particular franchise system. Be careful. Earnings projections can be misleading. Insist upon written substantiation for any earnings projections or suggestions about your potential income or sales.

Franchisors are not required to make earnings claims, but if they do, the FTC's Franchise Rule requires franchisors to have a reasonable basis for these claims and to provide you with a document that substantiates them. This substantiation includes the bases and assumptions upon which these claims are made. Make sure you get and review the earnings claims document. Consider the following in reviewing any earnings claims.

Sample Size. A franchisor may claim that franchisees in its system earned, for example, $50,000 last year. This claim may be deceptive, however, if only a few franchisees earned that income, and it does not represent the typical earnings of franchisees. Ask how many franchisees were included in the number.

Average Incomes. A franchisor may claim that the franchisees in its system earn an average income of, for example, $75,000 a year. Average figures like this tell you very little about how each individual franchisee performs. Remember, a few very successful franchisees can inflate the average. An average figure may make the overall franchise system look more successful than it actually is.

Gross Sales. Some franchisors provide figures for the gross sales revenues of their franchisees. These figures, however, do not tell you anything about the franchisees' actual costs or profits. An outlet with a high gross sales revenue on paper actually may be losing money because of high overhead, rent, and other expenses.

Net Profits. Franchisors often do not have data on net profits of their franchisees. If you do receive net profit statements, ask whether they provide information about company-owned outlets. Company-owned outlets might have lower costs because they can buy equipment, inventory, and other items in larger quantities, or they may own, rather than lease, their property.

Geographic Relevance. Earnings may vary in different parts of the country. An ice cream store franchise in a southern state, such as Florida, may expect to earn more income than a similar franchise in a northern state, such as Minnesota. If you hear that a franchisee earned a particular income, ask where that franchisee is located.

Franchisee's Background. Keep in mind that franchisees have varying levels of skills and educational backgrounds. Franchisees with advanced technical or business backgrounds can succeed in instances where more typical franchisees cannot. The success of some franchisees is no guarantee that you will be equally successful.

Source: FTC Consumer Guide to Buying a Franchise, *http://www.ftc.gov/bcp/edu/pubs/consumer/invest/inv05.shtm* (Accessed February 14, 2008).

figure **14.4**

The Twelve Worst Franchise Agreement Provisions

Do not sign a franchise agreement until you get these provisions changed!

1. **Gag Rules.** Some franchise agreements now prohibit franchisees from discussing any aspect of their franchise experience with anyone outside the system. This defeats the FTC rule and other state disclosure laws which require lists of terminated franchisees to be provided to prospective franchisees.

2. **Franchisor Venue Provisions.** These provisions require franchise disputes to be litigated or arbitrated in the home state of the franchisor. This not only increases costs for the franchisee, but also allows the franchisor to litigate, arbitrate or even mediate on their home turf.

3. **Lack of Reciprocal Cure Periods.** Many franchise agreements give the franchisor 30, 60, or 90 days to cure any alleged defaults; some even do not allow the franchisee any remedy if the franchisor defaults. On the other hand, some franchise agreements provide for no cure periods for any alleged default by the franchisee. What is good for the goose is certainly good for the gander.

4. **Nonreciprocal Noncompetition Covenants.** Many franchise agreements have oppressive post-term noncompetition covenants, both in terms of duration and geographical scope. At the same time, many franchise agreements allow the franchisor to place competing units pretty much where they want. If the franchisor wants protection from the franchisee after the agreement expires or terminates, why shouldn't the franchisee be entitled to the same protection during the franchise agreement?

5. **Sole Sourcing Requirements.** Many product-oriented franchise systems require franchisees to purchase products solely from the franchisor or from suppliers designated by the franchisor. No allowance is given to purchase from alternate sources even if quality standards are upheld. This leaves the determination of the gross margin achieved by the franchisee solely in the hands of the franchisor.

6. **Mandatory Subleases with Rent Overrides.** Many franchise systems require the franchisee to sublease the franchised premises from the franchisor who has in turn leased the premises from the landlord. This places the franchisor in the real estate business and able to net a profit essentially without risk. In addition, the fact of these overrides and the amount of them are rarely disclosed in franchise offering circulars.

7. **Lack of Accountability of Advertising Fund.** Over the years, franchise agreements have increasingly been drawn in a manner to give the franchisor maximum discretion over the use and application of advertising funds. Agreements are often drafted in such a way as to allow franchisors to not spend advertising dollars in the market where franchisees have contributed to ad funds.

8. **Lack of Reciprocal Legal Fee Provisions.** Many franchise agreements require the franchisee to pay all of the franchisor's legal expenses in the event of litigation between the parties. However, if the franchisee wins the litigation, the franchise agreement does not provide or legal fees. The only way a franchisee can obtain legal fees is if a state statute allows such recovery or in the unlikely event the franchisee prevails on a RICO claim.

9. **Kickbacks.** Some franchise agreements openly acknowledge that the franchisor has the right to make deals with vendors who sell goods and services to franchisees that are mandated by the franchise agreement Very often, these vendors provide kickbacks, promotional fees, and commissions to the franchisor in return for being allowed to sell their products and services to a captive market. Instead of passing these kickbacks, promotional fees and commissions on to franchisees to reduce their cost of goods sold and increase their margins, these payments are pocketed by the franchisors.

10. **Mandatory Arbitration Provisions.** While arbitration is a faster and presumably cheaper, it has major disadvantages to franchisees. Arbitration is private, with the resulting decisions not creating any precedents. In addition, the ability of a franchisee to obtain documents from the franchisor and to take depositions is severely limited.

11. **Radically Different Franchise Agreements on Renewal.** Many franchisees find that when it is time to renew, they are not really renewing their existing franchise agreement, but entering into a wholly new franchise agreement, often with materially different financial and operational terms.

12. **Unilateral Amendments to the Franchise Agreements.** Many franchise agreements provide that the franchisor can change its operations manual or other company policies from time to time without notice to or with the consent of the franchisee. Thus, the franchisor has the right to unilaterally change the franchise agreement. Moreover, the franchisee is rarely given an opportunity to inspect the franchisor's operating manual in advance of the sale of the franchise.

Source: *http://www.franchisee.org/Buying%20a%20Franchise.htm* (Accessed April 20, 2008).

ADDITIONAL FRANCHISEE ISSUES AND CONCERNS

Note the following pitfalls that plague franchising in general, along with the concerns in Figure 14.4.

1. Intense competition with franchisors of fast-food outlets, quick-printing shops, and service businesses often oversaturate markets; this causes **encroachment**, which results in many failures. Talk with current and past franchisees concerning this extremely important point. Some very successful franchisees have found their sales and profits have plummeted when faced with competition from within their own organization. More and more organizations also are migrating sales to the Internet, and you need to understand how this will affect local retail outlets.

2. Multilevel distributorships and pyramid sales schemes oftentimes only benefit the promoters.

3. Typically, current franchisees are offered new locations before they are offered to outsiders, meaning that the best opportunities are seldom offered to outsiders. Rarely is a new player offered a sure thing. New players may be offered those locations that have already been passed over or franchises that are being resold.

4. Termination clauses may be ambiguous. Thoroughly understand item #17 in the FDD before proceeding. Failure is a possibility, so consider the financial consequences before signing.

5. "Franchises that have closed or been sold back to the franchiser in the past five years or more than 5 to 10 percent in one year could mean many franchisees have become disgruntled or unprofitable," according to Kelly Spors, small-business writer for the *Wall Street Journal*.

6. Litigation, which is contained in the FDD, should be a concern; look closely at this FDD element. It can be a warning signal or a flashing red light.

7. Brokers sell franchises with very little regulatory control, and buyers need to recognize that these brokers are compensated by the franchisor and thus may have the franchisor's best interest in the forefront, not the buyer's. See Key Points on page 406 for more on this subject.

8. Legal recourse against the franchisor may be difficult. Be sure you understand what legal recourse you will have in case of a problem. Examine your contract carefully with your franchise attorney to determine if your legal recourse will be limited by the contract.

9. Royalties are based on gross sales, not net profits; if franchisors require you to sell specials at very low prices, you may find yourself losing a great deal of money on those sales. Tough times lead to low prices, price wars, and lower profits.

10. Freedom of association amongst franchisees may be discouraged by franchisors.

11. Noncompete clauses may be part of your contract. If you work hard but choose to terminate your contract or are terminated by the franchisor, you may not be able to compete as an independent business owner in a similar business.

12. In 38 states, franchisees have no "private right of action" and thus are required to go to the government if the franchisor violates the FTC rule.

13. Beware of "ground-floor" franchise opportunities; it is risky to be an early franchisee. A franchisor offering such an "opportunity" would be experimenting with *your money*. You want to buy a recognized brand name, a proven Business Plan, excellent field support, and experience that demonstrates the particular franchise will work in your location.

14. Voluntary chains such as True Value and Ace hardware stores are often a more desirable option to purchasing a franchise. Members of **voluntary chains** remain independent and pay no royalty or franchise fee. Look for more such organizations in the near future.

15. The management and owners of the franchise should be thoroughly investigated as occasionally new franchisors have questionable backgrounds.

Encroachment Entry into another's territory

Action Step 60

Investigate Franchisors and Franchisees

Use the questions throughout the chapter, especially those in Figure 14.2, and the questions that follow as you explore franchising by interviewing franchisors and franchisees:

1. **Franchisors:** Leave your checkbook at home and interview at least three franchisors. Here are some questions to start you off:
   What is included in the franchise fee?
   What is the duration of the agreement?
   How can the agreement be bought back?
   What are the royalty fees and other assessments?
   What level of training and service can I expect?
   Is the territory well defined?
   Under what circumstances can the franchisor change the territory?
   What is the turnover rate of the franchisees?
   How much help can I expect with advertising and promotion?

2. **Franchisees:** Now interview several franchisees. Try these questions:
   What do they wish they would have known before purchasing the franchise?
   Are they happy with the support and training they receive?
   What problems are the hardest for them to deal with in the business?
   How helpful was the franchise in site selection and development?
   What about financing?
   What about protected territories?
   And most important: What about profitability?
   How long did it take them to become profitable?

Voluntary chain Organization (consortium) formed by individual wholesalers or retailers to gain purchasing power and other economies of scale

You may not be comfortable operating by the rules and regulations set down by franchisors; many entrepreneur-types are not. Nonetheless, it makes good sense to check out franchise opportunities—especially those in your selected industry—because the search will give you a better picture of the marketplace and your competition. Complete Action Step 60 to expand your horizons about this option. You may find your dream business! Before going any further, ask if you can work in one of the franchises for 2 to 4 weeks to get a feel for daily operations and responsibilities.

In Chapter 13 we presented a checklist to use in evaluating an ongoing business you are considering buying. That checklist applies to franchises as well. To supplement it, we are giving you an additional checklist in Figure 14.5, prepared specifically for evaluating franchise opportunities. The questions will help you generate a profile of the franchise and make a wise decision. In franchising, you are not only investigating the actual franchise you are purchasing but the franchisor as well. Complete Figure 14.5 now. After reading the chapter, complete Action Step 61, which summarizes your thoughts and research.

figure **14.5**

Federal Trade Commission's Franchise Evaluation Checklist

General

1. Is the product or service: **yes**   **no**
   a. considered reputable?   _____   _____
   b. part of a growing market?   _____   _____
   c. needed in your area?   _____   _____
   d. of interest to you?   _____   _____
   e. safe,   _____   _____
      protected,   _____   _____
      covered by guarantee?   _____   _____
2. Is the franchise:
   a. local?   _____   _____
      regional?   _____   _____
      national?   _____   _____
      international?   _____   _____
   b. full-time?   _____   _____
      part-time?   _____   _____
      possible full-time in the future?   _____   _____
3. Existing franchises
   a. Date the company was founded _____
      Date the first franchise was awarded _____
   b. Number of franchises currently in operation or under construction
      _____
   c. References _____
      Franchise 1: owner _____
                   address _____
                   telephone _____ date started _____
      Franchise 2: owner _____
                   address _____
                   telephone _____ date started _____
      Franchise 3: owner _____
                   address _____
                   telephone _____ date started _____
      Franchise 4: owner _____
                   address _____
                   telephone _____ date started _____
   d. Additional franchises planned for the next twelve months _____
      _____

4. Failed franchises
   a. How many franchises have failed? _____
      How many in the last two years? _____
   b. Why have they failed? _____
      Franchisor reasons: _____
      Better Business Bureau reasons: _____
      Franchisee reasons: _____
5. Franchise in local market area
   a. Has a franchise ever been awarded in this area? _____
   b. If so, and if it is still in operation:
      owner _____
      address _____
      telephone _____ date started _____
   c. If so, and if it is no longer in operation:
      person involved _____
      address _____
      date started _____ date ended _____
      reasons for failure _____
   d. How many inquiries have there been for the franchise from the
      area in the past six months? _____
6. What product or service will be added to the franchise package
   a. within 12 months? _____
      _____
   b. within 2 years? _____
      _____
   c. within 2 to 5 years? _____
      _____
7. Competition
   a. What is the competition? _____
      _____
8. Are all franchises independently owned?
   a. Of the total outlets, _____ are franchised, and _____ are
      company-owned. _____
   b. If some outlets are company owned did they start out this way,
      _____ or were they purchased from a franchisee? _____
   c. Date of most recent company acquisition _____

(continued)

figure **14.5**

Federal Trade Commission's Franchise Evaluation Checklist (continued)

9. Franchise operations
    a. What facilities are required, and do I lease or build?

	build	lease
office	____	____
building	____	____
manufacturing facility	____	____
warehouse	____	____
_____	____	____

    b. Getting started—Who is responsible for:

	franchisor	franchisee
feasibility study?	____	____
design?	____	____
construction?	____	____
furnishings and equipment?	____	____
financing?	____	____
employee training?	____	____
lease negotiation?	____	____

Franchise Company

1. The company
    a. Name and address of the parent company, if different from the franchise company:
       name _____
       address _____
    b. Is the parent company public or private? _____
    c. If the company is public, where is the stock traded?

New York Stock Exchange	_____
American Stock Exchange	_____
over-the-counter	_____

2. Forecast of income and expenses can only be presented in UFOC. The franchisor should not give you any other estimates.
3. What is the best legal structure for my company?

proprietorship	_____
partnership	_____
corporation	_____
limited liability company	_____

4. The franchise contract
    a. Is there a written contract? _____ (Get a copy for lawyer and accountant to review.)
    b. Does it specify

	yes	no
franchise fee?	____	____
termination?	____	____
selling and renewal?	____	____
advertising and promotion?	____	____
patent and liability protection?	____	____
home office services?	____	____
commissions and royalties?	____	____
training?	____	____
financing?	____	____
territory?	____	____
exclusivity?	____	____

Source: Federal Trade Commission.

Legal Assistance

We cannot emphasize enough the importance of using an attorney who is experienced in dealing with franchisors and franchisees. To locate a franchise attorney, contact the International Franchise Association's Council of Franchise Suppliers at *http://www.franchise.org* and network with colleagues and other franchisees. If you have any friends or family members who own franchises, ask them to also review the FDD as well. They may spot issues and concerns based on their franchise experience, which may save you money and heartache.

According to Kay Marie Ainsley and Michel H. Seid, franchise consultants, "Regardless of what has been said or implied during your discussions with the franchisor, or with other franchisees in the system, as you go through the approval process, what is written in the contract is what will rule your relationship with the franchisor. The value of having an attorney review a franchise contract lies not in their ability to beat up the franchisor and 'get a better deal' for you, but in their ability to make sure you fully understand what you are getting into when you sign the contract. They can explain the different provisions, compare the provisions in the contract you are about to sign to what are considered 'best practices' in the industry, and tell you how the courts have interpreted similar provisions in other cases. *Everything* in the franchise agreement is important."

Action Step 61

Summarize Your Insights and Research

After you have perused several information packets from various franchisors, completed your Internet research, contacted past and present franchisees, and completed Figure 14.5 for several franchises, take up your pen and write a couple of paragraphs that answer the following questions:

1. What do you like about franchising?
2. What do you dislike about franchising?
3. What additional information do you need?
4. Is this the franchise for you? If so, why?
5. Can you make the amount of money you desire from this franchise?
6. If not, could owning an area franchise provide you with enough income?
7. What will you like most about owning this franchise?
8. What do you think you will like least?
9. Will you like running the day-to-day operation, or are you still in love with the idea of "owning a business" and "being your own boss"?
10. Where do you see this franchisor in 5 years?
11. Where do you see yourself and your franchise in 5 years?
12. Will you be able to sell this business easily?
13. Will you be able to hire a manager to take over day-to-day responsibilities?
14. Can you grow in this business?
15. How responsive has the franchisor been to change in the marketplace?
16. What questions still remain?

Don't be afraid to share your feelings with others: "I love this franchise because ..." or "This franchise packet gives me the shakes because ..."

PROCESS INVOLVED IN PURCHASING A FRANCHISE

If you have explored and investigated franchising and believe it is the right fit for you, and if you have worked through the Action Steps, the process truly begins. After contacting the franchise and prequalification, you will need to complete your due diligence as suggested above by researching the franchisor, franchisees, and profit potential. Begin by completing Action Step 60.

When analyzing the franchise packet, recognize that you are reading primarily advertising that's meant to sell you on the franchise. Try to read between the lines. Many of the packets will include an application for additional information such as Subway's in Figure 14.6, which you can fill out and return. We have used Subway as our example because we know there are few readers who are unfamiliar with their sandwiches and salads, which are served in more than 29,000 outlets in 86 countries.

If the franchise is large, a local sales manager or area franchisee will contact you after reviewing your application. You will meet to discuss capital requirements and locations further. If you will be purchasing a franchise through an area franchisor, you must also complete your due diligence, not only on the franchisor but on the area franchisor as well. Spend time and ask the questions we have presented throughout the chapter and those that have arisen from your discussions with franchisees. Inside the franchisor's packet, you will find information on capital requirements like those provided in Figure 14.7, which highlights Subway's requirements for their traditional restaurants.

Contact the American Franchisee Association at *http://www.franchisee.org* to determine if there is a local association of franchisees for your selected franchise in your local area. If so, contact them and delve as deeply as necessary, and for as long as you need to, until all your questions are answered. The more contact you have with franchisees, the better equipped you will be to make a final buying decision. As recommended earlier in the chapter, attempt to find a franchisee that will allow you to shadow him or her in their franchise for 2 to 4 weeks to better understand the operation before handing over any fees to the franchisor. Knowing what goes on in a franchise on a daily basis is essential before committing your funds, blood, sweat, and tears. After shadowing a franchisee and exploring your options, complete Action Step 61.

If your experience working in the franchise proves to you that you want to explore the franchise further, work with the franchisor to determine the best site or area for you. They should provide you with demographic, geographic, and psychographic information to support the numbers required for a successful franchise in selected areas. Deposits may be required before the site-selection process begins. If you are beginning to look at offices or retail space, involve your attorney immediately.

An accountant should also be called in to review material and point out financial issues that need to be discussed with the franchisor. Your accountant, if he or she has franchise experience, may help you assess the financial possibilities and feasibility of the venture and will help you compare it to other options. Review the Business Plan that the franchisor provides you and then work through the areas of the Business Plan that you need to adjust to fit your particular location, utilizing the appropriate Action Steps.

With the advice of your accountant, attorney, past and current franchisees, and banker, you are finally ready to negotiate with the franchisor to complete the sale. Be sure you understand your role and the franchisor's responsibilities.

figure **14.6**

Subway Application for Additional Information

Application for Additional Information

The filing of this form does not obligate the applicant to purchase or the franchisor to sell a franchise. Complete in full and do not use abbreviations. Please print clearly or type.

YOUR PERSONAL INFORMATION

Date ___ MM / DD / YYYY ___ Where did you hear about the SUBWAY® franchise? _____

Name _____ Citizen of _____
First   Last   Middle Initial

Date Of Birth ___ MM / DD / YYYY ___ Tax ID/Social Security Number _____ Gender - Male ❏ Female ❏

Other names known by _____ Are you of legal age in your State/Province/Residence Area? Yes ❏ No ❏

| Have you ever been convicted of a felony? Yes ❏ No ❏ | Have you ever been associated directly or indirectly with terrorist activities? Yes ❏ No ❏ | Have you been involved in any litigation proceeding within the last 5 years? Yes ❏ No ❏ | (If yes, on a separate sheet of paper provide the following for each proceeding: names of the parties involved, date filed, court where filed and nature of the proceeding.) |

Telephone(Home) _____ (Fax) _____ (Mobile) _____
area code / country & city code   area code / country & city code   area code / country & city code

Residence Address _____

City _____ State/Province _____ Zip/Postal Code _____

Country _____ Email Address _____

SPOUSE PERSONAL INFORMATION (Use A Separate Application for Partners)

Spouse's Name _____ Citizen of _____
First   Last   Middle Initial

Date Of Birth ___ MM / DD / YYYY ___ Tax ID/Social Security Number _____ Gender - Male ❏ Female ❏

Other names known by _____ Are you of legal age in State/Province/Residence Area? Yes ❏ No ❏

| Have you ever been convicted of a felony? Yes ❏ No ❏ | Have you ever been associated directly or indirectly with terrorist activities? Yes ❏ No ❏ | Have you been involved in any litigation proceeding within the last 5 years? Yes ❏ No ❏ | (If yes, on a separate sheet of paper provide the following for each proceeding: names of the parties involved, date filed, court where filed and nature of the proceeding.) |

EDUCATIONAL BACKGROUND

Highest Education Achieved	Schools Attended	Years	Grade or Degree Attained
❏ College Degree or higher ❏ Some College ❏ High School/GED ❏ Didn't Complete High School			

BUSINESS INFORMATION (Complete All Questions)

❏ Self Employed   ❏ Employed By _____

No. Years _____ Nature of Business _____

Title _____ Describe Position _____

Address _____

City _____ State/Province _____ Zip/Postal code _____

Telephone (Bus.) _____ Telephone (Alt.) _____
area code / country & city code   area code / country & city code

Select Your Business Experience Level

❏ Restaurant Mgmt.
❏ Other Business Mgmt.
❏ Restaurant Non-Mgmt.
❏ No Business Experience

May we contact you at work?
Yes ❏ No ❏

FINANCIAL INFORMATION (Please List Figures in US Dollars)

Income from current occupation $_____ / yr.

Income from other sources $_____ / yr.

Pls. explain other income_____

Personal Bank(s)/Branch   Address

Individual Liquid Assets (Cash, Stocks etc.) a)$_____

Individual Fixed Assets (Home, Car etc.)   b)$_____

Individual Total Assets   (a + b) c)$_____

Individual Liabilities (Mortgages, Loans etc.)d)$_____

Your Individual Total Net Worth (c - d) e)$_____
Excluding any financing listed below.

Would this business be your sole income source? Yes ❏ No ❏

Is there other financing not included in (e) above? Yes ❏ No ❏

If yes, how much financing is available? $_____

Application © 2005 Doctor's Associates Inc.

(continued)

figure **14.6**

Subway Application for Additional Information (continued)

REFERENCES (Excluding Relatives)

Name	Address	Telephone (area code/country & city code)

PARTNERS (All partners should fill out a separate Application)

Will you have partner(s)? ❑ Yes ❑ No   If not, you may skip this section. Otherwise, please complete all relevant sections below.

% Ownership

Partner's Name: _____ ❑ Active ❑ Silent _____ ❑ Male ❑ Female
First   Last   Middle Initial

Partner's Name: _____ ❑ Active ❑ Silent _____ ❑ Male ❑ Female
First   Last   Middle Initial

Partner's Name: _____ ❑ Active ❑ Silent _____ ❑ Male ❑ Female
First   Last   Middle Initial

Partner's Name: _____ ❑ Active ❑ Silent _____ ❑ Male ❑ Female
First   Last   Middle Initial

To include a partner's financial information, ensure they complete a separate Application for Additional Information

---

RESTAURANT OPERATIONS

If qualified, when will you invest in a franchise?	How involved will you be in operating the restaurant?	Preferred Geographic Franchise Area
❑ Now ❑ Within 6 months ❑ 6 months to 1 year ❑ Over 1 year	❑ 0% Not Involved At All ❑ 50% Somewhat Involved ❑ 100% Completely Involved	1st Pref. _____ 2nd Pref. _____ Estimated training date should you choose to invest: _____

I understand that the granting of a franchise is at the sole discretion of the Franchisor (Doctor's Associates Inc., Subway Franchise Systems of Canada, Ltd., Subway Systems Australia Pty. Ltd., Subway Systems do Brasil, Ltda., Subway Partners Colombia, C.V., Sandwich and Salad Franchises of South Africa (Pty.) Ltd., or Subway International B.V. or similarly situated franchising affiliate of Subway International B.V. or Doctor's Associates Inc.)

I understand that any information I receive from the Franchisor or from any employee, agent or franchisee of the Franchisor is highly confidential ("Confidential Information"), has been developed with a great deal of effort and expense to the Franchisor, and is being made available to me solely because of this Application. I agree that I shall treat and maintain all Confidential Information as confidential, and I shall not, at any time, without the express written consent of the board of directors of the Franchisor, disclose, publish, or divulge any Confidential Information to any person, firm, corporation or other entity, or use any Confidential Information, directly or indirectly, for my own benefit or the benefit of any person, firm, corporation or other entity, other than for the benefit of the Franchisor.

I authorize the procurement of an investigative consumer report, a general background search and an investigation in accordance with anti-terrorism legislation, such as the USA Patriot Act and Executive Order 13224 enacted by the US Government (collectively referred to as "Investigations"). I understand that these Investigations may reveal information about my background, character, general reputation, mode of living, association with other individuals or entities, creditworthiness, litigation history and job performance. I understand that, upon written request, within a reasonable period of time, I am entitled to additional information concerning the nature and scope of these Investigations. I hereby release a representative of the Franchisor, a credit bureau, security consultant or other investigative service provider selected by the Franchisor, its officers, agents, employees, and/or servants from any liability arising from the preparation of these Investigations.

This authorization for release of information includes but is not limited to matters of opinion relating to my character, ability, reputation, association with others and past performance. I authorize all persons, schools, companies, corporations, credit bureaus, law enforcement agencies or other investigative service providers to release such information without restriction or qualification to a representative of the Franchisor, a credit bureau, security consultant or other investigative service provider selected by the Franchisor and any of its officers, agents, employees and/or servants. I voluntarily waive all recourse and release them from liability for complying with this authorization. This authorization/release shall apply to this as well as any future request for these Investigations by the above named individuals or entities. I authorize that a photocopy or facsimile of this release be considered as valid as the original.

I agree that I will settle any and all previously unasserted claims, disputes or controversies arising out of or relating to my application or candidacy for the grant of a SUBWAY® franchise from Franchisor, exclusively by final and binding arbitration at a hearing to be administered by a neutral arbitrator in accordance with the Commercial Rules of the American Arbitration Association and to be held at Bridgeport, Connecticut, USA, unless my local laws require otherwise. Such claims include, but are not limited to, claims under federal, state, provincial or common law, such as employment law, civil rights law, contract law and tort law.

Everything that I have stated in this application is true and I understand that the information provided by me will be relied upon by the Franchisor. In accordance with anti-terrorism legislation, I understand that I will not be approved to purchase a franchise if I have ever been a suspected terrorist or associated directly or indirectly with terrorist activities. I read, understand, and agree to all of the above. Additionally, I understand that the Franchisor may require me to pass a standardized Math and English exam, unless I fall under one of the exemptions set forth in the Franchisor's Offering Circular.

Date_____Applicant's Signature (required)_____

Date_____Spouse's Signature (required)_____

Submit your completed application in one of the 3 convenient ways listed -	◆ **Online** - at http://www.subway.com/apply ◆ **By Fax** - to +1.203.783.7332 or +1.203.876.6688 ◆ **By Mail** - to SUBWAY HQ, 325 Bic Dr., Milford CT 06460, USA - attn: Franchise Sales

Application © 2005 Doctor's Associates Inc.

Source: Subway Franchise Packet.

figure **14.7**

Subway Franchise Capital Requirements

Effective: 4/2007 USA

SUBWAY® Franchise Capital Requirements
Traditional Restaurants

USA
US Dollars

General Breakdowns For:	Lower Cost	Moderate Cost	Higher Cost	When Due
Initial Franchise Fee	$15,000	$15,000	$15,000	upon signing Franchise Agreement
Real Property*	2,000	5,000	12,000	upon signing Intent to Sublease
Leasehold Improvements	42,000	78,750	105,000	pro rata during construction
Equipment Lease Security Deposit**	3,500	5,500	7,500	before equipment is ordered
Security System (not including monitoring costs)	1,000	2,500	6,000	when you place order
Freight Charges (varies by location)	2,750	3,750	4,000	on delivery
Outside Signs	2,000	4,000	8,000	when you place order
Opening Inventory	4,000	4,750	5,500	within 1 week of opening
Insurance	800	1,500	2,500	before opening
Supplies	500	900	1,300	before opening
Training Expenses (including travel and lodging)	1,500	2,500	3,500	during training
Legal and Accounting	500	2,000	3,500	before opening
Opening Advertising	2,500	3,250	4,000	around opening
Miscellaneous Expenses (business licenses, utility deposits, small equipment and surplus capital)	4,000	6,000	8,000	as required
Additional Funds - 3 Months	12,000	26,000	42,000	as required
Estimated Total Investment**	$94,050	$161,400	$227,800	

* This amount is the estimated deposit of 2 months rent payable upon signing the Intent to Sublease.
** If you do not select the equipment leasing program or it is not available, you should substitute the costs for Equipment Lease Security Deposit with $49,500 to $72,000 U.S. (including U.S. buffer of 10%). The amount of Additional Funds for the 3 months operating expenses would also be adjusted to reflect that you will not have to make 3 monthly equipment lease payments. This will cause your total initial investment to be substantially higher. (REFER TO GRAPH BELOW)

		Lower Cost	Moderate Cost	Higher Cost
The costs without an equipment lease, excluding any applicable taxes, including sales taxes, are estimated at:	USA	$149,050	$216,400	$282,800

THESE FIGURES ARE ESTIMATES OF THE COMPLETE INVESTMENT IN SETTING UP A SUBWAY® RESTAURANT AND OPERATING IT FOR 3 MONTHS. IT IS POSSIBLE TO SIGNIFICANTLY EXCEED COSTS IN ANY OF THE AREAS LISTED ABOVE.
Some costs will vary in relation to the physical size of the restaurant. A lower cost restaurant is one that would require fewer leasehold improvements, less seating and fewer equipment expenditures. Moderate and higher cost restaurants may require extensive interior renovations, extensive seating and additional equipment. If you are purchasing a franchise for another location opportunity, such as a non-traditional, satellite or school lunch program location, the above listed capital requirements may vary and could be substantially lower depending upon the necessary equipment you must acquire or changes in leasehold improvements you must make. The above figures do not include extensive exterior renovations.

Source: *http://world.subway.com/countries/developmentfiles/capital_int_trad_04_2005.pdf*

Once you have negotiated your contract, you may be on your own, or you may have a strong franchise organization behind you, helping you with site selection, store design, training, advertising, marketing, and possibly a grand-opening celebration. The story does not end upon opening—it has just begun! **Good luck!**

A Franchising Success Story

Susan Moore and her husband were lucky when it came time to investigate franchises; they had a source of inside information right in the family. They were also lucky because the franchisor they chose provided excellent support. Corporate support, which varies greatly among franchisors, was more important than brand-name recognition to Susan and her husband.

"Three years ago, my husband had to travel a lot in his job, and I was working very hard for a large company. While we were both drawing good salaries, we felt we had what it took to succeed on our own but wanted support. We decided to go the franchising route.

"We were both interested in the printing industry, and we chose a medium-sized national chain that seemed to have a franchise package

we could live with. We did have some inside information on this particular franchisor. My brother had been with them for 3 years, in the Pacific Northwest area, and he was making a good living.

"While we were interested in the quick-print industry, we weren't experts, so the 2 weeks of intense training was incredibly valuable. In addition, corporate helped us with site selection, market analysis, negotiating the lease, and the layout and design of our shop. There are so many details to think of when you're starting a business; it's very helpful to have experts take over some of the tasks.

"Another good feature of this franchise is that corporate will allow you to finance up to 80 percent of your start-up costs. This particular franchise can run as high as $200,000 up front, so that helped us.

"We opened a second shop last January, and both stores are doing nicely. We're developing a reputation for being on time in an industry known for being perpetually late."

BUYING AN EXISTING FRANCHISE

Turnover of existing franchises may happen due to divorce, health issues, retirement, relocation, or unhappiness of the owners, and it may provide an excellent way for you to enter the franchising world. Due diligence of both the franchisor and the franchise for sale should be undertaken as rigorously as if you were purchasing a new franchise location. Along with the information in this chapter, conduct the due diligence suggested in Chapter 13 for ongoing businesses.

Purchasing an existing franchise will shorten the required time to full operation; and if the business is currently successful, positive cash flow should come much quicker for you. You also will not have opening expenses and may be able to purchase used equipment at a reasonable price.

You may inherit the current employees, which may or may not be positive. If you are purchasing a retail establishment, shop the store frequently to assess the quality of the current employees. If they are outstanding, you will be a very lucky business owner. Also, if the business has been operating for several years, financial data should be available for you and your accountant to assess. Follow Myron's experience below.

Two Wins, One Loss

Michael Long completed a Regional Occupational Program (ROP) in healthcare and then earned his personal training certificate and worked at several health clubs for a few years. When he was 24, his great uncle died and left him $100,000. Feeling flush with cash, he considered buying a house or taking a trip around the world, but his parents encouraged him to purchase a franchise. Looking around, he realized his passion for fitness would be best realized if he purchased The Blitz franchise for his town. Michael opened the fitness center two months later in a strip center.

After successfully operating one franchise for two years, he was offered two more within a 40 mile radius. Seeing this as a way to increase his income substantially, Michael decided to purchase both franchises. One of the store's exercise studios had been losing money, but Michael felt he would be able to turn it around shortly.

Michael recognized after operating all three centers for another year that he was spending over 50% of his time at the losing studio and was afraid his time spent there was beginning to affect the other studios. Try as he would, he couldn't make money on the third center. He called the franchisor and explained that the one loser was draining too much of his time, energy and capital, and that he needed assistance in unloading it. The franchisor found several prospective buyers and together they chose the one they thought was the best. Michael now devotes all his time to working with his winners.

THE OTHER SIDE OF FRANCHISING: REASONS FOR NOT PURCHASING

If, after reading this chapter and exploring franchising, you are not convinced this is the correct path for you, you will join the many other entrepreneurs who have decided against buying a franchise. Whether rightly or wrongly, here are some of the reasons they have given:

1. I know the business as well as they do.
2. My name is as well known as theirs.
3. Why pay a franchise fee?
4. Why pay a royalty fee and advertising fee?
5. My individuality would have been stifled.
6. I didn't want others to tell me how to run my business.
7. I didn't want a ground-floor opportunity where I'd be the guinea pig.
8. It felt like I would have been committed for the rest of my life.
9. There were restrictions on selling out.
10. If I didn't do as I was told, I would lose my franchise.
11. The specified hours of business did not suit my location or desires.
12. The franchisor's promotions and products did not fit my customers' needs or tastes.
13. They offered no territory protection.
14. I would not be in control of my business.

But wait: maybe you do not want to own a franchise, but you have developed a winning business formula; maybe you can become a franchisor yourself. Many entrepreneurs have done this. This is another reason to learn all you can about franchising now.

CAN YOU FRANCHISE YOUR IDEA AND BECOME THE FRANCHISOR?

Paul and Lori Hogan have built a network of more than 700 Home Instead franchises (see Passion Box) throughout the United States and abroad, providing caregivers to the elderly, allowing them to remain independent. From their first office in Paul's mother's house in 1994, they knew they had a successful formula and could meet a growing need for home-care assistance. With previous experience in franchising, they searched out passionate franchisors interested in caring for others as they built Home Instead. Their focus on a rapidly growing market has propelled them to be named one of the top 100 franchise companies by *Success* and *Entrepreneur* magazines, and recently Mr. Hogan was named Entrepreneur of the Year by *Franchising World* magazine. Their success is incredible; according to *Franchising World,* the Hogans built "one of the first organizations to apply the franchising model to the home-care industry and take that concept international."

According to Francorp, a consulting firm in Olympia Fields, Illinois, the odds do not favor successfully franchising your business: "Fewer than 1 percent of franchise ideas ever get off the ground." Francorp suggested in an *Inc.* article, "Too Much Too Soon," that before you think of franchising, you first ask yourself the following questions:

1. Can someone learn to operate your business in 3 months or less?
2. How profitable are you? To attract high-quality franchisees, a franchise needs to generate at least $500,000 in annual revenue and earn the owner an income of at least 15 percent.

Consider reading books by Fred DeLuca, the founder of Subway, and articles by other major franchisors. Learning from their experiences and losses can be an excellent first step in exploring becoming a franchisor. Take time to talk to others who have started franchises—both the successful and the unsuccessful.

One former franchisor advises that franchising takes a substantial amount of money to start up, with no payoff guarantees, and recommends building a successful and profitable business model and replicating it several times before attempting to sell any franchises. Also, consider the time and effort entailed in developing your franchisees, and be careful not to provide additional concessions and finances to help them financially beyond what is reasonable.

⭐ *Passion* ⭐

Home Instead Franchisee Fulfills Her Dream

Altruism, honed through 15 years in the health care industry and 2 years as administrator of finance for her church, led April Moon Willingham to seek a franchise that would allow her to express her desire to help others and make a profit at the same time. After reviewing several franchise opportunities, she selected a Home Instead franchise, which specializes in providing non-medical-care services to seniors. Companionship, meal planning and preparation, coordinating household activities, light housekeeping, and help with transportation to doctors are just a few of the services offered by her caregivers.

Even with unemployment running below 4 percent, April was able to recruit excellent caregivers by reaching out to an untapped market of 50- to 70-year-olds who choose to work part- or full-time and enjoy helping others. Each client visit lasts a minimum of 3 hours, and visits can be arranged to meet the needs of the clients with weekly to daily visits.

A great deal of April's time is spent in the community visiting senior centers, assisted living centers, and nursing homes to discuss the firm's services with professionals who can recommend Home Instead to their clients as they transition. In addition, April meets each client personally to complete a needs assessment and returns once again to introduce the caregiver she has selected. If the match between caregiver and receiver does not work out for any reason, a new caregiver is assigned.

Her franchise fee in 2004 of $17,500 and a royalty fee of 5 percent, are, in her opinion, well worth the cost. Because long-term insurers now cover services such as those provided by Home Instead, April foresees continued and steady growth. In addition, Home Instead is developing alliances with senior organizations throughout the United States that provide additional clientele. April's passion for helping seniors has been realized through her Home Instead franchise.

Mark Siebert, CEO of iFranchise Group in Homewood, Illinois, warns potential franchisors, "If you truly love that small store of yours, prepare for a tearful farewell. You won't be a retailer anymore. You'll be advertising, marketing, selling, and serving the needs of your franchisees by providing them with operations manuals, training tools, and other assistance. It requires a different skill set."

Keep your idea simple and make sure you can train franchisees within a short period of time. Depending on the type of business, franchisees may only have 2 or 3 days time to learn the business. In addition, consider the amount of time that will be expended to assist the franchisees, not only in their start-up phase but also in the first year of operation. Personnel as well as personal and financial resources can be drained by demanding and unsuitable franchisees. Because of this, selecting your early franchisees is incredibly important for initial success. During the start-up phase, you just want to sell franchises; but do not get caught up in the selling, because it is the *success* of the franchises that will grow your business—not just the numbers.

Franchisors need to be aware that not all franchise ideas are transferable to other physical locations. Also, you need to make sure the concept can be replicated and is not dependent on the product or economic cycle. In addition, the success of many businesses is based on the personality of the owners and the employees. For a franchise, the success must not be dependent on the owner's personality but on the systems and the franchise's products or services.

Before becoming a franchisor, consider if you are willing to fulfill primarily the needs of your franchisees rather than the needs of your customers directly. Being a franchisor means working with many different personalities and setting up systems, operations, and training. In addition, you must be willing to watch others grow "your baby." Be aware that there are many consultants on the prowl for companies who think they can be the next Subway, and they will do their best to convince you that you are that next company.

FRANCHISING TRENDS AND FINAL FRANCHISING THOUGHTS

As you look for the right franchise opportunity, bear in mind that the best opportunity may lie with a young franchise that has proven its concept, has 50 to 60 winners, and is looking for growth in an area with which you are familiar. Many of these franchises currently are capitalizing on providing services such as home health care, tutoring, meal preparation and delivery, diet and fitness coaching, cleaning, handyman services, party planning, catering, teen activities, computer training or repair, and Web-based businesses.

Also, one of the most important elements in evaluating a franchisor is to assess whether they continually change and update their products and services to meet the changing marketplace. One of the strengths of a strong franchise should be a marketing research department that continually scans the environment to determine what steps will be necessary to capitalize on economic, social, technological, and demographic changes. Select the franchisor who is an innovator.

If you are really interested in making money as a franchisee, research becoming an area franchisee, where your territory could be as small as a section of town or as large as several states. Many individuals with strong business backgrounds have found area franchises to be quite lucrative. If you truly believe in the company's concept and have experience, explore the possibility of an area franchise. One Kentucky Fried Chicken franchisee now owns more than 50 stores.

Another growing trend in franchising today is the operation of multiple franchises housed and operated under the same roof. To research such franchise opportunities, interview key people at several multiple-franchise operations. Save yourself time, money, and maybe even some heartache by spending time visiting several successful and unsuccessful multiple-franchise operations.

Selling franchises is a numbers game. You, the potential franchisee, are a "lead." You will be told what you want to hear. If you have a few business skills and perhaps some business experience, then your chances of succeeding are far greater as a franchisee. A franchisor with a well-developed Business Plan will keep you on track. Ask to see it. Even if the franchisor has a well-developed Business Plan, you still need to complete one for your particular franchise location.

The key here is gut feeling. Look at franchising as an option—an example to learn from and maybe start with—and then, if you desire in the future, blend that knowledge and experience into a unique business that explores the gaps exposed in Chapters 2 and 3.

If you are not ready to be totally on your own yet, or you just want the assurance and support, franchising may be the way for you to start. With minimal financial investment, another alternative may be network marketing discussed in Figure 14.8, which presents both the pros and cons of multilevel marketing.

figure **14.8**

Network Marketers: Pros or Cons?
Microsoft Small Business Center

Network marketing adheres to a fundamental tenet: Lotions, potions and a slew of other products can be better sold face-to-face, without stores or middlemen.

The industry got its start in the early 1900s, and became popular in recent years through companies such as Amway. Network marketers sold door to door for years, with varying degrees of success.

The Internet era hasn't done anything to change this. However, the Web has revolutionized some marketing and distribution practices within the industry. It has made it faster and less costly for legitimate network-marketing companies to get the attention of potential customers.

Unfortunately, the Internet also has made it easier for illegal companies — mostly the skilled perpetrators of pyramid schemes and related scams — to get in the face of consumers as well. Many of these scam artists portray themselves as honest network marketers.

If you are interested in this high-risk but potentially lucrative industry, read on. You'll find some background on network marketing, as well as eight tips to help you distinguish a legitimate business opportunity from a fraud.

Amway spearheaded industry growth

First, some background on network marketing, which is also known as multi-level marketing (many people use the terms interchangeably).

Among its founding principles:

- A direct selling process lets distributors of certain products "educate" consumers more successfully (and more economically) on the products' merits than catchy TV ads or fancy store displays.

- Customers who are sold on a certain product can be motivated to sell it themselves and to recruit others to become sellers as well (forming a business "pyramid" of sorts over time).

- Sellers will have an incentive to sell and to recruit others, as they'll be paid commissions both on their own sales and their recruits' sales. In other words, the earlier you get in to the network, the more money you can make.

- Last, but not least, success is not guaranteed, and only the best products and services — and the best network marketers — will survive in the business.

Founded in 1959, Amway has built a multi-billion-dollar business on these basic premises. In the late 1970s, it successfully fought off claims by the federal government that it was an illegal pyramid scheme. In prevailing in court, Amway proved the key test of a legitimate business — that even the last person recruited into its networks can make money. (In a pyramid scheme, large numbers of people at the bottom end up paying money to only a few people at the top.)

(continued)

figure **14.8**

Today, legitimate network marketing companies span the globe, with several hundred in the U.S., including recognizable names such as Avon, Mary Kay, NuSkin, Unicity Network (formerly Rexall) and Herbalife. The products they sell range from vitamins and weight-loss plans to skin-care lotions to software and even dental insurance. Together, network marketing companies generated $28.7 billion in U.S. sales in 2002, according to the Direct Selling Association (DSA), a lobbying association that represents network marketers and other companies who sell directly to consumers.

'Technology a two-edged sword'

How pervasive is fraud in the industry? More pervasive than ever before, say many industry experts, although the Federal Trade Commission does not have statistics to quantify the impact. "I can tell you that, in the last 10 years, with the growth of the Internet, we have seen a significant growth in the number of apparent pyramid schemes," says Jim Kohm, the FTC's assistant director of marketing practices.

The low cost of entry into the industry long has encouraged scam artists. But the Internet has enabled them to market their schemes to consumers as successfully as it has legitimate network marketers, Kohm says. "Technology has proven to be a two-edged sword," notes Keith Laggos, an Amway veteran and industry expert who publishes Money Maker's Monthly (www.mmmonthly.com) and Direct Sales Journal (www.directsalesjournal.com).

8 fraud detectors

So how can you tell a scam or a shady business from a legitimate money-making opportunity? Here are eight things to consider before you take the plunge.

1. **Make sure that a solid product or service figures prominently in the business.** Sounds simple, but in many pyramid schemes, the product or service is a mere "fig leaf" to an illegal source of revenue — often the signup or membership fees required just to join a network. (Most will never see their money again.) Be convinced the product or service is not a gimmick or a throwaway, but one you'd buy yourself. A related scam, the Ponzi scheme, involves no products at all, but rather promises of investment or insurance windfalls. Most network marketers do charge a nominal signup fee of $30 to $60. But if there is no product being sold, keep your money — don't be swayed by the "benefits" of becoming part of a network.

2. **Confirm that the commission structure is supported by product sales.** Note that you are not becoming an "employee," but rather an independent business operator earning sales commissions. In illegal businesses, you can sell well but have your commissions diluted by other costs or obligations. For example, the FTC in 2000 shut down a Las Vegas-based company operating in eight states, because it required participants to pay excessively for seminars and desk space. Only a handful ever made any money.

3. **Don't pay more than $500 in initial "buy-in" costs.** Most network marketing companies require you to buy a certain amount of product to get started. If joining the company means you have to buy $500 in products or services, or if you see excessive product inventory costs, period, watch out. And again, if you are asked to fork over money without getting any product at all, flee as fast as you can.

4. **Beware of high earnings claims.** Many convicted pyramid schemers have been charged with misrepresenting the potential earnings of participants. You should expect reasonable commissions and growth opportunities, but nothing grandiose. Be wary of inordinate product and earnings hype. A rule of thumb: If it sounds too good to be true, it probably is.

5. **Don't participate unless the company is willing to buy back inventory.** Many scams — and some legitimate businesses—will refuse to buy back the leftover inventory you've purchased, even if you decide within a year that network marketing is not for you. In its membership requirements, the DSA mandates that network marketers be willing to buy back unused inventory, for at least 90% of the sale price, within a year of the sale.

6. **Find out if the network marketer is a DSA member.** The nine-decade-old association is the closest thing to a governing body for network marketers. The Direct Sales Association has about 150 U.S. member companies and some 50 others undergoing an intense application process for membership, says Joseph Mariano, executive vice president and legal counsel. All members are listed on its Web site. While less than half the U.S. network marketers are members, if the company you're interested in is a member, that's a good sign.

7. **Find out how long the company has been in business.** At least 90% of all network marketers fail within three years. About 80% fail within the first year, notes Bill Rodgers, a veteran Seattle-area network marketer who served as president of the Mercer Island Chamber of Commerce. If the company you're interested in has been around for more than three years, it is likely not only legitimate, but viable.

8. **Do your due diligence.** While you want to stay away from scam artists, you also want to avoid wasting time and money with a loser company. In Rodgers' own guidelines for assessing network marketing opportunities, he comments:

   "The FTC has been quick to identify and act on the companies engaging in illegal practices," says Rodgers, a marketer for Unicity Network. "Unfortunately, it takes a number of people to be swindled before the problem surfaces."

Source: http://www.microsoft.com/smallbusiness/resources/marketing/privacy-spam/network-marketers-pros-or-cons.aspx (Accessed April 20, 2008).

SUMMARY

There are two good reasons to consider buying a franchise: if the brand name is respected, you will already be positioned in the marketplace; and if the franchisor is strong, you will inherit a Business Plan that works. Examine the franchise's appeal with consumers carefully; you want to get a marketing boost from the name. Depending on the franchise, you may also receive other services for your money; for example, you may receive help with site selection, interior layout, and vendor connections, but the main thing you are buying is brand-name recognition. Earnings claims are not legal unless they appear in the Franchise Disclosure Document.

Just as if you were investigating an ongoing, independent business, study the opportunity thoroughly. Examine the financial history, and compare what you would make if you bought the business to what you would make if you invested the same money elsewhere or started a similar business without the franchise.

Know what drives the business and what factors are important for operating a potential franchise. The territory size you purchase and its demographics in relation to the product or service will help to determine your success and profitability. Information in Chapters 4 and 6 on demographics and site selection should be reviewed. In addition, all the appropriate Action Steps should be completed as you investigate possible franchise opportunities.

Buying a franchise does not ensure success. The ultimate responsibility for the success or failure of the business lies with the franchisee. Along with a name brand, you are purchasing a system to follow. Follow it carefully.

THINK POINTS FOR SUCCESS

- Avoid ground-floor opportunities. "Grow with us" should signal *caveat emptor* ("let the buyer beware").
- Talk to franchisees, especially those who have left the system. Franchisees who have left the fold are listed in the FDD. Keep in mind, current franchisees sometimes receive a finders fee, so they may not be totally honest with a potential buyer.
- Remember you are purchasing a job, and you *have* to do it their way, not your way.
- The franchisor gets a percentage of gross sales for advertising and royalty fees whether the franchisee is profitable or not.

- Consider carefully whether you really need the security blanket of a franchise.
- Read the proposed agreements carefully. They are airtight, favor the franchisor, and are usually nonnegotiable.
- Ask yourself if you can be comfortable relinquishing your independence.
- If you like to break rules, be creative, and stretch things to the limit, do not buy a franchise—you will very likely end up in court.

KEY POINTS FROM ANOTHER VIEW

Franchise Matchmakers' Real Clients

Kelly K. Spors

Start shopping for a franchise to buy, and you'll likely soon realize there are hundreds to choose from—some with flashy names like "Extreme Pita" or "Pilates Joe" that you've probably never heard of.

It's no wonder so many aspiring franchisees feel they need help choosing the right franchise. Just be careful where you turn.

There's a thriving industry of so-called franchise brokers, referral networks, or consultants offering prospective franchisees free help finding a franchise system that meets their needs. All these brokers—including bigger operations like FranChoice, FranNet, and the Entrepreneur's Source—essentially do the same thing: they interview prospective franchisees and recommend a short list of supposedly compatible franchises.

Conflict of Interest

But what's often lost in all this "free help" is a screaming conflict of interest: brokers get paid by the franchise systems that want to be promoted to potential franchisees—not by you.

The extensive interviewing process "gives a prospect a sense of false assurance that the broker is really working for them," says Michael Seid, a West Hartford, Connecticut, franchise adviser. In reality, "the broker's job is to bring as many good leads to the franchisors it represents as possible."

And there's great financial incentive to do just that. Brokers, Mr. Seid says, often make flat commissions of around $20,000, or 50 percent of the franchise fee, for every prospect who buys a franchise they recommended. They generally negotiate their commissions with each franchise system separately, so they might even get more money by recommending one over another.

Another potential drawback to using a broker, he adds, is that some represent only a small group of franchise companies—sometimes fewer than ten. So prospective franchisees may assume brokers are giving them recommendations from a vast pool of options, when they're only pitching the same five franchises again and again. There are no federal requirements for the brokers to disclose the franchises they represent or their compensation, though some states may carry their own disclosure rules.

A 2007 survey by Franchise Update Media Group, an industry resource, found that 14 percent of franchise sales were initiated through brokers. Some franchise systems that use brokers heavily, however, get more than 30 percent of their leads through them, industry experts say.

What the Brokers Do

Here's how the broker relationship usually works: A prospective franchisee hears about a broker through an acquaintance or a Web site and arranges a call or face-to-face meeting. The broker interviews the prospective franchisee and sometimes administers personality tests to gauge what kind of franchise system is best suited for that person. The interview process often involves questions about lifestyle needs, interests, managerial experience, risk tolerance and finances.

The broker then provides a list of three or four franchises for the prospect to further examine. The broker doesn't finalize sales for franchises, but instead leads clients their way.

Many brokers say that despite being paid by the franchises they promote, they only represent systems they've thoroughly vetted and believe are financially sound. The valuable service they can offer, they say, is the ability to help prospective franchisees home in on what they want in a franchise.

Kim and Rich Paul of Bel Air, Maryland, originally thought they wanted to buy a fast-food franchise. But after 4 hours of phone consultations with a FranChoice broker last year, they realized they preferred a franchise in which they didn't need to have employees or a storefront, one allowing them a more flexible schedule. "Using a broker was probably the best thing we did, because we really didn't know what we wanted," says the 51-year-old Mr. Paul.

After researching the four franchises the broker recommended, the Pauls bought a V2K window-treatment service franchise with $59,500 in start-up costs.

Marc Kiekenapp, a Scottsdale, Arizona, broker who represents six franchise systems including LA Sunset Tan and Right At Home, says brokers can also offer clients more details about the franchises they represent, how they operate, and what to expect.

Many of his prospects are referred to him by franchisors wanting to make sure franchisee candidates really understand the business and are well suited before signing up. He provides more information about the franchise and then, if clients are interested, they fly out to the franchisor's headquarters and perform their own due diligence to ensure the franchise really feels like a good fit.

Still, some say the inherent conflict of interest makes the value of using brokers questionable. Mr. Seid estimates that only a few hundred of 1,500 to 2,000 U.S. franchise systems work with brokers. Moreover, some of the best-known ones, like McDonald's, don't.

Careful Approach

Prospective franchisees hoping to use brokers may want to work with several to get the widest pool of possibilities, says Mark Siebert, chief executive of iFranchise Group, a Homewood, Illinois, franchisor consultant.

They should also ask brokers questions to discover how many franchise systems they represent, the fees they get paid, and how they conduct due diligence on the franchises they recommend.

Source: *http://online.wsj.com/article/SB120805177002210647. html* (Accessed April 20, 2008).

- Gather all your information together into one coherent unit; it will become a portable show-case for your business.
- Understand the importance of completing your Business Plan.
- Review the advantages and disadvantages of Business Plan software.
- Review a sample Business Plan to discover how one pair of entrepreneurs defined and show-cased their business.

- Understand that words can talk but numbers show it can be done.
- Review the Notes section for the financial information.
- Recognize the importance of providing all back-up data for your readers.
- Match or surpass the sample Business Plan in power and effectiveness.
- Put your finished Business Plan to work with passion.

chapter 15

Pull Your Plan Together
Launching with Passion

You may be closer to completing your Business Plan than you think. If you have completed the Action Steps in the preceding chapters, you already possess the major components of your plan. If you have not, return to Chapter 1 and work through the Action Steps. Through the past chapters, you have found gaps in the market, researched your Target Customer, defined your business, developed marketing and promotional ideas, and completed basic financial research and projections. As you develop your Business Plan using the Action Steps you have completed, you may recognize areas that need further attention and research. Also, some of the first Action Steps may need to be revised, as you have developed more knowledge of the market. Chapter 15 provides you with the structure to put your facts, figures, ideas, dreams, passion, and intuition into a workable plan.

Your Business Plan could be one of the most important documents you will ever pull together. If you need to start with your business immediately, consider using the Fast-Start Business Plan in Appendix A. Particularly if your business is less complex and has very low capital needs and low risk, this may be the alternative for you.

If you are completing a Business Plan for a high-tech company and seeking venture capital and angel investors, you will need to access additional Business Plans, as the specific requirements may go beyond what is covered in the basic Business Plan presented in this text. For new high-tech products, lenders and investors are most interested in how you plan to introduce a new concept and where specifically you will locate the early adopters for your product. For new ventures, the traditional channels of distribution may not work for your product, and you will therefore need to develop and substantiate how you will develop a new distribution method. Investors will focus on past accomplishments of the major players.

With a completed Business Plan in hand, you will have something to present to the people who are important to your business: bankers, lenders, relatives, venture capitalists, vendors, suppliers, key employees, friends, the SBA, and others. The plan is portable, so make as many copies as needed to share with people who can help you succeed. You can either mail it to contacts across the country or post it on the various Internet sites that link investors with entrepreneurs.

Planning is hard work. You will stay up nights, lose lots of sleep, and miss too many meals; but in the end, you will have saved time. Just as a pilot would not consider flying without a flight plan, neither should you consider a business venture without a Business Plan.

Occasionally, on completion of the plan, you may decide that the costs—in terms of money, time, effort, stress, and risk—are not justified. If this happens to you, congratulations! You have learned a valuable lesson, and it has only cost you time, not money. And you have learned how to research and write a Business Plan, so the next time opportunity knocks you will be ready to act.

Your plan should become a working, breathing, living document for your business dreams. Share your plan with others; they may have ideas, insights, or recommendations. Listen to their comments with an open ear. Chapter 6 introduced you to networking, and in Chapter 11, we encouraged you to find a mentor. It is now time to draw on these resources; review their input, and revise your plan as necessary. Business Plan reviewers sometimes ask for further details or back-up data that, when added to your plan, will make it stronger and more effective. Sometimes, we become so close to our Business Plan that we omit important and relevant details and information.

PREPARING TO WRITE YOUR BUSINESS PLAN

It is now time for your passion to come to the forefront and spill out into every section of your Business Plan. If your plan does not shout passion and confidence, you cannot expect your Business Plan readers to read further than the executive summary. Before you begin, gather in one place all your completed Action Steps and back-up data. Outline your plan, fill in the information from your Action Steps, refine the plan, ask knowledgeable people to review your plan, refine further, and prepare to present the plan to potential investors or lenders. Ask yourself, "Is it profitable to go forward with this plan?"

Remember, your reader and you should be looking at where you are now, where you are going, and how you are going to get there. Planning is an on-going process. Your Business Plan is a road map, but it should be one for a fast-growing area where new roads and new opportunities and challenges constantly present themselves.

If you are a creative thinker, chances are your thought processes do not always follow a linear sequence. That is great—it will help you as an entrepreneur. Nonetheless, the Action Steps in this chapter do follow a linear sequence: the sequence of the parts of a completed Business Plan. This is a matter of convenience—you will see an example of each part as it would appear in the finished product. Bear in mind, however, that we do not expect you to write each part sequentially. Also, depending on the type of business you are starting, one or two areas may be much more relevant than the other areas.

The best way to begin writing a Business Plan is to start with the material with which you feel most comfortable. For example, if you really enjoyed interviewing Target Customers, you might begin with "The Market and the Target Customers."

In this chapter, the Action Steps will serve as a checklist for keeping track of which parts of the plan you have written. For example, in practice you would probably write the cover letter last, but that is the first Action Step we present. Think of the writing of this first cover letter as a valuable exercise. After completing Chapter 15 and your Business Plan, rewrite your cover letter. The more cover letters you write, the easier it becomes to write them effectively. Reading through the plan will give you a good idea of what information lenders are looking for and the type of research you should conduct before writing your plan.

⭐ *Passion* ⭐
Entrepreneur Essentials

Radiate Passion and Energy

I have never seen an entrepreneurial situation, no matter how good the Business Plan or product, succeed without the infusion of personal passion and commitment by the people at the top of the organization. A great leader has the capacity not only to be motivated to an extraordinary degree but to share that passion, commitment, and vision with others. Venture capitalists, or anyone else funding new businesses, will look for passion and energy in the founders.

Passion and energy rule Wall Street. Those who can't communicate passion have a hard time getting funding. Investors care more about commitment and passion than they do about expertise or intelligence.

To succeed, entrepreneurs must avoid complacency and focus on a sense of urgency to get the job done. One of the worst things that can happen to a small business after it hits the initial "seed" round of funding is to lose its sense of crisis and urgency. Founders often get a little funding and think it's sufficient. They don't realize that a little bit of funding is setting itself up for a larger disaster if they don't make it work. Entrepreneurs have to refuse unacceptable reality and create new reality. That requires a lot of energy and time to move forward. If founders don't have passion or the ability to communicate that passion, they should find somebody to work with who does.

Don't Allow Your Organization to Politicize

In other words, insist on absolute integrity in behavior and information flows. Small organizations don't have the luxury in terms of cash flow and products to get bogged down in politicization, secondary turf fights, or policy or strategic fights. These conflicts drain the critical energy required for passion to move forward. It is incredibly easy to fall into this crippling morass of backbiting and positioning fights that characterize many, if not most, business organizations.

Every time I interview new job candidates, the first question I ask is how they view themselves on a scale of one to ten as a political infighter. If they brag about their expertise and how good they are, I take it as a red flag. That means they're wasting energy.

Managers and entrepreneurs should make it clear to new hires that they will not tolerate politicization nor unproductive time spent trying to position oneself, one's career, one's strategies, or one's preferences. Many good organizations are crippled by internal politicization.

Focus Tightly, Early, and Continuously

Entrepreneurial organizations face the biggest temptations during the second round of funding. A company receives its first million, goes through the steps, has a good Business Plan, and then receives an additional $15 million. Some entrepreneurs then say, "I have the resources to do what I really want to do. I can get outside that original focused Business Plan and rule the world." As a result, many entrepreneurs dilute their limited resources and never achieve their preliminary objectives.

If you are focused, you should be able to explain briskly and succinctly the essence of your business core competency and how you are unique in one sentence. If you don't have a rigorous enough focus to explain this in one sentence, you are probably not going down the right path. You can't spread limited human and financial resources over multiple objectives in most start-up companies. You have to be tightly focused and have a robust core competency.

Your focus should include gaining domain experience. You must have knowledge of the industry you are trying to dominate. Experience-measured capitalists and seed capitalists will first burrow in on whether or not you and your management team have a credible amount of domain experience in the industry you are targeting. Do you know the key decision makers? Do you know the key industry leaders? Are you on a first-name basis with them? Can you call them up and ask for help? That kind of domain experience is incredibly important. Right now the only Internet plays that are being funded are plays where the management team has heavy-duty domain market experience, not just technology experience.

Look yourself in the mirror before you go to someone with a Business Plan, and apply the one-sentence rule. Crisply and succinctly define what your core competence is, what differentiates you, and what makes you fundable to a potential investor or to potential employees whose lives will be your moral responsibility when they come on and accept your business partnership.

Link Up with Marketplace Decision Makers

You must have internally cultivated product advocates and thought leaders inside the company whose interests align with product thought leaders and market buyers outside the company. This should be done in a matrix of market orientation so you have a one-on-one relationship to move products through the organization.

(continued)

(continued)

Companies should have clear, unambiguous ownership of every major subgroup of internal products. Organizations need an internal ethic responsible for pushing that product forward and working with thought leaders on the outside. Often companies have an amorphous responsibility matrix, where the marketing department is responsible for four or five market areas and a vice president of sales is responsible for four or five product areas. No one really owns or has unit leadership or responsibility for different segmented market areas. Cultivate internal advocates and line them up internally in product groups.

Structure Decisions so One Bad Decision Won't Destroy the Company

Don't gamble on one fundamental premise. I know that sounds like a very conservative thing to do, but most successful entrepreneurs are not wild characters. Most entrepreneurs are actually extraordinarily conservative individuals who want to make things work. These entrepreneurs are not going to gamble the entire company on one rash strategic or marketing initiative.

Never have sink-or-swim moments when there is no contingency plan if the first one fails. Very little in life works out the way the business model said it would initially. You need to have resources left to react if something goes wrong. The company's entire future should never be fundamentally dependent on one decision.

Develop a Culture that Encourages Creative Failure

It's important to have a little bit of risk taking in the culture. This is the opposite of taking one big ego-ridden roll of the dice. Prudent failures on individual product initiatives should be encouraged to avoid a crippling politicization of company culture that could result in no one wanting to take initiative again. It's essential to instill courage. Everyone congratulates those who devote energy and take time to execute ideas and avoid failure.

Try not to destroy the integrity of future innovations of the company by doing anything to discourage well-formulated thinkers. It's more important to allow people the opportunity to experiment in a controlled fashion.

Empower Employees at Multiple Levels

Successful corporate leaders have ego security and self-confidence. They don't have to micromanage everyone's day-to-day lifestyle and situation, which tends to be a natural human tendency. Once given responsibility for an entity, organization, or division, people realize they will be assessed and held responsible. As a result, they overcompensate, get in everyone's faces, and keep people on too short a leash.

Experience has taught me that the best thing to do is hire extraordinarily talented people—if possible, people who are better than you are at what you are hiring them for. Find people who are so skilled that you can walk away from that responsibility on a daily basis and empower them with the sense of decision making. You must be unambiguous in your sense of strategic direction. You've got to give them a clear sense of mission, direction, limits, and resources. Once those are established, don't get in the way of good people. Make sure they feel confident enough to take good risks and move ahead.

Many good people leave organizations because they don't feel they have enough latitude to express their talents due to insecure and crippling micromanagement. Don't undercut the people you've hired. Avoid making detailed office decisions. If you hired them in the first place, it must be because you thought they were pretty good. Let them flourish, and empower them to go forward.

Moderate Your Greed

It's important to share generously with key employees who helped build the business. Blowing up wealth selfishly on topside options or ownership sends a very crippling message to employees about their relative importance and fundamental contributions to the economy. Go as deep as you possibly can with stock options. However, make sure that those stock options, which are essential portions of motivation and corporate ownership, are intimately linked to quantifiable performance and behaviors at the beginning of every year.

Don't toss around equity—it is sacred and is the ultimate motivator. I've never had to encourage my employees to work really hard. I already know that they work hard because their interests are aligned with my interests. They've got stock options. If they succeed, we all succeed. I don't worry about manipulation, mind games, or tricks. They know they're going to make out well if we all make out well.

If you set up a rigorous culture where people know that their incentive package is established fairly at the beginning of every fiscal year, the system runs itself. With quantifiable goals, you don't have to decide whether employees made or missed the objectives. I've never had to argue with people at the end of the fiscal year about whether we met goals or whether the costs per year went down 5 or 10 percent. It is already set up at the beginning of the year. Employees can sit down and write out their own bonus goal check and their own option check, because it is all rigorously quantitative and linked to personal performance.

In an entrepreneurial environment, you must link rewards to personal behavior. Group behavior is too amorphous. If you allow group achievements to define the primary incentive goal pool, you will not get the most out of every individual. It is best if at least 50 percent of a compensation package is linked to personal quantitative goal achievement.

This system takes an extraordinary investment of time and effort by senior entrepreneurial management. It means that you and two or three of your top-level colleagues will have to sit down with each employee and go through an exhausting interlinked, cross-related, mutually supported goal matrix that reflects the operational

(continued)

(continued)

realities of the company. That's hard work. It is difficult to make goals relevant to the operational reality of the company. But it's work that, if done well, will generate rich rewards for you, your employees, and your investors, who are very intimately concerned with the return on your investment.

Consistently Communicate Your Vision and Mission

It is astounding how many young employees will recite the general goal of the organization once or twice, adhere to it for 6 months, and then not reinforce it. It's essential that you work the organization on a handshake basis. Go from cubicle to cubicle, if necessary, and communicate precisely the objectives of the organization. People will not be as cognitive in that as you assume. They easily get out of focus. People need to be reminded on a personal basis clearly, briefly, and often of what your vision is for the entity in that period of time. Don't do it via e-mail. Walk around and make sure that you personally communicate your sense of mission and objectives.

Be Humble

What do I mean by "be humble"? I mean have a correct and realistic assessment of your organization's skills and competencies. People, when they receive a little funding, get a wildly inflated view of their capabilities and their organization's capabilities and misassess how to spend those limited human and capital resources in the short window of time available.

It's important that you're humble not only with regard to your internal capabilities but that you're exceedingly humble and realistic about your assessment of your competitors' strengths. Humble in this sense is almost a synonym for realistic and pragmatic. Do a real-world, ego-shrunken assessment of who your competitors are, where they're strong, where they're well positioned, where you should hit them hard, and where you should not even confront them. Humility is the key to an objective assessment of your own and your competitors' strengths. More mistakes are made in entrepreneurial businesses by those who have not narrowly focused their business mission and who have refused to assess their strengths and their competitors' strengths correctly. It is easy to make such mistakes. The most important vision of an entrepreneurial manager is to humbly assess exactly where you are relative to competitive strengths.

I see on average three to four new Business Plans a week. Ninety percent of them have not taken the time to objectively assess the competitive market environment in which they exist. Somebody gets a bright idea, a new biotechnology pops up, and they obtain access to the patent that they want to license. In their burst of enthusiasm for the new intellectual property or the new technology, they don't take the time to make a competitive assessment with people in similar areas. This can lead to really tragic mistakes—misallocations of people's lives as well as misallocations of capital. Entrepreneurs need humility.

Entrepreneurs who survive learn from other people's mistakes, not just their own. These ten entrepreneurial essentials are time-tested and will help you avoid many of the pitfalls awaiting new ventures. These tips will help you create a strong business model built to outlive the downturn in the economy. Investors not only seek companies that promise great returns, but also those that come equipped with the essentials.

About the Author: Gary L. Crocker has started, funded, or managed numerous ventures including: Crocker Ventures, LLC., a firm that develops high-tech health care and medical technology; Trainseek.com, a web site for corporate trainers and managers; ARUP Laboratories, an esoteric diagnostic blood and tissue testing company; Research Medical, Inc., a publicly traded manufacturer and marketer of cardiac catheters and devices used in open-heart surgery; and Theratech, Inc., a drug delivery firm. Crocker's Research Medical, Inc., was recognized by Forbes magazine for six consecutive years, 1991–1996, as one of "America's Best 200 Small Growth Companies." In 1995 Crocker was named Utah's "High-Technology" Entrepreneur of the Year, and in 1999 he was named Utah's Entrepreneur of the Year. Crocker earned his MBA and BS in economics from Harvard University. He gave this speech at the Marriott School's Entrepreneur Lecture Series 15 September 2000.

Source: Gary L. Crocker, *http://www.marriottschool.byu.edu/marriottmag/summer01/features/crocker4.cfm?10c=feature* (Accessed Feb 14, 2008).

To jump-start your writing skills, review the Business Plans for Yes, We Do Windows (Appendix A) and Annie's (Appendix B). In addition, you can log on to the Internet and access a wide variety of Business Plans online. A great deal of assistance and advice on the referenced sites will help you write a winning Business Plan. One of the best sites, *http://www.bplans.com*, offers a wide selection of sample Business Plans. Even if one of their plans does not exactly fit your business idea or model, you will get an idea of the Business Plan format for your particular type of business. The example we have provided in the text is for an educational facility; if you are opening a restaurant, Internet business, or manufacturer, the outline and requirements may be a little different, and you should tweak your plan accordingly. Thus, you may need to add additional sections to your Business Plan.

Three-Part Structure: Words, Numbers, and Appendices

Your Business Plan tells the world what kind of business you are in and where you are going. For ease of handling, divide your plan into two sections, and provide the needed documentation in appendices at the end.

In Section I use *words:* introduce your strategies for marketing and management. Try to hook your reader with the excitement of creating a business, assessing the competition, designing a marketing plan, targeting customers, finding the right location, and building a team—all those human things that most people can relate to, even if they are not in business. Clearly point out your firm's uniqueness and ability to compete and handle change.

In Section II and the appendix, present *numbers:* projected income statements, cash flows, break-even points, and balance sheets. This section is aimed primarily at bankers, credit managers, venture capitalists, vendors, small-business investment companies, and commercial-credit lenders. Projected income statements for 3 to 5 years are usually included in the appendix. Numbers should be accessible to the casual reader who is searching for the bottom line.

Support Sections I and II with *appendices.* This is where you place résumés, maps, diagrams, photographs, tables, reprints from industry journals, letters from customers and vendors, credit reports, personal financial statements, traffic studies and counts, bids from contractors, and other documentation that demonstrates the viability of your plan.

Note that in most cases, material in the appendices comes from existing sources. You are not stating anything new here; you are merely supporting what you have already said.

Appendices vary for each type of business; for that reason, sample appendices are not included in this book. If you followed and completed the Action Steps in the previous chapters, you will have in hand most of the components and appendices you will need to write a winning Business Plan.

Business Plan Software

Freeware, shareware, and "payware" for Business Planning are widely available on the Internet. Business Plan software only serves as a guide. Only through completing an incredible amount of work, such as you have done through the Action Steps, will you be able to "fill in the blanks" of a software program. The following are among the sources available on the Internet:

http://www.virtualrestaurant.com: Virtual Restaurant displays sample restaurant Business Plans and access to their software for sale.

http://www.toolkit.com: Business Owner's Toolkit offers sample Business Plans for small manufacturers, service providers, and retailers and a wealth of information.

http://www.bplans.com: Palo Alto software offers the Business Plan Pro software program, and the site displays more than 100 sample plans free, ranging from bed and breakfasts, horse resellers, engineering services, and multisport complexes.

http://www.business-plan.com: Automate Your Business Plan software—in combination with a book, *Anatomy of a Business Plan*—provides downloadable software for under $100.

http://www.inc.com: *Inc.*'s excellent site will link you to online Business Planning software and a wealth of Business Plan information.

http://www.bizplanit.com: BizPlanIt provides excellent resources for Business Planning.

http://www.jian.com: Jian offers a suite of business-planning products, which include BizPlan Builder, Builder Financials, Marketing Builder, Loan Builder, and Agreement Builder.

http://www.brs-inc.com/pwrite.html: PlanWrite is an award-winning software program published by Business Resource Software.

http://www.bptools.com: For under $100, you will have access to an excellent step-by-step software tool, Ultimate Business Planner. Software includes access to over 1,000 Business Plans.

http://agecon.purdue.edu/planner/login.asp: Business Planner guide and online tutorial from Purdue University's Agricultural Innovation and Commercialization Center.

http://www.morebusiness.com: Provides access to over 100 sample Business Plans, including those for an organic restaurant, a salsa manufacturer, and a motel/hunting lodge.

Software programs and the sites above facilitate Business Plan preparation, but they do not replace the work required. They serve as consultants as you write your plan, suggesting appropriate Web sites, prodding you for further explanation, and posing relevant questions. Business Planning software is a standardized tool; you must tweak it to make your plan appear unique. There is no one, magic Business Plan program or template that guarantees success. Only your hard work and passion, and an element of luck, can accomplish this.

Outside Assistance in Writing a Business Plan

Many people ask, "Should I hire a pro to write my Business Plan?" Our response is always, "*You* are the pro!" If you do not want to put the time and effort into writing your own Business Plan, it is doubtful that you will have the energy and drive to develop a business. Also, only *you* can put the passion you feel into your plan.

The information you have collected by completing the Action Steps now allows you to complete your Business Plan. We do suggest that on finishing your initial plan, you look for several business owners and possible investors to review it. In addition, attorneys, marketing specialists, accountants, and manufacturing experts may improve your plan with their review; they will show you what areas need additional clarification or support data. Take all of their comments to heart, and rework your plan where necessary.

Hiring a business consultant to refine your plan is acceptable, but do not allow him or her to dream your dream for you. Also, if you do not have total control over input to your plan, you may embarrass yourself by not being able to explain the details of your plan to investors and bankers.

Reminders

Completing a Business Plan helps reduce the risk of failure. No plan can guarantee success, but a well-researched plan will help acknowledge issues, anticipate problems, and determine the resources available to correct them.

The plan should be easy to read, with each number and figure well documented. Use bullets, graphs, and appendices to support the plan's strongest points. Be sure there are no typographical errors and that the plan is well written. If you are not comfortable with your writing skills, hire an editor to read and review your plan.

Action Step 62

Write a Draft Cover Letter

Address your letter to a specific person who can help your business. Be brief; aim for about 300–600 words. State the reason you are sending the plan. If you are asking for money, tell the person what you want if for, how much you need, and how you will repay the loan. Several well-written paragraphs should be all you need to do this.

You purpose in writing the cover letter is to open the door gently and prepare the way for further negotiations. The cover letter is bait on your hook. If you are contributing funds toward the business, or have already done so, indicate the amount. Most investors and lenders want to see that you are investing your own money into your business.

The tone you are after in this opening move is confident and slightly formal. You want to appear bright, organized, and in control of your venture and ready to capitalize on market needs. Refer to The Entrepreneurs' Hub.

Action Step 63

Write a Draft Executive Summary

Imagine you have 3-5 minutes to explain your business venture to a complete stranger. This gives you an idea of what information you need to include in your executive summary.

Limit yourself and practice explaining your venture to friends, colleagues, potential customers, and strangers. Ask them to raise questions, and use their questions to guide you as you revise and hone your presentation.

When you are satisfied with your oral summary, type it up. It should not exceed three typed pages. (The Entrepreneurs' Hub's executive summary that serves as our example was less than one single-spaced page.) This may constitute a very small portion of your Business Plan, but it may be the most important part. Refine your executive summary again after completing your Business Plan.

The goal of your executive summary is for the reader to ask, "Tell me more".

Focus on the potential opportunities the business provides for investors. Tie together—with a clear, consistent message—all elements of the plan. Include possible risks as well; a business without risks does not exist.

The plan should consist of about 15 to 25 pages with additional pages for appendices. The plan should be easy to read and visually appealing so that the reader can move quickly through the document. Make the plan easy for your reader to write notes on, and include how the reader can reach you—fax, e-mail, Web site, mailing address, telephone, pager, and so on.

In this chapter, we illustrate the steps involved in completing a Business Plan, along with providing you samples of each step as completed by a hypothetical business, the Entrepreneurs' Hub. The Hub has been in operation for 6 months and has been self-financed by the owners, who are now seeking to expand and need additional outside financing. Read through this chapter once and then reread, completing the Action Steps. Action Steps 62 and 63, writing a draft cover letter and executive summary, would normally be completed after Action Steps 64 through 70, but we suggest you complete draft copies of these two documents to jump start your Business Plan and keep you focused. When you have completed your Business Plan, revise both your cover letter and executive summary.

The Cover Letter

To aim your plan so it will achieve the most good, focus your cover letter on each individual reader's interests, needs, and concerns. The cover letter introduces the excitement of your plan and tells the person specifically why you have chosen to send it to him or her. This may be your only shot at making the reader want to review your Business Plan, so make your letter strong—prove you know who you are, where you are going, and how you are going to get there with passion and hard work.

Read the sample cover letter for the Entrepreneurs' Hub:

Sample Cover Letter

47 Dogwood Lane, Suite 108–9
Oak Ridge, TN 37953
Jackson@net.com
(865) 555–5555

June 5, 2008

River Bank
Ms. Nancy Hopp
Vice President, Lending
1400 Market Lane
Knoxville, TN 37944

Dear Ms. Hopp,
Thank you for the insight you shared with me on reviewing my Business Plan. Your thought-provoking questions in the marketing area led me to research additional advertising avenues. In addition, I have revamped the financial section by adding additional notes to the pro formas and reworking several of the figures. Your suggestions and the subsequent changes make our plan stronger. Everyone here at the Entrepreneurs' Hub appreciates the care you took reading over earlier drafts of our Business Plan.

The positive response to our entrepreneurial services over the past 6 months requires that the school expand to offer additional services to our entrepreneurs. As the economy slows, consumers with substantial severance checks and retirement plan funds in hand are reaching out for the dream of owning a business and the interest in entrepreneurship is very strong among the 20–28 year old market. To help make their dreams come true as quickly as possible, we provide our *Fast-Start* training using the most popular Business Planning software and Web site development software in conjunction with our consulting. Most of our clients have a good working knowledge of computers and basic software but seek advanced training that focuses on their particular entrepreneurial needs.

We feel passionate about our business and our entrepreneurs. We have watched many of our clients develop Web sites through our e-commerce courses and have aided in the preparation of more than 30 Business Plans to date. We serve not only the start-up businesses in the community, but also have found a market for our services among entrepreneurs whose businesses have been open 2 to 4 years, and who are now interested in expanding or making their business more professional.

Each of the founders has contributed $100,000 to launch the Entrepreneurs' Hub. We are currently in the market for a loan of $60,000 to be used for tenant improvements. The location we have in Oak Ridge is built out but will require additional wi-fi, electrical wiring, furniture, and appropriate lighting to enable us to provide a second classroom. We would appreciate your guidance concerning sources of capital available through your bank or additional avenues.

We plan to repay our loan from profits generated over the next 3 years as we grow to full capacity. For more information, please refer to the financial section.

Again, thank you for your assistance. We couldn't have done it without you.

Cordially,

Danielle Jackson
President

Let us summarize what is good about our sample cover letter. We can see that:

1. The writer is making use of a previous contact.
2. The writer tells the reader—the manager of a bank—that she is in the market for a loan. She does not put her on the spot by asking for money. Instead, she asks for advice on where to find sources of capital.
3. The writer shares her passion for her business and her customers with the reader.
4. The writer strikes the right tone. This often requires several revisions.

You can do as well or better—and it is well worth the effort. As you draft your cover letter, remember that the reader will pass judgment on your Business Plan, and on your business acumen, on the basis of the letter. Do you want your small business to appear profitable? Attractive? Exciting? Welcoming? Your cover letter needs to give the same impression. A well-written cover letter will make its readers want to become involved in your venture. Action Step 62 will help you write your draft cover letter now. Revise and finalize your cover letter once you have completed your plan. A good cover letter will lead the reader to your Business Plan, and a poor cover letter may be the only thing that gets read.

ELEMENTS OF A BUSINESS PLAN
The Table of Contents

Our sample table of contents provides a quick overview of a finished Business Plan. In practice, the table of contents is prepared last. Please note, as previously discussed, that the outline for your particular plan may vary. Review online Business Plans that are most similar to your type of business to discover what additional areas need to be covered and also what appendices might be appropriate. Depending on your business, certain areas will be more relevant to your success and should be treated as such in the plan.

Table of Contents

Executive Summary

I. Description of the Business
  A. Company Analysis and Services
  B. Market and Target Customers
  C. Competitive Analysis
  D. Marketing Strategy
  E. Facility Location and Operations
  F. Management and Personnel
  G. Exit Strategy

II. Financial Section
  A. Pro Forma Income
  B. Balance Sheet

III. Appendices*
  A Market Research
  B. Quotes from Hardware and Software Suppliers
  C. Personal Résumés
  D. Personal Financial Statements
  E. Pro Forma Cash Flows Forecasted for 3 Years
  F. Letters of Reference
  G. Bids from Contractors
  H. Floor Plan for Expansion
  I. Map with Competitors' Locations
  J. Census Data
  K. Pro Forma Income Statements Forecasted for 3 to 5 Years
  L. Break-Even Analysis
  M. Equipment Estimates

*The need for specific appendices varies greatly from Business Plan to Business Plan. For that reason, we have not included sample appendices. As you draft your plan, you will recognize items that require further documentation to substantiate your business strategies; the most logical place for this kind of documentation is in appendices. In addition, include references, consultants, or technical advisors who have assisted you.

Action Step 64

Describe Your Company, Product, and Services

Excite your reader about your business; excitement is contagious. If you can get your reader going, there is a good chance you will be offered money. Investors love hot ideas.

If this is a start-up, explain your product or service fully. What makes it unique? What industry is it in? Where does the industry fit in the big picture? Pull in the relevant information from your past Action Steps.

Mention numbers whenever you can. Percentages and dollar amounts are more meaningful than words like *lots* and *many.*

If this is an ongoing business, your records of sales, costs, and profit and loss will substantiate your need for money. Keep the words flowing and the keyboard smoking. You need to convince the reader to continue reading.

EXECUTIVE SUMMARY

The executive summary serves as an introduction to the Business Plan. Its function is similar to that of a preface in a book. It is written to 1) acquaint the reader with the subject matter of the material that follows, 2) direct the reader's attention to whatever strengths the author (entrepreneur) wants to emphasize, 3) define the market and your plan to reach the market, and 4) make the reader want to turn the pages and keep reading. Because the executive summary reviews the entire Business Plan, it is usually written last, but we have included it here to help you first focus on the most important parts of your Business Plan. We want you to write a two to three page draft executive summary and when your plan is completed, revise the original. Pay special attention to the *business description, current position and future outlook, management, uniqueness,* and—if you need financing—*funds sought, how they will be used, when they will be repaid,* and *how they will be repaid.* This summary appears right after the table of contents and should be able to stand on its own.

As a preview to your plan, the executive summary should excite, entice, and draw the reader into the plan. A well-written executive summary captures the reader's attention and makes him or her eager to explore further.

Because many readers never go further than the executive summary, it is important to expend a great deal of effort to make your executive summary an excellent selling tool—it may be your only chance to sell your idea.

As you write your executive summary, remember that lenders prefer hard numerical data and facts. Therefore such phrases as "30 percent return on the original investment" and "secured training agreements from three retail computer stores in the area" make the following example a *strong* executive summary. The words help to paint a picture of good management and solid growth for the Entrepreneurs' Hub.

You, too, can write an effective two to three page executive summary. Action Step 63 will help you decide which facts and numbers portray you and your business venture as credible and promising, and it will also help you summarize these facts in writing. At this point, draft your executive summary using the Action Step. Upon completion of your Business Plan, revise your executive summary.

Executive Summary of Entrepreneurs' Hub

The Entrepreneurs' Hub is a user-friendly, state-of-the-art software, e-commerce, and entrepreneurial training center. We are tapping into the growing need for entrepreneurs to have classes focused specifically on their entrepreneurial needs. But our main focus is providing a center for budding entrepreneurs to dream with others. We have found that our entrepreneurs thoroughly thrive on interaction with others. After each class, we provide coffee and snacks so that they can meet in our comfortable conference room area. Our market area is growing quickly today because of the expansion of the following groups:

- People retiring early and starting new businesses
- Entrepreneurs who are ready to expand their current businesses
- Individuals wanting to take advantage of opportunities the Internet can provide
- Young people who see entrepreneurship as an alternative to working in a corporate world
- People who run businesses in addition to their full-time jobs
- Individuals seeking franchising opportunities

We market our seminars and services exclusively to entrepreneurs and those dreaming of entrepreneurship. In addition to the software classes we offer, we will be presenting specialized seminars in writing Business Plans, developing Web sites, and franchising as an alternative. Instructors will all be asked to incorporate the students' business ideas into each class. The Entrepreneurs' Hub's sophisticated smart classroom provides hands-on education and support. We adapt packaged software to meet each participant's needs.

We are currently operating with one classroom and a conference room and hope to add an additional classroom within the next 6 months. This expansion will allow us to attain sales of $660,000 by the end of the fiscal year. At that time, our pretax profits will have reached almost $168,000.

According to our research and experience, entrepreneurs have an insatiable appetite for education and the support of fellow entrepreneurs. They generally have strong computer backgrounds and are attending our classes for advanced training and advice. We anticipate an annual sales growth rate of 30 percent over the next 3 years.

Our competitors have recently declined as many individuals have learned to master standard software, and the traditional software training schools have served their purpose. We are inclined to believe our competition is now the traditional educational system and their offerings. We hope to capitalize on our distinct differences from area school offerings.

We will contract with marketing consultants, attorneys, financial advisors, and accountants to provide specialized courses at our center, including:

- Patent protection
- Selling to the federal government
- Bringing a product to market
- Pricing strategies

Throughout the past 6 months, we have demonstrated that we offer superior training at competitive prices. Our plans for the future include developing additional training centers. Research and customer surveys indicate that we have just begun to tap the ever-increasing need for entrepreneurial education and services.

Danielle Jackson will continue to focus on sales and marketing in addition to developing and teaching courses with Robert Wojchik. Curriculum for more than 20 courses has been developed with another 10 courses in development. As the needs of our students change, we will be able to adapt accordingly. Robert Wojchik will also manage the technical aspects of keeping the hardware and software up to date and the computers functioning.

We are seeking funding of $60,000 to cover the remodeling costs required to equip an additional classroom. Funds will also be used for license fees, wi-fi, furniture, and equipment costs for our second classroom. The appendix contains contractor, computer, and furniture estimates. We plan to purchase refurbished classroom furniture; many businesses have gone under, so excellent buys are available at potential cost savings of $15,000 to $20,000.

Bank loans will be paid back from the operating profits of the business over the next 3 years.

SECTION I: DESCRIPTION OF THE BUSINESS

How well do you know your business? You need to prove it with words and numbers. By the time your reader finishes reading your Business Plan, you should have an ally on your side. To give you a sample to follow, we provide key sections from the Business Plan for the Entrepreneurs' Hub, a business that is seeking financing for remodeling and equipment expenses. Regardless of whether your business is ongoing or just starting up, the goals of Section I and II are the same: to demonstrate that you know your business and that you are a winner.

A. COMPANY ANALYSIS AND SERVICES

Include your unique qualifications, company history, and past accomplishments in this section. Review how the Entrepreneurs' Hub tackled this part. The Hub is likely to receive its funding because the writer of the plan proves that the business is a winning concern. The writer has:

- Let the facts speak for themselves.
- Supported all claims with numbers.
- Avoided hard-sell tactics.
- Refused to puff-up the product.
- Projected a positive future.

The writer does a terrific selling job. Now it is your turn. Complete Action Step 64 after reviewing the Entrepreneur Hub example.

Business Description of Entrepreneurs' Hub

The Entrepreneurs' Hub is an entrepreneurial center in Oak Ridge, Tennessee, near the rapidly growing area of West Knoxville. The vast number of scientists and engineers in the area make it ripe for entrepreneurial activity.

Students are drawn to our teaching method because we provide hands-on experience and incorporate their business ideas into our seminars and software usage. In addition, our entrepreneurs are busy, and a student can upgrade a given software skill by 50 percent in a three-hour class.

With our Fast-Start entrepreneurial program, a twelve-session program presented in 6 weeks, each student will produce a finalized Business Plan that has been reviewed by one of the owners as well as by fellow classmates. We will use Internet postings of Business Plans for students to review and comment on through our secure server. We will also help our students who are seeking funding to find the appropriate sources and possible Internet postings as well.

Our center will also provide resources for patent and copyright protection, as many of the entrepreneurs will require legal assistance in this area. In addition, lawyers well versed in Internet law will be available to help our clients through an ever-changing and ever-challenging quagmire of developing laws.

Most of our seminars and training will be offered in either 3-hour classes or 6-hour weekend classes. In contrast, the average college course—which emphasizes concepts, rather than hands-on experience—takes 12 to 18 weeks. Our price is $100 for most 3-hour courses and $200 for 6-hour classes. Our entrepreneurs have business to attend to and have requested short classes. In addition, we will limit our Fast-Start program, at $1250 for six weeks, to 20 students so that students build working relationships with their classmates. Our hope is for these relationships to continue after the formal 6-week class has ended. Entrepreneurs' Hub will have monthly meetings for all Fast-Start graduates with speakers and time for feedback and support on current issues and projects.

As a service business, we sell seats, skills, support, and information. We constantly survey our current customers for additional classes they would like to see offered. One area we hope to offer in the future is having a graphic artist available who can perform design work for clients, including logos, stationary, flyers, Web sites and so on. We would have space available on Saturdays to provide this service, and the graphic artist could make appointments to work with our clients on a fee basis. We will consider renting the artist space.

We are open Tuesday through Friday from 12 to 9 PM and Saturdays from 8 AM to 5 PM. This allows us to offer single-day, 6-hour courses, as well as short, 3-hour evening courses, thus maximizing the use of our facility. Seminars and guest speakers will be offered at least monthly.

The Entrepreneurs' Hub is in the business of jump-starting an individual's Business Plan and increasing productivity by providing the following:

- Sales-force automation software training
- Manufacturing software training
- Inventory-control software training
- Assistance with writing Business Plans, loan proposals, marketing plans, and employee manuals, using the most popular software programs
- Assistance with refining PowerPoint presentations
- Web page and Web store design
- Additional proposed seminars are listed in the appendix.

As a sales promotional tool, we plan to offer free training to several salespeople from each of the major stores that sell computers. The salespeople in turn will likely refer their customers to us for training. Computer retailers have learned they can sell upgraded systems if they can provide or offer software training. Although one store in our area offers in-house training, the training is generic, and students as young as 10 years of age participate in the classes. Those stores are in the business of selling systems, and we are in business of building entrepreneurs.

Our equipment is top quality. Our staff combines excellent training skills with attention to entrepreneurs and their needs. We have launched a solid start-up with a plan to continue our growth and success.

B. INDUSTRY AND MARKET OVERVIEW AND TARGET CUSTOMERS

Knowledge is power, especially in the Information Age. The Entrepreneurs' Hub—a service business—capitalizes on expert knowledge to define the marketplace. In the same way, if your research is sound, your niche will be evident in your writing. Depending on your business, this area could be divided in to two sections.

Use your industry research from the Action Steps in Chapters 2–4 to give your reader an overview of the industry. The reader needs to know the size of

Action Step 65

Describe the Market and the Target Customers

Bring all your marketing research into this section from past Action Steps, and wow your reader with a picture of your Target Customers just sitting there waiting for your product or service. Use data from secondary sources to give credibility to the picture you are painting. Provide any back-up research data in the appendix.

the market, trends in the marketplace, how the industry is segmented, where the industry is headed, and what specific part of the market you are aiming your product or service toward. In addition, briefly discuss any technological advances that are changing the industry and how you will capitalize on these changes. Address economic, social, legal, and global changes that may affect the industry and your target market.

Prove to your reader that you understand the market and are meeting a customer need. Discuss market segmentation. Define your Target Customers in great detail. Provide research data to back up your assumptions on demographics, psychographics, market size, and buying patterns. Return to your Action Steps from Chapter 4 to assist you in describing your Target Customers.

The reader should have a clear idea as to how your product or service will be capable of capturing a unique position in the marketplace. An in-depth explanation should be provided in the competition section of your Business Plan.

Complete Action Step 65 to show that you know the industry and your Target Customers. Review what the Business Plan for the Entrepreneurs' Hub says about its industry and Target Customers. Be sure to use secondary sources—documents, tables, and quotes—to give this section credibility. The following industry and market review is minimal, but for many entrepreneurs this section will need to focus on changes within an industry and how your firm will accommodate those changes.

Industry/Market Overview and Target Customers of Entrepreneurs' Hub

---

Industry and Market Overview

Today's seminar and classroom offerings for entrepreneurs are limited primarily to community colleges and universities. In addition, several national organizations offer one-day entrepreneurial boot-camp programs. Many entrepreneurs need to learn programs quickly and expect to be productive in a short time.

With the sales flurry of hardware and emphasis on speed, many are being left behind because they do not know how to fully utilize the software. A computer can be your best friend, but only if you learn how to maximize its capabilities. Entrepreneurs' Hub is on the cutting edge of providing services focused solely on entrepreneurs.

Target Customers

Geographically, our target area encompasses Knoxville, Oak Ridge, and Harriman. Realistically, most of our customers originate within a 25-mile radius of our location. We are looking ahead to possible future expansion throughout Tennessee over the next 5 years. Nashville, Memphis, and Chattanooga are three areas we are especially interested in exploring.

Anderson County's population is expected to grow an additional 10 percent over the next 5 years. Our entrepreneurial students are primarily college educated, 25 to 55, with annual incomes of $50,000 to $125,000. Our area has one of the highest concentrations of PhDs in the United States. Several of the leading scientists and researchers from the Oak Ridge National Laboratory have taken business-planning courses, developed excellent Business Plans and are currently seeking funding. The Tennessee Valley Authority employs a large group of engineers and biological scientists, many of whom are interested in developing their expertise into profit-making ventures, with several looking at Green technology. Our research indicates that 50 percent of our Target Customers will be women.

We hope to also reach individuals who are social entrepreneurs, looking to start nonprofit organizations with a business model, some of which choose to offer items for sale to support the nonprofit.

Our entrepreneurs, split fairly evenly between manufacturing, service, and retailing businesses, are dreamers first and foremost—our job is to help make their dreams come true as quickly as possible. We have found through our experience that entrepreneurship can be very lonely, because others may not be dreaming the same dream. We hope to reduce the loneliness by providing opportunities for our entrepreneurs to gather together and share their dreams.

All sales and marketing efforts are tracked, which aids us in refining our Target Customer profile and focusing our marketing efforts on the strongest and most profitable markets.

C. COMPETITIVE ANALYSIS

Obviously, if you know who your competitors are and how they fail to meet market needs, you are well on your way to developing your niche. You need to persuade your reader that your competitive tactics are effective. Reread Chapters 4–5 and review your Action Steps.

If your competitive strength derives from patents, copyrights, or trademarks, include information about them in this area. Provide copies of any patents or copyrights received or pending in the appendix. Include the attorney contact information.

How tough do your competitors look? As you read the Hub's assessment of its competition, note that the writer takes a cool, objective look at the competition. She does not belittle them, and she certainly does not underestimate them. The Hub's plan leaves no doubt that management is exploiting a market gap ignored by the competition: entrepreneurial training.

This is more than a matter of writing skill. Early on, the entrepreneurs who founded the Hub did the right research, so they could make decisions ahead of time—just as you were asked to do in the earlier chapters.

How will you handle your competition? Your readers will expect you to provide an honest appraisal of each of your major competitors. Now you are ready to complete Action Step 66.

Action Step 66

Describe Competitors

1. Briefly profile the businesses that compete with you directly. Be objective as you assess their operations.
2. What are their strengths? Weaknesses? What can you learn from them?
3. What makes your product or service unique in the eyes of your customers?
4. After you have described your competitors, indicate how you are going to ace them out of the picture or develop a niche you can own by presenting your competitive positioning strategy. Provide primary and secondary research back-up data in the appendix.

Competitive Analysis of Entrepreneurs' Hub

We hope to capitalize on the need for *entrepreneurial education and software training*, which our competitors are not currently providing. On reviewing our competitors, we discovered that major players in the industry have developed specific niches in the marketplace. A brief review of our two major competitors follows:

- **Roane State Community College:** Headquartered in Harriman, Tennessee, serving a seven-county area of East Tennessee. Classroom facility in Oak Ridge, Tennessee, offers primarily traditional classes, although recently they have begun to offer online and hybrid classes to meet the needs of busy students. They do not focus on entrepreneurial programs, but occasionally they offer a small-business class. We do recognize the school could possibly compete with us directly if they were to begin offering more short-term or online classes, but we do not see this happening in the near future. Most of our students have told us that completing classes in a short period of time is their primary goal. Classes at Roane State cost approximately $350 per semester for 48 classroom hours. Thus, our cost of $1250 for our Fast-Start 36-hour program is definitely more costly than our competitors but our clients have told us they are willing to pay this amount as it will bring them to market faster than a 16 week class.
- **University of Tennessee (UT):** Excellent large university located in Knoxville with easy freeway access. Courses are primarily taught in a traditional classroom manner. Being close to a leading research and teaching institution will provide our Hub and its students with highly trained experts in many different fields, which we will hire for short presentations and seminars. We are hoping to bring in experts at an approximate cost of $300 to $600 per evening seminar. We may not always make a profit on these specialized classes, but we hope to at least break even. Traditional classes at UT cost about $750 each. At this time, their extension program does not appear to be offering any entrepreneurial training.

Action Step 67

Describe Marketing Strategy Work Through the Four Ps

1. Now that you have profiled your Target Customers and assessed your competition, take time to develop the thrust of your marketing strategy. Which techniques will reap the most cost-effective responses?

2. Because pricing is such an important consideration, you might start with what your Target Customers see as a good value, and then develop your marketing mix further. Prepare back-up data for the appendix.

- **SBA Office in Knoxville:** Occasional classes are offered at the SBA office, but these are infrequent; we hope that the office will actually feed students to us, and we are beginning to develop relationships with the director.

Our business is geared to offer $100, $200 seminars, and the Fast-Start program at $1250. We will also offer our monthly meetings, with speakers and support, at $30 per evening. Again, we are stressing constant support from peers and advisors, e-mail advice, chat rooms, online blogs, and access to experts who have been screened.

D. MARKETING STRATEGY

Now it is time to describe your marketing strategy and pull together your work on your Action Steps from Chapters 4–7. You will be highlighting the four Ps: *price, product, promotion,* and *place.* The reader wants to understand how your firm will position itself in the marketplace. Also, demonstrate how you plan to retain your customers and you will impress readers with your forethought.

The marketing strategy excerpt from the Entrepreneurs' Hub's Business Plan demonstrates a carefully reasoned approach, and it describes conscious marketing policies that will help this small business be competitive. If you were to read a Business Plan in which the writer does not demonstrate this care and deliberation, how much faith would you have in the writer's business abilities?

Note that the Entrepreneurs' Hub uses a four-pronged approach to reaching the public. This business understands the importance of finding a good promotional mix.

In your Business Plan, include distribution channels, selling methods, and public relations. If your firm has plans to sell products or services internationally, discuss those plans in this section. Present a list of potential customers or clients and a sales forecast. If these are extensive, present them briefly in the body, and add further information in the appendices. Action Step 67 will help you refine your marketing strategy.

Marketing Strategy of Entrepreneurs' Hub

We use a wide range of strategies to let our customers know about our class offerings, including targeted mailers, special promotions, Internet advertising, personal selling, and networking. We are in the productivity and information business, and toward that end, we have developed an Internet site that will provide a community for budding Knoxville-area entrepreneurs. A new entrepreneur will be highlighted each week on our site, and we will send out weekly newsletters and ask our readers to forward them to their entrepreneurial friends. New class offerings and speakers will also be posted. In addition, we are considering posting, at our clients' request, Business Plans online for potential angel investors to review.

Networking
Each owner belongs to four professional organizations within a 20-mile radius. In addition, each owner has joined a local chamber of commerce organization to network. Both owners have also joined separate BNI networking groups and have found them to contain a wealth of contacts and students. The owners serve as guest speakers to civic and educational organizations as often as possible. A discount program will be designed for entrepreneurs in venture-training programs, such as SBDCs.

Radio Program
We plan to host and sponsor a ten-minute talk show each morning during drive time on a local radio station, KBIC. Our show will be called "The Entrepreneurs' Hub." We hope that by highlighting our Web site and programs on the show, as well as providing advice and encouragement, entrepreneurs will log on and contact us for further information.

Personal Selling

Fortunately, our owners have experience and talent in the area of personal selling. Each owner spends 5 to 15 hours per week talking with potential entrepreneurs and responding to emails. In addition, phone selling is an important aspect of our business. Converting phone and email queries into sales is a major goal of each person. Logging all calls and emails and making sure they are followed up on in a timely matter is essential for our success. Hub training programs are being developed for local stores, such as Staples and Office Max, to offer at a discount to their business customers.

Creative Promotions/Free Ink

We will sponsor a yearly Business Plan competition for the Junior Achievement (JA) chapters in the Oak Ridge/Knoxville area. In addition, we will sponsor one Business Plan competition for our clients each year. The prizes will include classes at our center and a small college scholarship for the JA winner. We hope to offer the Business Plan competition in conjunction with Roane State Community College or the University of Tennessee. Once a month we will have special speakers on site free for our current and potential clients as well as speakers where there will be a $30 charge. It is hoped that these will be promoted in the *Knoxville Business Journal, Knoxville Sentinel,* and the *Oak Ridge News.*

E. FACILITY LOCATION AND OPERATIONS

The next part of your Business Plan concerns location, site selection, and physical facilities. You may want to review your work from Chapter 6 now.

If you are planning a retail store or distributorship, this area is critical and should include extensive research data to back up your site-selection decision. Discuss the accessibility and visibility of the site and the demographics and psychographics of the surrounding population. Download graphics from the many online databases showing roads, competition, and potential customers for support data, which should be placed in the appendix but referenced in the text.

If you are in manufacturing, explain thoroughly your site selection, which may be based on energy costs, employee costs, and governmental incentives. In addition, provide your facility layout and information on equipment to help support your operations plan. Provide supporting data.

For a retail business that will be located in a shopping center or strip center, discuss the retail market mix and how it will help draw customers into your store. Drawings of the actual facility and store layout may help your reader visualize the store as well. Use professional quality photographs to enhance your Business Plan.

You need to paint an attractive picture of your business site and, at the same time, keep your reader interested by inspiring confidence in your choice. Location takes a tremendous amount of analysis. The Entrepreneurs' Hub writer gives himself a subtle pat on the back by describing the lease arrangements and by identifying the need for a second classroom.

Your plan will become very real when you showcase your physical facility. The operational plan, which supports your financial numbers, should clearly represent how you see the growth of your business. Read how the Entrepreneurs' Hub shows off its location, and complete Action Step 68.

Action Step 68

Show Off Your Facility/ Location and Operations

The great thing about a location is that it is so *tangible*. A potential lender can visit your site and get a feel for what is going on. Bankers often visit a client's business site if the Business Plan is to be considered further. That is good news for you, because now the banker is on your turf. Clean up the place before your banker arrives; make it shine!

1. In this section, you want to persuade potential lenders to visit your site. Describe what goes on there. Use photographs, diagrams, and illustrations to make the facility as real to the reader as possible.
2. If you have a manufacturing facility, discuss how you selected the building and equipment. You may need to discuss utility costs, insurance issues, employment costs, and possibly workers' compensation.
3. If your business will be operating in shifts, you may want to discuss those issues here as well.

Facility and Operations of Entrepreneurs' Hub

The Entrepreneurs' Hub has secured a 5-year lease at 47 Dogwood Lane, Oak Ridge, Tennessee. The facility is all on the ground floor and occupies 2,000 square feet. The area, which is zoned for business use, is near a hotbed of high technology and entrepreneurial activity. Within a 20-mile radius of the facility are three growing industrial parks, where there are many start-ups we hope to reach out to.

Action Step 69

Introduce Your Management Team and Personnel

Use this section to highlight the *positive* qualities of your management team. Focus on quality first—accomplishments, education, training, flexibility, imagination, tenacity. Be sure you weave in experience that relates to your particular business.

Remember—dreamers make terrific master builders, but they may make lousy managers. Your banker knows this, and potential investors will sense it. A great team can help you raise money, and the key to a great team is balance. Describe the kinds of people you will need as employees and how they fit into your plan. What skills will they need? How much will you have to pay them? Will there be a training period? If so, how long will it be? What fringe benefits will you offer? How will you handle overtime? Describe the work environment you hope to create.

Provide short résumés for each of the major players, and highlight their past successes. Full résumés should be placed in the appendix.

If you have not yet written job descriptions, do that now. Job descriptions will help you avoid potential problems with the people who work for you, although they are not necessary for your Business Plan.

Our location has easy freeway access, is close to the rapidly growing West Knoxville area, and offers well-lit and abundant parking.

During our lease negotiations, we persuaded the landlord to make extensive improvements to the interior and to spread the cost out over the term of the lease. The décor—blue carpet, white walls, and gray furniture—gives the effect of a solid, logical, somewhat plush business-learning environment.

The building is currently divided into four areas: a reception and lounge area (150 square feet), a director's office (150 square feet), a classroom (600 square feet), a conference room (500 square feet), and a current storage area (600 square feet).

The principals envision the storage area as a future second classroom (see diagram in the appendix) and are requesting funds to expand into this area. Each classroom will have 20 networked computers, comfortable chairs, printers, and video screens.

F. MANAGEMENT AND PERSONNEL

Management will make or break a small business. You are a member of the management team, and you want this Business Plan to inspire confidence in your investors that you have a winning team. Writing this section will help you focus on your management team members. Review your work from Chapter 11 now. Many plan reviewers read the management section first. If you have a high-tech business, the team and its past successes will be key, and therefore this section should be placed at the beginning of the Business Plan. Investors want to have confidence not only in the business idea but also in the team that will take the concept to reality. Now is the time to discuss the legal form of business you have chosen. Include applicable agreements and legal papers dealing with partnerships or corporations in the appendix.

Read how the Entrepreneurs' Hub introduced its management team. The Hub's team demonstrates balance, diversity, experience, some interesting track records, and the will to succeed. Danielle Jackson's experience in training and entrepreneurship combined with Robert Bennett's extensive curriculum development are strong selling points.

Highlight the balance and experience of your team with short résumés. Longer and more detailed résumés should be included in the appendix. The reader looks for financial skills, marketing skills, technical and operational skills, and management and entrepreneurial experience. In addition, many readers will focus on the teams' people skills.

The Hub was wise to include short résumés of the directors. In this case, the background of the directors enhances the balance of the team. All have admirable depth in their business careers, sharing a combined 45 years of experience in the corporate world.

The listing of the legal counsel, accounting firm, insurance broker, and advertising agency also adds to the impression of solid business practices. Nothing is more important than the people who will make your business successful. Present their pedigrees and focus on their track records and accomplishments as you complete Action Step 69.

For a start-up business, you are peering into the future with confidence—doing informal job analyses for key employees who will help you to succeed. For an ongoing business, you need to list your present employees and anticipate your future personnel needs. If you currently employ five people but want to indicate growth, try projecting how many jobs you will be creating in the next 3 years. Describe the work environment you plan to implement as your grow you business. Discuss what steps you will take to retain your employees as well.

When you start thinking about tasks and people to do them, review your work from Chapter 11. Preparing this part of your plan is important, because it gives you one more chance to analyze job functions before you begin interviewing, hiring, and paying benefits—all of which are very expensive.

Note that the Entrepreneurs' Hub gives a very brief rundown of the personnel situation. In describing their lean operation, the owners who run the Hub keep their job descriptions lean. They show good sense when they express a commitment to hold down operating costs. Their decision reflects business discipline and foresight. If you were a potential investor in this business, you would appreciate some tight purse strings and sweat equity.

Every person on your team is important. Action Step 69 will help you to describe the kinds of people you will need and how you will help them become productive.

Management and Personnel of Entrepreneurs' Hub

Owners
Danielle Jackson was born in Shaker Heights, Ohio, in 1960. She earned her BS degree in Industrial Engineering at Purdue University. After graduation, she spent 8 years in the Marine Corps, where she was a flight instructor and check pilot. While in the service, Jackson completed her MBA at the University of California in Irvine.

Following military service, Jackson was employed as a pilot for United Airlines for 5 years. Wanting a change, she purchased a firm exporting software and sold it 4 years later for $3 million. Serving on regional training committees and as a director of a local Small Business Development Center, she recognized a need for a for-profit center for entrepreneurial support and training.

Robert Wojchik was born in Dallas, Texas, in 1980. He has a BS degree in Information Science from the University of Oklahoma. After graduation, he worked for Procter and Gamble for several years. For 2 years he worked developing curriculum and training materials and presented classes for Microsoft, Quest, and Oracle. For the past 2 years, he has worked to develop specialized small-business programs for Microsoft. His vast exposure to entrepreneurs and software knowledge are an invaluable asset to the Entrepreneurs' Hub training center.

Directors
Cheryl Hughes Smith, born in Corpus Christi, Texas, in 1973, has an MBA from Harvard and a law degree from the University of Texas at Austin. Ms. Smith is a partner in Smith, Jones, and Schultz, a Knoxville law firm. She is the author of numerous articles in the field of small-business tax planning.

Phil Carpenter was born in Duluth, Minnesota, in 1968. He graduated from Purdue University with a BS in Management and a minor in Operations Management. Mr. Carpenter then worked for a large accounting firm for 5 years before attending Indiana University for his MBA. His research projects during his Master's program focused on entrepreneurship. Mr. Carpenter is currently Professor of Business at Roane State Community College, a general partner in two businesses, and a small-business consultant. He has published and lectured widely in the area of small business.

Other Available Resources
The Entrepreneurs' Hub has retained the legal firm of Farney and Shields and the accounting firm of Hancock and Associates. Our insurance broker is Sharon Mandel of Fireman's Fund. Our advertising agency is Friend and Associates.

Personnel
During our first 6 months of operations, we had one full-time employee, but we have found that an additional employee is necessary to facilitate our expansion and to serve our customers properly. Most of the initial classes will be taught by one of the owners. Additional instructors for specialized seminars will be hired on a contract basis. We need to run a lean operation, and the owners are willing to put in additional sweat equity.

G. EXIT STRATEGY

As discussed in Chapter 12, many readers of your plan will be interested in your exit strategy. The more money involved, the more likely they will want to know your particular plans. The Entrepreneurs' Hub founders plan on continuing for at least 5 years in their business.

Exit Strategy of Entrepreneurs' Hub

After we build out our Oak Ridge location, we hope to build two additional locations in Tennessee over the next 5 years. On successful completion, and when we are able to show a strong profit in each center, we plan to sell all three training facilities, either to the managers running the individual centers or to one entrepreneur wishing to run a small chain of centers.

SECTION II: FINANCIAL SECTION

Good Numbers

The financial section is the heart of your Business Plan. It is aimed at lenders—bankers, credit managers, venture capitalists, vendors, SBICs, commercial-credit lenders—people who think and dream in numbers. Lenders are skeptics by trade; they will not be swayed by the enthusiasm of your writing in Section I, so your job now is to make your numbers do the talking. This is easier than you might believe, since you are prepared.

In Chapter 8 you projected cash flow and income. You have tested your numbers on real lenders in the real world. If you have not already done so, you need to organize your numbers into standard instruments:

1. Pro forma income and cash-flow statements, pricing scenarios, and so on
2. Balance sheet

Examples from the Entrepreneurs' Hub will serve as models for you; adapt them to suit your business type. The idea is to know where every dime is going. You need to show when you will make a profit and in so doing appear neat, orderly, in control, and conservative. You will know you have succeeded when a skeptical lender looks up from your Business Plan and says, "You know, these numbers look good."

Good Notes

One way to spot a professional lender is to hand over your Business Plan and watch to see which sections he or she reads first. Most lenders first study the notes that accompany income and cash-flow projections. Knowing this allows you to prepare accordingly. Use these notes to tell potential lenders how you generated your numbers (for example, "Advertising is projected at 5 percent of sales") and to explain specific entries (for example, "Leased Equipment—monthly lease costs on computer equipment"). Make these notes easy to read with headings that start your readers off in the upper left-hand corner and march them down the page, step by step, to the bottom line. Some projections use tiny footnotes on the same page. We recommend *large* notes on a separate page with a "Notes" heading. Notes are important, so they should be big.

Creating your Business Plan takes a lot of time. It is only natural for you to hope that lenders will read it, become enthusiastic, and ask questions. The notes to your plan help you accomplish that, even if you have not yet started up and the numbers are projections into the future.

If your business has been going for some time, a detailed financial history should be included. For those seeking funding, the financial statements will be significant. You need to describe which type of funding you are seeking and include specific details on how that funding will be used and repaid. Completing your financial statements requires business finance and accounting knowledge.

A. PROJECTED INCOME

Your next task is to put together your projected income statement, also called a *profit and loss statement*. With the information you have gathered so far, it should not be too difficult. In fact, it will be enjoyable if the numbers look good. If they do not, reconsider before you commit.

Review the Entrepreneurs' Hub's projected income statement and the careful documentation of items (Table 15.1). Action Step 70 will help you project your own monthly profits and losses for 12 months. You should also include a projected income statement for the next 2 to 5 years for your business. Although a cash-flow projection has not been included for the center, many lenders will require one. Refer back to the numbers and scenarios you prepared back in Chapter 8 and revise and place them into your Business Plan.

B. BALANCE SHEET

Professional lenders look at your balance sheet, also called a statement of financial position, to analyze the state of your finances at a given point in time. They are looking at liquidity, which shows how easily your assets can be converted into cash, and capital structure—what sources of financing have been used, how much was borrowed, and so on. Professional lenders use such factors to evaluate your ability to manage your business.

The Entrepreneurs' Hub (see Table 15.2) did not provide notes to its balance sheets because in their case, no notes were needed. In conjunction with the income statement in the body of the text and cash-flow projections in the appendix, all the entries in the balance sheet should make sense to readers who are professionals. Under some circumstances, you would want to note unusual features of a balance sheet for an actual fiscal year, but in most cases—and in most projections—this will not be necessary. Complete Action Step 71 to help you prepare and include a balance sheet in your Business Plan.

Action Step 71 is the last Action Step for Chapter 15. It is the end, yes, but also the beginning.

All our best wishes go with you as you embark on your great adventure. We hope that this book and its Action Steps have convinced you that you can achieve success—whatever it means to *you*—and have *fun* at the same time. Good luck! Work smart, and enjoy your adventure with passion.

Ending Thoughts

Top 7 Myths About Starting a Business
From our experience consulting to entrepreneurs, start-ups, and small businesses over the past ten years, we've gained much exposure to the realities of starting and growing businesses. We thought it would be interesting—and hopefully instructive—to lay out some of the myths and assumptions of aspiring entrepreneurs.

1. **It Is All Dependent on Hard Work.** Hard work is an absolutely necessary, but not sufficient, condition for starting and growing a business. It is the given, but without a solid Business Plan and compelling value proposition for customers and partners, all of the hard work in the world will be for naught. The world is filled with overworked, overstressed, and not terribly successful small-business people who

Action Step 70

Project Your Income Statement and Cash Flow

What you are driving at here is *net profit*—what is left in the kitty after expenses—for each month and for the year.

First, figure your *sales and cost of goods sold*. The first big bite out of that figure is the *cost of goods sold*. (In a service business the big cost is labor.) Subtracting that gives you a figure called *gross margin*.

Now add up all your *expenses*—rent, utilities, insurance, and so on—and subtract them from gross margin. This gives you your *net profit before taxes*. (Businesses pay taxes in quarterly installments.) Subtract taxes to arrive at your net profit.

In some cases, the income statement and cash-flow statement can be combined as one. In other instances, two separate statements will be used. Either format is usually acceptable.

Action Step 71

Complete Your Balance Sheet

A balance sheet is a snapshot of your financial position at a certain point in time.

1. Add up your assets. For convenience, divide these into *current* (cash, notes receivable, etc.), *fixed* (land, equipment, buildings, etc.), and *other* (intangibles like patents, royalty deals, copyrights, goodwill, contracts for exclusive use, etc.). You will need to depreciate fixed assets that wear out. As value, show the net of cost minus the accumulated depreciation.
2. Add up your liabilities. For convenience, divide these into *current* (accounts payable, notes payable, accrued expenses, interest on loans, etc.) and *long-term* (trust deeds, bank loans, equipment loans, balloons, etc.).
3. Subtract liabilities from assets.

You now have a picture of your net worth. Are you in the red or in the black?

table 15.1

Entrepreneurs' Hub's Pro Forma Income Statement

	Total	1st Month	2nd	3rd	4th	5th
Sales Revenue	$607,329.22	$46,570.00	$47,268.55	$47,977.58	$48,697.24	$49,427.70
Expenses						
1. Advertising - 7%	$42,513.05	$3,259.90	$3,308.80	$3,358.43	$3,408.81	$3,459.94
2. Licenses/fees - 6%	$36,439.75	$2,794.20	$2,836.11	$2,878.65	$2,921.83	$2,965.66
3. Payroll Taxes - 10%	$4,159.20	$346.60	$346.60	$346.60	$346.60	$346.60
4. Salaries	$38,126.00	$3,466.00	$3,466.00	$3,466.00	$3,466.00	$3,466.00
5. Bank Charges - 0.4%	$18,219.88	$1,397.10	$1,418.06	$1,439.33	$1,460.92	$1,482.83
6. Dues and Subscriptions	$600.00	$50.00	$50.00	$50.00	$50.00	$50.00
7. Insurance	$18,000.00	$1,500.00	$1,500.00	$1,500.00	$1,500.00	$1,500.00
8. Janitorial - 0.7%	$4,251.30	$325.99	$330.88	$335.84	$340.88	$345.99
9. Office Supplies - 3.5%	$21,256.52	$1,629.95	$1,654.40	$1,679.22	$1,704.40	$1,729.97
10. Phone/Cable - 3%	$18,219.88	$1,397.10	$1,418.06	$1,439.33	$1,460.92	$1,482.83
11. Professional Fees	$12,000.00	$1,000.00	$1,000.00	$1,000.00	$1,000.00	$1,000.00
12. Rent	$46,680.00	$3,890.00	$3,890.00	$3,890.00	$3,890.00	$3,890.00
13. Repairs & Maint. - 3%	$18,219.88	$1,397.10	$1,418.06	$1,439.33	$1,460.92	$1,482.83
14. Travel & Entertain - 1%	$6,073.29	$465.70	$472.69	$479.78	$486.97	$494.28
15. Interest - 9%	$5,400.00	$450.00	$450.00	$450.00	$450.00	$450.00
16. Utilities - 3.0%	$18,219.88	$1,397.10	$1,418.06	$1,439.33	$1,460.92	$1,482.83
17. Misc. Expense - 3.0%	$6,443.93	$1,397.10	$425.42	$431.80	$438.28	$444.85
18. Lease Equipment	$24,000.00	$2,000.00	$2,000.00	$2,000.00	$2,000.00	$2,000.00
19. Contract Instructors (3)	$96,567.05	$7,200.00	$7,344.00	$7,490.88	$7,640.70	$7,793.51
20. Depreciation	$12,000.00	$1,000.00	$1,000.00	$1,000.00	$1,000.00	$1,000.00
Total Expenses	$450,855.60	$36,363.84	$35,747.12	$36,114.51	$36,488.14	$36,868.13
Net Income Before Taxes	$156,473.61	$10,206.16	$11,521.43	$11,863.07	$12,209.10	$12,559.57

Notes for Pro Forma Income Statement

Sales Revenue: Approximately 20 Fast-Start workshops sold at $1250 each (income spread over 6 weeks), 80 Saturday workshops at $200 each, 110 weeknight workshops at $100 each, and misc. Seminar income

Advertising: Based on 7% of sales

Licenses/fees: Software license fees estimated at 6% of sales

Payroll Taxes: 10% of salaries

Salaries: 2 full-time secretarial employees earning $9 per hour

Bank Charges: 75% of sales will be charged to credit cards at a cost of 4% of sales.

Dues and Subscriptions: Subscriptions for owners and classrooms

Insurance: Quote provided by our insurance broker, Sharon Mandel of Fireman's Fund

Janitorial: Cleaning will be provided by janitorial service for less than the normal rate as the owner has traded janitorial services for software training.

Office Supplies: 3.5% of sales

struggle not because of lack of appropriate effort, but rather for lack of appropriate planning.

2. **If Your Product or Service Is Compelling Enough, Customers Will Beat a Path to Your Door.** Unless you are building a business based upon intellectual property and/or technology that provides and creates a competitive advantage and compelling customer value proposition, the early success of your business will be based as much on your ability to market and sell your product and service as it will on the product or service offering itself. Remember: in a capitalistic marketplace there is NO distinction between value and perceived value.

3. **If Your Product or Service Is Compelling Enough, Investors Will Beat a Path to Your Door.** Those who identify themselves as prospective investors in earlier-stage, small companies are mostly INUNDATED with investment opportunities. As such, no matter how good and unique your business opportunity, there is always a strong, initial prejudice AGAINST investment that needs to be overcome.

4. **It Is All About You.** The myth of the charismatic, "do and be everything" entrepreneur is just that—a myth. Any and all companies of value are great teams much more than they are the by-product of a highly talented individual. The best entrepreneurs and business leaders inspire the mission, values, and philosophy of a company by their own example. This inspiration is then communicated to all of the business' stakeholders—employees, customers, investors, partners, vendors, and its wider community.

6th	7th	8th	9th	10th	11th	12th
$50,169.12	$50,921.65	$51,685.48	$52,460.76	$53,247.67	$54,046.39	$54,857.08
$3,511.84	$3,564.52	$3,617.98	$3,672.25	$3,727.34	$3,783.25	$3,840.00
$3,010.15	$3,055.30	$3,101.13	$3,147.65	$3,194.86	$3,242.78	$3,291.42
$346.60	$346.60	$346.60	$346.60	$346.60	$346.60	$346.60
$3,466.00	$3,466.00	$3,466.00	$3,466.00	$3,466.00	$3,466.00	$3,466.00
$1,505.07	$1,527.65	$1,550.56	$1,573.82	$1,597.43	$1,621.39	$1,645.71
$50.00	$50.00	$50.00	$50.00	$50.00	$50.00	$50.00
$1,500.00	$1,500.00	$1,500.00	$1,500.00	$1,500.00	$1,500.00	$1,500.00
$351.18	$356.45	$361.80	$367.23	$372.73	$378.32	$384.00
$1,755.92	$1,782.26	$1,808.99	$1,836.13	$1,863.67	$1,891.62	$1,920.00
$1,505.07	$1,527.65	$1,550.56	$1,573.82	$1,597.43	$1,621.39	$1,645.71
$1,000.00	$1,000.00	$1,000.00	$1,000.00	$1,000.00	$1,000.00	$1,000.00
$3,890.00	$3,890.00	$3,890.00	$3,890.00	$3,890.00	$3,890.00	$3,890.00
$1,505.07	$1,527.65	$1,550.56	$1,573.82	$1,597.43	$1,621.39	$1,645.71
$501.69	$509.22	$516.85	$524.61	$532.48	$540.46	$548.57
$450.00	$450.00	$450.00	$450.00	$450.00	$450.00	$450.00
$1,505.07	$1,527.65	$1,550.56	$1,573.82	$1,597.43	$1,621.39	$1,645.71
$451.52	$458.29	$465.17	$472.15	$479.23	$486.42	$493.71
$2,000.00	$2,000.00	$2,000.00	$2,000.00	$2,000.00	$2,000.00	$2,000.00
$7,949.38	$8,108.37	$8,270.54	$8,435.95	$8,604.67	$8,776.76	$8,952.30
$1,000.00	$1,000.00	$1,000.00	$1,000.00	$1,000.00	$1,000.00	$1,000.00
$37,254.58	$37,647.60	$38,047.32	$38,453.84	$38,867.29	$39,287.79	$39,715.45
$12,914.54	$13,274.05	$13,638.16	$14,006.92	$14,380.38	$14,758.60	$15,141.63

Professional Fees: Estimates received from our attorneys, Farney and Shields, and our accounting firm of Hancock and Associates

Rent: Based on $2.57 per square foot

Repairs and Maintenance: 3% of sales

Travel and Entertainment: 1% of sales; includes dues for professional and service organizations

Utilities: 3% of sales; based on discussions with utility providers and past experience

Misc. Indirect Expense: 3% of sales

Lease Equipment: Set monthly rate estimate provided by vendors

Contract Instructors: Three instructors each working 60 hours per month at $40 per hour

Interest: 9% per year on $60,000; 12 payments per year

Depreciation: Depreciation charges estimated by accountant

5. **The Government Is Your Friend.** We are constantly astounded by the regulatory and paperwork maze that a start-up company needs to negotiate and constantly monitor to both start and maintain a business. It is a significant time, money, and energy drain that detracts from the main value-creation intent of a new business. Our best advice in this regard—as resources are available—is to find competent legal and accounting counsel, to both advise upon and outsource the regulatory burden, so you can focus on business building.

6. **The Government Is Your Enemy.** Having said the above, in the mixed economy in which we live, government revenue opportunities on a local, state, federal, and international level have never been greater for small business. While slow, meandering, and confusing to approach, governments have much to recommend them as clients and customers, not the least of which is that once sold, government clients pay well and are not bad debt risks. A somewhat trite but very important credo to remember when selling to governments, even more so than in business, is that "it is not as much what you know but who you know."

7. **It Is Only Worth Doing if You Become the Next Google.** The vast majority of small businesses will always remain just that—small businesses. The odds of starting a business and have it become the next Google or a publicly traded company are very, very small. While we would never discourage entrepreneurs for aiming for the stars, it is also important to have success metrics grounded in probability. An expectation of a minimum of 2 years of very, very hard work with little financial return but with a lot of learning (and some fun hopefully as well) involved is a good starting point. From this first milestone, then and only then should there start

table **15.2**

The Entrepreneurs' Hub's Balance Sheet

Balance Sheet

	ACTUAL (After first 6 months)
Current Assets	
Cash	$13,970
Books/Materials	2,500
Total Current Assets	$16,470
Leasehold Improvements	81,000
Furniture	15,100
Equipment	40,600
Total Fixed Assets	$146,700
Other Assets	
License	25,000
TOTAL ASSETS	$178,170
Debt and Equity	
Current Debt	
Accounts Payable	7,060
Accrued Wages	2,500
Loan Payment	
Total Current Debt	$9,560
Long Term Debt	
Bank Loan	0
TOTAL DEBT	$9,560
Equity	
Owners' Net Worth	$168,610
TOTAL DEBT AND EQUITY	$178,170

to be an expectation of significant wealth building. Find that balance between the long-term vision and the Monday morning action plan—and success, while not guaranteed, is very likely.

Source: Jay Turo, *http://www.growthink.com* (Accessed February 20, 2008).

EPILOGUE

Act on What You Know

Well, do you feel like you are ready? You are. You have thoroughly researched your product or service, your industry, your Target Customers, your competition, your marketing strategy, and your location. You have discovered how to prepare for surprises you cannot afford; how to handle numbers; how to pursue financing; when and why you should incorporate; how to build a winning team; and whether you should buy an ongoing business, become a franchisee, or strike out on your own. And you have written it all up in a showcase: your winning Business Plan.

SUMMARY

It has been a long haul. When you visit vendors, bankers, and potential lenders, take your portable showcase, your Business Plan, to speak for you and demonstrate to all that you have a blueprint for success.

Begin writing by starting with the material you feel most comfortable with. Once you have completed one portion of the plan, the other parts will fall into place more easily. Fortunately, your work in earlier chapters has prepared you for each section.

Make sure your Business Plan has answered the following questions:

- What is your mission?
- How are you going to market your product or service?
- Who is going to purchase your product or service?
- How will you reach your Target Customers?
- What makes your firm unique?
- How will you support the financial needs of your growing firm?

After you have completed the plan, rewrite your cover letter and executive summary, highlighting the most relevant information and data for your readers. *Good luck and go forth with passion!*

THINK POINTS FOR SUCCESS

- The executive summary should read like advertising copy. Keep revising it until it is tight and convincing.
- Section I should generate enthusiasm for your business.
- Section II should substantiate the enthusiasm with numbers.
- Be sure footnotes sufficiently explain the numbers in your financial statements.
- Do not inflate numbers to impress.
- Use your Business Plan as a road map to success.
- Your Business Plan is a working, living document; revise it every 6 to 12 months.

KEY POINTS FROM ANOTHER VIEW

35 Biz Planning Tips—Best Practices for Practical Success

1. Clearly define your business idea, and be able to succinctly articulate it. Know your mission.
2. Develop a personal financial evaluation. Determine your net worth and your annual, personal cash-flow needs.
3. Examine your motives. Make sure that you have a passion for owning a business and for this particular business.
4. Be willing to commit to the hours, discipline, continuous learning, and the frustrations of owning your own business.
5. Understand that your primary responsibility is the proper use of capital and that you are in business to make a profit.
6. Test the economics of your product or service. Make sure that it is profitable and that the gross profit percentage is in line with that of the industry.
7. Determine who your customers are and what their wants or needs are. Know how your product or service satisfies their wants or needs.
8. Know how customers will buy from you. Plan how you will make your product or service available to them—wholesale, retail, direct, or Internet.
9. Know how you will finance your business. Visit lenders (banks) prior to seeking financing to gather information. Ask your lenders what they will want to see before you apply for a loan.
10. Conduct a competitive analysis in your market, including products, prices, promotions, advertising, distribution, quality, and service, and be aware of the outside influences that affect your business.
11. Test the reality of your business—know why it will work and how you will make it work. Think your business through step by step.
12. Write a Business Plan with a complete financial and marketing plan.
13. Determine your primary business unit—units sold, customers sold, average order, hours billed, and so on. Know what drives your business.
14. Develop meaningful sales forecasts in terms of basic business units. Predict weekly sales for the first few months and monthly sales for the first year. Consider possible scenarios, such as a 10 percent rise or fall in sales.
15. Develop realistic financial forecasts for income statements, cash flow, and balance sheets for 3 years. Forecast monthly for the first year.
16. Establish an annual operating plan. Review it and update it monthly with appropriate employees.

17. Carefully select your place of business. Review guidelines for locations on type of business, customer convenience, traffic, safety, and so on.

18. Develop profiles for your products or services, customers, and markets.

19. Conserve capital. Do not commit cash or capital until necessary. Don't buy services before you need them. Lease instead of buying when possible.

20. Carefully determine your inventory needs. Don't overstock or get oversold by eager vendors.

21. Know and use your suppliers, including your banker. They can be a great source of training, information, and support.

22. Select the proper business structure for your business. Consider taxes, liability, capital needs, costs, entry, and exit. Know the benefits and drawbacks of your legal structure.

23. Seek help from other small businesses, vendors, professionals, government agencies, employees, trade associations, and trade shows. Be alert, ask questions, and visit your local SCORE office.

24. Advertising is expensive, so know why you are advertising and what you want to accomplish. Evaluate your advertising carefully and measure its effectiveness.

25. Develop appropriate sales promotion tools such as flyers, brochures, and signs. Carefully review each item for its effectiveness, and evaluate what these tools say about your business.

26. Establish an accurate, timely, and meaningful accounting and financial system to enable proper management of the business.

27. Maintain strict separation of personal and business accounts.

28. Employees are your most important assets, so hire the best, provide training and growth opportunities, and recognize good performance.

29. Examine your own skills carefully. Know your strengths and weaknesses and hire to complement your skills, not duplicate them.

30. Have a meaningful, concise, realistic job description for each employee. Make sure you review it with the employee and that it is understood.

31. Be sure employees know what is expected of them. Establish high standards of performance and morality, but be realistic and practical and communicate effectively.

32. Instill and practice the concept of continuous quality improvement and quality customer service as a way of life in your business.

33. Study your business and stay abreast of what's going on in your industry. Read newspapers, periodicals, trade journals, and so on.

34. Get involved in your community. Join the chamber of commerce, business organizations, service clubs, and charities. Network and keep your antennae up.

35. Allow 3 to 4 hours every week for thinking and planning. Do not allow anything to interfere with this time. You run the business. Don't let it run you.

Provided by SCORE Business Counselor Richard Benner of Kansas City, Missouri, an experienced strategic and business manager.

Source: Richard Benner, *http://www.score.org/35ann/ success.html* (Accessed August 13, 2001).

appendix a

Fast-Start Business Plan

The Fast-Start Plan allows you to start *now*—a good option if you have been in business before and know the footwork of entrepreneurship. With the Fast-Start Plan, you are using the business as a probe into the marketplace. You can start quickly, because you have an instinct for beating out the competition. You have a sense of the market and a good feel of the business you are starting.

The Fast-Start Plan is *not* a substitute for preparing a full-fledged plan. Use the Fast-Start Plan for a specific venture that is easy to start, carrying minimal risk. Also use it for a business that is breaking new ground, where there is little data available and speed to the market is imperative. Or use the Fast-Start Business Plan if you need money now and have a good idea.

In addition, to check out a business idea quickly, you can prepare a Fast-Start Business Plan and then complete a full-fledged plan if the Fast-Start Plan looks promising, or if the business grows quickly and needs additional financing. Read through the Yes, We Do Windows Business Plan at the end of Appendix A before you begin writing your Fast-Start Plan.

If you are going it alone with money you can afford to lose ($1,000; $5,000; $10,000; $100,000), and if the loss of that money will not jeopardize your loved ones and make wolves howl at your door, the Fast-Start Plan may work for you; or it may work if you just want to try out an idea before exploring the business idea further.

If other people are involved—investors, bankers, advisors, company officers—then return to Chapter 15 and write a comprehensive plan that will give you a blueprint to follow month by month through the first year.

Gather up all the information from your past action steps. For additional assistance, use one of the online Business Plan templates discussed in Chapter 15 or develop the Fast-Start Plan on your own.

QUICK CHECKLIST

Below is a quick checklist for implementing the Fast-Start Plan:

1. Can you afford to lose your dollar investment? How much money can you afford to lose at the slots in Reno or Las Vegas or Atlantic City? Can you lose $100? $500? $1,000? $25,000? More? What is your deductible on your car insurance, your boat insurance, or your major medical insurance? Write down the amount you can afford to lose. If you have excess money to speculate with, then the Fast-Start Plan may be for you.

2. How easy is it to enter this business? Is it easy to talk to other owners? Are role models in abundance? Do the prospective customers have a clear understanding of the goods and services provided? Examples of businesses with wide-open doors include window washing, auto detailing, landscape maintenance, arts and crafts, selling on eBay, vacation pet sitting, and house sitting.

3. Can you start this business on a part-time basis? Starting part-time decreases your risk. You have a chance to prove the business and see how much you really like it. Keep a running tally of customer responses, but keep your other job and the income and possible benefits it provides.

4. How tough is it to gather needed data to formulate a Fast-Start Business Plan? In breaking new ground, be careful. In such a venture, the market is not clearly defined. There are very few competitors. Pricing is not clear, so you must make certain you have a market out there that is willing to pay. The opportunities may be endless. Take a chance!

5. Can you start using only your own funds? Bill Gates, the founder of Microsoft, could use the Fast-Start Plan for a business start-up costing billions. A single parent of two with rent and a car loan can afford much less. Be honest with yourself. Be honest with your family.

STRUCTURING YOUR PLAN

Use these questions and all of the Actions Steps you have completed to structure your Fast-Start Plan:

- How do you describe your business?
- What business are you really in?
- Who is your competition, and how are they doing?
- What is your pricing strategy?
- Who is your Target Customer?
- Why should Target Customers buy from you?
- How will you market your product or service?
- What are your start-up costs?
- What are your sales goals for the first three months?
- What is your break-even point?
- What are your operating expenses for the first three months?
- If you crash and burn, what can you salvage for cash?
- What have you forgotten?

A GREAT DREAM CAN EQUAL A GREAT BUSINESS

It's late, and the family has gone to bed. The house is quiet. The pets are snoozing. And in your head, a dream is brewing.

Your dream has given you a jump-start into a new world, a business of your own. Now you need to add in the details and make it happen.

You want to be proud of being in business. You want to care. You want your customers to care that you care. People love to do business with people who care about what they are doing. Such people take pride in a job well done, and it shows.

WHO ARE MY COMPETITORS?

How do you find them? If you are hunting for retailers or restaurant owners, hop in your car and drive around. Eat in the restaurants. Shop at the stores. Continue to network with your friends and neighbors if you are looking at a local business. If you are starting an Internet or distribution business, network your way to reviews and information on the Internet. Check out blogs, Web sites, and online customer reviews.

You know a business must communicate with potential customers, so turn on your entrepreneurial radar. Check Yellow Pages, area newspapers, and Web sites; look for business cards in copy centers, in service stations, in local food stores, and on kiosks.

What can you learn from your competitors? Each will probably have one or two elements at which they excel; look hard to find those elements, and do *not* discount your competitors' strengths.

Once you find your competitors, take a closer look. Were they easy to find? How visible was their advertising? As you study their advertising strategy, what kind of a customer profile can you draw? Are they spending a lot on their advertising? Are they working on a shoestring?

What can you tell from their pricing? Are prices firm or negotiable? Are they high? Low? Competitive? Which Target Customers will purchase at these prices? Who will get shut out? Do your competitors understand the marketplace? Is their pricing structure positioned properly?

Are your competitors zeroed in on a specific Target Customer, or are they using the shotgun approach? Profile the Target Customer of your competitors. Later you will be profiling your customer, and you may want to find a niche that is not being served.

Which of your competitors are successful? Can you tell why? Which are just hanging in there? Why? If a business has been operating for some time, there is a good chance the owner is doing something right. What is it? Nose around. What customer benefits do they offer? Fast service? Quality work? Free delivery? Low prices?

Take the time to talk with the customers of your competitors. Are they satisfied? If not, why not? How do they see the competition? What image does the competition project? How do customers feel about price, quality, and timeliness?

Even the most successful business overlooks something. Find out what your competitors missed. Are they overlooking a market segment? Are they sloppy with their advertising? Are their services actually limited? Is inventory sparse? Is their service poor? Thousands of businesses have been built on the weaknesses of the competition.

Take time to chat with competitors outside your area. Is there a gap no one has thought to close? If there is, you may be on your way faster than you thought!

WHO ARE MY TARGET CUSTOMERS?

Who will receive the biggest benefit from your business? Who can pay the price? Who can you affordably target? Where do they live? What is their income range? What do they need? What work do they do? Are they married, single, divorced, or retired?

To profile your customers, become a marketplace detective. To practice, study the customers that buy from your competitors.

Do women outnumber men? What is the average age? What cars do they drive? How are the customers dressed? How expensive are their shoes? If you can get inside, check out methods of payment. Do they use cash? Debit? Credit? How expensive are the items they are buying?

Practice trains your new eyes to consider the person as a prospect.

HOW CAN I CONNECT WITH MY CUSTOMERS?

Before you spend a bundle on Internet advertising, or three months knocking on doors of houses along Golf Course Drive, take time to refine your message.

What image do you want to project? How do you want the marketplace to receive your product or service? What position do you want to assume among your competitors? What are the key benefits your business will offer customers? How soon do you want to start?

Once you answer these questions, design your business card. Use a logo that offers an insight into your business. If you are starting an auto-detailing business, use something along the lines of "On Time Quality Service." If you are thinking of house cleaning: "Only Sparkle—Not a Speck of Dust." Always carry lots of business cards. They are inexpensive memory seeds, handy reminders, and often your most cost-effective advertising.

Once your business cards are done, research ways of reaching your customers. Do they gather at church, at school, at football games, or at Little League? What do they read, watch, and listen to? Could you reach them best through the Yellow Pages, radio, or billboards? What can you afford? Match that amount with the most effective communications channel.

For almost all businesses at the beginning, positive word of mouth propels the business forward fastest. As you develop your business you will need to determine what are the best ways to spread the word. Your current customers are your best promotional tool, and encouraging them to spread the word on your behalf is the cheapest and most effective way to promote your business. How can you use the Internet to spread the word?

Stay visible. If your Target Customers gather in groups, try to reach them there. Attend their meetings. Get on their list of speakers. Give a demonstration. Hand out business cards. Offer freebies.

If you must find your customers one at a time, spend a few hours each day knocking on doors. Telephone prospects. Work your mailing list. If you use mail contacts, be sure you do phone follow-ups.

Join the local chamber of commerce. If you are lucky, your chamber will run a short piece about you, the newcomer, in their newsletter. Stay visible at chamber meetings. Do not get pushy with your business cards, but have them handy.

While you are connecting with customers, do not overlook organizations that might act as your sales force. For example, let us say you have found a school where the parents' group is trying to raise funds to support an athletic endeavor. Put together a flyer for students to take home. In return for each sale from the flyer, your business will donate 10 percent to 15 percent to the fund-raising group. Consider the donation a part of your promotional budget.

HOW MUCH SHOULD I CHARGE?

Find out what is important to the customers. It is probably time or dependability or quality or convenience. Learn to see the value of your product or service through your customers' eyes. Answer this question: What is most important to your customer, and how can you meet their needs?

Pricing is one key. Do not be misled by thinking you can whisk customers away from established competitors by charging less for the same thing. It did not work for now-bankrupt department stores, and it will not work for you.

WHAT ARE MY START-UP COSTS?

At your local office supply store, make these purchases: a mileage log, an expense journal, and a folder to hold receipts. You can deduct mileage and expenses related to your business start-up only if you keep good records for the IRS.

Next, list everything that you need to open your business. Do not worry if the list would cost a bundle. You are brainstorming at this point. The key here is not to overlook anything. A visit to your competitors will add ideas to your list. An interview with an owner will trigger new items. When you are chatting with businesspeople, ask questions: What software do you find most helpful? What was the cost of start-up inventory? What items are essential to start this type of business? When your list is fat, add price tags to each item.

In the beginning, borrow everything you can. When you have to purchase, buy used. Although used equipment might be scratched or dented, you stand to save 50 percent to 90 percent. Check newspapers and online classifieds. Talk with potential suppliers—they usually know someone who is going out of business. You can find good deals from an owner who is folding or upgrading.

When you start purchasing, check the large discount stores. If one company in your area can supply most of your needs, focus on trying to get a package deal, and develop a long-term relationship.

You should also consider leasing your equipment. As your business grows and your leases expire, decide whether to replace by buying new or used. Leasing provides you a lot of up-front flexibility, because you are able to hold on to your capital a little longer. Divide your start-up list into two columns: Column 1 contains items that are absolutely necessary. Column 2 contains "nice-to-haves."

Check Column 1. Is there anything you can borrow from home, parents, or friends? Scrape to the bottom of the barrel here. Your goal is to cut costs so you will have cash to *run* the business. Many entrepreneurs sink themselves before they even open their doors by thinking it is necessary to have the latest and best. There will be plenty of time for that type of thinking later, but only if you are conservative at the beginning.

WHAT ARE MY SALES GOALS FOR THE FIRST THREE MONTHS?

How much would you like to sell the first month, the second, and the third? How much can you afford to sell? What is a realistic target for your new business?

Sales goals provide the information you need to forecast your variable expenses, which are those expenses forced to change in relation to sales volume. If you are selling a product or service, sales goals will allow you to estimate the cost of goods sold.

Sales goals provide the driving force for you and your team. They help you focus on your target for the month. When the month is finished, compare how you did with your initial sales goals. Did you make it? If not, why not? Did you exceed your goal by 25 percent? Why? What worked well? What did not? As you evaluate, decide how to improve each subsequent month. To chart a reasonable sales goal, focus on three factors:

1. **The weight of your marketing program.** Do you plan a wide-area campaign? Will you start by calling on friends and neighbors, counting on

them to spread the word slowly? How much energy are you putting into this? Will you start full-time? Will you keep your job? If you are in school, will you stay enrolled?

2. **The experience of entrepreneurs in businesses like yours who operate in a noncompeting area.** How much effort does Entrepreneur A have to put out to make a $100 sale in his or her area?

3. **The capacity you have to deliver the product or service.** What do you need to make this venture go? If it costs you $500 for materials to build one custom table, and you only have $500 worth of capital, then you will be limited to building one table at a time.

Or let us say you are starting a part-time business detailing automobiles. Detailing one automobile takes three hours. In addition, driving to the clients, collections, and scheduling take approximately one hour per car. Your maximum sales activity per week will be based on the number of hours you can devote to your business after you put in your hours at your full-time job, if you are still employed. If you can devote 24 hours a week your potential gross income would be:

$$24/4 = 6 \text{ autos per week maximum sales volume}$$
$$\text{Your charge per auto} = \$120$$
$$6 \times \$120 = \$720 \text{ per week potential gross income}$$

Make a list of your friends and relatives. Find out how many of them have their cars detailed. Add the repeat factor. How often do they want detailing—once a month, once every quarter, or once a year? When your list is finished, and you have 24 prospects, recognize that you may have a realistic shot at 18 of those prospects. For your business, that is enough for a start-up.

As a wise entrepreneur, you know that your first few jobs will take longer than later ones. You are new, and you are learning the business, so you must make sure you do a superb job so you can count on referrals. You have four prospects who want monthly detailing, and six more want it quarterly. Start with these ten prospects, and lay out a chart.

WHAT ARE MY FORECASTED EXPENSES?

List everything you will need to pay for on a regular basis to operate your business: for example, phone, supplies, truck, advertising/promotion, and so on. Next, list everything you can think of under each heading. If you have a competitor you know well out of your market territory, sit down with him and have him help you develop your list. Also, look to your associations as they may have help for you as well.

YOUR TO-DO LIST

Now that your plan is complete, it is time to follow through. The next step is to finalize your to-do list and begin. You need this list for at least three reasons:

1. It provides steps to follow.
2. It keeps you on target.
3. It provides realistic goals.

YOUR TURN NOW!

The key to any business, and to any Business Plan, is how well you understand the needs of your Target Customer. Find an itch that is not being scratched, and you can ace your competitors. Reread the Yes, We Do Windows Business Plan which follows, and gather your Action Steps. Read the instructions, complete your Fast-Start Plan, and become the entrepreneur you know you can be.

Once you write your own Fast-Start Plan, keep it handy, and refer to it often. Use it to keep your business on track in those early months of operation. When you have been in business for 3 months, use your Fast-Start Plan as a launching pad for your next 9 months of operation. For your second year, write a full-fledged Business Plan.

May your Business Plan, hard work, sweat, long hours, and passion lead to your success.

Congratulations!

YES, WE DO WINDOWS

Fast-Start Business Plan

1. Business Definition
2. Competition
3. Target Customers
4. Marketing Plan
5. Pricing
6. Start-up Costs
7. Sales Goals and Expenses (three months)
8. To-do list

1. Business Definition Providing sparkling clean windows which allow homeowners to enjoy their home, protect their investment, and deepen their pride of ownership utilizing only eco-friendly, fragrance-free products.

A home is a person's most expensive investment. Many homes today in my target market are supported by dual-incomes and few of these homeowners have the time or desire to do their own window cleaning.

2. Competition At this time, there are five window cleaning services listed in my area Yellow Pages—three franchisees and two independents The marketing research I undertook by making phone calls to my competitors indicated that there was room for another professional window cleaning firm in the area. Many of these firms did not return calls, did not seem interested, and were unable to provide phone bids. My research shows three of these operations are not reliable according to former clients. Although, one independent operating as a one-man shop is very reliable and will be my major competitor. As not to cannibalize on his business and acknowledging there is an ample market available I will try not to compete in the exact same neighborhoods as he does.

Research shows window cleaning services and pricing offered by the competitors are very similar. Thus, I have decided I will not compete on price but will try hard to offer exceptional, timely, guaranteed and professional service. Most window cleaners are in and out of business quickly and do not present a professional image. Thus, I plan to present a very professional appearance at all times; always wearing a clean shirt with my company name and logo, driving an immaculate truck with professional signage, and placing professional signs in each yard as I clean the windows.

My research also shows several of my competitors do not clean windowsills and tracks and thus these services will be added. In addition, all screens will be removed and scrubbed. Clients will be charged for these additional services.

Evaluating the competition has given my start-up a real advantage. Since I will be doing all the work myself, I can continue to gather customer data as I work. Many clients mentioned they were uncomfortable with different people working on their homes at each service. Since I will do all the work myself for at least six months this will definitely be a competitive advantage at the beginning. As I add employees I will go by and check their work each day to assure consistency and contact with my clients in the future. A home is a private place. It is a place where one goes to escape from the day. One does not want it invaded by strangers. My plan is to expand only when I find the right employees.

I see two additional "musts" for my business: a) bids must be firm and b) phone skills must be customer-oriented with calls returned within a few hours. The image I hope to present, "I aim to please. I'm interested in servicing your home and making you and your windows shine on a continuing basis."

3. Target Customers   I am focusing my business on ten large subdivisions. Within each of these subdivisions there are approximately 5–7 floor plans. When clients call for a bid, I will be able to ask them the model of their home and provide a quick estimate based on their information.

The majority of my clients will be dual career families with 1–2 children. Clients are primarily upper-middle class in this area with incomes of $80–100K. Spare time is at a premium and is reserved for recreation and entertainment. Homeowners drive primarily small SUV's and sedans. The homeowners take great pride in their homes and are very concerned with keeping up with their neighbors.

4. Marketing Plan

- I will maintain an image of high visibility and professionalism. My white truck with blue lettered signs will be washed weekly. All signs on the truck will be kept in perfect condition.

- All my advertising will be in navy blue and white. Business cards are blue with white lettering. On the reverse side is a list of my services. Whenever I hand out a business card I aim to gain one in return. Data from these cards will be placed in to my data base immediately for further marketing efforts.

- My attire will include a white shirt with my navy blue logo, navy blue pants and white tennis shoes.

- All my work equipment will be maintained in perfect shape so I present a professional image at all times.

- I acknowledge that I must compete with individuals operating illegally who offer bids 20–40% lower than the reputable licensed and bonded window cleaners. My challenge will be to turn this problem into an advantage rather than a disadvantage. Thus, clients will be presented with copies of my business license and proof of insurance and bonding. In addition, my insurance firm has a one-page statement that clearly delineates possible financial and legal consequences of using unlicensed businesses operating illegally and I will attach the statement to each bid. I will provide references for each of the neighborhoods where I serve.

- For the first three months, I will spend approximately three to four hours each weekend walking the neighborhoods with door hangers announcing my services. Also, while walking the neighborhoods on the weekend in my uniform, I hope to meet and talk with many of the homeowners who will be working in their yards or playing with their children. As people respond to the door hangers, I will continue my market research by asking the following: Whom did you use in the past? What did you like or dislike about their services? What additional services would you like?

- I will purchase my domain name for a future Web site where I will have an online calculator which will provide potential clients quick estimates. In addition, there will be a scheduling calendar onsite as well. I would like to set up a PayPal account to accept payments online as well.

- I will contact each client within 48 hours after I have completed my services and clear up any problems immediately. As I believe word of mouth will be my best marketing tool, I will do everything to keep my clients satisfied.

- I will contact each client every three months to try to develop repeat clientele.

- Company signs with my phone number will be displayed on client's property while window cleaning takes place.

- I will purchase small ads in the neighborhood association newsletters and will also post small ads on their association Web sites. These ads are very inexpensive and aimed directly at my clients.

- I will also donate window cleaning services for my daughter's private school on a monthly basis, hoping my efforts will be mentioned in the PTA newsletter.

- I will join a very successful BNI networking group which meets on a weekly basis. All members are required to market others' businesses.

5. Pricing Pricing will be competitive and within close range of my major competitors. I will not compete on price with the illegal operators.

Basic Rates for Window Cleaning	Fee
Windows-in and out/tracks/sills	
Plain	$4.00–$8.00 per window
Sliding Glass Doors	$5.00 per door
French Doors	$7.00 per door
Screens	$1.00 per screen
Mirrors	$4.00 each
Chandeliers	quote upon request
Car windows (inside and out)	$10 sedan/$20 SUV
Average cost per home	$120.00–$150.00

6. Start-up Costs

Insurance (car and business)	700
Truck*	
Bond (initial cost)	750
Ladders	350
Legal advice (1 hour)	150
Bookkeeper advice (2 hours)	100
Supplies	300
Signs for truck	295
Advertising	1000
Cell phone with Internet access/scheduler	500
P.O. Box per month—first and last month	40
Networking group (initiation fee)**	300
Fictitious business name filing	85
City business license	155

Used desk and chair	375
Supplies and file system	50
Computer accounting and billing software***	195
Bank account (order checks)	125
Total Estimated Start-up Expenses	5470

*I currently own a white 2005 Ford truck in excellent condition.
**Networking weekly meetings will cost $80.00 a month.
***Currently own computer and printer.

7. Sales Goals and Expenses, First Three Months   I plan to work six days per week for the first three months. I plan to work Monday through Friday completing window cleaning jobs and Saturday will be devoted to marketing and managing the business. I am assuming the first month that I will complete 20 window cleaning jobs, the second month 30, and the third month 40 at an average of $135.00 each.

table A.1

Proforma Income Statement— Yes, We Do Windows

	Sales Goals and Expenses		
	1st Month	2nd Month	3rd Month
Sales (1)	2700	4050	5400
Expenses:			
Gas (2)	400	500	600
Maintenance (3)	160	160	160
Insurance (4)	600	600	600
Phone (5)	100	100	100
Advertising (6)	200	200	200
Supplies (7)	200	300	400
Credit Card (8)	300	300	300
Network lunches	80	80	80
P.O. Box	40	40	40
Miscellaneous	400	500	600
Expense Total	2480	2780	3080
Gross Profit	220	1270	2320

Assumptions for Table A.1
1. Average customer $135 (20 – 1st month, 30 – 2nd month, 40 – 3rd month).
2. Gas, ($400 – 1st month, $500 – 2nd month, $600 – 3rd month)
3. Maintenance—mainly a reserve for tires, repairs, oil changes, $40 per week.
4. Auto and business liability, $1,500 per year.
5. Apple iPhone cell phone charges (currently own iPhone).
6. Approximately $200 for ads in association newsletters and Web sites and door hangers.
7. Approximately $10 per job.
8. Credit card payment for start-up expenses. Used $4,000 of cash on hand for expenses and cash advance of $3,000 which I intend to pay back before the end of the year.

8. To-Do List

1. Talk with experienced window cleaners.
2. Stay organized.
3. Choose a business name.
4. File for fictitious business name.
5. Determine specific geographical area to service.
6. Order cell phone service.

7. Check out several banks as fees and services vary. Set up business checking account and line of credit.

8. Locate, evaluate, and select suppliers and order initial supplies.

9. Check city and county business license regulations and apply.

10. File for a federal ID number—needed by all employers.

11. Locate an insurance agent and purchase insurance.

12. Set up a meeting with an accountant/bookkeeper.

13. Complete advertising for association newsletters and Web sites.

14. Join a discount warehouse club.

15. Order business cards, door hangers, thank you notes, and yard signs.

16. Set up P.O. Box

17. Record all income and expenses and mileage daily.

18. Meet with attorney for an hour to determine if there are any legal issues, which I need to consider.

19. Network with friends and relatives, encourage them to spread the word about my new business.

20. Order signs for vehicles.

21. Purchase accounting and billing software.

22. Arrange bond.

23. Obtain *Tax Guide for Small Business* (IRS Publication 334).

24. Obtain *Taxpayers Starting a Business* (IRS Publication 583).

25. Obtain *IRS's Tax Calendar for Small Business*.

26. Join International Window Cleaners Association.

27. Finish Fast-Start Business Plan.

appendix b

Annie's Business Plan Proposal

COVER LETTER FOR ANNIE'S

Business Plan Proposal for Specialty Chocolates and Candy Concession at Sea World

Annie's
27898 Palm Tree Lane
Escondido, CA 92677

Oct. 1, 2008

Sea World
Ms. Janet Wilkes
2 Sea World Drive
San Diego, CA 92888

Dear Ms. Wilkes,

We are pleased to offer our proposal to operate a chocolate and candy concession at Sea World with an August opening date. With thirteen years of retailing experience throughout San Diego, and our excellent reputation as a provider of one of the largest selections of candies and chocolates, we believe Annie's will be an excellent addition to Sea World's concession offerings.

Annie's is thrilled to offer your national and international tourists the opportunity to shop at San Diego's finest chocolate and candy store. Sea World's long and successful run as one of the premiere attractions in San Diego offers Annie's a great opportunity to expand our business.

Our firm is self-financed, and our strong balance sheet allows Annie's to expand into Sea World without outside financing. Thus we will be able to open within 8 weeks following acceptance of our proposal.

On review of our proposal, please contact us to clarify any points. We look forward to a long and profitable association with Sea World.

Sincerely,

Casey Johnson
President (Annie's)

ANNIE'S BUSINESS PLAN PROPOSAL

Business Plan Contents

Note: Due to the fact this Business Plan is a proposal for operating a concession within Sea World, primary emphasis is on store operations, experience, and product. Location is clearly defined, marketing is limited primarily to in-store promotions, and competition is limited to other concessionaires, none of whom are direct competitors.

EXECUTIVE SUMMARY

Annie's specialty shop will feature fine chocolates and candy as a concessionaire for Sea World. Annie's unique stores strive to create an atmosphere that is entertaining and fun for the customer to browse and shop in, upscale yet casual, and a place where employees enjoy working. We are known to provide high-quality, fresh products and intimate customer service. Annie's owners like it when people get excited in their stores and remember Annie's as a place that they want to return to. As owners, we are customer-driven and love retailing.

We have been successful candy retailers for the past thirteen years and believe we do an excellent job selling bulk candy, chocolates, and candy gift packages. Few other operations offer such a complete selection of confections from hundreds of manufacturers under one roof. Many of the items offered for sale are very different and unusual. Because of this wide selection, Annie's is able to offer many different price points to meet the needs of most customers. Your customers will also consider our candies and chocolates ideal gifts.

Our proposal for a candy concession at Sea World comes after thorough research into the make-up of the other vendors and our belief that Annie's will complement the other stores and not cannibalize sales. Candy is considered an "extra," one that tourists and families gladly splurge on during their vacations. Many visitors will pass our store as they exit Sea World and will want something sweet before they get on the road back to their homes or hotels.

Upon Sea World's acceptance of our proposal, we could be open within 8 weeks. Our strong balance sheet and available cash on hand will allow us to act immediately. Annie's staff will thoroughly train all Sea World store staff in our other stores prior to opening in Sea World. On opening day, we will offer trained personnel ready and willing to serve Sea World's customers with our legendary customer service.

Our creative store layout is designed to accommodate a large number of customers at one time, and at the busiest times of the day and year, we will be able to operate two computer registers. Through our thirteen years in business, we have refined our store layout to best serve our customers and employees.

We believe our retail experience, strong balance sheet, excellent reputation throughout the Southern California area, and tasty chocolate product offerings will be a wonderful addition to Sea World.

MANAGEMENT AND STAFFING

Retail Experience and History

Since its inception in 1995, Annie's has been a successful retailer of bulk candy and chocolates, top-of-the-line gourmet boxed chocolates and truffles, domestic and foreign product lines, sugar-free products, novelty and nostalgia candies, dried fruit gifts, gourmet food gifts, gift baskets, Kosher confections, difficult-to-find items, seasonal merchandise, and related gift items that complement the packaged food products. Annie's is well known by consumers in Southern California as having the largest and most complete selection of confections in the area at our five store locations.

SKU Stock Keeping Unit barcode

Through the years as owners, we have identified the best sources for over 2000 SKUs. We not only know where and how to purchase the merchandise, we also know, for each item, the turnover when reasonably priced, the shelf life, and the gross margin. We know how to purchase in both large and small quantities, depending on the candy, the weather, the store location, and the time of year. We know which vendors are able to keep freight costs under control and pack without excessive damage. Our company "cherry picks" the best from many distributors and manufacturers. We also carry nearly the entire line of those suppliers who do an excellent job; for example, Lindt, Joseph Schmidt, Asher's, Ghiradelli, Goelitz, Laymon, and so on.

Annie's does not manufacture any of its own chocolates. In the store, employees dip strawberries and other fresh and/or glazed fruit, Oreo cookies, pretzels, Rice Krispie treats, Gummi bears, and so on in chocolate. Sometimes empployees make gift baskets for holidays and special events, and the customers have great fun watching this and purchasing these great gifts.

Our five store locations throughout Southern California include Dana Point, Carlsbad, Fallbrook, Escondido, and downtown San Diego. We have opened one store every other year with our own funds. All stores are profitable, and we have more than 30 employees on the payroll.

Annie's opened in 1995 as an LLC in Escondido, California. The principal owner and manager of our company is Casey Johnson whose three adult children, Troy, Samantha, and Max, all play major roles in the management and daily operations of the business. Annie's owns the service mark and trademarks.

Management

1. Casey Johnson (see résumé) began working in her aunt's 15,000-square-foot retail department store business at the age of 13. Through the years working in this third-generation business, she learned many of the fine details of operating a successful retail business. She opened her own branch store of the family chain at 22.

   Casey worked her way through the ranks at several retail chains, Sears, and The Gap. In addition, she completed her undergraduate degree in economics at the University of California in Santa Barbara. After 20 years working for other's, Casey opened Annie's in 1995. Casey Johnson serves as a guest lecturer at several colleges and is a frequent guest speaker at retail association meetings.

2. Troy Johnson is currently site manager. He monitors inventory levels, develops staffing schedules, deals with day-to-day operational issues, and supervises personnel. He worked for several years as a shift supervisor for the Cheesecake Factory. He has been actively involved in all aspects of Annie's since its inception.

3. Samantha Johnson, an English graduate of Indiana University, helped develop all Annie's operation manuals. With six years of retail experience at Hallmark, K-Mart, and Nordstrom, Samantha brought wide exposure to various training methods and store layout and design. She is also responsible for all ad layouts.

4. Max Johnson holds an Information Management degree from UC Riverside. His primary focus with Annie's has been computer operations and information systems. He has assisted with all new store start-ups.

If awarded this concession, Casey Johnson will oversee overall operations of the business. Troy Johnson will provide on-site management under the close supervision of Casey Johnson. Other company members may also provide on-site management and support with members of the company reporting directly to Casey Johnson. Max Johnson will assist with store start up. Day and evening charge persons will be hired and trained.

Staffing Plan

1. Organizational chart for proposed operations:
   a. Casey Johnson: Responsible for the overall operations and management of the concession.
   b. Troy Johnson: Responsible for on-site, 24-hour management and supervision of the concession. Reports to Casey Johnson.
   c. Casey, Troy, and Samantha Johnson: Consultation and support.
   d. Day charge person (to be hired), reporting to Troy Johnson.
   e. Evening charge person (to be hired), reporting to Troy Johnson.
   f. Four additional sales people will be hired.

2. Staffing plan: There will be two employees to service the customers at all times. During busy seasons, there will be three to four employees. This number includes the charge person.

3. Résumés: see Business Plan Appendix.

Exit Strategy

Casey Johnson and her children will continue to run Annie's as a family company for the next 5 to 10 years, at which time Casey plans to step back from day to day operations and turn over the business to her children The company has been developed to support and provide a good living for the entire family. Each of the children enjoys retailing and finds opening and running new stores an exciting part of the business. Casey and her family hope to grow Annie's to 10 stores within the next 5 years.

STORE OVERVIEW

Floor Plan

A Ghirardelli merchandising tower will be near the right front window and a floor-standing sucker rack near the left window. These may be moved to other areas of the store periodically. Window displays will be seasonal and kept low to enhance visibility into the store. As the customers enter the store, they will face an 8-foot curved glass chocolate showcase merchandised with truffles, turtles, pecan rolls, English toffee, and similar chocolate items. On both sides of the chocolate case will be various packaged candies.

Both the right and left walls will be mirrored. Along the lower right wall will be acrylic Jelly Belly dispensers. Above these dispensers will be staggered glass shelves to display gift items. Along the back wall will be custom-made acrylic bulk candy bins. Gift items will be displayed along the top shelves of these bins, and the rear wall will be painted white. Neon will be installed across the rear wall above the bulk candy. Across from the bulk candy bins, on the back side of the service counter, will be shelves for novelty candy items and bins filled with taffy along the top shelf.

The left wall will have open cabinet shelves, the highest at 36 inches, for boxed chocolates. Above these shelves will be staggered glass shelves for displays of gift items. In the center of this wall will be an 8-foot section of custom slat wall to hang packaged items.

The service counter will be in the center of the store. There will be a 6-foot long, 36-inch high, flat glass counter showcase on both the right and left sides of the service area. The left side will hold sugar-free chocolates, and the right side will hold fudge and other bulk chocolates. A center island will be used to do chocolate dipping, to construct baskets, and so on. There will be one register and one scale on each side of the service counter.

Behind the rear wall of the store is the required hand sink, three-basin sink, mop sink, water heater, microwave, small refrigerator, and shelving. It is estimated that this area is approximately 140 square feet.

Floor Space

Approximately 250 square feet of retail floor space is allocated to merchandise fixtures. Based on this area, the square footage for each category follows:

1. Bulk candy: 84 sq. ft
2. Bulk chocolates: 38 sq. ft

3. Edible gifts: 66 sq. ft
4. Sugar-free and/or fat-free items: 15 sq. ft
5. Nonedible gifts: 10 sq. ft
6. Novelty candy: 37 sq. ft

However, because there are multiple levels of shelves, the percentage of products carried to actual square footage would be quite different. For example, the right wall would have 22 square feet of Jelly Belly Bean fixtures; but above the beans, there would be four levels of glass shelves, with approximately 15 square feet for each level, for packaged gift items. It is estimated that 90 percent of all revenue would be from edible food and gift products and less than 10 percent from nonedible gift products. Aisles would be 5 feet wide to allow for wheelchair access, backpacks, and comfortable movement for customers.

See detailed floor plan drawings in the appendix.

Visual Presentation of Merchandise

The colorful world of candy always lends itself to great displays and store designs. The stores are merchandised and decorated to reflect the numerous holidays and seasons throughout the year. The summer season is followed by fall, Halloween (great fun!), Thanksgiving, Hanukah, Christmas, Valentine's Day (the prettiest), St. Patrick's Day, Easter, Mother's Day, graduation, Memorial Day, Independence Day, and Labor Day. Colors and store decor are changed to match these events and holidays. Organdy and other beautiful ribbons are used to dress up packages and displays, and gift wrap paper is changed to match the seasons and holidays.

With the exception of very high-turnover products and products that are always carried, few single items are purchased in large quantities. Rather, many different items are purchased in smaller quantities, thus giving the customer a wider selection of products to choose from, and giving the company the ability to bring in new merchandise and change displays often. Most importantly, this ensures freshness of the products.

Unique gift items are incorporated into the merchandising themes. Many times the company purchases their own supplies to create these unusual gifts. For example, the employees may take small watering cans painted with sunflowers, insert cello bags printed with sunflowers, fill the bags with bulk lemon drops, and tie a silk sunflower into the organdy bow, or attach a small plush item or sunflower button doll. All of the Easter baskets sold by Annie's are custom made.

Bulk chocolates, including sugar-free items, are sold from the chocolate cases. Through the years, the company has identified those items that are in high demand and those companies who manufacture the best products. Annie's knows who makes the best truffles, the best turtles, the best honeycomb, and so on.

The bulk candy bins are very colorful; the customers love them—and they generate nice revenue. The bins will be segmented by types of candy: licorice, sour, gummi, sugar-free, and so on. Approximately 10 percent of the bulk bin space is allocated to candies that have a lower demand, such as horehound lumps and Bit O' Honey. Annie's believes that they maintain a competitive edge by carrying some of these more difficult-to-find items.

Individual shelves within the store may be merchandised with different themes; for example, all sea-item gifts, or all teacher gifts, or all dried-fruit packages. A certain shelf, for example, may be merchandised with the Shamu theme, including such items as suckers and stick candy with a Shamu on them, plush Shamus, and Shamu mugs filled with black and white Jelly Bellies. Product displays are changed frequently, so things do not become boring.

Products

The product lists in the appendix are examples of many products we carry; they are arranged by merchandise category. Not all items are carried at all times; new companies, such as Joseph Schmidt, never repeat their seasonal packaging from year to year, and they frequently change their product lines. Annie's is vigilant about staying on top of the market.

There are six major merchandise categories:

1. Bulk candy in self-serve bins
2. Bulk chocolates in the chocolate cases
3. Packaged, edible gift items (boxed chocolates, mugs filled with candy, etc.)
4. Sugar-free and/or fat-free items (incorporated throughout the store)
5. Nonedible gift items (collectible plush bears, candy dishes, candy tins, etc.)
6. Packaged novelty candy (War Heads, Pop Rocks, etc.)

Estimate of approximate quantities:

1. Bulk candy: 175 bins including 18 taffy and 54 Jelly Belly bins
2. Bulk chocolates: 500 different pieces
3. Edible gifts: 500 to 600 different items
4. Sugar-free items: 100 different items
5. Nonedible gifts: 200 different items
6. Packaged novelty: 300 to 400 different items

Pricing

Most packaged and gift items are now street priced at a 39 to 42 percent margin, which is monitored on the computer with every invoice. Since this was done, the average ticket increased, perhaps because customers feel they can afford to purchase more. Customers are happier now, product turnover is higher, and the problems with transferring product among stores have decreased significantly.

Estimate of price ranges:

1. Bulk candy: $1.79 per 1/4 lb.
2. Bulk chocolates: $2.98 per 1/4 lb. to $4.98 per 1/4 lb., average $3.98 per 1/4 lb.
3. Edible gifts: $1 to $150, average $10 to $30 range
4. Sugar- and/or fat-free items: Same as 1, 2, and 3 above
5. Nonedible gifts: $1 to $150, average $10 to $30 range
6. Packaged novelty candy: $0.99 to $25, average $1 to $3 each

MARKETING

Retail Trends

To keep abreast of retail trends, Annie's frequently attends the following trade shows:

1. The International Fancy Food Show—twice yearly
2. The Philadelphia Candy Show
3. The LA Gift Show
4. The Denver Gift Show
5. The Phoenix Gift Show

6. The New York Gift Show
7. The Seattle Coffee Fest

Annie's subscribes to trade journals and is in constant communication with both vendors and customers. Annie's frequently visits all competitors to monitor prices and look for new items.

Customer Service Philosophy/Programs

The customer service goal of Annie's is to meet customer needs in the most efficient and pleasant manner possible. The employees are expected to do whatever is necessary to make the purchase easy for the customer. This may mean gift wrapping a package, wrapping an item in bubble wrap so that it does not break, holding an item for a customer, or processing a special order.

Annie's accepts all credit cards for customer convenience.

Returns are processed cheerfully, efficiently, and without question. The customer is offered replacement merchandise or a refund. A refund/complaint form is completed, and all employees have the authority to process refunds so that the customer is taken care of immediately.

Customers are often in a hurry and like their purchases processed quickly. This requires employees who are well-trained, know the merchandise, and are swift, accurate, helpful, friendly, and courteous, especially under pressure. Annie's occasionally employs mystery shoppers and uses this feedback for coaching employees. Feedback on employee behavior is solicited from regular customers, employees from other businesses, business acquaintances, and friends whenever possible. Annie's business card is always out on the counter for customers who wish to call or email.

Employees are taught the following concepts of customer service:

1. Always, whenever possible, acknowledge the customer as they enter the store.
2. Offer assistance but also respect customers' wishes to be left alone.
3. Smile—all the time.
4. Do not ignore customers or turn your back on them.
5. Do not talk or gossip among yourselves when customers are in the store.
6. Do not talk badly about any customer, especially in front of other people, not even outside of work hours.
7. Do not complain about anything, or talk about personal problems, religion, or politics to customers or among yourselves when customers are in the store. Save this chatter for after hours, when you are away from the workplace.
8. Try to never leave a customer once you are engaged in a transaction.
9. Process refunds and/or complaints cheerfully and efficiently. Never argue. Listen and hear the customer out. Resolve the problem on the spot whenever possible.
10. Always say thank you.
11. The customer is your real boss, so treat each customer accordingly.

Employees are taught about candy and chocolate, because they are expected to be knowledgeable and conversant. They are also taught how to gift wrap, tie bows, construct gift baskets, dip chocolate, process special orders, and process charges. They are trained to handle cash accurately. They all learn how to process shipments from invoices and price products.

White aprons, red shirts with our blue logo, and name tags are required at all times.

Marketing Plan

1. An advertisement will be placed in the local Yellow Pages candy section of the major area phone books. This advertisement will promote corporate/quantity orders and special orders.

2. Entertainment retail: Most customers find it very entertaining just to browse the store. Employees dip chocolate-covered strawberries, caramel apples, and other items where customers can watch. Customers like to watch the employees mold chocolate items, such as Easter Bunnies. They also tend to stand and watch gift baskets being made.

3. Employees often dress up as a Mr. Jelly Belly or as a witch at Halloween or an Easter Bunny at Easter, and so on.

4. Controlled food sampling is used to promote sales.

STORE OPERATIONS

Stocking

Food products will be stored in the shop, and nonfood items will be stored in the storeroom. The storeroom area is inadequate and unsafe for storing food products that are not sealed in cans or glass bottles. The temperature is too warm, and it would be nearly impossible to have adequate pest control. There are storage shelves under the bulk candy bins, under the chocolate bins, and under the service counters. There is limited storage area near the sinks.

During slow periods or off hours, employees will replenish bulk candy bins and other products. Each candy bin is removable and can be replaced with a bin that is full. Employees will do pricing and stocking daily during quiet periods. During busy periods, such as Christmas, Valentines, and Easter, an employee will be brought in to adjust the price of merchandise and replenish shelves. All items will be individually priced, even if bar coded.

The owners may find it necessary to rent off-site storage. If this occurs, a part-time stocker will be hired to accept deliveries at the off-site location and price merchandise before transporting it to the store. During hot weather, merchandise will be transported only at night.

Logistics and Frequency of Deliveries

1. Delivery schedule of new goods: Most goods are delivered by UPS or similar common carrier. UPS can deliver daily. These shipments are generally not very large, and the on-site manager will be responsible for coordinating deliveries. Large freight shipments will come in approximately every 10 days and may have to go to off-site storage for processing. Most manufacturers only ship out UPS on Monday or Tuesday, so product does not sit in a UPS warehouse over the weekend.

2. Replenishment of on-site stock: Par levels are established for items that are carried all the time (e.g., malt balls). Orders are placed at least weekly and more often if needed. Seasonal items are replenished only if they turn over quickly and early. It is impossible to order replacement candy late into the holiday season. While stores are selling Christmas, the manufacturers are processing Valentine's orders, and so on.

Facility Maintenance Plan

1. Policy for maintenance and repairs: A preventative maintenance program will be implemented for the refrigerated chocolate case and the

under-counter refrigerator per manufacturer's recommendations. All repairs will be made in a timely manner and as needed.

2. Frequency of cleaning: Glass shelves are cleaned daily and more often if necessary. Employees mop the floors nightly, and floors are professionally cleaned quarterly. Windows are washed weekly and touched up daily. The store is dusted daily. It is management's expectation that the store be kept spotless.

3. Disposal of trash: Trash is emptied at least 8 times per day and sometimes more often.

4. Replacement of equipment, displays, fixtures, and flooring: No replacement is anticipated during the life of this lease. If the need occurs, items will be replaced accordingly.

FINANCIAL MANAGEMENT AND FINANCIALS

System of Internal Controls

Sales and Cash Receipts

a. Computer registers—Two point-of-sale computer terminals, which are capable of recording sales by stock-keeping units (SKUs), will be used. They will be equipped with sales-totalizer counters for all sales categories; the counters are locked, constantly accumulating, and cannot be reset. Beginning and ending sales-totalizer counter readings will be recorded daily.

b. Sales will be entered into one of five departments:

Bulk Candy (self-serve out of the bins)

Chocolates/Candy (all other food and/or items containing food)

Nonfood Gifts

Gift Certificates

Shipping Costs

c. Sales transactions will be cash, debit or credit card. No personal checks will be accepted. Credit cards will be processed through one of two terminals for electronic authorization and capture. All transactions will be entered into the computer terminals.

d. At the end of each day, the daily journals (Z tapes) will be removed from the registers and placed with the cash receipts for the day. A $200 bank will be left in each register, and a coin bank of $300 will be maintained on the premises. Each morning, for the previous day, Troy Johnson or his designee will prepare the night-drop deposit and deposit it at the bank.

e. The information from the daily journal tapes will be entered onto the weekly sales summary form. At the end of each week, the weekly totals will link to the monthly sales summary form. All Z tapes and any other paper transactions pertinent to the gross and/or net sales for each day (void slips, refund forms, cash paid-out receipts, employee discount receipts, credit card batch slips, deposit slips, etc.) will be attached together by day and stored by month in the storeroom.

f. Weekly and monthly records will be faxed to the CPA, who will prepare the monthly compiled financial statements for the location. The original Z tapes and other paper transactions will be submitted to the CPA, who will prepare the annual audited sales report. Once returned by the CPA, the original Z tapes and report forms will be stored in the storeroom.

g. The CPA performing the annual audit will review the system of internal controls semiannually.

h. Gross sales will only be offset by customer refunds, voids (documented employee errors during sales transactions), shipping expenses when an item is shipped for a customer (customer will only be charged actual cost of shipping), and Annie's employee discounts.

i. Annie's employees are allowed a 30 percent discount on all purchases daily and a 50 percent discount on Christmas Eve and Easter Sunday. All employee purchases will be entered into the registers by management. The sales receipt will be initialed by the manager and the employee and placed with the daily cash receipts. If management is not available, purchases will be documented in a Tab Book and paid for by the employee at a later date. Employees will not be allowed to ring up their own purchases.

j. Sea World employees will be allowed a discount of 10 percent on any total sale of $5 or more. The employee must be in uniform or be able to show some form of proof that he or she is an employee. The person receiving the discount must write where he or she works on the receipt and sign it. This receipt is placed with the daily cash receipts.

k. Employees are not allowed to make change from the register without a sale. There is no exception to this rule. Change is also only made up to the amount of cash tendered to complete the transaction.

l. Cash is bled from the cash drawers at frequent intervals throughout the day and transferred to a locked, built-in cash-drop drawer.

m. Voids: The cash register receipt tape showing the void will be stamped with the void stamp and initialed by the person making the error. Sometimes the customer just changes his or her mind after a sale is rung up. This is also treated as a void. The void slips are placed with the daily cash receipts.

n. Refunds/Returns: The refund/return form will be completed. The customer must present the merchandise and proof of purchase. The receipt will be attached to the refund/return form. If the item was charged, a credit will be processed. If the customer paid cash, a cash refund will be given. If there is no proof of purchase, but it can be determined that it was a valid purchase from Annie's, a refund will still be given. If the customer eats the merchandise and then attempts to get a refund, the request will be denied.

o. Discounts: It is not anticipated that any promotional discounts will be given.

p. Keys: One set of Annie's storeroom keys will be kept on a large key ring in the store, and a key log will be used. One set of keys will also be issued to Casey Johnson and Troy Johnson. Store keys will be issued to those hired to open and close the store. Delivery people and others will never be left unattended in the storeroom.

q. Badging: Only key personnel will be badged, such as the day and evening charge persons and Annie's management.

r. Secret Shoppers: To be used periodically. Employees will be informed of this when they are hired. Video cameras may be installed.

Inventory and Accounts Payable

a. Shipments will be checked at delivery for evidence of damage. Any damage will be documented with the carrier. Shipments will be checked against the packing slip/invoice. Internal damage and/or shortages will be documented and the vendor notified immediately.

b. Extensions on all invoices, including computer-generated invoices, will be checked before payment. Amounts for damaged merchandise will be deducted from payment.

c. COD shipments are not accepted by Annie's under any circumstances. It is anticipated that all purchases will be paid for by check or credit card and not by cash on hand.

d. All invoices for payment are to be approved by Casey Johnson. Checks will be prepared and signed by Casey Johnson or other management in her absence. Invoices will be paid when due and stored by month of payment in Annie's storeroom.

e. Inventory counts will be completed monthly.

f. A review of the actual cost of physical inventory will be compared to the inventory on the financial statement. Any significant variations will be investigated, especially for theft of inventory.

g. Transfer of inventory among Annie's locations will be documented, at cost, on a duplicate transfer form. A copy of each transfer form will be kept at both the sending and receiving store. These forms will be stored in Annie's storeroom.

ANNIE'S PROJECTED RENTAL REVENUES AND ANNUAL MINIMUM GUARANTEE

Proposer's Name	Annie's
Store Concept	Full line bulk and packaged chocolates, novelty candy, related gift-packaged fancy food, gift baskets, related gifts, bulk candy
Merchandising Theme	Fine chocolates and candy

Established Tenant Rental Rate: 12.5%

Projected Gross Sales ($)		Percentage Rent	Projected Rental Revenues	Rental Revs. Per Sq. Ft.
A. Year 1	$600,000	12.5%	$75,000	$71.43
B. Year 2	$660,000	12.5%	$82,500	$78.57
C. Year 3	$726,000	12.5%	$90,750	$86.43
D. Year 4	$798,600	12.5%	$99,825	$95.07
Total/ 4 years	$2,784,600		$348,075	

ANNIE'S ESTIMATED CAPITAL INVESTMENT

I. Retail Opportunity
  A. Proposer's Name   Annie's
  B. Store Concept: Full line bulk and packaged candy and chocolates, related gift-packaged fancy foods, gift baskets, and gifts
  C. Merchandising Theme   Fine Chocolates and Candy

II. Proposer's Estimated Capital Investment
  A. Architectural and Engineering Fees $5,000
  B. Equipment, Furnishings, and Fixtures[1][2]   20,000
  C. Leasehold Improvements[2]   40,000

D. Working Capital		15,000
E. Initial Inventory		25,000
F. Improvements Completion Bond		2,500
G. Total Investment (Sum of II-A. through II-F.)		$107,500

III. Source of Investment

A. Amount Financed	$75,000	70%
B. Cash	32,500	30%
C. Total Investment (III-A. + III-B.)	$107,500	100%
(Should equal II-G. above)		

IV. Facility Improvements/Sq. Ft. $57.14
    (II-B. + II-C.)/I-D.

---

(1) Items removable at end of lease term.

(2) The sum of these two categories (Equipment, Furnishings, and Fixtures and Leasehold Improvements) shall not be less than $55 per square foot.

ASSUMPTIONS USED IN DEVELOPING INCOME AND CASH FLOW PROJECTIONS

1. Statistics for this store are similar to the statistics for other stores in similar locations.
2. Five-year historical sales record for the former See's candy concession.
3. Current monthly sales should closely parallel historical record of former See's candy concession.
4. Growth projections provided by owner.
5. Historical record of growth.
6. Current economic growth.
7. Price increases in product over time.
8. U.S. Department of Commerce Confectionery Report shows a steady, consistent increase in per-capita consumption of candy (in pounds) since 1984.
9. Confection sales are predominantly impulse purchases; therefore, the higher the foot traffic, the higher the sales.

ANNIE'S APPENDIX*

A. Balance Sheet
B. Break-Even Analysis
C. Store Layout
D. Facility Design
E. Complete Store Design Details
F. Résumés
G. Legal References
H. Business References
I. Product Lists
J. Market Research Statistics

(*Appendices A-J would be provided to Sea World but are not included in the text.)

ANNIE'S

Projected Annual Income and Cash-Flow Statement for Proposed Store

Proposer's Name   Annie's
Store Concept   Packaged and bulk confections and related gift and food items
Merchandising Theme   Fine chocolates and candy

Category	Year 1 Amount	Year 1 % of Gross Sales	Year 2 Amount	Year 2 % of Gross Sales	Year 3 Amount	Year 3 % of Gross Sales	Year 4 Amount	Year 4 % of Gross Sales
Gross Sales	$600,000.00		$660,000.00		$726,000.00		$798,600.00	
Cost of Goods	$216,000.00	36%	$237,600.00	36%	$261,360.00	36%	$287,496.00	36%
Gross Profit	$384,000.00	64%	$422,400.00	64%	$464,640.00	64%	$511,104.00	64%
Operating Expenses:								
Salaries/Wages/Benefits	$84,000.00	14.0%	$92,400.00	14.0%	$101,640.00	14.0%	$111,804.00	14.0%
Utilities and Telephone	$1,200.00	0.2%	$1,320.00	0.2%	$1,452.00	0.2%	$1,597.00	0.2%
Maintenance/Cleaning/Supplies	$14,400.00	2.4%	$15,840.00	2.4%	$17,424.00	2.4%	$19,166.00	2.4%
Insurance	$6,000.00	1.0%	$6,600.00	1.0%	$7,260.00	1.0%	$7,986.00	1.0%
Marketing/Advertising	$6,000.00	1.0%	$6,600.00	1.0%	$7,260.00	1.0%	$7,986.00	1.0%
Licensing Fees	$18,900.00	3.2%	$20,790.00	3.2%	$22,869.00	3.2%	$25,156.00	3.2%
Rent	$75,000.00	12.5%	$82,500.00	12.5%	$90,750.00	12.5%	$99,825.00	12.5%
General and Administration	$36,000.00	6.0%	$39,600.00	6.0%	$43,560.00	6.0%	$47,916.00	6.0%
Interest Expense	$9,600.00	1.6%	$9,600.00	1.5%	$9,600.00	1.3%	$9,600.00	1.2%
Other Misc. Expenses	$1,800.00	0.3%	$1,980.00	0.3%	$3,630.00	0.5%	$3,993.00	0.5%
Total Expenses	$252,900.00	42.2%	$277,230.00	42.1%	$305,445.00	42.1%	$335,029.00	42.0%
Depreciation	$7,600.00	1.3%	$7,600.00	1.3%	$7,600.00	1.3%	$7,600.00	1.3%
Net Income	$123,500.00	20.6%	$137,570.00	20.8%	$151,595.00	20.9%	$168,475.00	21.1%
Add Back: Depreciation	$7,600.00		$7,600.00		$7,600.00		$7,600.00	
Cash Flow From Operations	$131,100.00	—	$145,170.00	—	$159,195.00	—	$176,075.00	—
Beginning Cash Balance	$10,000.00		$131,100.00		$251,170.00		$385,365.00	
Plus: Cash Flow from Operations	$131,100.00		$145,170.00		$159,195.00		$176,075.00	
Minus: Debt Service (Principal Only)	$10,000.00		$25,000.00		$25,000.00		$15,000.00	
Minus: On-Going Annual Capital Expenditures	$ —	—	$ —	—	$ —	—	$ —	—
Ending Cash Balance Available to Proposer	$131,100.00	—	$251,170.00	—	$385,365.00	—	$546,440.00	—

See list of assumptions made to create these sales projections and figures on the previous page.

appendix c

Forms, Forms, Forms

1. Family Budget
2. Personal Financial Statement
3. Application for Employer Identification Number: SS-4
4. Profit or Loss from Business: Schedule C
5. Net Profit from Business: Schedule C-EZ
6. Self-Employment Tax: Schedule SE
7. Employment Eligibility Verification: Form I-9
8. Application for Business Loan: SBA Form 4
9. Franchise Disclosure Document: An Overview

FAMILY BUDGET

INCOME   ———————————

EXPENSES   ———————————

Taxes

   Social Security   ———————————

   Federal State and Local   ———————————

Food

   Home   ———————————

   Away from home   ———————————

     Breakfasts   ———————————

     Lunches   ———————————

     Dinners   ———————————

Housing

   Rent or Mortgage Payments   ———————————

   Property taxes   ———————————

   Maintenance   ———————————

   Furniture/Household goods   ———————————

Insurance

   Life   ———————————

   Health   ———————————

   Car   ———————————

   House   ———————————

   Other   ———————————

Credit Card Payments   ———————————

School Loans   ———————————

Clothing   ———————————

Transportation

   Loan/Lease Payment   ———————————

   Gas/Oil   ———————————

   Maintenance   ———————————

   Licenses   ———————————

   Public transportation   ———————————

Child Care   ———————————

Health Care

   Insurance   ———————————

   Medical Services   ———————————

   Dentist/Orthodontist   ———————————

   Medicine/Supplies   ———————————

Entertainment

   Weekend/Dates   ———————————

   Hobbies (Personal, childrens) ———————————

   Other   ———————————

Personal Care (haircut, etc.) ———————————

Education (tuition, books, etc.) ———————————

Charitable Contributions ———————————

Utilities

   Phone   ———————————

   Electricity/Gas   ———————————

   Internet   ———————————

   Cable   ———————————

   Water/Garbage   ———————————

   Cell phone   ———————————

Spending Money   ———————————

Children's Allowances ———————————

Gifts   ———————————

Vacations   ———————————

Monthly Memberships (gym, etc.) ———————————

Retirement Contributions ———————————

Savings   ———————————

Other   ———————————

TOTAL EXPENSES   ———————————

INCOME MINUS EXPENSES ———————————

OMB APPROVAL NO. 3245-0188
EXPIRATION DATE:3/31/2008

PERSONAL FINANCIAL STATEMENT

U.S. SMALL BUSINESS ADMINISTRATION   As of _____ , _____

Complete this form for: (1) each proprietor, or (2) each limited partner who owns 20% or more interest and each general partner, or (3) each stockholder owning 20% or more of voting stock, or (4) any person or entity providing a guaranty on the loan.

Name	Business Phone
Residence Address	Residence Phone
City, State, & Zip Code	
Business Name of Applicant/Borrower	

ASSETS	(Omit Cents)	LIABILITIES	(Omit Cents)
Cash on hand & in Banks	$_____	Accounts Payable	$_____
Savings Accounts	$_____	Notes Payable to Banks and Others	$_____
IRA or Other Retirement Account	$_____	(Describe in Section 2)	
Accounts & Notes Receivable	$_____	Installment Account (Auto)	$_____
Life Insurance-Cash Surrender Value Only	$_____	Mo. Payments $_____	
(Complete Section 8)		Installment Account (Other)	$_____
Stocks and Bonds	$_____	Mo. Payments $_____	
(Describe in Section 3)		Loan on Life Insurance	$_____
Real Estate	$_____	Mortgages on Real Estate	$_____
(Describe in Section 4)		(Describe in Section 4)	
Automobile-Present Value	$_____	Unpaid Taxes	$_____
Other Personal Property	$_____	(Describe in Section 6)	
(Describe in Section 5)		Other Liabilities	$_____
Other Assets	$_____	(Describe in Section 7)	
(Describe in Section 5)		Total Liabilities	$_____
		Net Worth	$_____
Total	$_____	**Total**	$_____

Section 1. Source of Income		Contingent Liabilities	
Salary	$_____	As Endorser or Co-Maker	$_____
Net Investment Income	$_____	Legal Claims & Judgments	$_____
Real Estate Income	$_____	Provision for Federal Income Tax	$_____
Other Income (Describe below)*	$_____	Other Special Debt	$_____

Description of Other Income in Section 1.

*Alimony or child support payments need not be disclosed in "Other Income" unless it is desired to have such payments counted toward total income.

Section 2. Notes Payable to Banks and Others.   (Use attachments if necessary. Each attachment must be identified as a part of this statement and signed.)

Name and Address of Noteholder(s)	Original Balance	Current Balance	Payment Amount	Frequency (monthly,etc.)	How Secured or Endorsed Type of Collateral

SBA Form 413 (3-05) Previous Editions Obsolete   (tumble)

This form was electronically produced by Elite Federal Forms, Inc.

Section 3. Stocks and Bonds. (Use attachments if necessary. Each attachment must be identified as a part of this statement and signed).

Number of Shares	Name of Securities	Cost	Market Value Quotation/Exchange	Date of Quotation/Exchange	Total Value

Section 4. Real Estate Owned. (List each parcel separately. Use attachment if necessary. Each attachment must be identified as a part of this statement and signed.)

	Property A	Property B	Property C
Type of Property			
Address			
Date Purchased			
Original Cost			
Present Market Value			
Name & Address of Mortgage Holder			
Mortgage Account Number			
Mortgage Balance			
Amount of Payment per Month/Year			
Status of Mortgage			

Section 5. Other Personal Property and Other Assets. (Describe, and if any is pledged as security, state name and address of lien holder, amount of lien, terms of payment and if delinquent, describe delinquency)

Section 6.   Unpaid Taxes.   (Describe in detail, as to type, to whom payable, when due, amount, and to what property, if any, a tax lien attaches.)

Section 7.   Other Liabilities.   (Describe in detail.)

Section 8.   Life Insurance Held.   (Give face amount and cash surrender value of policies - name of insurance company and beneficiaries)

I authorize SBA/Lender to make inquiries as necessary to verify the accuracy of the statements made and to determine my creditworthiness. I certify the above and the statements contained in the attachments are true and accurate as of the stated date(s). These statements are made for the purpose of either obtaining a loan or guaranteeing a loan. I understand FALSE statements may result in forfeiture of benefits and possible prosecution by the U.S. Attorney General (Reference 18 U.S.C. 1001).

Signature: Date: Social Security Number:

Signature: Date: Social Security Number:

PLEASE NOTE: The estimated average burden hours for the completion of this form is 1.5 hours per response. If you have questions or comments concerning this estimate or any other aspect of this information, please contact Chief, Administrative Branch, U.S. Small Business Administration, Washington, D.C. 20416, and Clearance Officer, Paper Reduction Project (3245-0188), Office of Management and Budget, Washington, D.C. 20503. **PLEASE DO NOT SEND FORMS TO OMB.**

Form **SS-4**	**Application for Employer Identification Number**	OMB No. 1545-0003
(Rev. July 2007)	(For use by employers, corporations, partnerships, trusts, estates, churches, government agencies, Indian tribal entities, certain individuals, and others.)	EIN
Department of the Treasury Internal Revenue Service	▶ See separate instructions for each line. ▶ Keep a copy for your records.	

Type or print clearly.

1 Legal name of entity (or individual) for whom the EIN is being requested

2 Trade name of business (if different from name on line 1)	**3** Executor, administrator, trustee, "care of" name

4a Mailing address (room, apt., suite no. and street, or P.O. box)	**5a** Street address (if different) (Do not enter a P.O. box.)
4b City, state, and ZIP code (if foreign, see instructions)	**5b** City, state, and ZIP code (if foreign, see instructions)

6 County and state where principal business is located

7a Name of principal officer, general partner, grantor, owner, or trustor	**7b** SSN, ITIN, or EIN

8a Is this application for a limited liability company (LLC) (or a foreign equivalent)? . . . . ☐ Yes ☐ No	**8b** If 8a is "Yes," enter the number of LLC members . . . . ▶

8c If 8a is "Yes," was the LLC organized in the United States? . . . . ☐ Yes ☐ No

9a **Type of entity** (check only one box). **Caution.** If 8a is "Yes," see the instructions for the correct box to check.

☐ Sole proprietor (SSN) _____
☐ Partnership
☐ Corporation (enter form number to be filed) ▶ _____
☐ Personal service corporation
☐ Church or church-controlled organization
☐ Other nonprofit organization (specify) ▶ _____
☐ Other (specify) ▶ _____

☐ Estate (SSN of decedent) _____
☐ Plan administrator (TIN) _____
☐ Trust (TIN of grantor) _____
☐ National Guard   ☐ State/local government
☐ Farmers' cooperative ☐ Federal government/military
☐ REMIC   ☐ Indian tribal governments/enterprises
Group Exemption Number (GEN) if any ▶

9b If a corporation, name the state or foreign country (if applicable) where incorporated	State	Foreign country

10 **Reason for applying** (check only one box)

☐ Started new business (specify type) ▶ _____
☐ Hired employees (Check the box and see line 13.)
☐ Compliance with IRS withholding regulations
☐ Other (specify) ▶

☐ Banking purpose (specify purpose) ▶ _____
☐ Changed type of organization (specify new type) ▶ _____
☐ Purchased going business
☐ Created a trust (specify type) ▶ _____
☐ Created a pension plan (specify type) ▶ _____

11 Date business started or acquired (month, day, year). See instructions.	**12** Closing month of accounting year
	14 Do you expect your employment tax liability to be $1,000 or less in a full calendar year? ☐ Yes ☐ No (If you expect to pay $4,000 or less in total wages in a full calendar year, you can mark "Yes.")

13 Highest number of employees expected in the next 12 months (enter -0- if none).

Agricultural	Household	Other

15 First date wages or annuities were paid (month, day, year). **Note.** If applicant is a withholding agent, enter date income will first be paid to nonresident alien (month, day, year) . . . . ▶

16 Check **one** box that best describes the principal activity of your business.
☐ Construction ☐ Rental & leasing ☐ Transportation & warehousing ☐ Health care & social assistance ☐ Wholesale-agent/broker
☐ Real estate   ☐ Manufacturing   ☐ Finance & insurance   ☐ Accommodation & food service   ☐ Wholesale-other ☐ Retail
                                                                     ☐ Other (specify)

17 Indicate principal line of merchandise sold, specific construction work done, products produced, or services provided.

18 Has the applicant entity shown on line 1 ever applied for and received an EIN? ☐ Yes ☐ No
If "Yes," write previous EIN here ▶

Third Party Designee	Complete this section **only** if you want to authorize the named individual to receive the entity's EIN and answer questions about the completion of this form.	
	Designee's name	Designee's telephone number (include area code) ( )
	Address and ZIP code	Designee's fax number (include area code) ( )

Under penalties of perjury, I declare that I have examined this application, and to the best of my knowledge and belief, it is true, correct, and complete.

Name and title (type or print clearly) ▶ | Applicant's telephone number (include area code) ( )

Signature ▶   Date ▶ | Applicant's fax number (include area code) ( )

For Privacy Act and Paperwork Reduction Act Notice, see separate instructions.   Cat. No. 16055N   Form **SS-4** (Rev. 7-2007)

Do I Need an EIN?

File Form SS-4 if the applicant entity does not already have an EIN but is required to show an EIN on any return, statement, or other document.[1] See also the separate instructions for each line on Form SS-4.

IF the applicant...	AND...	THEN...
Started a new business	Does not currently have (nor expect to have) employees	Complete lines 1, 2, 4a–8a, 8b–c (if applicable), 9a, 9b (if applicable), and 10–14 and 16–18.
Hired (or will hire) employees, including household employees	Does not already have an EIN	Complete lines 1, 2, 4a–6, 7a–b (if applicable), 8a, 8b–c (if applicable), 9a, 9b (if applicable), 10–18.
Opened a bank account	Needs an EIN for banking purposes only	Complete lines 1–5b, 7a–b (if applicable), 8a, 8b–c (if applicable), 9a, 9b (if applicable), 10, and 18.
Changed type of organization	Either the legal character of the organization or its ownership changed (for example, you incorporate a sole proprietorship or form a partnership)[2]	Complete lines 1–18 (as applicable).
Purchased a going business[3]	Does not already have an EIN	Complete lines 1–18 (as applicable).
Created a trust	The trust is other than a grantor trust or an IRA trust[4]	Complete lines 1–18 (as applicable).
Created a pension plan as a plan administrator[5]	Needs an EIN for reporting purposes	Complete lines 1, 3, 4a–5b, 9a, 10, and 18.
Is a foreign person needing an EIN to comply with IRS withholding regulations	Needs an EIN to complete a Form W-8 (other than Form W-8ECI), avoid withholding on portfolio assets, or claim tax treaty benefits[6]	Complete lines 1–5b, 7a–b (SSN or ITIN optional), 8a, 8b–c (if applicable), 9a, 9b (if applicable), 10, and 18.
Is administering an estate	Needs an EIN to report estate income on Form 1041	Complete lines 1–6, 9a, 10–12, 13–17 (if applicable), and 18.
Is a withholding agent for taxes on non-wage income paid to an alien (i.e., individual, corporation, or partnership, etc.)	Is an agent, broker, fiduciary, manager, tenant, or spouse who is required to file Form 1042, Annual Withholding Tax Return for U.S. Source Income of Foreign Persons	Complete lines 1, 2, 3 (if applicable), 4a–5b, 7a–b (if applicable), 8a, 8b–c (if applicable), 9a, 9b (if applicable), 10 and 18.
Is a state or local agency	Serves as a tax reporting agent for public assistance recipients under Rev. Proc. 80-4, 1980-1 C.B. 581[7]	Complete lines 1, 2, 4a–5b, 9a, 10 and 18.
Is a single-member LLC	Needs an EIN to file Form 8832, Classification Election, for filing employment tax returns, **or** for state reporting purposes[8]	Complete lines 1–18 (as applicable).
Is an S corporation	Needs an EIN to file Form 2553, Election by a Small Business Corporation[9]	Complete lines 1–18 (as applicable).

[1] For example, a sole proprietorship or self-employed farmer who establishes a qualified retirement plan, or is required to file excise, employment, alcohol, tobacco, or firearms returns, must have an EIN. A partnership, corporation, REMIC (real estate mortgage investment conduit), nonprofit organization (church, club, etc.), or farmers' cooperative must use an EIN for any tax-related purpose even if the entity does not have employees.

[2] However, do not apply for a new EIN if the existing entity only (a) changed its business name, (b) elected on Form 8832 to change the way it is taxed (or is covered by the default rules), or (c) terminated its partnership status because at least 50% of the total interests in partnership capital and profits were sold or exchanged within a 12-month period. The EIN of the terminated partnership should continue to be used. See Regulations section 301.6109-1(d)(2)(iii).

[3] Do not use the EIN of the prior business unless you became the "owner" of a corporation by acquiring its stock.

[4] However, grantor trusts that do not file using Optional Method 1 and IRA trusts that are required to file Form 990-T, Exempt Organization Business Income Tax Return, must have an EIN. For more information on grantor trusts, see the Instructions for Form 1041.

[5] A plan administrator is the person or group of persons specified as the administrator by the instrument under which the plan is operated.

[6] Entities applying to be a Qualified Intermediary (QI) need a QI-EIN even if they already have an EIN. See Rev. Proc. 2000-12.

[7] See also *Household employer* on page 4 of the instructions. **Note.** State or local agencies may need an EIN for other reasons, for example, hired employees.

[8] Most LLCs do not need to file Form 8832. See *Limited liability company (LLC)* on page 4 of the instructions for details on completing Form SS-4 for an LLC.

[9] An existing corporation that is electing or revoking S corporation status should use its previously-assigned EIN.

SCHEDULE C
(Form 1040)

Department of the Treasury
Internal Revenue Service   (99)

Profit or Loss From Business
(Sole Proprietorship)

▶ Partnerships, joint ventures, etc., must file Form 1065 or 1065-B.

▶ **Attach to Form 1040, 1040NR, or 1041.**   ▶ See Instructions for Schedule C (Form 1040).

OMB No. 1545-0074

20**07**

Attachment
Sequence No. **09**

Name of proprietor

Social security number (SSN)

A   Principal business or profession, including product or service (see page C-2 of the instructions)

B Enter code from pages C-8, 9, & 10
▶

C   Business name. If no separate business name, leave blank.

D Employer ID number (EIN), if any

E   Business address (including suite or room no.) ▶
    City, town or post office, state, and ZIP code

F   Accounting method: **(1)** ☐ Cash   **(2)** ☐ Accrual   **(3)** ☐ Other (specify) ▶

G   Did you "materially participate" in the operation of this business during 2007? If "No," see page C-3 for limit on losses   ☐ Yes   ☐ No

H   If you started or acquired this business during 2007, check here   . . . . ▶ ☐

Part I   Income

1	Gross receipts or sales. **Caution.** If this income was reported to you on Form W-2 and the "Statutory employee" box on that form was checked, see page C-3 and check here . . . . . . ▶ ☐	**1**	
2	Returns and allowances	**2**	
3	Subtract line 2 from line 1	**3**	
4	Cost of goods sold (from line 42 on page 2)	**4**	
5	**Gross profit.** Subtract line 4 from line 3.	**5**	
6	Other income, including federal and state gasoline or fuel tax credit or refund (see page C-3). . .	**6**	
7	**Gross income.** Add lines 5 and 6 . . . . ▶	**7**	

Part II   Expenses. Enter expenses for business use of your home **only** on line 30.

8	Advertising	**8**		18 Office expense	**18**	
9	Car and truck expenses (see page C-4)	**9**		19 Pension and profit-sharing plans	**19**	
10	Commissions and fees . .	**10**		20 Rent or lease (see page C-5):		
11	Contract labor (see page C-4)	**11**		**a** Vehicles, machinery, and equipment .	**20a**	
12	Depletion	**12**		**b** Other business property. . .	**20b**	
13	Depreciation and section 179 expense deduction (not included in Part III) (see page C-4)	**13**		21 Repairs and maintenance . .	**21**	
				22 Supplies (not included in Part III)	**22**	
				23 Taxes and licenses	**23**	
				24 Travel, meals, and entertainment:		
				a Travel	**24a**	
14	Employee benefit programs (other than on line 19). .	**14**		**b** Deductible meals and entertainment (see page C-6)	**24b**	
15	Insurance (other than health) .	**15**		25 Utilities	**25**	
16	Interest:			26 Wages (less employment credits) .	**26**	
a	Mortgage (paid to banks, etc.) .	**16a**		27 Other expenses (from line 48 on page 2)	**27**	
b	Other	**16b**				
17	Legal and professional services	**17**				

28	**Total expenses** before expenses for business use of home. Add lines 8 through 27 in columns . ▶	**28**	
29	Tentative profit (loss). Subtract line 28 from line 7	**29**	
30	Expenses for business use of your home. Attach **Form 8829**	**30**	
31	**Net profit or (loss).** Subtract line 30 from line 29.		
	• If a profit, enter on both **Form 1040, line 12,** and **Schedule SE, line 2,** or on **Form 1040NR, line 13** (statutory employees, see page C-7). Estates and trusts, enter on Form 1041, line 3.	**31**	
	• If a loss, you **must** go to line 32.		
32	If you have a loss, check the box that describes your investment in this activity (see page C-7).		
	• If you checked 32a, enter the loss on both **Form 1040, line 12,** and **Schedule SE, line 2,** or on **Form 1040NR, line 13** (statutory employees, see page C-7). Estates and trusts, enter on Form 1041, line 3.	**32a** ☐ All investment is at risk.	
	• If you checked 32b, you **must** attach **Form 6198.** Your loss may be limited.	**32b** ☐ Some investment is not at risk.	

For Paperwork Reduction Act Notice, see page C-8 of the instructions.   Cat. No. 11334P   Schedule C (Form 1040) 2007

Schedule C (Form 1040) 2007

Page **2**

Part III **Cost of Goods Sold** (see page C-7)

33 Method(s) used to value closing inventory: **a** ☐ Cost **b** ☐ Lower of cost or market **c** ☐ Other (attach explanation)

34 Was there any change in determining quantities, costs, or valuations between opening and closing inventory? If "Yes," attach explanation . . . . ☐ **Yes** ☐ **No**

35 Inventory at beginning of year. If different from last year's closing inventory, attach explanation . .	**35**	
36 Purchases less cost of items withdrawn for personal use	**36**	
37 Cost of labor. Do not include any amounts paid to yourself	**37**	
38 Materials and supplies	**38**	
39 Other costs	**39**	
40 Add lines 35 through 39	**40**	
41 Inventory at end of year	**41**	
42 **Cost of goods sold.** Subtract line 41 from line 40. Enter the result here and on page 1, line 4 . .	**42**	

Part IV **Information on Your Vehicle.** Complete this part **only** if you are claiming car or truck expenses on line 9 and are not required to file Form 4562 for this business. See the instructions for line 13 on page C-4 to find out if you must file Form 4562.

43 When did you place your vehicle in service for business purposes? (month, day, year) ▶ _____/_____/_____

44 Of the total number of miles you drove your vehicle during 2007, enter the number of miles you used your vehicle for:

a Business _____ **b** Commuting (see instructions) _____ **c** Other _____

45 Do you (or your spouse) have another vehicle available for personal use?. . . . . ☐ **Yes** ☐ **No**

46 Was your vehicle available for personal use during off-duty hours? . . . . ☐ **Yes** ☐ **No**

47a Do you have evidence to support your deduction? . . . . ☐ **Yes** ☐ **No**

b If "Yes," is the evidence written? . . . . ☐ **Yes** ☐ **No**

Part V **Other Expenses.** List below business expenses not included on lines 8–26 or line 30.

_____		
_____		
_____		
_____		
_____		
_____		
_____		
_____		
48 **Total other expenses.** Enter here and on page 1, line 27	**48**	

Printed on recycled paper

Schedule C (Form 1040) 2007

SCHEDULE C-EZ (Form 1040) Department of the Treasury Internal Revenue Service	**Net Profit From Business** (Sole Proprietorship) ▶ **Partnerships, joint ventures, etc., must file Form 1065 or 1065-B.** ▶ **Attach to Form 1040, 1040NR, or 1041.** ▶ **See instructions on back.**	OMB No. 1545-0074 20**07** Attachment Sequence No. **09A**

Name of proprietor	Social security number (SSN)

Part I   General Information

You May Use Schedule C-EZ Instead of Schedule C Only If You:

- Had business expenses of $5,000 or less.
- Use the cash method of accounting.
- Did not have an inventory at any time during the year.
- Did not have a net loss from your business.
- Had only one business as either a sole proprietor or statutory employee.

And You:

- Had no employees during the year.
- Are not required to file **Form 4562,** Depreciation and Amortization, for this business. See the instructions for Schedule C, line 13, on page C-4 to find out if you must file.
- Do not deduct expenses for business use of your home.
- Do not have prior year unallowed passive activity losses from this business.

A Principal business or profession, including product or service

B Enter code from pages C-8, 9, & 10 ▶

C Business name. If no separate business name, leave blank.

D Employer ID number (EIN), if any

E Business address (including suite or room no.). Address not required if same as on page 1 of your tax return.

City, town or post office, state, and ZIP code

Part II   Figure Your Net Profit

1	**Gross receipts. Caution.** If this income was reported to you on Form W-2 and the "Statutory employee" box on that form was checked, see **Statutory Employees** in the instructions for Schedule C, line 1, on page C-3 and check here . . . . ▶ ☐	**1**
2	**Total expenses** (see instructions). If more than $5,000, you **must** use Schedule C.	**2**
3	**Net profit.** Subtract line 2 from line 1. If less than zero, you **must** use Schedule C. Enter on both **Form 1040, line 12,** and **Schedule SE, line 2,** or on **Form 1040NR, line 13.** (Statutory employees **do not** report this amount on Schedule SE, line 2. Estates and trusts, enter on Form 1041, line 3.)	**3**

Part III   Information on Your Vehicle. Complete this part **only** if you are claiming car or truck expenses on line 2.

4 When did you place your vehicle in service for business purposes? (month, day, year) ▶ .... / .... / ....

5 Of the total number of miles you drove your vehicle during 2007, enter the number of miles you used your vehicle for:

a Business .... **b** Commuting (see instructions) .... **c** Other ....

6 Do you (or your spouse) have another vehicle available for personal use? . . . . ☐ Yes ☐ No

7 Was your vehicle available for personal use during off-duty hours? . . . . ☐ Yes ☐ No

8a Do you have evidence to support your deduction? . . . . ☐ Yes ☐ No

b If "Yes," is the evidence written? . . . . ☐ Yes ☐ No

For Paperwork Reduction Act Notice, see page 2.   Cat. No. 14374D   Schedule C-EZ (Form 1040) 2007

Instructions

Before you begin, see General Instructions *in the 2007 Instructions for Schedule C.*

You can use Schedule C-EZ instead of Schedule C if you operated a business or practiced a profession as a sole proprietorship or you were a statutory employee and you have met all the requirements listed in Schedule C-EZ, Part I.

Line A

Describe the business or professional activity that provided your principal source of income reported on line 1. Give the general field or activity and the type of product or service.

Line B

Enter the six-digit code that identifies your principal business or professional activity. See pages C-8 through C-10 of the instructions for Schedule C for the list of codes.

Line D

You need an employer identification number (EIN) only if you had a qualified retirement plan or were required to file an employment, excise, estate, trust, or alcohol, tobacco, and firearms tax return. If you need an EIN, see the Instructions for Form SS-4. If you do not have an EIN, leave line D blank. Do not enter your SSN.

Line E

Enter your business address. Show a street address instead of a box number. Include the suite or room number, if any.

Line 1

Enter gross receipts from your trade or business. Include amounts you received in your trade or business that were properly shown on Forms 1099-MISC. If the total amounts that were reported in box 7 of Forms 1099-MISC are more than the total you are reporting on line 1, attach a statement explaining the difference. You must show all items of taxable income actually or constructively received during the year (in cash, property, or services). Income is constructively received when it is credited to your account or set aside for you to use. Do not offset this amount by any losses.

Line 2

Enter the total amount of all deductible business expenses you actually paid during the year. Examples of these expenses include advertising, car and truck expenses, commissions and fees, insurance, interest, legal and professional services, office expenses, rent or lease expenses, repairs and maintenance, supplies, taxes, travel, the allowable percentage of business meals and entertainment, and utilities (including telephone). For details, see the instructions for Schedule C, Parts II and V, on pages C-4 through C-8. If you wish, you can use the optional worksheet below to record your expenses. Enter on lines **b** through **f** the type and amount of expenses not included on line **a**.

If you claim car or truck expenses, be sure to complete Schedule C-EZ, Part III.

Line 5b

Generally, commuting is travel between your home and a work location. If you converted your vehicle during the year from personal to business use (or vice versa), enter your commuting miles only for the period you drove your vehicle for business. For information on certain travel that is considered a business expense rather than commuting, see the Instructions for Form 2106.

Paperwork Reduction Act Notice. We ask for the information on this form to carry out the Internal Revenue laws of the United States. You are required to give us the information. We need it to ensure that you are complying with these laws and to allow us to figure and collect the right amount of tax.

You are not required to provide the information requested on a form that is subject to the Paperwork Reduction Act unless the form displays a valid OMB control number. Books or records relating to a form or its instructions must be retained as long as their contents may become material in the administration of any Internal Revenue law. Generally, tax returns and return information are confidential, as required by Internal Revenue Code section 6103.

The time needed to complete and file this form will vary depending on individual circumstances. The estimated burden for individual taxpayers filing this form is included in the estimates shown in the instructions for their individual income tax return. The estimated burden for all other taxpayers who file this form is approved under OMB control number 1545-1973 and is shown below.

Recordkeeping . . . . 45 min.
**Learning about the law
or the form** . . . . 4 min.
Preparing the form . . . . 35 min.
**Copying, assembling,
and sending the form to the IRS** . . . . 20 min.

If you have comments concerning the accuracy of these time estimates or suggestions for making this form simpler, we would be happy to hear from you. See the instructions for the tax return with which this form is filed.

Optional Worksheet for Line 2 (keep a copy for your records)

a Deductible business meals and entertainment (see page C-6)	**a**	
b --	**b**	
c --	**c**	
d --	**d**	
e --	**e**	
f --	**f**	
g **Total.** Add lines **a** through **f**. Enter here and on line 2	**g**	

SCHEDULE SE
(Form 1040)

Department of the Treasury
Internal Revenue Service

Self-Employment Tax

▶ **Attach to Form 1040.** ▶ **See Instructions for Schedule SE (Form 1040).**

OMB No. 1545-0074

20**07**

Attachment
Sequence No. **17**

Name of person with **self-employment** income (as shown on Form 1040)	Social security number of person with **self-employment** income ▶		

Who Must File Schedule SE

You must file Schedule SE if:

- You had net earnings from self-employment from **other than** church employee income (line 4 of Short Schedule SE or line 4c of Long Schedule SE) of $400 or more, **or**

- You had church employee income of $108.28 or more. Income from services you performed as a minister or a member of a religious order **is not** church employee income (see page SE-1).

Note. Even if you had a loss or a small amount of income from self-employment, it may be to your benefit to file Schedule SE and use either "optional method" in Part II of Long Schedule SE (see page SE-4).

Exception. If your only self-employment income was from earnings as a minister, member of a religious order, or Christian Science practitioner **and** you filed Form 4361 and received IRS approval not to be taxed on those earnings, **do not** file Schedule SE. Instead, write "Exempt–Form 4361" on Form 1040, line 58.

May I Use Short Schedule SE or Must I Use Long Schedule SE?

Note. Use this flowchart **only if** you must file Schedule SE. If unsure, see Who Must File Schedule SE, above.

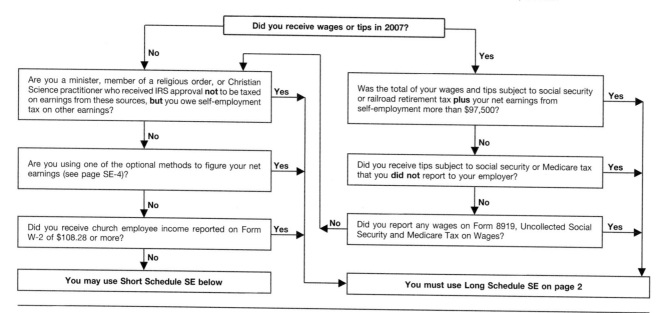

Section A—Short Schedule SE. Caution. Read above to see if you can use Short Schedule SE.

1	Net farm profit or (loss) from Schedule F, line 36, and farm partnerships, Schedule K-1 (Form 1065), box 14, code A	**1**	
2	Net profit or (loss) from Schedule C, line 31; Schedule C-EZ, line 3; Schedule K-1 (Form 1065), box 14, code A (other than farming); and Schedule K-1 (Form 1065-B), box 9, code J1. Ministers and members of religious orders, see page SE-1 for amounts to report on this line. See page SE-3 for other income to report	**2**	
3	Combine lines 1 and 2	**3**	
4	**Net earnings from self-employment.** Multiply line 3 by 92.35% (.9235). If less than $400, **do not** file this schedule; you do not owe self-employment tax . . . . ▶	**4**	
5	**Self-employment tax.** If the amount on line 4 is: • $97,500 or less, multiply line 4 by 15.3% (.153). Enter the result here and on **Form 1040, line 58.** • More than $97,500, multiply line 4 by 2.9% (.029). Then, add $12,090 to the result. Enter the total here and on **Form 1040, line 58**	**5**	
6	**Deduction for one-half of self-employment tax.** Multiply line 5 by 50% (.5). Enter the result here and on **Form 1040, line 27**	**6**		

For Paperwork Reduction Act Notice, see Form 1040 instructions.   Cat. No. 11358Z   **Schedule SE (Form 1040) 2007**

Schedule SE (Form 1040) 2007   Attachment Sequence No. **17**   Page **2**

Name of person with **self-employment** income (as shown on Form 1040)	Social security number of person with **self-employment** income ▶	⋮ ⋮

Section B—Long Schedule SE

Part I   Self-Employment Tax

Note. If your only income subject to self-employment tax is **church employee income,** skip lines 1 through 4b. Enter -0- on line 4c and go to line 5a. Income from services you performed as a minister or a member of a religious order **is not** church employee income. See page SE-1.

A   If you are a minister, member of a religious order, or Christian Science practitioner **and** you filed Form 4361, but you had $400 or more of **other** net earnings from self-employment, check here and continue with Part I . . . . . . ▶ ☐

1 Net farm profit or (loss) from Schedule F, line 36, and farm partnerships, Schedule K-1 (Form 1065), box 14, code A. **Note.** Skip this line if you use the farm optional method (see page SE-4)	**1**	
2 Net profit or (loss) from Schedule C, line 31; Schedule C-EZ, line 3; Schedule K-1 (Form 1065), box 14, code A (other than farming); and Schedule K-1 (Form 1065-B), box 9, code J1. Ministers and members of religious orders, see page SE-1 for amounts to report on this line. See page SE-3 for other income to report. **Note.** Skip this line if you use the nonfarm optional method (see page SE-4)	**2**	
3 Combine lines 1 and 2	**3**	
4a If line 3 is more than zero, multiply line 3 by 92.35% (.9235). Otherwise, enter amount from line 3	**4a**	
b If you elect one or both of the optional methods, enter the total of lines 15 and 17 here . . .	**4b**	
c Combine lines 4a and 4b. If less than $400, **stop;** you do not owe self-employment tax. **Exception.** If less than $400 and you had **church employee income,** enter -0- and continue. . . . . . ▶	**4c**	
5a Enter your **church employee income** from Form W-2. See page SE-1 for definition of church employee income **5a**		
b Multiply line 5a by 92.35% (.9235). If less than $100, enter -0- . . .	**5b**	
6 **Net earnings from self-employment.** Add lines 4c and 5b	**6**	
7 Maximum amount of combined wages and self-employment earnings subject to social security tax or the 6.2% portion of the 7.65% railroad retirement (tier 1) tax for 2007	**7**	97,500 00
8a Total social security wages and tips (total of boxes 3 and 7 on Form(s) W-2) and railroad retirement (tier 1) compensation. If $97,500 or more, skip lines 8b through 10, and go to line 11 . . . . **8a**		
b Unreported tips subject to social security tax (from Form 4137, line 10) **8b**		
c Wages subject to social security tax (from Form 8919, line 10) . . . **8c**		
d Add lines 8a, 8b, and 8c	**8d**	
9 Subtract line 8d from line 7. If zero or less, enter -0- here and on line 10 and go to line 11 . ▶	**9**	
10 Multiply the **smaller** of line 6 or line 9 by 12.4% (.124)	**10**	
11 Multiply line 6 by 2.9% (.029)	**11**	
12 **Self-employment tax.** Add lines 10 and 11. Enter here and on **Form 1040, line 58** . . .	**12**	
13 **Deduction for one-half of self-employment tax.** Multiply line 12 by 50% (.5). Enter the result here and on **Form 1040, line 27** **13**		

Part II   Optional Methods To Figure Net Earnings (see page SE-4)

Farm Optional Method. You may use this method **only if (a)** your gross farm income[1] was not more than $2,400, **or (b)** your net farm profits[2] were less than $1,733.

14 Maximum income for optional methods	**14**	1,600 00
15 Enter the **smaller** of: two-thirds (⅔) of gross farm income[1] (not less than zero) **or** $1,600. Also include this amount on line 4b above	**15**	

Nonfarm Optional Method. You may use this method **only if (a)** your net nonfarm profits[3] were less than $1,733 and also less than 72.189% of your gross nonfarm income,[4] **and (b)** you had net earnings from self-employment of at least $400 in 2 of the prior 3 years.

Caution. You may use this method no more than five times.

16 Subtract line 15 from line 14	**16**	
17 Enter the **smaller** of: two-thirds (⅔) of gross nonfarm income[4] (not less than zero) **or** the amount on line 16. Also include this amount on line 4b above	**17**	

[1] From Sch. F, line 11, and Sch. K-1 (Form 1065), box 14, code B.

[2] From Sch. F, line 36, and Sch. K-1 (Form 1065), box 14, code A.

[3] From Sch. C, line 31; Sch. C-EZ, line 3; Sch. K-1 (Form 1065), box 14, code A; and Sch. K-1 (Form 1065-B), box 9, code J1.

[4] From Sch. C, line 7; Sch. C-EZ, line 1; Sch. K-1 (Form 1065), box 14, code C; and Sch. K-1 (Form 1065-B), box 9, code J2.

Schedule SE (Form 1040) 2007

For form instructions, see the IRS Web site.

OMB No. 1615-0047; Expires 06/30/08

Department of Homeland Security
U.S. Citizenship and Immigration Services

Form I-9, Employment Eligibility Verification

Please read instructions carefully before completing this form. The instructions must be available during completion of this form.

ANTI-DISCRIMINATION NOTICE: It is illegal to discriminate against work eligible individuals. Employers CANNOT specify which document(s) they will accept from an employee. The refusal to hire an individual because the documents have a future expiration date may also constitute illegal discrimination.

Section 1. Employee Information and Verification. To be completed and signed by employee at the time employment begins.

Print Name: Last	First	Middle Initial	Maiden Name

Address *(Street Name and Number)*	Apt. #	Date of Birth *(month/day/year)*

City	State	Zip Code	Social Security #

I am aware that federal law provides for imprisonment and/or fines for false statements or use of false documents in connection with the completion of this form.

I attest, under penalty of perjury, that I am (check one of the following):

☐ A citizen or national of the United States
☐ A lawful permanent resident (Alien #) A _____
☐ An alien authorized to work until _____
(Alien # or Admission #)

Employee's Signature	Date *(month/day/year)*

Preparer and/or Translator Certification. *(To be completed and signed if Section 1 is prepared by a person other than the employee.)* I attest, under penalty of perjury, that I have assisted in the completion of this form and that to the best of my knowledge the information is true and correct.

Preparer's/Translator's Signature	Print Name

Address *(Street Name and Number, City, State, Zip Code)*	Date *(month/day/year)*

Section 2. Employer Review and Verification. To be completed and signed by employer. Examine one document from List A OR examine one document from List B and one from List C, as listed on the reverse of this form, and record the title, number and expiration date, if any, of the document(s).

List A	OR	List B	AND	List C
Document title: _____		_____		_____
Issuing authority: _____		_____		_____
Document #: _____		_____		_____
Expiration Date *(if any)*: _____		_____		_____
Document #: _____				
Expiration Date *(if any)*: _____				

CERTIFICATION - I attest, under penalty of perjury, that I have examined the document(s) presented by the above-named employee, that the above-listed document(s) appear to be genuine and to relate to the employee named, that the employee began employment on *(month/day/year)* _____ **and that to the best of my knowledge the employee is eligible to work in the United States. (State employment agencies may omit the date the employee began employment.)**

Signature of Employer or Authorized Representative	Print Name	Title

Business or Organization Name and Address *(Street Name and Number, City, State, Zip Code)*	Date *(month/day/year)*

Section 3. Updating and Reverification. To be completed and signed by employer.

A. New Name *(if applicable)*	B. Date of Rehire *(month/day/year) (if applicable)*

C. If employee's previous grant of work authorization has expired, provide the information below for the document that establishes current employment eligibility.

Document Title: _____	Document #: _____	Expiration Date (if any): _____

I attest, under penalty of perjury, that to the best of my knowledge, this employee is eligible to work in the United States, and if the employee presented document(s), the document(s) I have examined appear to be genuine and to relate to the individual.

Signature of Employer or Authorized Representative	Date *(month/day/year)*

LISTS OF ACCEPTABLE DOCUMENTS

LIST A	LIST B	LIST C
Documents that Establish Both Identity and Employment Eligibility	Documents that Establish Identity	Documents that Establish Employment Eligibility
OR		**AND**
1. U.S. Passport (unexpired or expired)	1. Driver's license or ID card issued by a state or outlying possession of the United States provided it contains a photograph or information such as name, date of birth, gender, height, eye color and address	1. U.S. Social Security card issued by the Social Security Administration *(other than a card stating it is not valid for employment)*
2. Permanent Resident Card or Alien Registration Receipt Card (Form I-551)	2. ID card issued by federal, state or local government agencies or entities, provided it contains a photograph or information such as name, date of birth, gender, height, eye color and address	2. Certification of Birth Abroad issued by the Department of State *(Form FS-545 or Form DS-1350)*
3. An unexpired foreign passport with a temporary I-551 stamp	3. School ID card with a photograph	3. Original or certified copy of a birth certificate issued by a state, county, municipal authority or outlying possession of the United States bearing an official seal
4. An unexpired Employment Authorization Document that contains a photograph (Form I-766, I-688, I-688A, I-688B)	4. Voter's registration card	4. Native American tribal document
	5. U.S. Military card or draft record	5. U.S. Citizen ID Card *(Form I-197)*
5. An unexpired foreign passport with an unexpired Arrival-Departure Record, Form I-94, bearing the same name as the passport and containing an endorsement of the alien's nonimmigrant status, if that status authorizes the alien to work for the employer	6. Military dependent's ID card	6. ID Card for use of Resident Citizen in the United States *(Form I-179)*
	7. U.S. Coast Guard Merchant Mariner Card	
	8. Native American tribal document	7. Unexpired employment authorization document issued by DHS *(other than those listed under List A)*
	9. Driver's license issued by a Canadian government authority	
	For persons under age 18 who are unable to present a document listed above:	
	10. School record or report card	
	11. Clinic, doctor or hospital record	
	12. Day-care or nursery school record	

Illustrations of many of these documents appear in Part 8 of the Handbook for Employers (M-274)

U.S. Small Business Administration
APPLICATION FOR BUSINESS LOAN

OMB Approval No: 3245-0016
Expiration Date: 11/30/04

Individual	Full Address

Name of Applicant Business	Tax I.D. No. or SSN

Full Street Address of Business	Tel. No. (inc. A/C)

City	County	State	Zip	Number of Employees (Including subsidiaries and affiliates)

Type of Business	Date Business Established	At Time of Application ____

Bank of Business Account and Address	If Loan is Approved ____
	Subsidiaries or Affiliates (Separate for above) ____

Use of Proceeds: (Enter Gross Dollar Amounts Rounded to the Nearest Hundreds)	Loan Requested		Loan Request
Land Acquisition		Payoff SBA Loan	
New Construction/ Expansion Repair		Payoff Bank Loan (Non SBA Associated	
Acquisition and/or Repair of Machinery and Equipment		Other Debt Payment (Non SBA Associated)	
Inventory Purchase		All Other	
Working Capital (including Accounts Payable)		Total Loan Requested	
Acquisition of Existing Business		Term of Loan - (Requested Mat.)	____ Yrs.

PREVIOUS SBA OR OTHER FEDERAL GOVERNMENT DEBT: If you or any principals or affiliates have 1) ever requested Government Financing or 2) are delinquent on the repayment of any Federal Debt complete the following:

Name of Agency	Original Amount of Loan	Date of Request	Approved or Declined	Balance	Current or Past Due
	$			$	
	$			$	

ASSISTANCE List the name(s) and occupation of anyone who assisted in the preparation of this form, other than applicant.

Name and Occupation	Address	Total Fees Paid	Fees Due
Name and Occupation	Address	Total Fees Paid	Fees Due

Note: The estimated burden completing this form is 12.0 hours per response. You will not be required to respond to any collection of information unless it displays a currently valid OMB approval number. Comments on the burden should be sent to U.S. Small Business Administration, Chief, AIB, 409 3rd St., S.W., Washington, D.C. 20416 and Desk Office for Small Business Administration, Office of Management and Budget, New Executive Office Building, room 10202 Washington, D.C. 20503. OMB Approval (3245-0016). **PLEASE DO NOT SEND FORMS TO OMB.**
SUBMIT COMPLETED APPLICATION TO LENDER OF CHOICE

Federal Recycling Program   Printed on Recycled Paper

ALL EXHIBITS MUST BE SIGNED AND DATED BY PERSON SIGNING THIS FORM

BUSINESS INDEBTEDNESS: Furnish the following information on all installment debts, contracts, notes, and mortgages payable. Indicate by an asterisk (*) items to be paid by loan proceeds and reason for paying them (present balance should agree with the latest balance sheet submitted).

To Whom Payable	Original Amount	Original Date	Present Balance	Rate of Interest	Maturity Date	Monthly Payment	Security	Current or Past Due
Acct. #	$		$			$		
Acct. #	$		$			$		
Acct. #	$		$			$		
Acct. #	$		$			$		
Acct. #	$		$			$		

MANAGEMENT (Proprietor, partners, officers, directors, all holders of outstanding stock – <u>100% of ownership must be shown</u>). Use separate sheet if necessary.

Name and Social Security Number and Position Title	Complete Address	%Owned	*Military Service From	To	*Sex
Race*: American Indian/Alaska Native ☐ Black/African-Amer. ☐ Asian ☐ Native Hawaiian/Pacific Islander ☐ White ☐	**Ethnicity*** Hisp./Latino ☐ Not Hisp./Latino ☐				
Race*: American Indian/Alaska Native ☐ Black/African-Amer. ☐ Asian ☐ Native Hawaiian/Pacific Islander ☐ White ☐	**Ethnicity*** Hisp./Latino ☐ Not Hisp./Latino ☐				
Race*: American Indian/Alaska Native ☐ Black/African-Amer. ☐ Asian ☐ Native Hawaiian/Pacific Islander ☐ White ☐	**Ethnicity*** Hisp./Latino ☐ Not Hisp./Latino ☐				
Race*: American Indian/Alaska Native ☐ Black/African-Amer. ☐ Asian ☐ Native Hawaiian/Pacific Islander ☐ White ☐	**Ethnicity*** Hisp./Latino ☐ Not Hisp./Latino ☐				

*This data is collected for statistical purpose only. It has no bearing on the credit decision to approve or decline this application. One or more boxes may be selected.

THE FOLLOWING EXHIBITS MUST BE COMPLETED WHERE APPLICABLE. ALL QUESTIONS ANSWERED ARE MADE A PART OF THE APPLICATION.

For Guarantee Loans please provide an original and one copy (Photocopy is Acceptable) of the Application Form, and all Exhibits to the participating lender. For Direct Loans submit one original copy of the application and Exhibits to SBA.

1. Submit SBA Form 912 (Statement of Personal History) for each type of individual that the Form 912 requires.

2. If your collateral consists of (A) Land and Building, (B) Machinery and Equipment, (C) Furniture and Fixtures, (D) Accounts *Receivable*, (E) Inventory, (F) Other, please provide an itemized list (labeled Exhibit A) that contains serial and identification numbers for all articles that had an Original value of greater than $500. Include a legal description of Real Estate Offered as collateral.

3. Furnish a signed current personal balance sheet (SBA Form 413 may be used for this purpose) for each stockholder (with 20% or greater ownership), partner, officer, and owner. Include the assets and liabilities of the spouse and any close relatives living in the household. Also, include your Social Security Number. The date should be the same as the most recent business financial statement. Label it Exhibit B.

4. Include the financial statements listed below: a,b,c for the last three years; also a,b,c, and d as of the same date, - current within 90 days of filing the application; and statement e, if applicable. Label it Exhibit C (Contact SBA for referral if assistance with preparation is wanted.) **All** information must be signed and dated.

a. Balance Sheet
b. Profit and Loss Statement (if not available, explain why and substitute Federal income tax forms)
c. Reconciliation of Net Worth
d. Aging of Accounts Receivable and Payable (summary not detailed)
e. Projection of earnings for at least one year where financial statements for the last three years are unavailable or when SBA requests them.

5. Provide a brief history of your company and a paragraph describing the expected benefits it will receive from the loan. Label it Exhibit D.

6. Provide a brief description similar to a resume of the education, technical and business background for all the people listed under Management. Label it Exhibit E.

ALL EXHIBITS MUST BE SIGNED AND DATED BY PERSON SIGNING THIS FORM

7. Submit the names, addresses, tax I.D. number(EIN or SSN), and current personal balance sheet(s) of any co-signers and/or guarantors for the loan who are not otherwise affiliated with the business as Exhibit F.

8. Include a list of any machinery or equipment or other non-real estate assets to be purchased with loan proceeds and the cost of each item as quoted by the seller as Exhibit G. Include the seller's name and address.

9. Have you or any officers of your company ever been involved in bankruptcy or insolvency proceedings? If so, please provide the details as Exhibit H. If none, check here:

          Yes   No

10. Are you or your business involved in any pending lawsuits? If yes, provide the details as Exhibit I. If none, check here: Yes [No

11. Do you or your spouse or any member of your household, or anyone who owns, manages or directs your business or their spouses or members of their households work for the Small Business Administration, Small Business Advisory Council, SCORE or ACE, any Federal Agency, or the participating lender? If so, please provide the name and address of the person and the office where employed. Label this Exhibit J. If none, check here:

12. Does your business, its owners or majority stockholders own or have a controlling interest in other businesses? If yes, please provide their names and the relationship with your company along with a current balance sheet and operating statement for each. This should be Exhibit K.

13. Do you buy from, sell to, or use the services of any concern in which someone in your company has a significant financial interest? If yes, provide details on a separate sheet of paper labeled Exhibit L.

14. If your business is a franchise, include a copy of the franchise agreement and a copy of the FTC disclosure statement supplied to you by the Franchisor. Please include it as Exhibit M.

CONSTRUCTION LOANS ONLY

15. Include as a separate exhibit (Exhibit N) the estimated cost of the project and a statement of the source of any additional funds.

16. Provide copies of preliminary construction plans and specifications. Include them as Exhibit O. Final plans will be required prior to disbursement.

EXPORT LOANS

17. Does your business presently engage in Export Trade? Check here: Yes [No

18. Will you be using proceeds from this loan to support your company's exports? Check here: Yes [No

19. Would you like information on Exporting? Check here: Yes   No

AGREEMENTS AND CERTIFICATIONS

Agreements of non-employment of SBA Personnel: I agree that if SBA approves this loan application I will not, for at least two years, hire as an employee or consultant anyone that was employed by SBA during the one year period prior to the disbursement of the loan.

Certification: I certify: (a) I have not paid anyone connected with the Federal Government for help in getting this loan. I also agree to report to the SBA office of the Inspector General, Washington, DC 20416 any Federal Government employee who offers, in return for any type of compensation, to help get this loan approved.

(b) All information in this application and the Exhibits are true and complete to the best of my knowledge and are submitted to SBA so SBA can decide whether to grant a loan or participate with a lending institution in a loan to me. I agree to pay for or reimburse SBA for the cost of any surveys, title or mortgage examinations, appraisals, credit reports, etc., performed by non-SBA personnel provided I have given my consent-

(c) I understand that I need not pay anybody to deal with SBA. I have read and understand SBA Form 159, which explains SBA policy on representatives and their fees.

(d) As consideration for any Management, Technical, and Business Development Assistance that may be provided, I waive all claims against SBA and its consultants.

If you knowingly make a false statement or overvalue a security to obtain a guaranteed loan from SBA, you can be fined up to $10,000 and/or imprisoned for not more than five years under 18 usc 1001; if submitted to a Federally insured institution, under 18 USC 1014 by Imprisonment of not more than twenty years and/or a fine of not more than $1,000,000. I authorize the SBA's Office of Inspector General to request criminal record information about me from criminal justice agencies for the purpose of determining my eligibility for programs authorized by the Small Business Act, as amended.

If Applicant is a proprietor or general partner, sign below:

By: _____

If Applicant is a Corporation, sign below:

_____

Corporate Name and Seal   Date

By: _____
             Signature of President

Attested by: _____
        Signature of Corporate Secretary

SUBMIT COMPLETED APPLICATION TO LENDER OF CHOICE

APPLICANT'S CERTIFICATION

By my signature, I certify that I have read and received a copy of the "STATEMENTS REQUIRED BY LAW AND EXECUTIVE ORDER" which was attached to this application. My signature represents my agreement to comply with the approval of my loan request and to comply, whenever applicable, with the hazard insurance, lead-based paint, civil rights or other limitations in this notice.

Each proprietor, each General Partner, each Limited Partner or Stockholder owning 20% or more, each Guarantor and the spouse of each of these must sign. Each person should sign only once.

Business Name: _____

By: _____

Signature and Title _____   Date _____

Guarantors:

_____   _____
Signature and Title   Date

_____   _____
Signature and Title   Date

_____   _____
Signature and Title   Date

_____   _____
Signature and Title   Date

_____   _____
Signature and Title   Date

_____   _____
Signature and Title   Date

_____   _____
Signature and Title   Date

THE FRANCHISE DISCLOSURE DOCUMENT: AN OVERVIEW

January 2008

Disclosure Obligations   A Federal Trade Commission (FTC) Rule and the laws in 15 states require franchisors to provide a disclosure document (usually referred to as a "Franchise Disclosure Document" or "FDD") to prospective franchisees before granting a franchise. The latest version of the FTC Franchise Rule (issued in 2007), which largely follows the Uniform Franchise Offering Circular (UFOC) Guidelines used by the 15 states that have presale disclosure laws, will be the only permitted disclosure format as of July 1, 2008.

An Overview of the Required Disclosures

The Franchise Rule identifies 23 items that must be addressed in the Franchise Disclosure Document. These items cover the franchisor, the franchised system, the parties' contractual relationship, and other obligations of the parties. Specifically, the FDD must include the following information:

Item 1—The franchisor must describe its business, its business experience, and the franchise offered. The franchisor must provide information about its parents, predecessors, and affiliates and their business experience. In addition, information must be disclosed about regulations specific to the franchisor's industry.

Item 2—The franchisor must include employment history for the last five years for directors, principal officers, general partners, trustees, and other executives who will have management responsibility in connection with the sale or operation of the franchise. Franchise brokers do not need to be disclosed.

Item 3—The franchisor must disclose certain litigation filed against the franchisor, any predecessor, any affiliate that offers franchises under the franchisor's principal trademark, and the persons identified in Item 2. The franchisor must disclose litigation involving a parent who guarantees the franchisor's performance. The franchisor must also disclose actions that it initiated against franchisees in the last fiscal year that were material to the franchise relationship (such as royalty collection suits).

Item 4—The franchisor must disclose any bankruptcy filings in the last 10 years involving the franchisor, any predecessor, any affiliate, and any person identified in Item 2.

Item 5—The franchisor must disclose any payments that the franchisee is required to make to the franchisor or its affiliates prior to opening.

Item 6—The franchisor must disclose all other isolated or recurring fees that the franchisee is required to pay to the franchisor or its affiliates.

Item 7—The franchisor must estimate the initial investment that the franchisee must make to begin operations of the franchised business.

Item 8—If the franchisee is required to purchase or lease any goods or services from sources designated or approved by the franchisor or based upon the franchisor's specifications, the franchisor must identify those goods and services. The franchisor also must disclose any supplier in which it owns an interest and must describe the approval process for new suppliers. The franchisor must state whether, and if so, precisely how, the franchisor or its affiliates will derive income from the franchisee's purchases from approved suppliers.

Item 9—The franchisor must list the franchisee's principal obligations under the franchise and related agreements.

Item 10—The franchisor must describe any financing offered directly or indirectly to the franchisee by the franchisor or its affiliates and any payments received by the franchisor or its affiliates as a result of the placement of financing.

Item 11—The franchisor must describe the services it is contractually obligated to provide to the franchisee. In addition, the franchisor must describe the process for selecting a location for the franchisee's business; the typical length of time between contract signing and unit opening; the franchisor's advertising programs; general information about computer system requirements; and the franchisor's training programs.

Item 12—The franchisor must describe any exclusive territory granted to the franchisee and warn the franchisee about intrabrand competition if the franchisee does not receive an exclusive territory. The franchisor must also disclose whether it has established, or may establish, another distribution outlet for products or services under the same trademark, or whether its affiliates have established or may establish other franchises or distribution outlets for similar products or services under a different trademark. The franchisor must disclose any rights it or its affiliates have to use alternative channels of distribution within the franchisee's territory and any right of the franchisee to use alternative channels of distribution to make sales outside its territory.

Item 13—The franchisor must provide information about the principal trademarks and service marks to be licensed to the franchisee and any limitations on the franchisee's use of these marks. The franchisor must provide a specific warning if its principal trademarks have not been registered with the United States Patent and Trademark Office.

Item 14—The franchisor must disclose information regarding any patents, copyrights, confidential information, or trade secrets relevant to the franchise.

Item 15—The franchisor must disclose whether the franchisee must personally participate in the operation of the franchised business.

Item 16—The franchisor must disclose any restrictions on the goods or services offered by the franchisee, any restrictions on the customers to whom the franchisee may sell goods or services, and whether the franchisor has the right to change the types of goods and services that the franchisee is authorized to offer.

Item 17—The franchisor must disclose (in tabular form) information about the term of the franchise relationship, modification, termination, renewal, and transfer of the franchise and dispute resolution. The franchisor also must describe what the term "renewal" means in the system, and whether franchisees could be required to sign a renewal contract with materially different terms and conditions.

Item 18—If a public figure endorses or recommends the purchase of the franchise, or the public figure is used in the franchise name or logo, the franchisor must disclose the compensation given to that public figure, the extent of the public figure's involvement in the management of the franchisor, and the total investment by the public figure in the franchisor.

Item 19—If a franchisor wants to provide any information to a franchisee about potential sales, expenses, or profits, the franchisor must include that information (known as a *financial performance representations*) in this Item.

Item 20—The franchisor must identify the name, address, and phone number of at least 100 current franchisees and their franchised businesses; the number of franchises it anticipates selling in the next year; the number of franchises in the last three fiscal years that have been transferred, canceled, terminated, not renewed, or reacquired by the franchisor; and the name, home address, and phone number of every franchisee who voluntarily or involuntarily ceased to be a franchisee during the last year, or who has not communicated with the franchisor within 10 weeks of the application date; and provide information about the number of company units that have been opened or closed during the last three years.

Item 21—The franchisor must include audited balance sheets as of the end of its last two fiscal years and statements of operations of stockholders' equity and of cash flow for its last three fiscal years. The financial statements must be prepared according to generally accepted accounting principles (GAAP). The franchisor may use its parent's consolidated financial statement and must include the parent's financial statement if the parent has postsale performance obligations or guarantees the franchisor's performance.

Item 22—The franchisor must include a copy of every contract that the prospective franchisee will or may be required to sign.

Item 23—The franchisor must include two copies of an acknowledgement of receipt to be signed by the prospective franchisee (one for the franchisee, and one for the franchisor).

The Franchise Rule allows the franchisor to provide disclosure electronically. Under the Rule, franchisors must update their disclosure document annually within 120 days of the close of the company's fiscal year.

What Is a Franchise?

Although the definition of a franchise varies by jurisdiction, as a general rule, a business will be considered a franchise and be subject to presale registration and disclosure obligations if it meets three criteria:

1. The franchisee's business is identified or substantially associated with the franchisor's trademark.

2. The franchisor exerts sufficient control over the franchisee's business or there is interdependence between the franchisee's business and the franchisor's system. There are three alternative tests used for this element. First, the Federal Trade Commission uses the "significant control" or "significant assistance" test, which is applicable in the majority of the states. This test focuses on the franchisor's level of control or assistance over the franchisee's entire business. Second, under the "marketing plan" test, which is used by 12 states, a franchise exists when the franchisor prescribes a marketing plan that the franchisee must follow. Third, under the "community of interest" test, which is used in three states, a franchise exists when there is a sufficient level of interdependence between the franchisee and the franchisor.

3. The franchisee is obligated to pay money to the franchisor or its affiliates for the right to engage in the business. Almost any monies paid to the franchisor or its affiliates can satisfy this element, except for the purchase of inventory at *bona fide* wholesale prices.

Some jurisdictions exclude from registration and disclosure certain business relationships that meet the definition of a franchise. Examples of excluded relationships are general partnerships, employment relationships, and fractional franchises (where the franchisee has experience in the franchised business and the new franchised business will account for less than 20% of the franchisee's total sales).

A number of states require certain franchisors to provide disclosure but do not require registration. The most common registration exemption is for a franchisor whose net worth exceeds a certain level (generally $5 million), and who is experienced in the franchised business.

Since the definition of a "franchise" and the applicable exclusions and exemptions vary, a business relationship may be considered a franchise in some jurisdictions but not in other jurisdictions.

For more information, please call 202-719-3157.

This is a publication of Wiley Rein LLP and should not be construed as legal advice or a legal opinion on any specific facts or circumstances. The contents are intended for general informational purposes. You are urged to consult your lawyer concerning your own situation and any specific legal questions.

Source: Wiley Reing LLP, *http://wileyrein.com/publication.cfm?pf=1&publication_id=8531* (Accessed February 23, 2008).

index